The Renaissance of Shiʿi Islam

The Institute of Ismaili Studies
Shiʿi Heritage Series, 9

Editorial Board: Farhad Daftary (general editor), Maria De Cillis (managing editor), Gurdofarid Miskinzoda (managing editor), Mohammad Ali Amir-Moezzi, Hermann Landolt, Wilferd Madelung, Orkhan Mir-Kasimov, Andrew Newman, Sabine Schmidtke, Paul E. Walker

Previously published titles:
1. Daftary, Farhad. *A History of Shiʿi Islam* (2013).
2. Daftary, Farhad, and Gurdofarid Miskinzoda, ed. *The Study of Shiʿi Islam: History, Theology and Law* (2014).
3. Mir-Kasimov, Orkhan. *Words of Power: Ḥurūfī Teachings Between Shiʿism and Sufism in Medieval Islam* (2015).
4. Asatryan, Mushegh. *Controversies in Formative Shiʿi Islam: The Ghulat Muslims and their Beliefs* (2017).
5. De Cillis, Maria. *Salvation and Destiny in Islam: The Shiʿi Ismaili Perspective of Ḥamīd al-Dīn al-Kirmānī* (2018).
6. Mir-Kasimov, Orkhan, ed. *Intellectual Interactions in the Islamic World: The Ismaili Thread* (2020).
7. Hermann, Denis and Matthieu Terrier, ed. *Shiʿi Islam and Sufism: Classical Views and Modern Perspectives* (2020).
8. Esots, Janis. *Patterns of Wisdom in Safavid Iran: The Philosophical School of Isfahan and the Gnostic of Shiraz* (2021).

The Renaissance of Shiʿi Islam

Facets of Thought and Practice

Edited by
Farhad Daftary and Janis Esots

I.B.TAURIS
in association with
The Institute of Ismaili Studies
LONDON, 2022

I.B. TAURIS
Bloomsbury Publishing Plc
50 Bedford Square, London, WC1B 3DP, UK
1385 Broadway, New York, NY 10018, USA
29 Earlsfort Terrace, Dublin 2, Ireland

In association with The Institute of Ismaili Studies
Aga Khan Centre, 10 Handyside Street, London N1C 4DN
www.iis.ac.uk

BLOOMSBURY, I.B. TAURIS and the I.B. Tauris logo are trademarks
of Bloomsbury Publishing Plc

First published in Great Britain 2022

Series design by Positive2
Front cover image: View of Shah Abbas Mosque, inside courtyard with iwan,
Esfahan, Iran. (© Zdenar Adamsen/Adobe Stock)
Back cover image: Steel plaque from a shrine, inscribed with the shahada and
?Ali wali Allah; Iran, 11th/17th century. Aga Khan Museum, Toronto, AKM617.

A catalogue record for this book is available from the British Library.

A catalog record for this book is available from the Library of Congress.

ISBN: HB: 978-0-7556-4943-3
PB: 978-0-7556-4944-0
ePDF: 978-0-7556-4945-7
eBook: 978-0-7556-4946-4

Series: Shiʿi Heritage Series

Typeset by RefineCatch Limited, Bungay, Suffolk

To find out more about our authors and books visit www.bloomsbury.com
and sign up for our newsletters.

The Institute of Ismaili Studies

The Institute of Ismaili Studies was established in 1977 with the object of promoting scholarship and learning on Islam, in the historical as well as contemporary contexts, and a better understanding of its relationship with other societies and faiths.

The Institute's programmes encourage a perspective which is not confined to the theological and religious heritage of Islam, but seeks to explore the relationship of religious ideas to broader dimensions of society and culture. The programmes thus encourage an interdisciplinary approach to the materials of Islamic history and thought. Particular attention is also given to issues of modernity that arise as Muslims seek to relate their heritage to the contemporary situation.

Within the Islamic tradition, the Institute's programmes promote research on those areas which have, to date, received relatively little attention from scholars. These include the intellectual and literary expressions of Shiʿism in general, and Ismailism in particular.

In the context of Islamic societies, the Institute's programmes are informed by the full range and diversity of cultures in which Islam is practised today, from the Middle East, South and Central Asia, and Africa to the industrialized societies of the West, thus taking into consideration the variety of contexts which shape the ideals, beliefs and practices of the faith.

These objectives are realised through concrete programmes and activities organized and implemented by various departments of the Institute. The Institute also collaborates periodically, on a programme-specific basis, with other institutions of learning in the United Kingdom and abroad.

The Institute's academic publications fall into a number of inter-related categories:

1. Occasional papers or essays addressing broad themes of the relationship between religion and society, with special reference to Islam.
2. Monographs exploring specific aspects of Islamic faith and culture, or the contributions of individual Muslim thinkers or writers.
3. Editions or translations of significant primary or secondary texts.
4. Translations of poetic or literary texts which illustrate the rich heritage of spiritual, devotional and symbolic expressions in Muslim history.
5. Works on Ismaili history and thought, and the relationship of the Ismailis to other traditions, communities and schools of thought in Islam.
6. Proceedings of conferences and seminars sponsored by the Institute.
7. Bibliographical works and catalogues which document manuscripts, printed texts and other source materials.

This book falls into category six listed above.

In facilitating these and other publications, the Institute's sole aim is to encourage original research and analysis of relevant issues. While every effort is made to ensure that the publications are of a high academic standard, there is naturally bound to be a diversity of views, ideas and interpretations. As such, the opinions expressed in these publications must be understood as belonging to their authors alone.

Shiʿi Heritage Series

Shiʿi Muslims, with their rich intellectual and cultural heritage, have contributed significantly to the fecundity and diversity of the Islamic traditions throughout the centuries, enabling Islam to evolve and flourish both as a major religion and also as a civilisation. In spite of this, Shiʿi Islam has received little scholarly attention in the West, in medieval as well modern times. It is only in recent decades that academic interest has focused increasingly on Shiʿi Islam within the wider study of Islam.

The principal objective of the *Shiʿi Heritage Series*, launched by The Institute of Ismaili Studies, is to enhance general knowledge of Shiʿi Islam and promote a better understanding of its history, doctrines and practices in their historical and contemporary manifestations. Addressing all Shiʿi communities, the series also aims to engage in discussions on theoretical and methodological issues, while inspiring further research in the field.

Works published in this series will include monographs, collective volumes, editions and translations of primary texts, and bibliographical projects, bringing together some of the most significant themes in the study of Shiʿi Islam through an interdisciplinary approach, and making them accessible to a wide readership.

In memoriam Janis Esots (1966–2021)

Contents

Contributors xiii
Abbreviations xv
Preface xvii
Farhad Daftary

1. The Shiʿi Milieu of Post-Mongol Persia 1
Farhad Daftary

PART ONE: ISMAILISM IN THE CONTEXT OF SHIʿI-SUFI COALESCENCE

2. A Reconsideration of Post-Alamūt Nizārī Ismaili Literature in Iran: Prose and Poetry 17
S. J. Badakhchani

3. The Scent of the Scarlet Pimpernels: Ismaili Leaders of the 11th/17th Century 29
Shafique N. Virani

4. Ismaili Doctrines in a Late Safavid Work: Quotations from the *Risālat al-Jāmiʿa* in Quṭb al-Dīn Ashkivarī's *Maḥbūb al-Qulūb* 75
Daniel De Smet

PART TWO: SHIʿI MESSIANISM AND THE SYMBOLISM OF LETTERS

5. The Resurrection of Shah Ismāʿīl in Alevi-Bektashi Literature 95
Amelia Gallagher

6. Ḥurūfism after Faḍl Allāh's Execution: Revisiting *Ṣaḥīfat al-Istikhlāṣ* 115
Fatih Usluer

7. Nuqṭavīs, Safavids and Shiʿism in the 9th–11th/15th–17th Centuries 131
Orkhan Mir-Kasimov

PART THREE: *ḤADĪTH* AND *FIQH*

8. Majlisī the Second, Ambiguous Architect of the Shiʿi Revival in Safavid Iran 179
Mohammad Ali Amir-Moezzi

9. The Akhbārī Movement and Literary Production in Safavid Iran 195
Devin J. Stewart

10. Postclassical Legal Commentaries: The Elaboration of Tradition in the Twelver Shiʿism of Safavid Times 241
Robert Gleave

11. A View from the Periphery: The *Ijāza* as Polemic in Early 10th/16th-Century Twelver Shiʿism 271
Andrew J. Newman

PART FOUR: PHILOSOPHY, THEOLOGY AND INTELLECTUAL HISTORY

12. Mīr Dāmād's 'Wisdom of the Right Side' (*al-ḥikma al-yamāniyya*) 305
Janis Esots

13. Some Aspects of the Reception of Suhrawardī's Philosophy by Mullā Ṣadrā 323
Christian Jambet

14. A *Symphonia* of Shiʿism, Philosophy and Sufism from the Late Safavid Period: Quṭb al-Dīn Ashkivarī's Epistle on the Imaginal World (written in 1077/1667) 341
Mathieu Terrier

15. Shah Ṭahmāsp's View of Nature, as Reflected in his *Shāhnāma* 369
Sheila R. Canby

Selected Bibliography 377
Index 387

Contributors

Mohammad Ali Amir-Moezzi	EPHE-PSL-LEM/The Institute of Ismaili Studies
S. J. Badakhchani	The Institute of Ismaili Studies
Sheila R. Canby	Metropolitan Museum of Art
Farhad Daftary	The Institute of Ismaili Studies
Daniel De Smet	CNRS – PSL – LEM, UMR 8584
The late Janis Esots	The Institute of Ismaili Studies
Amelia Gallagher	Niagara University, NY
Robert Gleave	University of Exeter
Christian Jambet	EPHE
Orkhan Mir-Kasimov	The Institute of Ismaili Studies
Andrew J. Newman	The University of Edinburgh
Devin J. Stewart	Emory University
Mathieu Terrier	CNRS – PSL – LEM
Fatih Usluer	Ankara University
Shafique N. Virani	University of Toronto

Abbreviations

AEPHE-SSR	Annuaire de l'École Pratique des Hautes Études. Section des Sciences Religieuses
BJMES	British Journal of Middle Eastern Studies
BSOAS	Bulletin of the School of Oriental and African Studies
EI	*Encyclopaedia of Islam*, ed. M. Th. Houtsma et al. 1st edition, Leiden, 1913–1938; reprinted, Leiden, 1987
EI2	*Encyclopaedia of Islam*, ed. H.A.R. Gibb et al. New edition, Leiden, 1960–2004
EI3	*Encyclopaedia of Islam*, ed. Kate Fleet et al. 3rd edition, Leiden and Boston, 2007–
EIr	*Encyclopaedia Iranica*, ed. E. Yarshater. London, and New York, 1982–
EIs	*Encyclopaedia Islamica*, ed. W. Madelung and F. Daftary. London, 2008–
IS	Iranian Studies
IJMES	International Journal of Middle East Studies
JFR	Journal of Folklore Research
JIP	Journal of Islamic Philosophy
JIS	Journal of Iranian Studies
JPS	Journal of Persianate Studies
JRAS	Journal of the Royal Asiatic Society
JSAI	Jerusalem Studies in Arabic and Islam
JSIS	Journal of Shia Islamic Studies
MW	The Muslim World
RSO	Rivista degli Studi Orientali
SSR	Shii Studies Review

Preface

After almost a millennium of marginalisation in the Muslim world, Shiʿi Islam entered an era of renaissance at the end of the 9th/15th century. This renaissance had multiple facets, probably the most important of them being the spread of Shiʿi sentiments and ʿAlid loyalism through the Sufi orders, the coalescence of Shiʿism and Sufism and the resurgence of Shiʿi messianism. Another significant facet was an increased interest in lettrism (*ʿilm al-ḥurūf*). During the 9th–11th/15th–17th centuries, magnificent monuments of Shiʿi scholarship and art imbued with the spirit of regained self-confidence were produced not only in transmitted and rational sciences, but also in literature, art and architecture.

The Nizārī Ismailis began to experience their own renaissance with the commencement of the imamate of Mustanṣir bi'llāh (II) around 868/1463–1464: this date marks the beginning of the so-called Anjudān revival in Ismaili history. Around the same time, several Shiʿi messianic movements, probably not unrelated to the Ismailis, as well as a number of Sufi orders, emerged in Iran and spread to the neighbouring countries. One of these, the Safavids, was particularly successful: in 906/1500, led by the youthful Ismāʿīl I, the Safavid forces defeated the army of the Aq-Qoyunlu, and a year later, in the summer of 907/1501, took their capital Tabrīz, thus establishing the Safavid state which became the first major Shiʿi power since the fall of the Fatimids in 567/1171.

The Institute of Ismaili Studies held an international conference on 3–5 October 2018 with the aim of investigating and evaluating the complexities of the roles of different groups, movements and currents of thought in the sophisticated multifaceted process that may be described as 'the Renaissance of Shiʿi Islam in the 9th–11th/15th–17th centuries'. The conference addressed, in particular, the following issues:

- What were the common characteristics of Shiʿi messianic movements of those centuries? Why was one of them, the Safavids or Qizil-bāsh, particularly successful?
- What was the substance of the Anjudān revival of the Nizārī Ismailis?
- Which developments of *kalām* (speculative theology) and Sufism in this era can be described as the 'Shiʿitisation of Sunnism'?
- How did the intellectual movement known as the School of Isfahan emerge? What were its principal manifestations in different fields of knowledge?
- How did different Shiʿi groups interact with Sufis?
- What were the defining characteristics of Shiʿi exegesis, theology, law and gnosis during this period?

The present volume brings together a selection of the revised versions of the papers presented at this conference. In accordance with the principal facets of the phenomenon explored, the volume consists of four parts.

Farhad Daftary's keynote article outlines the principal developments in the Shiʿi milieu of post-Mongol Persia (Iran) and establishes the landmark figures of the period.

Part One discusses Ismailism in the context of the coalescence of Shiʿism and Sufism in the post-Mongol period. It consists of three contributions. Jalal Badakhchani's paper provides a brief survey of post-Alamūt Nizārī Ismaili literature in the Persian language, introducing a hitherto unknown compendium of poetry by the 11th/17th-century Iranian Ismaili poet, Darwīsh Quṭb al-Dīn. Shafique Virani's contribution represents an analysis of a long poem written by another 11th/17th-century Persian Nizārī Ismaili poet Khālū Maḥmūd ʿAlī who flourished during the imamate of Nūr al-Dahr ʿAlī (d. 1082/1671). In his poem, Khālū Maḥmūd ʿAlī identifies numerous contemporary Ismaili leaders, listing their names and the areas of their activity (in Iran, Central Asia and the Indian subcontinent), and distinguishing them by their ranks (*pīr*, *dāʿī* and *muʿallim*). The poem also sheds some light on the Nizārī Ismaili doctrine of the time. By establishing and cataloguing the quotations from the *Rasāʾil Ikhwān al-Ṣafāʾ*, and from the *Risālat al-Jāmiʿa*, in Quṭb al-Dīn Ashkivarī's *Maḥbūb al-qulūb*, Daniel De Smet reflects on the presence of Ismaili doctrines in the latter work and its impact on late Safavid thought. De Smet argues that the manner in which Ashkivarī introduces the selected quotations shows that he had a clear understanding of their doctrinal implications. He concludes that the investigation of the influence of the *Jāmiʿa*, due to its explicit Ismaili character, is the best way to evaluate the importance of Ismaili traces in the works of Safavid philosophers.

Part Two, which deals with Shiʿi messianism and lettrism, consists of three papers. Amelia Gallagher examines the 'resurrection' of Shah Ismāʿīl in Alevi-Bektashi literature through the oral transmission of the corpus of his poetry, under the pen-name Khaṭāʾī, that continued to expand for several centuries after his death, becoming a major channel for the spread of Shiʿi attitudes and motifs in the Ottoman empire. The author demonstrates why and how this process was crucial for the development of esoteric Shiʿi Islam. Fatih Usluer presents an account of the fate of the Ḥurūfiyya after the execution of their founder Faḍl Allāh Astarābādī in 796/1394, based on a detailed analysis of a letter written by Amīr Ghiyāth al-Dīn in Jumāda I 836/ January 1433, a few months after he escaped from the prison of Shākhrukh. Orkhan Mir-Kasimov revisits Nuqṭavī-Safavid relations during the reign of Shah ʿAbbās I (r. 996–1038/1588–1629). He argues that the Nuqṭavī group in Qazvīn that attracted the attention of Shah ʿAbbās was part of a learned Nuqṭavī tradition which was closely aligned with the original texts of Maḥmūd Pasīkhānī. The author proposes a new understanding of the role of Nuqṭavī ideas in the evolution of Shah ʿAbbās's religious and political thinking.

Part Three, which consists of four papers, discusses the manifestations of the Shiʿi renaissance in the fields of *ḥadīth* and *fiqh*. Mohammad Ali Amir-Moezzi examines the role of Muḥammad Bāqir Majlisī (d. 1110/1699), the compiler of the monumental collection of Shiʿi *ḥadīth*, *Biḥār al-anwār*, in the formation of the religious policy of the state in Safavid Iran. The author points out that some of Majlisī's actions contradicted certain teachings found in the sayings attributed to the Ithnā ʿasharī imams, while he himself posed as the reviver of these teachings. Amir-Moezzi wonders whether Majlisī's actions should be interpreted as a voluntarily ambiguous attitude, or as an attempt to maintain the balance between safeguarding the Tradition and establishing Twelver Shiʿism as the state religion. Building on a number of disparate studies dealing with Akhbārī influence in particular genres, Devin J. Stewart investigates the role that the Akhbārīs played in shaping Safavid literary production. The author particularly focuses on the intersection of the production of learned works during the Safavid period and the contours and effects of the Akhbārī movement. Robert Gleave presents a study on the post-classical legal literature of Twelver Shiʿism. Drawing on a history of scholarship, he establishes the ways in which the legal works he examines are distinctively Twelver Shiʿi and demonstrates that, in many ways, they display characteristics which are not specifically 'legal', whereas in other ways they are deeply involved in expounding legal principles. Gleave argues that the post-classical legal tradition of the Ithnā ʿasharī Shiʿis reveals a dynamic of commentary which can be identified across scholarly disciplines. In this sense, it is both distinctive and conventional in the Islamic post-classical scholarly milieu. Andrew J. Newman's paper examines Ibrāhīm b. Sulaymān al-Qaṭīfī's (d. after 945/1539) *ijāzāt* preserved in Muḥammad Bāqir al-Majlisī's *Biḥār al-anwār* in order to establish how their style and substance contribute to the understanding of al-Qaṭīfī's debate with ʿAlī al-Karakī (d. 940/1534) and to the discussions on Twelver Shiʿi *ijāzāt* in general. The author concludes that al-Qaṭīfī's discourse in these *ijāzāt* might be viewed as both jurisprudential and personal, whereas al-Qaṭīfī himself cannot be described as either Uṣūlī or Akhbārī. Newman points to al-Qaṭīfī's deep anxiety about the developments in Twelver Shiʿism after it became the state religion of Safavid Iran.

Part Four, consisting of four papers, focuses on philosophy, theology and intellectual history. The late Janis Esots's paper presents a concise account of Mīr Dāmād's 'Wisdom of the Right Side' (*al-ḥikma al-yamāniyya*). First he discusses Mīr Dāmād's metaphysics, in particular, the pivotal concepts of perpetuity and perpetual inception, and then briefly examines the impact of the philosopher's metaphysical doctrine on his physics, psychology and eschatology. Christian Jambet looks at some aspects of Mullā Ṣadrā's reception of Suhrawardī's philosophy. Building his argument on a number of passages in Ṣadrā's commentary on Suhrawardī's *Ḥikmat al-ishrāq*, Jambet concludes that Mullā Ṣadrā's reaction to *ishrāqī* doctrine may be described as an exegesis which sets Suhrawardī's theses in a new metaphysical perspective. To demonstrate this, Jambet discusses such issues as

Ṣadrā's reinterpretation of the human caliphate of God, the dispute between philosophy and religious dogma regarding the eternity of the world and the definition of the human soul (as the rational soul that descends to the sensible world). Sheila Canby discusses Shah Ṭahmāsp's (r. 930–984/1524–1576) view of nature as reflected in his *Shāhnāma*, a magnificent manuscript consisting of 759 folios and 258 illustrations, which he commissioned soon after his accession to the throne. After investigating how the illustrations reflect the actual environment of Iran in the 10th/16th century and the Safavid attitude to the land and its stewardship, Canby attempts to establish to what extent the paintings reflect the Safavids' Shiʿi faith. Mathieu Terrier introduces Quṭb al-Dīn Ashkivarī's (d. between 1088 and 1095/1677 and 1684) treatise *Fānūs al-khayāl fī irā'at ʿālam al-mithāl* ('The Lantern of Imagination concerning the Presentation of the World of Image'), written in 1077/1667. Terrier's paper, based on the study of the sole extant manuscript of the treatise (MS 1615, Malek Library, Tehran), is a preliminary to its critical edition. It gives a useful overview of the work, focusing first on the concept of imaginal world, then on the convergence between Shiʿism, Sufism and philosophy.

Our esteemed colleague Janis Esots died unexpectedly in June 2021, shortly after he had finished assembling the first draft of the papers published in this volume. He had been with The Institute of Ismaili Studies for some eight years and was embarking on what would undoubtedly have been an important series of publications. He was held in high respect throughout the field of Islamic studies and will be greatly missed by all who knew him and worked with him, not least his friends and fellow academics at the Institute. This volume is dedicated to his memory.

Farhad Daftary

1

The Shiʿi Milieu of Post-Mongol Persia

Farhad Daftary

The Mongol invasions of southwestern Asia changed the political map of Persia and other parts of that region. After Chingiz Khan's death in 624/1227, the Mongols made new efforts, under Chingiz's son and first successor, Ögedei, to conquer all Persia, a task completed in the reign of the Great Khan Möngke (r. 649–658/1251–1260). By 654/1256, Möngke's brother Hülegü had destroyed the Nizārī Ismaili state of Persia before he entered Baghdad in 656/1258 and murdered the last Abbasid caliph, al-Mustaʿṣim (r. 640–656/1242–1258). By then, the Mongols had indeed completed their conquest of southwestern Asia.

It was during the same eventful period in Islamic history that Khwāja Naṣīr al-Dīn al-Ṭūsī (597–672/1201–1274), one of the most eminent Shiʿi scholars of all time, lived amongst and benefited from the patronage of the Nizārī Ismaili Shiʿis of Persia in their fortress communities, before attaching himself to the court of the Mongol Īlkhānid rulers of Persia and Iraq, a dynasty (654–754/1256–1353) founded by Hülegü himself. Al-Ṭūsī played a significant role in the political events of his time, under both the Ismailis and the Mongols. Born into a Twelver Shiʿi family, it was around 624/1227 that al-Ṭūsī entered the Ismaili fortresses of Persia, first in Quhistān, southern Khurāsān, and subsequently at Alamūt, the central headquarters of the Nizārī Ismaili state. During that period, al-Ṭūsī also converted to Ismailism, as related in his spiritual autobiography,[1] and made important contributions to Ismaili thought.

[1] Naṣīr al-Dīn al-Ṭūsī, *Sayr wa sulūk*, ed. and tr. S. J. Badakhchani as *Contemplation and Action: The Spiritual Autobiography of a Muslim Scholar* (London, 1998). See also Naṣīr al-Dīn al-Ṭūsī, *Rawḍa-yi taslīm*, ed. and tr. S. J. Badakhchani as *Paradise of Submission: A Medieval Treatise on Ismaili Thought* (London, 2005), which remains our major primary source on the Ismaili teachings of the Alamūt period.

On the surrender of the fortress of Alamūt, in northern Persia, to the Mongols in 654/1256, al-Ṭūsī became a trusted adviser to Hülegü and accompanied the Mongol conqueror to Baghdad and witnessed the demise of the Abbasid caliphate. Subsequently, Hülegü built a great observatory for al-Ṭūsī at Marāgha, Ādharbāyjān. Al-Ṭūsī, who had by then reverted back to Twelver Shiʿism,[2] also served Hülegü's son and successor Abaqa (r. 663–681/1265–1282) in the Īlkhānid dynasty, while engaged in his theological, philosophical and scientific enquiries. He now produced major works on Imāmī Shiʿi theological principles, notably the *Qawāʿid al-ʿaqāʾid* and the *Tajrīd al-ʿaqāʾid*, which became the most widely used *kalām* text in Persia and the eastern lands. Al-Ṭūsī was also the first Twelver scholar to have been at once a theologian and a philosopher, having been particularly influenced by Ibn Sīnā's (d. 428/1037) philosophy. This represented a tradition of philosophical theology elaborated earlier in Fatimid times by a number of Iranian *dāʿīs*, and more fully developed later in Persia under the Safavids.

Be that as it may, al-Ṭūsī may be considered to have initiated a new phase in the intellectual history of Twelver Shiʿism. In fact, al-Ṭūsī and his disciple Ibn Muṭahhar al-Ḥillī represented the last school of original thought in Twelver *kalām* theology. Subsequently, Twelver Shiʿi scholars produced mainly works of the genre of commentary (*sharḥ*) on, or restatements of, the earlier treatises. Meanwhile, close relations were also developing between Twelver theology and the Sufism of Ibn al-ʿArabī (d. 638/1240), while the Nizārī Ismailis of Persia and Central Asia were beginning to develop their own relationships with Sufism (*taṣawwuf*).

Similarly to Naṣīr al-Dīn al-Ṭūsī, al-Ḥasan b. Yūsuf Ibn Muṭahhar al-Ḥillī (d. 726/1325) gained eminence at the court of the Īlkhānid rulers. It was, in fact, under his influence that Öljeitü (r. 703–716/1304–1316), better known in the Islamic sources as Muḥammad Khudābanda, converted to Twelver Shiʿism in 709/1310 and minted coins to that effect. Ibn Muṭahhar al-Ḥillī, called ʿAllāma or the 'most learned one',

---

[2] On al-Ṭūsī's search for different patrons and his changing religious affiliations, see H. Dabashi, 'The Philosopher/Vizier: Khwāja Naṣīr al-Dīn al-Ṭūsī and the Ismaʿilis', in F. Daftary, ed., *Mediaeval Ismaʿili History and Thought* (Cambridge, 1996), pp. 231–245.

and his uncle Jaʿfar b. al-Ḥasan al-Ḥillī (d. 676/1277), known as al-Muḥaqqiq al-Ḥillī or al-Muḥaqqiq al-Awwal, were two major scholars from Ḥilla, in Iraq, which had superseded Qum and Baghdad as the stronghold of Twelver Shiʿi learning in the aftermath of the Mongol conquests. These scholars had significant impacts on the direction of Imāmī Shiʿi law that was to prevail. In particular, ʿAllāma al-Ḥillī, the author of numerous legal treatises, had a lasting influence on the foundations of Twelver Shiʿi jurisprudence. He argued against the reliability of *ḥadīth* and reorganised jurisprudence so as to make reason (*ʿaql*) its central focus. He also introduced new principles of legal methodology adapted from Sunni practices. Building on the work of his uncle, ʿAllāma al-Ḥillī provided a theoretical foundation for *ijtihād*, the principle of legal ruling by the jurist (*faqīh*) through reasoning (*ʿaql*). He argued that the jurist could arrive at valid judgements in religious law using reason and the principles of jurisprudence (*uṣūl al-fiqh*).[3]

Al-Ḥillī's acceptance of *ijtihād*, exercised by jurists known as *mujtahids*, represents a crucial step towards the enhancement of the juristic authority of the *ʿulamāʾ* in Twelver Shiʿism in the absence of a manifest imam, even though the *mujtahids*, in contrast to imams, are fallible. In the absence of the infallible imams, any ruling by a qualified *mujtahid* is nevertheless binding. These ideas, propounded by ʿAllāma al-Ḥillī, also provided the antecedents of the concept of *taqlīd*, or emulation, by those who are not qualified to exercise *ijtihād*, accounting for the bulk of the Twelver community. The emulators, or *muqallids*, seek the opinions of the *mujtahids* and are expected to abide by their judgements. It should be noted that *ijtihād* also gained importance within the Zaydī Shiʿi communities, even earlier than its adoption by the Twelvers, but was rejected by the Ismailis.

Īlkhānid rule effectively ended with Abū Saʿīd (r. 717–736/1317–1335), the last great member of that Mongol dynasty. Subsequently, until the advent of the Safavids, Persia became increasingly fragmented,

[3] ʿAllāma Jamāl al-Dīn al-Ḥasan b. al-Muṭahhar al-Ḥillī, *Mabādiʾ al-wuṣūl ilā ʿilm al-uṣūl*, ed. ʿA. M. ʿAlī (Najaf, 1390/1970), especially pp. 240–252. See also S. Schmidtke, *The Theology of ʿAllāma al-Ḥillī (d. 726/1325)* (Berlin, 1991) and Andrew J. Newman, *Twelver Shiism: Unity and Diversity in the Life of Islam, 632 to 1722* (Edinburgh, 2013), pp. 122–137.

with the exception of certain periods during the reign of Tīmūr (d. 807/1405), and that of his son Shāhrukh (r. 807–850/1405–1447). During this turbulent and confusing period in Persian history, in the absence of any strong central authority, different parts of the country were held by various local dynasties, including the minor Īlkhānids, the later Tīmūrids, the Jalāyirids, the Qara-Qoyunlu and the Aq-Qoyunlu, based on federations of Turkoman tribes. The post-Mongol political fragmentation of Persia provided more favourable conditions for the activities of various religio-political movements, most of which were now essentially Shiʿi or influenced by Shiʿi ideas. These conditions were indeed conducive to the rising tide of Shiʿism in post-Mongol Persia. Under the circumstances, the Nizārī Ismailis and certain Shiʿi-related movements with millenarian aspirations, such as those of the Ḥurūfīs, the Nuqṭavīs, the Sarbadārs and the Mushaʿshaʿ, as well as a number of Sufi *ṭarīqa*s or orders, now found a respite in Persia during the 8th/14th and 9th/15th centuries. As a result, these communities, movements or orders could actively organise themselves, though they were still occasionally persecuted by different local rulers who detected messages of opposition in their religio-political campaigns and agendas.

In the meantime, Shiʿi tendencies had been spreading in Persia and Central Asia since the 7th/13th century, creating a more favourable religious milieu in many predominantly Sunni regions for the activities of the Shiʿi communities (both Twelvers and Ismailis) as well as a number of Shiʿi-related extremist movements. These movements, as noted, normally entertained millenarian or Mahdist aspirations for the deliverance of the oppressed and the economically underprivileged, who rallied in large numbers, especially after Tīmūr's death in 807/1405, to lend support to their leaders, who often hailed from Shiʿi-Sufi backgrounds.

In this context, particular reference should be made to the Ḥurūfīs founded by the Shiʿi-Sufi Faḍl Allāh Astarābādī (d. 796/1394), whose doctrines were later adopted by the Bektashi dervishes of Anatolia, and the Nuqṭavīs who split off from the Ḥurūfīs under the initial leadership of Maḥmūd-i Pasīkhānī (d. 831/1427). From early on, Ḥurūfī teachings spread to Anatolia due to the missionary activities of ʿAlī al-Aʿlā' (d. 822/1419), one of Faḍl Allāh's original disciples and the author of numerous Ḥurūfī texts. In fact, Anatolia soon became the main stronghold of Ḥurūfism, and the Ḥurūfī doctrines were adopted by the Bektashi and several other Sufi orders. Subsequently, Ḥurūfism disappeared from Persia, but its teachings have continued to be upheld by the Bektashi dervishes of Turkey, who have also preserved the early literature of the community.

The Nuqṭavī movement became very popular in Persia, and by the early Safavid times it had numerous followers in the Caspian regions of northern Persia and in the Persian cities of Qazvīn, Kāshān, Iṣfahān and Shīrāz. The Nuqṭavīs were influenced by the Nizārī Ismaili doctrines of the Alamūt period. At least some eminent Nuqṭavīs may even have been crypto-Ismailis. The Nuqṭavīs disbanded completely in Persia under Safavid persecutions, while many of them, including a number of poets, sought refuge in India. By contrast to Ḥurūfism, which emphasised the secret of the letters of the alphabet (*ḥurūf*), Maḥmūd-i Pasīkhānī elaborated a system based on points (singular, *nuqṭa*).[4]

There was also the Twelver-related Mushaʿshaʿ of Khūzistān, in southwestern Persia, founded by Ibn Falāḥ (d. ca. 866/1461), who claimed Mahdism. The Mushaʿshaʿ ruled over parts of Iraq, and under their persecution policies Ḥilla lost its prominence as a centre of Twelver Shiʿi learning to Jabal ʿĀmil in Lebanon.

Instead of propagating any particular form of Shiʿism, a new syncretic type of popular Shiʿism was now arising in post-Mongol Persia, Central Asia and Anatolia. Expressed largely through Sufi orders, this popular Shiʿism ultimately culminated in early Safavid Shiʿism. Marshall Hodgson (1922–1968) designated this popular Shiʿi phenomenon as '*ṭarīqa* Shiʿism', as it was transmitted mainly through a number of Sufi orders.[5] The Sufi orders in question, most of which

[4] On the Ḥurūfīs and the Nuqṭavīs, see Ṣādiq Kiyā, *Nuqṭawiyān yā Pasīkhāniyān* (Tehran, 1320 Sh./1941); A. Amanat, 'The Nuqṭawī Movement of Maḥmūd Pisīkhānī and his Persian Cycle of Mystical-Materialism', in F. Daftary, ed., *Mediaeval Ismaʿili History*, pp. 281–297; K. Babayan, *Mystics, Monarchs and Messiahs: Cultural Landscapes of Early Modern Iran* (Cambridge, MA, 2002), pp. 57–108; S. Bashir, *Fazlallah Astarabadi and the Hurufis* (Oxford, 2005) and O. Mir-Kasimov, *Words of Power: Ḥurūfī Teachings Between Sufism and Shiʿism in Medieval Islam* (London, 2015).

[5] M. G. S. Hodgson, *The Venture of Islam: Conscience and History in a World Civilization* (Chicago, 1974), vol. 2, pp. 493 ff.

were formed in post-Mongol Persia, remained outwardly Sunni for quite some time, following one of the Sunni schools of law (*madhhab*), usually the Shāfiʿī school, while being particularly devoted to ʿAlī b. Abī Ṭālib and the Prophet Muhammad's family (*ahl al-bayt*). ʿAlī was in fact included at the head of their *silsila*s or chains of spiritual masters.

Among the Sufi orders that played a leading role in spreading this eclectic type of popular Shiʿism mention may be made of the Nūrbakhshiyya and the Niʿmat Allāhiyya orders. Both of these orders, as well as the most effective, the Ṣafaviyya, eventually became fully Shiʿi. Be that as it may, in this milieu of religious eclectism, ʿAlid loyalism soon became more widespread, beyond the Sufi orders, and Shiʿi elements began to be superficially imposed on Sunni Islam. By the 9th/15th century, the general outlook of predominantly Sunni Persia and its adjacent regions was increasingly moulded by this type of Sufi-disseminated Shiʿi-Sunni syncretism. Claude Cahen (1909–1991) has referred to this curious process as the 'Shiʿitisation of Sunnism', as opposed to the conscious propagation of Shiʿism of any particular form, Twelver or otherwise.[6] It was through such a complex process that Persia was gradually prepared for the official adoption of Shiʿism under the Safavids.

Amongst the Sufi orders that contributed to the 'Shiʿitisation' of Persia, the most direct role was played by the Ṣafavī *ṭarīqa*, because of the unique position it occupied in terms of the political ambitions of its masters.[7] The political and military successes of this order

---

[6] Claude Cahen, 'Le problème du Shîʿisme dans l'Asie Mineure turque préottomane', in T. Fahd, ed., *Le Shîʿisme Imâmite. Colloque de Strasbourg* (Paris, 1970), pp. 118 ff. See also M. Molé, 'Les Kubrawiya entre Sunnisme et Shiisme aux huitième et neuvième siècles de l'hégire', *Revue d'Études Islamiques*, 29 (1961), pp. 61–142; S. Amir Arjomand, *The Shadow of God and the Hidden Imam* (Chicago, 1984), pp. 66–84; B. Scarcia Amoretti, 'Religion in the Timurid and Safavid Periods', in *The Cambridge History of Iran*, Volume 6, *The Timurid and Safavid Periods*, ed. P. Jackson and L. Lockhart (Cambridge, 1986), pp. 610–634 and H. Halm, *Shiism*, tr. J. Watson (Edinburgh, 1991), pp. 71–83.

[7] On the Ṣafavī Sufi order and the background to the establishment of Safavid rule in Persia, see Michel M. Mazzaoui, *Origins of the Ṣafawids: Šīʿism, Ṣūfism, and the Ġulāt* (Wiesbaden, 1972), pp. 41–63, 71–82; R. Savory, *Iran under the Ṣafavids* (Cambridge, 1980), pp. 1–26; H. R. Roemer, 'The Safavid Period', in *The Cambridge History of Iran*, Volume 6, *The Timurid and Safavid Periods*, ed. P. Jackson and L. Lockhart (Cambridge, 1986) pp. 189–212 and Babayan, *Mystics*, pp. 3–7, 121–196.

eventually culminated in the accession of the Ṣafavī master (*shaykh*) to the throne of Persia. The Ṣafavī order was founded by Shaykh Ṣafī al-Dīn (d. 735/1334), an eminent Sufi master of the Īlkhānid period and a Sunni Muslim of the Shāfiʿī *madhhab*. It was after the establishment of the Safavid state that the dynasty claimed an ʿAlid genealogy, tracing Shaykh Ṣafī's ancestry to Mūsā al-Kāẓim (d. 183/799), the seventh imam of the Twelver Shiʿis.

The Ṣafavī order, initially centred at Ardabīl, spread rapidly throughout Ādharbāyjān, eastern Anatolia, Syria and Khurāsān. Most significantly, the order acquired a deep influence over several Turkoman tribes in Ādharbāyjān and adjacent regions. With Shaykh Ṣafī's fourth successor, Junayd, the Ṣafavī order was transformed into a militant revolutionary movement. The order's *murīd*s, or ordinary members, mainly from amongst the Turkomans, were gradually organised into a dedicated fighting force of Sufi soldiers. Junayd was also the first *shaykh* of the order to display Shiʿi sentiments combined with radical religious notions of the type held by the Shiʿi *ghulāt*. Shaykh Junayd was killed in 864/1460 in a battle against Caucasian Christians around Ādharbāyjān. However, his policies and ambitions were retained by his son and successor, Shaykh Ḥaydar, who also lost his life in 893/1488 in one of the numerous battles he fought. Shaykh Ḥaydar was responsible for instructing his followers to adopt the scarlet headgear with twelve gores, commemorating the Twelve imams of the Twelver Shiʿis, which led to their being designated by the Turkish epithet, Qizil-bāsh (Red-head). Sulṭān ʿAlī, Ḥaydar's son and successor, also fell in battle in 898/1493.

By then, the Ṣafavī order had acquired a strong military organisation, supported by many local adherents and powerful Turkoman tribes, which constituted the backbone of the Qizil-bāsh Sufi-soldiers. With these assets, Sulṭān ʿAlī's youthful brother and successor, Ismāʿīl, readily succeeded in seizing Ādharbāyjān from the Aq-Qoyunlu dynasty of Turkoman rulers. Thereupon, Ismāʿīl entered Tabrīz, the capital of the deposed dynasty, in 907/1501 and proclaimed himself Shah Ismāʿīl, the first member of the new Safavid dynasty, which was to last until 1135/1722.

The popular and eclectic Shiʿism of the Qizil-bāsh Turkomans manifested itself more clearly under Shah Ismāʿīl (r. 907–930/1501–1524), who portrayed himself to his Qizil-bāsh followers as the representative of the hidden Twelfth imam-Mahdi of the Twelvers, or even as the expected Mahdi himself, also claiming divinity. This type of Shiʿi extremism, characterised by Mahdist or chiliastic expectations, and even the deification of the Ṣafavī order's masters, had very little in common with the 'orthodox' doctrines of Twelver Shiʿism. However, this extremist, eclectic type of Shiʿism was gradually disciplined and brought into conformity with the tenets of Twelver Shiʿism. Be that as it may, Shah Ismāʿīl, who brought all of Persia under his control, inaugurated a new era for Shiʿism and the activities of the various Shiʿi movements in Persia.

It was under such circumstances that close relations had developed between Twelver Shiʿism and Sufism, as well as between Nizārī Ismaili Shiʿism and Sufism in Persia. Naṣīr al-Dīn al-Ṭūsī had already composed a treatise entitled *Awṣāf al-ashrāf* on the mystical path or *ṭarīqa*. However, one of the earliest Twelver-Sufi associations is reflected in the works of Sayyid Ḥaydar Āmulī, the eminent theologian, theosopher and gnostic (*ʿārif*) who died not long after 787/1385.[8] He hailed from Āmul in the Caspian region and served for some time as vizier to the local Bāwandid rulers there, before emigrating to Baghdad where he studied under ʿAllāma al-Ḥillī's son. Strongly influenced by the Sufi teachings of Ibn al-ʿArabī (d. 638/1240), Sayyid Ḥaydar combined the latter's mystical ideas with his own Shiʿi theology into an original synthesis in his *Jāmiʿ al-asrār* and other works. More than anyone else before him, he emphasised the common grounds between Shiʿism and Sufism and prepared the ground also for the doctrines held by many of the Persian Sufi orders.

---

[8] On Ḥaydar Āmulī, and relations between Shiʿism and Sufism in general, see H. Corbin, *En Islam Iranien. Aspects spirituels et philosophiques* (Paris, 1971–1972), vol. 1, pp. 74–85, and vol. 3, pp. 149–213; Kāmil M. al-Shaybī, *Tashayyuʿ va taṣawwuf*, tr. ʿAlī R. Dh. Qaraguzlū (Tehran, 1359 Sh./1980), pp. 64–71, 112–125; S. H. Nasr, 'Le Shîʿisme et le Soufisme', in Fahd, ed., *Le Shîʿisme Imâmite*, pp. 215–233; idem, *Ideals and Realities of Islam* (New rev. ed., Cambridge, 2001), pp. 115–140 and J. van Ess, 'Ḥaydar-i Āmulī', *EI2*, vol. 12, Supplement, pp. 363–365. See also M. Terrier, 'The Defence of Sufism among Twelver Shiʿi Scholars of Early Modern and Modern Times: Topics and Arguments', in D. Hermann and M. Terrier, ed., *Shiʿi Islam and Sufism: Classical Views and Modern Perspectives* (London, 2020), pp. 27–63.

According to Sayyid Ḥaydar Āmulī, a Muslim who combines *sharīʿa* with *ḥaqīqa* and *ṭarīqa*, the spiritual path followed by the Sufis, is not only a believer but a believer put to the test (*al-muʾmin al-mumtaḥan*). Such a gnostic Muslim, at once a Sufi and a true Shiʿi, would preserve a balance between the *ẓāhir* and the *bāṭin*, equally avoiding the literalist interpretations of Islam undertaken by the jurists (*fuqahāʾ*) as well as the antinomian (*ibāḥī*) tendencies of the radical groups such as the Shiʿi *ghulāt*.[9]

The efforts at integrating Sufism and Twelver Shiʿism, initiated by Ḥaydar Āmulī, were continued by others, notably the Twelver scholar Muḥammad b. ʿAlī al-Aḥsāʾī (d. after 904/1499), better known as Ibn Abī Jumhūr. This scholar hailed from al-Aḥsāʾ in Bahrain and later taught in Najaf and Mashhad in Persia. Thus, in his *Kitāb al-mujlī*, anticipating the contributions of the so-called 'School of Iṣfahān', Ibn Abī Jumhūr al-Aḥsāʾī offers a synthesis of Twelver *kalām* theology, Avicennan Peripatetic (*mashāʾī*) philosophy, the illuminationist (*ishrāqī*) thought of Shihāb al-Dīn Suhrawardī (d. 587/1191) and the gnostic-mystical teachings of the school of Ibn al-ʿArabī.[10]

Indeed, aspects of interactions between Twelver Shiʿism and gnosis (*ʿirfān*), in combination with different philosophical/theosophical traditions, later culminated in the works of Mīr Dāmād (d. 1040/1630), Mullā Ṣadrā (d. 1050/1640), and other Shiʿi gnostic theosophers belonging to the 'School of Iṣfahān'. Members of this school, who produced a metaphysical synthesis of a variety of philosophical, theological and gnostic traditions within a Shiʿi perspective, elaborated

---

[9] See, for instance, Sayyid Ḥaydar Āmulī, *Jāmiʿ al-asrār wa manbaʿ al-anwār*, ed. H. Corbin and O. Yahya, in their collection of Āmulī's works entitled *La philosophie shiʿite* (Tehran and Paris, 1969), pp. 2–617, at pp. 47, 116–117, 216–217, 220–222, 238, 388, 611–615 and Āmulī's *Asrār al-sharīʿa wa anwār al-ḥaqīqa*, ed. M. Khwājawī (Tehran, 1360 Sh./1982), pp. 5 ff., 23 ff.

[10] Ibn Abī Jumhūr al-Aḥsāʾī, *Mujlī mirʾat al-munjī fiʾl-kalām waʾl-ḥikmatayn waʾl-taṣawwuf*, ed. R. Y. Fārmad (Beirut, 2013). See also W. Madelung, 'Ibn Abî Ĝumhûr al-Aḥsâʾî's Synthesis of *kalām*, Philosophy and Sufism', in *La signification du Bas Moyen Age dans l'histoire et la culture du monde Musulman: Actes du 8ème Congrès de l'Union Européenne des Arabisants et Islamisants (Aix-en-Provence, 1976)* (Aix-en-Provence, 1978), pp. 147–156; reprinted in his *Religious Schools and Sects in Medieval Islam* (London, 1985), article XIII.

an original intellectual tradition of 'philosophical Shiʿism' designated as *al-ḥikma al-ilāhiyya* (Persian, *ḥikmat-i ilāhī*), generally translated as divine wisdom or theosophy.[11] It may be noted here that with the persecution of the Sufi orders in early Safavid times, the advocates of the mystical experience in Islam adopted the term *ʿirfān* (gnosis) in preference to *taṣawwuf* (Sufism).

In the meantime, the Nizārī Ismailis of Persia and Central Asia had developed their own coalescence with Sufism in post-Mongol times. In the aftermath of the demise of their state at the hands of the Mongols in 654/1256, the Nizārī Ismailis espoused a diversity of religious and literary traditions in different languages. Research difficulties here stem from the scarcity of primary sources as well as the widespread practice of *taqiyya* adopted by the Nizārīs during the early post-Mongol times in order to safeguard themselves against rampant persecution. It was during the same obscure period that Persian Nizārī Ismailis disguised themselves under the cover of Sufism, without establishing formal affiliations with any of the Sufi *ṭarīqa*s then spreading across Persia and Central Asia. This phenomenon soon gained wide currency among the Nizārī Ismailis of Central Asia and Sind as well. By the middle of the 9th/15th century, Ismaili-Sufi relations had indeed become well established in the Iranian world.

The origins and early development of the complex association between Persian Ismailism and Sufism remain rather obscure in the absence of adequate sources and studies. Be that as it may, better understanding of the history of Sufism in Persia and our access to post-Alamūt Ismaili literature in modern times have greatly enhanced our knowledge of the relations between Sufism and Persian Ismailism, the two independent esoteric traditions in Islam with common

---

[11] On the 'School of Iṣfahān', see H. Corbin, *Histoire de la philosophie Islamique* (Paris, 1986), pp. 462–475; English tr., *History of Islamic Philosophy*, tr. L. Sherrard (London, 1993), pp. 338–348; S. H. Nasr, 'The School of Iṣpahān', in M. M. Sharif, ed., *A History of Muslim Philosophy* (Wiesbaden, 1963–1966), vol. 2, pp. 904–932 and H. Dabashi, 'Mīr Dāmād and the Founding of the "School of Iṣfahān"', in S. H. Nasr and O. Leaman, ed., *History of Islamic Philosophy* (London, 2001), vol. 1, pp. 597–634. See also *Patterns of Wisdom in Safavid Iran: The Philosophical School of Isfahan and the Gnostic of Shiraz* (London, 2021) by the late Janis Esots for the most recent assessment of this important subject.

doctrinal grounds. It has now become rather clear that after the fall of Alamūt, Nizārī Ismailism became increasingly infused in Persia with Sufi teachings and terminology. At the same time, the Sufis themselves, who relied on *bāṭinī taʾwīl* or esoteric exegesis like the Ismailis, began to use ideas which were more widely ascribed to the Ismailis. As part of this coalescence, the Nizārī Ismailis began to adopt Sufi ways of life even externally. Thus, the post-Alamūt Nizārī imams, starting with Shams al-Dīn Muḥammad (d. ca. 710/1310), lived clandestinely for the most part as Sufi *pīr*s, while their followers adopted the typically Sufi designation of *murīd* or disciple.[12]

It is due to the close relationships between Persian Ismailism and Sufism that it is often difficult to ascertain whether a certain post-Alamūt Persian treatise was written by a Nizārī author influenced by Sufism, or whether it was written in Sufi circles exposed to Ismaili teachings. As an instance of Ismaili-Sufi interactions, mention may be made of the celebrated Sufi treatise entitled *Gulshan-i rāz* (The Rose-Garden of Mystery) and a later esoteric commentary on it by a Nizārī author. This versified work was composed by Maḥmūd-i Shabistarī (d. after 740/1339), a Sufi *shaykh* from Ādharbāyjān. He was a contemporary of Nizārī Quhistānī (d. 720/1320), probably the first Nizārī Ismaili to express his religious ideas in the guise of Sufi expressions and poetry,[13] a model adopted by many later Nizārī authors of Persia, Afghanistan and Central Asia. Nizārī Quhistānī was the first post-Alamūt Nizārī Ismaili to use Sufi terminology such as *khānaqāh*, *darvīsh* (dervish), *qalandar* (wandering dervish) as well as *pīr* and *murshid*, terms used by Sufis in reference to their spiritual

[12] F. Daftary, 'Ismāʿīlī-Sufi Relations in Early Post-Alamūt and Safavid Persia', in L. Lewisohn and D. Morgan, ed., *The Heritage of Sufism*: Volume III, *Late Classical Persianate Sufism (1501–1750)* (Oxford, 1999), pp. 275–289; reprinted in his *Ismailis in Medieval Muslim Societies* (London, 2005), pp. 183–203; idem, 'Khayrkhwāh-i Harātī and the Post-Mongol Revival in Nizārī Ismaili Literary Activities in Persia', in M. A. Amir-Moezzi, ed., *Raison et quête de la sagesse. Hommage à Christian Jambet* (Turnhout, 2020), pp. 215–227 and H. Landolt, "Aṭṭār, Sufism and Ismailism', in L. Lewisohn and C. Shackle, ed., *ʿAṭṭār and the Persian Sufi Tradition: The Art of Spiritual Flight* (London, 2006), pp. 3–27.

[13] Nadia Eboo Jamal, *Surviving the Mongols: Nizārī Quhistānī and the Continuity of Ismaili Tradition in Persia* (London, 2002), especially pp. 57–146.

guide.[14] Maḥmūd-i Shabistarī produced his *Gulshan-i rāz*, in 717/1317, in reply to a number of questions put to him on Sufi teachings by a Sufi master in Herat. This treatise gained much popularity in Sufi circles, and numerous commentaries have been written on it. However, the Nizārī Ismailis of Persia and Central Asia consider this work part of their own literary heritage and, as such, it was commented upon in Persian by at least one Nizārī author. This anonymous Ismaili commentary consists of esoteric interpretations (*ta'wīlāt*) of selected verses of the *Gulshan-i rāz*.[15]

As a result of their close relationship with Sufism in post-Alamūt times, the Nizārī Ismailis have regarded some of the most prominent mystic poets of Persia as their co-religionists, and selections of their works have been preserved by the Persian-speaking Nizārī communities of Central Asia, Afghanistan and Persia. Among these appropriated personalities, mention may be made of Sanā'ī (d. ca. 535/1140), Farīd al-Dīn ʿAṭṭār (d. ca. 627/1230), and Jalāl al-Dīn Rūmī (d. 672/1273).[16] The Nizārīs of Badakhshān, now divided between Afghanistan and Tajikistan, also regard ʿAzīz al-Dīn Nasafī as a co-religionist. This celebrated Central Asian Sufi master and author emigrated to Persia and died there around 661/1262. His Sufi treatise entitled *Zubdat al-ḥaqā'iq* has been preserved in Badakhshān as an Ismaili work.[17] The

---

14 Nizārī Quhistānī, *Dīwān*, ed. M. Muṣaffā (Tehran, 1371–1373 Sh./1992–1994), vol. 1, pp. 583–584, 617, 632–633, 634–635, 642–643, 660, 674–675, 724–725, 753–754, 795, 860, 866, 880, 881, 966–968, 994–995, 1359–1360. See also L. Lewisohn, 'Sufism and Ismāʿīlī Doctrine in the Persian Poetry of Nizārī Quhistānī (645–721/1247–1321)', *Iran*, 41 (2003), pp. 229–251.

15 An early critical edition of Shabistarī's work, together with a prose English version, was produced by Edward H. Whinfield (1836–1922) under the title of *Gulshan i Raz: The Mystic Rose Garden* (London, 1880). The anonymous Ismaili commentary, entitled *Baʿḍī az ta'wīlāt-i Gulshan-i Rāz*, has been edited and translated into French by Henry Corbin in his *Trilogie Ismaélienne* (Tehran and Paris, 1961), text pp. 131–161, translation pp. 1–174.

16 W. Ivanow, *Ismaili Literature: A Bibliographical Survey* (Tehran, 1963), pp. 129–131, 164, 185, and idem, 'Sufism and Ismailism: *Chirāgh-nāma*', *Revue Iranienne d'Anthropologie*, 3 (1338 Sh./1959), pp. 53–70.

17 See A. Bertel's and M. Bakoev, *Alphabetic Catalogue of Manuscripts found by 1959–1963 Expedition in Gorno-Badakhshan Autonomous Region* (Moscow, 1967), pp. 63–64, 81–82 and F. Daftary, *Ismaili Literature: A Bibliography of Sources and Studies* (London, 2004), p. 166.

Nizārī Ismailis of Persia, Afghanistan and Central Asia have continued to use verses of these and other mystic poets of the Iranian world in their social and religious ceremonies.

By the middle of the 9th/15th century, the Nizārī Ismaili imams had established their seat at the village of Anjudān near Qum and Maḥallāt in central Persia, initiating the so-called Anjudān revival in Nizārī *daʿwa* and literary activities.[18] Taking advantage of the changing religio-political milieu of post-Mongol Persia, including the spread of ʿAlid loyalism and Shiʿi tendencies through Sufi orders, the imams now successfully began to reorganise and reinvigorate their *daʿwa* activities to win new converts and reassert their central authority over various Nizārī communities. However, the Nizārīs were still obliged, in Sunni-majority Persia, to observe *taqiyya* under the guise of Sufism.

The Anjudān period in Nizārī history, lasting until the end of the 11th/17th century, also witnessed a revival in the literary activities of the Nizārīs. In the context of Ismaili-Sufi relations during the Anjudān period, valuable details are preserved in the *Pandiyāt-i javānmardī* (Admonitions on Spiritual Chivalry), containing the religious sermons of Imam Mustanṣir bi'llāh (II), the first Nizārī imam who established his residence in Anjudān and died there in 885/1480.[19] Permeated with Sufi ideas, the imam's admonitions in the *Pandiyāt* start with the *sharīʿat-ṭarīqat-ḥaqīqat* categorisation of the Sufis, and depicting *ḥaqīqat* as the *bāṭin* of *sharīʿat* which could be attained by the faithful (*mu'minīn*) through the spiritual path or *ṭarīqat*. Other doctrinal works of the period were written by Abū Isḥāq Quhistānī (d. after 904/1498) and Khayrkhwāh-i Harātī (d. after 960/1553), among others.

By the time of the establishment of Safavid rule, the Shiʿi milieu of Persia had developed significantly, although Persia and adjacent regions still remained mainly Sunni. At any rate, the founder of the Safavid dynasty, as noted, adopted Twelver Shiʿism as the official religion of his realm. However, it took more than a century to transform the initial

[18] F. Daftary, *A Short History of the Ismailis* (Edinburgh, 1998), pp. 170–177.

[19] Mustanṣir bi'llāh, *Pandiyāt-i javānmardī*, ed. and tr. W. Ivanow (Leiden, 1953). See also Shafique N. Virani, *The Ismailis in the Middle Ages* (Oxford, 2007), pp. 122–126, 140 ff., 159–164, 180–182.

extremist, eclectic Safavid form of Shiʿism into what could be designated as the 'orthodox' Twelver form of Shiʿi Islam; and all this renaissance of Shiʿism occurred with the help of the Twelver jurists brought to Persia from Arab lands, notably Jabal ʿĀmil (in today's Lebanon), Iraq and Bahrain. It is also to be noted that the early Safavids soon adopted persecutionary policies against all Shiʿi communities or Shiʿi-related popular movements that fell outside the confines of Twelver Shiʿism, in addition to suppressing the majority of the Sufi orders.

It was under such circumstances that by the time of Shah ʿAbbās I (r. 995–1038/1587–1629), the greatest member of the dynasty who established his capital at Iṣfahān, the Persian Ismailis had widely and successfully adopted what was the now 'politically correct' Twelver Shiʿism as another form of disguise. Needless to add that in due course, the bulk of the Persian Nizārī Ismailis were in fact assimilated into the Twelver Shiʿi milieu of their surroundings. Meanwhile, Zaydī rule in the Caspian regions of northern Persia was ended in 1000/1592 by the Safavids, by which time all Zaydī communities in the Caspian provinces as well as in the Persian regions of Rayy, Fārs and Khurāsān had also disintegrated or converted to Twelver Shiʿism.[20]

Thus, the highly complex and gradual process of the 'Shiʿitisation' of Sunni Persia, initiated during the early post-Mongol times, eventually led to the emergence of Twelver Shiʿism as the prevailing religion of Persia – a position retained into modern times, making Iran the single most important Twelver Shiʿi country of the world.

---

[20] For a brief history of Zaydī Shiʿism in the Caspian regions, see F. Daftary, *A History of Shiʿi Islam* (London, 2013), pp. 151–162.

PART ONE

ISMAILISM IN THE CONTEXT OF SHIʿI-SUFI COALESCENCE

2

A Reconsideration of Post-Alamūt Nizārī Ismaili Literature in Iran: Prose and Poetry

S. J. Badakhchani

The remarkable Ismaili tradition of producing religious literature in both prose and poetry, despite a lessening of momentum after the fall of Alamūt, continued to be a dynamic mean of expressing the religious identity, the tenets of faith, the history and above all of highlighting the lineage of the Nizārī Ismaili imams. With reference to new discoveries in the field, this study aims at producing a brief survey of the bulk of post-Alamūt Nizārī Ismaili literature in the Persian language and introduces a hitherto unknown compendium of poetry by the 11th/17th-century Iranian Ismaili poet known as Darvīsh Quṭb al-Dīn.

In general terms, the Ismaili written heritage, has not enjoyed treatment equal to the majority of the Muslim written heritage of which it constitutes an important part. In the eventful course of Ismaili history, the main repositories of their literature were destroyed twice: first by the Ayyubids, under the command of Ṣalāḥ al-Dīn at the fall of the Fatimid caliphate in 567/1171,[1] and again by Hülegü the Mongol warlord at the fall of Alamūt in 654/1256.[2] In the case of the Fatimids, the celebrated Ismaili *dāʿī* al-Muʾayyad fiʾl-Dīn al-Shīrāzī, foreseeing the volatile political conditions that were to come, or

[1] Ṣalāḥ al-Dīn founded the Ayyubid dynasty in Egypt in 569/1174 and ordered the destruction of the Dār al-ʿIlm and the renowned Fatimid libraries. For details see Farhad Daftary, *The Ismāʿīlīs: Their History and Doctrines* (2nd ed., Cambridge, 2007), pp. 253–254.

[2] On Hülegü's confrontation with the Nizārī Ismailis, see Daftary, *The Ismāʿīlīs*, pp. 380–402 and Shīrīn Bayānī, *Dīn va dawlat dar Īrān-i ʿahd-i Mughul* (Tehran, 1367 Sh./1988), vol. 1, pp. 196–256.

perhaps seeking to elevate and strengthen the Ismaili mission, transferred part of the Ismaili literature to Yemen which at the time was governed by the Ṣulayḥids as part of the Fatimid empire.[3] This collection seems to have been preserved up to the present time among the Mustaʿlian Ismailis.[4] The Nizārī Ismailis on the other hand, possessing invincible fortresses, did not take the precautionary measure of transferring their written heritage to an alternative safe place and consequently when they surrendered to the Mongols a sizable bulk of their written heritage was put to the fire.[5]

At the turn of the 7th/13th century, the Ismaili imam, Jalāl al-Dīn Ḥasan (d. 618/1221), in his effort to improve good relations with neighbouring Sunni rulers, forged a rapprochement with the Abbasid caliphate, ordered his followers to abide by the prescripts of Sunni religious law and in the process invited Sunni dignitaries from Qazvīn, the city closest to Alamūt, to inspect its library and destroy any books that in their opinion did not conform with their theology. As a result, a great number of treatises in support of the Nizārī Ismaili teachings composed by Ḥasan-i Ṣabbāḥ (d. 518/1124), Jalāl al-Dīn's father, Nūr al-Dīn Muḥammad II (d. 607/1210) and his grandfather Ḥasan II, better known as *ʿalā dikrihi'l-salām* (d. 561/1166) were destroyed.[6] Thus in all these cases, apart from any social or political motives, it seems that annihilation of the Ismaili written heritage by their opponents was considered an act of piety.[7]

---

[3] For al-Mu'ayyad's close relationship with the Ismaili mission in Yemen, see Daftary, *The Ismāʿīlīs*, pp. 203–207.

[4] In recent years a substantial part of this collection was donated to the Ismaili Special Collections Unit of The Institute of Ismaili Studies, now housed at the Aga Khan Centre. For more information and catalogues of the works see: 1) Delia Cortese, *Arabic Ismaili Manuscripts: The Zāhid ʿAlī Collection in the Library of The Institute of Ismaili Studies* (London, 2003), and 2) François de Blois, *Arabic, Persian and Gujarati Manuscripts: The Hamdani Collection in the Library of The Institute of Ismaili Studies* (London, 2013).

[5] ʿAlā' al-Dīn ʿAṭā Malik b. Muḥammad Juwaynī, *Tārīkh-i Jahāngushā*, ed. M. Qazvīnī (Leiden, 1912–1917), vol. 3, pp. 269–270.

[6] Juwaynī, *Tārīkh-i Jahāngushā*, vol. 3, p. 244.

[7] The case of the Fatimids and the annihilation of their written heritage has resulted in some controversy since it was not considered an official act and was executed gradually. For details, see Fozia Bora, 'Did Ṣalāḥ al-Dīn Destroy the Fatimid Books: A Historiographical Enquiry', *JRAS*, 25 (2014), pp. 21–39. For the case of Nizārī Ismailis, see Juwaynī, *Tārīkh-i Jahāngushā*, vol. 3, p. 270.

There are, however, other factors that have played a decisive role in limiting the production of the Ismaili written heritage: the first in the order of importance, and a classical one, would be the alternation between the periods of concealment (*satr*) and those of manifestation (*kashf*). In a period of *satr*, direct communication between the imam and his followers was severed, the imam's identity being known only to a few trusted members of the community, and consequently his followers had to practise religious dissimulation (*taqiyya*). In this context we need to look at the corollaries of *satr* and *taqiyya* which at times had a positive effect on the production of religious literature and at others a negative one. The positive corresponds to those times when the community was striving to gain political power, as in the case of the pre-Fatimid Ismailis and the beginning of the Nizārī Ismaili mission in Iran, when there was a surge in the production of the written heritage. The negative effect appeared when the community was defeated politically and an 'obligatory' *satr* and *taqiyya* was enforced. It was during such a period that a tradition of oral transmission of religious knowledge arose and became the main channel of communication and, as might be expected, the slightest resemblance in the work of a famous scholar to Ismaili tenets of faith would be sufficient reason to consider it as an Ismaili work compiled under the disguise of religious dissimulation.[8]

Apart from the points highlighted above, we can add another two factors that played a role in the production of the Nizārī Ismaili written heritage of post-Alamūt times. The first would be a consequence of the Mongol invasion and the simultaneous fall of Alamūt and Baghdad within a short span of time resulting in the diminishment if not the end of Abbasid political power, when the arena of Sunni theological writing contracted and the surviving written heritage of the Nizārī Ismailis in a

[8] The subject requires detailed study which is beyond the scope of the present article. Famous poets and scholars like Rūdakī, Firdawsī, Kasā'ī, Khayyām, Sanā'ī, Sa'dī, Jalāl al-Dīn Balkhī (Mawlānā), as well as Ibn Sīnā, al-Shahrastānī and Afḍal al-Dīn Kāshānī, to name but a few, are included in the list. In a number of cases the resemblance is compelling and such assumptions may not be utterly implausible. The case of Mawlānā is an exemplar since his devotion to Shams-i Tabrīz is well known and indisputable, and Shams, according to the oral tradition of the Iranian Ismailis, is in fact their 28th imam. For a general overview on the subject, see 'Aṭā Allāh Tadayyūn, *Mawlānā wa ṭūfān-i Shams* (Tehran, 1372 Sh./1993), pp. 558–584.

subtle manner was claimed by various Sufi circles, by Twelver Shiʿism[9] and, in some cases, utilised as a substratum of thought by religious movements that appeared at this time.[10] The second phenomenon is interpolation, carelessness and defective corrections by the scribes. Take for example a qualified Nizārī Ismaili author who wrote a treatise, or in rare cases a book. For some reason the original copy cannot be traced, the scribe rarely mentions preparing his copy from the original and consequently among the existing manuscripts of the same work one can hardly find two closely similar copies. Manuscript variants and interpolations are so numerous that when W. Ivanow (1886–1970) started his pioneering work of editing Persian Nizārī Ismaili texts, in the majority of cases, he preferred to correct them, that is, in a way producing another manuscript of the text.[11]

---

[9] To name a few, the *Āghāz wa anjām* and *Akhlāq-i Muḥtashamī* by Naṣīr al-Dīn al-Ṭūsī and some of the works by Muḥammad b. ʿAbd al-Karīm al-Shahrastānī such as *Mafātīḥ al-asrār* and *Majlis-i maktūb-i Khwārazm*.

[10] Shīrīn Bayānī. *Dīn va dawlat*, vol. 1, p. 256 and Abbas Amanat's remark: 'The dynamics of dissent inherent in Ismailism could not have remained dormant infinitely, however. The eighth/fourteenth and ninth/fifteenth centuries witnessed one of the most intense, yet diffuse, phases of "heterodox" resurgence in the Iranian world, with doctrinal features and political consequences akin to Nizari Ismailism. Ranging from Niʿmat Allahi and Nurbakhshi Sufi orders to Hurufi and Nuqtavi heresies, these movements shared a doctrinal pattern founded on the ideas of cyclical renewal of sacred time, anticipation of a messianic advent, and hermeneutical (*batini*) interpretation of the text'; see Abbas Amanat, *Apocalyptic Islam and Iranian Shiʿism* (London, 2009), p. 74.

[11] Continuing the remarkable efforts of W. Ivanow (1888–1970), after joining The Institute of Ismaili Studies in 1979, and while organising its library and teaching various courses, the editing and translation of Alamūt and post-Alamūt Nizārī Ismaili written heritage became part of my own assignments. Circumstances then also gave me the opportunity to edit and translate all the major Ismaili works of Naṣīr al-Dīn al-Ṭūsī, namely the *Sayr va sulūk* as *Contemplation and Action* (London 1998); the *Rawḍa-yi taslīm* as *Paradise of Submission* (London, 2005), and a collection of his short treatises, namely the *Āghāz wa anjām*, *Tawallā wa tabarrā* and *Maṭlūb al-mu'minīn* as *Shiʿi Interpretations of Islam* (London, 2010). Further, Ḥasan-i Maḥmūd-i Kātib's compendium of poems known as 'Poems of the Resurrection' (*Dīwān-i Qā'imiyyāt*) was published in 2011 and his prose treatise known as *Haft bāb* was published as *Spiritual Resurrection in Shiʿi Islam* in 2017. For the new edition of *Haft bāb*, 30 manuscripts were consulted, compared with 19 for Ivanow's edition and the final text was based on 6 manuscripts. For more information see my introduction to *Spiritual Resurrection in Shiʿi Islām: An Early Ismaili Treatise on the Doctrine of Qiyāmat* (London, 2017), pp. 37–42.

In the Persian-speaking territories, that is, Iran, Afghanistan, Tajikistan and the northern provinces of Pakistan, for almost 100 years – apart from the works of Nizārī Quhistānī (d. 720/1320) who seems to have been well informed about Ismaili teachings and actually was born around the last years of Alamūt period – we do not have any literary work worth mentioning. It was in the second half of the 7th/13th century, that Qāsim Shāh, the 31st imam authorised Abū Isḥāq-i Quhistānī to produce a book on the Ismaili mission (*daʿwat*). Entitled the *Haft bāb-i Abū Isḥāq* this work soon became the source for a number of books and treatises produced at the time of the rise of the Safavid dynasty and the beginning of the renaissance of Shiʿi Islam, when the Nizārī Ismaili imams had also regained sufficient political power to revive the community and establish themselves in Anjudān.[12] The appearance of *Haft bāb-i Abū Isḥāq* meant that the period of *satr* or concealment of the Nizārī Ismaili imams, begun at the fall of Alamūt in 654/1256, was practically over.

Farhad Daftary in his comprehensive work, *Ismaili Literature*, classifies the Nizārī Ismaili written heritage of the post-Alamūt period into four main categories, namely, the Persian, the Badakhshānī or Central Asian, the Syrian and the South Asian, and highlights the obstacles that the Nizārī Ismailis were facing in the production of their literature.[13] This classification defines the scope of the present paper, which is concerned with the Persian and Central Asian production, since the Arabic and a large component of the Nizārī Ismaili literature produced in various vernacular languages of South Asia have their own story which cannot be covered here.

The scope and extent of Persian Nizārī Ismaili literature

In 1997, while preparing a tentative list of the Nizārī Ismaili literature in Persian by comparing almost all the bibliographical sources available

---

[12] For more information, see Daftary, *The Ismāʿīlīs*, pp. 422–442.

[13] Daftary, *Ismaili Literature: A Bibliography of Sources and Studies* (London, 2004), pp. 61–62.

at the time,[14] an inventory containing 224 titles was compiled. The list included extant original manuscripts or their photocopies housed at the library of The Institute of Ismaili Studies (IIS); titles whose existence were somehow certain but which had not yet been procured by the IIS library, doubtful titles and titles that had been recorded but whose whereabouts are not known and titles that may not be genuine Ismaili works. Out of 224 titles, 51 belonged to the Alamūt and the rest to the post-Alamūt period, of which 22 titles are specifically in praise of Ismaili imams. Although an updated catalogue of Persian Ismaili works held at the Ismaili Special Collections Unit of the IIS has not yet been published, from a tentative survey of the existing works and being mindful of the on-going discovery of new titles, the inventory of Persian Ismaili literature may well exceed three hundred titles.[15]

Content, Reflection of Faith and Religious Identity

Having at our disposal reliable editions of the Ismaili literature of the Alamūt period and Ivanow's edition of the *Haft bāb-i Abū Isḥāq* that reflects the main trend of the Ismaili teachings of the post-Alamūt period, it is possible to confirm that there were no major changes in the basic tenets of faith and the religious identity of the Nizārī Ismailis. A brief scrutiny of the contents of *Haft bāb-i Abū Isḥāq* shows that not only is it a reiteration, but sometimes an elaboration and commentary upon two major works composed during the Alamūt period, namely the *Haft bāb* of Ḥasan-i Maḥmūd-i Kātib and Naṣīr al-Dīn al-Ṭūsī's *Rawḍa-yi taslīm*. The only genuine addition in Abū Isḥāq's work is the description of the ceremonies of the *qiyāma*, an event that took place at Alamūt in

[14] The main bibliographical sources at the time were Ivanow's *Guide to Ismaili Literature* (London, 1933) and his *Ismaili Literature: A Bibliographical Survey* (Tehran, 1963); *Fihrist al-Majdūʿ* by Ismāʿīl b. ʿAbd al-Rasūl al-Ujjainī (Tehran, 1344 Sh./1966), Appendix iii, pp. 305–352 provides a list of 1344 titles out of which 122 are in the Persian language; A.E. Bertel's and M. Bakaev, *Alphabetic Catalogue of Manuscripts found by 1959-1963 Expedition in Gorno-Badakhshan Autonomous Region* (Moscow, 1967) and Ismail K. Poonawala, *Biobibliography of Ismāʿīlī Literature* (Malibu, CA, 1977).

[15] This inventory did not include small fragments and a substantial number of Blessed Directives (*taʿlīqa-yi mubārak*) issued by the imams after their migration to the Subcontinent.

559/1164.[16] The interpolations, in the majority of cases, were aimed at presenting the work as a counter-balance to Twelver Shiʿi religious manuals (*Risāla-yi ʿamaliyya*).[17] Examples of this approach are visible in the various manuscripts of Abū Isḥāq's work. The Ismaili Special Collection Unit holds eight manuscripts of the text, and earlier copies are in tune with the Alamūt style of authorship without interpolations, but later copies contain detailed additional material that gives the work a new outlook. To highlight the point, a cursory word-count of two chapters in the existing manuscripts of the *Haft bāb* is given below:

Catalogue number	Date	Chapter One	Chapter Four
MS BT 270	1968	124 lines, 928 words	96 lines, 846 words
MS BT 118	No date	134 lines, 1206 words	109 lines, 981 words
MS BA 229	1989	114 lines, 1250 words	111 lines, 1124 words
MS BA 63	No date	124 lines, 1488 words	114 lines,1368 words
MS BA3	1903	112 lines, 1120 words	158 lines,1422 words
MS BA 48	1870	138 lines, 1074 words	223 lines 1784 words
MS BA 107	No date	217 lines, 1736 words	185 lines,1665 words
MS BT 117	No date	123 lines,1107 words	102 lines, 918 words
MS 60	1935	257 lines, 3598 words	112 lines, 1568 words

16 *Haft bāb-i Bū Isḥāq*, ed. and tr. W. Ivanow (Bombay, 1959), pp. 40–42.

17 In a broad sense, if we consider Twelver Shiʿism as a representative of juristic and Ismailism of gnostic Islam, then, *Haft bāb-i Abū Isḥāq* can be considered as a religious manual or handbook, similar to the religious manuals of the *marājiʿ-i taqlīd* authorities in Twelver Shiʿism.

The word-count[18] comparison shows that chapter one in BT270 has 928 words, while it has 3598 in MS 60 and chapter four in BT270 has 846 words, while it has 1784 words in BA48.

In the preamble to his edition of Abū Isḥāq's work Ivanow speaks of its close resemblance to *Kalām-i pīr*, a text by Khayrkhwāh Harātī, a prolific writer and poet who unscrupulously plagiarised the writings of Abū Isḥāq and to enhance the work's authenticity attributed its authorship to Nāṣir-i Khusraw.[19] In the matter of attribution Ivanow is correct, but a comparison of *Kalām-i pīr* with eight manuscripts of Abū Isḥāq's work tells a different story about the plagiarising of the contents. Undoubtedly, the main skeleton of both the *Haft bāb-i Abū Isḥāq* and the *Kalām-i pīr* comes from al-Ṭūsī's *Rawḍa-yi taslīm* and Ḥasan-i Maḥmūd's *Haft bāb*.[20] The popularity of the *Haft bāb* by Ḥasan-i Maḥmūd, which was composed during the imamate of Nūr al-Dīn Muḥammad II, was probably later suppressed due to it being *qiyāma* literature. But in the month of Shaʿbān 633/April 1236, after almost fifty years, permission was given to the chief *dāʿī* Muẓaffar b. Muʾayyad to read the sacred chapters (*Fuṣūl-i muqaddas*) of Ḥasan *ʿalā dhikrihi al-salām*,[21] and this probably paved the way for the return of the *Haft bāb* to the main arena of Ismaili scholarship. The popularity of *Haft bāb-i Ḥasan-i Maḥmūd* was further enhanced when al-Ṭūsī incorporated large segments of it in the *Rawḍa-yi taslīm*[22] and introduced it as a work of reference in theological matters.

---

18 Since page size and the writing style of each scribe differs, I have counted the number of lines per chapter, multiplied by the average number of words per line, therefore figures are approximate.

19 Ivanow, preface to *Haft bāb-i Bū Isḥāq* (Bombay, 1959).

20 Based on newly found manuscripts of the *Haft bāb-i Bū Isḥāq* which are compared with the *Haft bāb-i Ḥasan-i Maḥmūd* and the Ismaili writings of Naṣīr al-Dīn al-Ṭūsī, I have prepared a new edition and English translation of the *Haft bāb of Abū Isḥāq*, in which Abū Isḥāq's sources are highlighted. This is to be published in the *Ismaili Texts and Translations* series of The Institute of Ismaili Studies.

21 See Ḥasan-i Maḥmūd-i Kātib, *Dīwān-i Qāʾimiyyāt* (Tehran, 1395 Sh./2016), ode 90, pp. 251–253.

22 al-Ṭūsī, *Rawḍa-yi taslīm*, ed. and tr. by S. J. Badakhchani as *Paradise of Submission: A Medieval Treatise on Ismaili Thought* (London, 2005), pp. 136, 191–194.

In the aftermath of the fall of Alamūt, it seems that a new style of authorship developed among the Persian-speaking Ismailis of the Quhistān and Badakhshān regions who were left with only a handful of reliable texts from their ancestors and the *Haft bāb* of Ḥasan-i Maḥmūd, due to its unsophisticated language became the main source of their compilations. According to Ivanow, Abū Isḥāq compiled his *Haft bāb* towards the beginning of 10th/16th century, during the imamate of Gharīb Mīrzā, that is, Mustanṣir bi'llah III (d. 904/1498).[23] The fact that this work was itself based on the writings of Naṣīr al-Dīn al-Ṭūsī and Ḥasan-i Maḥmūd, allowed Khayrkhwāh to improve on it without any intentional forgery; in other words, by adding further material that he felt was important to his milieu, he produced an updated version of the book. Among the eight manuscripts entitled *Haft bāb-i Abū Isḥāq*, MS 60 also starts in so different a fashion that it cannot be said to be a copy of either *Kalām-i pīr* or the *Haft bāb* of Abū Isḥāq. As has been pointed out, the only original segment in Abū Isḥāq's work is his description of the *qiyāma* ceremonies. This segment is summarised in MS 60 and partly deleted in the *Kalām-i pīr* which leads us to conclude that apart from the possibility of being a copy, there are also some versions like *Kalām-i pīr* and MS 60, which it would be more appropriate to speak of as independent works or editions with amendments to Abū Isḥāq's work.

Having briefly touched upon some features of the post-Alamūt Nizārī Ismaili literature, it would be appropriate here to mention a unique component of the bulk of this collection that deals with eulogy, praise and exaltation of the imams. As mentioned earlier in the listings of Nizārī Ismaili literature, there are 22 odes in praise of the imams which differ remarkably from those of the Fatimid and Alamūt periods. If we take the eulogies by Ibn Hāni'[24] and Ḥasan-i Maḥmūd-i

[23] In the oldest manuscript at our disposal, MS BA48, f. 20, the author specifically mentions that he met the Ismaili imam, Qāsim Shāh and was appointed by him as a *ma'dhūn* to write works. But the composition of the book actually took place after the imam's demise.

[24] Muḥammad b. Hāni' al-Andalusī al-Azdī (d. 362/973), was the chief court poet to the Fatimid Imam-caliph, al-Muʿizz.

Kātib[25] as representatives of the Fatimid and Alamūt periods, we find many exaggerated expressions, while the post-Alamūt odes serve instead as historical narratives and occasionally end up with the reiteration of the names of the imams up to the one contemporary with the poet. Information of this nature could be used for substantiating dates, the real names of the imams and above all the trend towards using Sufi terminology that found its way into the Nizārī Ismaili written heritage.

The inroads made by Sufi terminology were indeed concomitant to the close relationship the Ismaili imams had with Sufi circles after the Mongol invasion and the revival of Twelver Shiʿi juristic Islam. A good example of this phenomenon in the post-Alamūt Nizārī Ismaili written heritage would be the hitherto unknown compendium of poetry by Darvīsh Quṭb al-Dīn of Yahn, a village some 50 kilometres from Bīrjand in southern Khurāsān. Little is known about his life apart from certain oral traditions and the recording of his name as a major Ismaili *dāʿī* in 11th/17th-century Quhistān.[26] Three manuscripts of the text are currently available. It is a compilation of approximately 2300 lines of poetry arranged in semi-*ghazal* style with seven lines in each *ghazal*. The terminology follows a hermeneutic style of expression. Without a background knowledge of Ismaili teachings, it is difficult to decipher an Ismaili orientation here. As an example, the text and translation of a *ghazal* from the oldest manuscript, which seems to be the autograph copy, is reproduced here. In this poem, Darvīsh not only re-caps Ḥasan-i Ṣabbāḥ's doctrine of *taʿlīm* (in the last couplet), but also describes a specific type of relationship that exists between the imam and his followers which is invoked repeatedly in the *Qāʾimiyyāt* of Ḥasan-i Maḥmūd-i Kātib.

---

[25] Ḥasan-i Maḥmūd-i Kātib was contemporary with three imams of the Alamūt period, that is, Nūr al-Dīn Muḥammad II, Jalāl al-Dīn Ḥasan and ʿAlā al-Dīn Muḥammad. For more information on him see my introduction to the *Dīwān-i Qāʾimiyyāt*, pp. 7–20.

[26] *Qaṣīda-yi Maḥmūd dar Madḥ-i dāʿīyān*, scribe Ghiyāth al-Dīn Mīrshāhī, Ismaili Special Collections Unit, Acc. No 14708 (به جو درویش قطب الدین که در یهن است قطب دین طریقت دان حقیقت بین، چه غم از خارجی دارم). 'Look for Darvīsh Quṭb al-Dīn who is the pole of faith in Yahn. He knows the path, he sees the truth. How can (our) enemies cause (us) grief?'

آنها که آشنائی خود با خدا کنند
آیا بود که پیش خدا یاد ما کنند

پرواز داده از قفس جسم مرغ روح
منزل فراز عالم لا منتها کنند

آن قوم از عنایت لطف خدای خویش
در دم سما زمین و زمین را سما کنند

یابند اگر ز جانب جانان اشارتی
فی الحال جان خود به تمامی فدا کنند

مستی کنند بر سر کویش ز شوق او
دانی که در حریم وصالش چه ها کنند

با خویش تا به چند نشینیم بی ملال
ایشان مگر که ما و من از هم جدا کنند

کس قطب الدین بخود بخدا آشنا نشد
ایشان مگر ترا به خدا آشنا کنند

Will it be possible for those who recognise God
To remember us in His presence?

They who have liberated the bird of [their] soul from the cage of the body,
Are denizens of the higher world!

In one breath, by Divine Grace and Bounty,
They can change heaven into earth and earth into heaven! [and],

If they receive but an indication from the Beloved,
Instantly, they sacrifice their soul for it entire!

Within His precincts they ecstatically yearn for Him,
Imagine what they will do within the sanctity of His union!

On our own, how long shall we sit unafflicted [by our isolation],
Could it happen that they separate the 'I' and 'us'?

O Quṭb al-Dīn, no one on his own can recognise God,
Unless they familiarise you with God.

3

The Scent of the Scarlet Pimpernels: Ismaili Leaders of the 11th/17th Century*

Shafique N. Virani

A servant of ʿAlī, king of men, am I. What have I to fear of his foe?
Submissive to God's command am I. What have I to fear of a rebel?
Khālū Maḥmūd ʿAlī

A. Introduction: The Scarlet Pimpernel and the Ismaili *Dāʿīs*

'The Scarlet Pimpernel?' said Suzanne, with a merry laugh. 'Why! what a droll name! What is the Scarlet Pimpernel, Monsieur?' She looked at Sir Andrew with eager curiosity. The young man's face had become almost transfigured. His eyes shone with enthusiasm; hero-worship, love, admiration for his leader seemed literally to glow upon his face. 'The Scarlet Pimpernel, Mademoiselle,' he said at last 'is the name of a humble English wayside flower; but it is also the name chosen to hide the identity of the best and bravest man in all the world, so that he may better succeed in accomplishing the noble task he has set himself to do.'

Baroness Orczy, *The Scarlet Pimpernel*[1]

---

* This article is dedicated to the memory of Mīrzā Ḥasan b. ʿAbd al-Ghaffār (d. ca. 1305/1887) of the village of Sidih, near Bīrjand. I would like to express my gratitude to Dr Faquir M. Hunzai, the late Dr Janis Esots, Dr Rahim Gholami and Russell Harris for their valuable and detailed input on a draft of this article, to Dr Maryam Muʿizzī for her kind correspondence and sharing the material she had available, and to Kiana Mozayyan Esfahani, Parnian Haeri Hindi, Seoren A'Garous and Pouya Ebrahimi for their excellent insights.

[1] (New York, n.d.), pp. 35–36.

In 1939, Wladimir Ivanow wrote, 'The Bāṭinī (i.e., Ismaili) *dāʿī* already at an early date becomes a prominent figure in the annals of Islam' and the redoubtable Russian author went on to paint a vivid picture of how their foes depicted these Ismaili emissaries or 'inviters':

> As elusive and omnipresent as the 'Scarlet Pimpernel', as malicious, ruthlessly cruel, and unscrupulous in farfetched diabolical schemes as the leader of a criminal gang in any detective best seller, as superhumanly clever, brave, persevering, and daring as any detective hero of the best American cinema film, — the *dāʿī* appears as the chief 'villain of the plot', responsible for many failures and defeats which the corrupt and incapable Abbasid administration had to suffer.[2]

Naturally, Ismaili depictions of their *dāʿīs* contrast sharply with this kind of characterisation. For example, in his treatise on the etiquette expected of Ismailis in leadership positions, al-Nīsābūrī (fl. ca. 4th/10th century) provides extensive details on the conduct of the *dāʿīs*:

> We hold that the *dāʿī* must be firmly grounded in the principles of the religion to which he invites with a sincerity and certainty untainted or mixed with another purpose, loyal to the Imam for whom he appeals and to the Messenger who is the foundation of the religion on whom, to whom, and by whom the invitation is based. . . . He should be God-fearing in his piety and that cannot happen without knowledge of both the exterior and the interior. . . . The *dāʿī* must be chaste and upright. It is as God said: 'The good word ascends unto Him and the pious deed exalts it' (Q 35: 10). . . . He must be kind to the believers, merciful and forgiving. As God has said: 'We sent you not but as a mercy for the worlds' (Q 21: 108). . . . A *dāʿī* should be humble, not haughty with the believers. . . ., intelligent, with a perfect wisdom and knowledge. . . ., generous and not miserly. . . ., truthful in what he says. . ., chivalrous, for chivalry is an aspect of faith. . . ., modest, for modesty is also a part of faith. . . ., sound of opinion and skilled in administration. . ., and firm in his word, for religion is the fulfilment of the covenant. He must keep secret what is secret. Religion is based on the preservations of secrets that need

[2] Wladimir Ivanow, 'The Organization of the Fatimid Propaganda', *Journal of the Bombay Branch of the Royal Asiatic Society*, New Series, 15 (1939), p. 1.

> to be kept from those who are not worthy of them. If the secrets are lost, religion is lost. At times, the divulging of a secret connected to a matter of religion has led to the destruction of a nation or the ruin of a province.[3]

Despite the dramatic contrast between the two depictions, a common feature is the emphasis on the exercise of discretion and prudence by the *dāʿī*s, not drawing attention to themselves and maintaining secrecy when necessary, particularly when working in hostile milieus.[4]

In Ivanow's words, the *dāʿī* was something of a 'Scarlet Pimpernel', the hidden protagonist of Baroness Orczy's perennial bestselling novels. In these tales as much as the Pimpernel is admired and adored by his proteges who help him save victims from the guillotine, he is feared and despised by the French revolutionaries. Notably, his symbol was 'a humble English wayside flower', a plant as inconspicuous as it is anonymous. Ivanow's reference also imaginatively depicts, unsurprisingly, how little we know about the lives of even some of the most distinguished Ismaili luminaries. As the eminent Islamicist Henry Corbin wrote with regard to the Ismailis, 'Over the course of centuries, the secret was so well kept that the names of great thinkers and titles of monumental works remain completely absent from our repertoires.'[5]

Detailed information on the community's dignitaries is rare in Ismaili literature, and in this respect, the 11th/17th-century poem examined here is unusual. Written by a certain Khālū Maḥmūd ʿAlī, the work

---

[3] Aḥmad b. Ibrāhīm al-Naysābūrī, *al-Risāla al-mūjaza al-kāfiya fī ādāb al-duʿāt*, ed. and tr. Verena Klemm and Paul E. Walker as *A Code of Conduct: A Treatise on the Etiquette of the Fatimid Ismaili Mission* (London, 2011), pp. 27–36 (Arabic), 49–55 (English). Translation slightly modified. On the meaning of Q 35: 10, see Nāṣir-i Khusraw, *Wajh-i dīn*, ed. Ghulām Riḍā Aʿwānī (Tehran, 1398/1977), p. 114.

[4] For example, in describing the departure of a *dāʿī* and his disciple from a religious gathering, Jaʿfar b. Manṣūr al-Yaman (d. ca. 346/957) wrote, 'Then the two of them took their leave and left together, cautiously and in secret', Jaʿfar b. Manṣūr al-Yaman, *al-ʿĀlim wa'l-ghulām*, ed. and tr. James Winston Morris as *The Master and the Disciple: An Early Islamic Spiritual Dialogue* (London, 2001), p. 115 (English).

[5] Henry Corbin, 'Étude préliminaire', in Nāṣir-i Khusraw, *Kitab-e Jamiʿ al-Hikmatain: Le livre réunissant les deux sagesses; ou harmonie de la philosophie Grecque et de la théosophie Ismaélienne*, ed. Henry Corbin and M. Moʿin (Tehran and Paris, 1953), p. 4, my translation. All translations are by the author, unless otherwise indicated.

invokes dozens of the poet's contemporaries who were in positions of community leadership dispersed across many lands: 'I shall speak the name of every guide (*rahbar*), of the teachers (*muʿallim-hā*) of every land.' He enumerates Ismaili notables in locations scattered throughout Khurāsān, Quhistān, Badakhshān, Iraq, Turkistān and Hindūstān, and in this candidness his composition is highly unconventional.[6]

With the death of the Prophet Muhammad, the Muslims adopted diverse interpretations of his message, and various schools emerged. The Imāmī Shiʿa accepted the privileged position of the hereditary imams of the Prophet's family, adhering closely to their guidance. Following the death of Imam Jaʿfar al-Ṣādiq in 148/765, the Imāmī community divided. Among other groups, one group eventually recognised the imamate of his son Mūsā al-Kāẓim, while others held to al-Ṣādiq's designation of his elder son, Ismāʿīl al-Mubārak. Over time, the adherents of this elder lineage were designated as Ismailis, while the younger lineage came to be known as the Ithnāʿasharīs, or Twelvers, after the occultation of their Twelfth imam. In common with many other Shiʿis, the Ismailis championed intellect's role in religion and disavowed exclusively literal understandings of scripture. Thus, their enemies dubbed them the people of inner meaning (*bāṭin*), as opposed to those of outward form (*ẓāhir*).[7]

---

[6] Of currently extant literature, perhaps only modern works, such as some of the 'Rules of the Shia Imami Ismailia Councils' promulgated in various parts of the world from 1905 onwards, which were the predecessors of the Ismaili 'Constitutions', give details of those appointed to community leadership. See, for example, *Rules of the Shia Imami Ismailia Councils of Kathiawar, Kāṭhīyāvāḍanī Shīyā Imāmī Īsmāīlīā Kāunsīlnanā kāyadā*, Revised ed. (Rajkot: Alijehan Esmail Virji Madhani J.P. President, Shia Imami Ismaili Kathiawar Supreme Council (Ālījahāṃ Ismaīl Vīrajī Mādhāṇī Je.Pī., Presīḍenṭ, Shīyā Īmāmī Ismaīlī Kāṭhiyāvāḍ Suprīm Kāunsīl), 1928), F-G, 2–19, which lists the 32 members of the Ismaili Supreme Council of Kathiawar, and 785 locales in the region with an Ismaili presence. With regard to leadership specifically charged with religious guidance, *Rules of the Shia Imami Ismailia Missions of Bombay* (Mumbai, 1922) bears some similarities to Khālū Maḥmūd ʿAlī's account. Works such as *Khojā Ismāilī kelenḍar ane ḍīrekṭarī: 1910* (Mumbai, 1910) are similarly informative about leadership in the community. But even these modern examples, when taken individually, do not have the geographical scope of Khālū Maḥmūd's poem.

[7] It was a name in which many Ismailis took pride. See, for example, Shafique N. Virani, 'The Right Path: A Post-Mongol Persian Ismaili Treatise', *JIS*, 43 (2010), pp. 200, 205, 213.

In 297/909, the Ismaili imam ʿAbd Allāh al-Mahdī (d. 322/934) established the Fatimid caliphate. At the height of their power, the Fatimids ruled over much of North Africa, the Arabian Peninsula, the Levant and Sicily, patronising numerous scientific, literary and artistic endeavours. Following the death of the Fatimid Imam-caliph al-Mustanṣir in 487/1094, there was a succession struggle between two of his sons, Nizār al-Muṣṭafā li-Dīn Allāh and al-Mustaʿlī bi'llāh, leading to a split in the Ismaili community. Shortly before this rupture, Ḥasan-i Ṣabbāḥ (d. 518/1124), one of al-Mustanṣir's most senior dignitaries, successfully had acquired the fortress of Alamūt, which was to become the headquarters of the followers of Imam Nizār.[8] Under the able leadership of Ḥasan-i Ṣabbāḥ and his successors, Ismailism spread throughout the domains of its sworn enemies, the Turkish Saljūqs. The Saljūqs governed with the blessing of the Abbasid caliphs, who were now largely reduced to being the titular heads of Sunni Islam. Repeated massacres were perpetrated against Shiʿi Ismaili communities living in the Saljūq empire.[9] They were burned alive or put to the sword in Aleppo, Baṣra, Baghdad, Damascus, Qazvīn, Rayy, Iṣfahān, south Khurāsān and elsewhere. Unable to confront the empire's considerable military superiority head-on, they defended themselves in their remote fortresses which constituted an independent state both opposed to and within the Saljūq state.[10] However, at the start

---

[8] Hasan-i Sabbah held the position of 'proof' (*ḥujja*) in the Ismaili religious hierarchy. See, for example, the work of his near contemporary Muḥammad b. ʿUbayd Allāh Abu'l-Maʿālī, *Bayān al-adyān: Dar sharḥ-i adyān wa madhāhib-i jāhilī wa Islām*, ed. ʿAbbās Iqbāl Āshtiyānī and Muḥammad Taqī Dānishpazhūh (Tehran, 1376 Sh./1997), p. 55. For more details on his position and activities, see Shafique N. Virani, 'Alamūt, Ismailism and Khwāja Qāsim Tushtarī's *Recognizing God*', *SSR*, 2 (2018), pp. 194–197; Farhad Daftary, 'Hasan-i Sabbah and the Origins of the Nizari Ismaʿili *Daʿwa* and State', Chapter 7 in his *Ismailis in Medieval Muslim Societies* (London, 2005).

[9] For details and sources, see Marshall G.S. Hodgson, *The Order of Assassins: The Struggle of the Early Nizārī Ismāʿīlīs against the Islamic World* (The Hague, 1955), pp. 78, 85, 88, chart following p. 89, pp. 93–94, 101, 105, 144–146, 215; Farhad Daftary, *The Ismāʿīlīs: Their History and Doctrines* (2nd ed., Cambridge, 2007), pp. 329–330, 335–336; Bernard Lewis, *The Assassins: A Radical Sect in Islam* (London, 1967), pp. 50, 52, 70; Bogdan Smarandache, 'The Franks and the Nizārī Ismāʿīlīs in the Early Crusade Period', *Al-Masaq*, 24 (2012), pp. 227–231.

[10] On this dynamic, see Hodgson, *Order of Assassins*, pp. 111–112; Daftary, *Ismāʿīlīs*, pp. 328–329. On depictions of the Ismailis at Alamūt, see Shafique N. Virani, 'An Old Man, a Garden, and an Assembly of Assassins: Legends and Realities of the Nizari Ismaili Muslims', *Iran* (2021), pp. 1–15 https//doi.org/10.1080/0578967.2021.1901062.

of the 7th/13th century the Mongols, an adversary of far greater destructive ability, appeared on the horizon. After these invaders captured Alamūt in 654/1256, they hunted down Ismailis and slaughtered them indiscriminately. The destruction of the Ismaili state ushered in an era so nebulous and hazy that the first half a millennium after the Mongol conquest has had to be classified by researchers under the amorphous title of 'post-Alamūt history'.[11] In the first edition of his landmark work, *The Ismāʿīlīs: Their History and Doctrines*, Farhad Daftary echoed the sentiments of earlier scholarship in describing this period as 'the darkest phase' in the annals of the community.[12]

In the wake of this wholesale slaughter, the Ismailis resorted to *taqiyya*, or pious circumspection, to survive.[13] However, as Khālū Maḥmūd ʿAlī's poem demonstrates, there were different degrees of circumspection, and times when and regions where the community had the wherewithal to be more public about its identity. This was most likely the outcome of policies implemented in the previous century. The writings of Khayrkhwāh-i Harātī (d. after 960/1553) allude to this situation. He explains that hitherto 'a veil was drawn over the visage of truth', but that the imam had now 'allowed the veil to be lifted', permitting written communication.[14] The unpublished poetry

---

[11] Daftary, *Ismāʿīlīs*, p. 403; Farhad Daftary, *Ismaili Literature: A Bibliography of Sources and Studies* (London, 2004), p. 59.

[12] Farhad Daftary, *The Ismāʿīlīs: Their History and Doctrines* (1st ed., Cambridge, 1990), p. 435. He was preceded in this regard by Edward Irving Howard, *The Shia School of Islam and its Branches, Especially that of the Imamee-Ismailies: A Speech Delivered by E.I. Howard, Esquire, Barrister-at-Law, in the Bombay High Court, in June, 1866*, ed. H. Wynford Barrow (Bombay, 1866); Syed Mujtaba Ali, *The Origin of the Khojāhs and their Religious Life Today* (Bonn, 1936), p. 55; Hamid Algar, 'The Revolt of Āghā Khān Maḥallātī and the Transference of the Ismāʿīlī Imamate to India', *Studia Islamica*, 29 (1969), p. 55.

[13] On this phenomenon, see Shafique N. Virani, '*Taqiyya* and Identity in a South Asian Community', *Journal of Asian Studies*, 70 (2011) and 'Surviving Persecution: Ismailism and *Taqiyyah* after the Mongol Invasions', in Leonard Lewisohn and Reza Tabandeh, ed., *Sufis and their Opponents in the Persianate World* (Irvine, CA, 2020), pp. 205–236.

[14] Shafique N. Virani, 'Khayrkhwāh-i Harātī: The Epistle (Risāla)', in Hermann Landolt et al., ed., *An Anthology of Ismaili Literature: A Shiʿi Vision of Islam* (London, 2008), pp. 247–249; Shafique N. Virani, 'Khayrkhvāh-i Harātī', *EI3*.

of a certain Ustād Manṣūr supports this. Writing in the year 1052/1642 during the reign of Imam Nūr al-Dahr ʿAlī, also known as Nūr al-Dīn ʿAlī (d. 1082/1671), he proclaims:

digar bu-g(u)dhasht ān dawrī kih pinhān būd sirr-i ḥaqq
sar āmad ẓulmat-i shab-hā bu-shud layl ū nahār āmad[15]
Passed has the age when God's secret was hidden
The oppressive darkness has waned. Night has departed and day has arrived!

However, such writings were held strictly within the confines of the community and they were not shared with outsiders. Works written in the period immediately preceding Khayrkhwāh's emphasise prudence and discretion. Thus, in his *Pandiyāt-i javānmardī*, Imam Mustanṣir bi'llāh of Anjudān also known as Gharīb Mirzā (d. 885/1480), cautioned his followers not to reveal the identities of their imams to non-Ismailis.[16] The verses of Ḥusayn, an Ismaili poet and contemporary of this imam, mirror this sentiment: 'The time has come to express love openly, we expound the secrets of faith to the lovers. After this we shall sit together in probity, concealing the path of the invitation from the enemies of faith.'[17] That this mindset still prevailed in Khālū Maḥmūd's time can be seen in the compositions of his near contemporaries. Many of them invoked the tragic figure of Ḥusayn b. Manṣūr al-Ḥallāj (d. 309/922), whom the Abbasid caliph al-Muqtadir (r. 295–320/908–932) had executed after he publicly disclosed his convictions. For example, in a poem in praise of Imam Dhu'l-Faqār ʿAlī (d. 1043/1634), Mullā ʿAzīz Allāh Qummī wrote:

---

[15] Ustād Manṣūr (pseud.), 'Dar bāb-i tashrīf āwardan-i Shāh ʿAbbās-i thānī wa Āqā-yi Buzurg', incipit, بحمد الله كه بازم نخل اميدى ببار آماد, accession number 14713, Ismaili Special Collections Unit, The Institute of Ismaili Studies, London.

[16] Mustanṣir bi'llāh, *Pandiyāt-i Javānmardī*, ed. and tr. Wladimir Ivanow (Leiden, 1953), p. 56 (Persian), p. 35 (English). On the authorship of this text, see Shafique N. Virani, *The Ismailis in the Middle Ages* (New York, 2007), pp. 122–126.

[17] For the text of the poem from the manuscript, see Virani, *The Ismailis in the Middle Ages*, p. 251, n. 13. On this poet, see Virani, *Ismailis in the Middle Ages*, pp. 26, 112, 115, 129–139, 136, 172–174.

tū ham imām-i zamān-rā bi-dān ū wāfiq bāsh
agar zi ahl-i yaqīn-ī az ū ma-kun inkār
ma-gūy sirr-i ḥaqīqat bi-jāhil-i munkir
mithāl-i Khwāja-yi Manṣūr mī-shawī bar dār[18]

You, too, must know and follow the Imam of the time
Deny him not, if you be of the people of certainty
Tell not the secret of reality to the ignorant deniers
Lest you mount the gallows like Khwāja Manṣūr!

The poetry of the most senior representative of Imam Nūr al-Dahr ʿAlī, Ṣūfī b. Ṣādiq, also uses this precise imagery:

ma-gūy Ṣūfī az īn ramz-i khāṣṣ bā ḍiddān
kih mī-barand sarat-rā bih dār chūn Ḥal(l)āj[19]

Speak not to rivals of this special mystery, Ṣūfī,
Lest like Ḥallāj they make off to the gallows with your head!

During the reign of this imam, authors widely used the Ḥallājian trope to caution their audiences against revealing the inner mysteries of the faith. For example, in his lengthy *Nigāristān* (Gallery of Paintings), Khākī Khurāsānī (d. after 1056/1646), the Ismaili poet of the village of Dīzbād, apportioned God's creatures to three realms: the law (*sharʿ*), the way (*ṭarīq*), and the reality (*ḥaqīqat*). The people of the law cannot understand the way, and the people of the way cannot understand the reality. Gnostics like Manṣūr meet their end on the gallows when

[18] Cited in Muḥammad b. Zayn al-ʿĀbidīn Fidāʾī Khurāsānī, *Hidāyat al-muʾminīn al-ṭālibīn*, ed. Aleksandr Aleksandrovich Semenov (Moscow, 1959), p. 138. It is in one of the most common Persian metres, and particularly favoured by Saʿdī, see Finn Thiesen, *A Manual of Classical Persian Prosody: With Chapters on Urdu, Karakhanidic and Ottoman Prosody* (Wiesbaden, 1982), pp. 145–146, *mujtath-i muthamman-i makhbūn-i aṣlam (musbagh)* ˘ – ˘ – | ˘ ˘ – – | ˘ – ˘ – | – –. The word *wāfiq* is unusual, and one wonders if the original word may have been *wāqif*, and the letters *qāf* and *fā* were transposed. If this is so, the translation of the first line would be 'You, too, must know the Imam of the time and be aware.'

[19] Cited in Maryam Muʿizzī (Moezi), *Ismāʿīliyān-i Īrān: Az suqūṭ-i Alamūt tā imrūz bā takya bar dawrān-i muʿāṣir* (MA, Dānishgāh-i Firdawsī-yi Mashhad, 1372 Sh./1993), p. 350, n. 60. The metre is ˘ – ˘ – | ˘ – – – | ˘ – ˘ – | ˘ –, hence the gemination of the letter *lām* in Ḥallāj is eliminated.

[20] Imām Qulī Khākī Khurāsānī, *An Abbreviated Version of the Diwan of Khaki Khorasani*, ed. Wladimir Ivanow (Bombay, 1352/1933), p. 115.

they utter words incomprehensible to others.[20] Given the prevailing sentiment, we can assume that Ismailis carefully guarded their literature from outsiders. However, as evidenced by the testimony of Khayrkhwāh Harātī, and the revelation of the identities of Ismaili leaders in Khālū Maḥmūd's poem, the imam had permitted his appointees to commit the faith's teachings to writing for circulation within the community.

Through an analysis of the known elements of Khālū Maḥmūd's biography and work, and a critical edition and translation of 'A servant of 'Alī', this study uncovers aspects of the Ismaili *daʿwa* and its *dāʿīs* in the 11th/17th century. This will help us in, as it were, detecting the 'scent of the scarlet pimpernel' at that time. Following this introduction, the article continues with section B, 'Manuscripts and Studies', which documents our sources, including the discovery of a new manuscript that helps us to resolve several ambiguities in the text. Section C, '*Di Dam Dam Dam*: Prosody in Khālū Maḥmūd's Composition', examines the poem's rhythm and how this affects the understanding of its contents. Sections D, *Ghulām-i Shāh-i mardān-am* and E, 'A servant of 'Alī, King of Men, am I', contain the critical edition and translation, respectively. Section F, 'Prayers of Proximity in Ismaili and Sister Communities', places the poem in the context of its genre. It is followed by section G, 'Whose Uncle Was He?', which analyses what can be deduced about the author, primarily from his own writings. Finally, section H, 'Afterword', concludes the piece and outlines further areas for exploration.

B. Manuscripts and Studies

A number of years ago, when I had an exhibition of my work, the people in charge who came to pick up my manuscripts saw them piled up haphazardly in the garage, and were shocked. 'What?! They'll grow mold like this!' they said. People who do things properly apparently make a dedicated manuscript room, where they can control humidity.

–Akira Toriyama, Japanese manga artist[21]

---

[21] Akira Toriyama and Masanori Nakamura, *WIRED Japan*, 1997 https://www.kanzenshuu.com/translations/wired-japan-1997-akira-toriyama-interview/ (accessed on 10 October 2019).

I first encountered Khālū Maḥmūd ʿAlī's writings many years ago when researching the manuscript archives of the library of The Institute of Ismaili Studies, London. A photocopied text with the accession number 14708 contained a poem that was of immense importance. I was given to understand that the paper copy reproduced photographs of an original manuscript that belonged to an unnamed Ismaili in Iran. It began:

> *Ghulām-i shāh-i mardānam chih bāk az khārijī dāram?*
> *Muṭīʿ-i amr-i Yazdānam chih bāk az khārijī dāram?*[22]

> A servant of ʿAlī, king of men, am I. What have I to fear of his foe?
> Submissive to God's command am I. What have I to fear of a rebel?

It was copied by Ghiyāth al-Dīn Mīrshāhī, originally from the village of Dīzbād in the province of Khurāsān. At the time of this writing, he resides in Mashhad, where he was formerly a congregation leader (*mukhī*) of the Ismaili community (*jamāʿat*). The handwriting was familiar to me. The text occupies pages 51 to 66 of what was apparently a larger manuscript, but the remainder, which may have included a colophon, was not present.

In her 1993 MA thesis, 'Ismailis of Iran' (*Ismāʿīliyān-i Īrān*), Maryam Muʿizzi identified three manuscripts of this poem coming from three different villages. None of these indicated the scribe or date of copying. No further information about the manuscripts was provided, except that she used the text with the greatest number of verses as her source.[23] Farhad Daftary later wrote that in 1985 the leaders of the Nizārī Ismaili community in Khurāsān gave him copies of this and other poems of Khālū Maḥmūd.[24] In 2015, Maryam Muʿizzī published an important Persian article on the subject entitled *Qāsim-shāhiyān dar shʿir-i*

[22] Khālū Maḥmūd ʿAlī, incipit, 'غلام شاه مردانم چه باک از خارجی دارم', accession number 14708, Ismaili Special Collections Unit, The Institute of Ismaili Studies, London.

[23] Muʿizzī, *Ismāʿīliyān-i Īrān*, p. 47.

[24] Daftary, *Ismāʿīlīs: History and Doctrines*, pp. 438–439. I am grateful to Dr Daftary for checking his collection to try to locate these manuscripts of Khālū Maḥmūd ʿAlī's poetry. They were not currently available to him, and so I was unable to consult them. Personal communication, 20 January 2020.

Maḥmūd.[25] Lamenting the fact that years of searching had failed to yield exemplars of greater antiquity than those she had discovered previously, she resolved to conduct her study based on the replicas produced by two contemporary Ismaili scribes. The aforementioned Mukhī Ghiyāth al-Dīn Mīrshāhī also transcribed the first exemplar available to her, and the second was by Ṣadr al-Dīn Mīrshāhī.[26] The latter, also of Mashhad, is a grandson of the prominent Ismaili scholar, the late Muḥammad b. Zayn al-ʿĀbidīn 'Fidāʾī' Khurāsānī, known as Hājjī Ākhūnd (d. 1342/1923). Dr Muʿizzī kindly corresponded with me about these two manuscripts, but as her copies were in Iran while she was in the United States, she could not provide me with them. However, her edition based on these is available in her article.

Fortunately, I was able to identify an older and better copy of the poem, which served as the primary manuscript for preparing the new critical edition provided here. It occupies folios 82 verso to 87 verso of a volume entitled *Gul-chīn-i ahl-i ʿirfān*, (The Rose-Gatherer of the Gnostics) copied by a certain Murtaḍā b. Muṣṭafā on 1 Rabīʿ I 1328/13 March 1910. The original, numbered 55, is in the Ismaili Special Collections Unit of the Institute of Ismaili Studies, London. I have used this number as its siglum.[27] The scribe does not distinguish between the letters *kāf* and *gāf*, generally omits the letter *wāw*, meaning 'and', uses the *alif khanjariyya* rather than the *madda* for the long *ā* sound, and normally abbreviates the *radīf* or recurrent rhyme words *chih bāk az khārijī dāram* to *chibāk*. That the copyist checked his work is evident from the correction he makes in verse 44, changing *dil āgāh* to *Mīr Nūr Allāh*.

The secondary manuscript used is the copy made by Mukhī Ghiyāth al-Dīn Mīrshāhī, with the siglum 14708. While produced by the same

---

[25] Maryam Muʿizzī, 'Qāsim-shāhiyān dar shiʿr-i Maḥmūd (Qasim Shahi Communities in the Poem of Mahmud)', *Muṭāliʿāt-i taʾrīkh-i Islām*, 7 (Autumn 1394 Sh./2015).

[26] Muʿizzī, 'Qāsim-shāhiyān', p. 153. I am grateful to Dr Jalal Badakhchani for the information he has provided on these two contemporary Ismailis.

[27] Khālū Maḥmūd ʿAlī, 'Ashʿār-i durr nithār-i Maḥmūd Khālū Maḥmūd ʿAlī', incipit, 'غلام شاه مردانم چباك از خارجی دارم', in manuscript 55, Ismaili Special Collections Unit. Dr Karim Jawan kindly informed me of the existence of this manuscript, and Dr Wafi Momin and Dr Nour Nourmamadchoev of the Unit were kind enough to provide copies of the relevant pages for me.

scribe, it is not identical to the document available to Maryam Muʿizzī. Her text has the title 'From the Poetry of Khālū Maḥmūd ʿAlī' (*min ashʿār-i Khālū Maḥmūd ʿAlī*) and has scribal glosses that are absent in mine. There are also several variants in the text.[28] For example, verses 8 and 34, present in the manuscripts I consulted, are missing in the two manuscripts to which Muʿizzī had access, while verses 53 and 54, available in other manuscripts, are not included in the manuscript with siglum 14708. Verse 26, present in other manuscripts, is not found in manuscript 55. Drawing on all the manuscripts, the critical edition presented here has 78 verses. As the Muʿizzī edition does not record variants, where the readings differ, the siglum *mīm* identifies them in the critical apparatus.

C. *Di Dam Dam Dam*: Prosody in Khālū Maḥmūd's Composition

For rhetoric, he could not ope
  His mouth, but out there flew a trope;
And when he happened to break off
  I' th' middle of his speech, or cough,
H' had hard words ready to show why,
  And tell what rules he did it by;
Else, when with greatest art he spoke,
  You'd think he talked like other folk.
For all a rhetorician's rules
  Teach nothing but to name his tools.
  Samuel Butler, *Hudibras*[29]

Khālū Maḥmūd ʿAlī composed 'A Servant of ʿAlī, king of men, am I' in *baḥr-i hazaj*, the so-called 'trilling metre', an infrequent cadence in both Arabic and Persian.[30] Nevertheless, several poets employed it to

[28] Muʿizzī, 'Qāsim-shāhiyān', p. 153.

[29] Samuel Butler, *Hudibras* (Boston, MA, 1866 [originally published 1684]), pp. 18–19.

[30] Chris Golston and Tomas Riad, 'The Phonology of Classical Arabic Meter', *Linguistics*, 35 (1997), pp. 113–114; Ashwini Deo and Paul Kiparsky, 'Poetries in Contact: Arabic, Persian, and Urdu', in Maria-Kristiina Lotman and Mihhail Lotman, ed., *Frontiers in Comparative Prosody* (Bern, 2011), p. 156.

impressive effect, including Ḥāfiẓ in his famous *ghazal, Agar ān Turk-i Shīrāzī bih-dast ārad dil-i mā-rā*, (Were that Turk of Shīrāz to capture my heart).

Similarly, a popular composition by Sanāʾī, *Ma-kun dar jism ū jān manzil kih īn dūn ast ū ān wālā*, (d. ca. 525/1131) is in this metre. Notably, the Ismaili luminary Ḥasan-i Maḥmūd-i Kātib (d. 645/1246) extolled it in his *Dīwān-i qāʾimiyyāt* (Poems of the Resurrection):

ma-kun dar jism ŭ jān manzil kih īn dūn ast ŭ ān wālā
'Abide not in body and soul, for this one's sordid and that sublime'[31]

In Khālū Maḥmūd's poem, each foot (*rukn*) has a short (*kūtāh*) syllable, followed by three long (*buland*) syllables, traditionally articulated by the mnemonic device, *mafāʿīlun*. In breve-macron notation, this is ˘ – – –, or what Western analysis refers to as a first epitrite. The foot repeats four times in each of two hemistiches (sg. *miṣrāʿ*), for a total of eight feet in each verse (i.e., *baḥr-i hazaj-i muthamman-i sālim*).

Most of Khālū Maḥmūd's verses follow the rules of prosody. However, he often resolves overlong (*darāz*) syllables as long (*buland*), even when these are not the final syllable of a hemistich. Jalāl al-Dīn Rūmī (d. 672/1273) also took liberties of these kinds in his poetry.[32]

Occasionally, I have introduced minor emendations to the text for metrical reasons. For example, in verse 47 مطیعِ امرِ الرّحمٰن, present in all manuscripts, needs to be read in a highly convoluted manner to scan correctly: *muṭīʿ-i amr-i ar-Raḥmān*. It is preferable to conjecture a reading along the lines of *muṭīʿ-i amr-i Raḥmān [khwān]*, which satisfies the metre and does not significantly change the meaning. Meanwhile, I have provided the original reading of the manuscripts in the critical apparatus. Similarly, verse 38 appears in the manuscripts as follows:

Buwad dar ʿĀrak ū dar Afkisht

[31] Abu'l-Majd Majdūd b. Ādam Sanāʾī Ghaznawī, *Dīwān-i Ḥakīm Sanāʾī Ghaznawī bar asās-i muʿtabartarīn nuskha-hā*, ed. Parwīz Bābāʾī and Badīʿ al-Zamān Furūzānfar (Tehran, 1381 Sh./2002), p. 58; Ḥasan-i Maḥmūd-i Kātib, *Dīwān-i qāʾimiyyāt*, ed. Sayyid Jalāl Badakhchānī (2nd ed., Tehran, 1395 Sh./2016), no. 3, p. 44. In this regard, see *JRAS*, Series 3, 29 (2019), p. 36.

[32] Thiesen, *Classical Persian Prosody*, pp. 15–18.

The second *dar* breaks the metre and we can easily remove it without affecting the meaning. Once again, the manuscript renderings are available in the critical apparatus.

Prosody lapses in five verses particularly draw the attention as all involve proper names. It is possible the scribes did not correctly record these names, or that the poet himself erred in his prosody.

The first hemistich of verse 20 reads:

Ham az Bābā ʿAlī Kūhsārī ṭalab kun himmat ū yārī

As is readily apparent to a Persian speaker, an extraneous long syllable in the second foot spoils the rhythm. One could, of course, recompose the line to fit the metre:

Ham az Bābā-yi Kūhsārī ṭalab kun himmat ū yārī

However, this reading is entirely speculative and leads to little else but a poem that is easier to recite.

A similar issue can be seen in verses 23, 51 and 62, where the third syllable is short where it should be long:

Ghulām ʿAlī bih Kūhābād (23)
ʿAzīz Amīr kī bāshad (51)
Muḥib(b) ʿAlī'st dar Ghūrī (62)

In verse 51, one might hazard that originally ʿAzīz Amīr (عزيز امير) was ʿAzīz al-Mīr (عزيز المير), thus solving the metrical problem, though remaining entirely hypothetical. There are, however, occasional instances in Persian poetry in which the composer doubles a consonant for the sake of metre. Therefore, technically, it is unnecessary to make a change, and ʿAzīz Amīr may be the correct name.[33]

Finally, in verse 59, a syllable is missing in the second foot, most likely in the third position:

digar az jūy-naw wa'z ʿAlī Khwāja bayād āwar

33 For examples of this, see Thiesen, *Prosody*, pp. 59–60.

D. *Ghulām-i Shāh-i mardān-am*[34]

غلام شاه مردانم چه باک[35] از خارجی دارم
مطیع امر یزدانم چه باک از خارجی دارم
به قلبم سکّهٔ شاهی ز دل جو هرچه[36] می‌خواهی
بیا گر مرد این راهی چه باک از خارجی دارم

[34] In the main, this edition follows the 'Guidelines for Editors of Scholarly Editions' promulgated by the Modern Language Association; see Robert Hirst, Dirk Van Hulle, and MLA Committee on Scholarly Editions, *Guidelines for Editors of Scholarly Editions*, New York, Modern Language Association of America, access date: March 29, 2018, https://www.mla.org/Resources/Research/Surveys-Reports-and-Other-Documents/Publishing-and-Scholarship/Reports-from-the-MLA-Committee-on-Scholarly-Editions/Guidelines-for-Editors-of-Scholarly-Editions. It takes into account, however, the criticisms levelled at the Committee on Scholarly Editions, such as those directed towards editions of non-English language texts; see D.C. Greetham, 'Textual Scholarship', in Joseph Gibaldi, ed., *Introduction to Scholarship in Modern Languages and Literatures* (New York: Modern Language Association, 1992), p. 107. The spelling conventions adopted reflect the guidelines provided in Farhangistān-i zabān ū adab-i Fārsī, *Dastūr-i khaṭṭ-i Fārsī* (Tehran, 1394 Sh./2015). These guidelines, however, are for prose, and so some recommendations do not apply to poetry.

The basic format of the critical apparatus is as follows.

Lemma: variant, siglum

Additional sigla are separated by commas. Additional variants are separated by semicolons. Additional lemma are separated by periods.

a. <angle brackets> indicate lacunae

b. [square brackets] are the editor's interpolations

c. + means this lemma was added by the scribe

d. – means this lemma was omitted by the scribe

The following example illustrates a typical entry in the critical apparatus:

معمور: مأمور، ۱۴۷۰۸

This indicates that the lemma معمور used in the critical edition is represented by مأمور in the manuscript with siglum ۱۴۷۰۸.

In the critical edition, the doubling or gemination (*tashdīd*) of letters is only indicated where required by poetic metre. Thus, occasionally the same word may appear in some places with the *shadda* and other places without. For example, we find *ḥad* (حد) in verses 43, 48 and 51, but *ḥadd* (حدّ) in verse 60, since here the word requires a doubled consonant for the metre to be correct.

[35] چه باک: چباک، ۵۵

[36] جو هرچه: جوهر چه، م

شب معراجِ پیغمبر که بود دربان [او][37] بر در
بغیر از[38] خواجهٔ قنبر؟ چه باک از خارجی دارم
رسولی[39] چون نبی دارم به دل مهر علی دارم
نظررا بر وصی دارم چه باک از خارجی دارم

شب معراج کز بستر نبی شد جانب داور
ندید آنجا به جز حیدر چه باک از خارجی دارم
هزاران پند گفتم من ترا[40] از[41] رهبر[42] سالک
بکن گوش ار نه‌ای هالک چه باک از خارجی دارم
مرو دنبال نام و[43] ننگ سگ نفس آور اندر بند
ز مردان این شنیدم[44] پند چه باک از خارجی دارم
به مرد[45] حق تمنّا کن ز غیر او تبرّا کن
تو آنگه رُو به مولا[46] کن چه باک از خارجی دارم
اگر مولا شود یارم نسازد مرد حق خوارم[47]
خبر از مؤمنان آرم چه باک از خارجی دارم

معلّم‌های هر کشور بگویم اسم هر رهبر
شفیع خود کنم یک سر چه باک از خارجی دارم
به اوّل[48] از خراسان گو ز پیر و[49] رهبر آن[50] گو
دمادم ذکر ایشان گو چه باک از خارجی دارم
تو یعقوب شاه داعی دان [و امرش][51] امر شاهی دان
ملازم‌هاش راهی دان چه باک از خارجی دارم
مقام و منزلش پترو خدا خواهی[52] به امرش[53] رو

---

37 بود دربان [او]: بوده راهبان، ۵۵، ۱۴۷۰۸، م
38 از: ــ، ۱۴۷۰۸
39 رسولی: رسول، ۵۵
40 ترا: تورا: ۵۵
41 از: ای، ۵۵
42 رهبر: هر، ۱۴۷۰۸
43 و: ــ، ۵۵
44 شنیدم: شنودم، ۱۴۷۰۸
45 به مرد: بمرد، ۵۵
46 مولا: <بحورا>، ۱۴۷۰۸
47 خوارم: خارم، ۵۵
48 به اوّل: باول، ۵۵
49 و: ــ، ۵۵
50 رهبر آن: رهبران، ۵۵؛ رهبر او، ۱۴۷۰۸
51 [و امرش]: امورش، ۵۵، ۱۴۷۰۸، م
52 خواهی: خاهی: ۵۵
53 به امرش: بامرش، ۵۵

ز من این نکته‌ها[54] بشنو چه باک از خارجی دارم
خدایا نقد صوفی‌را نگهدار از همه آفات
بدین و[55] مذهبش صلوات[56] چه باک از خارجی دارم

دگر از ایل بیچاره تو ذکر میر حیدر گو
ز صدقش سر بسر برگو چه باک از خارجی دارم
تو شمس‌الدّین علی‌را[57] دان که باشد مسکنش غوریان[58]
ز لطفش جان و[59] دل شادان چه باک از خارجی دارم
میان لاخیان ره بین بجو ملاّ کمال‌الدّین
کند بیگانه‌را تلقین چه باک از خارجی دارم
دگر مرزا[60] علی‌را دان که باشد ایل شیبانی
اگر دانای مردانی چه باک از خارجی دارم
کنیم[61] از میر رستم یاد کو ساکن به جاجرم است
ز عشّاقان دل گرم است چه باک از خارجی دارم

هم از بابا علی کوهساری طلب کن همّت و[62] یاری
طلب زان بندهٔ[63] باری چه باک از خارجی دارم
یکی عارف که در جام است و[64] محمود است نام او
مطهّر جسم و جان[65] او چه باک از خارجی دارم
[و][66] الله‌داد[67] خلق او که باشد در فره ساکن
بُوَد از زمرهٔ باطن چه باک از خارجی دارم
غلام‌علی به کوه‌آباد[68] دلش از «مَا سِوَىٰ» آزاد

---

54 نکته‌ها: نکتها، ۵۵

55 و: —، ۵۵

56 On the Persian pronunciation *ṣalwāt* rather than *ṣalawāt*, required here for metre, see ʿAlī Akbar Dihkhudā, Muḥammad Muʿīn and Jaʿfar Shahīdī, *Lughat-nāma* (2nd ed., Tehran, 1377 Sh./1998), s.v. صلوت.

57 را: —، ۱۴۷۰۸

58 Here, the letter *wāw* in the word غوریان must be pronounced as a short vowel to maintain the metre. Regarding the shortening of this vowel in Persian poetic license, see Thiesen, *Classical Persian Prosody*, p. 64.

59 و: —، ۵۵

60 مرزا: میرزا

61 کنیم: کنم، ۱۴۷۰۸

62 و: —، ۵۵

63 بندهٔ: بندهٔ، ۵۵

64 و: —، ۵۵

65 جسم و جان: جان و جسم، ۱۴۷۰۸

66 [و]: ز، ۵۵، ۱۴۷۰۸، م

67 و: +، ۱۴۷۰۸، م

68 کوه‌آباد: کوآباد، ۵۵

شوند عشّاق ازو[69] دل‌شاد چه باک از خارجی دارم
کند مرغ دلم پرواز به مولدگاه خویشم باز
شود با مؤمنان همراز چه باک از خارجی دارم

بیا پیک صبا برسان سلام من به صد[70] دستان
به درویشان قوهستان چه باک از خارجی دارم
به ماهوسک[71] نعمت‌الله است غلام خاصّ الله است
به سوی حق ورا راه است چه باک از خارجی دارم
به رایک ساکن[ش][72] عارف که اسمش شاه حسین آمد
محبّان‌را چه[73] عین آمد چه باک از خارجی دارم
ز میرزگ یادگار است آن منوّر دین و ایمانش[74]
کزان روشن بُوَد[75] جانش چه باک از خارجی دارم
بجو درویشِ قطب‌الدّین که در یهن است قطب دین
طریقت‌دان حقیقت‌بین چه باک از خارجی دارم

ورا[76] بی‌شک ولی می‌دان به خلقش چون نبی می‌دان
محبّ متّقی می‌دان چه باک از خارجی دارم
چه ملّا قاسمِ بورنج که نقد خواجه جان آمد[77]
محبّ خاندان آمد[78] چه باک از خارجی دارم
در اصل مسک[79] مرد حق یقین سلطان علی باشد
اخویم چون ولی باشد چه باک از خارجی دارم
مرا مولود از آن خاک است و دایم جسته‌ام همّت
ز روح خواجه‌ها[80] همّت چه باک از خارجی دارم
یکی زان خواجه جان باشد که آسو جای آن[81] باشد
دلیل مؤمنان باشد چه باک از خارجی دارم

---

69 ازو: <او>، ۱۴۷۰۸

70 به صد: بصد

71 ماهوسک: م؛ مایوسک، ۱۴۷۰۸

72 او: +، ۵۵

73 چه: چو، ۱۴۷۰۸

74 و ایمانش: ایمانش، ۵۵؛ و دنیایش، ۱۴۷۰۸

75 بود: —، ۵۵

76 ورا: —، ۱۴۷۰۸

77 آمد: باشد، ۱۴۷۰۸

78 آمد: باشد: ۱۴۷۰۸

79 در اصل مسک: بکسکک، ۱۴۷۰۸؛ به بسکک، م

80 خواجه‌ها: خواجها، ۵۵

81 آن: او، ۱۴۷۰۸

ز سلطان بازگو آن به به نزد اهل که تا مه
بُوَد در خُنگ و[82] در نوده چه باک از خارجی دارم
ملک اندر سده رهبر به امر داعی سرور
خدایش حافظ و[83] یاور چه باک از خارجی دارم
چه گویم[84] وصف از کُنذُر رضا ساکن در او[85] چون دُر
دلش از مهر مولا پر چه باک از خارجی دارم
بُوَد در عارک و[86] افکشت امینِ[87] امن با ایمان
ثنا گویم ورا از جان چه باک از خارجی دارم
به سرخیج دوست محمّدرا دعا گوییم در هردم
نه اندوه بیند و نه غم چه باک از خارجی دارم

ز جازارِ ولی گویم هم از میرزا علی گویم
ورا کلب علی گویم چه باک از خارجی دارم
بشو سوی عراق ای دل بشکرت روز هر منزل
که گردد مدّعا حاصل چه باک از خارجی دارم
جماعات[88] عطاءاللّهیان‌را[89] صد صفا باشد
معلّمشان رضا باشد چه باک از خارجی دارم
معلّم در حد کرمان تو ملّا شاه بیکـرا[90] دان
بُوَد از جملهٔ مردان چه باک از خارجی دارم
معلّم در سرقو[91] دان ز احشاماتِ دل آگاه
همی‌دان میر نورالله چه باک از خارجی دارم

به[92] عشّاقان هندوستان مجالس‌شان[93] بُوَد بستان
بگویم صدق آن مستان چه باک از خارجی دارم
حسن‌شاه است در لاهور داعی سوی مولانا
در این اسرار با معنا چه باک از خارجی دارم
ابل[94] بین ساکن ملتان[95] اخویش پیر محمّد دان

82 و: —، ۵۵
83 و: —، ۵۵
84 چه گویم: چگویم، ۵۵
85 در او: در آن: ۱۴۷۰۸
86 در: +، ۵۵، ۱۴۷۰۸
87 و: +، ۱۴۷۰۸
88 جماعات: جماعت، ۱۴۷۰۸
89 عطاءاللّهیان‌را: عطاللّهیان‌را، ۵۵
90 بیکـرا: بیکا، ۱۴۷۰۸
91 سرقو: سبرقو: ۱۴۷۰۸
92 به: ز، ۱۴۷۰۸
93 مجاجلسشان: مجلّسشان، ۵۵
94 ابل: امین ۱۴۷۰۸؛ ایل، م
95 ملتان: بلتان، ۵۵؛ مولتان، ۱۴۷۰۸، م

مطیعِ امر رحمان [خوان][96] چه باک از خارجی دارم
معلّم در حد گجرات پیر فاضل علی باشد
چه آن[97] فاضل ولی باشد چه باک از خارجی دارم
خضر خان ساکن دیول به دیول نیستش مُبْدل
خبیر و عالم و[98] اکمل چه باک از خارجی دارم

بُوَد اندر جلاله‌پور کسکه نام آن[99] دانا
غلام خاص[100] مولا[نا] چه باک از خارجی دارم
عزیز امیر کی[101] باشد معرّف[102] در حد کابل
غلام صاحب دلدل چه باک از خارجی دارم
ز بک توت[103] میر محمّدرا دعا خواندن بُوَد رخصت
خداوندش دهد فرصت[104] چه باک از خارجی دارم
یکی در چاریک کار است که اسمش رحمت‌الله است
محبّ خاص الله است چه باک از خارجی دارم
دگر اندر فریضه آن مَلِک حاجی معلّم دان
بُوَد حق‌دان بُوَد حق‌خوان چه باک از خارجی دارم

به لیهان کرده است[105] آن حیدرِ قاسم بحق گویا
از او[106] روشن شود دل‌ها چه باک از خارجی دارم
مرادِ[107] طاهری‌را هم[108] ارس خان کنکنش[109] داده
بُوَد ساقی[110] این باده چه باک از خارجی دارم
ارس خان داعی[111] حق‌دان که اندر درّهٔ نور است

---

96 امر رحمٰن [خوان]: امرِالرّحمٰن، ۵۵، ۱۴۷۰۸، م
97 آن: او، ۱۴۷۰۸
98 و: –، ۵۵
99 آن: او، ۱۴۷۰۸
100 خاص: خوٰصهٔ، ۵۵؛ خاصه، ۱۴۷۰۸، م
101 کی=که
102 معرّف: معروف، ۱۴۷۰۸
103 ز بک توت: به یک توت، ۱۴۷۰۸
104 فرصت: رخصت، ۵۵
105 کرده است: کرد، ۱۴۷۰۸
106 او: آن، ۱۴۷۰۸
107 خان: +، ۱۴۷۰۸
108 هم: –، ۱۴۷۰۸
109 کنکنش: گنگنش، م
110 از: +، ۵۵، ۱۴۷۰۸، م
111 داعی: دعی، ۵۵

از او[112] آن گوشه معمور[113] است چه باک از خارجی دارم
بُوَد درویش علی در اصل سبز از[114] عارفِ حیدر
به صدق و[115] خلق چون قنبر چه باک از خارجی دارم
دگر از جوی نو[116] از علی[117] خواجه بیاد آور[118]
ارس خانش بُوَد رهبر[119] چه باک از خارجی دارم

کُتل یک موضعی باشد محمّد رهبر است آنجا
در آن حدّش بُوَد مأوا چه باک از خارجی دارم
شنو ز اقلیم ترکستان و حق‌دانان آن کشور
ز[120] یک یک گویم ای رهبر چه باک از خارجی دارم
محبّ علی است در غوری که امرش هست دستوری
بگویم ار نه دل کوری[121] چه باک از خارجی دارم
بُوَد حق‌داد دُرِ قندز معلّم بر سر جمعی
دل تاریک‌را شمعی چه باک از خارجی دارم
بدیع آن عارف حق‌دان که ساکن در بدخشان است
به تحقیق از محبّان است چه باک از خارجی دارم

بحقّ این معلّم‌ها بحقّ این خدادان‌ها
گناهم‌را عفو فرما چه باک از خارجی دارم
الٰهی فردی و اکبر پناه کهتر و[122] مهتر
ز تقصیرات من بگذر چه باک از خارجی دارم
کنی ز اسرار آگاهم نمایی سوی خود راهم
کمینه کلب درگاهم چه باک از خارجی دارم
الٰهی بی‌نیازی تو الٰهی کار سازی تو
یقین دانای رازی تو[123] چه باک از خارجی دارم
بحقّ آدم و حوّا بحقّ صالح و[124] یحیی

---

112 او: آن، ۱۴۷۰۸
113 معمور: مأمور، ۱۴۷۰۸
114 سبز از: سبزار، ۵۵
115 و: –، ۵۵
116 و: +، ۵۵، ۱۴۷۰۸، م
117 علی: اعلی، ۵۵
118 آور: آر، ۱۴۷۰۸
119 رهبر: سرور، ۱۴۷۰۸
120 ز: که، ۱۴۷۰۸
121 دلکوری: دلکور، ۵۵
122 و: –، ۵۵
123 تو: –، ۱۴۷۰۸
124 و: –، ۵۵

ببخشایی گناه ما چه باک از خارجی دارم

بحقّ نوح و[125] طوفانت به اسماعیل و[126] قربانت
شدم در امر و[127] فرمانت چه باک از خارجی دارم
بحقّ موسیٰ و عیسیٰ رسول الله نبیّ ما
شفیع آخرت فردا چه باک از خارجی دارم
به سیّدنا و رای او به اعجاز و[128] دعای او
رئیسان[129] با رضای او چه باک از خارجی دارم
بحقّ صوفیِ[130] صادق علومش بر همه فایق
که غمگین باد نالایق چه باک از خارجی دارم
به یعقوب‌شاهٔ پیر ما[131] و آن[132] دست دعای او
رضای حق رضای او چه باک از خارجی دارم

چرا اندیشهٔ باطل[133] از این ضدّان[134] کنی محمود
چه نورالدّهر شد یارم[135] چه باک از خارجی دارم
شفیع جرم من باشند این مردان راه دین
بزرگان‌را است این آیین چه باک از خارجی دارم
شفیع ما ستمکاران بسویت[136] حق‌شناسان‌اند
غلامش‌را غلامان‌اند چه باک از خارجی دارم
بحقّ ذات نورالدّهر بزرگ آن قایم[137] اعظم
بُوَد با این [همه][138] همدم چه باک از خارجی دارم

125 و: –، ۵۵
126 و: –، ۵۵
127 و: –، ۵۵
128 و: –، ۵۵
129 رئیسان: رائیان، ۵۵
130 و: +، ۱۴۷۰۸
131 پیر ما: ما پیرو، ۵۵
132 آن: بآن، ۵۵
133 باطل: باطن، ۱۴۷۰۸
134 ضدان: مندان، ۵۵
135 یارم: یاور، ۱۴۷۰۸
136 ما ستمکاران بسویت: هاشم والدان بوند، ۵۵
137 بزرگان قایم: بزرگان خالق، ۵۵؛ بزرگ آن قائم، ۱۴۷۰۸
138 این [همه]: این‌ها، ۵۵، ۱۴۷۰۸

E. A Servant of ʿAlī, King of Men, am I

A servant of ʿAlī, king of men, am I. What have I to fear of his foe?
Submissive to God's command am I. What have I to fear of a rebel?[139]
Stamped on my soul is his royal die. From my heart, seek what you will.
Come hither if you be a man of this path. What have I to fear of a rebel?
On the night of the Prophet's heavenly ascent, who stood guard by the gate?
It was none save ʿAlī, master of Qanbar. What have I to fear of a rebel?[140]
I have a prophet like Muhammad, love for ʿAlī fills my heart.
I set my sights upon the legatee (*waṣī*). What have I to fear of a rebel?
When the Prophet from where he slept, ascended to the Judge Divine,
He saw none there save ʿAlī, the lion. What have I to fear of a rebel?

---

[139] The rhythm of the poem in Persian is such that each hemistich is further divided by a caesura. This pause in the rhythm often indicates a transition in the meaning as well. The translation frequently reflects these caesurae with punctuation marks in mid-hemistich, even if these are not requisite in English.

[140] Abu'l-Shaʿthā' Qanbar b. Kādān al-Dawsī is celebrated in many stories for his unswerving fidelity and devotion as the servant of Imam ʿAlī. For references to him in Ismaili poetry written by a contemporary of Khālū Maḥmūd ʿAlī, see Khākī Khurāsānī, *Muntakhab-i dīwān*, pp. 35, 94. For references to Qanbar in Fatimid times, see al-Qāḍī al-Nuʿmān, *Daʿāʾim al-Islām*, tr. A. A. A. Fyzee and completely revised by Ismail K. Poonawala as *The Pillars of Islam: Acts of Devotion and Religious Observances* (New Delhi, 2002–2004), vol. 1, p. 64, with bibliographical references in n. 168 and vol. 2, pp. 444, 474, 486. A general sense of the traditions circulating about Qanbar at the time of Khālū Maḥmūd ʿAlī's writing may be gleaned from Muḥammad Bāqir al-Majlisī (d. 1110/1698), *Biḥār al-anwār*, ed. ʿAbd al-Zahrā' ʿAlawī (Beirut, 1403/1983), vol. 42, pp. 121–140. Some examples of the relationship between Qanbar and Imam ʿAlī as a trope in Persian poetry may be found in Habibeh Rahim, 'Perfection Manifested: ʿAlī b. Abī Ṭālib's Image in Classical Persian and Modern Indian Muslim Poetry' (PhD, Harvard University, 1989), pp. 296–298.

Thousands of counsels I related to you, from the guide of the traveller on the spiritual path.
If you're not destined for perdition, take heed! What have I to fear of a rebel?
Chase not name and fame. Leash the dog of ego.
This counsel have I heard from the brave. What have I to fear of a rebel?
Long for the man of God alone. Disavow all save him,
Then turn your face towards the Imam. What have I to fear of a rebel?[141]
If the Imam aids me, the man of God won't debase me.
I bring you tidings of the faithful. What have I to fear of a rebel?

10

I shall speak the name of every guide (*rahbar*), of the teachers (*muʿallim-hā*) of every land,
Taking them together as my intercessors. What have I to fear of a rebel?
Speak first of Khurāsān, tell of its sage (*pīr*) and guide.
Remember them with every breath. What have I to fear of a rebel?
Know Yaʿqūb Shāh to be the inviter (*dāʿī*). His command is the Imam's.
Know his attendants to be emissaries (*rāhī*). What have I to fear of a rebel?[142]

---

[141] In Ismaili writings, *mard-i ḥaqq* generally refers to the imam or the Prophet as the 'man of God', or *mard-i Khudā*, i.e., God's representative on earth, who is also the *mard-i ḥaqīqat*, the 'true man', i.e., the sole human being in his time who conveys knowledge but does not need to receive it from any earthly source. With regard to the latter meaning, see Nāṣir-i Khusraw, *Wajh-i dīn*, pp. 289, 295. Khālū Maḥmūd ʿAlī, however, seems to use it for someone appointed by the imam as a member of the religious hierarchy (*ḥudūd-i dīn*), as becomes clear in couplet 32, in which his brother Sulṭān ʿAlī of Mask is also referred to as the *mard-i ḥaqq*.

[142] On the *rāhīs*, see Virani, *Ismailis in the Middle Ages*, pp. 41, 213 n92. While all manuscripts read امورش, 'his affairs', this is almost certainly the result of the transposition of the letter *wāw* and should be read و امرش, 'and his command'. Cf. couplet 74, *riḍā-yi Ḥaqq riḍā-yi ū*. Among Central Asian Ismailis, there is a common expression *amr-i muʿallim amr-i imām-i zamān*, 'the command of the teacher is the command of the Imam of the time', a formula that directly parallels one found among South Asian Ismailis, *amar mukhī sāheb amar hāzar imām*. See His Highness Prince Aga Khan Shia Imami Ismailia Supreme Council for Europe, Canada, U.S.A. and Africa, ed., *Religious Rites and Ceremonies* (Nairobi, 1981), p. 2.

Patraw is his home and hearth. Follow his commands if you seek God.
  Harken to my pithy hints. What have I to fear of a rebel?
O God, from every trial and tribulation, guard the son of Ṣūfī.
  Benedictions be upon his faith and fold. What have I to fear of a rebel?[143]

Recall Mīr Ḥaydar of the Bīchāra tribe.
  Tell of his honesty from start to finish. What have I to fear of a rebel?[144]
Know Shams al-Dīn ʿAlī who dwells in Ghūriyān.
  Heart and soul rejoice at his grace. What have I to fear of a rebel?
Seek Mullā Kamāl al-Dīn, who knows the path among the people of Lākhī.
  It is he who instructs strangers. What have I to fear of a rebel?
Next, if you are wise among men, know Mīrzā ʿAlī,
  Who is of the Shaybānī tribe. What have I to fear of a rebel?
We shall recall Mīr Rustam, for he lives in Jājarm.
  Our heart is stirred by the lovers. What have I to fear of a rebel?

Seek courage and support from Bābā ʿAlī of Kūhsār.
  Seek from that servant of the Creator. What have I to fear of a rebel?
A gnostic named Maḥmūd lives in Jām.
  How pure his body and soul! What have I to fear of a rebel?
And Allāh-dād of his flock who lives in Farah
  Is among the company of inner meaning. What have I to fear of a rebel?
Ghulām ʿAlī of Kuhābād, his heart is free of ʻall else but (God)ʼ.
  The hearts of the lovers rejoice at him. What have I to fear of a rebel?

---

[143] On the translation of *naqd* as ʻsonʼ in this context, see Dihkhudā, Muʿīn, and Shahīdī, *Lughat-nāma*, s.v. نقد where the following verse is cited as an example:

بس است این دو صاحبقرانرا همین
که این نقد آن است و آن جد این

The verse may also be read, ʻguard the treasure of Ṣūfīʼ, etc.

Once again, to my birthplace, the bird of my heart takes flight,
Sharing secrets with the faithful. What have I to fear of a rebel?

25
Come, O footman of the zephyr, convey my salutation with a hundred tales
To the dervishes of Quhistān. What have I to fear of a rebel?
In Māhūsk is Niʿmat Allāh, a special servant of God.
He has a path towards the Truth. What have I to fear of a rebel?
There dwells a gnostic in Rāyak named Shāh Ḥusayn.
What a spring came to the true lovers. What have I to fear of a rebel?
He is a memento of Mīrzag. May his religion and faith be resplendent.
Thus is his soul illumined. What have I to fear of a rebel?
Seek Dervish Quṭb al-Dīn, who is the pole of religion in Yahn
A knower of the path (*ṭarīqat*), a seer of the truth (*ḥaqīqat*). What have I to fear of a rebel?

30
Without doubt, know him as a saint (*walī*), whose nature is like the Prophet's.
Know him to be a pious lover. What have I to fear of a rebel?[145]

[144] Muʿizzī regards *Bīchāra* here as a corruption of *Jabbāra*, the name of an Arab tribe. There seems to be no compelling reason to modify the word *Bīchāra* though. It is found in all manuscripts and, as Aḥmad ʿAlī Khān Vazīrī informs us, the Bīchāra tribe in Kirmān is closely connected with the Ismaili ʿAṭāʾ Allāhī tribe, see his, *Jughrāfiyā-yi Kirmān*, ed. Muḥammad Ibrāhīm Bāstānī Pārīzī (Tehran, 1376 Sh./1997), p. 317. Interesting information about the Bīchāra community in Gunābād, an important centre of the Niʿmat Allāhī community, which has historically had close connections with the Ismailis, may be found in Ḥājj Sulṭān-Ḥusayn Tābanda, *Taʾrīkh wa jughrāfiyā-yi Gunābād* (2nd ed., Tehran, 1379 Sh./2000), pp. 169–170. Elsewhere, I have pointed out that the scholarly consensus tracing Ismaili-Niʿmat-Allāhī connections to the fifteen-century is based on an incorrect reading of the sources. See Virani, *Ismailis in the Middle Ages*, p. 146. However, in Khālū Maḥmūd's 11th/17th-century poem, we may have the earliest known evidence of such a connection in the reference to the *Īl-i Bīchāra*.

[145] Or, 'For his people consider him like the Prophet'.

What about Mullā Qāsim of Būranj, who is the son of Khwāja Jān?
He is a lover of the Holy Family. What have I to fear of a rebel?[146]
From Mask, the man of God is certainly Sulṭān ʿAlī.
Like unto a saint is my brother. What have I to fear of a rebel?
I was born in that land and have constantly sought high-minded resolve.
Resolve comes from the spirit of the masters (*khwāja-hā*). What have I to fear of a rebel?
Among them is Khwāja Jān, who hails from Āsū.
He is the director (*dalīl*) of the faithful. What have I to fear of a rebel?
In the presence of great and small, it is best to speak of Sulṭān.
He is in Khung and in Nawdih. What have I to fear of a rebel?
Malik is the guide in Sidih, by the command of the master inviter (*dāʿī-yi sarvar*).
May God be his protector and helper. What have I to fear of a rebel?
How can I describe Kundur in which, like a pearl, resides Riḍā?
Love for the Imam fills his heart. What have I to fear of a rebel?
In ʿĀrak and in Afkisht is the faithful Amīn, protector of peace.
From the depths of my soul, I praise him. What have I to fear of a rebel?[147]
With every breath, we pray for Dūst Muḥammad in Sarkhīj.
May he witness neither grief nor sorrow. What have I to fear of a rebel?
I speak of Jāzār of Walī, and also speak of Mīrzā ʿAlī.
I call him the hound of ʿAlī. What have I to fear of a rebel?[148]

---

[146] It is likely that this is the Khwāja Jān from Āsū mentioned in couplet 34, below. Regarding the word *naqd*, see the note to couplet 14, above.

[147] It is likely that *amīn-i aman* is here used as a proper name, Amīn, and not in its root meaning of trustee or protector. Without detailed knowledge of the individuals mentioned, it is often difficult to determine whether particular words in the poem are to be understood as proper names.

[148] Or 'the saint's Jāzār', Jāzār probably being modern-day Gāzār in Khurāsān-i Junūbī.

Turn towards Iraq, O heart, to give thanks each day for every place,
That your desire be fulfilled. What have I to fear of a rebel?
May the congregations (*jamāʿāt*) of ʿAṭāʾ Allāhīs have a hundred joys.
Their teacher (*muʿallim*) is Riḍā. What have I to fear of a rebel?
Know Mullā Shāh Bīk to be the teacher in the boundary of Kirmān.
He is among the company of courageous men. What have I to fear of a rebel?
Know the teacher in Saraqū to be in the retinue of perceptive hearts.
Know him to be Mīr Nūr Allāh. What have I to fear of a rebel?

45
I speak of the rectitude of those intoxicated ones, the lovers of Hindūstān.
May their assemblies turn into gardens. What have I to fear of a rebel?
In these meaningful mysteries, it is Ḥasan Shāh in Lahore
Who is the inviter to our Imam. What have I to fear of a rebel?
Abal-bīn lives in Multān, know his brother to be Pīr Muḥammad.
Call him submissive to the will of the Merciful. What have I to fear of a rebel?[149]
The teacher in the bounds of Gujarāt is Pīr Fāḍil ʿAlī.
What a gifted saint is he. What have I to fear of a rebel?
Khiḍr Khān of Daiwal is peerless in that land,
Learned, a scholar, so perfect. What have I to fear of a rebel?

---

149 Here, in place of *Abal-bīn* (ابلبين) as found in manuscript 55, Muʿizzī has *Īl bīn*. However, this does not fit the metre. Manuscript 14708 has *Amīn bīn*. It is possible that this was an Indic name, which was incorrectly rendered by the scribes. *Abalājan* (ابلاجن, અબળાજન), for example, is a synonym of *abaḷā*, or helpless maiden, an epithet used by Pīr Ḥasan Kabīrdīn (fl. 9th/15th c.) to describe his humility before the imam. See, for example, his, ʻĀdam ād nıriñjan', in *100 Gınānani chopaḍi: Venati moṭi maher karo tathā Sat vachan ne Sataguranuranā vivānuṃ nānuṃ gınān tathā bijā gınāno vāli* (5th ed., Mumbai, 1990 VS/1934), vol. 1, no. 3, 6–14. It is also possible that bīn should be read separately, as a verb: 'Behold Abal . . .'

In Jalālahpūr Kaskah lives one named Dānā.
He is a special servant of our Imam. What have I to fear of a rebel?
ʿAzīz Amīr, known in the bounds of Kābul
Is the servant of Duldul's lord, ʿAlī. What have I to fear of a rebel?[150]
Mīr Muḥammad of Bik Tūt is granted leave to read the prayer.
May the lord give him ease. What have I to fear of a rebel?
There is one in Chārayak Kār named Raḥmat Allāh.
He is a special lover of God. What have I to fear of a rebel?[151]
Know also that in Farīḍa, Malik Ḥājī is the teacher.
A knower of God, an invoker of God. What have I to fear of a rebel?

He appointed that Ḥaydar, son of Qāsim, to speak the truth in Līhān
Through whom hearts are illuminated. What have I to fear of a rebel?
Aras Khān also gave his divining rod to Murād-i Ṭāhirī.
He is the cupbearer of this wine. What have I to fear of a rebel?[152]
Know that in Darra-yi Nūr is Aras Khān, the inviter, knower of God.
Through him, that corner flourishes. What have I to fear of a rebel?

---

[150] Duldul was the famous mount of ʿAlī. The *EI2* article provides some useful historical information, but is inadequate for understanding Duldul as a poetic trope. See Huart and Pellat, 'Duldul', *EI2*. https://doi.org/10.1163/1573-3912_islam_SIM_2151. For the poetic trope, see Habib Rahim, 'Perfection Manifested: ʿAlī b. Abī Ṭālib's Image in Classical Persian and Modern Indian Muslim Poetry', pp. 291–295.

[151] The name of the place must be read Chārayak Kār for the metre. It is likely this is modern-day Chārīkār.

[152] Muʿizzī suggests that Kankan may refer to the Kang district of Nīmrūz province, Afghanistan, Muʿizzī, 'Qāsim-shāhiyān', p. 164. I have followed Dihkhudā, who treats it as meaning *kān-kan* or *kahan-kan* in the sense of *chāh-kan*, *qanāt-kan*, or *muqannī*, the latter meaning 'skillful at finding water.' The hoopoe is sometimes referred to as *muqannī al-arḍ*. In this sense, I've tentatively rendered it with the English expression 'divining rod,' a forked tree branch that indicates to a skilled user the presence of water or treasure underground.

In reality, Darwīsh ʿAlī flourishes as Ḥaydar's gnostic.
In honesty and temperament, he's like Qanbar. What have I to fear of a rebel?[153]
Next, recall ʿAlī Khwāja from Jūy-Naw.
Aras Khān is his guide. What have I to fear of a rebel?
Kutal is a place in which Muḥammad is the guide.
In that realm of his, he lives. What have I to fear of a rebel?
Harken to the tale of the clime of Turkistān, and the knowers of God in that land,
For I shall speak of them one by one, O guide. What have I to fear of a rebel?
Muḥibb ʿAlī is in Ghūrī, where his command rules the land.
I shall speak if your heart isn't blind. What have I to fear of a rebel?
Haqq-dād is the pearl of Qunduz, the teacher at the head of a group.
He is a candle for the benighted heart. What have I to fear of a rebel?
Badīʿ, that God-knowing gnostic, who lives in Badakhshān,
Most assuredly, he is among the lovers. What have I to fear of a rebel?
For the sake of these teachers, for the sake of these knowers of God,
Forgive my sins. What have I to fear of a rebel?
O God, You are unique and greater, refuge of high and low.
Forgive all my transgressions. What have I to fear of a rebel?
Grant me knowledge of mysteries. Show me the path to You.
This humble creature is a dog at Your threshold. What have I to fear of a rebel?
O God, You are self-sufficient, beyond need. O God, You are my helper.
You are certainly the knower of the secret. What have I to fear of a rebel?
For the sake of Ādam and Ḥawwā (Eve), for the sake of Ṣāliḥ and Yaḥyā (John the Baptist),
Forgive our sins. What have I to fear of a rebel?

---

153 *Sabz az* might more fruitfully be read here as *Sibzār*, a place near Herat. The metre, however, would be broken and the translation would be a rather strained, 'originally Darwīsh ʿAlī is from ʿĀrif Ḥaydar's Sibzār'.

For the sake of Nūḥ (Noah) and Your flood, by Ismāʿīl (Ishmael)
and the sacrifice made for You,
I have submitted to Your command and will. What have I to
fear of a rebel?
For the sake of Mūsā (Moses) and ʿĪsā (Jesus), Rasūl Allāh, our
Prophet,
Is the intercessor in tomorrow's Judgment. What have I to
fear of a rebel?
By Sayyidnā [Ḥasan-i Ṣabbāḥ] and his vision, by his wonders
and prayer.
By the chieftains (*rā'īs-ān*) in accord with him. What have I
to fear of a rebel?
For the sake of Ṣūfī, son of Ṣādiq, whose knowledge is superior
to all,
May the unworthy be rent by sorrow. What have I to fear of a
rebel?[154]
By Yaʿqūb Shāh, our sage, and his hands (raised in) prayers.
His pleasure is God's pleasure. What have I to fear of a rebel?

Wherefore these futile cares of foes, Maḥmūd?
When Nūr al-Dahr has befriended me, What have I to fear of
a rebel?
These brave men, followers of the path of faith, will intercede
for my sins,
For such is the custom of the noble. What have I to fear of a
rebel?
Before you, the intercessors for us, the sinful, are those who
have recognised God.
His (Nūr al-Dahr's) slave has his own slaves. What have I to
fear of a rebel?
By the essence of Nūr al-Dahr, how great that resurrector
sublime!
United with all these, What have I to fear of a rebel?

---

[154] *Ṣūfī-yi Ṣādiq* may equally be translated as 'sincere Ṣūfī'. However, Ismaili oral tradition in Quhistān, as recorded by Maryam Muʿizzī, traces the family genealogy to this Ṣādiq. See Maryam Muʿizzī, 'Risāla-yi Ḥusayn bin Yaʿqūb Shāh', *Faṣl-nāma-yi muṭālaʿāṭ-i ta'rīkhī*, 3 (1370 Sh./1991–1992), p. 408.

F. Prayers of Proximity in Ismaili and Sister Communities

> *Tobho tobho takasīradār, bando sīr tā pā gunehagār, yā shāh tuṃ bakṣīe bakṣaṇahār. Dhuā to pīr paḍe, bando to venatī kare, sachcho shāh to kabul kare.*
>
> I repent, I repent! This sinner is a slave guilty from head to foot – forgive me O lord, for you are the clement. The *pīr* prays, this slave entreats, true Lord – yours is to pardon.
>
> Pīr Ṣadr al-Dīn, *The Primordial Prayer*[155]

In his poem, Khālū Maḥmūd seeks refuge in Imam Nūr al-Dahr, and the intercession of 'those who have recognised God'. These are the community's dignitaries in scattered lands, along with Adam, Eve and several prophets, culminating in the Prophet Muhammad. He also invokes Sayyidnā, i.e., Ḥasan-i Ṣabbāḥ, the imam's proof (*ḥujjat*) Ṣūfī son of Ṣādiq, 'whose knowledge is superior to all', and Yaʿqūb Shāh, the poet's own *pīr*, who was the son of Ṣūfī.[156] Entreaties that invoke the imams in general, and the imam of one's time in particular, in seeking sanctuary and proximity to God, are ubiquitous at every period of Ismaili history. We find direct parallels of this practice in many sister Muslim communities, such as the invocation of the Ithnāʿasharī imams in Twelver Shiʿi practice, or of the saints of various Sufi orders in their prayers, plentiful examples of which are documented by Constance Padwick in her *Muslim Devotions*.[157] These works, often

155 Pīr Ṣadr al-Dīn, *Asal Dhuā: Shiyā Īmāmi Isamāīlīnī traṇ vakhatanī bandagī* (4th ed., Mumbai, 1984 VS/1928), p. 2.

156 On Ḥasan-i Ṣabbāḥ, see Ali Mohammad Rajput, *Hasan-i-Sabbah: His Life and Thought* (revised ed., London, 2013); Farhad Daftary, 'Hasan-i Sabbah and the Origins of the Nizari Ismaili *Daʿwa* and State', in his *Ismailis in Medieval Muslim Societies* (London, 2005), pp. 124–148. On the family of Ṣūfī b. Ṣādiq, Yaʿqūb Shāh b. Ṣūfī and Ḥusayn b. Yaʿqūb Shāh, see Virani, 'Ḥusayn b. Yaʿqūb Shāh b. Ṣūfī: The Adornment of Assemblies', in *An Anthology of Ismaili Literature: A Shiʿi Vision of Islam*, pp. 296–297; Shafique N. Virani, 'Spring's Equinox: Nawrūz in Ismaili Thought', in Orkhan Mir-Kasimov, ed., *Intellectual Interactions in the Islamic World: The Ismaili Thread* (London, 2020), pp. 471–479; Muʿizzī, 'Ḥusayn bin Yaʿqūb Shāh', pp. 405–408. A manuscript of a poem by Khālū Maḥmūd ʿAlī, available to Muʿizzī but not to me, explicitly states that Ṣūfī held the rank of *ḥujjat*. See Muʿizzī, 'Ḥusayn bin Yaʿqūb Shāh', p. 405; Muʿizzī, *Ismāʿīliyān-i Īrān*, p. 351, n. 61.

157 Constance Evelyn Padwick, *Muslim Devotions: A Study of Prayer-Manuals in Common Use* (London, 1961), pp. 234–244 et passim.

called *istighātha* or 'imploring help' and *awrād* or 'litanies', regularly mirror the powerful rhythmical prose and stylistic elements of the Ismaili prayers, such as those found in the work of the 11th/17th-century author, Mīrzā Ḥusayn b. Yaʿqūb Shāh. His *Tazyīn al-majālis* (Adornment of Assemblies) contains the *Awrād al-mu'minīn* (Litanies of the Faithful) immediately followed by a section invoking the imams' names, entitled *Fi'l-istighātha* (On Imploring Help). Similarly, among several Sufi orders a practice known as the frock or chain of the litany (*khirqat* or *silsilat al-wird*) exists. This recounts the 'heads of the *ṭarīqa* [order] from the founder to the Prophet'.[158]

Such practices had already taken root by the early years of the Fatimid caliphate. In his *Daʿā'im al-Islām*, the Ismaili jurist al-Qāḍī al-Nuʿmān (d. 363/974) writes:

> ʿAlī related that the Messenger of God was wont to say, 'Surely, God will grant the wishes of those in my community who pass their right hand over their faces upon the completion of prayers and recite: "O God, praise belongs to You. There is no god save You, the knower of what is visible and what is unseen. O God, dispel my open and hidden sorrow, distress, and temptations."'
>
> The Imams related to us their decree to recite the prayer of drawing nigh (*taqarrub*) after every mandatory prayer. After ending the prayer with the salutations, the worshipper should raise his hands, palms exposed, and recite, 'O God, I approach You through Muhammad, Your Messenger and Prophet, and his legatee, Your sanctified authority, ʿAlī, and the pure Imams descended from him, namely al-Ḥasan, al-Ḥusayn, ʿAli b. al-Ḥusayn, Muḥammad b. ʿAlī, and Jaʿfar b. Muḥammad. . . .'
>
> The worshipper should name every Imam, one after the other, till he reaches the Imam of his time, and then he should say, 'O God, I approach You through them, and befriend them, and before You I disavow their enemies. I bear witness, O God, by the realities of sincerity and veracity of certainty that they are Your representatives on Your earth, and Your Proofs against Your creatures and the means of reaching You and the gates of Your Mercy. O lord, gather me with them and banish me not

158 J. Spencer Trimingham, *The Sufi Orders in Islam* (New York, 1971), p. 183, transliteration modified. See also Frederick Mathewson Denny, 'Wird', *EI2*; Louis Massignon, 'Wird', *EI*, vol. 4, p. 1139.

> from the circle of their friends, and make me firm in my covenant to them. O God, through them, dignify me before You in this world and the next, and make me among those drawn near to You. O lord, strengthen the certainty in my heart and increase my guidance and illumination. O Lord, bless Muhammad and the progeny of Muhammad. Grant me of the abundance you bestowed on Your faithful worshippers, by which I may be safe from Your punishment and be worthy of Your pleasure and mercy. By Your sanction, guide me aright when differences of opinion arise. Surely, You guide whom You will unto the right path. I beg You, lord, for Your grace in this world and the next, and I beseech You to save me from the torment of Hell.'[159]

Ismaili literature is replete with such prayers of proximity (*taqarrub*) in which the faithful draw nigh unto God by invoking the imams, generally in succession. This feature of the supplications, many in rhymed prose, is vividly depicted in the manuscripts. Generations of scribes sometimes crowd into the margins the names of the imams of their time, adding them to the list provided by the original author.[160] The Sufis were later

---

[159] Al-Qāḍī al-Nuʿmān, *Daʿāʾim al-Islām*, ed. Asaf A.A.Fyzee (Cairo, 1383/1963 [1st ed. 1951]), vol. 1, p. 171. My translation, which benefits from al-Nuʿmān, *Pillars of Islam*, vol. 1, pp. 214–215. The original Arabic has masculine singular in its address, which was regularly used in providing guidance of a general nature. As this is no longer common in English, I have used the plural, which does not show gender.

[160] Some good examples may be seen in the following manuscripts: Ḥusayn b. Yaʿqūb Shāh, 'Tazyīn al-majālis', accession number 7822, Ismaili Special Collections Unit, The Institute of Ismaili Studies, London, p. 134; Ḥusayn b. Yaʿqūb Shāh, 'Tazyin al-Majālis: Fi'l-istighāthah', accession number 15107, RK61, Ismaili Special Collections Unit, The Institute of Ismaili Studies, London. On the author of this work, see Muʿizzī, 'Ḥusayn bin Yāʿqūb Shāh', pp. 404–409. I am completing a critical edition and translation of the *Adornment of Assemblies*. For further details and extended excerpts, see Virani, 'Ḥusayn b. Yaʿqūb Shāh b. Ṣūfī: The Adornment of Assemblies', in *An Anthology of Ismaili Literature: A Shiʿi Vision of Islam*; Virani, 'Spring's Equinox'. The practice of adding the names of succeeding imams is present in Ismaili poetry as well. One may take, for example, the genealogy found in the poetry of Dāʿī Anjudānī (fl. 9th/15th c.), which ends with the name of the imam of his time, Mustanṣir bi'llāh (d. 885/1480), Dāʿī Anjudānī, '[Qaṣīda-yi dhurriyya]', accession number AG53, Ismaili Special Collections Unit. The poem was continued by ʿAbd al-Ṣamad Shāh, a great-grandson of Imam Ḥasan ʿAlī Shāh Aga Khan I (d. 1298/1881), who, writing under his penname 'Yaḥyā', extended the verses to the imam of his own time, Sulṭān Muḥammad Shāh Aga Khan III. On the poet Dāʿī, see Virani, *Ismailis in the Middle Ages*,

to adopt similar initiatic lines (*silsilas*), a development which, as Massignon and Trimingham observe, took place with the fall of the Shiʿi Fatimid and Būyid dynasties, and the Sufi adoption of the primarily Shiʿi custom of the pledge of allegiance (*bayʿa*).[161]

Prayers of proximity abound in the works of Khālū Maḥmūd's Ismaili contemporaries. Most of these remain unedited in yet to be catalogued manuscripts. For example, we may find elements in a poem entitled *The Seven Pillars of the Prophetic Dispensation* (*Haft arkān-i sharīʿat*) by the aforementioned Ṣūfī b. Ṣādiq, in the writings of his son Yaʿqūb Shāh b. Ṣūfī, such as his poem 'O lord, by my life, make my heart submissive to your command' (*Khudāwandā dil-i mā-rā bi-jān maʾmūr-i farmān kun*), and most elaborately in the *Tazyīn al-majālis* of the latter's son, Ḥusayn b. Yaʿqūb Shāh, and in the works of other contemporary Ismaili poets, such as 'Come hither, O sincere servant, invoke Shāh Nūr al-Dahr' (*Biyā ay banda-yi ṣādiq bu-gū yā Shāh Nūr al-Dahr*) by a certain Ustād Manṣūr, who composed it in 1052/1642 on the occasion of the imam's arrival in Mashhad.[162]

From at least the Fatimid period of Ismaili history, these invocations often incorporate the names of spiritual guides in a chain from the

---

pp. 25–26, 81–82, 86, 117–118, 174–175; Virani, 'Dāʿī Anjudānī: The Trusted Spirit', in *An Anthology of Ismaili Literature: A Shiʿi Vision of Islam*. On this poem of ʿAbd al-Ṣamad Shāh, see Muʿizzī, *Ismāʿīliyān-i Īrān*, p. 41. The *Qaṣīda-yi dhurriyya* was composed by Raqqāmī Khurāsānī (fl. 11th/17th), the son of the more famous Khākī Khurāsānī. His versified register of Ismaili imams was continued by a later poet to the time of Imam Sulṭān Muḥammad Shāh, Aga Khan III, who succeeded to the imamate in 1885. See A. A. Semenov, 'Ismailitskaya oda, posvyashchennaya voploshcheniyam ʿAliya boga', *Iran*, 2 (1928) and Wladimir Ivanow, 'Notes on the Ismailis in Persia', in *Ismailitica*, in *Memoirs of the Asiatic Society of Bengal*, 8 (1922), pp. 73–76. See also Paul E. Walker, 'Introduction', in his *Master of the Age: An Islamic Treatise on the Necessity of the Imamate* (London, 2007), p. 27 with regard to a similar phenomenon in the manuscripts of al-Kirmānī's *Lights to Illuminate the Proof of the Imamate* (*al-Maṣābīḥ fi'l-ithbāt al-imāma*).

161 Massignon, 'Wird', *EI*, p. 1139; Trimingham, *Sufi Orders*, p. 14.

162 'Haft arkān-i sharīʿat', incipit, 'ای دل طریق بندگی دوست کن شعار', accession number 14714, Ismaili Special Collections Unit; Anjuman-i taʿlīm u tarbiyat-i madhhabī-yi Shīʿa-yi Imāmiyya-yi Ismāʿīliyya-yi Khurāsān, ed. *Majmuʿa-yi ashʿār-i madhhabī az bayn-i jamāʿat-i Īrān* (Mashhad, 1374 Sh./1995), np; Ḥusayn b. Yaʿqūb Shāh, 'Tazyīn al-majālis', accession number 7822, Aga Khan Library; Manṣūr (pseud.), 'Dar bāb-i tashrīf āwardan-i Shāh ʿAbbās-i thānī wa Āqā-yi Buzurg', incipit, 'بحمد الله که باز م نخل امیدی ببار آماد', accession number 14713.

time of Adam onwards.[163] This trend of including figures from hoary antiquity as manifestations of a single divine light (*nūr*) continues in the Ginān s of the South Asian Ismailis, as in the *Primordial Canticle* (*Muḷ gāvantri*) of Sayyid Imām Shāh (fl. 9th–10th/15th–16th c.).[164] Indic Ismaili literature mirrors Khālū Maḥmūd's invocation of the imam's appointees 'who had recognised God'. Examples include the *Primordial Prayer* (*Asal dhuā*) of Pīr Ṣadr al-Dīn (fl. 8th/14th c.) and

163 See, for example, *Adʿiyat al-ayyām al-sabʿah* (Beirut, 1427/2006), p. 14.

164 Sayyid Imām Shāh, *Muḷ: gāvantri* (Mumbai, 1905), passim. On this figure, see Shafique Virani, 'The Voice of Truth: Life and Works of Sayyid Nūr Muḥammad Shāh, A 15th/16th Century Ismāʿīlī Mystic' (MA, McGill University, 1995), pp. 19–22. Similar compositions continued to be written in modern times. As an example, see the Gujarati poem *Jay jay Alī-oṃm nakalaṅk*, Ebrāhīm Jusab Varatejī, *Vedik Islām athavā Mī. Jīmane Jawāb: pahelo bhāg – Varatejīnuṃ Vīl, bijo bhāg – Īsmāīlīyā rahasy* (Mumbaī, 1339 AH/1977 VS/1921 CE), section 16, 1–3. For examples in Persian Ismaili literature, see, for example, the manuscript '[*Duʿā-yi taqarrub*]', accession number n.a., Ismaili Special Collections Unit, The Institute of Ismaili Studies, London, pp. 3–5, with the incipit [تـ]وکلت بمولانا توکلت بمولانا توکل کردم و بیزارم از خویش. This is a hitherto uncatalogued item with no visible accession number in the Ismaili Special Collections Unit of the IIS. It is a paper copy produced, I am told, from photographs taken in 1978 of a manuscript, the original of which was apparently in the possession of an unidentified Ismaili in Iran. Handwritten English numbers occur as later additions at the top right-hand corner of the first four pages. The extract available to me, unfortunately, does not include a colophon or other information that would allow us to identify the scribe or the year of writing. However, there is another item in the collection in precisely the same handwriting that does have a colophon. We can safely presume that manuscript نخ, used in S. J. Badakhchani's critical edition of the Poems of the Resurrection (*Dīwān-i qāʾimiyyāt*) of Ḥasan-i Maḥmūd-i Katib (d. 645/1246), was produced by one and the same hand. An image of the last page of نخ, reproduced in Badakhchani's edition indicates that the scribe was Muḥammad Ḥusayn b. Mīrẓā ʿAlī 'the fashioner of ʿArabī footwear of Sidih, who completed it on Tuesday, the 25th of the month of Muḥarram, 1101 AH', which corresponds to 1689 CE. S. J. Badakhshānī, 'Muqaddima-yi muṣaḥḥiḥ', in his edition of *Dīwān-i qāʾimiyyāt*, p. cxxviii. The Imam of the time in this manuscript is identified as 'Mawlānā Shāh Khalīl Allāh' (d. 1090/1680), however, certain indications in the text of the prayer suggest that it may originally have been written during the Alamūt period, and like other works of its genre, had the names of succeeding imams added each time it was recopied. Similarly, an anonymous *mathnawī* copied in 986/1560 recounts the names of the imams from the time of Adam to ʿAlī, and then from ʿAlī until the author's time. See Virani, *Ismailis in the Middle Ages*, pp. 81–82.

the *Prayer of the Vessel on the Dais* (*Ghāṭ pāṭ nī dhuā*), supplications in a combination of Arabic, Persian, Sindhi, Punjabi and Gujarati. While Khālū Maḥmūd ʿAlī identifies the imam's representatives in his own lifetime, these South Asian ismaili prayers invoke a lineage of representatives stretching back to the founding days of Islam.[165]

G. Whose Uncle Was He?

Āb-rā ū khāk-rā barham zadī
Z'āb ŭ gil naqsh-i tan-i Ādam zadī
Nisbat-ash dādī ŭ juft ū khāl ŭ ʿam
Bā hazār andīsha ū shādī ŭ gham
Together You cast water and dust
From clay and water, You moulded man's form
Giving him lineage, a mate, and uncles, maternal and paternal
With a thousand thoughts, and joys, and sorrows
Mawlānā Jalāl al-Dīn Rūmī, *The Spiritual Couplets* (*Mathnawī-yi maʿnawī*)[166]

We must deduce virtually everything we know about our poet from his own compositions, as no other works yet discovered mention him. In verse 78, he gives his penname (*takhalluṣ*) as 'Maḥmūd'. In verses 75 and 78 he identifies the imam of his time as Nūr al-Dahr, also known as Nūr al-Dīn ʿAlī. This imam held his position from 1043/1634 to 1082/1671 and thus he was contemporary with three Safavid sovereigns, Shah Ṣafī (d. 1052/1642), Shah ʿAbbās II (d. 1077/1666) and Shah Sulaymān I (d. 1105/1694):

chirā andīsha-yi bāṭil az īn ḍiddān kunī Maḥmūd
chih Nūr al-Dahr shud yār-am chih bāk az khārijī dāram. . . .
bi-ḥaqq-i dhāt-i Nūr al-Dahr buzurg ān qāyim-i aʿẓam
buwad bā īn hama hamdam chih bāk az khārijī dāram

---

165 Pīr Ṣadr al-Dīn, *Asal Dhuā: Shiyā Īmāmi Isamāīlīnī traṇ vakhatanī bandagī, Mānavantā bodhaguru Pīr Sadaradīn Sāhebe rachelī asal dhuā*, 1st [Gujarati] ed. (Mumbaī, 1975 VS/1919 CE), pp. 19–22 et passim; *Ghaṭapāṭanī dhuā*, 2nd [Gujarati] ed. (Mumbai, 1978 VS/1922 CE), pp. 47–51.

166 Jalāl al-Dīn Rūmī, *Mathnawī-yi maʿnawī*, ed. and tr. R. A. Nicholson (London, 1925–1940), vol. 1, p. 285. My translation, which benefits from Jalāl al-Dīn Rūmī, *Mathnawī*, ed. and tr. R. A. Nicholson, vol. 2, p. 257.

Wherefore these futile cares of foes, Maḥmūd?,
When Nūr al-Dahr has befriended me, What have I to fear of a rebel?. . .
By the essence of Nūr al-Dahr, how great that resurrector sublime!
United with all these, What have I to fear of a rebel?

Not found in the composition itself, however, is the poet's full name, 'Khālū Maḥmūd ʿAlī', which we must glean from elsewhere. Fortunately, manuscript 55 heads his composition with the words, "The Pearl Scattering Verses of Maḥmūd Khālū Maḥmūd ʿAlī' (*Ashʿār-i durr nithār-i Maḥmūd Khālū Maḥmūd ʿAlī*). Similarly, the Mukhī Ghiyāth al-Dīn Mīrshāhī manuscript available to Maryam Muʿizzī, includes the title 'From the verses of Khālū Maḥmūd ʿAlī' (*Min ashʿār-i Khālū Maḥmūd ʿAlī*).[167] A previously unknown poem of the author in a manuscript from Sidih, Iran, also begins with the words, 'Verses of Khālū Maḥmūd ʿAlī' (*ashʿār-i Khālū Māḥmūd ʿAlī*).[168]

This last manuscript is especially revealing. A cover label announces that the owner of the notebook (*bayāḍ*) was a certain Muḥammad Ḥasan b. ʿAbd al-Rashīd Rīsh Qirmiz of Sidih, Bīrjand district, Khurāsān.[169] It records the poetry of Ākhūnd Mawlānā Mīrzā Ḥusayn, an Ismaili luminary also mentioned in Khālū Maḥmūd's 'A servant of ʿAlī, king of men, am I'. It records compositions by several other poets as well, including such noted figures as Hilālī Astarābādī Jaghatāʾī (d. 936/1529) and Ṣāʾib Tabrīzī (d. 1087/1676). The label tells us the scribe wrote (i.e., copied) the text around 1112/1701, in other words, during the reign of Imam Shāh Nizār (d. 1134/1722), and that the accession number of the copy housed in the Ismaili Special Collections Unit is RK32. A researcher photographed the images on 24 December 1978 and apparently developed the film. The reproductions of the first

[167] Khālū Maḥmūd ʿAlī, 'Ashʿār-i durr nithār-i Maḥmūd Khālū Maḥmud ʿAlī', incipit, "غلام شاه مردانم چباك از خارجی دارم', in manuscript 55, 82v; Muʿizzī, 'Qāsim-shāhiyān', p. 153.

[168] Khālū Maḥmūd ʿAlī, 'Ashʿār-i Khālū Maḥmūd ʿAlī', incipit, 'ایدل بیا که وعدهٔ هنکام محشر است', accession number RK32, vol. 2, Ismaili Special Collections Unit, IIS, p. 35.

[169] Transliteration slightly modified.

three reels were available to me, though the label suggests that there were originally seven reels. The handwriting is very obscure and difficult to decipher in the copy. We can only hope that the original has survived in Sidih and will one day be available for scholarly research.

As explained above, our poet wrote during the reign of Imām Nūr al-Dahr ʿAlī (r. 1043–1082/1634–1671). Therefore, the copyist recorded the main portions of the Sidih manuscript a maximum of 66 solar years (69 lunar years) after Khālū Maḥmūd composed 'A servant of ʿAlī'.[170] Most importantly, Maḥmūd's poem in this collection reveals that he penned it during the campaign by the Safavid shah ʿAbbās II (d. 1077/1666) to retake Qandahār in the 1050s/1640s. The shah recaptured this important city from the Mughals in 1059/1649, after an immense struggle.[171] Khālū Maḥmūd composed the poem in the very popular metre *muḍāriʿ-yi makhbūn-i akhrab-i makfūf-i maḥdhūf*, that is, – – ˘ | – ˘ – ˘ | ˘ – – ˘ | – ˘ –.

ay dil biyā kih waʿda-yi hangām-i maḥshar ast
ṣad shūr ū ṣad futūr dar īn charkh-i akhḍar ast
Come hither, O heart, for arrived has the promised resurrection
Beneath earth's azure dome, pandemonium and upheaval reign

Both the sentiment and the rhythm of the composition are reminiscent of Muḥtasham Kāshānī's (d. 996/1588) famous and oft-imitated strophe (*tarkīb-band*) on the martyrdom of Imam Ḥusayn at Karbala, which may have been Khālū Maḥmūd's inspiration:

Bāz īn chih shūrish ast kih dar khalq-i ʿālam ast?
Bāz īn chih nawḥa ū chih ʿazā ū chih mātam ast?
Whence this tumult that again grips the world's people?
Whence this lament, this mourning, this weeping?

---

170 There appears, however, to have been more than one scribe of the Sidih manuscript, one of whom notes the year 1314/1896 on a page later numbered 10 in Latin script.

171 For a background to these events, see Rudi Matthee and Hiroyuki Mashita, 'Kandahar iv. From the Mongol Invasion through the Safavid Era', in *EIr* http://www.iranicaonline.org/articles/kandahar-from-the-mongol-invasion-through-the-safavid-era.

The composition depicts Khālū Maḥmūd being confronted by a hidden oracle, a man of God (*mard-i Khudā*). If we take *mard-i Khudā* in 'Come hither, O heart' to be synonymous with *mard-i ḥaqq* in verse 32 of 'A servant of ʿAlī', it is likely that it refers to a member of the religious hierarchy. The poet expresses his confusion about whether to support the Safavid campaign. 'Hush!' the figure replies, as this is an unrevealed secret. However, as Khālū Maḥmūd is among the people of unity, the oracle will guide him. He divulges that the time for the advent of ʿAlī's progeny is nigh and that Shah ʿAbbās should be supported, as he is a lover of ʿAlī and a Shiʿi. Khālū Maḥmūd concludes by seeking refuge in ʿAlī against all evil.

Verses 32–33 of 'A servant of ʿAlī' inform us that our poet was born in Mask in the Muʾmināb̄ād region, where there was a well-established Ismaili presence, and that his brother, Sulṭān ʿAlī, had an important leadership role there.[172] The wistful memory of his homeland reveals that he no longer lived in the village of his birth. He seeks the intercession of the community's various leaders, thereby confessing they hold a rank higher than his own. However, his detailed knowledge of the notables of his time and their geographical distribution indicates that he himself occupied a position in the hierarchy. In his poem 'Come hither, O heart', the allusion that he was among the people of unity (*ahl-i waḥdat*) to whom the oracle could confide information about the Safavid shah is suggestive. He does not use the phrase 'people of unity' (*ahl-i waḥdat*) here in the technical sense found in Naṣīr al-Dīn al-Ṭūsī and Ḥasan-i Maḥmūd's *Rawḍa-yi taslīm* (Paradise of Submission), where it refers to the imam's supreme proof (*ḥujjat-i aʿẓam*). It does, however, intimate that our poet played a role in the religious hierarchy and was not merely a lay believer, or 'respondent' (*mustajīb*).[173]

---

[172] The name of the locale is corrupted as 'Baskak' in the more recent manuscripts. Muʿizzī ably demonstrates that Mask (or alternatively, Gask) is more likely to be correct. That it is indeed Mask is established definitively in the newly discovered manuscript 55, used for this edition. Muʿizzī, 'Qāsim-shāhiyān', pp. 153–157.

[173] On the technical use of the phrase *ahl-i waḥdat*, see Naṣīr al-Dīn al-Ṭūsī and Ḥasan-i Maḥmūd-i Kātib, *Rawḍa-yi taslīm*, ed. S. J. Badakhchani (Tehran, 1393 Sh./2014), p. 69; Naṣīr al-Dīn al-Ṭūsī and Ḥasan-i Maḥmūd-i Kātib, *Rawḍa-yi*

I have encountered the penname 'Maḥmūd' associated with a handful of other poems in scattered Persian Ismaili manuscripts, mostly uncatalogued. At present, it is not possible to determine if these spring from the pen of our poet, but I document them here as the references may be useful for future researchers.

A short composition entitled the *Couplets of Maḥmūd* (*mathnawī-yi Maḥmūdī*) exists. It is in praise of the Prophet Muhammad and is an extended commentary on the famous mystical tradition (*ḥadīth*), *anā Aḥmad bilā mīm*, 'I am Aḥmad (i.e., Muhammad) without the letter *m*', i.e., Aḥad, 'One'.[174] It begins:

zabān-am qābil-i ḥamd-i Khudā shud
kih bā nām-i Muḥammad āshanā shud

Like Khālū Maḥmūd 'Alī's 'A servant of 'Alī, king of men, am I', this composition is also in a 'trilling metre' (*hazaj*), which is uncommon for a *mathnawī*.

Another poem explores the mystical meaning of the letters *'ayn* (ع) and *ghayn* (غ), and begins:

Ay chashm-i chirāgh-i qurrat al-'ayn
w'ay zubda-yi muqtadā-yi kawnayn

The type of letter symbolism present in these two compositions, however, strongly suggests that they are by Maḥmūd Pasīkhānī (d. 831/1428), the founder of the Nuqtawī movement in Iran.

---

taslīm, ed. and tr. S. J. Badakhchani as *Paradise of Submission: A Medieval Treatise on Ismaili Thought* (London, 2005), p. 85 (English). While continuing to use the phrase *ahl-i waḥdat* in the technical sense in his *Seven Chapters*, Ḥasan-i Maḥmūd also uses it with a broader meaning, making it synonymous with *mu'min, mūqin, 'ārifān, mustajīb, mujāhid, qā'imī, muḥiqqa, bāṭiniyya* and *arjāl-i qā'im*. See Ḥasan-i Maḥmūd-i Kātib, *Haft bāb*, ed. and tr. S. J. Badakhchani as *Spiritual Resurrection in Shi'i Islam: An Early Ismaili Treatise on the Doctrine of Qiyāmat* (London, 2017), pp. 42 (Per.), 83 (English).

[174] On the use of this *ḥadīth qudsī* in esoteric Islam, see Annemarie Schimmel, *Mystical Dimensions of Islam* (Chapel Hill, NC, 1975), pp. 224, 419–420; A. Schimmel, *And Muhammad is His Messenger: The Veneration of the Prophet in Islamic Piety* (Chapel Hill, NC, 1985), pp. 116–117 , 200, 202, 205, 212, 217, 240, 289 n66, 307 n138.

Āfāq-nāma-yi Maḥmūd (Maḥmūd's Tale of Horizons) is another composition, documented in Bertel's and Bakoev's *Alphabetic Catalogue* (*Alfavitnïy katalog*) and also found in private collections.[175] It begins:

ay giriftār dar man ū mā'ī
tā kay az bahr-i nafs bar pā'ī

However, the contents of this text and allusions to both Nāṣir-i Khusraw and the *Umm al-kitāb* strongly suggest that it was written in Central Asia, and not Iran.[176]

In trying to decipher our poet's identity, the Iranian scholar Maryam Muʿizzī said, 'It is not clear whose uncle (*khālū*) he was'. While the word *khālū* does, indeed, refer to an uncle in Persian, or more specifically, a mother's brother, the simplest explanation may be that it is also a common expression of respect. However, this interpretation itself begs the question of why the title is specific to Maḥmūd ʿAlī. To the best of our knowledge, the name *khālū* as a mark of esteem is not associated with any other Ismaili author.

There is a plausible explanation for this. When Imam Ḥasan ʿAlī Shāh Aga Khan I (d. 1298/1881) went to India, he took with him an entourage of Iranians, among whom were many Ismailis whose descendants, till today, are known as the 'Khālū' *jamāʿat*, i.e., the Khālū community. Referring to the larger group of Iranian émigrés that included this group, in his *Memoirs*, Aga Khān III wrote:

175 Andrei E. Bertel's and Mamadvafo Bakoev, *Alfavitnïy katalog rukopisey obnaruzhennïkh v Gorno-Badakhshanskoy Avtonomnoy Oblasti ékspeditsiey 1959-1963* gg., ed. Bobodzhon G. Gafurov and A.M. Mirzoev (Moscow, 1967), p. 23, no. 12.

176 On the special attachment of the Central Asian Ismailis to the memory of Nāṣir-i Khusraw, see Shaftolu Gulamadov, 'The Hagiography of Nāṣir-i Khusraw and the Ismāʿīlīs of Badakhshān' (PhD, University of Toronto, 2018); Daniel Beben, 'The Legendary Biographies of Nāṣir-i Khusraw: Memory and Textualization in Early Modern Persian Ismāʿīlism' (PhD, Indiana University, 2015) and Dagikhudo Dagiev, *Central Asian Ismailis, An Annotated Bibliography of Russian, Tajik and Other Sources* (London, 2022), pp. 15–23. For a partial bibliography of studies on the *Umm al-kitāb*, see Farhad Daftary, 'Omm al-ketāb', in *EIr* http://www.iranicaonline.org/articles/omm-al-ketab.

> My grandfather [Āghā Khān I] in his migration from Persia had brought with him more than a thousand relatives, dependents, clients, associates, personal and political supporters, ranging from the humblest groom or servant to a man of princely stature, a direct near-descendant of Nadirshah of Delhi fame, who had taken my grandfather's side in the disputes and troubles in Persia and with him had gone into exile.[177]

He referred more specifically to the Khālū *jamāʿat* in addresses to his Indian followers at Mañjevaḍī (Junāgaḍh) and Nāgalpur (Kachchh) in 1903, mentioning the difficulties of his Khālū disciples in Iran. They lived in circumstances where they could not openly practice their faith and publicly passed as Twelver Shiʿis.[178] In many ways, this scenario parallels that of the imam's 'Guptī' adherents in India, who blended with the majority Hindu population.[179] In another communication in the same year, this time to the Ismailis in Kerā (Kachchh), he distinguished between his 'Khurāsānī' and 'Khālū' followers. This suggests that like his Khwāja (also known as Khojā), Momnā, Shamsī and other Indian adherents, the Khālūs were one among several distinct Iranian Ismaili communities.[180] In 1923, the imam deputed Ālījāh (i.e., ʿĀlī-jāh) Dātū Merū of Gwādar (d. 1939) as an emissary to his Iranian devotees.[181] A manuscript with details of the journey in

[177] Sultan Mahomed Shah Aga Khan III, *The Memoirs of Aga Khan: World Enough and Time* (London, 1954), p. 9.

[178] Sulṭān Muḥammad Shāh Āghā Khān III, *Kalāme imāme mubīn: yāne avval imām Hajharat Maulā Muratujhā Alīthī nasal b nasal utarī āvelā imāmatanā 48 mā jomānā dhaṇī Maulānā Hājhar Imām Nur Sulatān Mohammad Shāh Āgākhān sāhebanā mubārak pharamāno (i. s. 1885 thī 1910 sudhīnā), Kalam E Imam E Mubin: Holy Firmans of Mowlana Hazar Imam Sultan Mohomed Shah the Agakhan (from 1880 [sic] A.D. to 1910 A.D.)* (1st ed., Mumbaī, 1950), vol. 1, pp. 180, 212–213.

[179] Virani, 'Taqiyya and Identity', pp. 99–139. On the Ismaili practice of *taqiyya* particularly in post-Mongol Iran, see Virani, 'Surviving Persecution', in *Sufis and their Opponents in the Persianate World.*

[180] Āghā Khān III, *Kalāme imāme mubīn*, vol. 1, p. 222. On the Khurāsānī Ismailis and their various tribes, see Ivanow, 'Ismailis in Persia', p. 51.

[181] Gwadar is today a port city on the southwestern coast of Baluchistan, Pakistan. Located on the shores of the Arabian Sea opposite Oman, it was at the time an overseas possession of Oman. On this figure, see Shihābuddīn A. Gvādrī, *Gohar-i Gvādar: Gvādar ke Ismāʿīlīoṉ kā tārīkhī jāʾizah* (Karāchī, 1994); Mumtaz Ali Tajddin Sadik Ali, *101 Ismaili Heroes: Late 19th century to Present Age*, vol. 1 (Karachi, 2003).

Khwāja Sindhi (Khojki) script and Sindhi language specifies that five of the imam's 'Khālū' followers, whose ancestors hailed from Iran, accompanied him. These were ʿAlī-khān Maʿṣūm-ʿalī, Qāsim Mukhī Yaʿqūb-ʿalī, Muḥammad Ḥusayn Ghulām-ḥusayn Sīrjānī, ʿAbbās Ibrāhīm Khurāsanī and Ḥasan-qulī ʿAbbās Khurāsānī. When romanised from the original Khwāja Sindhi, these are: Alikhān Māsumāli, Kāsam Mukhi Yākub-ali, Māmad Husenı Gulāmahusenı Sira<jā>nı, Abāsı Ebırāhem Khurāsānı and Hasana<ku>li Abāsı Khurāsānı.[182] That the manuscript identifies two of these figures as 'Khurāsānī' may suggest that there was no distinction between the Khālūs and the Khurāsānīs, or possibly that with time Indic Ismailis addressed all their Iranian coreligionists as 'Khālū'. Similarly, many Western scholars refer to the various groups of South Asian Ismailis simply as 'Khwāja' or 'Khojā', without realising the historical and ancestral distinctions among the imam's diverse followers in the Subcontinent. Rāʾī Shaʿbān Dādullāhī, the first president of His Highness Shia Imami Ismaili Council for Iran, originally from Shahr-i Bābak and currently a resident of Tehran, provides additional confirmation. According to the oral tradition of the area, Imam Ḥasan ʿAlī Shāh used to refer to his community in the area intimately as 'Khālū.' He also notes that the area of Shahr-i Bābak where the imam and his followers lived is still known as Maḥlah-yi Khālū-hā, 'the neighbourhood of the Khālūs.' A fortress and many other Ismaili antiquities are still in existence there.[183]

While the foregoing outlines the existence of an Iranian Ismaili community known as 'Khālū', no proper study yet exists of its history. It is, therefore, not possible to ascertain definitively how far back the use of this name goes.[184] However, it is certainly conceivable that

---

182 '*Sıri Mubaithi saphar Erān taraph ravānā. . .*', incipit, 'n.a.', personal collection of the late Abdul Aziz Gilani 'Sairab Abuturabi', Karachi. I am grateful to Mr Mumtaz Ali Tajddin for kindly sending me a scan of this manuscript.

183 I am grateful to Rāʾī Shaʿbān Dādullāhī for kindly providing this information and to Seddigheh Kardan for graciously conveying it to me. Maps of the area place this neighborhood at 30.1148° N 55.1165° E.

184 I have met and interviewed many members of the diaspora Khālū community in India in two of their historical centres, Vāḍī in Mumbai, and in Pune. See also Hamīr 'Sinnaph' (pseud.) Lākhā, *Kachchhanā Vāras Moledīna Meghajīnāṃ jīvan*

Khālū Maḥmūd ʿAlī may have been a member of the Khālū *jamāʿat*, and that this could be the reason for his unusual title.

H. Afterword

> *And so instinctively she walked along the terrace towards that more secluded part of the garden just above the river bank, where she had so oft wandered hand in hand with him in the honeymoon of their love. There great clumps of old-fashioned cabbage roses grew in untidy splendour, and belated lilies sent intoxicating odours into the air, whilst the heavy masses of Egyptian and Michaelmas daisies looked like ghostly constellations in the gloom.*
>
> Baroness Orczy, *The Elusive Pimpernel*[185]

For the Ismailis, the 11th/17th century was a time of both great promise and significant risk. Without providing details, Khālū Maḥmūd's poem suggests that a rebel threatened the community. However, it also expresses confidence in the imam's appointees to positions of spiritual leadership, the sages (*pīr*s), inviters (*dāʿī*s), guides (*rahbar*s), teachers (*muʿallim*s) and others stationed across much of the Near East. The poet seeks the intercession of these luminaries, along with the prophets, illustrious sages of the past, and most importantly, the Imam of the Age, Shāh Nūr al-Dahr. His approach is both rooted in centuries-old tradition and an innovation in its own right. Invoking the imams in 'prayers of proximity' is a practice recorded since at least Fatimid times and prevalent among Maḥmūd's Ismaili contemporaries, with analogous practices found in sister communities. We can find parallels to Maḥmūd's invocation of the

---

saṃsmaraṇo: Smṛti jhaṅkār (2nd ed., Karāchī, 1961), p. 24. Aḥmad ʿAlī Khān Vazīrī (d. 1295/1878) mentions a tribe of Turkic origins centred on Rābur and Shastfich in Kirmān, a region with significant Ismaili activity, which goes by the name Khālū. However, they apparently adopted this name because a leader of the Mihnī tribe named Fatḥ ʿAlī Khān (fl. 19th c.) married a woman of their tribe named Fāṭima Khānum. After this, they came to be known as Khālūs. See Vazīrī, *Jughrāfiyā-yi Kirmān*, p. 199; A.K.S. Lambton, 'Kirmān', *EI2*. If this is the same tribe from which the Ismaili Khālūs come, then the name is of too late an origin to have applied to Khālū Maḥmūd ʿAlī.

185 Baroness Emmuska Orczy, *The Elusive Pimpernel* (Mineola, New York, 2007), p. 97.

members of the spiritual hierarchy in the compositions of the author's coreligionists, including those of South Asia. Identifying dozens of spiritual officers of one's time by name and domain, however, is something that in hitherto known Ismaili literature is unique to Khālū Maḥmūd. From the author's own works, we have deduced facts about his identity, such as his full name and penname, a few details about his family, his place of origin, suggestions about his position within the spiritual hierarchy, and so on. Limitations of space, however, prevent an exploration of the richness of historical detail provided in the poem. This includes the identities and locations of the dignitaries recounted and the possible distinctions between the various leadership positions mentioned, which often differ from the nomenclature recorded in the better documented Fatimid and Alamūt periods.[186] I anticipate returning to these questions in a future publication.

Khālū Maḥmūd ʿAlī's poem reveals much about the so-called 'scarlet pimpernels' of his time, the members of the Ismaili invitation (*daʿwa*). In Baroness Orczy's *The Elusive Pimpernel* cited above, a sequel to her original novel, she writes not only of the demure pimpernel, but of cabbage roses, lilies, and Egyptian and Michaelmas daisies. As the evidence of Khālū Maḥmūd's 'A servant of ʿAlī, king of men, am I' demonstrates, the Ismaili leaders of the 11th/17th century counted figures scattered across much of the Muslim world, doubtless with myriad approaches to their tasks in the face of local circumstances. Future research will certainly reveal that the Ismaili *dāʿī*s included not just the 'scarlet pimpernels', of Ivanow's estimation, but were a kaleidoscopic garden of various hues.

[186] Some insightful work in this direction has already been accomplished by Muʿizzī in 'Qāsim-shāhiyān', pp. 157–169.

4

Ismaili Doctrines in a Late Safavid Work: Quotations from the *Risālat al-Jāmiʿa* in Quṭb al-Dīn Ashkivarī's *Maḥbūb al-Qulūb*

Daniel De Smet

The renaissance of Islamic philosophy in Safavid Iran was the fruit of a creative reflection on a wide range of sources, belonging to different traditions such as *falsafa* (al-Fārābī, Ibn Sīnā, al-Ghazālī), *ishrāq* (Suhrawardī, Shahrazūrī), Sufism (Ibn ʿArabī) and the Arabic Plotinus (the so-called *Pseudo-Theology of Aristotle*). That the *Rasāʾil Ikhwān al-Ṣafāʾ* were also part of these sources is attested by literal quotes, for instance in the works of Mullā Ṣadrā,[1] although the influence of the Brethren's thought on Safavid philosophy and the diffusion of their Epistles at that time in Iran still need to be investigated.

An initial contribution to this topic was provided by Mathieu Terrier in the annotation and commentary to his outstanding French translation of the first book of the *Maḥbūb al-qulūb*, an impressive universal history of wisdom and philosophy, from Adam to Mīr Dāmād (d. 1040/1631), compiled by the late Safavid philosopher, Quṭb

[1] Christian Jambet, *L'acte d'être. La philosophie de la révélation chez Mollâ Sadrâ* (Paris, 2002), pp. 238, 241, 251 (quotes from the *Rasāʾil* in Ṣadrā's *Asfār*); Mathieu Terrier, 'La représentation de la sagesse grecque comme discours et mode de vie chez les philosophes šīʿites de l'Iran safavide (XIe/XVIIe siècle)', *Studia graeco-arabica*, 5 (2015), p. 316 (quotes in Ṣadrā's *al-Mabdaʾ waʾl-maʿād*). However, in the hand-written catalogue of Ṣadrā's private library, the *Rasāʾil Ikhwān al-Ṣafāʾ* and the *Risālat al-Jāmiʿa* do not occur; for the 111 titles appearing in this list, see Sajjad Rizvi, *Mullā Ṣadrā Shīrāzī: His Life and Works and the Sources for Safavid Philosophy*, *Journal of Semitic Studies*. Supplement 18 (2007), pp. 117–135 (hence, in his study, Rizvi does not include the writings of the Ikhwān among the sources for Safavid philosophy).

al-Dīn Ashkivarī (who died ca. 1088/1677 and 1095/1684).[2] Among the large number of disparate sources Ashkivarī used, Terrier identified a few quotes from the *Rasāʾil Ikhwān al-Ṣafāʾ* and, more surprisingly, a long citation taken from the *Risālat al-Jāmiʿa*. In this study, I will first briefly examine the quotations from the *Rasāʾil*, before addressing the long passage from the *Jāmiʿa* occurring in the chapter on Adam and a second citation from the same work in the entry on Zoroaster, which apparently was not noticed by Terrier. As the quotes from the *Risālat al-Jāmiʿa* are directly linked to the main tenets of Ismaili doctrine, the question arises as to whether Ashkivarī consciously included them, although they were not common issues in Safavid philosophy.

Ashkivarī and the *Rasāʾil Ikhwān al-Ṣafāʾ*

In the second book of the *Maḥbūb al-qulūb*, devoted to the philosophers from the Islamic era, Ashkivarī has an entry about the Ikhwān al-Ṣafāʾ.[3] It opens with an explicit identification of the Brethren:

> The philosophers of the Ikhwān al-Ṣafāʾ [were]: Abū Sulaymān Muḥammad b. Maʿshar al-Bustī, known as al-Maqdisī, Abu'l-Ḥasan ʿAlī b. Hārūn al-Zanjānī, Abū Aḥmad al-Mihrajānī,[4] al-ʿAwfī al-Baṣrī and Zayd b. Rifāʿa al-Hāshimī. This group agreed to compose a book containing fifty-one treatises; fifty of them are about fifty branches of science, whereas the fifty-first is the summary (*jāmiʿa*) of all the other treatises in a concise and selective way.[5]

[2] Mathieu Terrier, *Histoire de la sagesse et philosophie shi'ite. "L'Aimé des cœurs" de Quṭb al-Dīn Aškevarī* (Paris, 2016); on Ashkivarī, his life and his works, see Terrier, *Histoire*, pp. 41–105; Terrier, 'Quṭb al-Dīn Ashkevarī, un philosophe discret de la renaissance safavide', *Studia Iranica*, 40 (2011), pp. 171–210; Terrier, 'Le *Maḥbūb al-qulūb* de Quṭb al-Dīn Ashkevarī: une œuvre méconnue dans l'histoire de l'histoire de la sagesse en islam', *Journal Asiatique*, 298 (2010), pp. 345–387.

[3] Quṭb al-Dīn al-Ashkivarī, *Maḥbūb al-qulūb, al-maqāla al-thāniyya fī aḥwāl ḥukamāʾ al-Islām*, ed. Ḥāmid Ṣidqī and Ibrāhīm al-Dībājī (Tehran, 1382 Sh./2003), pp. 133–137: n° 81 *ḥukamāʾ Ikhwān al-Ṣafāʾ*.

[4] The name appears in this form in the edition of the *Maḥbūb* and in Lippert's edition of Ibn al-Qifṭī (see note 6). However, in secondary literature, the form al-Nahrajūrī, which is attested in some manuscripts, is often used.

[5] Ashkivarī, *Maḥbūb*, vol. 2, pp. 133–134.

This information, along with the major part of Ashkivarī's entry, is taken from Ibn al-Qifṭī's chapter about the Ikhwān al-Ṣafāʾ, which in turn partly depends on Abū Ḥayyān al-Tawḥīdī's *Kitāb al-Imtāʿ wa'l-muʾānasa.*[6] In the beginning of his chapter, Ibn al-Qifṭī mentions different opinions about the identity of the Ikhwān al-Ṣafāʾ, including those who claim that the author was an imam from the offspring of ʿAlī b. Abī Ṭālib.[7] At first sight it looks strange that Ashkivarī, as a convinced Twelver Shiʿi, should have skipped this part of Ibn al-Qifṭī's entry, and he seems to accept the authorship of a Sunni group of scholars around Abū Sulaymān al-Maqdisī. Perhaps he was well aware of the fact that claims about (hidden) imam(s) as author(s) of the *Rasāʾil* were stemming from Ismaili circles,[8] which inevitably would arouse suspicion as to the orthodoxy of the Ikhwān al-Ṣafāʾ.

Ashkivarī further introduced a significant alteration in Ibn al-Qifṭī's text. He copied part of the conversation which al-Tawḥīdī had in 373/983-84 with the Būyid *amīr* Ṣamsām al-Dawla about two presumed members of the Ikhwān al-Ṣafāʾ: Zayd b. Rifāʿa and Abū Sulaymān al-Maqdisī. Questioned about the latter's opinion concerning the relationship between revealed law and philosophy, al-Tawḥīdī mentions, according to Ibn al-Qifṭī's version, al-Maqdisī's bold position in the following terms:

---

[6] Ibn al-Qifṭī, *Taʾrīkh al-ḥukamāʾ*, ed. Julius Lippert (Leipzig, 1903), pp. 82–88 (the passage of Ashkivarī translated above is a combination of Ibn al-Qifṭī, p. 83.15-16, with addition of the name Zayd b. Rifāʿ mentioned on p. 82.17, and Ibn al-Qifṭī, p. 82.2-5). On al-Tawḥīdī's and Ibn al-Qifṭī's famous 'witness' about the supposed authors of the *Rasāʾil Ikhwān al-Ṣafāʾ*, see Samuel M. Stern, 'The Authorship of the Epistles of the Ikhwān aṣ-Ṣafāʾ', *Islamic Culture*, 20 (1946), pp. 368–370; idem, 'New Information about the Authors of the "Epistles of the Sincere Brethren"', in his *Studies in Early Ismāʿīlism* (Jerusalem and Leiden, 1983), pp. 155–157; Ismail K. Poonawala, 'Why We Need an Arabic Critical Edition with an Annotated English Translation of the *Rasāʾil Ikhwān al-Ṣafāʾ*', in Nader El-Bizri, ed., *Epistles of the Brethren of Purity. The Ikhwān al-Ṣafāʾ and their* Rasāʾil. *An Introduction* (Oxford, 2008), pp. 51–54; Joel L. Kraemer, *Humanism in the Renaissance of Islam. The Cultural Revival during the Buyid Age* (Leiden, 1986), pp. 165–178; Godefroid de Callataÿ, *Ikhwan al-Safa'. A Brotherhood of Idealists on the Fringe of Orthodox Islam* (Oxford, 2005), pp. 4–8.

[7] Ibn al-Qifṭī, *Taʾrīkh*, p. 82.9-11.

[8] Daniel De Smet, 'L'auteur des *Rasāʾil Ikhwān al-Ṣafāʾ* selon les sources ismaéliennes ṭayyibites', *SSR*, 1 (2017), pp. 151–166.

> The *sharīʿa* is a medicine for the sick, whereas philosophy is a medicine for the healthy. The prophets only treat the sick with the aim that their diseases may not increase and sickness may be replaced by health. As to the philosophers, they protect the health of the healthy, so that disease never can affect them. Between the manager (*mudabbir*) of the sick and the manager of the healthy there is a manifest difference and [this is] an evident matter.[9]

Ibn al-Qifṭī introduces this passage with the following sentence: 'But al-Ḥarīrī, the *ghulām* of Ibn Ṭarrāra provoked him one day at the booksellers (*fiʾl-warrāqīn*) with such words that he [al-Maqdisī] rushed off and said. . .'. Although Ashkivarī mentions the same passage *verbatim*, he introduces it in a quite different way: 'But al-Mihrajānī said one day. . .'. The quotation is thus attributed to another presumed member of the Ikhwān al-Ṣafāʾ. It is repeated in the introduction to the first book of the *Maḥbūb*, where it is presented in such a way that the reader gets the impression that the quote is taken from the *Rasāʾil*: 'The philosopher al-Mihrajānī, who belongs to the philosophers of the Ikhwān al-Ṣafāʾ, said. . . .'.[10] In fact, it is not a literal quote, although the idea that philosophers and prophets both practice the medicine of the souls is common in the *Rasāʾil*.[11] It is also noteworthy that Ashkivarī adds a (personal?) note in Arabic, specifying that it is easier to preserve health than to cure sickness.[12] He thus implies that prophets are superior to philosophers, a subtle way of neutralising the heterodox undertone of the quotation.

According to Ashkivarī, in the introduction of the *Maḥbūb*, the 'true' philosophers are dependent on the prophets, as they derive their wisdom from the 'niche of prophecy and guardianship' (*mishkāt*

---

[9] Ibn al-Qifṭī, *Taʾrīkh*, p. 88.7-12 = Ashkivarī, *Maḥbūb*, vol. 2, pp. 135.19–136.2.

[10] Quṭb al-Dīn al-Ashkivarī, *Maḥbūb al-qulūb, al-maqāla al-ūlā*, ed. Ibrāhīm al-Dībājī and Ḥāmid Ṣidqī (Tehran, 1370 Sh./1999), p. 106.

[11] See, for instance, Ikhwān al-Ṣafāʾ, *Rasāʾil* (Beirut, 1958), vol. 2, p. 141; Carmela Baffioni, *Epistles of the Brethren of Purity. On the Natural Sciences. An Arabic Critical Edition and English Translation of Epistles 15-21* (Oxford, 2013), pp. 384–385 (Arabic), 301–302 (tr.); cf. Terrier, *Histoire*, p. 192.

[12] Ashkivarī, *Maḥbūb*, vol. 1, p. 106; vol. 2, p. 136.

al-nubuwwa wa'l-walāya).[13] There follows praise of the virtues of the true philosopher, the description of the scope of his learning (knowledge of the essence of things, their genus, their species and the individuals) and nine questions about their causes, the whole copied from Epistle 40 of the Ikhwān al-Ṣafā'.[14]

Ashkivarī closes his introduction with a long passage about the division of sciences, mainly copied from Epistle 7.[15] There are many differences between the two texts, partly due to corruption in the manuscripts and their modern editions.[16] More important is the fact that Ashkivarī distinguishes nine religious sciences, three more than the Ikhwān: the science of divine unity (*'ilm al-tawḥīd*), the science of the principles (*'ilm al-mabādi'*) and the science of the harmony between revelation (*tanzīl*) and (esoteric) exegesis (*ta'wīl*).[17] Finally, in Ashkivarī's version there are a number of phrases without parallel in the text of the

---

[13] The revealed origin of 'true' philosophy is one of the basic ideas in the *Maḥbūb al-qulūb*. The conviction that the first Greek philosophers took their wisdom from the 'niche of prophecy' goes back to Abu'l-Ḥasan al-'Āmirī's *Kitāb al-Amad 'ala'l-abad* and was shared by a large number of authors, not at least by al-Shahrastānī; see Daniel De Smet, *Empedocles Arabus. Une lecture néoplatonicienne tardive* (Brussels, 1998), pp. 39–45. Significantly, as a Shi'i, Ashkivarī adds the term *walāya* to the expression *mishkāt al-nubuwwa*, implying that the philosophers are not only the heirs of the prophets, but also of the imams. On *walāya*, see Mohammad Ali Amir-Moezzi, *La religion discrète. Croyances et pratiques spirituelles dans l'islam shi'ite* (Paris, 2006), pp. 177–207.

[14] Ashkivarī, *Maḥbūb*, vol. 1, p. 99.5-10, corresponding to Ikhwān, *Rasā'il*, vol. 3, p. 345.7-12; cf. Terrier, *Histoire*, p. 183.

[15] Ashkivarī, *Maḥbūb*, vol. 1, pp. 132.2–133.20, corresponding to Ikhwān, *Rasā'il*, vol. 1, pp. 266.14–268.13; cf. Terrier, *Histoire*, pp. 220–223.

[16] For instance, in Ashkivarī's version, there are four classes of science: the propaedeutic (*riyāḍiyya*), those pertaining to religious law (*shar'iyya*), the 'conventional' (*waḍ'iyya*) and the true philosophical (*al-falsafa al-ḥaqīqiyya*) (Ashkivarī, *Maḥbūb*, vol. 1, p. 132.2-3), whereas in the text of the Ikhwān, there are only three classes: *al-riyāḍiyya*, *al-shar'iyya al-waḍ'iyya* and *al-falsafiyya al-ḥaqīqiyya*, the label *waḍ'iyya* ('conventional' or rather 'imposed') being a qualification of the *sharī'a* (Ikhwān, *Rasā'il*, vol. 1, p. 266.14-15). Hence, it seems that Ashkivarī was misled by a textual corruption in his manuscript. On the division of the sciences according to the Ikhwān, see de Callataÿ, *Ikhwan al-Safa'*, pp. 59–68.

[17] Ashkivarī, *Maḥbūb*, vol. 1, p. 132.13-16, to compare with Ikhwān, *Rasā'il*, vol. 1, p. 267.4-7.

Ikhwān.[18] Hence, we cannot exclude the possibility that Ashkivarī relied on Epistle 7 only indirectly, copying from another source regarding the division of sciences that was dependent on the Ikhwān's *Risāla*.

In the opening part of his chapter concerning Pythagoras, Ashkivarī includes a long quotation from Epistle 32, about numbers as the principles of being, the presence of dyads, triads, tetrads, pentads . . . in different realms of reality, and the correspondence between the nine numbers of the decad and the nine levels of the universe.[19] In the last part of the quote, there is a significant difference between the text of the Ikhwān (at least in the 'uncritical' Beirut edition), who, in conformity with their usual doctrine, associate Matter (*hayūlā*) and Nature respectively with the numbers four and five (between three = the Soul and six = the Body), whereas Ashkivarī (and Walker's new edition of the Epistle) reverses the order: Nature, corresponding to four, precedes Matter, abased to the fifth level.[20] Ashkivarī's and Walker's versions look like an adaptation of the Ikhwān's cosmic hierarchy to more 'orthodox' Neoplatonic standards: the order Intellect, Soul, Nature and Matter.[21] As noted by Terrier, the first part of the quotation from Epistle 32 also occurs in Ḥaydar Āmulī's *Jāmiʿ al-asrār*, one of the many sources used by Ashkivarī in his *Maḥbūb*

---

[18] Ashkivarī, *Maḥbūb*, vol. 1, p. 132.3-5; 132.6-8; 132.15-21.

[19] Ashkivarī, *Maḥbūb*, vol. 1, pp. 209.9–210.6 and 210.7–211.3, which is a slightly abridged version of Ikhwān, *Rasāʾil*, vol. 3, pp. 178.15–180.7 and 181.5–182.4; Paul E. Walker, Ismail K. Poonawala, David Simonowitz and Godefroid de Callataÿ, ed., *Epistles of the Brethren of Purity. Sciences of the Soul and Intellect. Part 1. An Arabic Critical Edition and English Translation of Epistles* 32-36 (Oxford, 2015), pp. 5.11–7 ult., 8.14–10.6 (Arabic), pp. 17–19; cf. Terrier, *Histoire*, pp. 374–375.

[20] Compare Ikhwān, *Rasāʾil*, vol. 3, p. 181.20-21 with Walker, *Epistles*, p. 9.14-15. This inversion is not mentioned in Walker's *apparatus*.

[21] The usual cosmic hierarchy of the Ikhwān, with Prime Matter preceding Nature, appears in another passage of Walker's edition (*Epistles*, Arabic p. 20 Arabic, tr., p. 29); on Matter preceding Nature, see Yves Marquet, *La philosophie des Iḫwān al-Ṣafāʾ* (2nd corrected ed., Paris and Milan, 1999), pp. 82–84; de Callataÿ, *Ikhwan al-Safa'*, pp. 19–20; Daniel De Smet, *La quiétude de l'intellect. Neoplatonisme et gnose ismaéliene dans l'œuvre de Ḥamīd ad-Dīn al-Kirmānī (Xe/XIes)* (Leuven, 1995), pp. 258–259. For the part of Epistle 32 quoted by Ashkivarī, see Yves Marquet, *Les "Frères de la pureté" pythagoriciens de l'Islam. La marque du pythagorisme dans la rédaction des Épîtres des Iḫwān aṣ-Ṣafāʾ* (Paris, 2006), pp. 220–224.

al-qulūb. But as Āmulī's quotation, explicitly introduced as being taken from the *ṣāḥib [Rasāʾil] Ikhwān al-Ṣafāʾ*, is shorter than Ashkivarī's, it seems likely that the latter copied it directly from the *Rasāʾil.*[22]

This short examination of the citations from the *Rasāʾil Ikhwān al-Ṣafāʾ* in the *Maḥbūb al-qulūb* leads to the conclusion that Ashkivarī probably had at his disposal a copy of the *Epistles*, although the possibility that he found the quotes in other sources cannot be excluded. In any case, their content has no direct link with Ismaili doctrine. It is also striking that Ashkivarī avoids mentioning the Ikhwān al-Ṣafāʾ by name and that in the entry devoted to them in the second volume of the *Maḥbūb*, he remains silent about the possibility that the authors of the *Epistles* were Shiʿi, although this option is suggested in Ibn al-Qifṭī, his main source. Hence, the presence of the Ikhwān in Ashkivarī is rather discrete. If we restrict our investigation to the influence solely of the *Rasāʾil*, Terrier's statement 'La voix des Ikhwān al-Ṣafāʾ participe de l'originalité doctrinale du *Maḥbūb al-qulūb*'[23] looks somewhat exaggerated.

Ashkivarī and the *Risālat al-Jāmiʿa*

However, things are quite different with the *Risālat al-Jāmiʿa,* the so-called 'crown' (*tāj*) of the *Rasāʾil Ikhwān al-Ṣafāʾ*. This work presents itself as the quintessence of the *Rasāʾil*, of which it is supposed to reveal the esoteric meaning. It would thus have been reserved for an initiated elite. In reality, the text offers a rather incomplete summary of the *Rasāʾil*, which has been infiltrated by Ismaili concepts and doctrines (in particular concerning the transmigration of souls, the fall of the Universal Soul into matter and eschatology) that are absent from, or only discretely present in the *Rasāʾil*. Traditionally attributed variously to the same author(s) as the *Rasāʾil*, or to the Andalusian mathematician and astronomer Maslama al-Majrīṭī (d. 398/1007) or to the Ismaili imam Aḥmad, the

---

22 Ḥaydar Āmulī, *Jāmiʿ al-asrār*, ed. Henry Corbin, in his *La philosophie shiʿite* (Tehran and Paris, 1969), § 453-457, pp. 233–234; cf. Terrier, *Histoire*, p. 375 n. 2. This is the only quote from the Ikhwān al-Ṣafāʾ.

23 Terrier, *Histoire*, p. 149.

grandson of Muḥammad b. Ismāʿīl, the *Risālat al-Jāmiʿa* seems to have been written by an Ismaili author at a later date than was the *Rasāʾil*.[24]

The diffusion of the *Risālat al-Jāmiʿa* in Safavid Iran has never been studied. However, the first volume of Ashkivarī's *Maḥbūb al-qulūb* contains two longer citations from the *Jāmiʿa*, in the chapters on Adam and Zoroaster. They deserve a further investigation.

The Story of Adam

In Ashkivarī's history of philosophy, Adam is presented as the first sage, preceding Seth and Hermes. The long chapter devoted to Adam opens with a discussion about the nature of the names and the wisdom that God revealed to him, according to the Qur'an and Shiʿi tradition, and closes with some conventional material about the story (*qiṣṣa*) of Adam, his life and death.[25] In the central part of this chapter Ashkivarī copies almost *verbatim* two long passages from the *Risālat al-Jāmiʿa*, but reversing the order in which they appear there: he first copied what corresponds to pages 119 to 128 in Muṣṭafā Ghālib's edition of the *Jāmiʿa* and then immediately continued with pages 66 to 69.[26] Unlike the citations from the *Rasāʾil Ikhwān al-Ṣafāʾ*, those from the *Jāmiʿa* are mostly unabridged; Ashkivarī reproduces the entire text, without adding any comment.[27] The choice of these passages is remarkable for a Twelver Shiʿi author, as they address some central tenets of Ismailism; the reversing of the order in which they were copied even enhances their Ismaili flavour.

---

[24] Daniel De Smet, 'The Religious Applications of Philosophical Ideas', in Ulrich Rudolph, Rotraud Hansberger and Peter Adamson, ed., *Philosophy in the Islamic World. Volume 1: 8th – 10th Centuries* (Leiden and Boston, 2017), p. 755.

[25] Ashkivarī, *Maḥbūb*, vol. 1, pp. 135–157; cf. Terrier, *Histoire*, pp. 249–275.

[26] Ashkivarī, *Maḥbūb*, vol. 1, pp. 138.18–144.4, corresponding to Aḥmad b. ʿAbd Allāh b. Muḥammad b. Ismāʿīl b. Jaʿfar al-Ṣādiq (attr.), *al-Risāla al-Jāmiʿa*, ed. Muṣṭafā Ghālib (Beirut, 1984), pp. 119.16–128.12; *Maḥbūb*, vol. 1, pp. 144.6–146.4, corresponding to *Jāmiʿa*, pp. 66.11–69.13; cf. Terrier, *Histoire*, pp. 253–261.

[27] In fact, the first quote is interrupted (Ashkivarī, *Maḥbūb*, vol. 1 p. 143.6, corresponding to *Jāmiʿa*, p. 126.4) by some unidentified verses in Persian; then (p. 143.14) the citation goes on with *Jāmiʿa*, p. 127.13, introduced with 'one of the philosophers of Islam said. . .'. Thus, Ashkivarī skipped *Jāmiʿa*, pp. 126.4–127.13. In the second quote from the *Jāmiʿa* (pp. 144.6–146.4) there are some abridgements.

Following the example of the *Rasāʾil Ikhwān al-Ṣafāʾ*, the author of the *Risālat al-Jāmiʿa* was a master in *tabdīd al-ʿilm* ('dispersing the knowledge'), a well-known technique in esoteric writing: elements of a single doctrine are scattered throughout different parts of a book, introduced into the most unexpected places, so that the careful reader has to identify them, putting them together as pieces of a puzzle in order to understand their relationship. Hence, in the *Risālat al-Jāmiʿa*, there is not one chapter about Adam, but his story is told in different ways at different places, even in sections related to *Epistles* which have nothing to do with Adam.[28]

It is remarkable that Ashkivarī (or his source?) selected two passages and put them together in such an order as to provide a long Ismaili *taʾwīl* of Qurʾanic verses and *ḥadīth* about Adam, Iblīs, the forbidden Tree, Adam's fall and repentance. The esoteric interpretation of this well-known story is developed on four distinct levels, which are however somehow interwoven, thus creating a rather complex picture. We distinguish successively the cosmic, psychic, soteriological and epistemic levels.

Let us start with the cosmic level. In the passage of the *Jāmiʿa* immediately preceding the section quoted by Ashkivarī, we learn that the Universal Soul, given its intermediary position between Intellect and Nature, is unable to resist to the temptations of Nature. Given its inclination for the physical world the Soul partly gets entangled in matter; through its fall (*hubūṭ*) the partial soul (*al-nafs al-juzʾiyya*) is bound to corporeal envelopes (*hayākil jismāniyya*). The author calls this embodiment 'the hell of the world of generation and corruption'. Apparently, in this 'hell', there is a hierarchy of fallen souls and their respective bodies, the highest level being the 'human form': the human soul linked to a human body.[29]

It is with this evocation of the superiority of the human form that the passage quoted by Ashkivarī begins. Here, the author of the *Jāmiʿa*, after addressing the topic of man as a microcosm (see *infra* our second level of the *taʾwīl*), returns to the fall of the soul. This fall into the corporeal world is caused by the fact that the partial soul only receives

---

[28] For the location of all the passages about Adam, see al-Majrīṭī (attr.), *al-Risālat al-Jāmiʿa*, ed. Jamīl Ṣalībā (Damascus, 1949), vol. 2, pp. 409–410 (index, *s.v.* Ādam).

[29] *Jāmiʿa*, p. 119.

in an imperfect way the benefits (*fawāʾid*) of the Universal Soul and the infusions of the Intellect (*al-mawādd al-ʿaqliyya*). However, the body in which the soul is imprisoned after its fall is also an instrument for its salvation, as it is through the sense perception of the body that the soul can acquire the intellectual knowledge necessary for its escape from the material world and its ascent to Paradise (*jannat al-maʾwā waʾl-firdaws al-aʿlā*), which is the intelligible world, the realm of the Intellect.

At this stage, the *Risālat al-Jāmiʿa* establishes an explicit link with the story of Adam: 'The soul then repents, as did Adam when he repented from his disobedience after having fallen into error'.[30] Hence, the fallen soul corresponds to Adam; Nature, the cause of the fall, is similar to Iblīs; after the fall, the soul or Adam repents and is forgiven, allowing it to return to its home.

The fall of the Universal Soul into Nature, its division into a plurality of partial souls embodied in a corporeal envelope, and the valorisation of the body as a necessary instrument for the soul's salvation are central components of 4th/10th-century Ismaili Neoplatonism. The details of this doctrine, for instance the question of whether human souls are a 'part' (*juzʾ*) or rather an 'imprint' (*athar*) of the Universal Soul, were among the issues under discussion in the famous debate between opposing Persian *duʿāt* such as Muḥammad al-Nasafī, Abū Ḥātim al-Rāzī and Abū Yaʿqūb al-Sijistānī.[31]

This first, cosmic, level of the *taʾwīl* of Adam's story is intimately linked to the second level, which I called psychic, as it concerns the faculties of the human soul. Elaborating on the Ikhwān's conception of man as a microcosm and their comparison of the human body with the organisation of the state, the *Risālat al-Jāmiʿa* associates the rational soul (*al-nafs al-nāṭiqa*), which receives the effusions of the Universal Soul, with the king and with Adam: just as Adam was placed in Paradise, the rational soul is the noblest part of the human form, located close to the intelligible world, whose intellectual forms it is

---

30 Ashkivarī, *Maḥbūb*, vol. 1, pp. 140–141 = *Jāmiʿa*, p. 122.

31 Daniel De Smet, 'La doctrine avicennienne des deux faces de l'âme et ses racines ismaéliennes', *Studia Islamica*, 93 (2001), pp. 77–89; Daniel De Smet, *La philosophie ismaélienne. Un ésotérisme chiite entre néoplatonisme et gnose* (Paris, 2012), pp. 113–125. On this debate, see Ismail K. Poonawala, 'An Early Doctrinal Controversy in the Iranian School of Ismaʿili Thought and its Implications', *JPS*, 5 (2012), pp. 17–34.

able to conceive of. However, it has to struggle continuously against all kinds of forbidden bodily pleasures: these pleasures refer to the Tree the fruits of which Adam was forbidden to eat. The lower faculties of the soul – the concupiscent soul (*al-nafs al-shahwāniyya*) and the irascible soul (*al-nafs al-ghaḍabiyya*) – try to seduce the rational soul, so that it yields to bodily pleasures: they play the role of Iblīs. If they are successful, the rational soul falls down and the lights of the intellect (*al-anwār al-ʿaqliyya*) no longer reach it. In the same way Iblīs provoked the fall of Adam, who was expelled from Paradise, so deprived of the benefits emanating from the intelligible world.[32]

The soteriological level starts with Adam's repentance and God's mercy. The disobedience of Adam, by eating the forbidden fruit, not only caused his fall and expulsion from Paradise, but also the closing of the 'cycle of manifestation' (*dawr al-kashf*), during which the intelligible realm was directly accessible to all creatures, and the opening of a 'cycle of occultation' (*dawr al-satr*). Hence, the intelligible world could only be approached through the teaching of an uninterrupted succession of prophets and messengers sent by divine mercy in order to rescue the fallen souls. Adam, after his repentance, was the first of them: 'Every prophet, every messenger, was in his own time what Adam was in his period; the people of this period are his children.' However, Adam was not yet endowed with 'firm resolution' (*dhu'l-ʿazm*), the force to resist the temptations of Iblīs and to save mankind from the sin he committed. Only the prophets after Adam had this resolution.[33]

Although Iblīs had no longer a direct influence on the sinless prophets, he appeared at their side as an antagonist (*ḍidd*), similar to the concupiscent or irascible soul trying to corrupt the rational soul. In those cases where Iblīs succeeds in stirring up people against their prophet, he transforms their rational soul into a satan in potentiality

---

[32] Ashkivarī, *Maḥbūb*, vol. 1, pp. 139–140 = *Jāmiʿa*, pp. 120–122.

[33] Ashkivarī, *Maḥbūb*, vol. 1, pp. 141–142 = *Jāmiʿa*, pp. 122–123. Here again, the *Risālat al-Jāmiʿa* echoes a controversial issue in 4th/10th-century Ismailism: was Adam among the *ulū'l-ʿazm* and was he a prophet?; see Daniel De Smet, 'Adam, premier prophète et législateur? La doctrine chiite des *ulū al-ʿazm* et la controverse sur la pérennité de la *šarīʿa*', in Mohammad Ali Amir-Moezzi, Meir M. Bar-Asher and Simon Hopkins, ed., *Le shīʿisme imāmite quarante ans après. Hommage à Etan Kohlberg* (Turnhout, 2009), pp. 187–202.

(*shayṭān bi'l-quwwa*), which becomes a satan in actuality (*shayṭān bi'l-fiʿl*) after the death of the body. This means that the rational soul remains attached to the passions of the physical world, rejects the emanation coming from the intelligible realm and returns to the 'house of ignominy' (*dār al-hawān*), 'the place of sufferings and pains' (*maḥall al-asqām wa'l-ālām*), which is the world of generation and corruption. This allusion to metempsychosis is confirmed by the quotation of Q 4:56, a verse often invoked by the adepts of *tanāsukh*, including Ismaili authors: 'Surely those who disbelieve in Our signs – We shall certainly roast them at a Fire; as often as their skins are wholly burned, We shall give them in exchange other skins, that they may taste the chastisement' (Arberry's translation).[34]

In contrast, if the rational soul rejects the temptations of Iblīs (the bodily pleasures) and listens to the prophets (the messengers of the intelligible world), it becomes an angel in potentiality; after its separation from the body, having been purified and transformed into an angel in actuality, it undertakes its heavenly ascent. At the end of the cycle of manifestation, when the Resurrector (*qā'im*) will reveal all the truths (*kashf al-ḥaqā'iq*), Iblīs will be definitively neutralised.[35]

At this eschatological level, the prophets correspond to Adam and the rational soul; their antagonists to Iblīs and the concupiscent and irascible souls; the cycle of occultation is the result of Adam's fall; the cycle of manifestation refers to the initial paradisaical state before the fall; its reopening by the *qā'im* means the final redemption and the return to Paradise.[36]

Human souls turning into devils or angels in potentiality and in actuality, the succession of cycles of occultation and manifestation, and the final redemption by a Resurrector disclosing all 'truths', are well-known Ismaili concepts developed by 4th/10th-century authors, for instance in the *Kitāb al-Shajara* attributed to a *dāʿī* called Abū Tammām.[37]

---

[34] For the use of this verse, see Daniel De Smet, 'Ismaʿili-Shiʿi Visions of Hell. From the 'Spiritual' Torment of the Fāṭimids to the Ṭayyibī Rock of Sijjīn', in Christian Lange, ed., *Locating Hell in Islamic Traditions* (Leiden and Boston, 2016), pp. 248–249.

[35] Ashkivarī, *Maḥbūb*, vol. 1, pp. 142–143 = *Jāmiʿa*, pp. 124–126.

[36] Ashkivarī, *Maḥbūb*, vol. 1, pp. 143–144 = *Jāmiʿa*, pp. 127–128.

[37] This is in particular the case with the distinction between *al-shayṭān bi'l-quwwa / bi'l-fiʿl* and *al-malak bi'l-quwwa/ bi'l-fiʿl*; see Daniel De Smet, 'The Demon in Potentiality and the Devil in Actuality. Two Principles of Evil according to 4th/10th Century Ismailism', *Arabica*, 70 (2023), pp. 1–25 (forthcoming).

The fourth and last level in our *ta'wīl* is the *epistemic* one, as it concerns the transmission of knowledge from God to mankind. It is the highest level, and probably the most 'esoteric' one, as it explains the ultimate reason for Adam's fall and its consequences. Remarkably enough, Ashkivarī copied it from an earlier part of the *Risālat al-Jāmiʿa* (some 60 pages in Ghālib's edition) and inserted it immediately after his long quote discussed thus far, introducing it with: 'this sage (*hādhā al-ḥakīm*) said. . .'[38]

After Adam's creation, God established him in the garden of Paradise and concluded a pact with him: he was forbidden to approach a certain tree and to eat of its fruit. God even explained to him the reason for this interdiction. The fruit of the tree contained the remnants of the first cycle of manifestation (*dawr al-kashf al-awwal*). Throughout the entire cycle of occultation, of which Adam was the first lieutenant (*khalīfa*),[39] the fruit of the tree had to remain hidden, as it was reserved for the end of the cycle, when things would return to their origin. With the opening of the cycle of felicity (*dawr al-saʿāda*) by the 'pure soul' (*al-nafs al-zakiyya*, a denomination of the Resurrector), the tree, identified with the *sidrat al-muntahā* (Q 53:14), will appear, which is the sign of the advent of the second creation or final resurrection.

Iblīs tried to convince Adam and his wife Eve to violate their pact with God and to acquire the knowledge reserved for the *qā'im*, as the possession of this knowledge would make him equal to God. The devil aroused Adam's curiosity and avidity, by claiming that the knowledge was about the Resurrection, the second creation, and the 'appearance of spiritual forms without material bodies in the abode of permanence'. With this knowledge, Adam and Eve would become eternal angels. Blinded by Iblīs's words, Adam violently desired this knowledge, passionately aiming to proceed from potentiality to actuality, from the cycle of occultation to the cycle of manifestation. By the consumption of the forbidden fruit, he acquired a forbidden knowledge, which caused his fall and expulsion from Paradise.[40]

---

38 Ashkivarī, *Maḥbūb*, vol. 1, p. 144.6; cf. *Jāmiʿa*, p. 66.11

39 This contradicts what was said earlier, that Adam's disobedience and fall were the cause for the opening of a cycle of occultation: here Adam is from the outset the first 'lieutenant' of this cycle.

40 Ashkivarī, *Maḥbūb*, vol. 1, pp. 144–146 = *Jāmiʿa*, pp. 66–69.

Here Ashkivarī borrows the standard esoteric Ismaili interpretation of the fall of Adam from the *Risālat al-Jāmiʿa*, one which was considerably expanded (partly under the influence of the *Risālat al-Jāmiʿa* itself) by Ṭayyibī authors.[41] Hence, he included in the central part of his chapter on Adam what looks as an Ismaili treatise exposing a four-level *taʾwīl* of the story of Adam and his fall. By copying and inserting two longer passages that appear in a different order in the *Risālat al-Jāmiʿa*, Ashkivarī built a coherent whole, demonstrating that he was well aware of the underlying doctrine. Of course, it cannot be excluded *a priori* that he found this combination in an Ismaili (Ṭayyibī?) work dependent on the *Risālat al-Jāmiʿa*, but so far there is no evidence that Ismaili literature in the Arabic language (and thus belonging to the Fatimid and Ṭayyibī traditions) circulated freely in Safavid Iran.

Zoroaster and the origin of evil

That Ashkivarī had access to the *Risālat al-Jāmiʿa* is also clear from his chapter about Zoroaster, although he depends for the major part on al-Shahrastānī's *Kitāb al-Milal waʾl-niḥal.*[42] However, in the middle of al-Shahrastānī's exposition of Zoroaster's doctrine of Light and Darkness, in order to clarify and explain the link between Darkness and evil Ashkivarī introduces a longer passage defending the thesis that 'evil has no root in the first origination from the true Creator' (*al-sharr lā aṣl lahu fiʾl-ibdāʿ al-awwal min jihat al-mubdiʿ al-ḥaqq*). This passage, a quote from the *Risālat al-Jāmiʿa*,[43] attributes the origin

[41] Bernard Lewis, 'An Ismaili Interpretation of the Fall of Adam', *BSOAS*, 9 (1938), pp. 691–704; Daniel De Smet, 'L'Arbre de la connaissance du bien et du mal. Transformation d'un thème biblique dans l'ismaélisme ṭayyibite', in Stefan Leder, ed., *Studies in Arabic and Islam. Proceedings of the 19th Congress of the U.E.A.I., Halle 1998* (Leuven, 2002), pp. 513–521; De Smet, *La philosophie ismaélienne*, pp. 100–111.

[42] Ashkivarī, *Maḥbūb*, vol. 1, pp. 355–359, mainly based on al-Shahrastānī, *Kitāb al-Milal waʾl-niḥal*, ed. Muḥammad Sayyid Kaylānī (Beirut, n.d.), vol. 1, pp. 236–244; cf. Terrier, *Histoire*, pp. 643–649. The chapter about Zoroaster in the *Maḥbūb* was briefly studied by Henry Corbin, 'L'idée du paraclet en philosophie Iranienne', in *La Persia nel Medioevo* (Rome, 1970), pp. 56–59.

[43] Ashkivarī, *Maḥbūb*, vol. 1, pp. 357–358 = *Jāmiʿa*, pp. 49.5–50.15. The quote ends with Q 21:104. But before proceeding with al-Shahrastānī's text, Ashkivarī adds one sentence ending with the repetition that 'evil has no root in the origination' (Ashkivarī, *Maḥbūb*, vol. 1, p. 358). This sentence seems to belong to the *Risālat al-Jāmiʿa*, although it is absent in both Ghālib's and Ṣalība's (vol. 1, p. 76) editions.

of evil to the gradual loss of perfection in the scheme of emanation: if the Intellect proceeding from the Originator is at the highest level of perfection, imperfection increases with the successive emanation of the Soul, Nature and the composite beings. As evil is the result of the downward procession from the Intellect, it will disappear with the final reversion, the *reditus* or way up back to the Intellect.

In the previous *faṣl*, the *Risālat al-Jāmiʿa* uses the sentence 'evil has no root in the origination from the Creator' against the dualists (*al-thanawiyya*), who claim that Good and Evil are eternal ultimate principles.[44] This is also the case in the 25th 'wellspring' of the *Kitāb al-Yanābīʿ* by the Ismaili *dāʿī* Abū Yaʿqūb al-Sijistānī, a chapter entitled: *Fī anna al-sharr lā aṣl lahu fi'l-ibdāʿ*.[45] But here, the polemical tone against the dualists is even more explicit, mentioning Ahuramazda and Ahriman, the Magians and the followers of Bihāfarīd.[46] However, Ashkivarī uses his quote from the *Risālat al-Jāmiʿa* in the opposite way, not as an argument against the dualists, but rather as a clarification of Zoroaster's doctrine as he found it in al-Shahrastānī. And indeed, in the *Kitāb al-Milal wa'l-niḥal*, Zoroaster is presented as a monotheist, believing in a one and unique God, who created the two contrary principles of Light and Darkness. Evil only occurs in the composite things, as a result of the mixing of Light and Darkness, without which the world could not exist. In no case, can the Creator be considered as the origin of evil.[47] It is this Islamised picture of Zoroaster that allows

---

44 *Jāmiʿa*, pp. 48–49.

45 Abū Yaʿqūb al-Sijistānī, *Kitāb al-Yanābīʿ*, ed. Henry Corbin, in his *Trilogie ismaélienne* (Tehran and Paris, 1961), pp. 61–63; English translation by Paul E. Walker in his *The Wellsprings of Wisdom* (Salt Lake City, UT, 1994), pp. 85–87.

46 Al-Sijistānī, *Yanābīʿ*, § 121, pp. 61–62; Walker, *Wellsprings*, p. 85. Although the wordings are different, al-Sijistānī's argument against the dualists is similar to what is found in the *Risālat al-Jāmiʿa*. The relationahip between these texts requires further investigation.

47 Al-Shahrastānī, *Milal*, vol. 1, pp. 237–238; al-Shahrastānī, *Livre des religions et des sects*, tr. by Daniel Gimaret and Guy Monnot (Paris and Leuven, 1986–1993), vol. 1, pp. 643–644. On the transformation of Iranian dualist systems into monotheist religions more or less compatible with Islam, see Daniel De Smet, 'Le combat mythique entre le Roi de la Lumière et le Prince des Ténèbres selon le Mani arabe: une lecture Islamisée du dualisme?', in Marie-Anne Persoons, Christian Cannuyer and Daniel De Smet, ed., *Les combats dans les mythes et les littératures de l'Orient* (*Acta Orientalia Belgica*, 31) (Brussels, 2018), pp. 293–304.

Ashkivarī to include him among the sages and philosophers who took their knowledge from the 'niche of prophecy'.

The same passage of the *Risālat al-Jāmiʿa*, with the sentence *al-sharr lā aṣl lahu fi'l-ibdāʿ*, is often quoted by Ṭayyibī authors in a similar way, although without explicit reference to Persian dualism. The dualistic opposition between light and darkness, good and evil, which permeates the Ṭayyibī worldview, is absent here from the highest levels of the intelligible world, as it is the result of the gradual loss of perfection and brightness in the process of emanation.[48]

Conclusion

If occasional quotes from the *Rasāʾil Ikhwān al-Ṣafāʾ* by Iranian Twelver Shiʿi authors of the Safavid era are quite common (although still unstudied), Ashkivarī's use of the *Risālat al-Jāmiʿa* is, to the best of my knowledge, unique. In contrast with his citations from the *Rasāʾil*, which have few doctrinal consequences, the two longer quotes from the *Jāmiʿa* in the chapters on Adam and Zoroaster contain Ismaili teachings, which were already present in 4th/10th-century authors, but were extensively elaborated on in the later Ṭayyibī system: the fall of the Universal Soul (or the third Intellect) to Nature and the fall of the individual 'partial' souls into bodily envelopes; the dualist opposition between good and evil, light and darkness as a result of this fall, but occurring at a lower level in the scheme of emanation; the gradual disclosure of the knowledge leading to salvation by an uninterrupted chain of prophets and imams; the transmigration of unpurified human souls into new bodily envelopes; the final redemption of souls and the victory of light over darkness with the advent of the Resurrector.

There is no evidence that Ashkivarī was aware of the Ismaili origin of these doctrines, as they are exposed in the *Risālat al-Jāmiʿa*. It is clear

---

[48] Daniel De Smet, 'La *Risāla al-Jāmiʿa* attribuée aux Ikhwān al-Ṣafāʾ: un précurseur de l'ismaélisme ṭayyibite?', in Antonella Straface, Carlo De Angelo and Andrea Manzo, ed., *Labor Limae. Atti in onore di Carmela Baffioni* (Naples, 2018), vol. 1, pp. 278–279, 295; Daniel De Smet, '"Le mal ne s'enracine pas dans l'instauration". La question du mal dans le shiʿisme ismaélien', *Oriens*, 49 (2021), pp. 181–215.

from his *Maḥbūb al-qulūb* that he was a master in copying and inserting material. But the quotes he selected from the *Jāmiʿa* and the intelligent way he introduced them into his chapters on Adam and Zoroaster, show that he had a quite correct understanding of their doctrinal implications. It is also noteworthy that Ashkivarī, who embellished his book with numerous traditions attributed to the Ithnāʿasharī Shiʿi imams and explicit references to Twelver Shiʿi ideas, never establishes a link with any Shiʿi tradition when quoting material related to the Ikhwān al-Ṣafāʾ. In the entry about them in the second volume, he only refers to Ibn al-Qifṭī on the Sunni opinion about the attribution of authorship to Abū Sulaymān al-Maqdisī and his circle. Can this be seen as a form of *taqiyya*? Even if he ignored the Ismaili background of the *Risālat al-Jāmiʿa*, he must have been aware that the book contains 'heterodox' material according to the standards of contemporary Twelver Shiʿi views. But he also adopted an unconventional position towards radical forms of Sufism, which brings Mathieu Terrier to the conclusion that he was 'un esprit indépendant de toute orthodoxie'.[49] The same can be said about his treatment of the citations from the *Risālat al-Jāmiʿa*.

Ashkivarī's use of the *Risālat al-Jāmiʿa* shows in any case that the work circulated in 11th/17th-century Iran, raising the question about its influence on Safavid thought. More than the possible use of the *Rasāʾil Ikhwān al-Ṣafāʾ* by authors such as Mullā Ṣadrā or Mīr Dāmād, the investigation of the influence of the *Jāmiʿa*, with its explicit Ismaili character, seems the best way to evaluate the importance of Ismaili traces in the works of Iranian philosophers from the Safavid era.

---

[49] Mathieu Terrier, 'Apologie du soufisme par un philosophe shīʿite de l'Iran safavide. Nouvelles remarques sur le *Maḥbūb al-qulūb* d'Ashkevarī', *Studia Islamica*, 109 (2014), pp. 240–273; the quote is on p. 272.

PART TWO

SHIʿI MESSIANISM AND THE SYMBOLISM OF LETTERS

5

The Resurrection of Shah Ismāʿīl in Alevi-Bektashi Literature

Amelia Gallagher

Introduction: Shah Ismāʿīl and the Renaissance of Shiʿi Islam

While the title of my chapter declares a 'Resurrection' of Shah Ismāʿīl Ṣafavī (d. 930/1524), literary history points more to his 'immortality' among the Qizil-bāsh (Turkish: Ḳızılbaş), the main descendant communities of which today are referred to as Alevi, or Alevi-Bektashi.[1] Considering the large scope of the attributions to his pen-name Khaṭā'ī, Shah Ismāʿīl can be said to have gone on, after his death, to compose a varied corpus perhaps well into the 20th century.[2] Of course, there are logical explanations for this supra-human feat. We can see this resurrection through a literary dynamic, one that is not fully understood because of its oral transmission. Yet this literary process is crucial for the development of what we have been characterising as a 'broader esoteric' Shiʿi Islam during the period of time we would like to discuss here. The corpus of Shah Ismāʿīl's poetry

[1] Although communities with a historical relationship to the Safavids include the Ahl-i Ḥaqq and the Shabak, this study confines itself to the Alevi-Bektashi of Anatolia and the Balkans. On related communities, see Irène Mélikoff, 'Le problème Bektaşi-Alévi: quelques dernières considérations', *Turcica*, 31 (1999), p. 27.

[2] According to Vladimir Minorsky, Shah Ismāʿīl probably derived his *makhlaṣ* from the medieval Persian name for China, 'Khaṭā(y)'. Vladimir Minorsky, 'The Poetry of Shāh Ismāʿīl I', *BSOAS*, 4 (1942), p. 1028. A more recent anthology of his work relates a tradition in which Shah Ismāʿīl styled his pen-name to mimic the name of the Chaghatay poet Mīr ʿAlī Shīr Navāʾī (d. 906/1501). See İbrahim Arslanoğlu, *Şah İsmail Hatayî: Divan, Dehnâme, Nasihatnâme ve Anadolu Hatayîleri* (Istanbul, 1992), p. 14.

that continued to generate after his death was a major way in which esoteric Shiʿi Islam spread in the Ottoman empire, including not only Anatolia, but also the Balkans – in Albania and Bulgaria and other places where descendant communities of the Qizil-bāsh still live today.

As we are aware, the young Shaykh Ismāʿīl inherited the leadership of the Ṣafavī Sufi order sometime after the death of his father Shaykh Ḥaydar (d. 893/1488).[3] By this time, Ḥaydar had outfitted and militarised his 'devotee-soldiers' into loyal and disciplined troops as he and his followers became major players in the power struggles of the Turkoman dynasties.[4] In 907/1501, Ismāʿīl was crowned and seated on the Aq-Qoyunlu throne in Tabrīz, founding the Safavid empire, the dynastic state responsible for the establishment of Ithnāʿasharī Shiʿism in Ādharbāyjān and the rest of Iran. As the first ruler of an important Shiʿi state, Ismāʿīl stands as a central figure in this broader context. His has become one of the iconic voices of the transformation of Iran and of this renaissance of Shiʿi Islam during the 9th/15th, 10th/16th and 11th/7th centuries.

What role did Shah Ismāʿīl play in this renaissance of Shiʿi Islam, which saw both Ismailis and Twelvers enter the arenas of power after centuries of marginalisation? It is difficult to deny that the establishment of Twelver Shiʿism as the religion of his nascent state was his crowning political and religious achievement. But modern Safavid historiography has placed an even more profound emphasis on the role of Ismāʿīl in the triumph of the Safavids. In a quest to account for how such a young leader of a dervish order managed to become the shah of an empire, modern scholarship analysed Ismāʿīl through Max Weber's understanding of the concept of 'charisma'. In this way, the Safavids, by elevating their *pīr* to the throne, were held up as the most successful

---

[3] On the history of succession from Ḥaydar to Ismāʿīl, see A. H. Morton, 'The Early Years of Shah Ismaʿil in the *Afżal al-Tavārīkh* and elsewhere', in Charles Melville, ed., *Safavid Persia: The History and Politics of an Islamic Society* (London, 1996), p. 33.

[4] Although Ḥaydar's 'soldier-devotees' donned red headdresses, the term Qizil-bāsh (red-head) became identified with these tribes only after the establishment of the dynasty. See Shahzad Bashir, 'The Origins and Rhetorical Evolution of the Term Qizilbāsh in Persianate Literature', *Journal of the Economic and Social History of the Orient*, 57 (2014), pp. 364–369.

of all of the messianic movements of the post-Mongol period.[5] And in discerning the role of Ismāʿīl's personal charisma in this achievement, we have his own words as evidence; words which, from the point of view of Safavid historiography, seemed to be a gift from God himself.

Shah Ismāʿīl's Poetry: The Question of a Messiah

Every student of Safavid history has an image of Ismāʿīl as a leader that is gleaned from his own words, his own poetry. This verse became known to international academia through Vladimir Minorsky's publication, 'The Poetry of Shāh Ismāʿīl', which included poems from the Paris manuscript of Ismāʿīl's *Dīwān*, at that time evaluated as the oldest and most authentic of his formal collections. Presenting this vivid imagery as an articulation of the young shah's theocratic mission, Minorsky was the first to see that the poetry of Shah Ismāʿīl had profound historical consequence. To demonstrate this, Minorsky curated and translated about twenty poems of various forms from the original Turkic or Azeri verses. In these selections, Ismāʿīl seems to be speaking directly to his soldiers as an ethereal military commander, 'My name is Shah Ismāʿīl. I am God's mystery', with orders to 'Prostrate yourselves before the shah'.[6] Declaring himself the 'Eye of God,' the poet would transmute into an alignment with the divine speaking as the 'Essence of Divine Truth' (*aṣl-i ḥaqq*).[7]

At times Khaṭāʾī seemed to be preparing his audience for the coming of the Mahdi, at times announcing the revelation of the awaited one, using language taken directly from Shiʿi apocalyptic tradition. This apocalyptic expression is used carefully, however. Subsequent critical analysis of Shah Ismāʿīl's *Dīwān* of poetry has established that in his

---

[5] See Said Amir Arjomand, *The Shadow of God and the Hidden Imam: Religion, Political Order and Societal Change in Shiʿite Iran from the Beginning to 1890* (Chicago, 1984); Roger Savory, *Iran Under the Safavids* (Cambridge, 1980); Hans Roemer, 'The Safavid Period', in *The Cambridge History of Iran*, Volume 6, *The Timurid and Safavid Periods*, ed. P. Jackson and L. Lockhart (Cambridge, 1986), pp. 189–350.

[6] Translations taken from Minorsky, 1042, 1047 and 1043, corresponding to Turhan Gandjeï, ed., *Il Canzoniere di Šāh Ismāʿīl Ḫaṭāʾī* (Naples, 1959), nos. 16, 198 and 20.

[7] *Dīvān-i Khaṭāʾī*, MS, n.d., Arthur M. Sackler Gallery Preserve, ff. 38v–39r. For the full *ghazal* and translation, see Amelia Gallagher, 'The Apocalypse of Ecstasy: The Poetry of Shah Ismāʿīl Revisited', *IS*, 51 (2018), pp. 363–366.

poetic assertions he consistently stops short of taking the presumptuous last step of declaring himself to be the Mahdi.[8] More likely, Ismāʿīl aimed to present himself as a major herald in the return of the eschatological Mahdī, certainly the most rightful of his generation's contenders.[9] In any event, it became almost inevitable to view his words as reflections of Safavid political aspirations, as the circumstantial evidence tends to corroborate. Perhaps the Safavid soldier-devotees did see Ismāʿīl as immortal, just as they had deemed his father and grandfather before him, according to the Aq-Qoyunlu historian Rūzbihān Khunjī (d. 927/1521).[10] Or perhaps he saw himself as divine chastisement for the Ottomans, just as the contemporary European observers portrayed him, reporting that he was 'reverenced as a god'. However, both Aq-Qoyunlu courtiers and Venetian informants had reasons to project their fears and expectations upon the Safavids and their partisans. Influenced by their own political aims, the sensational Italian accounts at least should be regarded with caution as 'entertaining anecdote' and 'rumour' rather than objective witness.[11]

Elsewhere, I have analysed the poetic strategies of Shah Ismāʿīl's *Dīwān* as apocalyptic in a revelatory and literary sense, as opposed to eschatological in a literal sense.[12] One could further argue a wider

---

[8] According to A. T. Karamustafa, Shah Ismāʿīl does not present himself as the Mahdi, but rather 'the supreme enabler of the 'Alid mission on earth.' See, 'In His Own Voice: What Hatayi Tells us about Şah İsmail's Religious Views', in M. A. Amir-Moezzi, ed., *L'Ésotérisme shi'ite, ses racines et ses prolongements* (Turnhout, 2016), p. 608.

[9] Erika Glassen was the first to argue for Shah Ismāʿīl's role as the forerunner of the Mahdi in her 'Schah Ismāʿīl, ein Mahdī der anatolischen Turkmenen?', *Zeitschrift der Deutschen Morgenländischen Gesellschaft*, 121 (1971), pp. 61–69. More recently, Rıza Yıldırım has also analysed Shah Ismāʿīl's poetic persona along these lines. See his 'In the Name of Hosayn's Blood: The Memory of Karbala as Ideological Stimulus to the Safavid Revolution', *JPS*, 8 (2015), pp. 127–154.

[10] 'They openly called Shaykh Junayd "God" (*ilāh*) and his son "the son of God (ibn-Allāh)" . . .'. See John E. Woods, ed., *Faḍlullāh b. Rūzbihān Khunjī-Isfahānī, Tārīkh-i ʿĀlam-ārā-yi Amīnī* (London, 1992), p. 57.

[11] Palmira Brummett, 'The Myth of Shah Ismail Safavi: Political Rhetoric and 'Divine' Kingship', in John Victor Tolan, ed., *Medieval Christian Perceptions of Islam: A Book of Essays* (New York, 1996), p. 333.

[12] A. Gallagher, 'The Apocalypse of Ecstasy: The Poetry of Shah Ismail Revisited', pp. 361–397.

capacity for interpretation on the part of the audiences of this poetry, as the entire premise of *ghazal* poetry rested on a foundation of allegory. One of the assumptions regarding the potency of the lyrics was that later copies of the *Dīwān* had toned down Ismāʿīl's blasphemous self-regard. Minorsky speculated that concerns of orthodox Shiʿi propriety were in mind as later editions of Ismāʿīl's *Dīwān* (dating from the reign of Shah Ṭahmāsp onwards) were cleansed of their original excess.[13] However, it is difficult to regard any of the later Safavids as unaware of Ismāʿīl's strident self-imaging, since a representative selection of his poetry appears in a later genealogy of the Safavid dynasty.[14] It is also difficult to imagine how later audiences would take such imagery seriously. Gradually, as more copies of Shah Ismāʿīl's *Dīwān* have been discovered, we have seen the extent to which it was copied throughout the 10th/16th and 11th/17th centuries, although critical analysis of the contents of a newly discovered manuscript awaits comparison.

The elevated language of Ismāʿīl's descriptions of himself accompanied by the graphic violence of his poetic images has gained attention in a way that perhaps has masked other literary influences and references. Ismāʿīl's indebtedness to the Ḥurūfi poet and martyr Nesīmī (d. 820/1417) and the towering figure of Manṣūr al-Ḥallāj (d. 309/922) in his own ecstatic pronouncements ('I am the Divine Truth') could have been interpreted as literary expression of the poet's own achievement of mystical union had they been written by anyone else. Furthermore, a common assumption held in both historical and literary circles was that not only was his poetry primarily political propaganda, but sub-standard art as well. However, Azeri literary historians consistently defended his status as an early standard of Azeri poetics, in a literary canon which also includes Nesīmī and Fużūlī (d. 963/1556).[15] In the modern republic of Azerbaijan, where

---

13 Minorsky, 'The Poetry of Shāh Ismāʿīl I', p. 1026.

14 A. Gallagher, 'Shah Ismaʿil's Poetry in the *Silsilat al-Nasab-i Safaviyya*', *IS*, 44 (2011), pp. 895–911.

15 See Azizaga Memedov, 'Le plus ancien manuscrit du *dīvān* de Shah Ismail Khatayi', *Turcica*, 6 (1972), pp. 8–23.

large civic statues place the pen as well as the sword in his hands, Ismāʿīl has been resurrected as a proto-nationalist literary giant.

Even if the verse is divorced from Ismāʿīl's status as a revolutionary, he cultivates a formidable poetic persona in the midst of an imminent reckoning for the opponents of the ʿAlid loyalists. The awaited parties of this event are at once vague and all encompassing: ʿAlī, Ḥusayn, the Mahdi, 'the Shah'. As seen in the following *ghazal* taken from the Paris *Dīwān*, the poet presents the return of the entire line descending from ʿAlī as a collective event that has been fulfilled. The Mahdi has come to the battlefield (*maydān*) in the successive line of the Twelve imams, followed directly by the shah-poet himself in the final succession and couplet:

1. Praise be to God that the gate of the world, the manifest of the saints has come,

The lantern of Islam has ignited so that the religion of Muṣṭafā has come.

2. To the hypocrites' destruction, to the partisans of Yazīd numerous blows have come,

The Shah of the world, ʿAlī Murtaḍa, again has come.

3. ʿAlī is the shah of the holy lineage (*wilāyat*), the secret of spiritual guidance (*hidāyat*),

To manifest the secret of the saints, ʿAlī has come.

4. Ḥasan is as magnificent as the Mahdi is generous,

Still wielding his sword, Ḥusayn of Karbala has come.

5. Zayn al-ʿĀbid, Bāqir and Jaʿfar Ṣādiq have decreed,

The venerable imams, Kāẓim and ʿAlī Mūsā Riḍā, have come.

6. Taqī is the sultan of the world, Naqī is the firmament of faith,

After them, to battlefield, Ḥasan has come.

7. Muḥammad the Mahdi, the righteous guide, became the master of the faith,

Demons who reject the path to the battlefield have come.

8. Awake, be not prodigal, for Shah Ismāʿīl has come,

On this path, sacrifice your life for the guiding Imam who has come.[16]

Although Minorsky did not cite this particular poem, it seems to express the sort of militancy which characterised the loyalty of the Safavids' followers. The beginning of the poem predicts destruction for the partisans of Yazīd, and later, the presence of demonic minions in battle against 'Muḥammad the Mahdi'. The royal title 'Shah Ismāʿīl' in the signature couplet inserts a physical identity into the company of sacred presences. Against the conventions of a genre that favours pen-names, this brazen revelation of the 'real' author would support the theory that Ismāʿīl used his art for political ends. But this should not detract from the main objective of the verse, which is adoration of the Twelve imams. Embedded in the body of the poem and taking up the majority of its lines, is a structured litany of praise to the Twelve imams named in sequence. While Shah Ismāʿīl's poetry is often cited as primarily a vehicle for his own praise, many more of his poems bear themes of pious devotion, including this one. Perhaps these poems in which the central strategy consists of expressing reverence for sacred Shiʿi figures such as the Twelve imams have been overlooked despite their prominence in the *Dīwān* because of their formulaic constructions and conventional piety. And yet it is likely that these kinds of approach were more influential in the literary evolution of the Qizil-bāsh and related groups than any of Ismāʿīl's flights of grandiose self-expression.

We have reached an important limitation as to the extent to which Shah Ismāʿīl's bold and complex verse affected political history. However, despite the correctives, we cannot yet claim a complete revision of Minorsky's original premise of the poetry's historical value.

---

[16] Gandjeï, *Il Canzoniere di Šāh Ismāʿīl Ḫaṭāʾī*, no. 19.

With three *Dīwān* manuscripts that were probably produced during Ismāʿīl's lifetime and many more afterwards, his historical body of work, that is, the material produced during his life along with subsequent copies, will be a source for future reflection on the foundational generations of Safavid rulers.[17] Although no longer deemed the 'mass of authentic facts'[18] it was once assumed to be, Ismāʿīl's *Dīwān* should be subject to comprehensive interpretation as much as any literary source in consideration of both poetic interpretation and socio-political context. While we cannot be confident that Shah Ismāʿīl's poetry played a role in bestowing on him the contested Turkoman throne, it certainly contributed to the Renaissance of Shiʿi Islam, especially when we see this rebirth as a phenomenon beyond the defeat of opponents and seizing of political power.

Shah Ismāʿīl's Resurrection in 'Broader Esoteric' Shiʿi Islam

One of the more obscure aspects of Shah Ismāʿīl's literary legacy has to do with the people among whom he was resurrected. Important questions still surround the development of the Qizil-bāsh tribes into a stable sectarian community in the Ottoman empire. Subject to persecution because of their suspect loyalty, the Ottoman Qizil-bāsh were bound to the Safavids, at least in the eyes of the Ottoman authorities, until the 11th/17th century.[19] By modern times, when these communities came to be identified as 'Alevi', they had preserved and

---

17 For a detailed examination of the existing manuscripts of Shah Ismāʿīl's *Dīwān*, see Ferenc Csirkés, 'Messianic Oeuvres in Interaction: Misattributed Poems by Shah Esmāʿīl and Nesimi', *JPS*, 8 (2015), pp. 155–194. On several recently discovered manuscripts, see, Mehmet Fatih Köksal, 'Şah İsmail Hatâyî'nin Şiirlerinde Kullandığı Vezin Meselesi', *Türk Kültürü ve Hacı Bektaş Velî Araştırma Dergisi*, 66 (2013), pp. 169–185; Muhsin Macit, 'Şah İsmail'in Eserleri ve Şairliği Üzerine', *Yeni Türkiye*, 72 (2015), pp. 623–630.

18 Minorsky, p. 1025.

19 On the complex evolution of Qizil-bāsh leadership during the Ottoman period, see Ayfer Karakay-Stump, *Subjects of the Sultan, Disciples of the Shah: Formation and Transformation of the Kizilbash/Alevi Communities in Ottoman Anatolia* (PhD, Harvard University, 2008).

developed a faith distinct from that of 'orthodox' Shiʿi Islam as regards theology, law, ritual, philosophy and clerical authority. However, any discussion of Qizil-bāsh-Alevi history in Turkey today, especially their development throughout the pivotal Safavid period in the 10th/16th century is often political, even polemical. This tension can be sidestepped to an extent: given their Twelver identification, it is common for Alevi accounts of their own religious history to begin with the Prophet's family and ʿAlī, going through each of the imams in an unbroken chain and revived in the fervent ʿAlid mysticism of medieval Anatolia. It is also common to go back further still and seek the origins of Qizil-bāsh beliefs in pre-Islamic Turkic religion. This was the dominant nationalist position in modern Turkish academia.[20] When modern eyes turned to the Alevi-Bektashi faith and started to study it in its own right, it became commonplace in Turkey and beyond to attribute the 'heterodox' beliefs and practices of the Qizil-bāsh to pre-Islamic Turkic belifs ('shamanism'), and to emphasise the ancient Central Asian basis of their tribal culture. Whether or not this was the intention, this orientation had the effect of claiming Qizil-bāsh communities for the modern nation-state of Turkey, despite the demographic reality that a large portion of Alevis are Kurdish (native speakers of Zaza and Kurmanji).[21] In recent decades, there has been a renewed interest in these questions of origin, one of the results of which is that Alevis are writing their own histories, published in both the academic and popular press, with a pronounced presences in digital media. Shah Ismāʿīl, both as a heroic figure and an influential *pīr*, has been a central figure of these communally-conscious narratives of Alevi history.[22]

---

[20] Associated with the modern pioneer of Turkish studies, Fuad Köprülü, this approach is extensively analysed in Markus Dressler, *Writing Religion: The Making of Turkish Alevi Islam* (Oxford, 2013).

[21] For an overview of the issue of Kurdish Alevism, see Martin van Bruinessen, 'Between Dersim and Dâlahû: Reflections on Kurdish Alevism and the Ahl-i Haqq religion', in Shahrokh Raei, ed., *Islamic Alternatives: Non-Mainstream Religion in Persianate Societies* (Wiesbaden, 2017), pp. 65–93.

[22] Several recent examples include: Tufan Gündüz, *Son Kızılbaş: Şah İsmail* (Istanbul, 2018); Ahmet Taşgin, Ali Yaman and Namiq Musalı, ed., *Safevîler ve Şah İsmail* (Istanbul, 2014), which was published to commemorate the 500th anniversary of the battle of Chaldirān, and Mustafa Ekinci, *Şah İsmail ve İnanç Dünyası* (Istanbul, 2010).

Connected to this fundamental historical question outlined above is the issue of the relationship between the Bektashi order and the Qizil-bāsh-Alevi. Of course, the Bektashi order pre-dates Qizil-bāsh formation in Anatolia. With their mythical beginnings in the 7th/13th century, the Bektashi dervishes seem to have been granted a privileged position by the Ottoman sultans as their historic association with the Janissary units attests. However, during in the 10th/16th century, the order went through profound structural transformations. While most histories indicate that this structural change accompanied a theological transformation of the order due to an alignment with the Qizil-bāsh and other non-conformist elements, major aspects of this alignment remain obscure.[23] For example, it is now common to speak of 'Alevi-Bektashi' as a fused religious identity of shared beliefs and practices, but two distinct social structures survived into the Republican period: a centralised dervish order on the one hand, and a trans-regional set of communities under the authority of local hereditary lineages on the other.[24] While historically speaking it would make sense to disentangle the two traditions, their unity is evidenced in a body literature held in common which is often paralleled in and even claimed as Turkish folk literature, with which it shares many stylistic features.

This collection of religious literature is a central aspect of the cohesion between the Alevi and Bektashi, as it is a major conduit of their religious thought. In this way, literature must be understood in the broadest sense, including long periods dominated by oral-musical transmission. And inasmuch as Alevi scholars are discussing the possibility and process of a written canonisation of the literary tradition, Shah Ismāʿīl's poetry is chief among the bodies of work for consideration.[25] But at

[23] As a result of the Bektashi order's mandate to neutralise 'extremist' Shiʿi groups such as the Qizil-bāsh, it 'assimilated the heterodox trends it was intended to change' (Thierry Zarcone, 'Bektaşiyye', *EI3*) https://referenceworks-brillonline-com.iij.idm.oclc.org/entries/encyclopaedia-of-islam-3/bektasiyye-COM_24010?s.num=1&s.f.s2_parent=s.f.cluster.Encyclopaedia+of+Islam&s.q=zarcone (accessed on 24 January 2021)

[24] Officially banned by the Republic along with other dervish orders, the Bektashis' central organisation moved to Albania. See Zarcone, 'Bektaşiyye'.

[25] On the question of discerning and canonising Alevi written sources, see Rıza Yıldırım, 'Literary Foundations of the Alevi Tradition: Mainstream, Canon, and Orthodoxy', in Benjamin Weineck and Johannes Zimmermann, ed., *Alevism between Standardisation and Plurality: Negotiating Texts, Sources and Cultural Heritage* (Berlin, 2018), pp. 61–96.

which precise point Shah Ismāʿīl's poetic persona was transferred to a later literary stream or tradition is difficult to measure, for like many of the authoritative figures of this tradition, we have to assume major developments took place during periods of orality. But in the early written examples of pious attributions to Shah Ismāʿīl a disjuncture with his *Dīwān* of poetry is evident.[26]

In this subsequent Khaṭāʾī tradition, new strategies, themes and concerns emerge in the poetry, while the poetic forms, metres, and dialects diverge significantly from the contents of Shah Ismāʿīl's *Dīwān*.[27] Furthermore, these works are designated as performance pieces marking specific episodes in a variety of rituals – communal, initiatory and funerary, as well as informal prayer or supplication. Folklore studies which trace the way in which oral literature develops, view the pen-name essentially as a collective identity composing in the original poet's name. Khaṭāʾī is not the only poet who has enjoyed a literary afterlife through this process of pseudo-epigraphy, as this phenomenon is associated with other poetic figures of the tradition, such as Pīr Sulṭān Abdal, and those outside the Alevi-Bektashi tradition proper, including Yunus Emre (d. 720/1320).[28] This growing body of poetic attributions not only served to express ritual and theological teachings, it also served to perpetuate the poet's legacy.

Often dismissed in academic histories as 'pseudo-Khaṭāʾī,' in these later attributions scant memory of the notorious demagogue so closely associated with the poetry in Shah Ismāʿīl's *Dīwān* remains. Self-references become relegated to the signature couplet where they are generally self-depreciating as a final statement of the poet's humility.

---

[26] On these early written poems attributed to Khaṭāʾī, see Gallagher, 'Poetry Attributed to Shah Ismail in the Study of Anatolian Alevism', *Turcica*, 49 (2019), pp. 61–83. These early written examples from the 'pseudo-Khaṭāʾī' tradition are included in an 11th/17th-century Qizil-bāsh manuscript of a text known as the *Buyruk* ('Order'). As a category, the *Buyruk* consists of written teachings traditionally attributed to either the Sixth imam, Jaʿfar al-Ṣādiq, or the first Safavid shaykh, Ṣafī al-Dīn (d. 735/1334). On these written sources, see Ayfer Karakaya-Stump, 'Documents and Buyruk Manuscripts in the Private Archives of Alevi Dede Families: An Overview', *BJMES*, 37 (2010), pp. 273–286.

[27] I am referring to the three oldest copies of his *Dīwān*: the manuscripts of Paris, Tashkent and the Sackler Gallery.

[28] See Paul Koerbin, 'Pir Sultan Abdal: Encounters with Persona in Alevi Lyric Song', *Oral Tradition*, 26 (2011) https://muse.jhu.edu/ (accessed June 21, 2019).

This not only in accordance with convention, but is a trait associated with the voice of Khaṭā'ī and his role in the transmission of teachings. Even the meaning of the pen-name 'Khaṭā'ī', which Minorsky had assumed derived from *khaṭā'* (the one from Cathay), becomes understood in this subsequent tradition to mean 'The Culpable One', based on the slightly different root *khaṭā* (offence, transgression). It is tempting to see this as literary evidence of political vicissitudes among the descendants of the Anatolian partisans of the Safavids. Did the Qizil-bāsh become disenchanted with the idea of Ismā'īl as an immortal saviour after his defeat by the Ottomans in 920/1514? That is a difficult theory to prove, but Shah Ismā'īl as a figure at the head of a messianic dispensation is not a trope that was carried through in the later Khaṭā'ī poetic tradition. While this fascinating aspect of Shah Ismā'īl is relegated to his *Dīwān*, Khaṭā'ī was regenerated in Alevi-Bektashi culture as a sage.

Düvaz Imam

For over a century, Turkish literary specialists have regarded Shah Ismā'īl's historical *Dīwān* collections and the corpus of his attributions known in the Alevi-Bektashi context, as two separate bodies of work. Both folklorists and literary historians who study the Alevi-Bektashi characterise Ismā'īl as a revered figure, but one that has little connection to the historical shah apart from a pen-name. Within the community, however, there is a strong cultural memory of Ismā'īl's historical achievements as shah. And despite the stylistic disjuncture, common themes run throughout all of the poetry attributed to Shah Ismā'īl, from the distinctly Alevi-Bektashi ritual songs ('Hatayileri'), back to the historical *Dīwāns*, that is, the material which was collected before 930/1524.

In this regard, poems dedicated to the Twelve imams stand out as the most prominent examples of a strategy indebted to Shah Ismā'īl's original *Dīwān* of poetry. An important structural transformation was necessary, however, in order for these themes to fulfil a new ritual purpose: the poetry became recast in the metre of song. In Alevi-Bektashi literature and musicology, poetic-lyric categories are identified according to their content, or strategy, rather than their formal structure. Poetry or hymns in praise of the Twelve imams, for example, are simply referred to as '*düvaz imam*'. Moreover, there is little distinction in content between poetry, song or prayer in this wisdom tradition which for most of its history and for most of its adherents, was inherited orally as ritual song. As a discernable approach, the *düvaz imam* is a prayer that parallels earlier litany like supplications (*duʿā*) in which the Twelve imams are iterated, invoked and praised for their divine-like attributes. These supplications were originally in Arabic, and of course the names of the imams are Arabic. For this reason, it is possible that the earliest *düvaz imam* in the Qizilbāsh milieu were originally composed as mnemonic songs for a Turkic-speaking audience.[29]

Literary evidence shows that these hymns dedicated to the Twelve imams proliferated among the Alevi-Bektashi bearing both devotional and ritual content. *Düvaz imam* are intended for both formal communal ritual and informal rites, as before a meal or *sofra*, as a verbal amulet or apotropaic, or to elicit intercessory healing (*shifāʾ*).[30] Although the earliest poetic eulogies of the *düvaz imam* type are traced to the earlier Ḥurūfī and Bektashi contexts of the 9th/15th century, the form became fully developed in the ritual poetry attributed to Khaṭāʾī in the 10th/16th century.[31] Again, like so many other aspects of the tradition, Shah Ismāʿīl is cited as the innovator of the *düvaz imam* form itself in the secondary literature. This is due to the fact that a majority of *düvaz imam* poems that have come down to us are attributed to Khaṭāʾī and, as will be shown, a clear precedent of the *düvaz imam* form is present in his original works.

Therefore, it is helpful to turn to the poetry contained in Shah Ismāʿīl's historical *Dīwān* collection when establishing the basis of the *düvaz imam* poetry that flourished later. Out of the numerous poetic invocations of the Twelve imams in Shah Ismāʿīl's formal collections,

---

[29] Rıza Yıldırım, 'Red Sulphur, the Great Remedy and the Supreme Name: Faith in the Twelve Imams and Shiʿi Aspects of Alevi-Bektashi Piety', in Denis Hermann and Mathieu Terrier, ed., *Shiʿi Islam and Sufism: Classical Views and Modern Perspectives* (London, 2020), pp. 255–290.

[30] Fatih İyiyol, 'Alevî-Bektaşî Geleneğinde Düvâzlar-Düvâzimamlar', *Uluslararası Sosyal Araştırmalar Dergisi*, 6 (2013), p. 235.

[31] Rıza Yıldırım, 'Red Sulphur, the Great Remedy and the Supreme Name'; İyiyol, 'Alevî-Bektaşî Geleneğinde Düvâzlar', p. 231.

the following *qaṣīda* is chosen because of its rich theological and mythical references. Its inclusion in the Sackler Gallery's manuscript, which is one of the *Dīwāns* which has been assessed as dating from the lifetime of Ismāʿīl, is also a factor in its selection, despite the fact that the text in the original manuscript is damaged, rendering some lines illegible.[32] The ubiquitous presence of ʿAlī dominates the poem, with his sacred name terminating each couplet. Accompanied by the prophet Muhammad and Fāṭima in the opening section, ʿAlī is manifested through the main body of the poem as the spirit behind the sacred lineage, the source of its heart, soul, faith and knowledge.

1. The mine deep in the ocean of Najaf is ʿAlī,

That Balas ruby within the mine is ʿAlī.

2. Emanating from its gems are two lights,

The sun is Muḥammad and the luminous moon is ʿAlī.

3. The two worlds came into existence by his command,

[ʿAlī illuminated what was concealed in its heart].[33]

4. It was Muḥammad who made the ascent (*miʿrāj*) from below,

[Within the *dargāh*, he saw the divine lion who was ʿAlī].[34]

5. In Islam, the blessed Fāṭima is the 'Best of all women',

---

32 *Dīvān-i Khaṭāʾī*, MS, Arthur M. Sackler Gallery, ff. 59r–50v. On the dating of the Sackler Gallery manuscript, see Wheeler Thackston, 'The Diwan of Khata'i: Pictures for the Poetry of Shah Isma'il I', *Asian Art*, 1 (1989), p. 39.

33 Here, the Sackler Gallery manuscript is damaged. As this couplet is absent in the Paris *Dīwān*'s version of this poem, the second line from this couplet is taken from Ekber Necef and Babek Cavanşir, ed., *Şah İsmail Hatâî Külliyatı: Türkçe Divanı, Nasihat-name, Tuyuğlar, Koşmalar, Geraylılar, Varsağılar ve Bayatılar* (Istanbul, 2006).

34 This line in the Sackler MS is damaged. The translation is completed based on the Paris *Dīwān* in Gandjeï, *Il Canzoniere di Šāh Ismāʿīl Ḫaṭāʾī*, no. 17.

He who who embodies all faith is ʿAlī.

6. I am the servant of the Shah Ḥasan, the ruler of the age,

The heart on the sultan's throne is ʿAlī.

7. Become a Sufi and martyr and sacrifice your life for the love of Ḥusayn,

Come, abandon your doubt for the Shah of the brave is ʿAlī.

8. Go to the street of Zayn ʿAbā and proclaim, 'I am the Truth' (*anā al-ḥaqq*),

Bāqir is the body, and the soul of the holy one is ʿAlī.

9. In the letters of Jaʿfar's visage (*yüz*) I learn 100 (*yüz*) lessons,

With his every look (*ṣūrat*), I see that the Sura Raḥmān is ʿAlī.

10. Like the seven wonders, the divine attributes manifest in Mūsā Kāẓim,

He became the sea and the ocean was ʿAlī.

11. The doors of paradise open through the sanctity of Mūsā Riḍa,

The Shah of Khurāsān is ʿAlī.

12. In the verses of the Qur'an, Taqī takes the most beautiful form,

Do not be scrupulous in piety, for true knowledge (*ʿirfān*) is ʿAlī.

13. You will find the Imam Naqī present in Baghdad,

Turning, revolving under his dome is ʿAlī.

14. Trust in God and clutch the cloak of ʿAskar,

The cure of suffering for the faithful is ʿAlī.

15. The sultan became manifest behind the palace curtain just like the Mahdi,

As it was revealed, the Shah of the age is ʿAlī.

16. Khaṭāʾī abandon your doubt and unbelief,

Just Solomon knows every cursed demon, know [the reality] is ʿAlī.

The poem is remarkable not only as an early precedent for the *düvaz imam* form, but as expression of an esoteric theology which would become fully developed in Alevi-Bektashi teachings. This ʿAlī-centred theology is present throughout Shah Ismāʿīl's *Dīwāns*, but here he carries this theological reality through the succession of the Twelve imams, in an unbroken chain of *walāya*. This is a hidden reality, of course, and the poet also considers the privileged nature of this understanding. To do this, the poem begins by setting up the dichotomous 'Two Worlds', with Muhammad as the visible daylight of the sun, and ʿAlī as the moon, which is no less luminous, but hidden except for those who possess true knowledge. Revelation of this hidden truth is addressed directly in the fourth couplet, which tells of Muhammad's recognition of ʿAlī as the divine lion (*ḥaqq aṣlān*) appearing to him during the celestial ascent (*miʿrāj*). This obscure, yet pivotal episode describes the Prophet's ascent as culminating in the realisation of ʿAlī's omnipresent divinity, becomes fully elaborated in mythic-poetic narratives (*miraçlama*) as part of the later Alevi-Bektashi poetic complex.[35]

The sacred names of the imams, however, establish the rhythmic pace and constitute each step of the poem's steady progression. This historical arc begins with their Eve and matriarch, Fāṭima, and culminates with the Mahdi unveiled, who is likened to a sultan hidden behind the palace curtain. In the intervening couplets, the poet

[35] See A. Gallagher, 'Shāh Ismāʿīl Ṣafevī and the *Miʿrāj*: Ḫaṭāʾī's Vision of a Sacred Assembly', in Christiane Gruber and Frederick Colby, ed., *The Prophet's Ascension: Cross-Cultural Encounters with the Islamic Miʿrāj Tales* (Bloomington, IN, 2010), pp. 313–329.

acknowledges each of the Twelve imams by their divine attributes, their battles, their thrones, sepulchres and teachings, with ʿAlī as the divine presence behind these visible and material aspects of their history. This is a history that does not culminate, as one has come to expect, in the triumphalism of the worldly shah-poet. Rather, the poet uses the concluding lines to confess his weakness of faith and doubt, invoking King Solomon as the legendary demonologist for his discernment of the occult. Other cursory self-references in the poem are similarly modest. The Sufi-martyr sacrifices his life, not for the commanding shah, but for the love of Ḥusayn, just as the author declares himself the servant of the elder brother, Ḥasan.

It may seem radically revisionist to speak of Shah Ismāʿīl's humility, but self-effacing statements are present even in the original poetic sources. These are easy to attribute to a false affectation, seeking the real voice of the Ismāʿīl in his statements of military and spiritual supremacy. However, it is the subservient Khaṭāʾī that is preserved in the later esoteric tradition. For that reason, we must assume a degree of nuance in Shah Ismāʿīl's image of himself and interpret his persona of the humble servant as more than perfunctory conformity to poetic convention.

To demonstrate the resonance of this voice for later generations, the following *düvaz imam* attributed to Khaṭāʾī will be considered. This version of the poetic prayer (*nefes*) is taken from a recently published version of the Alevi compendium of teachings, therefore its dating is not precise.[36] Nevertheless, *düvaz imam* poems that are attributed to Khaṭāʾī predominate in pious sources. As stated, *düvaz imam* poems serve a variety of ritual and devotional functions, and this piece serves to mark specific death rites in the Alevi ritual cycle. Recited as a prayer of supplication, it serves as a final plea for forgiveness recited by the community on behalf of the deceased.

> I have transgressed, for the sake of God (*Khudā*), forgive,
> For Muḥammad Muṣṭafā, forgive.
>
> I know my sin has violated the boundary,
> For ʿAlī Murtaḍā, forgive.

---

[36] Mehmet Yaman, ed., *Buyruk: Alevî İnanç-İbâdet ve Ahlâk İlkeleri* (Mannheim, 2000), p. 200. The orthography of the text cited has been retained in this translation.

For Fāṭima-i Zahrā, for 'The Great Khadīja',
For their dignity, forgive.

Entering the field (*maydan*) for the love of Ḥasan,
For Ḥusayn of Karbala, forgive.

Forgive for [the sake of] Imams Zayn al-ʿĀbid, Muḥammad
Bāqir,
Câfer, Kâzīm and Ali Musâ Rızâ.

For Muḥammad Taqī and Aliyyün-Naqī,
For the person of Ḥasan-i Askari, forgive.

Muḥammad Mahdi, the Lord of Time,
For the beggar at his threshold, forgive.

Khatâyî, the Shah, the Twelve imams,
Come all, and for the light of God, forgive.

This invocation of the Twelve imams stands as a typical example of Shah Ismāʿīl's later attributions, in which plays on the root of his pen-name, *khaṭā*, are commonplace. Here, the connection to Shah Ismāʿīl's image as a penitent sinner is even more pronounced, as the entire intention of the poem is to seek forgiveness. Again, in this *düvaz imam*, the author eschews mention of his own illustrious lineage in favour of the sacred lineage of the Twelve, summoned here for the sake of the sinner's appeals in their final hour.

Numerous attributions to Khaṭāʾī such as this circulate as litanies usually in the form of lyric song, with succinct iteration of the sacred names, producing the effect of a *dhikr*. We can surmise the proliferation of these poetic invocations of the Twelve imams attributed to Khaṭāʾī are early, perhaps from the 10th/16th century, given the strong presence of similar works in his *Dīwān*. This connection between the historical works and the enduring tradition, moreover, suggest a conscious custodianship of Shah Ismāʿīl's poetic legacy, beyond mere attribution. This poetic process by which devotion to the Twelve imams was instilled among the Qizil-bāsh helped to define Qizil-bāsh Shiʿism as it contracted from Safavid Shiʿism both in space and in time. For the descendent communities of the Qizil-bāsh, this poetry did not usher in a radical and new dispensation. Rather, it restored the sacred presence of the imams who had grown more distant with the advance of time.

Conclusion

We should revisit certain interpretations regarding Shah Ismāʿīl when considering his role in the Renaissance of Shiʿi Islam: did the Safavids come to power based on the personal charisma of their leaders? Did Shah Ismāʿīl command the sort of loyalty and devotion that was based on the reverencing of a personal cult, as his original verse seems to demonstrate? And further still, did Shah Ismāʿīl play a role in establishing the foundations of Qizil-bāsh belief, the most prominent form of esoteric Shiʿi Islam in the Ottoman lands, which then spread throughout the empire and its successor states?

Revisiting these sorts of questions, and questioning these common assumptions often leads to the diminishing of a particular figure's role during the analysis of a broad cultural transformation. Further investigation of the influence of Shah Ismāʿīl's *Dīwān* of poetry on the rise of the Safavids may well result in ascribing a more proportionate historical role to him. However, we must also consider Shah Ismāʿīl's rebirth for successive generations in poetry and beyond. He is a subject of various traditional literary vehicles such as romantic folktales and heroic narratives in Persian, Azeri and Turkish.[37] His persona continued to be a source of religious and political inspiration in the 20th century through new genres and media, including opera and the historical novel.[38] The lyrics attributed to him became more widespread than ever, being performed in *maykhāna*, broadcast on radio and posted on youtube. And finally, his poetry, a major conduit by which esoteric Shiʿi Islam re-emerged during the Renaissance, continues to generate new meanings for each of his many lives.

---

[37] On later Persian heroic narratives about Ismāʿīl, see Barry Wood, 'The *Târîkh-i jahânârâ* in the Chester Beatty Library: An Illustrated manuscript of the "Anonymous Tales of Shah Ismaʿil"', *IS*, 37 (2004), pp. 89–107; On the Turkic folktales, see A. Gallagher, 'The Transformation of Shah Ismail Safevi in the Turkish *Hikâye*', *JFR*, 46 (2009), pp. 173–195.

[38] On the Azeri opera based on Shah Ismāʿīl's *destan*, see Aida Huseynova, *Music of Azerbaijan: from Mugham to Opera* (Bloomington, 2016), p. 133; Reha Çamuroğlu's, *İsmail* (Istanbul, 1999) is the most notable of the novels about Ismāʿīl's reign.

Conclusion

6

Ḥurūfism after Faḍl Allāh's Execution: Revisiting *Ṣaḥīfat al-Istikhlāṣ*

Fatih Usluer

Introduction

When Tīmūr died, eleven years after Faḍl Allāh's execution in 796/1394, his sons and grandsons became involved in a struggle for the throne. In the end, most of the brothers and cousins of Shāhrukh were defeated, and in 811/1409 Shāhrukh, Tīmūr's eldest son, took the throne.

Certain Turkoman ruling clans, such as those of the Qara-Qoyunlu and Aq-Qoyunlu, sought to attain power during Tīmūr's era, strengthening their positions in Ādharbāyjān before Shāhrukh took the throne. There were also potential alternative focal points of power, such as the Jalāyirids and Muẓaffarids.

After taking control of the vast area that now constitutes Iran and Afghanistan (his son Ulug Beg reigned over Samarqand and Bukhara), Shāhrukh asked the Qara-Qoyunlu khān, Qarā Yūsuf, to acknowledge his suzerainty. Qarā Yūsuf refused, and Shāhrukh marched his army from Herat to Tabrīz, arriving on 15 Sha'bān 823/25 August 1420.[1] Despite the defeat and death of Qarā Yūsuf, Shāhrukh's seizure of lands in Ādharbāyjān and Eastern Anatolia and the acknowledgment of his authority by the local *amīrs*, there were no fundamental changes in the balance of power in western Iran because Shāhrukh returned to Khurāsān about a year later in Shawwāl 824/October 1421.[2]

[1] İsmail Aka, *Tīmūr ve Devleti* (Ankara, 2000), p. 62; Faruk Sümer, *Karakoyunlular* (Ankara, 1992), pp. 105–108.

[2] Aka, *Timur*, p. 63; Sümer, *Karakoyunlular*, p. 121.

After Shāhrukh returned to Herat, Iskandar, the son of Qarā Yūsuf, starting his campaign from Tabrīz, captured and looted cities such as Akhlāt, Van, Shirvān and Sulṭāniyya, punishing the local governors who had submitted to Shāhrukh.[3]

Inevitably, Shāhrukh embarked on a second expedition to Ādharbāyjān. He left Herat on 5 Rajab 832/10 April 1429. On 17 Dhu'l-Ḥijja 832/17 September 1429, in the valley of Salmas near Tabrīz, Iskandar and his brother, Jahānshāh, were defeated in a battle and retreated to Eastern Anatolia. After Shāhrukh left the region on 15 Shaʿbān 833/9 May 1430, Iskandar began recapturing the places he had lost.[4] Finally, in 837/1434, he marched his army to Shirvān and looted it. The cry for help from the Shirvānshāh, the conflicts between the princes of the Qara-Qoyunlu and the capture of Erzurum by Qarā Yuluk of the Aq-Qoyunlu forced Shāhrukh to embark on yet another expedition.[5]

Shāhrukh left Herat on 2 Rabīʿ II 838/5 November 1434 on a third expedition to Ādharbāyjān. This time he had Iskandar's brother Jahānshāh on his side and made him a governor of Ādharbāyjān.[6] The conflict between Jahānshāh and Iskandar ended only when the latter was killed in 841/1438.[7] Following Shāhrukh's death in 850/1447, Jahānshāh organised expeditions against the Tīmūrids as sultan, taking the throne of Tīmūr by entering Herat.[8] Jahānshāh was killed in battle with the Aq-Qoyunlu in 872/1467.[9]

After Faḍl Allāh left Tabrīz in 787–788/1385–1386, he travelled to Samarqand and Iṣfahān and, after a long journey, settled on an island near Baku on the Caspian Sea. After Faḍl Allāh's execution, his grandson Amīr Nūr Allāh was staying in Faḍl Allāh's *zawiya*, Valī-yi Dulaq, in Tabrīz which changed hands between the Tīmūr and the

---

[3] Sümer, *Karakoyunlular*, p. 127.

[4] Aka, *Timur*, p. 68; Sümer, *Karakoyunlular*, pp. 128–131.

[5] Sümer, *Karakoyunlular*, pp. 131–132.

[6] Aka, *Timur*, p. 71.

[7] Sümer, *Karakoyunlular*, pp. 139–140.

[8] ʿAlī Baṣīrī Pūr, 'Ashʿār-i bāz-mānda az Dīwān-i Ḥaqīqī', *Āyina-yi Mīrāth*, 45 (1388 Sh./2009), p. 54.

[9] Qandīm Qurbānof; Yūsuf Qucaq, 'Jahānshāh-i Ḥaqīqī', *Shiʿr*, 21 (1376 Sh./1997), p. 228.

Qara-Qoyunlu. The expansion of the Ḥurūfīs into new areas, such as Bitlis, the Black Sea coast and Anatolia, took place during this era.

The Shāhrukh Era

Faḍl Allāh never had any direct contact with Shāhrukh or the leaders of the Turkoman confederacies mentioned above. However, when he interpreted Sayyid ʿAbd al-Ḥayy's dream in Mashhad, he hinted at Shāhrukh without actually mentioning his name.[10]

A year after the death of ʿAbd al-Ḥayy in 829/1425-6, who was known for his closeness to both the Ḥurūfīs and Shāhrukh, Aḥmad Lūrī attempted to assassinate Shāhrukh. This event and the accounts of it in the the chronicles of that era have been analysed in detail by Evrim Binbaş,[11] however some comments are in order here.

The historians of the Shāhrukh era, Ḥāfiẓ-i Ābrū (d. 833/1430), Muḥammad Ṭūsī (d. 869/1464), Faṣīḥ Khwāfī (d. 845/1441), ʿAbd

---

[10] During his last journey to the south, as Faḍl Allāh was passing through Mashhad, Sayyid (Niẓām al-Dīn) ʿAbd al-Ḥayy (d. 829/1425), (see Faṣīḥ Khwāfī, *Mujmal-i Faṣīḥī*, ed. Sayyid Muḥsin Nājī Naṣrābādī (Tehran, 1386 Sh./2007), vol. 3, p. 1112), a prominent individual in Mashhad, had a dream and he invited Faḍl Allāh for dinner to have his dream interpreted. Faḍl Allāh told him that the dream had many interpretations, one of which he recounted. When ʿAbd al-Ḥayy asked about the other interpretations, Faḍl Allāh answered that they were in a chapter of 'the Book'. As explained more explicitly in the Persian version of the *Khwāb-nama*, it is the book in which Faḍl Allāh wrote about the significant events that would take place in the next 30 years. According to the notes, the king of the era would send ʿAbd al-Ḥayy to the governor of Gīlān. The interpretation ends here. The report continues in ʿAbd al-Ḥayy's own words: *Ḥaḍrat-i khilāfat-panāh, amīr-i sulṭān-zāda Shāhrukh khallada Allāhu salṭanatahū* (referred to only as *Shāhrukh* in the Turkish translation) sent Sayyid ʿAbd al-Ḥayy to Lāhijān, one of the townships in Gīlān, to Sayyid Riḍā Kiyā, the governor of Gīlān. This dervish (Sayyid Riḍā Kiyā in the translation) asked Sayyid ʿAbd al-Ḥayy for the Book in order to study it. ʿAbd al-Ḥayy told him that the Book was very precious and valuable to them, and they therefore had placed it in Imam Riḍā's shrine, but a fire broke out in the treasury, so that it was burnt along with the other items. (Sayyid Isḥāq, *Khwāb-nama*, Millet Library, ʿAlī Amīrī, Persian, No. 1042, ff. 25b–26b; ʿAbd al-Majīd b. Firishta, *Tarjuma-yi Khwāb-nama*, ff. 46b–47a.)

[11] Ilker Evrim Binbaş, 'The Anatomy of a Regicide Attempt: Shāhrukh, the Ḥurūfīs, and the Tīmūrid Intellectuals in 830/1426–27', *JRAS*, 23 (2013), pp. 391–428. See also Ṣādiq Kiyā, *Wāzhanāma-yi Gurgānī* (Tehran, 1330 Sh./1951), pp. 9–14; Yaʿqūb Āzhand, 'Ḥurūfiyān wa bīdād-i Tīmurī', *Kayhān-i farhangī*, 61 (1368 Sh./1989), pp. 52–54.

al-Razzāq Samarqandī (d. 887/1482) and Mīr Khwānd (d. 903/1498), give the following information regarding the attempted assassination of Shāhrukh:

> On 23 Rabīʿ II 830/ 21 February 1427,[12] Shāhrukh went to the royal mosque of Herat for the Friday prayer. After the prayer, he mounted his horse and left the mosque. Aḥmad Lūrī, a follower of Mawlānā Faḍl Allāh Astarābādī, wearing a *kepenek* (a gown worn by Sufis), stopped him, making a request. Shāhrukh asked someone from his retinue to find out what the man wanted. Taking advantage, Aḥmad Lūrī leapt forward and stabbed Shāhrukh in his abdomen. One of Shāhrukh's *amīrs*, ʿAlī Sulṭān Quchin, killed Aḥmad Lūrī on the spot. It turned out that Shāhrukh's wound was not fatal: he recovered after receiving treatment. Shāhrukh's son, Mīrzā Bāysunghur, and his *amīrs* established which inn Aḥmad Lūrī had stayed in by dint of a key they found in his belongings; the inn-keeper told them that Lūrī made caps and also gave them the name of Mawlānā Maʿrūf Khaṭṭāṭ.

Mawlānā Maʿrūf Khaṭṭāṭ was a Sufi in a long coat and hat who carried an *alifī namad* around his neck. Previously he had been Sulṭān Aḥmad Jalāyirī's companion in Baghdad but then came to despise Aḥmad Jalāyirī and went to Shīrāz, where he met Mīrzā Iskandar and became a calligrapher in his private library. After Shāhrukh captured Shīrāz, he sent him to Herat, where he worked as a calligrapher in the palace library. Mīrzā Bāysunghur sent him a letter, proposing that he prepare a copy of Niẓāmī's *Khamsa*. Maʿrūf Khaṭṭāṭ returned the letter to Bāysunghur a year later without fulfilling the request. Based on the claim that Maʿrūf Khaṭṭāṭ was a friend of Aḥmad Lūrī, Bāysunghur decided to execute him. However, Maʿrūf Khaṭṭāṭ was not executed, despite being taken to the gallows three times, but was imprisoned in the dungeon in the castle of Ikhtiyār al-Dīn. After torture he said that the name of the person who had attempted the assassination was Aḥmad Lūrī, who was one of the followers of Faḍl Allāh Astarābādī, and that a person named ʿAḍud (the son of Mawlānā Majd al-Dīn Astarābādī) was the instigator.

---

[12] Cf. Binbaş, 'The Anatomy', p. 398. For the date of '23 Jumāda II 830' see Muḥammad Yūsuf Vāleh Iṣfahānī Qazvīnī, *Khuld-i Barrīn: Sections 6–7*, ed. Mīr Hāshim Moḥaddith (Tehran, 1380 Sh./2001), p. 469.

Khwāja ʿAḍud al-Dīn (the son of Faḍl Allāh's daughter) and the comrades of Aḥmad Lūrī were captured and put on trial. Initially, they argued that their conviction was a slander. However, after being tortured and beaten with sticks, they confessed. According to their statements, while they had been discussing a conspiracy against one of the sultan's servants, Aḥmad Lūrī had acted precipitately. Since they had confessed, they were executed in the marketplace and put to death by fire with wood put together the people. The smell of the burning spread throughout the city.

We do not know whether Aḥmad Lūrī was a Ḥurūfī or the extent to which he was devoted to the Ḥurūfī cause. Among the books found in his room, it is said, were works about Ḥurūfism and also Qāsim Anwār's *Dīwān*, and probably other lettrism-related books or esoteric works, as a result of which, such people as Ṣā'in al-Dīn Turka, Qāsim Anwār,[13] his disciple Amīr Makhtūm Nīshābūrī and Mawlānā Maʿrūf Khaṭṭāṭ[14] whom we know was not a Ḥurūfī, were treated as suspects; yet this event was not related to Ḥurūfism, and the authorities had a very superficial knowledge of Ḥurūfism.

Though Ṣā'in al-Dīn is not mentioned in the chronicles among those tortured and exiled after the attempt to assassinate Shāhrukh, he also had problems with the authorities.[15] Ṣā'in al-Dīn responded to the accusations of the *ʿulamā'* that his faith was improper by compiling the treatises *Nafsat al-maṣdūr-i awwal* and *Iʿtiqādāt*, and so was pardoned. *Nafsat al-maṣdūr-i thānī* was written during his exile in the

---

[13] Faḍl Allāh's grandson Nūr Allāh said that Qāsim Anwār was viewed by the Ḥurūfīs as a believer in the unity of existence and thus they had many conflicts. Amīr Ghiyāth al-Dīn, *Ṣaḥīfat al-istikhlāṣ*, Millet Library, ʿAlī Amīrī, Persian no. 825, f. 14a. Nevertheless, one of the dream interpretations of Faḍl Allāh in the *Khwāb-nāma* was narrated by Qāsim Anvār which shows clearly that he was attending Faḍl Allāh's gatherings. See Sayyid Isḥāq, Ibid., f. 24b.

[14] In the *Khwāb-nāma* Sayyid Isḥāq includes hearsay about a 'peaceful calligrapher living in Herat'. This calligrapher, named Mawlānā Badr al-Dīn Astarābādī, said to Sayyid Isḥāq that a person had gone to Faḍl Allāh to recount his dream and mentioned Faḍl Allāh's interpretation. It was understood that this calligrapher was living in Marv, like Maʿrūf Khaṭṭāṭ, and had visited the Ḥurūfī circle. Sayyid Isḥāq, *Khwāb-nāma*, ff. 68a–68b.

[15] *Chahārdah risāla-yi fārsī az-Ṣā'in al-Dīn ʿAlī b. Muḥammad Turka-yi Iṣfahānī*, ed. S. A. M. Bihbahānī, S. I. Dībājī and Taqī Sharīf Riḍā'ī (Tehran, 1351 Sh./1972), pp. 205–206.

aftermath of the assassination attempt as a plea for his innocence.[16] From his writings on the science of letters, it was clear that Ṣāʾin al-Dīn was not a Ḥurūfī.

Most notably in *Nafsat al-maṣdūr-i thānī*, Ṣā'in al-Dīn covertly vilified 'the group' (*īn ṭāʾifa*), whom he had had many occasions to meet. He accused them of two things in particular: they disregarded the laws of Islam, and they believed that the end of the era of sainthood (*khatm-i walāyat*) would arrive in two years' time.[17] However, according to Ḥurūfism, the era of sainthood came to an end with Faḍl Allāh's death, some claiming that a new era of divinity (*dawr-i ulūhiyat*) had already begun.

The information about Ṣāʾin al-Dīn's attitude towards this group is not related to the Ḥurūfīs. He could not have been so ignorant of Ḥurūfism as to claim that the Ḥurūfīs believed the end of the era of sainthood would take place in the near future. Undoubtedly, Ṣā'in al-Dīn knew more than these stereotypical accusations. We know that, following Faḍl Allāh's advice, his brother Ṣadr al-Dīn, abandoned the idea of writing a book interpreting Islamic law through philosophy, and that his father, Afḍal al-Dīn, became a Ḥurūfī and was encouraged by Faḍ Allāh to wear the conical head-dress. As a result, Ṣāʾin al-Dīn faced difficulties for nine months following the assassination attempt before he was admitted into the presence of Shāhrukh. He said that he was fortunate enough to kiss Shāhrukh's hand and the hem of his garment and had been permitted to attend an audience with him twice a week.[18]

As mentioned above, some contemporary chronicles said that Faḍl Allāh's grandson and his companions were burned alive, the stench spreading across the entire city. However, we have a letter written by a certain Amīr Ghiyāth al-Dīn addressed to another Ḥurūfī, refuting this, in which those who elsewere were said to have been burnt

---

16 *Chahārdah risāla-yi fārsī*, pp. 197–217.

17 *Chahārdah risāla-yi fārsī*, p. 212. Here, and on the previous page, he claims that the group disregarded the rules of Islam (*takālīf-i sharʿiyya*). Binbaş understands *takālīf-i sharʿī* (Islamic rules/duties) to mean the Islamic taxes by saying that 'he demanded the easing of the *sharʿī* taxes (*takālīf-i sharʿī*) levied upon dervishes like him. These were probably the taxes that had been imposed upon them after the assassination attempt.' Binbaş, 'The Anatomy', p. 415.

18 *Chahārdah risāla-yi fārsī*, p. 207.

discussed the trial. This letter, which we believe to be the most important document regarding the extent of the Tīmūrids' knowledge about the Ḥurūfīs, demonstrates the nature of their relations with the *'ulamā'* and the Tīmūrid statesmen. One and a half years after the assassination attempt, Amīr Ghiyāth al-Dīn was among those who were detained.

This letter was first published by Abdülbaki Gölpınarlı and later also by Alyārī.[19] Notwithstanding this, Alyārī, like Gölpınarlı, does not reflect on the nature of the letter. Parts of it, however, were taken into consideration by Bashir[20] and Binbaş[21] in their discussions regarding the assassination attempt.

The importance of this letter is undeniable, as it is a significant example of internal Ḥurūfī correspondence. The criticism of certain Ḥurūfīs, the consistency of the names mentioned and dates of events, given the information we have, are the most significant proof of the authenticity of this letter.[22]

---

[19] Ḥusayn Alyārī, 'Nāma'ī az pisar-i Faḍl Allāh-i Ḥurūfī', *Pazhūhishhā-yi falsafī-yi dānishkada-yi adabiyyāt wa 'ulūm-i insānī-yi Tabrīz*, 82 (1346 Sh./1967), pp. 175–197.

[20] Bashir believes that 'the letter was written five years after the arrest (ca. 836/1432–33), while they were still in captivity and Amir Nūr Allāh was probably executed in the end' (*Fazlallah Astarabadi and the Ḥurūfīs*, p. 105). In fact, it was written after their escape from prison during their stay in Bā 'anqaba (probably Baquba, near Baghdad), on 16 Jumādā I 836/17 January 1433.

[21] However, there are some mistakes in the readings of Binbaş. For example, he says: 'Khvāja Pīr Aḥmad alleged that some tax irregularities were discovered in the books of Amīr Nūr Allāh. The defiant Amīr Nūr Allāh rejected the first allegation, but conceded that he was not in a position to respond to the question of his tax records, but he promised to check his records when he returned to Tabrīz.' (Binbaş, 'The Anatomy', p. 408). In fact, the original text says that Khwāja Pīr Aḥmad told the person accusing Amīr Nūr-Allāh that, in the case that the slander was not proved, he would be fined 50 *tenges*, and reminded him that he had already paid such an amount in the past. He slandered readily saying that 'he found the treasury', implying that he was rich enough to pay the penalty for slander (f. 3b). Binbaş uses this argument as one of the main proofs of his argument in his article. There are some other misreadings too. For example, while Binbaş mentions that the captured Ḥurūfīs were tried in Herat in the presence of Ulugh Beg (p. 409), the encounter with Ulugh Beg actually took place in Samarqand (ff. 10b–11a).

[22] Amīr Ghiyāth al-Dīn, *Ṣaḥīfat al-Istikhlāṣ*, Millet Library, 'Alī Amīrī, Persian, No. 825.

An Analysis of *Ṣaḥīfat al-istikhlāṣ*

The author of this letter, Amīr Ghiyāth al-Dīn, was one of the leading thinkers of the Ḥurūfīs and is best known for his *Istiwā-nāma*. We also know that he was the son of ʿAlī al-Aʿlā's sister.[23]

Ghiyāth al-Dīn and Amīr Nūr Allāh (the son of Makhdūmzāda) were detained in Māzandarān, and were handed over to soldiers of Shāhrukh, who at that point having left Herat had arrived in Baḥrābād. The family tree documenting the children and grandchildren of Faḍl Allāh and his testament reveal that the name of the second daughter of Faḍl Allāh, nicknamed Makhdūmzāda, was ʿĀisha. Since ʿAlī al-Aʿlā (d. 822/1419) mentions the death of Makhdūmzāda in his *Mahshar-nāma*,[24] it is obvious that Makhdūmzāda was not party to the assassination attempt. Therefore, we can confidently say that the person who in the letter is called 'Ḥaḍrat-i Amīr', is Nūr Allāh, who appears in the family tree of Faḍl Allāh as Makhdūmzāda's son. Additionally, since the letter says that 'two persons of bad *madhhab*, who are non-believers and infidels, have been caught and will be executed', (f. 8a), we can conclude that only two persons figured in the case, namely Amīr Ghiyāth al-Dīn and Amīr Nūr Allāh.

Even though the events in the letter focus on the fates of two people, we understand that there were two other Ḥurūfīs involved, Darvīshzāda ʿAbd al-Wahhāb and Darvīsh Najm al-Dīn, who were imprisoned and joined Amīr Ghiyāth al-Dīn and Amīr Nūr Allāh later. The names of these two dervishes were first mentioned when the prisoners travelled to Samarqand. While Amīr Nūr Allāh and Amīr Ghiyāth al-Dīn were travelling by horse, these two dervishes accompanied them on foot. When the two escaped from Suleymānī Castle, the dervishes were with them.

According to the letter, the first interrogation of Amīr Ghiyāth al-Dīn and Amīr Nūr Allāh by Shāhrukh and his religious scholars took place in Baḥrābād, and the second in Herat one year and seven months later (when Amīr Nūr Allāh alone was present). The

---

[23] Ishqurt Dede, *Ṣalāt-nāma*, Millet Library, ʿAlī Amīrī, Persian, No. 1043, f. 50.

[24] ʿAlī al-Aʿlā, *Maḥshar-nāma*, Millet Library, ʿAlī Amīrī, Persian, No. 139, f. 219a.

subsequent interrogations or disputes also took place in Herat, at the Gawharshād Madrasa and Bāgh-i Naw. Subsequently, Ulugh Beg questioned them in Samarqand on five different days, one during the Ramaḍān.

During these interrogations, Amīr Nūr Allāh insisted that he had not been involved in the assassination plot because at the time of the assassination they were travelling from Tabrīz to Bitlis and Kurdistān, and they had not sent any assassins (f. 2b). Another charge against them was that they had been preparing for a war against Shāhrukh as allies of Mirzā Iskandar. As there were no witnesses to support this second charge, and Khwāja Sayyidī Muḥammad, who was declared a witness by the person claiming their involvement in the assassination plot, did not testify regarding this charge, subsequent hearings focused on their alleged unbelief.

As the jurists of Shāhrukh could not prove their unbelief through their statements regarding Ḥurūfism, their persuasion, religion and the principles of faith, and their status as *sayyid*s, were all questioned. When they could not find any evidence against the accused, they accused them of drinking alcohol and/or proclaiming that drinking alcohol was permitted. When they could not find any witness for this charge too, all the charges were dropped and the case was forwarded to Ulugh Beg.

It was obvious that without any witnesses the charge of assassination could not be maintained. Therefore, Ulugh Beg then questioned them about Ḥurūfism. At one point, he asked if it was true that they drank wine. Eventually, it could not be concluded from their answers that they were infidels. In view of this, Ulugh Beg refused to punish them and sent them back to his father Shāhrukh.

The letter contains some information between the lines about Ḥurūfism. For example, during the initial interrogation in Bahrabad, Amīr Nūr Allāh said that, at the time of the attempted assassination, they were travelling from Tabrīz to Bitlis and Kurdistān (f. 2b).[25] We

---

[25] On another occasion Amīr Nūr Allāh sent Amīr Ghiyāth al-Dīn to Bitlis. See Amīr Ghiyāth al-Dīn, *Istiwā-nāma*, Millet Library, ʿAlī Amīrī, Persian, No. 269, f. 38a.

can conclude that the Ḥurūfis travelled north to Anatolia and Kurdistan and south to the island of Hurmūz (f. 16b).

In the first interrogation, Amīr Fīrūzshāh said that Sayyid Shahrastānī and Khwāja Sayyidī Muḥammad had visited Amīr Nūr Allāh's *zāwiya* in Tabrīz (ff. 2b–3a). This tells us that after Faḍl Allāh left Tabrīz his lodges continued to function, and literati and statesmen continued to visit them. The letter of denunciation which Amīr Fīrūzshāh presented as evidence allows us to conclude that people with bad intentions also visited the lodges, as was the case already in the time of Faḍl Allāh (f. 3a).

One of the important points of the letter is that Shāhrukh, Ulugh Beg and the learned men present at the interrogations were ignorant of Ḥurūfism. The strongest evidence in support of our conclusion is: 1) 'Shāhrukh raised his eyebrow and asked "Which letter is this?"'; 2) Amīr Nūr Allāh asked the religious scholars 'in which part of the Qur'an are the *rakʿat*s of the prayer (one of the basic themes of Ḥurūfism) mentioned' but they could not answer; everyone present heard the basic tenets of Ḥurūfism for the first time.

We can arrange the events that followed the capture of Amīr Nūr-Allāh and his companions chronologically as follows: We know that Shāhrukh left Herat on 5 Rajab 832/19 April 1429 for a military campaign in Ādharbāyjān, arriving in Baḥrābād on 27 Rajab 832/14 May 1429.[26] As Amīr Ghiyāth al-Dīn and Amīr Nūr Allāh were detained in Mazandaran and handed over to Shāhrukh's soldiery, he in the meantime having left Herat and arrived at Baḥrābād, we can ascertain that their first interrogation took place either at the end of the month of Rajab or at the beginning of Shaʿbān 832/May 1429.

After that, the two prisoners were held in separate fortresses, and it took Shāhrukh a year and seven months to return from Tabrīz. When on returning from the expedition to Ādharbāyjān, Shāhrukh had reached the city of Turbat-i Jam in Dhu'l-Hijja 833/September 1430, Amīr Nūr Allāh was then dispatched from the castle of Sarakhs, arriving in Herat on 8 Muḥarram 834/26 September 1430.

[26] According to Samarqandī, *Matlaʿ*, vol. 3, part 2, p. 390. In Khwāfī, *Mujmal*, vol. 4, p. 1117, Shāhrukh arrived in Baḥrābād on 27 Rajab 831/12 May 1428.

Amīr Ghiyāth al-Dīn and Amīr Nūr Allāh travelled to Samarqand to Ulugh Beg before Ramaḍān 834/May 1431. After several interrogations, they broke their fast with Ulugh Beg.

Then they left Samarqand and reached Herat in twelve days on 3 Muḥarram 835/20 September 1431. Upon the arrival, they were imprisoned in a well, or oubliette. Hence, we can conclude that they stayed in Samarqand with Ulugh Beg until 20 Dhu'l-Hijja 834/7 September 1431.

On 9 Muḥarram 835/26 September 1431, after six days they were taken out of the well, and were then sent to Kirmān.

After a month in Kirmān, they were taken to the Castle of Sulaymānī and imprisoned there in Rabīʿ I 835/November 1431.

On 8 Jumādā II 835/20 February 1432, they escaped from the Castle of Sulaymānī.

They hid in a well for twenty-two days, until 30 Jumādā II 835/12 March 1432.

On 10 Rajab 835/22 March 1432, after travelling for nine days, they arrived in Hurmūz and, after a few days there, continued on to Shīrāz, and from there, to Baghdad. Their travels had lasted, all in all, eight months.

So, after eight months, they reached Baghdad in Rabīʿ II 836/ December 1432, and had an audience with Shāh Muḥammad, the son of Qarā Yūsuf.

They left Baghdad and went to Bā ʿanqaba[27] (probably Baquba, near Baghdad), where the letter was written on 16 Jumādā I 836/17 January 1433.

In the introduction we said that, according the material contained in the chronicles of the period, after being tortured, Mawlānā Maʿrūf named ʿAḍud, the son of Mawlānā Majd al-Dīn, as the instigator of the attempted assassination. According to the chronicles, Khwāja ʿAḍud al-Dīn and Aḥmad Lūrī, companions of Faḍl Allāh's nephew, were detained and interrogated; after being subjected to torture, they pleaded guilty. As a result, they were executed in the bazaar and were burned alive with firewood brought by the people.

---

[27] In *Istiwā-nāma,* f. 43b this place is referred to as Bāgh Qupa.

However, ʿAḍud al-Dīn was not the nickname of Amīr Nūr Allāh; in fact, none of the children and grandchildren of Faḍl Allāh were called ʿAḍud al-Dīn.[28] Conversely, if, as has been claimed, ʿAḍud al-Dīn confessed that he was the instigator of this assassination attempt and was punished, it is pointless to search for clues pointing to any other instigators in the above letter; it contains no information on this matter. Hence, we must conclude that the information in the chronicles of the period is unreliable.

Another point that we want to underscore is the absence of any indication that the imprisoned persons who were accused of 'instigating an assassination' were tortured other than being restrained by a ball and chain and imprisoned in a dungeon or well. Furthermore, because in this letter, we see that the persons so charged were interrogated and investigated such that their conviction was beyond any doubt and they were not executed summarily.

According to the information provided by Ḥasan Rūmlū (d. 985/1577), the Ḥurūfīs rebelled in 835/1431 in Iṣfahān under the leadership of Ḥājī Surkh, and killed two sons of ʿAbd al-Ṣamad, one of the *amīr*s of Shāhrukh. Eventually, the Ḥurūfīs involved were caught, and Ḥājī Surkh was executed.[29] No chronicler writing before Rūmlū mentions such an event. Since Rūmlū places this information in an appendix to the events of 835, it is likely that his source was rumours circulating among the people.

The Qara-Qoyunlu

The Qara-Qoyunlu state, established by Bayrām Ḥoja (d. 782/1380) and which included the cities of Mosul, Mush, Akhlat and Erzurum, initially fought against the Jalāyirid rulers, Sulṭān Uways and Sulṭān Ḥusayn. At this time, when Faḍl Allāh was in the Jalāyirid lands, Ḥurūfī sources make no mention of Bayrām Ḥoja or his successor and nephew, Qarā Meḥmed (d. 791/1389).

[28] For Faḍl Allāh's relatives see Fatih Usluer, 'Ḥurūfism: The Faḍlallāh Family, Children, and Testament', *IS*, 54 (2021), pp. 605–631.

[29] Yaʿqūb Āzhand, *Ḥurūfiyya dar tārīkh* (Tehran, 1369 Sh./1990), p. 87; Rawshan Khiyāvī, *Ḥurūfiyya* (Tehran, 1378 Sh./1999), p. 235.

The first contacts between the Ḥurūfīs and the Qara-Qoyunlu that can be identified took place during the reign of Qarā Yūsuf (d. 822/ 1420), the son of Qarā Meḥmed. Amīr Nūr Allāh, the grandson of Faḍl Allāh, said that he, Nūr Allāh, drank wine in the assembly of Qarā Yūsuf. Amīr Nūr Allāh cited the ignorance of Qarā Yūsuf as the justification for his behaviour. Fearing for his life if he disobeyed Qarā Yūsuf by abstaining from alcohol, he had drunk wine in his presence (f. 14b).

However, ʿAlī al-Aʿlā in his elegy for his brother praised Qarā Yūsuf, saying: 'The fortunate sultan, loyal Yūsuf, who, with the help of God, obtained the throne, since Yūsuf killed Mīrānshāh.' According to ʿAlī al-Aʿlā, Mīrānshāh was responsible for killing Amīr Nūr Allāh.[30] Ritter argued that ʿAlī al-Aʿlā wrote the Kursī-nāma after Qarā Yūsuf's victory in Tabrīz.[31]

We know that when Qarā Yūsuf died, of his five sons, Jahānshāh, Shāh Meḥmed and Iskandar were in contact with the Ḥurūfīs.

In the letter, when narrating the imprisonment and interrogation of Amīr Ghiyāth al-Dīn and Amīr Nūr Allāh over the attempted assassination, the names of Mīrzā Iskandar and Shāh Meḥmet, the Qara-Qoyunlu princes, are mentioned. While Amīr Fīrūzshāh was questioning Amīr Ghiyāth al-Dīn and Amīr Nūr Allāh (f.3a), we learn that the Ḥurūfīs were accused of planning a rebellion, and because they had slaughtered many people on the way to Sulṭāniyya, Mīrzā Iskandar expelled them from Tabrīz. Even though these charges could not be proved and Amīr Nūr Allāh denied them, they may contain factual information albeit presented in an exaggerated and distorted way. Thus, it may be argued that the Ḥurūfīs and Mīrzā Iskandar were close during a particular period but, after a while, disagreements arose between them.

---

[30] ʿAlī al-Aʿlā, Firāq-nāma, Istanbul University Library, No. 1158, f. 58b.

[31] Hellmut Ritter, 'Studien zur Geschichte der Islamischen Frömmigkeit: Die Anfange der Ḥurūfīsekte', Oriens, 7 (1954), pp. 1–54; Persian tr. by Ḥ. Muʾayyad in Farhang-i Īrān Zamīn, 10 (1341 Sh./1962), p. 362. See also B.S. Amoretti, 'Religion in the Timurid and Safavid Periods', in The Cambridge History of Iran, Volume 6, The Timurid and Safavid Periods, ed. P. Jackson and L. Lockhart (Cambridge, 1986), pp. 610–656, but in particular p. 624.

The most substantial evidence for Amīr Nūr Allāh attending meetings with Mīrzā Iskandar is found in his statements. In fact, during the trial, Khwāja Ghiyāth al-Dīn, the son of Iskandar's vizier, and Besīḥaq, claimed that in Iskandar's presence Amīr Nūr Allāh had said, 'I sent someone to stab Mīrzā Shāhrukh.' In his response to this accusation, Amīr Nūr Allāh said that they should confirm whatever he said in the meeting with Iskandar, or at another meeting, by asking Sulṭān Ghāzān Mīrzā.

After the name of Amīrzāda Iskandar the expression *zādat nuṣratuhu* ('may God increase his victory!'), is added. Fīrūzshāh, one of the commanders of Shāhrukh who fought against Amīrzāda Iskandar, is given the sentence in which this expression is inserted. But it is obvious that Amīr Fīrūzshāh did not actually say these interpolated words. We do not know who added the expression, either Amīr Ghiyāth al-Dīn or a copyist.

After Amīr Ghiyāth al-Dīn and Amīr Nūr Allāh escaped from prison, they travelled to a number of places and had an audience with the son of Qarā Yūsuf, Shāh Muḥammad, in Baghdad on Rabīʿ II 836/ December 1432.[32] Shāh Muḥammad showed them much affection. However, because of problems with Shāh Muḥammad's faith, they left Baghdad without his permission (f. 16b).

The daughter of Faḍl Allāh and a dervish called Yūsuf or Pīr Turābī increased adherence to Ḥurūfism in Tabrīz during the reign of Jahānshāh (d. 872/1467). Allegedly, the *faqīh*s who were afraid of the Ḥurūfī influence on Jahānshāh, forced the mufti, Uskūyī, to give a *fatwā* on the subject and eventually in 845/1441–2 Jahānshāh ordered the execution of five hundred Ḥurūfīs, including the daughter of Faḍl Allāh.[33] However, the earliest source for this information is Ḥāfiẓ

[32] Shāh Muḥammad (Shāh Meḥmed) was the eldest of the five sons of Qarā Yūsuf. He governed Baghdad, which he had conquered on 5 Muḥarram 814/29 April 1411, until he was killed by Amīr Baba Ḥājī Hamadānī on 18 Shaʿbān 836/9 April 1433. See Samarqandī, *Matlaʿ*, vol. 3, part 1, p. 155 and vol. 3, part 2, p. 429.

[33] See Shahzad Bashir, 'Enshrining Sainthood: The death and memorialization of Faḍlallāh Astarabadi in Ḥurūfī Thought', *MW*, 90 (2000), p. 302; Ṣādiq Kiyā, 'Āgāhīhā-yi tāza az Ḥurūfiyān', *Majalla-yi dānishkada-yi adabiyyāt-i dānishgāh-i Tihrān*, 2 (1333 Sh./1954), pp. 39–42.

Ḥusayn Tabrīzī's (d. 997/1589) *Rawḍāt al-jinān wa jannāt al-janān* dated 975/1567.[34] Subsequently Ḥaṣrī Tabrīzī repeated this account in his *Rawḍa-yi aṭhār* (1011/1602).[35] Thus, the earliest source describing this incident dates to one and half centuries later. Before that, no chronicler referred to the execution of five hundred Ḥurūfīs. On the other hand, the original source relies only on the tales heard from the locals living near the Ḥurūfī shrine in Tabrīz. The author visited the city, catalogued its shrines and collected the legends associated with the shrine.

However, we have Jahānshāh's *Dīvān* (he wrote poetry under the penname Ḥaqīqī) which reveals to us the intellectual dimensions of Jahānshāh's contacts with Ḥurūfīs.

When Jahānshāh learned that Nesīmī had been killed, he found a copy of Nesīmī's *Dīvān* with the help of his assistant, Bashīr Baghdādī; he read it and was influenced by it, and composed eulogies on the death of Nesīmī.[36]

Even though this information can be disputed, we can confidently state that the poems of Jahānshāh are similar to those of Nesīmī. It is beyond the scope of this article to evaluate his poems as literary works. Let us just say that many of Ḥaqīqī's poems abound with images related to Ḥurūfism. In addition, there are some allusions to Faḍl Allāh in Ḥaqīqī's poems. Like all Ḥurūfī works, these are used with a double meaning related to those of both 'the grace of God' and 'Faḍl Allāh':

> *O Ḥaqīqī, God helped you through his grace (Faḍl).*
> *If you die in that way, that is eternal life (jāvidān* here refers to the *Jāvidān-nāma).*[37]

[34] Ḥāfiẓ Ḥusayn Tabrīzī b. al-Karbalā'ī, *Rawḍāt al-jinān wa jannāt al-janān*, ed. Ja'far Sulṭān al-Qurrā'ī (Tehran, 1344–44 Sh./1965-70), vol. 1, pp. 478–481.

[35] Mullā Muḥammad Amīn Ḥaṣrī Tabrīzī, *Rawḍa-yi aṭhār* (Tabrīz, 1371 Sh./1992), p. 74.

[36] Qurbānof; Qucaq, 'Jahānshāh', p. 228.

[37] Macit, *Karakoyunlu Hükümdarı Cihanşah ve Türkçbayna ale Şiirleri* (Ankara, 2002), p. 84. See also pp. 87, 94, 102, 105, 121, 131, 143.

Conclusion

After the death of Faḍl Allāh, his grandson Amīr Nūr Allāh was arrested and imprisoned because of an assassination attempt made against Shāhrukh by a person called Aḥmad Lūrī, someone who was not proved to be a Ḥurūfī. Even though he was imprisoned for a serious crime, namely instigating a murder, he was not convicted as a result of the interrogations carried out separately by both Shāhrukh and Ulugh Beg. Even though Shāhrukh and his subordinates were certain that Amīr Nūr Allāh was the instigator, since it could not be proved, they were content to punish him with imprisonment. We see that, in fact, according to the account given, a trial process in the 9th/15th century was very close to the concept of 'a fair trial'.

Another conclusion that can be drawn from the trials of Amīr Nūr Allāh is that outsiders, including the *ʿulamāʾ* of the era, lacked any substantive knowledge of Ḥurūfism. What circulated outside Ḥurūfī circles were rumours, misinterpretations and defamation. Thus, we conclude that we should not give credence the chronicles regarding the beliefs or the fate of the Ḥurūfīs in the 8th/14th and 9th/15th centuries.

The Qara-Qoyunlu Turkomans, who were becoming more and more powerful in the region of Eastern Anatolia and Ādharbāyjān in this period, established close relations with the Ḥurūfīs. We see the Ḥurūfīs present at the assemblies of Qarā Yūsuf and his sons. There may be two basic explanations for this: first, the Qara-Qoyunlu Turkomans, who were neither completely nomadic nor settled, were not greatly Islamised. Second, the Ḥurūfīs hated the Tīmūrids, who were the enemies of the Qara-Qoyunlu.

Jahānshāh represented the acme of this rapprochement. It is obvious that Jahānshāh understood the basic tenets of Ḥurūfism better than any of the *ʿulamāʾ* at the courts of Shāhrukh and Ulugh Beg. Indeed, he often referred to them in his poems. The claim that during his reign five hundred Ḥurūfīs were executed may have emerged as a popular myth long after his death. Even if some real event lies behind this myth, we must interpret in pragmatic terms, rather than in political and religious ones – for example, in the light of Jahānshāh's submission to Shāhrukh in order to receive support in his conflict with his brother, Iskandar.

7

Nuqṭavīs, Safavids and Shiʿism in the 9th–11th/15th–17th Centuries

Orkhan Mir-Kasimov

Much scholarly attention has been paid recently to the relationships between the Safavids, and more specifically Shah ʿAbbās I (r. 996–1038 /1588–1629), and the Nuqṭavīs, a mystical and messianic movement founded by Maḥmūd Pasīkhānī (d. 830/1427). This interest is mostly due to the importance of the Safavid-Nuqṭavī connection in our understanding of the Safavid religious policies. However, many aspects of these policies, as well as issues related to the balance of political forces within the Safavid structure of power, remain insufficiently explained.[1]

It should be noted that all existing studies relied heavily on historical sources written by non-Nuqṭavī authors, most of whom were indeed openly hostile to the Nuqṭavīs. The input of Nuqṭavī sources has been disproportionately low and is generally limited to excerpts from an unidentified Nuqṭavī treatise published by Ṣādiq Kiyā as an appendix

[1] Kathryn Babayan has conducted in-depth research and addressed this topic in several publications, most extensively in her *Mystics, Monarchs, and Messiahs: Cultural Landscapes of Early Modern Iran* (Cambridge, MA, and London, 2003), pp. 1–117. Other scholars who have proposed various theoretical frameworks for the Safavid-Nuqṭavī relationships are Said Amir Arjomand and Abbas Amanat. See S. A. Arjomand, *The Shadow of God and the Hidden Imam: Religion, Political Order, and Societal Change in Shiʿite Iran from the Beginning to 1890* (Chicago and London, 1984), pp. 198–199; Abbas Amanat, 'The Nuqṭawī Movement of Maḥmūd Pisīkhānī and his Persian Cycle of Mystical-Materialism', in Farhad Daftary, ed., *Mediaeval Ismaʿili History and Thought* (Cambridge and New York, 1996), pp. 281–297.

to his ground-breaking monograph.[2] To this has been added some information about Nuqṭavī doctrinal views derived from the *Dabistān-i madhāhib,* an Adhar-Kayvānī source composed in India in the 11th/17th century.[3]

This almost complete dearth of information about the Nuqṭavī doctrinal positions has inevitably caused some distortion in the analysis of Safavid-Nuqṭavī relationships. First, it led to inaccurate and sometimes simply erroneous assumptions – based mainly on non-Nuqṭavī sources – regarding the theoretical basis of the Nuqṭavī ideology, as well as the confessional identity and possible political aspirations of this group. Consequently, some potentially important factors in the evaluation of the motivations of the Safavid-Nuqṭavī relationships have been overlooked. Second, hostile historical accounts have drawn scholarly attention to the negative aspect of the Safavid-Nuqṭavī relationship, namely, the rejection and persecution of the Nuqṭavīs as dangerous heretics. No serious exploration has taken place of the positive aspect of this relationship, that is, the Nuqṭavī doctrinal points that could have found favour with the Safavid rulers as politically viable ideologies.

A rebalancing of this relationship by modern scholarship started at the end of the twentieth century with a series of studies by the Iranian scholar ʿAlī Riḍā Dhakāvatī Qarāguzlū which were devoted to the foundational Nuqṭavī texts, including the major works of Maḥmūd Pasıkhanı, such as *Kitāb-i mīzān* and *Mafātīḥ al-ghuyūb*.[4] In addition, we are now equipped with a better knowledge of the intellectual background of the Nuqṭavī works due to progress in the

---

[2] Ṣādiq Kiyā, *Nuqṭaviyān yā pāsīkhāniyān* (Tehran 1320 Sh./1941–42, repr. 1392 Sh./2013–14), pp. 76–125. The incipit of the untitled manuscript cited by Kiyā (p. 73) is the same as MS 4761 of the Majlis Library in Tehran, which is catalogued under the title *Mafātīḥ al-ghayb* and attributed to Maḥmūd Pasīkhānī. However, several other texts with this title are attributed to the same author in various manuscript collections. Further research is needed in order to confirm the titles and authorship of these works.

[3] It is remarkable that one of 12 chapters of the *Dabistān* is entirely devoted to the Nuqṭavīs. On this work, see Azfar Moin, 'Dabistān-i madhāhib', *EI3*.

[4] Some of these studies have been now conveniently brought together in a book titled *Junbish-i Nuqṭaviyya* (Qum, 1383 Sh./2004–05). Unfortunately, Dhakāvatī does not seem to address the issue of the textual identification of a work known as *Mafātīḥ al-ghuyūb* or *Mafātīḥ al-ghayb*. This is probably because he was aware only of one manuscript with this title. Cf. *Junbish-i Nuqṭaviyya*, p. 175, where he mentions 'the only manuscript copy of that [work]' (*tanhā nuskha-yi khaṭṭī-yi ān*).

study of Ḥurūfī doctrinal literature, which was doubtless one of the main sources that inspired Maḥmūd Pasīkhānī's thought.[5] Even if critical editions and comprehensive studies of the Nuqṭavī and Ḥurūfī texts are still desiderata, we are now in a position to attempt a preliminary revision of the previous studies, taking into account the new doctrinal evidence. Therefore, the purpose of the present paper is to use the Nuqṭavī texts themselves in order to introduce a more balanced representation of the Nuqṭavī voice in the Safavid-Nuqṭavī relationship. When necessary, Nuqṭavī doctrinal points will be clarified with reference to the works of Maḥmūd Pasīkhānī's teacher and the founder of the Ḥurūfī doctrine, Faḍl Allāh Astarābādī (d. 796/1394).

It must be mentioned that – by using the foundational Nuqṭavī texts (composed at the latest in the first half of the 9th/15th century) to represent the thought of the Nuqṭavīs mentioned in the Safavid chronicles contemporary to Shah ʿAbbās I, that is, those chronicles composed at the end of the 10th/16th and in the first half of the 11th/17th centuries – we make an assumption that the core ideas of the Nuqṭavī doctrine were preserved over almost two centuries without significant modifications. In other words, we assume that the Nuqṭavī groups that came into contact with Shah ʿAbbās were aware of, and adhered to, the learned Ḥurūfī/ Nuqṭavī tradition as developed in Pasīkhānī's works.[6]

---

[5] Maḥmūd Pasīkhānī was an excommunicated disciple of Faḍl Allāh Astarābādī (d. 796/1394), the founder of the Ḥurūfiyya. On the Ḥurūfīs and their doctrine, see Shahzad Bashir, *Fazlallah Astarabadi and the Hurufis* (Oxford, 2005) and, more recently, Orkhan Mir-Kasimov, *Words of Power: Ḥurūfī Teachings between Sufism and Shiʿism in Medieval Islam* (London and New York, 2015).

[6] We are poorly informed about the evolution of the Nuqṭavī groups and their doctrines after the death of the movement's founder. However, in case of the Ḥurūfī tradition, we know that the doctrinal uniformity of the movement was compromised shortly after the death of Astarābādī in 796/1394. Different Ḥurūfī groups emphasised different aspects of the original doctrine, and its further evolution was influenced by other mystical and intellectual currents. Therefore, the doctrinal identity of groups described as Ḥurūfīs in later sources is uncertain. See Mir-Kasimov, *Words of Power*, pp. 17–18. The same kind of division and doctrinal divergence could very well also have taken place with the Nuqṭavīs. By the 'learned' tradition we understand the tradition based on doctrinal works building on the thought of the movement's founder, as opposed to what can be called the 'popular' tradition combining some salient elements of the foundational theories with beliefs and rituals not necessarily linked to the movement's original doctrine.

The soundness of this approach can be contested, however, on the grounds that we have no first-hand information about the doctrines professed by the Nuqṭavī circle of Qazvīn at the time of Shah ʿAbbās I. If this group produced any texts, they have not survived nor yet been recovered.[7] We cannot therefore compare their doctrines with the foundational Nuqṭavī texts. As mentioned, no detailed account of their beliefs is given in any of the available historical sources that mention Shah ʿAbbās I's interaction with the Nuqṭavīs. These sources either refer to the Nuqṭavīs as a group whose heresy is self-evident and does not require any explanation, or they provide a short list of non-specific heresiographical clichés.[8] Indeed, some accounts of the Nuqṭavīs do not mention the term 'Nuqṭavī' at all, referring to this group either as 'heretics' (*mulḥidān*), or simply 'that people' (*ān jamʿ*).[9]

However, historical chronicles and other non-Nuqṭavī sources do contain some evidence confirming the existence of the Nuqṭavī learned tradition at that time. What is more, these sources suggest that there existed a vast and influential Nuqṭavī intellectual network spread over Iran and India, which doubtless deserves further study. Prominent Nuqṭavī scholars, such as Mīr Aḥmad Kāshī in Kāshān, Sharīf Āmulī in India and others were part of this network and at least some of them were connected with Dervish Khusraw who led the Nuqṭavīs of

---

7 Two of the historical chronicles examined below say that the Nuqṭavī group in Qazvīn and their leader, Dervish Khusraw, possessed books. See Mullā Jalāl al-Dīn Munajjim Yazdī, *Tārīkh-i ʿAbbāsī*, ed. Sayf Allāh Vaḥīd-niyā ([Tehran], 1366 Sh./1987), p. 121; and Faḍlī Beg Khūzānī Iṣfahānī, *Afḍal al-tawārīkh*, ed. K. Ghereghlou (Exeter, 2015), vol. 1, p. 144.

8 For similar observations concerning the historical accounts of the Ḥurūfīs, see Orkhan Mir-Kasimov, '*Takfīr* and Messianism: The Ḥurūfī Case', in Camilla Adang et al., ed., *Accusations of Unbelief in Islam: A Diachronic Perspective on* Takfīr (Leiden and Boston, 2016), pp. 189–212.

9 This is the case of Maḥmūd b. Hidāyat Allāh Afūshta-yi Naṭanzī's *Naqāvat al-āthār fī dhikr al-akhyār dar tārīkh-i Ṣafaviyya*, ed. Iḥsān Ishrāqī (Tehran, 1373 Sh./1994) and of Yazdī's *Tārīkh-i ʿAbbāsī*. The editor had to add a footnote to Naṭanzī's text (p. 527) explaining that the 'heretics' mentioned in the chronicle are in fact a group known as the Nuqṭavīs.

Qazvīn.[10] There are only limited accounts of the Nuqṭavī teachings in the sources such as the already mentioned *Dabistān-i madhāhib* and perhaps these accounts even underwent some distortion in the process of being transmitted by non-Nuqṭavī authors. However, they do contain some recognisable traces of ideas found in the original Nuqṭavī texts. The survival of these original ideas might also be confirmed by the works of such thinkers as Muḥammad b. Maḥmūd Dihdār Shīrāzī (d. 1016/1607) who, according to Dhakāvatī, established links between Ibn ʿArabī's teachings, Nuqtavī theories and some Buddhist concepts.[11] The learned character of the Nuqṭavī teachings is also indirectly demonstrated by the fact, almost unanimously acknowledged in non-Nuqṭavī sources, that they attracted not only simple people but also elites, including nobles, statesmen and kings.[12]

---

[10] For the mention of the Nuqṭavī leaders connected with the circle of Qazvīn, see Naṭanzī, *Naqāvat*, pp. 523–527; Iskandar Beg Turkmān Munshī, *Tārīkh-i ʿālam-arā-yi ʿAbbāsī* (Tehran, 1350 Sh./1971), vol. 1, p. 476; Iṣfahānī, *Afḍal al-tawārīkh*, p. 145. In a letter addressed to Aḥmad Kāshī, the Mughal emperor Akbar (r. 963–1014/1556–1605) asks him to send his greetings to Dervish Khusraw, which also confirms that the Nuqṭavī leaders in various locations were in contact with each other. See Azfar Moin, *The Millennial Sovereign: Sacred Kingship and Sainthood in Islam* (New York, 2014), pp. 164–165 and references on p. 292, n. 131. Sharīf Āmulī was influential at the court of Akbar and is mentioned in several Indian texts, including ʿAbd al-Qādir Badaʾūnī's *Muntakhab al-tawārīkh*. See Moin, *The Millennial Sovereign*, pp. 165–166 and Kiyā, *Nuqṭaviyān yā pāsīkhāniyān*, pp. 11–12 and 32–35.

[11] See Dhakāvatī, *Junbish-i Nuqṭaviyya*, pp. 132–134 with reference to Dihdār's *Risāla-yi durr-i yatīm*. Excerpts from this and another of Dihdār's treatises titled *Risāla-yi nafāʾis al-arqām* are also cited in Kiyā, *Nuqṭaviyān*, pp. 24–32. Dihdār's criticism of the Nuqṭavī doctrinal views shows his close familiarity with the Nuqṭavī doctrinal positions, including some expressions (such as *markab al-mubīn*) from Pasīkhānī's foundational works. However, a closer reading of Dihdār's works is necessary to determine the extent of his familiarity with the original Nuqṭavī texts. Both works of Dihdār are available in the collection of his treatises titled *Rasāʾil-i Dihdār*, ed. Muḥammad Ḥusayn Akbārī Sāvī (Tehran, 1375 Sh./1996).

[12] Shah ʿAbbās himself is, of course, a salient example of this, and the interest of his courtiers and military commanders in Nuqṭavī teachings is noted in the chronicles analysed below. The Mughal Emperor Akbar also evinced an interest in Nuqṭavī doctrine, maintaining contact with various Nuqṭavī leaders in Iran and in India, as well as having prominent Nuqṭavī thinkers at his court. According to Iskandar Munshī, Akbar's advisor, Abu'l-Faḍl ʿAllāmī (d. 1011/1602) was a Nuqṭavī who converted him to Nuqṭavism. See *Tārīkh-i ʿālam-arā-yi ʿAbbāsī*, p. 476.

This evidence indicates both that the learned Nuqṭavī tradition not only survived but was thriving during the 10th–11th/16th–17th centuries in Iran and India, and that the Nuqṭavī group in Qazvīn which attracted the attention of Shah ʿAbbās I belonged to that tradition. Therefore, it seems safe to assume that the Nuqṭavī circle of Qazvīn adhered to teachings that were more or less closely aligned with the original texts of Maḥmūd Pasīkhānī.[13] This would justify our use of Pasīkhānī's foundational works as the main source for the doctrinal views of the Nuqṭavīs at the time of Shah ʿAbbās. Examining the historical accounts of the relationship of Shah ʿAbbās with the Nuqṭavīs against the background of doctrinal evidence from the Nuqṭavī texts may provide us with a new understanding of the role that Nuqṭavī ideas may have played in the evolution of the religious and political thinking of Shah ʿAbbās.

We shall start with a reflection on the nature of Safavid Shiʿism and on the situation of the Nuqṭavīs in the context of Shiʿi and Sufi trends in Safavid Iran. We shall then summarise the information available in the historical chronicles contemporary with Shah ʿAbbās I, along with a discussion of inconsistencies in the narratives and unanswered questions posed by these chronicles. This material will be collated with the doctrinal evidence contained in the Nuqṭavī texts to see if this can shed new light on the reasons for Shah ʿAbbās's interest in the Nuqṭavīs. In conclusion, we shall briefly discuss the fate of the Nuqṭavīs in Mughal India under the Emperor Akbar, comparing it to the narrative of their encounter with Shah ʿAbbās.

Twelver Shiʿi scholars, esoteric Shiʿism, mystico-messianic Shiʿi/Sufi trends and Safavid Shiʿism

Jean Aubin suggested that during the period preceding the rise of the Safavids, Iran was evolving towards some form of Shiʿism, and that the advent of the Safavids supported by the Qizil-bāsh Turkic tribes,

[13] Bada'ūnī in his *Muntakhab al-tawārīkh* explicitly refers to Sharīf Āmūlī's use of Pasīkhānī's books; see Kiyā, *Nuqṭaviyān*, pp. 32–33, and Moin, *The Millennial Sovereign*, p. 165.

originating in Anatolia and external to the Iranian religious landscape, restricted the rich diversity of various Shiʿi and Shiʿi-sympathising tendencies in Iran by subordinating them to the Qizil-bāsh interpretation of Shiʿism.[14] This observation doubtless reflects some aspects of the reality behind the radical change in the religious and political evolution of Iran that was introduced by the rise to power of the Safavids. However, we know that Safavid religious experimentation was not confined within the limits of Qizil-bāsh beliefs, and it arguably involved a broad range of existing religious orientations in the lands they conquered. Despite Safavid persecution of various religious groups, their religious politics were also influenced by the diversity of Shiʿi, and also Sufi and Sunni tendencies and doctrines which had developed in Iran and Iraq in the period preceding the Safavid conquest. Furthermore, many of these tendencies and doctrines continued to develop under the Safavids, creating new forms of philosophical and mystical thought and contributing to the 'Shiʿi renaissance' to which this volume is dedicated.

It is well known that Twelver Shiʿism did not immediately become the predominant religious paradigm in Iran when, upon his entry into Tabrīz in 907/1501, Shah Ismāʿīl I proclaimed it the official religion of his still-growing empire. This action by the fourteen-year-old king still puzzles historians. It is also difficult to say what kind of Twelver Shiʿism he had in mind, since it is unlikely that he or his supporters had any systematic knowledge of the theologico-jurisprudential Twelver

[14] Jean Aubin, 'La politique religieuse des Safavides', in *Le shîʿisme imâmite* (Paris, 1970), pp. 238–239. On the historical evolution of the meanings attributed to the term 'Qizil-bāsh', see Shahzad Bashir, 'The Origins and Rhetorical Evolution of the Term Qizilbash in Persianate Literature', *Journal of the Economic and Social History of the Orient*, 57 (2014), pp. 364–391. For the sake of simplicity, I use here the term 'Qizil-bāsh' to designate the Turkic tribes supporting the Safavids.

tradition at that time.[15] It is more likely that the Twelver Shiʿism of Shah Ismāʿīl, in his initial understanding, was just another name for the faith of his soldiers and disciples, the Qizil-bāsh. Focused on the cult of ʿAlī b. Abī Ṭālib and his descendants, the Qizil-bāsh faith included the veneration of the Prophet's family and of the imams of

---

[15] None of the best-known historical accounts of Shah Ismāʿīl's proclamation of Twelver Shiʿism, such as Khwāndamīr's *Ḥabīb al-siyar*, Yaḥyā b. ʿAbd al-Laṭīf Qazvīnī's *Lubb al-tawārīkh* or Ḥasan Beg Rūmlū's *Aḥsan al-tawārīkh*, specifies what kind of Twelver Shiʿism he intended to promote. A later, 11th/17th-century source, *ʿAlam ārā-yi ṣafavī*, mentions the support of ʿAlī that Shah Ismāʿīl received in a dream. For an analysis of these and other sources relevant to Shah Ismāʿīl's religious initiative see Rosemary Stanfield-Johnson, 'The Tabarra'iyan and the Early Safavids', *IS*, 37 (2004), pp. 47–71. It is remarkable that the religion proclaimed by Shah Ismāʿīl is also described in the sources as the 'religion of the *ahl al-bayt*', the 'Ḥaydarī religion' (*madhhab-i Ḥaydarī*) and the 'Jaʿfarī faith' (Stanfield-Johnson, 'The Tabarra'iyan', pp. 56 and 58, citing Qazwīnī, *Lubb al-tawārīkh* and Mīrzā Beg Junābadī, *Rawḍat al-Ṣafawiyya*). These expressions suggest that the proclamation of Twelver Shiʿism by Shah Ismāʿīl was in line with the beliefs of his father Ḥaydar and indeed with the doctrine of Jaʿfar al-Ṣādiq, the sixth Shiʿi imam and a foundational figure of the early Shiʿi thought. The idea that Shah Ismāʿīl was restoring the Twelver faith of the Būyid era after it was interrupted by the Saljūqs, or that he was a millennial reviver of the Shiʿi Islam is also mentioned in the sources; see Stanfield-Johnson, 'The Tabarra'iyan', p. 58, with reference to Rūmlū's *Aḥsan al-tawārīkh*; K. Ghereghlou, 'Chronicling a Dynasty on the Make: New Light on the Early Ṣafavids in Ḥayātī Tabrīzī's *Tārīkh*', *Journal of the American Oriental Society*, 137 (2017), p. 808, citing ʿAbdī Beg Qavāmī Shīrāzī (d. 988/1580), *Takmilat al-akhbār* and Qāsim Beg Ḥayātī Tabrīzī (fl. 961/1554), *Tārīkh*. Although he also had contacts with Shiʿi scholars at earlier dates, Shah Ismāʿīl's interest in the learned Twelver tradition was confirmed during his military campaigns in Iraq and his conquest of Baghdad in 914/1508, several years after his initial proclamation. In his *Tārīkh*, Ḥayātī Tabrīzī reports that in Baghdad Shah Ismāʿīl received a delegation from the Shiʿi shrines of Iraq, led by the prominent Shiʿi jurist, ʿAlī al-Karakī (d. 940/1535) (who was perhaps already known to the shah from their meeting in Iṣfahān in 910/1504–1505), and that Shah Ismāʿīl visited the centres of Shiʿi learning in Najaf and Ḥilla. See Ghereghlou, 'Chronicling', p. 830 and his edition of Ḥayātī Tabrīzī's *Tārīkh, A Chronicle of the Early Ṣafavids and the Reign of Shah Ismāʿīl (907–930/1501–1524)* (New Haven, CT, 2018), pp. 354–355 and 362–366. Three years later al-Karakī responded to Shah Ismāʿīl's invitation and moved to Iran where he became the main proponent of the Twelver Shiʿi scholarly tradition. On al-Karakī, see Wilferd Madelung, 'al-Karakī', *EI2*.

Twelver Shiʿi Islam, but otherwise had little in common with its normative tradition.[16]

However, whatever his initial idea of Twelver Shiʿism might have been, Shah Ismāʿīl soon turned to the normative Twelver Shiʿi tradition represented by Shiʿi scholars and jurists in Iran and Iraq, and invited them to preside over the establishment of Twelver Shiʿism in his realm.[17]

---

16 On Qizil-bāsh beliefs, see Markus Dressler, 'Alevīs', *EI3*, and references cited there. Although the Qizil-bāsh tradition includes the veneration of the 12 imams and several elements of the rituals linked with Shiʿi religious memory and values, it is unclear whether Shah Ismāʿīl or his followers identified themselves as Twelver Shiʿis prior to his declaration of Twelver Shiʿism as the official religion of his state in 907/1501. The literature also throws up the potential influence of other branches of Shiʿi Islam which could have influenced the Qizil-bāsh. The *Abū Muslim-nāmas*, the epic narratives devoted to Abū Muslim al-Khurāsānī (d. 137/755) – the leader of the movement that had overthrown the Umayyads and resulted in the Abbasids seizing caliphal power – were used by the early Safavids to attract followers among the Anatolian Qizil-bāsh. These narratives, which depicted Abū Muslim as the champion of the rights of the Prophet's family and of the ʿAlid cause, conveyed some information on the early Shiʿi sect of the Kaysāniyya, who supported the right of Muḥammad b. al-Ḥanafiyya, one of the sons of ʿAlī b. Abī Ṭālib. It is also known that at the initial stage of his career Shah Ismāʿīl and his followers were sheltered by the Zaydīs, and therefore might have been influenced by Zaydī Shiʿism. See, for example, Babayan, *Mystics, Monarchs, and Messiahs*, pp. 124 ff.; Andrew J. Newman, *Safavid Iran* (London and New York, 2009), p. 14, n. 3 and p. 151, n. 4. It should be kept in mind that, in the 8th/14th and 9th/15th centuries, the adoration of ʿAlī b. Abī Ṭālib, of the wider family of the Prophet and of the Twelver imams of the Twelver tradition was not an exclusively Shiʿi feature, it was also widespread in some Sunni circles. This phenomenon, which is probably rooted in the audacious religious reforms of the Abbasid caliph, al-Nāṣir li-Dīn Allāh (r. 575–622/1180–1225), is referred to in scholarly literature in varied terms, such as 'Alid loyalism' (Marshall Hodgson), 'Imamophilism' (Matthew Melvin-Koushki) or even 'Twelver Sunnism' (Rasūl Jaʿfariyān). For further references, see Orkhan Mir-Kasimov, 'Connaissance divine et action messianique : la figure de ʿAlī dans les milieux mystiques et messianiques (du Ve/XIe au Xe/XVIe siècle), in M.A. Amir-Moezzi, *Ali, le secret bien gardé* (Paris, 2020), pp. 325–352 and Angelika Hartmann, *An-Nāṣir li-Dīn Allāh (1180–1225) : Politik, Religion, Kultur im der späten ʿAbbāsidenzeit* (Berlin, 1975).

17 The nickname 'inventor of Shiʿism' (*mukhtariʿ al-shiʿa*) attributed to ʿAlī al-Karakī by his enemies, who resented his zeal in implementing the principles of Shiʿi jurisprudence, reflects the extent to which this form of Shiʿism was still perceived as something new and artificial at the time of Ismāʿīl's successor Shah Ṭahmāsp. For this nickname see, for example, Rula Jurdi Abisaab, *Converting Persia: Religion and Power in the Safavid Empire* (London and New York, 2004), p. 19.

Like his choice of Twelver Shiʿism as the official creed, the subsequent persecution of the Sunnis and other religious groups and the forced conversions, Shah Ismāʿīl's transition from the Qizil-bāsh creed to the theologico-jurisprudential version of Twelver Shiʿism has not, as yet, been convincingly explained. It can be argued that the learned, moderate Shiʿism of scholars and jurists was more suitable for the role of the state religion than the 'unruly' creed of the Qizil-bāsh, and also that the turn to the Twelver scholars was part of the Safavid plan to harness the power and messianic expectations of their Qizil-bāsh followers. That may well have been the case. It is true that, unlike the theologico-jurisprudential Twelver tradition, Qizil-bāsh Shiʿism did not possess any systematic doctrine that could be used as the basis of a state administration.[18] On the other hand, Twelver scholars had developed political theories that, at the first glance, could establish Safavid legitimacy on a more solid basis that appealed to a broader population.[19] Also, the Qizil-bāsh constituted a

---

[18] It should be recalled that before the Safavids, the Sarbadārs, a similar movement with Shiʿi leanings but apparently without any clearly articulated doctrine, took the same steps in inviting the prominent Twelver Shiʿi scholar, Muḥammad b. Makkī al-ʿĀmilī (d. 786/1384), to establish the theologico-jurisprudential form of Twelver Shiʿism in the short-lived polity that they founded in Khurāsān in the 8th/14th century. On the Sarbadārs, see C.P. Melville, 'Sarbadārids', *EI2*. Ibn Makkī wrote an important work on Imāmī law titled *al-Lumʿa al-Dimashqiyya* for the Sarbadārs. Michel Mazzaoui observed that 'in many ways, Šāh Ismāʿīl was the successor who put [the Sarbadār leader] ʿAlī Muʿayyad's attempt into effect a little more than a century later in Aḏarbaiǧān.' See Mazzaoui, *The Origins of the Ṣafawids: Šīʿism, Ṣūfism, and the Ġulāt* (Wiesbaden, 1972), p. 67.

[19] According to Twelver Shiʿi beliefs, only the imam, who is endowed with special knowledge, is the legitimate political and spiritual leader of the Islamic community. Since the occultation of the Twelfth imam, and especially since the beginning of the major occultation (329/940) when communication between the Hidden imam and the community was definitively severed, Twelver scholars developed various theories concerning the legitimacy of participation in government in the absence of the Hidden imam as well as the legitimacy of the ruler – depending on the ruler's adherence to Twelver beliefs and his treatment of the Twelver community. Some degree of legitimacy could be conceded to a ruler in the absence of the Hidden imam if that ruler was 'just'. For a concise outline of the evolution of the Twelver political theories see Mohammad Ali Amir-Moezzi and Christian Jambet, *Qu'est-ce que le shîʿisme?* (Paris, 2004), pp. 181–199; Moojan Momen, *An Introduction to Shiʿi Islam* (New Haven and London, 1985), pp. 191–196; and, for a short summary of Twelver attitudes towards Safavid legitimacy, see Abisaab, *Converting Persia*, pp. 15–16.

specific group determined by its tribal organisation and Turkic identity. The members of this group regarded the Safavid leaders as their spiritual masters. It is clear that applying this socially and ethnically limited Qizil-bāsh model with its unusual set of beliefs to a vast empire with its culturally and religiously diversified populations could have been a difficult task.[20]

However, Qizil-bāsh loyalty was also a substantial asset for the Safavid kings, and it is not clear whether this asset outweighed the benefits of the alliance with the Imāmī scholars or not. Qizil-bāsh beliefs focussed on the figure of the Safavid shah, investing him with quasi-divine spiritual authority. Consequently, for the Qizil-bāsh, the legitimacy of the Safavid shahs as political rulers was unquestionable. Conversely, in the doctrinal framework of the Imāmī Shiʿi tradition, the Safavid claim to religious and political authority could never be completely fulfilled in the absence of the Hidden imam. Even though Safavid genealogy was conveniently arranged to present them as descendants of the seventh imam of the Twelver line, Mūsā al-Kāẓim[21] and, starting from the beginning of the dynastic period, the traces of Qizil-bāsh 'deviations' in their past were progressively censored and removed, the most positive description of their legitimacy that the Safavids could obtain within the limits of Twelver political theory would have sounded more like a justification than a confirmation: since the imam, who is the only rightful ruler, was absent, and since the Safavids belonged to the ʿAlid and Fatimid line, it was conceivable to recognise them as rightful rulers, but only to the extent that they

---

[20] The Qizil-bāsh supporters of the Safavids belonged to a limited number of *oymāqs*, or tribes, and were bound by tribal loyalties. After the Safavids became a royal dynasty, a principle was introduced according to which it was no longer possible to become a Qizil-bāsh by conversion, and only people born into an *oymāq* were considered Qizil-bāsh. See Babayan, 'The Safavid Synthesis: From Qizilbash Islam to Imamite Shiʿism', *IS*, 27 (1994), p. 138.

[21] This apparently happened in the middle of the 9th/15th century. See Kazuo Morimoto, 'The Earliest ʿAlid Genealogy for the Safavids: New Evidence for the Pre-dynastic Claim to *Sayyid* Status', *IS*, 43 (2010), pp. 447–469.

could be regarded as executing the will of the Hidden imam.[22] This attitude constituted a sharp contrast to the central place that the Safavid kings occupied in the Qizil-bāsh mindset.[23]

It is reasonable to suppose that, despite their support of Twelver scholars and their self-imposed role as the champions of the Twelver Shiʿi cause, the Safavid shahs were aware of the limited scope of the authority and legitimacy that they could enjoy within the scholarly Twelver paradigm. Therefore, they were prepared to consider any reasonable means of legitimising their authority without either maintaining a privileged link with the Qizil-bāsh or sacrificing their religious charisma to the Twelver clergy in exchange for a half-hearted recognition.[24]

Seen from this perspective, Shah Ismāʿīl's proclamation of Twelver Shiʿism does not appear to be a watershed after which the Safavids' commitment to the scholarly form of Twelver Shiʿism was unwavering and from which point this form of Shiʿism was irrevocably bound to remain the official religion of the Safavid state. This event can be regarded rather as an experiment in the Safavids' search for a new

---

[22] 'As the ruler of the age and the Lord of Command is absent, it is rightful for a competent member of the exalted Fatimid, ʿAlid dynasty to execute the commandments of the Imam of the age among God's creatures . . .' ʿAbdī Beg Qavāmī Shīrāzī (historian under Shah Ṭahmāsp, d. 988/1580), *Takmilat al-akhbār*, cited in Saïd Amir Arjomand, 'The Rise of Shah Esmāʿil as a Mahdist Revolution', in his *Sociology of Shiʿite Islam* (Leiden and Boston, 2016), pp. 305–306.

[23] In the long term, the alliance with Twelver scholars proved to be rather a bad choice not only for the Safavids, but for Iranian monarchy in general.

[24] The potentially discordant aspects of the Safavid alliance with the juristic version of Twelver Shiʿism were present from the outset of this difficult relationship and, as we will see below, were soon transformed into open conflict. As noted by Ernest Tucker: 'Shah Isma'il I's 1501 enthronement in Tabrīz created a situation that would affect the Safavids for the rest of their time in power. It initiated an implicit tension between the monarch and the clergy over the definition of royal legitimacy.' See Tucker, *Nadir Shah's Quest for Legitimacy in Post-Safavid Iran* (Gainesville, FL, 2006), p. 17.

formula of religious and political authority.[25] There was nothing to prevent Shah Ismāʿīl's successors from being open to alternative choices, if these choices were beneficial to their quest for legitimacy and if they could be implemented without radically challenging the existing balance of political forces. The tentative character of the Safavid move towards the normative Twelver tradition seems to be confirmed by the swings in their religious policies, going even as far as a return to Sunni Islam. A realisation of the danger posed by the growing power of the Twelver scholars and jurists, sometimes in alliance with the Qizil-bāsh, was one of the possible motivations for the move towards Sunni Islam contemplated by Ismāʿīl II (r. 984–985/1576–1577), Ṭahmāsp's successor, early in Safavid history, and this led to a conflict between the Safavid shah and some groups of the Twelver clergy and the Qizil-bāsh.[26] Over a century and a half later, a fusion with Sunni Islam, by presenting Twelver Shiʿism as a legal school (*madhhab*) similar to the four Sunni schools, was advocated by Nādir Shah Afshār (r. 1149–1160/1736–1747), founder of the Afshārid dynasty that succeeded the Safavids.[27]

It is also worth noting that, in spite of their support for the Twelver scholars, theologians and jurists, the Safavid kings did not totally abandon their claims of mystico-messianic authority. Their attachment to their status as Sufi leaders is confirmed by the attention given by Ṭahmāsp I and ʿAbbās I to the shrine of the founder of the Safavid order, Shaykh Ṣafī al-Dīn (d. 735/1334) in Ardabīl, Iran, and the

---

[25] The effective 'watershed', when the consolidation of Twelver Shiʿi clergy and the conversion of the Iranian population reached the point of no return, must arguably be situated at the end of, or even after, Safavid rule. Alessandro Bausani observed, 'It is a fact that when the Safavids arrived the majority of the Persian population was Sunnite, and the change to Shiʿism was a conscious and deliberate policy carried out by the Safavids themselves... The effective conversion of the mass of the Persian people to Shiʿism probably occurred in the eighteenth century'; see Alessandro Bausani, *The Persians* (New York 1971), p. 139.

[26] See Michel Mazzaoui, 'The Religious Policy of Safavid Shah Ismaʿil II', in Michel Mazzaoui and Vera B. Moreen, ed., *Intellectual Studies on Islam: Essays Written in Honor of Martin B. Dickson* (Salt Lake City, UT, 1990), pp. 49–56; Abisaab, *Converting Persia*, pp 41–50.

[27] On Nādir Shah's religious policy, see Tucker, *Nadir Shah's Quest*.

preservation of elements of Sufi rituals at their courts.[28] Eschatological and messianic expectations were high at the time of Shah Ṭahmāsp, who was described by his court historian, ʿAbdī Beg Qavāmī Shīrāzī (d. 988/1580), as the king of the 'end of time'.[29] Shah Ṭahmāsp also expected the imminent return of the Hidden imam, as the eschatological saviour (Mahdi). A white horse was kept ready for the Mahdi, and Ṭahmāsp's favourite sister, Sulṭānim, remained unmarried as the Mahdi's fiancée.[30] Andrew Newman has argued that Shah Ṭahmāsp's declaration of ʿAlī al-Karakī as the 'deputy of the Twelfth imam' might suggest that the shah himself was identified as the imam.[31] Shah Ṭahmāsp's friendly disposition towards mystico-messianic groups, including the Nuqṭavīs, is attested in some sources.[32] A study of the anti-Abū Muslim literature in Safavid Iran also suggests a surge in the popularity of the mystico-messianic discourse after the death of Shah Ismāʿīl I, when Twelver scholars found themselves in a defensive position.[33]

[28] See Newman, *Safavid Iran*, pp. 32, 59; A.H. Morton, 'The Chub-i Tariq and Qizilbash Ritual in Safavid Persia', in Calmard, ed., *Études Safavides* (Tehran/Paris, 1993), pp. 225–245.

[29] Arjomand, 'The Rise of Shah Esmāʿil', p. 307, with reference to ʿAbdī Beg's *Takmilat al-akhbār*.

[30] Arjomand, 'The Rise of Shah Esmāʿil', p. 307, with reference to Michele Membré, *Relazione di Persia*.

[31] Newman, *Safavid Iran*, p. 37.

[32] Iṣfahānī, *Afḍal al-tawārīkh*, vol. 1, p. 142, notes that the father of Dervish Khusraw (who will be discussed further below), the Nuqṭavī leader of Qazvīn, was known to be a heretic (supposedly a Nuqṭavī like his son), that he was appreciated by Shah Ṭahmāsp and was often present at the royal meetings with scholars and learned men. This did not stop Ṭahmāsp from ruthlessly persecuting the Nuqṭavīs. The same love-hate relationship can also be observed between Shah ʿAbbās and the Nuqṭavīs. It is noteworthy that Qāsim Beg Ḥayātī Tabrīzī, mentioned above as the author of the chronicle of the early Safavids entitled *Tārīkh* and written at the time of Shah Ṭahmāsp, probably also had some Nuqṭavī proclivities. See Ghereghlou, 'Chronicling', p. 809.

[33] See Newman, *Safavid Iran*, pp. 31–33, and his 'The Limits of "Orthodoxy"? Notes on the Anti-Abū Muslim Polemic of Early 11th/17th Century Iran', in Denis Hermann and Mathieu Terrier, ed., *Shiʿi Islam and Sufism: Classical Views and Modern Perspectives* (London, 2020), pp. 65–119.

The Safavids' search for a new formula of religious and political authority inevitably brought them into contact with the milieu of Shiʿi and Shiʿi/Sufi mystical and messianic groups and movements in Iran and Iraq. Indeed, since the traditional balance of religious and political authority represented by the caliphate was disrupted by the Mongol invasions in the middle of the 7th/13th century, this milieu can be regarded as a testing ground for various doctrines that specifically addressed the issue of religious authority and its possible links to political power.

Modern scholarship has come to distinguish this milieu as a separate phenomenon of sorts, but its nature and the role it played in the socio-political transformations of the post-Mongol period have still not been sufficiently conceptualised. This is also visible in the somewhat confused terminology used to refer to the groups and movements that belonged to this milieu and combined Sufi and Shiʿi doctrinal elements with active political agendas. These groups and movements are most often described as 'messianic', 'antinomian' or 'extremist'. However, none of these terms conveys an accurate idea of their identity. The word 'messianic' is in general problematic in Islamic contexts and suggests the expectation of the imminent advent of an eschatological saviour,[34] something that none of these groups and movements

34 Following the Qur'anic use, the word 'Messiah' (*masīḥ*) generally refers, in Islamic context, to Jesus. The Islamic concept which comes closest to the Judaeo-Christian idea of the eschatological saviour is that of the Mahdī, 'the rightly guided one'. However, the Mahdī is not necessarily a saviour expected at the end of time, he can also be a millennial justifier who appears at the turn of every century or millennium in order to restore the pristine purity of Islam. In this sense, the Mahdī is a renovator (*mujaddid*). Obviously, a claim to be the saviour coming at the end of time would put the claimant in an embarrassing situation if the end of time did not occur as expected. Therefore, most of the leaders of the so called 'messianic' movements of the post-Mongol era did not claim to be eschatological saviours, but rather renovators initiating a new era, which might or might not lead to the coming of the eschatological Mahdī in a more or less distant and usually unspecified future. Presiding over a new era provided them with a broad degree of freedom in advocating new doctrinal and socio-political models without being concerned with preparations for an imminent end of time. It is in this sense that the term 'messianic' is used in this paper.

seemed to claim.[35] Two other concepts, 'antinomianism' and 'extremism', are doxographic clichés inspired by medieval polemical literature and correspond to the Arabic terms *ibāḥa/ilḥād* and *ghuluww* respectively. Again, as far as is known, none of these movements was 'antinomian' in the sense of medieval heresiology, that is, none of them explicitly advocated the abolition of Islamic religious law.

The last term, 'extremism' (*ghuluww*) is perhaps the most frequently employed to refer to the post-Mongol mystico-messianic groups and movements. This term originated in early Islamic doxological literature where it was used to refer, in particular, to the supporters of the Shiʿi imams who, according to their opponents, 'exaggerated' some aspects of the imams' esoteric teachings, the term being applied especially to those who allegedly deified the imams.[36] The occultation of the Twelfth imam in the middle of the 4th/10th century weakened the esoteric wing of the Twelver branch, and fostered the development of the rationalist theologico-jurisprudential tendency which became predominant. However, the esoteric elements of the Twelver line did not completely disappear. Apparently nurtured by other esoteric currents, especially Sufism and Ismaili Shiʿism, Twelver esotericism re-surfaced after the major disruption in the balance between various

[35] Faḍl Allāh Astarābādī's major work, *Jāvidān-nāma-yi kabīr,* does not contain any explicit claim. It can be deduced from its contents and from other works attributed to Faḍl Allāh that he saw himself as the inaugurator of the new era of hermeneutical disclosure leading to the final apocalypse presided over by Jesus. See Mir-Kasimov, *Words of Power*, pp. 13–15. Muḥammad b. Falāḥ (d. 870/1465–1466), founder of another influential post-Mongol mystico-messianic movement, the Mushaʿshaʿ, claimed the status of the representative of the Hidden imam rather than that of the imam himself. On him, see Michel Mazzaoui, 'Mushaʿshaʿiyān: A Fifteenth Century Shiʿi Movement in Khūzistān and Southern Iraq', *Folia Orientalia*, 22 (1981–1984), pp. 139–162, and ʿAlī Riḍā Dhakāvatī Qarāguzlū, 'Nahḍat-i Mushaʿshaʿī va gudhārī bar kalām al-Mahdī', *Maʿārif*, 37 (1375 Sh./1996), pp. 59–67. Muḥammad Nūrbakhsh (d. 869/1464), founder of the Nūrbakhshī Sufi movement, claimed the status of the Mahdī, but again, in the sense of renewer and inaugurator of a new era rather than eschatological saviour presiding over the end of time. See Shahzad Bashir, 'The Imam's Return: Messianic Leadership in Late Medieval Shiʿism', in Linda S. Walbridge, ed., *The Most Learned of the Shiʿa: The Institution of the Marjaʿ Taqlīd* (New York, 2001), pp. 21–33, p. 30.

[36] On this term, see Sean Anthony, 'Ghulāt (extremist Shiʿis)', *EI3*.

religious currents in Islam brought about by the Mongol invasions and Mongol rule. It was represented by such thinkers as Ḥaydar Āmulī (d. after 787/1385) and Rajab Bursī (d. 843/1411).[37] A great synthesis of Islamic theology, Shiʿism, Sufism, the illuminationist (*ishrāqī*) theosophy of Shihāb al-Dīn Suhrawardī (d. 587/1191) and Avicennian philosophy was attempted in the work of Ibn Abī Jumhūr al-Aḥsāʾī (d. after 906/1501).[38] At the same time, the boundaries between the juristic and esoteric currents of Twelver Shiʿism became more porous. Imāmī scholarly culture under the Safavids combined commitment to the juristic pattern with broad erudition and deep interest in philosophy and esotericism, a tendency exemplified by such prominent scholars as Shaykh Bahāʾī (d. 1030/1621), Mīr Dāmād (d. 1041/1631) and Mullā Ṣadrā Shīrāzī (d. 1050/1640) as well as many others.

Another part of Twelver Shiʿi esotericism, again closely linked to Sufism and implicitly nurtured by Ismailism and perhaps by other mystical Shiʿi trends, fed into mystico-messianic movements outside the fold of Twelver Shiʿism as such.[39] These groups were at the forefront

---

[37] The introduction of Shiʿi sensibilities to Sufi thought, and more specifically the Shiʿi reinterpretation of the work of Ibn al-ʿArabī (d. 638/1240) started in the 7th/13th century in the Shiʿi circles of Bahrain and was continued by Ḥaydar Āmulī. On the school of Bahrain, see Ali al-Oraibi, 'Shīʿī Renaissance: A Case Study of the Theosophical School of Bahrain in the 7th/13th Century' (PhD, McGill University, Montreal, 1992), especially pp. 172–217; and his 'Rationalism in the School of Bahrain: A Historical Perspective', in L. Clarke, ed., *Shīʿite Heritage* (Binghamton, NY, 2001), pp. 331–343. On Ḥaydar Āmulī, see Henry Corbin, *En Islam Iranien. Aspects spirituels et philosophiques* (Paris, 1971–1972), vol. 3, pp. 198–199. On Rajab Bursī, see Bursī, *Les Orients des lumières*, tr. H. Corbin (Paris, 1996) and Kāmil Muṣṭafā al-Shaybī, *al-Ṣila bayna al-taṣawwuf wa'l-tashayyuʿ* (Beirut, 1982), vol. 2, pp. 224–256.

[38] On him, see Sabine Schmidtke, *Theologie, Philosophie und Mystik im zwölferschiitischen Islam des 9./15. Jahrhunderts: die Gedankenwelten des Ibn Abī Ǧumhūr al-Aḥsāʾī (um 838/1434–35 – nach 906/1501)* (Leiden, Boston and Cologne, 2000).

[39] For possible Ismaili traces in the Ḥurūfī texts, see Orkhan Mir-Kasimov, 'The Nizārī Ismaili Theory of the Resurrection (*qiyāma*) and Post-Mongol Iranian Messianism', in O. Mir-Kasimov, ed., *Intellectual Interactions in the Islamic World: The Ismaili Thread* (London, 2020), pp. 323–352. For Ismaili-Nuqṭavī relations, see Farhad Daftary, *The Ismāʿīlīs: Their History and Doctrines* (2nd ed., Cambridge, 2007), pp. 421–422.

of experimentation with the Shiʿi and Sufi ideas of religious authority conferred by divinely inspired knowledge. In some cases, these ideas were combined with the theories of a new, messianic, age that required a new kind of leader, one commissioned from above to operate a radical renewal and re-unification of the Islamic community and/or to lead it to the final apocalypse. Some movements of this kind, such as the Ḥurūfīs, Nuqṭavīs and Nūrbakhshīs produced substantial and original doctrines including new conceptions of religious authority, but they failed to find political support for them. Others, like the Sarbadārs or Mushaʿshaʿ, were politically more successful, and were able to create distinct political entities in various locations in Iran and Iraq.[40] These political entities are seen as forerunners of the Safavid empire. Some of these groups, such as the Nūrbakhshīs and the Mushaʿshaʿ derived directly from the Twelver branch of Islam.[41] Others, like the Ḥurūfīs and the Nuqṭavīs, were apparently rooted in more syncretic Shiʿi/Sufi values which included veneration of the Prophet's family, and more specifically of ʿAlī b. Abī Ṭālib and of the Shiʿi imams, however, still with an arguably recognisable Shiʿi esoteric background.[42] It is remarkable that some of these movements evolved towards various formulations of confessional universalism that transcended the boundaries between various Islamic groups, especially that between the Shiʿis and Sunnis, in line with the messianic expectations of the re-unification of the Islamic community in the

[40] On the Sarbadārs, see C.P. Melville, 'Sarbadārids', *EI2*. On the Nūrbakhshīs and Mushaʿshaʿs, see n. 35 above.

[41] Ibn Falāḥ studied with Aḥmad b. Fahd al-Ḥillī (d. 841/1438), a well-known Twelver Shiʿi scholar with Sufi proclivities. On him, see al-Shaybī, *al-Ṣila*, vol. 2, pp. 257–265. A less plausible connection between al-Ḥillī and Muḥammad Nūrbakhsh is also mentioned in one source. More importantly, the Twelfth imam occupies a prominent position in the doctrines of Ibn Falāḥ and Muḥammad Nūrbakhsh.

[42] It will be argued further below that this esoteric Shiʿi background is most clearly attested to in the hermeneutical perspectives of these movements. Also, it is worth mentioning that Faḍl Allāh Astarābādī's genealogical tree makes him a descendant of the seventh imam of the Twelver line, Mūsā al-Kāẓim. For references regarding Astarābādī's genealogy, see Abdülbâki Gölpınarlı, *Hurûfilik metinleri kataloğu* (2nd ed., Ankara, 1989), pp. 4–5.

final age.[43] The Safavids maintained complex relationships, ranging from persecution to integration, with most of these groups.

To the extent that post-Mongol mystico-messianic movements incorporated elements of early Shiʿi esoteric lore, they can indeed be regarded as the heirs of those early Shiʿi esoteric groups which were designated as *ghulāt* by their opponents. Nevertheless, the term is still misleading for the following reasons. First, the term *ghulāt* has pejorative connotations. Most of the groups that were designated as *ghulāt* in the heresiographical sources neither called nor considered themselves 'extremists', and the perpetuation of this medieval terminology in modern scholarship is a moot point. Second, the post-Mongol mystico-messianic movements combined the heritage of Shiʿi esotericism with many other elements of Islamic mysticism, theology and philosophy. The inappropriateness of the term *ghulāt* has been recognised by modern scholars, but its use has nevertheless continued as no convincing or widely accepted alternative has emerged so far.[44] I prefer to use 'mystico-messianic movements' instead as, in a sense, these movements can be regarded as a form of generalisation and extension of the original esoteric Shiʿi substratum, and especially of the Shiʿi hermeneutical theories and doctrines of the imamate, through the incorporation of other mystical, philosophical and theological elements. In this sense, they could perhaps better be described as 'broader Shiʿi', or 'supra-Shiʿi'.

As the first Safavid kings were establishing themselves in lands they conquered in Iran and Iraq, they encountered these 'broader Shiʿi' mystico-messianic movements, and it seems reasonable to suppose that they considered these movements as possible substitutes for both

---

[43] This universalist ethos also recalls the spirit of the project of the Abbasid caliph al-Nāṣir li-Dīn Allāh (see n. 16 above). For the universalist dimension of Ḥurūfī thought, see Mir-Kasimov, *Words of Power*, pp. 427–433, for Muḥammad Nūrbakhsh, see Bashir, 'The Imam's Return', p. 30. Nuqṭavī universalism will be discussed further below.

[44] See, for example, a discussion of the term *ghulāt* and its application to the Qizil-bāsh in Arjomand, 'The Rise of Shah Esmāʿil', p. 303, and Babayan, 'The Safavid Synthesis', p. 136, n. 3.

Qizil-bāsh and theologico-jurisprudential Twelver ideology.[45] In any case, when Shah ʿAbbās ascended the throne, the issue of Safavid religious legitimacy was far from being solved.[46]

In the following sections we will discuss how Nuqṭavī doctrine addressed this issue, and the possibility that Shah ʿAbbās seriously considered the advantages of the Nuqṭavī option for some time, but then decided to reject it.

Safavi-Nuqṭavī relationships in historical sources: does the historical narrative make sense?

The importance attached to the relationship of Shah ʿAbbās I[47] with the Nuqṭavīs of Qazvīn during his reign is corroborated by the fact that this is discussed, sometimes at significant length, in most contemporary chronicles. These chronicles, which are hostile to the

---

45 The Safavids' progressive familiarisation with the Shiʿi and 'supra-Shiʿi' intellectual milieus of Iran and Iraq, and their engagement, either in the form of patronage or of persecution, with some of the groups and movements of these milieus and an official endorsement of one of them, namely the theologico-jurisprudential form of Twelver Shiʿism, can be regarded as one aspect of the gradual 'Iranisation' of the originally Turkic Safavid dynasty.

46 As Sholeh A. Quinn has put it: 'Safavid kings initially promoted their legitimate right to rule by presenting themselves as (1) the representative of the Hidden Imam, (2) the shadow of God on earth, in line with pre-Islamic Persian notions of kingship, and (3) the head of the Safavid Sufi order. By the time Shah ʿAbbās came to power, these three "pillars of legitimacy" were not functioning very well. The Shiʿi *ʿulama'* (religious clerics), initially brought to Iran from Jabal al-ʿAmil in Lebanon, elaborated on Shiʿi doctrines, thereby rendering it difficult for the king to claim to be the representative of the Hidden Imam. The Qizilbash, to whom the rulers appealed as head of the Sufi order, had become increasingly powerful and thus constituted a threat to the state. Shah ʿAbbās, therefore, had to pursue alternative legitimizing programs in order to maintain his power.' (Quinn, *Historical Writing During the Reign of Shah ʿAbbas: Ideology, Imitation and Legitimacy in Safavid Chronicles* (Salt Lake City, UT, 2000), p. 5. Aubin noted that Shah ʿAbbās's contact with the Nuqṭavīs was informed by his search for a form of religious authority alternative to Qizilbashism, however he linked this, in my opinion erroneously, with the alleged Persian nationalism of the Nuqṭavīs; see his 'La politique religieuse', p. 240.

47 For the sake of simplicity, the regnal number of this monarch is omitted in the rest of the chapter.

Nuqṭavīs, constitute our main source of information on this episode. In this section, we shall discuss information obtained from these sources in order to compare it with evidence from the Nuqṭavī doctrinal sources that will be presented in the next section.

The longest and the most detailed account of the encounter of Shah ʿAbbās with the Nuqṭavīs in Qazvīn at the onset of the second Islamic millennium (around the years 1001–1002/1592–1594) is found in Afūshta-yi Naṭanzī's (d. after 1008/1599) *Naqāvat al-āthār fī dhikr al-akhyār dar tārīkh-i Ṣafaviyya*, which was completed in 1007/1598.[48] Naṭanzī may have been employed at Shah ʿAbbās's court, and may have been a direct witness of the events he described, but this is not certain. It is possible that he disliked Shah ʿAbbās,[49] but this does not mean that he sympathised with the Nuqṭavīs. The description of the Nuqṭavī episode is given in the chapter on heretics (*malāḥida*). It is remarkable that the Nuqṭavīs appear in Naṭanzī's work as the supreme heretics of the time of Shah Ṭahmāsp and Shah ʿAbbās, following such arch-heretics as Mani and Mazdak in pre-Islamic Iran and Ḥasan-i Ṣabbāḥ in the time of the Saljūqs. With the exception of a short introduction, the whole of the chapter on heretics is devoted to them. Their status as the most prominent heresy is also emphasised by the fact that the name of the group is not mentioned in the chapter and they are referred to simply as 'the heretics'.[50]

According to Naṭanzī, Shah Ṭahmāsp was determined to uproot the Nuqṭavīs because they were spreading unbelief, transgressing the *sharīʿa* and misleading uneducated people. He arrested some of their leaders, had others killed, and the movement was silenced until the time of Shah ʿAbbās. At that time, an individual named Khusraw, dressed as a dervish, set up residence in Qazvīn and, in Naṭanzī's

[48] Naṭanzī, *Naqāvat*, pp. 515–528. On him, see Quinn, *Historical Writing*, p. 20, and K. Ghereghlou, 'Afušta'i Naṭanzī, Maḥmūd', *EIr.* Kathryn Babayan used this source extensively, along with Iskandar Beg Munshī's *Tārīkh-i ʿālam-arā-yi ʿAbbāsī*, in her analysis of the Nuqtavī episode; see her *Mystics, Monarchs, and Messiahs*, pp. 1–117.

[49] Quinn, *Historical Writing*, p. 20.

[50] It is also remarkable that neither Naṭanzī nor the authors of other chronicles hostile to the Nuqṭavīs explain in any detail what the doctrinal positions of the Nuqṭavīs were, and nor do they engage in any substantial polemic against their views. The Nuqṭavī 'heresy' is presented as a self-evident fact, which does not need to be demonstrated.

words, started the 'trade of deceit and hypocrisy' (*bāzār-i shayd va zarq*).[51] His influence grew fast, since people came to see him 'from far and near, Turks and Tajiks'.[52] This growing influence attracted the attention of Shah ʿAbbās. One day when the shah happened to pass near the residence of Dervish Khusraw, he came out and invited the king to enter. After this first visit, Shah ʿAbbās returned regularly to see Dervish Khusraw, and each time offered him large amounts of cash and other goods. Many military commanders and nobles (*umarā' va arkān*) joined the shah and became disciples (sing. *murīd*) of Dervish Khusraw.[53] In a short time, the number of his disciples increased dramatically.

Naṭanzī hastens to add that Shah ʿAbbās's interest in the Nuqṭavīs was motivated exclusively by his wish to 'understand the true identity' (*bi-taḥqīq-i ḥāl va kayfiyyat*) of Dervish Khusraw,[54] a suspected heretic. This does not seem consistent either with the lavish presents that the shah gave to the dervish, nor with him encouraging his military commanders and statesmen to become the heretic's disciples, thus promoting the heresy among his military and state apparatus and making it more influential. Also, it hardly makes sense to suppose that Shah ʿAbbās would personally infiltrate a suspect group and spend a sizeable amount of his time carrying out an investigation for the reasons of general piety only. Shah ʿAbbās's interest in Dervish Khusraw's teachings was most probably authentic, and clearly represented some goal that was extremely important to him.[55] This would explain the shah's support for the movement and the fact that he did not prevent his high-ranking officers and ministers from joining it. The popularity of Nuqṭavī teachings among the elite also obviously contradicts Naṭanzī's statement that the Nuqṭavī ideas appealed only to uneducated people. There was apparently something in these

[51] Naṭanzī, *Naqāvat*, p. 515.
[52] Ibid.
[53] Ibid., p. 516.
[54] Ibid.
[55] This was also noted by several scholars who examined the mentioned historical chronicles.

teachings that attracted people from all walks of life, and there was something that strongly attracted Shah ʿAbbās.

In the continuation of Naṭanzī's account, it is said that one of the persons occupying a high status in Dervish Khusraw's circle, Yūsifī Khurāsānī the quiver-maker (Tarkishdūz), often visited Shah ʿAbbās to deliver quivers he had ordered. Believing that Shah ʿAbbās could be unreservedly trusted, Yūsifī freely discussed with him the details of Nuqṭavī beliefs. Something in these discussions must have interested Shah ʿAbbās so intensely that he delayed his departure to Luristān, where he had to deal with a rebellion, and went to see Yūsifī in Dervish Khusraw's residence. At that point, he was told that if his journey to Luristān could not be cancelled, he must try and return to Qazvīn a few days before the month of Muḥarram of the year 1002/[1593–94], because at the beginning of that year, one of the 'masters of spirit' (*arbāb-i ḥāl*), that is, one of the Nuqṭavī dervishes, would reach the station of kingship and independence and become the ruler (*ṣāḥib-i amr*), combining spiritual and temporal power and marking the beginning of the Nuqṭavī cycle. 'Since the shah's capacity to exercise this [power] is more developed than [the capacity to rule] of that people who claim it, and it is the shah who presently holds the royal power, it would be preferable that the power should not be transferred to another person.'[56]

Considering the story of ruthless persecution of the Nuqṭavīs by Shah ʿAbbās's grandfather Shah Ṭahmāsp that Naṭanzī mentioned at the beginning of his account of the Nuqṭavī heretics, it sounds highly improbable that a high-ranking Nuqṭavī dervish such as Yūsifī the quiver-maker would have divulged any sensitive information to Shah ʿAbbās, even if he allegedly supposed that the shah was one of them. Does Naṭanzī's narrative reflect a proposal made by the Nuqṭavī leadership to Shah ʿAbbās to transform the nature of his rule by becoming the king who combines political and spiritual power and

[56] Naṭanzī, *Naqāvat*, pp. 517–518.

ushers in the new historical cycle informed by the Nuqṭavī ideals?[57] For the reasons discussed in the previous section, Shah ʿAbbās might have seen in Nuqṭavī teachings the possibility of finding a new basis of legitimacy for his rule.

However, Naṭanzī's story includes also an element of threat to Shah ʿAbbās's rule: Shah ʿAbbās is told that if he does not manage to return to Qazvīn by the date indicated, his rule will be transferred to another member of the group. According to Naṭanzī, it was this threat, combined with Dervish Khusraw's claim to be able to put together a strong army (which he offered to send to Shah ʿAbbās to help him defeat the rebellion in Luristān),[58] that convinced Shah ʿAbbās to take immediate action against the Nuqṭavīs. He entrusted this mission to his herald (*jārchī-bāshī*), who marched soldiers to the residence of Dervish Khusraw and eventually killed or arrested many dervishes.[59] This was followed by the episode of Yūsifī being put on the throne for

[57] Although some sources mention Qizil-bāsh involvement in the Nuqṭavī movement, however there seems to be insufficient evidence to demonstrate that this involvement was significant. Iskandar Beg Munshī reports that 'even some of the *qezelbāš* were members of this sect', giving as example Būdāq Beg Dīn-oğlū Ustājlū (Eskandar Beg Monshi, *Tārīḳ-e ʿAlamārā-ye ʿAbbāsī*, tr. R. Savory as *History of Shah ʿAbbas the Great* (Boulder, CO, 1930) vol. 2, p. 650), which suggests that Qizil-bāsh adherence to the Nuqṭavī movement was an exception rather than a rule. This would therefore discount Babayan's thesis that Nuqṭavī doctrine provided the Qizil-bāsh with an alternative to their original ideology and with a means of expressing their disillusionment with the Safavids, which links Shah ʿAbbās's anti-Nuqṭavī persecutions with his anti-Qizil-bāsh policies (cf. Babayan, 'The Safavid Synthesis'). Some features of Nuqṭavī doctrine also seem to make a large-scale Qizil-bāsh-Nuqṭavī alliance problematic. For example, although the figure of ʿAlī b. Abī Ṭālib plays an important role in the Nuqṭavī texts, it is far from occupying a place as central as that in Qizil–bāsh belief. Also, some sources report that the Qizil–bāsh were compared to dogs in Nuqṭavī teachings (cf. *Dabistān al-madhāhib*, tr. David Shea and Anthony Troyer as *The Dabistan, or School of Manners* (Paris and London, 1843), vol. 3, p. 21), an idea which, if proved true, would not have contributed to the popularity of Nuqṭavism among the Qizil-bāsh. It seems more plausible that Shah ʿAbbās was considering the Nuqṭavī ideology as a means of re-establishing his status as an absolutist spiritual and temporal ruler on a basis independent of the Qizil-bāsh.

[58] Munajjim Yazdī and Faḍlī Beg Khūzānī Iṣfahānī mention 50,000 and 40,000 men, respectively. See *Tārīkh-i ʿAbbāsī*, p. 121, and *Afḍal al-tawārīkh*, p. 143.

[59] Naṭanzī, *Naqāvat*, pp. 520–521.

three days in order to counter the effects of an ominous star, and then being executed.

It is difficult to make sense of the Nuqṭavī threat to Shah ʿAbbās. Dervish Khusraw's proposal to muster a powerful army and place it in support of Shah ʿAbbās is not consistent with the fact that the herald with a small detachment of 100 soldiers was able to surround the Nuqṭavī residence, and to arrest and kill the members of the group, including its leaders, apparently without any resistance. Considering the Nuqṭavī influence at court and among the population that Naṭanzī mentioned earlier in his account, and his claim that many army commanders and nobles were enrolled in the sect, the enthronement of a high-ranking Nuqṭavī, accompanied by all the formal rituals of the transmission of power from Shah ʿAbbās to Yūsifī, seems a dangerous thing to have done.[60] Does Naṭanzī not exaggerate the influence of the Nuqṭavīs and especially the threat they represented to Shah ʿAbbās's rule in order to justify their persecution, the real motivation of which could have been different?

Jalāl al-Dīn Munajjim Yazdī (d. 1028/1618), author of the *Tārīkh-i ʿAbbāsī* which was probably completed in 1020–21/1611–12, was directly involved in the Nuqṭavī episode (he was Shah ʿAbbās's court astrologer and it was he who suggested the three-day enthronement of Yūsifī the quiver-maker). His hostile stance towards the Nuqṭavīs could have been fostered by occultist rivalry and competition for influence over Shah ʿAbbās, since the Nuqṭavī theories, especially those concerning the advent of the new cycle, were also based on astrological predictions.[61] Similarly to Naṭanzī, Yazdī does not mention the name 'Nuqṭavī' in his account, referring to the Nuqṭavīs as 'heretics'

---

[60] Something of this concern transpires in Iskandar Beg Munshī's account: 'One of the functions of a king is to issue orders, and so far this artificial king issued no orders. Now that he knows you are out to kill him, if he decides to forestall you by issuing an order for your execution, the order must inevitably be carried out. You had better be careful for the next three days!' (*History of Shah ʿAbbas the Great*, vol. 2, p. 649). This warning, addressed to the court astrologer Jalāl al-Dīn Munajjim Yazdī, holds true for Shah ʿAbbās himself.

[61] For possible competition over political support between the Ḥurūfīs and other Tīmūrid and Ottoman trends focussed on astrology, alchemy and the science of letters, see Mir-Kasimov, *Words of Power*, p. 432. For the political ambitions of the 'occultist' intellectuals, see numerous publications by Matthew Melvin-Koushki.

or simply 'that lot' (*ān jamʿ*). As in other chronicles, Yazdī recognises that Shah ʿAbbās often visited Dervish Khusraw. He also is keen to emphasise that this interest was based uniquely on Shah ʿAbbās's intention to establish whether or not Dervish Khusraw was a heretic. And should the Nuqṭavīs' heresy be established, adds Yazdī, Shah ʿAbbās should act against them, reduce them to poverty, seize their false books and destroy them, since 'those people' (Dervish Khusraw's followers) are far from reason.[62] Yazdī's account of the reasons that led to the persecution of the Nuqṭavīs corroborates Naṭanzī's narrative but contains minor differences. He also mentions that some Nuqṭavīs divulged the secret teachings of their group to Shah ʿAbbās because they believed that he sincerely adhered to their creed. Moreover, they asked the shah to eliminate his attendants, including the *ʿulamāʾ* and the learned men (*fuḍalāʾ*) because, according to the Nuqṭavīs, 'those people' had completely lost their way. Shah ʿAbbās should not worry about the number of his attendants though, because the Nuqṭavīs would provide him with a force of nearly 50,000 devoted and battle-capable men, an army with which he would be able to conquer the world. An interesting point in Yazdī's narrative is that Shah ʿAbbās did not take immediate action against the Nuqṭavīs because he wanted to obtain their books. At that time, the shah had to leave Qazvīn in order to deal with an insurrection in Luristān. En route, he received a message from Dervish Khusraw containing certain claims. According to Naṭanzī's chronicle, it was the nature of these claims that apparently triggered a radical and secretly prepared punishment for the Nuqṭavīs. Shah ʿAbbās sent a robe of honour and some cash to Dervish Khusraw and simultaneously issued an order to his chief herald, Malak Sulṭān ʿAlī, to arrest the Nuqṭavīs. This is followed by the account of the ominous star and Yūsifī's enthronement.[63]

Iskandar Beg Munshī (d. ca. 1043/1633–34) was Shah ʿAbbās's secretary and could have personally witnessed the events that he describes in his *ʿAlam-ārā-yi ʿAbbāsī*. The second part of this work, which contains the description of the Nuqṭavī episode, was completed

[62] Yazdī, *Tārīkh-i ʿAbbāsī*, p. 121.

[63] Yazdī, *Tārīkh-i ʿAbbāsī*, pp. 121–122.

in 1038/1629, several decades after the events.[64] Munshī provides some additional details about Dervish Khusraw and his link to the Nuqṭavīs. According to Munshī, Dervish Khusraw 'came from a line of well-diggers and refuse collectors'. He became a wandering dervish and, at some point, met a group of Nuqṭavīs and studied their doctrine.[65] Dervish Khusraw was established in Qazvīn by the reign of Shah Ṭahmāsp. In spite of complaints from the Twelver *'ulamā'*, Shah Ṭahmāsp was not able to find anything heretical in Dervish Khusraw's beliefs and left him alone. When ʿAbbās became king, what caught his attention was the influence of Dervish Khusraw and his large following (described as 'luckless people and idlers').[66] Like Naṭanzī, Munshī also suggests that Shah ʿAbbās's interest in Dervish Khusraw was founded exclusively on the desire to establish whether or not Khusraw was spreading heretical views. He notes, however, that Shah ʿAbbās and Dervish Khusraw discussed mystical knowledge, since Shah ʿAbbās 'adopted the manner of speech used by travellers on the mystical way, and unfolded his own personal knowledge of God to him after the fashion of dervishes'.[67] Like Naṭanzī, Munshī reports that Shah ʿAbbās's decision to persecute the Nuqṭavīs was triggered by some 'extravagant claims' made by his followers, Yūsufī and Dervish Kūchek Qalandar, who, due to their 'complete lack of caution', exposed Dervish Khusraw's heresy to the shah. Unlike Naṭanzī, Munshī does not specify what this 'heresy' was, and nor does he mention the Nuqṭavī notion of a new cycle that would be initiated by the advent of a ruler in whom were combined temporal and spiritual powers. He simply notes that the shah decided to persecute them. His account of Yūsifī's enthronement displays no significant difference from Naṭanzī's account. The statement that Dervish Khusraw was eventually executed because wine was found in his residence sounds somewhat dubious, since wine drinking was part of Iranian culture of that time and Shah ʿAbbās himself drank it.[68]

---

64 See Quinn, *Historical Writing*, p. 22.

65 *History of Shah ʿAbbas*, vol. 2, p. 647.

66 Ibid.

67 *History of Shah ʿAbbas the Great*, vol. 2, p. 648.

68 For Shah ʿAbbās's drinking habits as an expression of his adherence to the model of Persian kingship, see Sholeh A. Quinn, *Shah ʿAbbās: The King Who Refashioned Iran* (London, 2015), pp. 77–78.

The rest of Munshī's account deals with the persecution of the Nuqṭavīs elsewhere in Iran, including the learned Nuqṭavī scholar, Mīr Sayyid Aḥmad Kāshī, Dervish Kamāl Iqlīdī and Dervish Biryānī, and is accompanied with a short summary of what the author thought were the core Nuqṭavī beliefs. We will return to Munshī's short outline of the Nuqṭavī presence in India in the conclusion.

The description of the Nuqṭavī episode in the third volume of Faḍlī Beg Khūzānī Iṣfahānī's (d. after 1049/1639) *Afḍal al-tawārīkh* (unfinished), is different from other historical accounts in that, as noted by Melville, Faḍlī Beg downplays Shah ʿAbbās's involvement with the Nuqṭavīs and emphasises the role of the shah's attendants, including the nobles and the *ʿulamāʾ*, in eradicating the Nuqṭavī heresy.[69] Faḍlī Beg spent most of his life in the Caucasus and there is no evidence to suggest that he could have directly witnessed the events in Qazvīn. However, his paternal uncle, ʿInāyat Allāh, surnamed "Ināyat the Bald' (*ʿInāyat-i kal*) served at Shah ʿAbbās's court and, according to Faḍlī Beg's chronicle, took an active part in dealings with the Nuqṭavī group in Qazvīn.[70]

According to Faḍlī Beg, Dervish Khusraw himself and his father had an inclination for learning and both Shah Ṭahmāsp and Shah ʿAbbās appreciated their company.[71] Dervish Khusraw had frequent discussions with Shah ʿAbbās, who eventually became his disciple. Since Dervish Khusraw attracted many followers, Shah ʿAbbās granted him a residence and a daily allowance. When Shah ʿAbbās left for Luristān, a certain Mawlānā Yūsifī, who was one of Dervish Khusraw's trusted vicegerents, promulgated the notion that if Shah ʿAbbās were to remove the people of wrong beliefs (meaning his courtiers and attendants) from his entourage, there would be 40,000 Sufis from among the followers of Maḥmūd [Pasīkhānī?] ready to serve him. ʿInāyat Kal suggested to Shah ʿAbbās that he should speak kindly to Mawlānā Yūsifī in order to obtain the list of those people from him.

[69] Charles Melville, 'New light on the Reign of Shah ʿAbbās: Volume III of the *Afżal al-tavarikh*', in A.J. Newman, ed., *Society and Culture in the Early Modern Middle East: Studies on Iran in the Safavid Period* (Leiden and Boston, 2003), pp. 83–85.

[70] For a more detailed account of Faḍlī Beg Khūzānī Iṣfahānī and his work, see Ghereghlou's introduction to his edition of *Afḍal al-tawārīkh*, vol. 1, pp. xi–lxvi.

[71] Faḍlī Beg Khūzānī Iṣfahānī, *Afḍal al-tawārīkh*, vol. 1, p. 142.

But when the list of Dervish Khusraw's trusted followers reached Shah ʿAbbās, ʿInāyat Kal took hold of it and tore it into pieces, because it contained many names of 'highly placed people and their sons' whose execution would be a disaster. It was ʿInāyat Kal who persuaded Shah ʿAbbās to arrest Mawlānā Yūsifī and other Nuqṭavīs.[72] At a later point, a commission of *ʿulamāʾ*, counting such prominent members as Mīr Dāmād and Shaykh Bahāʾ al-Dīn, interrogated Dervish Khusraw but found nothing contrary to the *sharīʿa* in his discourse. It was only when his books were found and examined that it appeared that he was a Nuqṭavī who practised dissimulation (*taqiyya*) of his true beliefs.[73] Like other authors of historical chronicles, Iṣfahānī does not specify what exactly the heretical doctrine of Dervish Khusraw was. Their heresy thus established, Dervish Khusraw and his followers were executed.

What sense can be made of the historical accounts discussed above? There are certainly some inconsistencies which indicate that the real situation was more complex than the narratives of the chroniclers. The claim that Nuqṭavī doctrine was so unsophisticated that it could only appeal to simple, uneducated people, contrasts with the attraction this doctrine had for Shah ʿAbbās and his high-ranking officers. The alleged Nuqṭavī military threat is not consistent with the fact that a small detachment of 100 soldiers easily dealt with the 'heretics'. This is another argument against any extensive Qizil-bāsh involvement in the Nuqṭavī movement, in which case the Nuqṭavīs could count on Qizil-bāsh military support. Therefore, it is more likely that the Nuqṭavīs sided with Shah ʿAbbās, as part of the monarch's plan to weaken the power of the Qizil-bāsh. It is less likely that Nuqṭavī ideology was used by the Qizil-bāsh as an alternative to their original beliefs which sustained their absolute allegiance to the Safavids. The enthronement of an influential Nuqṭavī leader by Shah ʿAbbās looks like a somewhat opportunistic and over-adventurous enterprise at a time when the Nuqṭavī movement had many followers and supporters in the army, in the state administration and at court. The conflict between the Nuqṭavīs and the *ʿulamāʾ* mentioned in all the chronicles may be a reflection of a struggle for influence over the shah.

---

[72] Faḍlī Beg Khūzānī Iṣfahānī, *Afḍal al-tawārīkh*, vol. 1, pp. 142–143.

[73] Ibid., pp. 143–144.

Finally, it seems quite obvious that Shah ʿAbbās had an authentic interest in Nuqṭavī teachings. Statements concerning his pious motivations – claiming that the only reason for his contact with the Nuqṭavīs was his wish to investigate the integrity of their faith – sound unconvincing, as does the alleged carelessness of the high-ranking Nuqṭavīs who 'divulged' the most secret points of their doctrine to the shah. The *Dabistān-i madhāhib*, a source less hostile to the Nuqṭavīs, claims that Shah ʿAbbās was a Nuqṭavī initiate, and that even his persecution of the Nuqṭavīs was not an expression of hostility, but was carried out in order to purify the movement of its unworthy members.[74] The truth is perhaps somewhere in the middle of the various rationales provided, at one extreme, by historical chronicles hostile to the Nuqṭavīs and, at the other, by sympathetic accounts like *Dabistān-i madhāhib.* It is unlikely that Shah ʿAbbās was a voluntary inquisitor animated by pious zeal and obsessed with rooting out heretics, or that he was a Nuqṭavī hero. It is more likely that, as a pragmatic ruler, he found something in the Nuqṭavī teachings that could serve his interests. Our chronicles hint at such a pragmatic point: the Nuqṭavīs apparently offered Shah ʿAbbās the status of a millennial leader combining spiritual and temporal authority, that is, the status of a charismatic king who was to usher in a new era in the history of mankind. How exactly was such a claim expressed in the Nuqṭavī theoretical framework, how could it be reconciled with Shah ʿAbbās's commitment to Shiʿi Islam, and how could it serve his wish to establish his religious and political authority on a basis independent of both Qizil-bāsh and legalist Twelver Shiʿi ideologies? These questions bring us to the next section where we propose to take a closer look at the relevant points of Nuqṭavī doctrine.

Nuqṭavī doctrinal positions: what the Nuqṭavīs had to offer to Shah ʿAbbās?

As noted, in the doxographical and historical literature hostile to the Nuqṭavīs this movement is described as a heresy *par excellence*, an antinomian group falling outside the fold of Islam, a description that has been perpetuated in modern scholarship that has drawn on these

---

74 *The Dabistān,* vol. 3, p. 23.

hostile accounts. Obviously, if the Nuqṭavīs unambiguously advocated a rupture with Islamic tradition and the inauguration of some sort of new religion, Shah ʿAbbās could not have considered their ideology as a possible source for his legitimacy, which was supposed to be not only Islamic, but specifically Shiʿi, even if not necessarily in complete accord with either Qizil-bāsh or normative Twelver interpretations of Shiʿism. But the evidence from the Nuqṭavī doctrinal works is significantly at odds with the image conveyed by the sources hostile to the movement. As mentioned, an in-depth systematic study of the Nuqṭavī texts is still a desideratum. However, even a cursory reading of the foundational Nuqṭavī texts shows that theirs is a complex and original doctrine with deep roots in Islamic scriptural material and in the intellectual substratum of various Islamic trends, including esoteric Shiʿism and Sufism as well as theological and legal schools of thought. Even if this doctrine did contain some authentically antinomian trends, we will try to demonstrate below that there is ample evidence in Nuqṭavī works supporting their adherence to Islamic law and the continuity of the religious tradition established by the Prophet Muhammad, as well as indicating links with Shiʿi, and more particularly Twelver, doctrinal views. This intellectual substratum, associated with the idea of a charismatic millennial leader – whose advent is determined by a particular configuration of stars, and who is expected to combine political and spiritual power and launch a new era in the history of the mankind – could understandably have attracted Shah ʿAbbās. And this is exactly what the Nuqṭavī group in Qazvīn offered Shah ʿAbbās according to Naṭanzī's account discussed above.

The perceived 'antinomianism' of the Nuqṭavīs might be explained by their understanding of the consecutive stages of the development of prophetic revelation, and more specifically of Qur'anic revelation. According to the Ḥurūfī theory, which was one of the main sources of Nuqṭavī doctrine, the meaning of the Qur'an unfolded in two different and complementary processes, the 'descent' (*tanzīl*) of the literal meaning and the 'return to its [metaphysical] origin' (*ta'wīl*). Faḍl Allāh Astarābādī, the founder of the Ḥurūfī doctrine, never claimed to abrogate the *sharīʿa* or to be a prophet of a new religion, but he may well have regarded himself as a herald of the era of *ta'wīl*, the era of spiritual hermeneutics leading to the apocalyptic disclosure of the innermost meaning of the Qur'an and of all preceding prophetic revelations. Along the same lines, Maḥmūd Pasīkhānī, the founder of the Nuqṭavī tradition and a former disciple of Faḍl Allāh Astarābādī, may well have believed that his mission was to initiate the last stage of *ta'wīl*. Such an evolution is in fact suggested by the very names of these groups and is also reflected in the diagram from Pasīkhānī's *Kitāb-i mīzān* (see fig. 7.1). According to the Ḥurūfīs, the disjointed letters (*ḥurūf*) are the instrument of the ultimate *ta'wīl* and the key to the metaphysical meanings of the Qur'an and to the metaphysical dimension of Islamic law, while the dot (*nuqṭa*) represents the same meanings but in a concentrated, undifferentiated form that is beyond the grasp of the human mind. It is possible that Pasīkhānī took one step further along that line and claimed to possess secret knowledge of that ultimate dot that leads to the deepest level of the hermeneutical process. While this would not involve any kind of rupture with Islam or with its religious law, it could involve a claim that new hermeneutical knowledge would lead to a different, deeper understanding of the Islamic scriptural sources and of the law based on them.

The evidence from Nuqṭavī texts would appear to confirm the idea that Maḥmūd Pasīkhānī perceived his mission as an expansion of the religious tradition introduced by the Prophet Muhammad and continued, according to Shi'i beliefs, through the line of the Shi'i imams. More precisely, like his former master Faḍl Allāh Astarābādī, Pasıkhānī arguably viewed his doctrine as an extension of the Shi'i idea of a hermeneutical cycle following the revelation (*tanzīl*) of the divine Word and of the divine Law by the Prophet and led by the imams endowed with special knowledge by virtue of their close relationship or 'friendship' (*walāya*) with God.[75] The mission of the imams does not include a new revelation, but the disclosure of the true meanings of the already existing one. In this perspective, both Ḥurūfīs and Nuqṭavīs may be qualified as 'broader Shi'i' or 'supra-Shi'i' movements in the sense discussed above. Let us now turn to the textual evidence that could support this view.

---

[75] This idea of an extension of the Shi'i idea of the imamate is arguably present already in Faḍl Allāh Astarābādī's work; see Orkhan Mir-Kasimov, 'Ummīs versus Imāms in Ḥurūfī Prophetology: An Attempt at a Sunni/Shī'ī Synthesis?', in O. Mir-Kasimov, ed., *Unity in Diversity: Mysticism, Messianism and the Construction of Religious Authority in Islam* (Boston and Leiden, 2013), pp. 221–246.

One of the main arguments cited in the scholarly literature as a proof of the Nuqṭavī rupture with Islam is the distinction between the Arab and the "Ajamī' cycles frequently mentioned in Nuqṭavī texts. We will explain in the following paragraphs the meaning of the term "Ajamī' in the context of Pasīkhānī's work and why we think it cannot be unequivocally translated as 'Persian'. At this point, let us note that the fact that the ʿAjamī cycle follows the Arab cycle does not necessarily mean that Islam, and the Arabic Qur'an are replaced by a new, ʿAjamī religion and a new revelation. The finality of Muhammad's prophetic dispensation, of the Qur'an, of the customs and religious law established by him, is stated rather explicitly in Pasīkhānī's *Kitāb-i mīzān*:

> Any [claim to] have a prophetic mission or to compose a [sacred] book after the seal of the prophets [has to be] obliterated and abolished. [Such a claim] is an innovation invented by a [heretical] innovator. It is an act of highway robbery which is against the order and the word of [the Prophet] Muhammad. The person who claims such a mission treats [the Prophet] Muhammad as a liar... And whoever claims to introduce new laws, customs and regulations after him is, like the previous person, an innovator, a highway robber and a dissident, [such a person] is discordant with the language of Muhammad... Whoever does not know that Muhammad, peace be upon him, is water, should know that *sharīʿat* means 'watering place,' [the place] where the animals can reach the source of water. That is to say, whoever reaches the *sharīʿat* reaches the source of the water of life, which alludes to [the person of] Muhammad.[76]

[76] *Kitāb-i mīzān*, ms. Malik library, Tehran, n. 6226, f. 52 a–b.: *baʿd az khātim-i rusul har ke risālatī rā inshā kunad yā kitābī rā taṣnīf kunad fi'l-jumla har inshā'ī ke bar sabīl-i risālat kitābat karde āyad ān inshā va risālat mansūkh va mundaris buwad... bal bidʿatī bāshad ke mubtadiʿyi badīʿ āvarde bāshad bal rahzanī bāshad ke be-khilāf-i silk va qawl-i Muḥammad ẓāhir āmade bashad va muṣannif-i īn risālat shakhsī bāshad ke lisān-i Muḥammad rā be-takdhīb dāshte bāshad... va har ke baʿd az sunan-i ū va baʿd az nahj va rasm-i ū rasmī va sunnatī rā ẓāhir kunad yā qāʿide-yi baʿd az qavāʿid-i ū biyāvarad īn shakhṣ nīz mithl-i shakhṣ-i avval mubtadiʿ va rahzan va mukhālif āmade bāshad va ham dar īn ẓuhūr nīz khilāf-i lisān-i Muḥammad karde bāshad... har ke nadānad ke Muḥammad ṣlm āb ast bāyad be-dānad ke har che sharīʿat be-maʿnā-yi jāyist ke ḥayvānāt bad-ānjā be-chashma-yi āb vurūd kunand va be-āb be-rasand tā har ke be-sharīʿat dar-āyad be-chashma-yi āb-i ḥayvān ke kināyat az Muḥammad ast be-rasad.*

Also, continuity with the prophetic mission of Muhammad and with the 'Arab cycle' is clearly emphasised in Pasīkhānī's works. Pasīkhānī described himself as the combined manifestation of Muhammad and ʿAlī b. Abī Ṭālib, who were a single light in pre-eternity and are focused again as a single power in the person of Maḥmūd Pasīkhānī.[77] Significantly, in Shiʿi thought, these figures are associated respectively with revelation (*tanzīl*) and its spiritual hermeneutics (*taʾwīl*). Maḥmūd Pasīkhānī's major works, and especially *Kitāb-i mīzān*, contain abundant citations of, and comments upon, Qurʾanic passages and various *ḥadīths*. Thus, Pasīkhānī's ʿAjamī cycle does not appear as a totally new prophetic dispensation representing a 'rupture' with Islam, with the revelation of Muhammad or with anything Arab.[78] It is, on the contrary, described as developing from and being the consequence of the preceding Arab cycle. The ʿAjamī cycle complements the cycle of Muhammad just as day complements night.[79] The number 28, which characterises the 'Arab' cycle (the number of the lunar phases and that of the letters of the Arabic alphabet), in conjunction with the number 12 which governs the ʿAjamī cycle (the number of the constellations of the Zodiac associated with Sun, and the number of dots under or over the four Persian letters added to the Arabic alphabet (*pe, che, zhe* and the *gāf*)),[80] produces 40, which is the number of temporal perfection and completion.[81] ʿ*Ajam* is from the Arab descent (ʿ*itrat*), and the dot

[77] *Kitāb-i mīzān*, ff. 54b–55a. For the description of Muhammad and ʿAlī as a single light in Islamic, and more specifically Shiʿi literature, see Uri Rubin, 'Pre-existence and Light: Aspects of the Concept of *Nūr Muḥammad*', *Israel Oriental Studies*, 5 (1975), pp. 62–119. In f. 15a Maḥmūd Pasīkhānī is described as the meeting point of prophethood (*nubuwwa*, associated with Muhammad) and sainthood (*walāya*, associated with ʿAlī).

[78] However, in the *Kitāb-i mīzān*, f. 12a, Maḥmūd Pasīkhānī's *Mafātīḥ* is included among the prophetic books.

[79] Kiyā, *Nuqṭaviyān yā pāsīkhāniyān*, p. 76.

[80] The Persian letters *pe, che* and *zhe* are written with three diacritic points each, and the line over the Persian letter *gāf* is interchangeable with three dots. Therefore, the dots associated with these four Persian letters add up to twelve.

[81] Kiyā, *Nuqṭaviyān yā pāsīkhāniyān*, p. 85. The idea that the number 40 represents perfect temporal duration is also expressed in the *Jāvidān-nāma* of Faḍl Allāh Astarābādī. See Mir-Kasimov, *Words of Power*, pp. 156–157.

(*nuqṭa*) is from the descent of letter (*ḥarf*). Maḥmūd is from the descendance of Muhammad.[82] Muhammad is the letter and Maḥmud the dot, and everything is composed of letters and dots.[83]

One of the reasons for the misunderstanding and misinterpretation of the Nuqṭavī relationship between the Arab and ʿAjamī cycles is the limiting of the meaning of the word *ʿajamī* to 'Persian' or 'Iranian', which led to far-fetched theories developed in modern scholarship on the Nuqṭavīs as the flag-bearers of Persian nationalism and of Persian/Arab antagonism.[84] While it is true that in the context of Ḥurūfī and the Nuqṭavī hermeneutical theories some degree of superiority is implicitly ascribed to the Persian alphabet, regarded as an extension of the Arabic alphabet with four added letters, this superiority is not accompanied by any ideological and still less nationalistic discourse. Furthermore, the word "*ajamī*" has a broader meaning in Nuqṭavī doctrinal works. In the *Kitāb-i mīzān*, ʿAjam is defined as the place that contains the seeds of every existing thing, and these seeds are likened to the diacritical dots with which the letters are provided. The dots represent the concentrated, undifferentiated potentialities of existents, the seeds from which the external forms of letters, objects and beings develop.[85] This interpretation of the dot (*nuqṭa*) is in line with Ḥurūfī thought.[86]

> *ʿAjam* in Arabic means 'seed', . . . and *ḥarf muʿjam* means 'a letter provided with a seed'. Therefore, the seed of every existing thing is contained in *ʿajam*, and the dot, which is the self of Maḥmūd, indicates [*ʿajam*] as well. Whoever does not reach *ʿajam* does not

82 Kiyā, *Nuqṭaviyān yā pāsīkhāniyān*, p. 91.

83 Ibid., p. 121. This relationship between the letter and the dot is also reflected in the diagram in fig. 7.1.

84 See, for example, Abbas Amanat, 'The Nuqṭawī Movement', pp. 282 ff.

85 The derivatives from the Arabic root *ʿJM* include 'seed' and 'diacritical dot'. Cf. Hans Wehr, *A Dictionary of Modern Written Arabic* (3rd ed., Beirut and London, 1980), p. 694: "*Ajam*: stone, kernel, seed; *Muʿjam:* dotted, provided with diacritical point (letter).'

86 See Mir-Kasimov, *Words of Power*, pp. 70 ff. and Glossary, pp. 454–455.

reach the seed, and whoever does not reach the seed cannot fully fulfil [the purpose of] his/her life.[87]

ʿAjam thus refers to the realisation of the innermost potentialities, the 'seeds' of existing things. It is the place of the dot which, in Ḥurūfi and in Nuqṭavī doctrines symbolises the highest, albeit undifferentiated, knowledge of divine metaphysical truths, the source of all possible realisations in the universe. As such, the dot is associated with the figure of ʿAlī b. Abī Ṭālib and with spiritual hermeneutics (*ta'wīl*).[88] Therefore, the distinction between the Arab and the ʿAjamī cycles in Pasīkhānī's works reflects neither the antagonism between the 'old' and 'new' religious dispensations, nor between the Arabs and the Persians, but the mutual complementarity of *tanzīl* and *ta'wīl*. In Shiʿi thought, *ta'wīl* is closely associated with *walāya*, the divine 'friendship' bestowed on the chosen ones, the imams. Hermeneutical knowledge is received by divine election only, which means that *ta'wīl* is impossible without *walāya*. The fact that elsewhere in the *Kitāb-i mīzān*, *ʿajam* is defined as the 'land of the *walāya*' could be an additional indication of the Shiʿi inspiration of Maḥmūd Pasīkhānī which, as we shall see, is also corroborated by other evidence from Nuqṭavī works.[89]

It is also possible that Pasīkhānī's idea of *ʿajam* as place where the 'seeds' of things are revealed is a reflection of Ibn ʿArabī's theory of the 'seal of sainthood,' which was influential among post-Mongol

[87] *Kitāb-i mīzān*, f. 59b: *dar kalam har che ʿajam ast be-muṣṭaliḥ-i ʿarab dāna ast ke be-pārsī tukhm-i mavīz va ḥarf muʿjam yaʿnī ḥarf-i dāna-dār aʿnā ḥarf-i tukhm-dār tā muḥaqqiq gardad ke tukhm-i kull va kuliyyāt be-juz-i ʿajam natavānad būd ke nuqṭa ishārat be-dūst ke nafs-i Maḥmūd khūd ūst tā har ke be-ʿajam narasad be-tukhm narasīda bāshad va har ke be-tukhm narasīda bāshad ū barkhūrdār-i ʿumr-i khūd be-hīch vajh nashuda bāshad.*

[88] See Mir-Kasimov, *Words of Power*, pp. 70 ff. The famous *ḥadīth* where ʿAlī is described as the dot under the letter *bā'* of the *bismi'l-Lāhi al-raḥmān al-raḥīm* ('In the name of God, the Beneficent, the Merciful', the opening formula of the Qur'an), the dot that contains all the meanings of the Qur'anic text, is cited in this context in the Ḥurūfi and Nuqṭavī texts. For references for this *ḥadīth*, see *Words of Power*, p. 466.

[89] *Kitāb-i mīzān*, f. 10b.

mystico-messianic movements.[90] If this is the case, this could also clarify the nature of Pasīkhānī's claim. According to Ibn ʿArabī, the seal of Muhammadan sainthood was manifested at Muhammad's time, while the seal of general sainthood was Jesus. Both seals introduced new eras. Elmore's observation that 'On the strength of the data in the *ʿAnqāʾ* it would be possible to construe Ibn al-ʿArabī's theory of the seals of prophecy/sainthood as a binary system alternating between the manifestation of Mosaic/Muhammadan (Semitic) *nubūʾa* and Christic/Akbarian (*aʿjamī* = "Aryan") *wilāya*'[91] seems perfectly applicable to Maḥmūd Pasīkhānī's works. Ibn ʿArabī also stated that 'The one who is worthy [of being the seal of sainthood] is a man... who is non-Arab (*ʿajamī*)', and that 'He is from a foreign people, not an Arab'.[92] And Jesus, an important, if not the key figure, in Islamic eschatological lore, and the seal of general sainthood according to Ibn ʿArabī, was obviously non-Arab, that is to say, an *ʿAjamī*. Pasīkhānī's familiarity with Ibn ʿArabī's theory of seals is corroborated by his use of expressions such as 'seal of the prophecy' (*khātam-i nubuwwa*) and 'seal of the sainthood' (*khātam-i walāyat*).[93]

As mentioned, Shah ʿAbbās was deeply engaged with Twelver Shiʿism, in its Qizil-bāsh form on the one side and its scholarly and legalist form, on the other. Only if he had wanted to make a revolutionary move could he have considered adhering to any new ideology that was completely disconnected from the fundamental tenets of Shiʿi Islam. We have already discussed some indications of Shiʿi influence on Nuqṭavī thought. Let us now turn to some more tangible evidence that suggests links between the Nuqṭavī and Twelver Shiʿi doctrines.

---

[90] For Ibn ʿArabī's theory of the seals of prophethood and sainthood, see Michel Chodkiewicz, *Le sceau des saints : prophétie et sainteté dans la doctrine d'Ibn Arabî* (Paris, 1986), and Gerald T. Elmore, *Islamic Sainthood in the Fullness of Time: Ibn al-ʿArabī's Book of the Fabulous Gryphon* (Leiden, Boston and Cologne, 1999). For an example of the interpretation of this theory in post-Mongol mystico-messianic milieus, see Muḥammad Nūrbakhsh, *Risālat al-hudā*, ed. Shahzad Bashir, *RSO*, 75 (2001), p. 107.

[91] Gerald T. Elmore, 'The "Millennial" Motif in Ibn al-ʿArabī's "Book of the Fabulous Gryphon"', *Journal of Religion*, 81 (2001), p. 431.

[92] See Gerald T. Elmore, 'The "Millennial" Motif', pp. 417, 418, with reference to Ibn ʿArabī's *al-Jawāb al-mustaqīm* and his *ʿAnqāʾ mughrib*, respectively.

[93] *Kitāb-i mīzān*, ff. 14b–15a.

The number 12 is prominent in Nuqṭavī works. It is associated with the *ʿajamī* cycle which, as we have seen, is that of *walāya.* More importantly, it is explicitly associated with the Twelfth imam of the Twelver Shiʿis. According to the *Kitāb-i mīzān,* there are 16 imams in the era of Maḥmūd Pasīkhānī, twelve of whom are those of the era of Muhammad, which is a clear allusion to the imams of the Twelver branch.[94] According to the Nuqṭavī work published by Kiyā, the cycle of Muhammad is associated with the number 28 and the Moon with its 28 phases, while the *ʿajamī* cycle of Maḥmūd is associated with the number 12 and with the Sun, which is the master of the 12 constellations of the Zodiac. The Twelfth imam is an allusion to this Sun.[95]

The figure of ʿAlī plays an important role in Nuqṭavī thought. The symbolism attributed to ʿAlī in Nuqṭavī texts echoes some Shiʿi motifs but is also embedded in the Ḥurūfī/Nuqṭavī context. ʿAlī is an intermediary between Muhammad's age of the letter (*ḥarf*) and the *ʿajamī* age of the dot (*nuqṭa*): 'That [morning] star is an allusion to ʿAlī, because [it is he who], after the setting of the full moon of Muhammad, announces the transition from the era of the letter, which is an allusion to the era of Muhammad, to [the era of the] dot, which is an allusion to the appearance of Maḥmūd.'[96] As in the Ḥurūfī works, ʿAlī's link with the dot is highlighted by the famous *ḥadīth* where ʿAlī states that he is the diacritical dot under the letter *bāʾ* of the basmala

[94] *Kitāb-i mīzān,* f. 51b. Thus, the era of Maḥmūd continues in the line of the 12 imams, which also corroborates the use of the term 'supra-Shiʿi' that we proposed earlier to describe the movements such as the Nuqṭavīs.

[95] Kiyā, *Nuqṭaviyān yā pāsīkhāniyān,* pp. 77, 81. Significantly, these statements are supported by references to the Qurʾanic verses.

[96] Kiyā, *Nuqṭaviyān yā pāsīkhāniyān,* p. 83: *ān sitāra-yi madhkūr kināyat az ʿAlī ast ke baʿd az ghurūb-i badr-i Muḥammadī khabar dād ke ʿahd-i ḥarf ke kināyat az ʿahd-i Muḥammad ast be-nuqṭa ke kināyat az ẓuhūr-i Maḥmūd ast badal shud.* As mentioned, this transition is most likely one from one hermeneutical stage to another, from the *tanzīl* to the consecutive stages of the *taʾwīl,* not from one prophetic dispensation to a new one. The association of Muhammad with the 'letter' echoes the Ḥurūfī idea that Muhammad was the only prophet to whom the meanings of the disjointed letters were revealed, which is reflected in the isolated letters that appear at the beginning of some Qurʾanic suras (*al-ḥurūf al-muqaṭṭaʿa*). A broader perspective of the hermeneutical transition from the more complex to the simpler elements of the language (speech – word – letter – dot) is represented in Fig. 7.1.

which contains all the meanings of the Qur'an.[97] ʿAlī's approach to the religious rituals, accomplished not out of weakness (*ʿajz*) and submission, but as an act of generosity (*karāmat*) and manliness (*muruwwat, javānmardī*), exemplifies the Shiʿi attitude.[98] ʿAlī is the seal of sainthood (*khātam-i walāyat*).[99]

Its universalism was another aspect of Nuqṭavī doctrine that may have appealed to Shah ʿAbbās and could be effectively used to attenuate frictions between various Islamic groups, especially between the Sunnis and the Shiʿis, and perhaps even to render his rule more attractive to religious minorities such as the Jews and the Christians. As in Ḥurūfī thought, the universalist dimension of the Nuqṭavī doctrine is directly linked to its claim to possess the keys to the ultimate hermeneutics (*ta'wīl*) leading to the direct perception of universal metaphysical truths which constitute the innermost meanings of the Qur'an and of all other prophetic books. This idea is expressed in the rectangular diagram found on f. 3b of the manuscript of the *Kitāb-i mīzān*.[100]

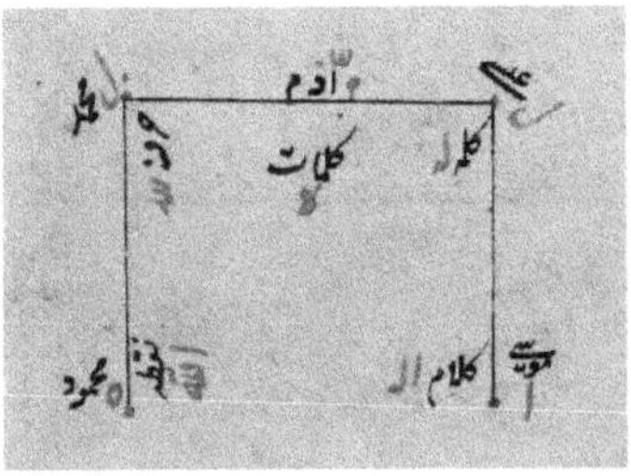

Figure 7.1. Rectangular Diagram (Maḥmūd Pasīkhānī, *Kitāb-i mīzān*, ms. Malek National Library and Museum Institution n. 6226, undated, f. 3b).

[97] Kiyā, *Nuqṭaviyān yā pāsīkhāniyān*, p. 83, see also n. 89.

[98] Kiyā, *Nuqṭaviyān yā pāsīkhāniyān*, pp. 119–120.

[99] *Kitāb-i mīzān*, f. 15a. This corresponds to the interpretation of Ibn ʿArabī's idea of the 'seal of the saints' by the Shiʿi thinkers of the School of Bahrain, such as ʿAlī b. Sulaymān (d. ca. 672/1273) and Maytham al-Baḥrānī (d. 689/1290), followed by the Iranian scholar Ḥaydar Āmulī (d. after 787/1385). See references in n. 37.

[100] Image courtesy of the Malek National Library and Museum Institution in Tehran. My thanks to Ms Marjan Afsharian and Mr Shahram Khodaverdian for helping me to obtain a high resolution copy of this image and for securing permission to reproduce it from the Malek Library.

The text surrounding the diagram (ff. 2b–3b) (fig. 7.1) explains that it represents the divine balance (*mīzān-i Allāh*), which encompasses every existent thing. Every letter of the name *Allāh,* including the *tashdīd* over the second *lām*, is associated with a prophet and with an element of the divine language. Thus Adam is associated with the *tashdīd* and with 'words' (*kalimāt*), Moses is associated with the *alif* and with speech (*kalām*), Jesus is associated with the *lām* and with the Word (*kalima*), Muhammad is associated with the *lām* and with 'letter' (*ḥarf*), and Maḥmūd is associated with the *hāʾ* and with the 'dot' (*nuqṭa*). Neither the order of the names nor the linguistic elements attributed to them are discussed in the text. But in the Ḥurūfī texts, Adam's knowledge of the 'words' is inspired by the Qurʾanic episode where God teaches to Adam the 'names of all things' (Q. 2:31); the attribution of 'speech' to Moses is based on the Qurʾanic episodes where Moses hears divine speech (on the Mount [Sinai] and from the Burning Bush); Jesus's identification with the Word of God is explicitly Qurʾanic (4:171); and Muhammad's 'lettrism' is an allusion to the famous disjointed letters of the Qurʾan (*al-ḥurūf al-muqaṭṭaʿa*). Maḥmūd Pasīkhānī's identification with the dot is, of course, his own idea.

Also with reference to the Ḥurūfī context, it is possible to offer an explanation for the order of the linguistic entities and related prophets. From right to left in the diagram, linguistic entities progress from complex to simple: the sum of all words, speech, word, letter, dot. This is also a progression from the specific to the universal: words can produce all possible speech, letters can produce all possible words, and dots can produce all possible letters, in all possible languages. A knowledge of the metaphysical meanings of the simpler linguistic units is the key to the interpretation of the more complex entities. Maḥmūd takes this schema one step further than his master, Faḍl Allāh Astarābādī, claiming the knowledge of the ontological dot, which is the source of all letters. The choice of prophets on the diagram indicates Pasīkhānī's ecumenical ambitions. Moses represents the Jews, Jesus represents the Christians and Muhammad represents the Muslims. By positioning himself as the most universal and the simplest linguistic element (the dot, of which the letters, words and larger linguistic entities of all languages are composed), Maḥmūd Pasīkhānī expresses the idea that he presides over the final stage of the hermeneutical process at which confessional divisions will be overcome and the followers of all religions will be brought together.

This idea of universality obtained at the highest point of the hermeneutical process is also expressed in the concept of a universal Nuqṭavī language (*lisān-i Nuqṭavī*):[101]

> The distinctive sign of Maḥmūd is that he speaks all the languages of the first and of the last. The condition of his speech is such that he speaks all these languages in one language of oneness which is the Nuqṭavī language. [This Nuqṭavī language] cannot be dual. For example, he [Maḥmūd] speaks the language of Moses to the Jews, but in the Nuqṭavī language; he speaks the language of Jesus to the Christians, but in the Nuqṭavī language, and he speaks the language of Muhammad to the Muslims, but in the Nuqṭavī language . . . All this is the language of the oneness which is the Nuqṭavī language . . . For every soul, it is the language of [this individual] soul. For the genies it is the language of genies, and for humans, it is the language of human beings. For every person, it is the language of [this] person. But for everything it is the language of oneness, the Nuqṭavī language that expresses the oneness: 'God hath given us speech, (He) Who giveth speech to everything' [Q. 41:21].[102]

The Nuqṭavī doctrinal positions analysed above suggest that the Nuqṭavī texts did not advocate any radical rupture with Islam or

---

[101] Here Pasīkhānī implicitly uses the idea of a universal language underlying all existing human languages and, in fact, all the sounds in the universe, produced either by inanimate objects, plants or animals, which was developed in the works of Faḍl Allāh Astarābādī. In Astarābādī's works, the return to this universal language, which is the direct and immediate expression of the metaphysical truths, is obtained at the end of the hermeneutical process. The Qurʾanic verse Q. 41:21 is used by Pasīkhānī in the passage cited below, which reports the speech of the skin of human beings in the Hereafter, to support the idea that everything is endowed with speech, figures prominently in the relevant passages of the *Jāvīdān-nāma* of Faḍl Allāh Astarābādī. For Astarābādī's theory of universal language see Mir-Kasimov, *Words of Power, passim.*

[102] *Kitāb-i mīzān*, ff. 21a–b.: *Har che ʿalāmat-i Maḥmūd ast dar ẓuhūr-i ānast ke be-jumla alsina-yi awalīn va ākhirīn khūd nāṭiq gardad va sharṭ-i nuṭq-i ū ān bāshad ke bedān jumla zabān ke ū nāṭiq āmade bāshad be-hamān yak lisān-i vāḥid nāṭiq āmade bāshad ke lisān-i nuqṭavī ast ke dū būdan-i ū muḥāl ast mithl-i ānke ū-rā bā yahūdī lisān-i Mūsā bāshad [valī] be-zabān-i nuqṭavī va bā naṣrānī lisān-i ʿIsā bāshad valī be-lisān-i nuqṭavī va bā musulmān lisān-i Muḥammad bāshad valī be-zabān-i nuqṭavī. . . valī jumla be-lisān-i vāḥid bāshad ke lisān-i nuqṭavī ast. . . va ū-rā bā kull-i nafs lisān-i kull-i nafs bāshad va bā jinn va ins lisān-i jinn va ins bāshad va bā kull shakhṣ lisān-i kull-i shakhṣ bāshad valī bā jumla lisān-i vāḥid dāshte bāshad ke lisān-i nuqṭavī ast be-iẓhār-i vāḥidī anṭaqanā Allāh alladhī anṭaqa kulla shay' . . .*

Islamic law. Nuqṭavī doctrine had some features that brought it close to Shiʿi and, more specifically, Twelver Shiʿi tenets. These features include recognition of the prominent role of ʿAlī as the harbinger of the ultimate hermeneutical cycle, the seal of sainthood and the upholder of the inner meaning of the external manifestations of the religion established by the Prophet Muhammad, as well as recognition of the Twelve imams. On the other hand, the idea that the doctrine of Maḥmūd Pasīkhānī is the extension and culmination of the hermeneutical mission of the Twelve imams, seems to corroborate the suggested description of the Nuqṭavīs as a 'broader Shiʿi' or 'supra-Shiʿi' movement. These features presented Shah ʿAbbās with the possibility of adopting the image of a Muslim ruler who adhered to the values of Twelver Shiʿism without any particular commitment to either its Qizil-bāsh or its theologico-jurisprudential interpretations.

In addition, both Ḥurūfī and Nuqṭavī doctrines promoted the idea of a leader possessing supreme religious authority based on the knowledge of the most fundamental hermeneutical principles (knowledge of the metaphysical meanings of the separate letters in Ḥurūfism and knowledge of the metaphysical meaning of the primordial dot in Nuqṭavī thought). In order effectively to open the new hermeneutical era associated with this knowledge, both the Ḥurūfīs and the Nuqṭavīs sought political support.[103] Shah ʿAbbās had the opportunity to explore this source of religious authority as a basis for the legitimisation of his temporal power, thus becoming independent of the uncomfortable paradigms of legitimacy offered by the Qizil-bāsh (who wanted the shah to remain their spiritual leader) or by the Twelver scholars (for whom the ultimate political authority belonged to the Hidden imam and therefore Safavid legitimacy was questionable). The universalist scope of Nuqṭavism combined with the status of a millennial charismatic king ushering in a new era could have, potentially, provided Shah ʿAbbās with a remarkable degree of authority in both the religious and the political spheres.

From the historical accounts, it seems that Shah ʿAbbās seriously considered this possibility but at some point decided to reject it. We can only speculate about the reasons that lay behind his decision, and

---

[103] For the Ḥurūfī political involvement see Mir-Kasimov, *Words of Power*, pp. 15 ff.

about what shape the history of the Safavid dynasty and of Iran might have taken had he decided to further experiment with Nuqṭavī ideas. But we do know that Shah ʿAbbās's decision to abandon the Nuqṭavīs and to support the Twelver Shiʿi clergy led to the Safavids' progressive loss of religious and then also of political authority to the clergy.[104] We also know that an experiment very close to that abandoned by Shah ʿAbbās was carried out by his contemporary, the Mughal emperor, Akbar. We will now briefly turn to Akbar's religious experimentation, which resulted in the successful application of principles close to, and probably directly inspired by, Nuqṭavī ideals.

Conclusion: Shah Akbar and the scenario of Nuqṭavī political success

That Safavid/Nuqṭavī relationships concerned the fundamental issue of power and legitimacy is perhaps indirectly confirmed by the positive turn that Nuqṭavī relations with rulers took in a different cultural, religious and political context, namely, in Mughal India.

It is interesting that the most prominent stage of Nuqṭavī political activity is contemporaneous with the reigns of two key figures of Safavid and Mughal state building, that is, Shah ʿAbbās I (r. 995–1038/1587–1629) and the Emperor Akbar (r. 963–1014/1556–1605). It is not surprising that the Nuqṭavī model of a universal millenarian charismatic ruler was one of great interest at a time when the rulers of these two Muslim empires were reflecting upon and developing the foundations of their religious and political legitimacy, a time replete in millenarian references with the completion of the first one thousand years of Islam.

We have seen how Shah ʿAbbās I considered and eventually rejected the Nuqṭavī model. He chose to support instead the Twelver Shiʿi scholars who, in the context of Safavid Iran, had several strong points in their favour in contrast to the Nuqṭavīs. First, the Twelver scholars were legal experts, they were able to introduce and guarantee the working of religious law and the administration of the Safavid state. This was an extremely important point in a state with a majority

104 The Shiʿi clergy survived the downfall of the Safavid dynasty, consolidated their power under the Qājārs (1789–1925) and, in the late 20th century, claimed political power in the Iranian revolution of 1979.

Muslim population. Second, the implementation of a form of juristic Islam would bring the Safavids, who emerged from the 'unruly' mystico-messianic milieux, into the fold of 'orthodox' Islam, thus creating bridges with their neighbours, in particular with the Sunni Ottomans. But this choice came at a price: the Safavid monarchs had to delegate a significant part of their religious authority to the jurists and scholars, which resulted in the laying down of the foundations of a powerful clergy which today holds the reins of power in Iran.

The situation in Mughal India was very different. Normative juristic Islam was arguably not the most effective tool of administration in the multi-ethnic and multi-religious context of the Indian subcontinent where Muslims constituted only a small minority. In contradistinction, a universalist doctrine founding the authority of a messianic millennial leader, such as that proposed by the Nuqṭavīs, was very much in line with the political philosophy of Akbar and was likely to find some resonance with the official ideology of the Mughal state in India.

Instead of devolving his religious authority to the clergy, Akbar emphasised his own spiritual authority, thus dominating the clergy. With the simultaneous elaboration of the doctrine of 'universal peace' (*ṣulḥ-i kull*), which advocated the tolerance of all religions based on their common inner truth, Akbar assumed the status of a universal spiritual and political leader. There is some evidence that the Nuqṭavīs and similar groups, some of which, such as the Ādhar Kayvānīs, were very probably influenced by the Nuqṭavīs, were part of the inner circles of Akbar and his adviser, Abu'l-Faḍl ʿAllāmī (d. 1011/1602). These groups took an active part in the construction of Akbar's image as a universal charismatic ruler.[105]

The Nuqṭavīs were apparently active at the court of Akbar even before Shah ʿAbbās came to the throne. Iskandar Beg Munshī notes that both Abu'l-Faḍl ʿAllāmī and Akbar had converted to Nuqṭavī beliefs.[106] As

[105] On possible Nuqṭavī influence on the Ādhar Kayvānīs, an Iranian religious group which thrived in India and was founded by Ādhar Kayvān (d. 1027/1618), see Daniel J. Sheffield, 'The Language of Heaven in Safavid Iran: Speech and Cosmology in the Thought of Āḏar Kayvān and His Followers', in Alireza Korangy and Daniel J. Sheffield, ed., *No Tapping around Philology: A Festschrift in Honor of Wheeler McIntosh Thackston Jr.'s 70th Birthday* (Wiesbaden, 2014), pp. 161–183.

[106] *History of Shah ʿAbbas the Great*, vol. 2, p. 650.

mentioned, there is evidence that Akbar corresponded with Mīr Aḥmad Kāshī, a well-known Nuqṭavī from Kāshān, and that he was aware of the existence of, and entertained friendly relationships with, the Nuqṭavī group in Qazvīn led by Dervish Khusraw.[107] Akbar's letter to Kāshī also suggests that Akbar used the widespread Nuqṭavī network to recruit followers in Iran. Further evidence concerning relationships between the Mughal rulers and the Nuqṭavīs is reported in *Muntakhab al-tawārīkh* of ʿAbd al-Qādir Bada'ūnī (d. ca. 1024/1615). Bada'ūnī was a scholar and historian at the court of Akbar known for his dislike of the Nuqṭavīs and of the religious experimentation of Akbar. Badā'ūnī describes the success of a prominent Nuqṭavī intellectual, Sharīf Āmulī, at the court of Akbar and Āmulī's contribution to the shaping of Akbar's messianic image.[108] Nuqṭavī ideas, combined with the doctrines of Ibn ʿArabī and apparently with some Indian, and more particularly Buddhist, substratum, were developed and promulgated in India in the works of intellectuals such as the *Risāla-yi durr-i yatīm* of Muḥammad b. Maḥmūd Dihdār Shīrāzī (d. 1016/1607).[109]

According to Moin, the partnership between Akbar and the Nuqṭavīs was 'built upon a shared adoration of pre-Islamic Persianate symbols.'[110] However, as we have seen, the Nuqṭavī works do not seem to display any specific focus on pre-Islamic Persianate symbols. What they do display, in continuation of Ḥurūfī doctrines, is a strong theoretical support for the image of a charismatic millennial leader initiating a new era in the history of Islam and in the history of mankind, and that this new era will be informed by a universalist ethos grounded in Islamic hermeneutical and eschatological beliefs. The use of this kind of theory as a possible ideology and source of legitimacy was seriously considered by the key figures of both the Safavid and Mughal dynasties. Rejected in Iran, this ideology realised at least a part of its political potential in India by feeding into intellectual milieus that supported Akbar's religious reforms.

---

107 See n. 10.

108 Moin, *The Millennial Sovereign*, pp. 165–166; the relevant passage is cited in Kiyā, *Nuqṭaviyān yā pāsīkhāniyān*, pp. 11–12, 32–35.

109 See n. 11.

110 Moin, *The Millennial Sovereign*, p. 165.

PART THREE

ḤADĪTH AND *FIQH*

8

Majlisī the Second, Ambiguous Architect of the Shiʿi Revival in Safavid Iran

Mohammad Ali Amir-Moezzi

Muḥammad Bāqir al-Majlisī (d. 1110/1699), also known as Majlisī the Second, one of the most important historical figures of Safavid Iran, needs no introduction, although a number of the important events of his life will be referred to in the course of this discussion.[1] By his time, the division of the Imāmī scholars between the Principlists (*uṣūliyya*) and the Traditionalists (*akhbāriyya*) was well established. From the sharp distinction made, in the 6th/12th century, by ʿAbd al-Jalīl al-Qazwīnī in his *Kitāb al-naqḍ* to the constitution of the Uṣūlī 'clergy' under the second Safavid king, Ṭahmāsp, in the 10th/16th century, and in particular after the decisive work of the 'neo-traditionalist' Muḥammad Amīn Astarābādī (d. 1030/1624) and his radical and methodical criticism of his principlist co-religionists, the rift, violent conflict even, between the two groups was clearly visible and attested

[1] Reliable studies on him are numerous, made by both Western and Shiʿi scholars. For the first category, see for example, Karl-Heinz Pampus, 'Die theologische Enzyklopädie *Biḥār al-anwār* des Muḥammad Bāqir al-Majlisī (1037–1110/1627–1699)' (PhD, Rheinische Friedrich-Wilhelms-Universität Bonn, 1970); Abdul-Hadi Hairi, 'Madjlisī, Mullā Muḥammad Bāḳir', *EI2*, vol. 5; Rainer Brunner, 'Majlesī, Moḥammad Bāqer', in *EIr* https://www.iranicaonline.org/articles/majlesi-mohammad-baqer (accessed on 26 January 2021); for the second group, see, for example: Muṣliḥ al-Dīn Mahdavī, *Zindagi nāmayi ʿAllāma Majlisī* (Isfahan, n.d.; repr. Tehran, 1378 Sh./1999); Ḥusayn Dargāhī and ʿAlī Akbar Talāfī Dāriyānī, *Kitāb shināsi-yi Majlisī* (Tehran, 1st ed. 1370 Sh./1991; repr. 1382 Sh./2003); Ḥasan Ṭāramī, *ʿAllāma Majlisī* (Tehran, 1375 Sh./1997).

to by both sides.[2] The divergences between the two groups were numerous and can probably be traced back to the differences between the original esoteric Shiʿism and the rationalist Shiʿism of the Būyid era.[3] Certain divergences that emerged later will be examined but as regards the general aim here in sum one can say that the Akhbārīs were the proponents of the exclusive recourse to the text of the Qurʾan and the *ḥadīth* (in its Shiʿi conception) and therefore opposed to the personal endeavour of interpretation in its various forms (*ijtihād, raʾy, qiyās*) and also opposed to participation in political activity. The Uṣūlīs, for their part, practised a critical reading of the scriptural sources, especially the *ḥadīth*, used *ijtihād* and the scholastic argumentation of *kalām* and often involved themselves in political

---

[2] On these two rival Shiʿi groups, see, for example, Gian Roberto Scarcia, 'Intorno alle controversie tra Akhbârî e Usûlî presso gli Imâmiti di Persia', *RSO*, 33 (1958), pp. 211–250; Etan Kohlberg, 'Ak̲bārīya', *EIr*, https://www.iranicaonline.org/articles/akbariya (accessed on 26 January 2021); Etan Kohlberg, 'Aspects of Akhbārī Thought in the Seventeenth and Eighteenth Centuries', in his *Belief and Law in Imāmī Shīʿism* (Aldershot, 1991), article XVII. Many of the works of Andrew J. Newman, for instance, are devoted to this subject: 'The Development and Political Significance of the Rationalist (Uṣūlī) and Traditionalist (Akhbārī) Schools in Imāmī Shīʿī History From the Third/Ninth to the Tenth/Sixteenth Century' (PhD, UCLA, 1986); 'The Nature of the Akhbārī/Uṣūlī Dispute in Late-Safawid Iran', *BSOAS*, 55 (1992), pp. 22–52 and 250–262; 'Anti-Akhbārī Sentiments among the Qājār *ʿUlamāʾ*: the Case of Muḥammad Bāqir al-Khwānsārī (d. 1313/1895)', in Robert Gleave, ed., *Religion and Society in Qajar Iran* (London-New York, 2005), pp. 155–173. Also Devin J. Stewart, see for example his *Islamic Legal Orthodoxy: Twelver Shiite Response to the Sunni Legal System* (Salt Lake City, UT, 1998); 'The Genesis of the Akhbārī Revival', in Michel Mazzaoui, ed., *Safavid Iran and Her Neighbors* (Salt Lake City, UT, 2003), pp. 169–193; and for Robert Gleave, especially his *Inevitable Doubt: Two Theories of Shīʿī Jurisprudence* (Leiden, 2000); *Scripturalist Islam. The History and Doctrines of the Akhbārī Shīʿī School* (Leiden, 2007).

[3] M.A. Amir-Moezzi, *Le Guide divin dans le shiʿisme originel. Aux sources de l'ésotérisme en islam* (Paris, 1992 (2005^2)), Introduction, pp. 13–48 (English translation *The Divine Guide in Early Shiʿism*, tr. D. Streight. New York, 1994). Ḥasan Anṣārī (= Hassan Ansari), 'Akhbāriyān wa aṣḥāb-i ḥadīth-i imāmiyya: nīm nigāhī bi tārīkhcha-yi taḥawwulāt-i fiqh-i imāmī', in his *Tashayyuʿ-i imāmī dar bastar-i taḥawwul. Tārīkh-i maktab-hā va bāvar-hā dar Īrān va Islām* (Tehran, 1395 Sh./2016), vol. 1, pp. 37–80.

activity, especially when power lay in Shiʿi hands. But what was Majlisī's position in Safavid Iran in the 11th/17th century? [4]

The *Uṣūlī* trend: Positions and activities

Having pursued a successful career as *mujtahid*, Majlisī reached the apex of the theological-political hierarchy as the *shaykh al-Islām* of the capital, Iṣfahān, during the reigns of Shah Sulaymān (r. 1077–1105/1666–1694) and Shah Sulṭān Ḥusayn (r. 1105–1135/1694–1722).[5] However, we know that in the traditions attributed to the Ithnā ʿasharī Shiʿi imams, they urged their followers, explicitly and insistently, to stay away from any political activity. Notably, the imams were particularly opposed to the quest for any form of political and religious leadership (*riʾāsa*) on the part of their followers, to any revolt against political power (*qiyām*) before the advent of the End of Time, or to any effective collaboration with the government (*ittibāʿ al-sulṭān*).[6]

There was an initial decisive break with this early tradition when the Shiʿi dynasty of the Būyids came to power in the 4th/10th century and the figure of the jurist-theologian, Principlist and collaborator with

[4] There has already been some debate about Majlisī's ideological adherance; see for example Ḥ. Ṭāramī, *ʿAllāma Majlisī*, chapters 3 and 6; ʿAlī Malikī Miyānjī, *ʿAllāma Majlisī, akhbārī yā uṣūlī?* (Qum, 1385 Sh./2006); Gleave, *Scripturalist Islam*, pp. 201 and 257. My study attempts to bring new elements of reflection and new historical perspectives to this debate.

[5] On the institution of *shaykh al-Islām*, a kind of ministry of religious affairs, and its relations with other important politico-religious positions such as *ṣadr, muftī, qāḍī, qāḍī ʿaskar*, see Rasūl Jaʿfariyān, *Dīn va siyāsat dar ʿaṣr-i Ṣafavī* (Qum, 1370 Sh./1991), pp. 90–92; Mahdavī, *Zindagī nāma*, vol. 1, pp. 275–277; Willem Floor, 'The *ṣadr* or Head of the Safavid Religious Administration, Judiciary and Endowments and Other Members of the Religious Institution', *Zeitschrift der Deutschen Morgenländischen Gesellschaft*, 150 (2000), pp. 461–500.

[6] On *ḥadīth* concerning these subjects, reported in particular by al-Kulaynī in his *Kāfī*, see Amir-Moezzi, *Guide divin*, pp. 170–171 and the Part III-1; also Amir-Moezzi and Hassan Ansari, 'Muḥammad b. Yaʿqūb al-Kulaynī (m. 328/939–940 ou 329/940–941) et son *Kitāb al-Kāfī*. Une introduction', *Studia Iranica*, 38 (2009), pp. 220–221.

rulers, began to replace that of the imam, who was still hidden.[7] The political and social weight of the Imāmī jurist-theologian became even more important thanks to the scholars of the School of Ḥilla during the 6th/12th and 7th/13th centuries, and especially after the turning point in the formalisation of Twelver Imamism as a state religion under the Safavids in the 10th/16th century. The most spectacular illustration of this evolution is the royal decree issued by the sovereign Ṭahmāsp I in Dhu'l-Ḥijja 939/July 1533, declaring the great *mujtahid*, ʿAlī b. al-Ḥusayn al-Karakī, 'the representative of the Hidden imam' (*nā'ib al-imām al-ghā'ib*).[8] In another undated decree, he also declared that the *mujtahids* were the representatives of all the infallible imams and opposition to them was equivalent to the associationism (*shirk*) and would be severely punished.[9]

It must be pointed out that even before becoming the *shaykh al-Islām* and being appointed as the official preacher at Shah Sulṭān Ḥusayn's coronation ceremony, Majlisī was closely involved socially and politically in the defence of official Shiʿism and the repression of the ideas and currents of belief deemed deviant: the doctrinal attacks on, and most probably the violent repression of, Sufism and the mystical orders;[10] the declaration of philosophy, as well as

[7] Amir-Moezzi, *Guide divin*, Appendix, pp. 319ff; Amir-Moezzi and Christian Jambet, *Qu'est-ce que le shi'isme?* (Paris, 2004; repr. 2014), part 3, chapters 1 to 3; English translation as *What is Shi'i Islam?* tr. E. Ormsby (Richmond, 2018).

[8] ʿAbd Allāh b. ʿĪsā Afandī/ Efendī, *Riyāḍ al-ʿulamā'* (Qum, 1401/1981), vol. 3, pp. 445–460.

[9] Muḥammad Bāqir al-Khwānsārī, *Rawḍāt al-jannāt* (Qum, 1390–1392/1970–1972), vol. 4, p. 363.

[10] For his doctrinal attacks see, for example, Majlisī, *ʿAyn al-ḥayāt*, ed. ʿAlī Muḥammad Rafīʿī (Tehran, n.d. [ca. 1993]), pp. 25ff, 52ff, 202ff, 233ff; idem, *Biḥār al-anwār*, 'Kumpānī''s edition (Beirut, 1403/1983), vol. 1, pp. 3ff; idem, *Mir'āt al-ʿuqūl*, ed. Sayyid Hāshim Rasūlī Maḥallātī (2nd ed., Tehran, 1404/1984), vol. 1, pp. 1–2. See also Baḥrānī, *Lu'lu'at al-Baḥrayn*, ed. Muḥammad Ṣādiq Baḥr al-ʿulūm (Qum, n.d.), p. 55; Laurence Lockhart, *The Fall of the Ṣafavī Dynasty and the Afghan Occupation of Persia* (Cambridge, 1958), pp. 70ff; Dhabīḥallāh Ṣafā, *Tārīkh-i adabiyyāt-i Īrān* (Tehran, 1370 Sh./1991), vol. 5, pp. 181, 205–209; Colin Turner, *Islam without Allah? The Rise of Religious Externalism in Safavid Iran* (Richmond, 2000), pp. 148ff. However, in the accounts of the repression of the Sufis, some scholars seem sometimes to have confused Muḥammad Bāqir al-Majlisī with Muḥammad Bāqir Khātūnābādī, mentor of Shah Sulṭān Ḥusayn; see Ṭāramī, *ʿAllāma Majlisī*, pp. 109ff and 218ff.

Sufism, as a false form of learning (*ʿilm bāṭil*) and a blameworthy innovation (*bidʿa*); [11] the violent denunciation of Shiʿi esotericism, as well as spiritual hermeneutics (*taʾwīl*) as 'extremism' or exaggeration (*ghuluww*);[12] the intermittent repression of non-Shiʿi religious communities epitomised by the destruction of the Hindu temple in Iṣfahān and the expulsion of Hindus from the city.[13] The rigour of Majlisī is manifested through his writings and his actions as a major politico-religious authority but also in his decrees as a religious judge (*qāḍī, ḥākim*) during the last twenty years of his life. The latter illustrates one of the many ambiguities of our man. Indeed, Majlisī was thoroughly acquainted with the *ḥadīths* of the imams emphasising the extreme difficulty of the profession of judge, the dangers it held for personal salvation as well as the problematic cases of religious jurisdiction (*ḥukūma*) and the application of the canonical punishments (*ḥudūd*) during the Occultation, i.e., in the physical absence of the infallible

---

[11] Majlisī, *Mirʾāt al-ʿuqūl*, vol. 1, p. 2; idem, *Biḥār*, vol. 1, pp. 3ff and 103ff; idem, 'Jawāb al-masāʾil al-thalāth', in Rasūl Jaʿfariyān, 'Rūyārūyī-yi faqīhān va ṣūfiyān dar ʿaṣr-i ṣafaviyān', *Kayhān-i andīsha*, 33 (1370 Sh./1991), pp. 101–127; Ṣafā, *Tārīkh*, vol. 5, pp. 181, 205–209.

[12] Majlisī, *Biḥār*, vol. 25, pp. 261–350 (against the *ghulāt*); *Biḥār*, vol. 5, pp. 260–261 and 267; vol. 6, pp. 201–202 and 255; vol. 54, p. 363; vol. 57, p. 149, also vol. 58, pp. 144–164 (and many other instances). It should be noted, however, that sometimes Majlisī's criticism of *taʾwīl* seems ambiguous in the sense that it is not directed against Shiʿi esotericists but against a certain kind of rationalist who illegitimately deflects the Qurʾan and the *ḥadīth* from their writings (see e.g. the critics against al-Shaykh al-Mufīd in *Biḥār*, vol. 6, pp. 249–252, or against al-Sharīf al-Murtaḍā –*Biḥār*, vol. 6, pp. 201–202).

[13] Majlisī speaks about it himself in *Biḥār*, vol. 102, p. 20; cf. ʿAbd al-Ḥusayn Khātūnābādī, *Waqāʾiʿ al-sinīn waʾl-aʿwām* (Tehran, 1352 Sh./1973), p. 540. On the repression of Sunnis, Zoroastrians and Jews see Edward G. Browne, *A Literary History of Persia* (Cambridge, 1908–1930), vol. 4, *Modern Times (1500–1924)*, pp. 403ff; Lockhart, *Fall of the Ṣafavī Dynasty*, pp. 54ff; Pampus, *Theologische Enziklopädie*, pp. 33–34. These acts of repression seem to have depended on social conditions and periods of political crisis. On the doctrinal side, Majlisī supports the usual position of Islamic law recognising the rights and duties of the People of the Book/the Protected people (*ahl al-kitāb/ahl al-dhimma*), see Majlisī, 'Ṣawāʿiq al-yahūd', in his *Bīst o panj risāla-yi fārsī*, ed. Sayyid Mahdī Rajāʾī (Qum, 1412/1991), pp. 515–522.

authority of the imam.[14] ʿAbd al-Ḥayy al-Riḍawī, who allegedly flourished in the 12th/18th century, in his *Ḥadīqat al-shīʿa* relates a sermon that Majlisī gave in a mosque in Iṣfahān in which after having wept lengthily he reportedly declared: 'People! How puzzled I am faced with my destiny. My father and I spent our lives spreading the faith and teaching the doctrinal foundations and practical applications [of Shiʿism] and this is how people from all over the region learned the chapters of the Law, what is licit and what is illicit. So how is it I came to be a judge?'[15]

Finally, effective collaboration with the political power of the day – which, as we have seen, was in contradiction to the teaching of the imams – reached a peak in Majlisī's career with the coronation sermon for Shah Sulṭān Ḥusayn in 1106/1694, referred to above.[16] Following many other Uṣūlī scholars, Majlisī sought to provide legal and theological justifications for a legitimate government during the Occultation. Presenting Safavid power as grounded in justice and fidelity to the imams in general and the Hidden imam in particular, he said that the best possible government was achieved through close collaboration between a just ruler (*sulṭān ʿādil*) and a learned jurist (*faqīh ʿālim*). Majlisī had already defended the legitimacy of Safavid

---

14 Amir-Moezzi, *Guide divin*, pp. 323–325; Amir-Moezzi and Jambet, *Qu'est-ce que le shi'isme?*, Part 3, chapter 2, n° 1.

15 Cited by R. Jaʿfariyān, *Dīn va siyāsat*, p. 351. On *Ḥadīqa al-shīʿa* and its author, see Andrew J. Newman, 'Sufism and Anti-Sufism in Safavid Iran: the Authorship of the *Ḥadīqat al-Shīʿa* Revisited', *Iran*, 37 (1999), pp. 95–108. It should be added that for another problematic case during the Occultation, namely the practice of Friday collective prayer, Majlisī opts for the lawfulness or even the obligatory nature of it in all situations, a position more often adopted by the Uṣūliyya (but also by some Akhbāriyya), see for example *Biḥār*, vol. 86, pp. 146, 221, 231, 319. Studies on this question, especially in Persian, are numerous; see for example Jaʿfariyān, *Dīn va siyāsat*, pp. 121–180 ; Andrew J. Newman, 'Fayḍ al-Kāshānī and the Rejection of the Clergy/State Alliance: Friday Prayer as Politics in the Safavid Period', in Linda S. Walbridge, ed., *The Most Learned of the Shiʿa*, pp. 34–52; idem, 'The *Vezir* and the *Mulla*: a Late Safavid Period Debate on Friday Prayer', in Michele Bernardini et al., ed., *Etudes sur l'Iran médieval et moderne offertes à Jean Calmard*, special issue of *Eurasian Studies*, 1–2 (2006), pp. 237–269.

16 A good manuscript of this sermon exists in the Majlis collection, n°1, majmūʿa n° 2721, ff. 352–359 ('Khuṭba dar julūs-i Shāh Sulṭān Ḥusayn-i Ṣafavī'); see an analysis of it in Ṭāramī, *ʿAllāma-yi Majlisī*, pp. 246–250.

rule and therefore the need to collaborate with it in his *Biḥār al-anwār*: first, by commenting on certain traditions of the imams which say that the Riser (*al-qāʾim*) begins his uprising in the province of Jīlān (Gīlān, in northern Iran), Majlisī declared that Shah Ismāʿīl I had started his movement in Jīlān before going to Ardabīl.[17] Elsewhere, he reported a *ḥadīth* of Imam Muḥammad al-Bāqir, taken from al-Nuʿmānī's (disciple of al-Kulaynī) *Kitāb al-Ghayba* where it says that in the future, seekers of the truth (*ṭalabat al-ḥaqq*, i.e. the faithful Shiʿa), after having suffered many defeats, will resort to arms and will eventually achieve power in order to entrust it to the imam of the Time (i.e. the Hidden imam). In his commentary Majlisī wrote: 'The *ḥadīth* is probably alluding to Safavid power. May God consolidate the pillars of this power and associate it with the government of the *qāʾim*.'[18] The position advocated by Majlisī is not readily defensible because it contradicts not only certain fundamental teachings of Twelver Shiʿism reported in the ancient corpus of Imāmī *ḥadīth*, but also a legal tradition of addressing the problems that collaboration with any power, by definition unjust (*jāʾir*), posed. Indeed, according to an old Imāmī dogma, all political power before the advent of the eschatological Saviour (the only just ruler) can only be unjust. This is the notion called *al-tawallī ʿan al-jāʾir*, 'dissociation with the unjust (power or sovereign)'.[19] Majlisī himself dedicated an entire chapter of his *ʿAyn al-ḥayāt* to the 'Corruptions related to the proximity with rulers' (*Mafāsid-i qurb-i pādshāhān*) where he enumerated a great number of perils that the faithful faced in their salvation when they collaborated with holders of political power. But, at the same time, he presented extensive arguments in defence of the point that when the government is in the hands of 'the religion of the truth' (*dīn-i ḥaqq*, i.e. Imāmī Shiʿism), it sometimes becomes necessary, even legally obligatory

---

[17] Majlisī, *Biḥār*, vol. 52, p. 236. Indeed, Ismāʿīl Mīrzā had begun his insurrectionist messianic movement in Gīlān around 903/1497 before moving to Ardabīl in 905/1499 at the age of 13 and taking command of his Sufi warrior adherents.

[18] Majlisī, *Biḥār*, vol. 52, p. 243. For other works relating some Imāmī eschatological *ḥadīth*s to the arrival of the Safavids see Āqā Buzurg al-Ṭihrānī, *al-Dharīʿa ʿalā taṣānīf al-shīʿa* (Beirut, 1403/1983), vol. 15, pp. 4–5.

[19] See for example Muḥammad Ḥasan al-Najafī, *Jawāhir al-kalām fī sharḥ sharāʾiʿ al-Islām* (Beirut, 1983), vol. 22, pp. 155–168.

(*wājib*), to collaborate with it.[20] Majlisi also defended this position in his 'Mirror for Princes' in Persian, entitled *Ādāb-i sulūk-i ḥākim bā raʿyat.*[21]

Some Akhbārī aspects

At the same time, Majlisī's life and works present many explicitly traditionalist aspects. Among those who had granted him permission to transmit from the sources, some of whom were undoubtedly his masters, we find some great Akhbārī names, such Mullā Ṣāliḥ Māzandarānī (d. 1080/1669), Muḥsin Fayḍ Kāshānī (d. 1091/1680), Ḥurr ʿĀmilī (d. 1096/1685) or Mullā Muḥammad Ṭāhir Qummī (d. 1098/1687).[22] To these must be added his own father, the great scholar Muḥammad Taqī Majlisī (d. 1070/1659), known as Majlisī the First, a scholar of mystical and Akhbārī proclivity and a great admirer of the aforementioned Muḥammad Amīn Astarābādī, the founder of so-called Neo-Akhbārism.[23]

It was especially in his *ʿAyn al-ḥayāt* that our author revealed his taste for mysticism. While criticising Ibn ʿArabī's doctrine of *waḥdat al-wujūd* and the spiritual hermeneutics (*ta'wīl*) of the Sufis who do not respect the letter of the scriptures, Majlisī declared that the legal religion has an esoteric dimension (*bāṭin*) that can be attained through the acquisition of knowledge (*maʿrifat*) and the purification of oneself

---

[20] Majlisī, *ʿAyn al-ḥayāt*, pp. 499–506.

[21] Majlisī, in *Bīst va panj risāla-yi fārsī*, pp. 135–179.

[22] Majlisī, *Biḥār*, vol. 107, pp. 103–106; idem, *Ijāzāt* (Qum, n.d.), p. 122; also al-Ḥurr al-ʿĀmilī, *Wasā'il al-shīʿa*, ed. Rabbānī Shīrāzī (Qum, 1403/1983), vol. 20, pp. 49ff; Nūrī Ṭabarsī/Ṭabrisī, *al-Fayḍ al-qudsī fī tarjamat al-ʿAllāma al-Majlisī*, edited in *Biḥār*, vol. 102, p. 80.

[23] On him, see the article of Rainer Brunner in *EIr* (2002), and in particular the monograph of Ḥamīd Mīr Khandān, *Muḥammad Taqī Majlisī* (Tehran, 1374 Sh./1995). On his admiration for Astarābādī and his work, see Majlisī I, *Lawāmiʿ-yi ṣāḥibqarānī* (Qum, 1416/1995), vol. 1, p. 47; it is a commentary in Persian of the *Kitāb man lā yaḥḍuruhu'l-faqīh* of Ibn Bābūya; in the Arabic version of this commentary entitled *Rawḍa al-muttaqīn* (Qum, 1399/1979), vol. 1, p. 21, Muḥammad Taqī Majlisī is less laudatory about the criticisms of the Principlists made by Astarābādī (we will come back to this later).

(*tahdhīb-i nafs*), while respecting the religious rules of conduct (*ādāb-i dīn*). The aim is to reach proximity to God (*taqarrub-i ḥaqq*) and its ultimate consequences, annihilation in God (*fanāʾ fī Allāh*) and the ability to perform miracles (*karāmāt*), on which it is advisable to remain silent.[24] Elsewhere in the same book, he readily referred to some of the great names of the Ithnā ʿasharī tradition – Raḍī al-Dīn ʿAlī b. Ṭāwūs, Ibn Fahd al-Ḥillī, 'the Second Martyr' Zayn al-Dīn b. ʿAlī and Ṣafī al-Dīn al-Ardabīlī, the eponymous founder of the Safavid dynasty – as 'Imāmī Sufis' (*ṣūfiyya-yi imāmiyya*), and presented their works as containing 'the subtleties of the secrets of Sufism' (*daqāʾiq-i asrār-i ṣūfiyya*).[25] In his responses to Mullā Khalīl Qazvīnī, Majlisī recounted how his father, Mullā Muḥammad Taqī, was introduced to the Sufi practices of *dhikr* and *fikr* by his spiritual master, the famous Bahāʾ al-Dīn Muḥammad ʿĀmilī or Shaykh Bahāʾī (d. 1031 or 1032/1622 or 1623). He then added that he himself had been initiated in the same practices and that he had repeatedly performed 'forty-day retreats' (*arbaʿīnāt*).[26] Finally, in another work of mystical tendency, *Kitāb al-arbaʿīn*, the great *mujtahid* severely criticised those Shiʿa, especially the scholars, who were content with the exoteric aspects (*ẓāhir*) of religion and who did not attempt to explore the subtle secrets of the teachings of the imams.[27]

But the Akhbārī tendencies (in the literal sense of the term) of Majlisī are most impressively manifested in his *magnum opus*, the monumental encyclopedia of Shiʿi traditions (*akhbār*), the famous *Biḥār al-anwār*.[28] In the most recent edition, known as the Kumpānī

---

24 Majlisī, *ʿAyn al-ḥayāt*, pp. 49–57.

25 Ibid., pp. 238ff.

26 A treatise on this is discussed by Rasūl Jaʿfariyān in 'Rūyārūyī-yi faqīhān va ṣūfiyān dar ʿaṣr-i ṣafaviyān', pp. 123ff.

27 Majlisī, *Kitāb al-arbaʿīn* or *Sharḥ-i ʿArbaʿīn* (Qum, 1358 Sh./1977), pp. 101, 179.

28 K.-H. Pampus, '*Die theologische Enzyklopädie* Biḥār al-anwār' (PhD, Bonn, 1970); Etan Kohlberg, 'Beḥār al-anwār', *EIr*, vol. 4, pp. 90–93; https://www.iranicaonline.org/articles/behar-al-anwar (accessed on 26 January 2021); Ḥasan Ṭāramī, *al-ʿAllāma al-Majlisī wa kitābuhu* Biḥār al-anwār (Tehran, 1378 Sh./1999). Ḥasan Anṣārī (= Hassan Ansari), 'Zindagī, āthār va andīsha-yi yak muḥaddith-i imāmī dar nīma-yi avval-i sada-yi sīzdahum-i hijrī', in his *Tashayyuʿ-i imāmī dar bastar-i taḥawwul* (see above footnote 3), pp. 81–120 (the article is about the Imāmī scholar Sayyid ʿAbd Allāh Shubbar but includes important studies on the structure and method of *Biḥār al-anwār*).

edition, the work is divided into 110 volumes with about 450 pages in each. Unique in all Shiʿi *ḥadīth* literature, it is the result of a heroic attempt to bring together all the teachings of the Fourteen Infallibles, the Prophet Muhammad, his daughter Fāṭima, and especially the Twelve imams of the Ithnā ʿasharī Shiʿa, as reported by all known sources. Most of the work seems to have been done by Majlisī himself, but he also sought help from other scholars, including two of his main disciples, Niʿmatullāh Jazāʾirī (d. 1112/1701) and ʿAbd Allāh b. ʿĪsā Afandī / Efendī (d. between 1130/1717 and 1140/1727) and a team of excellent scribes. The project was supported by the Safavid royal treasury, which financed many and sometimes extended journeys in search of manuscripts across the lands of Islam and paid the salaries of the scribes. Writing it took almost fifteen years, from 1077/1666 to 1091/1681. Etan Kohlberg has divided the innumerable sources of the *Biḥār* into five groups according to their era: from the time of the historical imams to the beginning of the Minor Occultation (which occurred in 260/874 according to Imāmī Tradition); from the time of the Minor Occultation to the beginning of the Major Occultation in 329/941 and then the Būyid period; thirdly, the period up to the Mongol invasion and the fall of Baghdad in 656/1258; fourthly, from the end of the Abbasid caliphate until the advent of the Safavids in the early 10th/late 15th century; lastly, the sources of Safavid period up to the time of Majlisī himself. The reported traditions relate to all religious issues, from fundamental doctrines to law, from prayers to sermons, from historical accounts to medical recipes, from ethics to ritual and canonical practice. What is remarkable and concerns our subject is that in the 'Oceans of Light', almost no source has been set aside, including compilations containing the most esoteric traditions or those whose authenticity or legitimacy have been questioned by Principlist scholars (works like Sulaym b. Qays's *Kitāb*, al-Mufaḍḍal's *Tawḥīd*, Ibn Shuʿba al-Ḥarrānī's *Tuḥaf al-ʿuqūl*, al-Khaṣībī's *al-Hidāya al-kubrā*, *Ithbāt al-waṣiyya* attributed to al-Masʿūdī and Rajab Bursī's *Mashāriq al-anwār*). No tradition, even the most 'subversive', seems to have been suppressed or censored, for example those concerning the theory of the falsification of the official text of the Qur'an (*taḥrīf al-Qurʾān*), those on the practice of anathematising the non-ʿAlid companions of the Prophet (*sabb al-ṣaḥāba*) or on the divine nature of the imams and their knowledge, and their miraculous powers (the notion of *tafwīḍ* and its implications); subjects that the Uṣūlī tradition always regarded as either embarrassing or pertaining solely to the Shiʿi *ghulāt* and therefore to be dismissed. At the same time, Majlisī often tried to justify his choices, anticipating the possible criticisms of his detractors.

It is true that certain historical circumstances may explain the choices that Majlisī made, such as the promotion of an aversion to Sunnism in the atmosphere of the incessant wars between the Safavids and Ottomans or the legitimisation of the divine nature of the imams and their miracles and therefore exhorting the faithful to undertake pilgrimage (*ziyāra*) to their graves, with the resultant economic benefits.[29] But it seems that his main objective was the collection and preservation of the heritage of Shiʿi *ḥadīth*, in its entirety and historical fullness, without taking into account any ideological or technical considerations. Indeed, on a technical level, Majlisī quite often did not comply with the criteria and rules of *ʿilm al-ḥadīth* – in particular, he did not take into account the factors that conventionally determine the reliability of the chains of transmitters (*sanad, isnād*).[30] The partial neglect of these purely technical aspects in favour of content made Majlisī the object of criticism (sometimes severe) by some Uṣūlī scholars. Thus, he was attacked by Muḥammad Ḥusaynī Mīr Lawḥī (who was also his political rival) in his *Kifāyat al-muhtadī*, and the criticism continued into recent times as can be seen in the *Aʿyān al-shīʿa* of Sayyid Muḥsin al-Amīn al-ʿĀmilī (d. 1952).[31]

Search for balance or voluntary ambiguity?

In *al-Ḥadāʾiq al-nāḍira*, Yūsuf al-Baḥrānī (d. 1186/1773) reported that Muḥammad Bāqir Majlisī was a convinced Akhbārī throughout his

---

29 E. Kohlberg, 'Beḥār', conclusion.

30 See what Majlisī himself says about this subject in *Biḥār*, vol. 1, pp. 10, 26–30, 42.

31 For the first source, see Muḥammad Taqī Dānishpažūh, *Fihrist-i kitābkhāna-yi ihdāʾī-yi āqā-yi Sayyid Muḥammad Mishkāt bi kitābkhāna-yi dānishgāh-i Tihrān* (Tehran, 1334 Sh./1956), vol. 3, pp. 1497–1507; Kathryn Babayan, *Mystics, Monarchs and Messiahs: Cultural Landscapes of Early Modern Iran* (Cambridge, 2002), pp. 465, 470–471; Rainer Brunner, 'Majlesī, Moḥammad Bāqer', *EIr*; Muḥsin al-Amīn, *Ayān al-shīʿa* (Beirut, 1403/1983), vol. 9, p. 183.

youth, with critical attitude towards the *mujtahids*. Then, after years of study, reflection and contact with the Uṣūlīs, he came to the conclusion that it was necessary to overcome the divisions and oppositions between the different Imāmī tendencies. Baḥrānī thus placed him among the precursors of those who try to establish a balance between scholars of both tendencies.[32] The above discussion indeed points in this direction. Majlisī attempted to achieve an equilibrium by including the most important Sunni or Muʿtazilī Qur'anic commentaries in the sources for his *Biḥār al-anwār*. Thus, he used works such as Fakhr al-Dīn al-Rāzī's *Mafātīḥ al-ghayb*, al-Bayḍāwī's *Anwār al-tanzīl*, al-Zamakhsharī's *al-Kashshāf*, al-Baghawī's *Maʿālim al-tanzīl* and al-Suyūṭī's *al-Durr al-manthūr*. One can also refer to the great compilations of Sunni *ḥadīth* and their commentaries (the *Ṣiḥāḥ sitta* and the commentaries of Ibn Ḥajar, al-Nawawī and al-Kirmānī), the Sunni books of history (al-Ṭabarī, Ibn al-Athīr, Ibn al-Jawzī, Ibn Khallikān etc) and the works of the great Sunni thinkers such as al-Ghazālī, al-Taftāzānī, Abu'l-Faraj al-Iṣfahānī, and many others.[33]

Moreover, Majlisī did not hesitate to express his admiration for the great Akhbārī thinker, Muḥammad Amīn Astarābādī, as his father had already done, calling him 'the chief of the transmitters of *ḥadīths*' (*ra'īs al-muḥaddithīn*), while criticising his attacks against the Principlists.[34] It can also be pointed out that like a typical Uṣūlī author, he sometimes dwelt on the critical methodology of the study of *ḥadīth*, examining in detail the criteria for authenticity or inauthenticity of traditions or those for the credibility of a compiler. At the same time, as already noted, he used several sources and reported thousands of traditions that only Akhbārīs or even only Shiʿi mystics treat as

---

[32] Yūsuf al-Baḥrānī, *al-Ḥadā'iq al-nāḍira* (Qum, 1363–1367 Sh./1985–1987), vol. 1, author's 2nd introduction.

[33] Majlisī, *Biḥār*, vol. 1, pp. 24ff (presentation of the sources of *Biḥār*).

[34] For the praise of Astarābādī, see Majlisī, *Biḥār*, vol. 1, p. 20; for his criticism, Majlisī, *Biḥār*, vol. 2, p. 284 (here Astarābādī is discreetly called *baʿḍ al-muta'akhkhirīn*, but the allusions are clear to those who know the work of the leader of the neo-Akhbārīs).

authentic.[35] Finally, like any authentic Usūlī thinker, Majlisī often resorted to the arguments of scholastic theology (*kalām*).[36]

At the same time, our author presented himself as a moderate Akhbārī according to what Yūsuf Baḥrānī calls 'the middle way' (*ṭarīq wusṭā*).[37] Indeed, in a treatise entitled 'Response to a question by a dear man' (*Pāsukh-i su'āl-i mard-i ʿazīzī*), edited by Rasūl Jaʿfariyān, Majlisī wrote:

> However, with regard to the way of the *mujtahid*s and the Akhbārīs, my method consists of choosing the middle gate (*bāb-i wasaṭ*) between the two groups. Exaggerations of any kind are reprehensible. I consider the opinion of those who accuse the Imāmī doctors of reductionism erroneous, because they were the great figures of our religion. In the same way, I dismiss those who consider these men as impeccable guides and sources of imitation and present their adversaries as good for nothing ... I firmly believe that the use of rational arguments not supported by the Qur'an and the *ḥadīth* is wrong; on the other hand, I think it is lawful to follow guidelines rationally deduced from the Qur'an and *ḥadīth* if they are not in contradiction with the letter of these sacred texts.[38]

Clearly, Majlisī sought to be the driving force behind the widest diffusion and expansion of Imāmī Shiʿism. The fact that he wrote a large number of his doctrinal works in Persian, especially his monumental encyclopedia of Shiʿi traditions, makes him one of the most important figures in the Shiʿi revival of the Safavid era, whether among the elite or the generality of the faithful. It is true that, it is due to Majlisī, a considerable number of fundamental doctrines – but also popular beliefs and even superstitions reported by all kinds of sources – were widely disseminated. In this respect, Ḥujjat Balāghī is

---

[35] See the analysis of Ḥ. Ṭāramī, *ʿAllāma Majlisī*, pp. 185–196; idem, *al-ʿAllāma al-Majlisī wa kitābuhu* Biḥār al-anwār, chapter 5.

[36] See, among many other citations, *Biḥār*, vol. 1, pp. 85, 124; vol. 3, pp. 144, 231–234; vol. 4, pp. 28–33, 62, 137; vol. 5, pp. 43, 223–226, 332–334; vol. 6, pp. 110, 326–328, etc.

[37] *Al-Ḥadā'iq al-nāḍira*, vol. 1, author's 2nd introduction.

[38] See R. Jaʿfariyān, 'Rūyārūyī-yi faqīhān va ṣūfiyān', pp. 120–125; see also long abstracts of this letter of Majlisī in Maʿṣūm ʿAlī Shāh, *Tarā'iq al-ḥaqā'iq*, ed. Muḥammad Jaʿfar Maḥjūb (Tehran, 1339 Sh./1961), vol. 1, pp. 280–284.

right when he says that Majlisī sought above all to collect, safeguard and transmit as many Shiʿi texts as possible even if he did not believe in the authenticity of some of them.[39] It is by pursuing this goal that Majlisī sought to establish the right balance between Uṣūlism and Akhbārism. But it is equally true that the search for a balance between two tendencies of unequal strength always serves better the one that is more powerful, in this case the Uṣūliyya. In such a situation, the balance borders on ambiguity: it was deemed necessary at one and the same time to protect Shiʿi spirituality based on individual reverence for the imams and the community dimension of religion, and to ensure that this community dimension remained under the control of its jurists or experts of religious law who were almost always Principlists.[40] This ambiguity becomes even more evident when one takes into account Majlisī's political life, his proximity to the Safavid rulers and his repressive severity, as we saw earlier, with regard to those groups of the Shiʿa which he perceived as deviant and vis-à-vis the non-Shiʿa, such as Sunnis, Jews or Hindus.

Two of Majlisī's texts are particularly symptomatic in this respect. The first is the sermon for the coronation of Shah Sulṭān Ḥusayn referred to earlier. In it, Majlisī tried to show that, contrary to what is stated in certain Imāmī traditions, government other than that of the Saviour of the End of Time (obviously he means that of the Safavid state) can be just.[41] Then, in his *ʿAyn al-ḥayāt*, he took up the same arguments adding that it is true that those responsible for such power are not infallible (*maʿṣūm, muṭahhar*), and obedience, or disobedience, to them is not equivalent to obedience or disobedience to God, but since they seek to establish justice (*ʿadāla, ʿadl*), their government represents that of the Hidden imam and is therefore legitimate. Majlisī

39 Ḥujjat Balāghī, *Gulzār-i Ḥujja* (sic) *Balāghī* (Tehran, 1350/1931), chapter on Majlisī.

40 I have already studied such ambiguity in Shaykh al-Mufīd, the 'founding father' of the rationalist tradition in 'Al-Shaykh al-Mufīd (m. 413/1022) et la question de la falsification du Coran', *RSO*, 87 (2014), pp. 155–176; also in Daniel De Smet and Mohammad Ali Amir-Moezzi, ed., *Controverses sur les écritures canoniques de l'islam* (Paris, 2014), pp. 199–229.

41 For this text, see above footnote 16. Also, R. Jaʿfariyān, 'Rūyārūyī-yi faqīhān va ṣūfiyān', pp. 124–125.

went on to speak about two kinds of 'right to power': that of the imams, based on their divine election and that of those who govern justly (*ḥākimān-i ʿadl*) who, as reason requires, seek to 'implement what is good for the city' (*riʿāyat-i maṣāliḥ-i madīna*).[42] Thus, he argued that the *sine qua non* of a just government is its absolute conformity to religious rules and laws which can only be possible in the presence of a strict control of power by the religious scholars (*ʿulamā-yi dīn*), i.e., the jurists.[43] In other words, according to Majlisī, a legitimate, and thus doctrinally acceptable power during the Major Occultation, is one founded and governed by two pillars: justice (*ʿadl*), guaranteed by the sovereign and his government, and law (*fiqh*) ensured by the jurist.[44]

Was Majlisī the Second aiming to establish balance and moderation or to maintain a strategic ambiguity? His approach must be considered in the historical context of the delicate balance that most of the Twelver Shiʿi scholars sought to reach after the Occultation of the Twelfth imam; the balance between the religion as an individual mystical relationship binding the believer to the imams, especially the 'hidden' one, and the safeguarding of a collective and institutional religion necessary for the survival of a community of believers.

42 Majlisī, *ʿAyn al-ḥayāt*, pp. 488–499.

43 Ibid., pp. 487, 490–491.

44 See also Majlisī, 'Ādāb-i sulūk-i ḥākim bā raʿyat', in Majlisī, *Bīst o panj risāla-yi fārsī*, pp. 176ff.

9

The Akhbārī Movement and Literary Production in Safavid Iran

Devin J. Stewart

The Islamic world witnessed two major periods of Shiʿi political expansion, one in the 4th/10th and 5th/11th centuries and one in the 10th/16th and 11th/17th centuries. The Shiʿi dynasties that ruled substantial regions of the Islamic world during those periods – the Būyids in Iran and Iraq, the Fatimids in North Africa, Egypt and Syria in the first period, the Quṭbshāhīs in southern India, the Safavids in Iran, and others in the second – had major and lasting effects, not only on political history but also on the religious, intellectual and literary history of the Islamic world. Of all these Shiʿi dynasties, it was the Safavids that produced what arguably have been the most profound long-term effects. Thanks to the Safavids, most of the population of Iran converted to Shiʿi Islam, with the result that Iranian culture and Twelver Shiʿism have become inextricably intertwined. Iran became the centre of gravity of the Shiʿi world in the 10th/16th century and has remained so ever since. The shrine of the eighth Ithnā ʿasharī imam ʿAlī Riḍā in Mashhad and that of his sister Fāṭima in Qum have been built up through centuries of donations and patronage and have become major centres of religious culture and learning. Shiʿi manuscripts from all over the Islamic world have been taken to Iran and are now in the major collections in Mashhad, Qum, Ardabīl and Tehran. The present study examines one facet of these varied historical effects, the production of works related to the Akhbārī movement, in the broader category of the production of Shiʿi literature during the Safavid period.

Safavid literary production has been the focus of significant scholarly attention. In some respects, the Safavid dynasty, including not only the shahs but also princes and princesses, as well as high officials of the realm, continued the patterns of patronage set by their predecessors. The lavishly illustrated *Shāhnāmas*, the *Khamsa* of Niẓāmī and other canonical works of Persian literature, the royal chronicles, the biographical-anthological *tadhkiras* of poets that had been popular at the courts of Herat, Tabrīz and elsewhere continued to be written and patronised. However, considerable effort was put into certain novel forms of literary production particularly having to do with Shiʿi Islam. This was part of the Safavid policy to promote Twelver Shiʿism as the religion of their empire. Works on all aspects of Shiʿi doctrine and practice were patronised by the Safavid shahs, including creeds, expositions of the Twelver Shiʿi theory of the imamate, basic religious devotions, collections of prayers connected with the Shiʿi religious calendar, Shiʿi prayers generally, Lives of the imams and other figures from Shiʿi history, and anti-Sunni polemic. Famous works from the Shiʿi tradition of the Islamic religious sciences were abridged or translated into Persian, and introductory works were written in both Persian and Arabic.

Scholars who had immigrated from Lebanon, Iraq and Bahrain to Iran played a particularly important role in this movement, both in writing accessible works in Arabic for aspiring students of Shiʿi religious studies and in translating popular works into Persian. As a result, a considerable number of works were produced. Particularly noteworthy are those that al-Muḥaqqiq al-Karakī (d. 940/1534) composed in support of the Safavid dynasty's pro-Shiʿi policies, such as his books on the legitimacy of collecting the *kharāj* or land tax, on the legitimacy of anathematising the companions of the Prophet, and on the performance of the Friday prayer in the absence of the Twelfth imam, all of which justified the ideological positions and practices favoured by the Safavid shahs. There were also Shiʿi doctrinal works dedicated to the monarchs, such as the *Jāmiʿ-i ʿAbbāsī*, the legal manual of Bahāʾ al-Dīn al-ʿĀmilī (d. 1030/1621), which was written in Persian and which was clearly intended to serve as an accessible standard reference work for a wide audience.[1] An important role in this sort of

[1] See Rula Jurdi Abisaab, *Converting Persia: Religion and Power in the Safavid Empire* (London, 2004).

production was played by scholars from Jabal ʿĀmil in Lebanon, who were specialists in Shiʿi religious traditions and had immigrated to Iran. Native Persian scholars more often produced similar works in Persian or translated fundamental works of the Shiʿi tradition from Arabic into Persian. The remarkable translation movement undertaken during the Safavid period is just beginning to be explored.[2]

Over the last several decades, considerable progress has also been made in the understanding of the history and thought of the Akhbārī movement, which constitutes a major facet of the intellectual history of Safavid Iran in its final century. Most of these studies have brought out aspects of the jurisprudential and hermeneutical theory of the Akhbārīs, refining the understanding of the ideological differences between the Akhbārīs and their opponents, the Uṣūlīs, providing a more substantial account of the adherents and salient works of the Akhbārī movement, and recognising the existence of considerable differences of opinion and approach among the Akhbārīs themselves.[3] One phenomenon

[2] For some examples, see Yusuf Ünal, 'Princesses, Patronage, and the Production of Knowledge in Safavid Iran', in Mirjam Künkler and Devin J. Stewart, ed., *Women's Religious Authority in Shiʿi Islam* (Edinburgh, 2021).

[3] Juan Cole, 'Shiʿi Clerics in Iraq and Iran, 1722–1780: The Akhbari-Usuli Conflict Reconsidered', *Iranian Studies*, 18 (1985), pp. 3–34; Etan Kohlberg, 'Aspects of Akhbārī Thought in the Seventeenth and Eighteenth Centuries', in Nehemia Levtzion and John O. Voll, ed., *Eighteenth Century Renewal and Reform in Islam* (Syracuse, 1987), pp. 133–160; Andrew J. Newman 'The Nature of the Akhbārī/Uṣūlī Dispute in Late Ṣafawid Iran. Part 1: ʿAbdallāh al-Samāhijī's "*Munyat al-Mumārisīn*"', *BSOAS*, 55 (1992), pp. 22–51; idem, 'The Nature of the Akhbārī/Uṣūlī Dispute in Late Ṣafawid Iran, Part 2: The Conflict Reassessed', *BSOAS*, 55 (1992), pp. 250–261; Devin J. Stewart, *Islamic Legal Orthodoxy: Twelver Shiʿi Responses to the Sunni Legal System* (Salt Lake City, UT, 1998), pp. 175–208; idem, 'The Genesis of the Akhbārī Revival', in Michel Mazzaoui, ed., *Safavid Iran and Her Neighbors* (Salt Lake City, UT, 2003), pp. 169–193; Mazlum Uyar, *Ahbârîlik Imami Şiasından Düşünce Ekolleri* (Istanbul, 2000); Robert Gleave, 'The Akhbārī-Uṣūlī Dispute in *Ṭabaqāt* Literature: An Analysis of the Biographies of Yūsuf al-Baḥrānī and Muḥammad Bāqir al-Bihbihānī', *Jusur: UCLA Journal of Middle Eastern Studies*, 10 (1994), pp. 79–109; Robert Gleave, 'Akhbārī Shīʿī *Uṣūl al-fiqh* and the Juristic theory of Yūsuf b. Aḥmad al-Baḥrānī', in Robert Gleave and E. Kermeli, ed., *Islamic law: Theory and Practice* (London, 1997), pp. 24–45; idem, *Inevitable Doubt: Two Theories of Shīʿī Jurisprudence* (Leiden, 2000); idem, 'The Qadi and the Mufti in Akhbari Shiʿi Jurisprudence', in Wolfhart Heinrichs, Peri Bearman and Bernard Weiss, ed., *The Law Applied: Contextualizing the Islamic*

that has not been satisfactorily explained hitherto is the broad role of the Akhbārī movement in shaping Safavid literary production. Overall, then, advances have been made in the understanding of both the production of learned works during the Safavid period and the contours and effects of the Akhbārī movement, but the intersection of these two phenomena has only been addressed in a piecemeal and incomplete fashion. The present essay is an attempt to provide an overview of the influence of Akhbārism on Safavid literary production, building on and expanding the work of a limited number of studies that mention the Akhbārī influence on particular works and genres.

The Akhbārī Movement

The beginning of the Akhbārī movement may be dated to the first half of the 11th/17th century and more precisely to 1031/1622, when Muḥammad Amīn al-Astarābādī (d. 1036/1626-27) published *al-Fawāʾid al-madaniyya*, in effect the movement's manifesto. Although the Akhbārīs claimed to be revitalising an earlier trend in Twelver Shiʿism, and despite the fact that the exact term *akhbārī* had been used in Twelver Shiʿi writings centuries earlier, such as in the manual of legal hermeneutics *Nihāyat al-uṣūl* by al-ʿAllāma al-Ḥillī (d. 726/1325), it is clear that this movement was a new phenomenon and not the continuation of an existing trend. It was not directly related to the thought of earlier thinkers labelled Akhbārīs in Twelver history. In *al-Fawāʾid al-madaniyya*, Muḥammad Amīn al-Astarābādī decried two historical developments in the history of Twelver jurisprudence and legal hermeneutics. One was the adoption of a system for grading

Shariʿa, Studies in Honor of Frank Vogel (London, 2007), pp. 235–258; idem, 'Questions and Answers in Akhbari Jurisprudence', in A. Christmann, Robert Gleave and Colin Imber, ed., *Studies in Islamic law* (Oxford, 2007), pp. 73–122; idem, *Scripturalist Islam: The History and Doctrines of the Akhbārī Shīʿī School* (Leiden, 2009); idem, 'Compromise and Conciliation in the Akhbārī–Uṣūlī Dispute: Yūsuf al-Baḥrānī's Assessment of ʿAbd Allāh al-Samāhījī's *Munyat al-Mumārisīn*', in Omar Alí-de-Unzaga, ed., *Fortresses of the Intellect: Ismaili and Other Islamic Studies in Honour of Farhad Daftary* (London, 2011), pp. 491–520; Rula Jurdi Abisaab, 'Was Muḥammad Amīn al-Astarābādī (d. 1036/1626-27) a Mujtahid?', *SSR*, 2 (2018), pp. 38–61; Etan Kohlberg, 'Akbārīya', *EIr*, vol. 1, pp. 716–718.

the authenticity of *ḥadīth* reports, including the levels of *ṣaḥīḥ* 'strong', *ḥasan* 'good' and *ḍaʿīf* 'weak'. The other was, as he put it, the division of Twelver Shiʿis into two groups, the members of which are termed *mujtahid* 'one who is capable of arriving at independent legal rulings' and *muqallid* 'one who submits to the opinion and authority of another'. According to al-Astarābādī, both of these developments were due to Sunni influence.

The Akhbārī movement was intended to right what the Akhbārīs viewed as a historical tragedy. In their view, Shiʿi jurists had, over centuries, assimilated their legal system to that of the Sunni legal *madhhab*s to an unacceptable degree. At the same time, they had adopted a view of the religion that assigned religious authority to an exclusive group of scholars who attained their authority through training in rationalist legal hermeneutics. One characteristic of the jurisprudence adopted by this group was that they were willing to override the evidence of a *ḥadīth* report, which they considered a scriptural text, with probative value, in favour of a variety of rational arguments. The Akhbārīs argued instead that, during the occultation of the Twelfth imam, when direct, intentional contact with the imam was cut off, Shiʿi believers had to rely on recourse to the oral reports, or *akhbār*, of the imams, as preserved in the canonical Twelver Shiʿi collections, and interpretive priority should be given to these texts over any rational considerations. Their designation as Akhbārīs derived from their insistence on the idea that religious authority inhered in the texts, the *akhbār* of the imams.

Developments in the field of *ḥadīth* criticism played a critical role in sparking the Akhbārī movement. Jamāl al-Dīn b. Ṭāwūs (d. 673/1274-75) and al-ʿAllāma al-Ḥillī had written on *ḥadīth* criticism, but the main impetus for al-Astarābādī's manifesto was a more recent work by Zayn al-Dīn al-ʿĀmilī (d. 965/1558) and the scholarly disputes it had engendered. By applying methods of *ḥadīth* criticism that he had adopted from Sunni works to the canonical Shiʿi *ḥadīth* works, Zayn al-Dīn had created what the Akhbārīs viewed as an epistemological threat to the entire Shiʿi *ḥadīth* corpus. It was this threat above all that drove al-Astarābādī to write *al-Fawāʾid al-madaniyya*. He was intent upon defending the integrity of the *ḥadīth* corpus and particularly concerned about the assimilation of Shiʿi learned institutions to Sunni norms. The *akhbār* of the imams, in his view, represented the surest, indeed for most intents and purposes the only, means of access to their guidance. The authenticity of the extant Shiʿi *ḥadīth* corpus had to be upheld *in toto*. Furthermore, religious authority did not lie in a class of jurists but rather in the texts themselves. The Akhbārīs, like Martin Luther with the famous dictum *sola scriptura*, sought to locate authority in the texts themselves. Even if this, in a practical sense, was impossible, the implication is that in order for scholars to participate in Shiʿi religious authority, they needed to consult *ḥadīth* reports above all other sources. One may argue that, in both cases, this was somewhat disingenuous attempt to argue that authority is not actually located in people. In the case of the Akhbārīs, it appears that, in essence, they were attributing religious authority to experts in *ḥadīth* above other categories of scholars.[4]

Zayn al-Dīn wrote two works on *ḥadīth* criticism, one of which has been lost, and one of which is extant. Zayn al-Dīn's student, Ibn al-ʿAwdī, lists in his master's bibliography the work *Kitāb Ghunyat al-qāṣidīn fī maʿrifat iṣṭilāḥāt al-muḥaddithīn*, and Zayn al-Dīn mentions it at the end of his extant work on *ḥadīth* criticism, suggesting that it was incomplete but would be more comprehensive.[5] As far as is known, this work is not extant. The work that has survived is a basic text along with its commentary, the title of which Ibn al-ʿAwdī gives as *al-Bidāya fī ʿilm al-dirāya*, 'and its commentary'.[6] This work has been published several times and translated into English once.[7] In the colophon Zayn al-Dīn records that he completed the work on the eve of Tuesday, 5 Dhu'l-Ḥijja 959/22 November 1552.[8] The commentary,

4 Stewart, 'The Genesis of the Akhbari Movement'.

5 ʿAlī al-ʿĀmilī, *al-Durr al-manthūr min al-maʾthūr wa-ghayr al-maʾthūr* (Qum, 1398/1978), vol. 2, p. 188; Zayn al-Dīn al-ʿĀmilī, *Sharḥ al-Bidāya fī ʿilm al-dirāya*, ed. Muḥammad Riḍā al-Ḥusaynī al-Jalālī (Qum, 1432/2011), pp. 141–142.

6 ʿAlī al-ʿĀmilī, *al-Durr al-manthūr*, vol. 2, p. 188.

7 Zayn al-Dīn al-ʿĀmilī, *al-Dirāya: Sharḥ al-Bidāya fī ʿilm al-dirāya* (Tehran, 1360 Sh./1981); *Sharḥ al-Bidāya fī ʿilm al-dirāya*, ed. ʿAbd al-Ḥusayn Muḥammad ʿAlī Baqqāl (Tehran, 1361–62 Sh./1982–83); Zayn al-Dīn al-ʿĀmilī, *al-Riʿāya li-ḥāl al-bidāya fī ʿilm al-dirāya wa al-Bidāya fī ʿilm al-dirāya* (Qum, 1381 Sh./2002); Zayn al-Dīn al-ʿĀmilī, *Dirāyat al-ḥadīth*, English translation followed by *Introduction to Ḥadīth* by ʿAbd al-Hādī al-Faḍlī, tr. Nazmina Virjee (London, 2002).

8 Zayn al-Dīn al-ʿĀmilī, *Sharḥ al-Bidāya*, ed. Muḥammad Riḍā al-Ḥusaynī al-Jalālī (2nd ed., Qum, 1389 Sh./2011), p. 142.

entitled *al-Riʿāya li-ḥāl al-Bidāya*, is an interwoven commentary (*sharḥ mazj*), in which the original text, distinguished by overlining, is written into the sentences of the commentary, rather than being presented separately, after sections of the original text.

Zayn al-Dīn's work on *ḥadīth* criticism soon influenced the teaching of religious learning in Iran. His student Ḥusayn b. ʿAbd al-Ṣamad (d. 984/1576), who studied with him and travelled and taught with him for decades, also became a proponent of the teaching of the subjects connected with *ḥadīth*. Ḥusayn reached the Safavid empire in 961/1554 and stayed there until 983/1575, the year before he died. The Safavid chronicler, Iskandar Beg Munshī, emphasises the point that Ḥusayn studied *taṣḥīḥ-i ḥadīth va-rijāl* with Zayn al-Dīn, in addition to instruction in the tools of legal interpretation.[9] Mīrzā ʿAbd Allāh al-Iṣfahānī reports that Ḥusayn played a pivotal role in promoting the study of the canonical Shiʿi *ḥadīth* works.[10] Shortly after arriving and settling in Iṣfahān in 961/1554, Ḥusayn wrote a work on *ḥadīth* criticism that is based closely on *al-Bidāya fī ʿilm al-dirāya*. It is essentially a rearranged, slightly expanded, version of the text. Ḥusayn reports that he completed the work in Mashhad, and he dedicated it to the reigning shah, Ṭahmāsp I (r. 930–984/1524–1576). It is possible that he completed the work later the same year, 961/1554, after undertaking a pilgrimage to Mashhad.

A third figure who was involved in the spread of the teaching of Shiʿi *ḥadīth* criticism was ʿAbd Allāh b. al-Ḥusayn al-Tustarī [or al-Shūshtarī] (d. 1021/1612). He was born in Shūshtar, and in his youth studied in the shrine cities of Iraq with al-Muqaddas Aḥmad b. Muḥammad al-Ardabīlī (d. 993/1585). In 987/1579-80 he made the *ḥajj*, and on the way back he stopped in the town of ʿAynāthā in Jabal ʿĀmil, where he received *ijāza*s from Niʿmat Allāh b. Aḥmad b. Muḥammad b. Khātūn al-ʿĀmilī and his son Aḥmad. One *ijāza* is dated 17 Muḥarram 988/4 March 1580 and the other to the middle decade of Muḥarram 988/ early March 1580. He apparently arrived in Iṣfahān after fleeing from

---

9 Iskandar Beg Munshī, *Tārīkh-i ʿālam-ārā-yi ʿAbbāsī* (Tehran, 1350 Sh./1971), vol. 1, p. 155.

10 Mīrzā ʿAbd Allāh al-Iṣfahānī, *Riyāḍ al-ʿulamāʾ wa-ḥiyāḍ al-fuḍalāʾ*, ed. Aḥmad al-Ḥusaynī (Qum, 1401/1980), vol. 2, p. 118.

Karbala around 1006/1598. Mīrzā ʿAbd Allāh al-Iṣfahānī suggests that he fled from Iṣfahān to Mashhad some time after this on account of some problem with the shah, but that he was restored to favour when the shah came to Mashhad, which must have been on the occasion of Shah ʿAbbās's famous barefoot pilgrimage in 1009/1601. Al-Tustarī supposedly played an instrumental role in convincing Shah ʿAbbās to make the extensive pious endowment called the *chahārdah maʿṣūm* 'The Fourteen Chaste Ones'. He returned to Iṣfahān with Shah ʿAbbās, who had a *madrasa* built for him where he reportedly taught hundreds of students. Many of the scholars of the next several generations who were trained in the *ḥadīth* sciences had him as their main teacher, including his son Ḥasan ʿAlī al-Tustarī (d. 1069/1658-59), and Mīr Muḥammad Qāsim Quhpā'ī (fl. 11th/17th c.), Mīrzā Rafīʿ al-Dīn al-Qā'inī (fl. 11th/17th c.), Muḥammad Taqī al-Majlisī (d. 1070/1660), ʿAbd Allāh b. Muḥammad al-Fāḍil al-Tūnī (d. 1071/1660-61), and Muṣṭafā al-Tafrishī (fl. 11th/17th c.). He died on 26 Muḥarram 1021/29 March 1612. Iskandar Beg Munshī reports in *Tārīkh-i ʿālam-ārā-yi ʿAbbāsī* that he had studied for thirty years with al-Muqaddas al-Ardabīlī.[11] His student, Muḥammad Taqī al-Majlisī, wrote that when al-Tustarī first arrived in Iṣfahān there were no more than fifty students of the religious sciences in the capital, but by the time he died, about fourteen years later, there were over a thousand.[12] As Abisaab and Gleave have noted, together with Ḥusayn b. ʿAbd al-Ṣamad, he was responsible for a surge in interest in *ḥadīth* scholarship before the Akhbārī movement, something that is particularly evident from the writings of his students. Robert Gleave has discussed al-Tustarī's teaching of *ḥadīth* and *ḥadīth*-based elaboration of the law, referring to his 'proto-Akhbārī *madrasa*' in Iṣfahān.[13]

---

[11] Iskandar Beg Munshī, *Tārīkh-i ʿālam-ārā-yi ʿAbbāsī*, vol. 2, pp. 859–860; Al-Ḥurr al-ʿĀmilī, *Amal al-āmil*, vol. 2, p. 159; Mīrzā ʿAbd Allāh al-Iṣfahānī, *Riyāḍ al-ʿulamā'*, vol. 3, pp. 195–205; Muḥammad Bāqir al-Khwānsārī, *Rawḍāt al-jannāt wa-aḥwāl al-ʿulamā' wa'l-sādāt* (Qum, 1390–1392/1970–1972), vol. 4, pp. 234–235.

[12] Muḥammad Bāqir al-Khwānsārī, *Rawḍāt al-jannāt*, vol. 4, p. 241, citing Muḥammad Taqī al-Majlisī's commentary on the *mashyakha* of *Man lā yaḥḍuruhu al-faqīh*. This would imply that he first arrived in Isfahan ca. 1006/1598.

[13] Abisaab, *Converting Persia*, p. 106; Gleave, *Scripturalist Islam*, pp. 163–165, 238–239.

In the next generation after Zayn al-Dīn, various scholars wrote several short works on *ḥadīth* criticism. Zayn al-Dīn's son al-Ḥasan b. Zayn al-Dīn al-ʿĀmilī (d. 1011/1602) wrote a short treatise on *ḥadīth* criticism as an introduction to his work on *ḥadīth*, *Muntaqā al-jumān*, which he completed in 1006/1597-98. Ḥusayn's son, Bahā' al-Dīn Muḥammad, wrote *al-Wajīza*, a similarly short work on *ḥadīth* criticism as an introduction to *al-Ḥabl al-matīn*, which he completed in Mashhad on 18 Shawwāl 1007/14 May 1599, and yet another similar short treatise as an introduction to his work *Mashriq al-shamsayn*, which he completed in Qum on 14 Dhu'l-Qaʿda 1015/13 March 1607.[14]

The application of *ḥadīth* criticism to the Twelver Shiʿi *ḥadīth* corpus posed an epistemological threat. According to Zayn al-Dīn and his student, Ḥusayn b. ʿAbd al-Ṣamad, many of the *ḥadīth* reports in the canonical Twelver Shiʿi *ḥadīth* books could not be categorised as 'sound' or even as 'good', because their chains of authority were defective in some way. Either not enough information was provided about the transmitters in the first place, since there were simply missing links in the chain, or the transmitters were unknown or not Imāmīs, or there was insufficient evidence of their probity and reliability as transmitters. This critical stance presented a problem for the elaboration of Islamic law from the Twelver Shiʿi perspective, because it threatened to remove from consideration many reports on which legal rulings had been based for centuries. With so much of the scriptural evidence removed, there was a chance that many traditional Twelver legal positions would be weakened or undermined.

It was in large part in response to this challenge that the Akhbārī movement emerged. They fundamentally opposed the *ḥadīth* criticism of Zayn al-Dīn al-ʿĀmilī and viewed it as a faulty and alien import from Sunni *ḥadīth* criticism inserted into the Shiʿi learned tradition. Their response to the epistemological threat was to champion the opposing view. They held that the canonical collections of Shiʿi *ḥadīth* were of unassailable authenticity *in toto*. It did not make sense to try to perform a triage, separating out layers of varying probability and reliability,

14 Stewart, 'Genesis', pp. 177–178.

when the whole corpus was guaranteed.[15] In their efforts to promote their views and to bolster the authority of the canonical Shiʿi *ḥadīth* collections, the Akhbārī movement exerted a tremendous influence on the production of works of Islamic religious learning, primarily in the Safavid empire and primarily in the 11th/17th and early 12th/18th centuries, but also extending beyond these parameters to lands outside Iran and into the late 12th/18th and the 19th century as well. The following is an attempt to outline the main genres that were strongly affected, building on and gathering together existing secondary scholarship but also examining particular primary texts in detail.

The Akhbārī Movement and Safavid Literary Production

A. *Akhbārī and Uṣūlī Legal Hermeneutics*

The first set of works that were engendered by the Akhbārī movement were direct polemical writings. These included, first and foremost, the work that inaugurated the movement, Muḥammad Amīn al-Astarābādī's *al-Fawāʾid al-madaniyya*.[16] Though this book touched on a large number of topics, including law, theology, *ḥadīth*, *tafsīr* and philosophy, the fundamental message of the text had to do primarily with legal hermeneutics. Above all, it aimed to refute the hermeneutical claims and methods of contemporary Twelver Shiʿi jurists. That this was the centre of Akhbārī thought and the basis of

[15] I have discussed these developments in Stewart, *Islamic Legal Orthodoxy*, pp. 175–208; Stewart, 'The Genesis of the Akhbari Movement'. Rula Jurdi Abisaab has criticised the views expressed there, and particularly the idea that the Akhbārī movement was motivated in part by resistance to the Shiʿi jurists' assimilation of Sunni norms. She argues instead that the movement arose primarily because of factors internal to Shiʿism and that the Akhbārīs and their opponents were drawing on various ideas found in the majority Islamic tradition. She stresses in particular the Akhbaris' scepticism regarding the epistemology and methods of the rationalist jurists and their rejection of Safavid legitimacy and the *mujtahids*' legal authority. See Rula Jurdi Abisaab, 'Shīʿī Jurisprudence, Sunnism, and the Traditionist Thought (Akhbārī) of Muḥammad Amīn Astarabādī (D. 1626-27)', *IJMES*, 47 (2015), pp. 5–23. I hope to address these criticisms in a future study.

[16] Muḥammad Amīn al-Astarabādī, *al-Fawāʾid al-madaniyya, wa-bi-dhaylihi al-Shawāhid al-makkiyya li-Nūr al-Dīn al-Mūsawī al-ʿĀmilī* (Qum, 1426/2005).

their movement may be understood from the fact that their opponents came to be known primarily as the 'Uṣūlīs', indicating their dependence on *uṣūl al-fiqh*, the 'roots of the law', that is, jurisprudence or legal hermeneutics. *Al-Fawā'id al-madaniyya* engendered a number of other works in the same category, such as *al-Shawāhid al-makkiyya*, a refutation of *al-Fawā'id al-madaniyya* by al-Sayyid Nūr al-Dīn ʿAlī b. ʿAlī b. al-Ḥusayn b. Abī al-Ḥasan al-Mūsawī al-Āmilī (d. 1068/1657-58). The most important continuations of *al-Fawā'id al-madaniyya* were written by Muḥsin Fayḍ al-Kāshānī (d. 1091/1680), *Safinat al-najāh* and *al-Uṣūl al-aṣīla*.

This category includes a number of specialised discussions that list subsidiary issues related to the hermeneutical stances espoused by the Akhbārīs and their opponents. Andrew Newman has discussed one important example of this genre of text, that of ʿAbd Allāh al-Samāhījī (d. 1135/1722-23), which was titled *Munyat al-mumārisīn*.[17] Robert Gleave has discussed a large number of other examples of such lists, both those that exist as independent works, like that of al-Samāhījī, and those that are embedded in larger works. He provides an appendix that identifies twenty-five of these texts, ranging in date from the 12th/18th century to the 20th century. A substantial chapter of his work, *Scripturalist Islam*, discusses the various ways in which these lists frame and portray the Akhbārī-Uṣūlī conflict.[18]

Other works address particular issues in the broader category of legal hermeneutics. A prominent doctrinal dispute in this area was that of *taqlīd al-mayyit*: whether one could adhere to, and base one's religious practice on, the opinions of a deceased authority. Zayn al-Dīn al-ʿĀmilī had written a work against this view, and his opinion represented a common view among the Uṣūlīs. Many Akhbārīs rejected this position, along with the ideas that *mujtahid*s had the exclusive right to interpret scriptural material having to do with law and theology and that non-*mujtahid*s were required to follow the opinions of a living *mujtahid*. Zayn al-Dīn's work rejecting adopting the opinion of a deceased jurist as authoritative, *Risāla fi ʿadam jawāz taqlīd al-mayyit*,

[17] Newman, 'The Nature of the Akhbārī/Uṣūlī Dispute in Late Ṣafawid Iran', parts 1 and 2.

[18] Gleave, *Scripturalist Islam*, pp. 177–215, 311–314.

was completed on 15 Shawwāl 949/22 January 1543. He dedicated it to his student al-Sayyid Ḥusayn b. Abi'l-Ḥasan (d. before 980/1572-73), who was also his father-in-law.[19] It is interesting that Zayn al-Dīn wrote the work in the year following his announcement of his status as a *mujtahid*, 948/1542, something which suggests that the treatise was meant in part to support his claim to have attained *ijtihād*. He was apparently arguing against contemporaries who were still following the opinions of al-Muḥaqqiq al-Karakī, who had died in 940/1534 and was widely recognised as the most important jurist of the previous generation.

A representative text on the Akhbārī side of the debate is *Manbaʿ al-ḥayāt*, by Niʿmat Allāh al-Jazāʾirī (d. 1112/1701). Robert Gleave has discussed this text briefly in his book on the history and doctrines of the Akhbārīs.[20] Niʿmat Allāh al-Jazāʾirī completed his treatise, entitled *Kitāb Manbaʿ al-ḥayāt wa-ḥujjiyyat qawl al-mujtahid min al-amwāt* in Shūshtar in southwestern Iran on 6 Jumādā II 1100/28 March 1689. Though the title does not refer to Zayn al-Dīn's treatise, it is clear from al-Jazāʾirī's introduction that he is undertaking a refutation of that work in particular. Al-Jazāʾirī's remark that he came to this question after reading widely in Twelver Shiʿi religious literature while writing his commentaries on *Tahdhīb al-aḥkām* and *al-Istibṣār* suggests he was presenting it as an attempt to correct a historical deviation from earlier Shiʿi positions, as is evident when studying the full span of Shiʿi legal texts.

These two works, however, are only a small part of the literary production on this question. Āqā Buzurg al-Ṭihrānī's catalogue of Shiʿi works, *al-Dharīʿa ilā taṣānīf al-shīʿa*, includes twenty-one works devoted to the topic of *taqlīd al-mayyit* or *taqlīd al-amwāt* that were written between the 10th/16th and the 20th century.[21] The works that are clearly meant to uphold Zayn al-Dīn al-ʿĀmilī's position on the topic, that it is forbidden to adopt the opinion of a deceased *mujtahid* and also obligatory for the layman to adopt the opinion of a living *mujtahid*, include the following:

---

19 ʿAlī al-ʿĀmilī, *al-Durr al-manthūr*, vol. 2, p. 188.

20 Gleave, *Scripturalist Islam*, pp. 194–202.

21 Muḥammad Muḥsin Āqā Buzurg al-Ṭihrānī, *al-Dharīʿa ilā taṣānīf al-shīʿa* (Qum, 1366 Sh./1987), vol. 4, pp. 390–393, vol. 11, p. 154.

Taqlīd al-mayyit, Zayn al-Dīn al-ʿĀmilī (d. 965/1558)
Taqlīd al-mayyit, Ḥasan b. Zayn al-Dīn (d. 1011/1601-2)
Taqlīd al-mayyit, Muḥammad b. Jābir b. ʿAbbās al-ʿĀmilī al-Najafī (11th/17th c.)
Taqlīd al-mayyit, Muḥammad Bāqir al-Bihbihānī (d. 1205/1791)

Treatises on the topic that espoused the opposite opinion, allowing laymen to adopt the opinion of a deceased authority, are the following:

Taqlīd al-mayyit, Faḍl Allāh al-Astarābādī (fl. 10th/16th c.)
Taqlīd al-mayyit, ʿAbd al-Laṭīf b. Nūr al-Dīn ʿAlī b. Aḥmad al-Jāmiʿī (11th/17th c.) *Taqlīd al-mayyit*, al-Ḥurr al-ʿĀmilī (d. 1104/1693)
Manbaʿ al-ḥayāt, Niʿmat Allāh al-Jazāʾirī (d. 1112/1701)
Taqlīd al-mayyit, Sulaymān b. ʿAbd Allāh al-Māḥūzī (d. 1121/1709-10)
Taqlīd al-mayyit, Mīrzā Muḥammad b. al-Ḥasan al-Shirwānī (d. 1098/1687)
Risāla fī taqlīd al-mayyit, Mullā Muḥsin b. Samīʿ (fl. early 12th/18th c.)
Taqlīd al-mayyit, Muḥammad b. ʿAbd ʿAlī b. Muḥammad b. Aḥmad Āl ʿAbd al-Jabbār al-Qaṭīfī (fl. 12th/18th c.)

Overall, scholarship on this topic began before the rise of the Akhbārī movement in the 11th/17th century. Both Zayn al-Dīn and his son evidently wrote on the topic. Indeed, it is suggested that refutations were also written before the rise of the Akhbārīs, by Faḍl Allāh al-Astarābādī, a contemporary of Zayn al-Dīn, and ʿAbd al-Laṭīf al-Jāmiʿī, a student of Zayn al-Dīn's son. However, it is clear from al-Jazāʾirī's *Manbaʿ al-ḥayāt* and from other works by al-Ḥurr al-ʿĀmilī and Sulaymān al-Māḥūzī that this topic was of significant concern to Akhbārīs generally. Moreover, the treatise by al-Bihbihānī shows that this issue was also one that the opponents of the Akhbārīs viewed as a crucial part of their general refutation of the Akhbārīs' legal hermeneutics.

B. *Commentaries on the canonical* ḥadīth *works*

A principal area of literary production that was spurred on by the Akhbārī movement was the publication of commentaries on the canonical Shiʿi *ḥadīth* works: *al-Kāfī* by Muḥammad b. Yaʿqūb al-Kulaynī (d. 329/941), *Man lā yaḥḍuruhu al-faqīh* by Muḥammad b. Bābawayh al-Qummī (d. 381/991), and *Tahdhīb al-aḥkām* and *al-Istibṣār* by Muḥammad b. al-Ḥasan al-Ṭūsī (d. 460/1067). In the 11th/17th century a large number of commentaries on these collections was produced in Iran. Aside from the obvious intention to explain and elaborate on difficult or complex passages in these collections, such commentaries reflected an aim to bolster the authenticity of the standard Shiʿi *ḥadīth* corpus, which had been called into question by the application of stringent *ḥadīth* criticism to the reports they contained. They also stressed the idea that the four canonical collections together form an integral whole that should not be split up or picked apart. The following lists of commentaries on the four canonical *ḥadīth* works represent those that are mentioned in *al-Dharīʿa ilā uṣūl al-sharīʿa*. I have excluded a number of works that al-Tihrānī included on the grounds that they were produced long after the Safavid period.[22]

Commentaries on *al-Kāfī*:[23]

1. *al-Rawāshiḥ al-samāwiyya*, by Mīr Muḥammad Bāqir-i Dāmād al-Astarābādī (d. 1041/1632).
2. Commentary by Rafīʿ al-Dīn Muḥammad b. Muʾmin al-Jīlānī (fl. 11th/17th c.), a student of Bahāʾ al-Dīn al-ʿĀmilī (d. 1030/1621).
3. *al-Ṣāfī fī sharḥ al-Kāfī*, by Mullā Khalīl al-Qazwīnī completed 1064-74/1653-64.
4. Commentary by Mīrzā Rafīʿ al-Dīn Muḥammad al-Nāʾīnī (d. 1082/1671).
5. Commentary by Muḥammad Ṣāliḥ al-Māzandarānī (d. 1086/1675).
6. *Mirʾāt al-ʿuqūl*, by Muḥammad Bāqir al-Majlisī (d. 1111/1699)
7. Commentary by Muḥammad Hādī b. Muḥammad Ṣāliḥ al-Māzandarānī (fl. late 11th/17th c.).
8. Commentary by Yaʿqūb b. Ibrāhīm b. Jamāl al-Ḥuwayzī (d. 1147/1734-35).

22 Robert Gleave is working on a study of commentaries on *ḥadīth* works in the Safavid and later periods.

23 Āqā Buzurg, *al-Dharīʿa ilā taṣānīf al-shīʿa*, vol. 14, pp. 26–28.

Commentaries on *Uṣūl al-Kāfī*:[24]

1. Muḥammad Amīn al-Astarābādī (d. 1036/1626-27).
2. Mullā Ṣadrā, Ṣadr al-Dīn Muḥammad b. Ibrāhīm al-Shīrāzī (d. 1050/1640), completed in Shīrāz in 1044/1634-35.
3. Anonymous, begun in Mecca in 1057/1647-48, uses philosophical language.
4. Ismāʿīl al-Khātūnābādī (fl. 11th/17th c.)
5. *Shawāhid al-Islām*, by Mullā Rafīʿā, Rafīʿ al-Dīn Muḥammad b. Ḥaydar al-Ḥasanī al-Nāʾīnī (d. 1082/1071).
6. Muḥammad Ṣāliḥ b. Aḥmad al-Sarawī al-Māzandarānī (d. 1086/1675), in four large volumes. He finished *Kitāb al-ʿAql wa-faḍl al-ʿilm* on 14 Ṣafar 1063/14 January 1563. In it, he refuted Mullā Ṣadrā's commentary. He also wrote a continuation, commenting on the next sections of *al-Kāfī*.
7. Muḥammad Maʿṣūm b. Mīr Faṣīḥ b. Mīr Awliyāʾ al-Tabrīzī al-Qazwīnī (d. 1091/1680-81).
8. ʿAlī b. Muḥammad b. al-Ḥasan b. Zayn al-Dīn (d. 1103/1692). He completed the commentary on the chapters of *al-ʿaql* and *al-ʿilm*, and gave it the title *al-Durr al-manẓūm min kalām al-maʿṣūm*.
9. . . . b. Muḥammad Shafīʿ (fl. late 11th/17th c.).
10. Muḥammad Ḥusayn b. Yaḥyā al-Nūrī al-Māzandarānī (d. after 1133/1720-21), student of Muḥammad Bāqir al-Majlisī.

Commentaries on *Man lā yaḥḍuruhu al-faqīh*, by Ibn Bābawayh al-Qummī:[25]

1. Commentary by Bahāʾ al-Dīn al-ʿĀmilī (d. 1030/1621).
2. *Maʿāhid al-tanbīh*, by Muḥammad b. al-Ḥasan b. Zayn al-Dīn (d. 1030/1621), grandson of al-Shahīd al-Thānī.
3. *Rawḍat al-muttaqīn*, in Arabic, by Muḥammad Taqī al-Majlisī (d. 1070/1659)
4. *al-Lawāmiʿ al-qudsiyya*, in Persian, by Muḥammad Taqī al-Majlisī (d. 1070/1659).

---

[24] Āqā Buzurg, *al-Dharīʿa ilā taṣānīf al-shīʿa*, vol. 13, pp. 94–100.

[25] Ibid., vol. 14, pp. 93–95.

5. Commentary by Mullā Ḥusām al-Dīn Muḥammad Ṣāliḥ b. Mullā Aḥmad al-Sarawī al-Māzandarānī (d. 1081/1670-71).
6. Mīr Muḥammad Ṣāliḥ b. Mīr ʿAbd al-Wāsiʿ al-Khātūnābādī (d. 1126/1714),
7. *Miʿrāj al-nabīh*, by Yūsuf al-Baḥrānī (d. 1186/1772).

Commentaries on *al-Istibṣār*, by al-Shaykh Muḥammad b. al-Ḥasan al-Ṭūsī:[26]

1. Muḥammad b. al-Ḥasan b. Zayn al-Dīn (d. 1030/1621).
2. Muḥammad Amīn al-Astarābādī (d. 1036/1626-27), incomplete.
3. Mīr Dāmād (d. 1041/1632), perhaps similar to *al-Rawāshiḥ al-samāwiyya*.
4. ʿAbd al-Laṭīf b. Abī Jāmiʿ al-ʿĀmilī (d. 1050/1640).
5. ʿAbd al-Rashīd b. Nūr al-Dīn al-Tustarī (d. ca. 1078/1667–68).
6. Niʿmat Allāh al-Jazāʾirī (d. 1112/1701). He first wrote a short commentary, then expanded it to form the work *Kashf al-asrār*.
7. Sayyid ʿAbd al-Riḍā b. ʿAbd al-Ṣamad al-Ḥusaynī al-Uwālī al-Baḥrānī (fl. late 11th/17th c.).
8. Muḥammad Ṣāliḥ b. ʿAbd al-Wāsiʿ al-Khātūnābādī (d. 1126/1714).
9. Sayyid Muḥsin b. al-Ḥasan al-Aʿrajī al-Kāẓimī (d. 1127/1715).

Commentaries on *Tahdhīb al-aḥkām*, by al-Shaykh al-Ṭūsī:[27]

1. Muḥammad b. ʿAlī b. Abī al-Ḥasan al-Mūsawī al-ʿĀmilī (d. 1009/1600-1)
2. al-Qāḍī Nūr Allāh al-Shushtarī (d. 1019/1610).
3. Mullā ʿAbd Allāh b. al-Ḥusayn al-Tustarī (d. 26 Muḥarram 1021/29 March 1612). Niʿmat Allāh al-Jazāʾirī quotes this work in his commentary.
4. Muḥammad b. al-Ḥasan b. Zayn al-Dīn (d. 1030/1621).
5. Muḥammad Amīn al-Astarābādī (d. 1036/1626-27), incomplete.
6. ʿAbd al-Laṭīf b. ʿAlī b. Aḥmad b. Abī Jāmiʿ al-ʿĀmilī (d. 1050/1640).

---

[26] Ibid., vol. 13, pp. 83–87.

[27] Āqā Buzurg, *al-Dharīʿa ilā taṣānīf al-shīʿa*, vol. 13, pp. 155–159.

7. *Iḥyā' al-aḥādīth*, by Muḥammad Taqī al-Majlisī (d. 1070/1659).
8. Muḥammad Ṭāhir b. Muḥammad Ḥusayn al-Shīrāzī al-Qummī (d. 1098/1686-87).
9. Muḥammad b. al-Ḥasan al-Shīrwānī (d. 1099/1687-88).
10. ʿAbd Allāh b. Muḥammad Taqī al-Majlisī (fl. 11th/17th c.).
11. *Malādh al-akhyār fī fahm Tahdhīb al-akhbār*, by Muḥammad Bāqir al-Majlisī (d. 1111/1699).
12. An extensive commentary by Niʿmat Allāh b. ʿAbd Allāh al-Jazā'irī (d. 1112/1701), in twelve volumes. Only parts of it are extant.
13. *Ghāyat al-marām*, by Niʿmat Allāh b. ʿAbd Allāh al-Jazā'irī (d. 1112/1701), an abridged version of the previous work, in eight volumes.
14. Anonymous commentary which cites the works of Muḥammad Bāqir al-Majlisī and Niʿmat Allāh al-Jazā'irī.
15. Aḥmad b. Ismāʿīl al-Jazā'irī al-Najafī (d. 1149/1136-37).

Even though Āqā Buzurg was a very careful scholar, it is likely that important examples have been missed because they were uncatalogued and not accessible to him, because they had individual titles that did not make it clear that they were commentaries on one of the four canonical *ḥadīth* books, or because they have simply been lost. The lists provided above represent an attempt to indicate the scope of production of these commentaries.

Not all of the authors of these works were Akhbārī jurists, but it is nevertheless true that the Akhbārī movement provided the main impetus for their production. Very striking is the fact that Āqā Buzurg al-Ṭihrānī does not record any such commentaries during the exceedingly long period between the 5th/11th century, by which time the canonical collections had been compiled, and the late 10th/16th century. But several commentaries were written before Muḥammad Amīn al-Astarābādī completed *al-Fawā'id al-madaniyya*. They include works by such authors as Ṣāḥib al-Madārik, Mullā ʿAbd Allāh b. al-Ḥusayn al-Tustarī, al-Qāḍī Nūr Allāh al-Shushtarī and Muḥammad b. al-Ḥasan b. Zayn al-Dīn al-ʿĀmilī.

In the 11th/17th century, there was an explosion in the writing of these works. Muḥammad Amīn al-Astarābādī started the trend, for he wrote commentaries on *Uṣūl al-Kāfī*, *al-Istibṣār* and *Tahdhīb al-aḥkām*, all listed in *al-Dharīʿa*, and a commentary on *Man lā yaḥḍuruhu al-faqīh* that has been discovered in manuscript as well.[28] The bulk of the works in these lists were written by Akhbārī scholars, or at least by scholars who were sympathetic to Akhbārī views and methods. Robert Gleave has discussed what may be taken as typical examples of this genre, the two commentaries on Ibn Bābawayh al-Qummī's *Man lā yaḥḍuruhu al-faqīh*, one in Arabic and one in Persian, by Muḥammad Taqī al-Majlisī (d. 1070/1659). The first work, written in Arabic, *Rawḍat al-muttaqīn fi sharḥ Man la yaḥḍuruh al-faqīh*, was completed in 1046/1636-37. The second, *Lawāmiʿ-i ṣāhib-qirānī*, also called *al-Lawāmiʿ al-qudsiyya*, and written in Persian, was completed in Shawwāl 1066/June 1656. Gleave has examined the *Lawāmiʿ* and argued on the basis of this work that Muḥammad Taqī al-Majlisī was thoroughly Akhbārī in his methodology, not only focusing on *ḥadīth* reports in this particular collection, but also arguing that the *ḥadīth* of the imams constituted the main basis of all Shiʿi doctrine, whether theology or law. Gleave noted, however, that al-Majlisī argued for the religious authority of the scholars on this basis, and also that he had close ties to the Safavid court and accepted royal patronage.[29] This conclusion is a little surprising, given what is generally understood regarding his academic background, and that he was a student of Bahāʾ al-Dīn al-ʿĀmilī, the leading legal authority of the previous generation, and regarding his more famous son, Muḥammad Bāqir al-Majlisī, who is renowned as a leading representative of the Uṣūlīs and a fierce proponent of the authority of the Twelver jurists.

---

28 Muḥammad Amīn al-Astarabādī, '*Ḥāshiya ʿalā* Tahdhīb al-aḥkām', Kitābkhāna-yi markazī-yi iḥyāʾ-i mīrāth-i islāmī, Qum, MS 2750, pp. 84–174; ʿAlī Fāḍilī, ed., 'al-Ḥāshiya ʿalā *Uṣūl al-Kāfī* li Muḥammad Amīn al-Astarabādī, jamaʿahā wa-rattabahā Mawlā Khalīl Qazwīnī (d. 1089AH/1678AD)', *Mīrāth-i ḥadīth-i shīʿa*, 8 (2001), pp. 229–410; ʿAlī Fāḍilī, 'Ḥāshiyat *Man lā yaḥḍuruhu'l-faqīh*, Mawlā Muḥammad Amīn Astarabādī (d. 1036)', *Mīrāth-i ḥadīth-i shīʿa*, 10 (2003), pp. 449–513; ʿAlī Fāḍilī, '*Ḥāshiyat al-Istibṣār*, Muḥammad Amīn Astarabādī (d. 1036/1626–7), Muḥammad Astarabādī (d. 1025/1616)', collected by Muḥammad b. Jābir Najafī', *Mīrāth-i ḥadīth-i shīʿa*, 13 (2005), pp. 35–125; ʿAlī Fāḍilī, '*Sharḥ Tahdhīb al-Aḥkām*', Kitābkhāna-yi ʿumūmī-yi Āyat Allāh al-ʿUẓmā Marʿashī Najafī, Qum, MS 3789, cited in Abisaab, 'Was Muhammad Amin Astarabadi a Mujtahid?, pp. 59–60.

29 Gleave, 'Muḥammad Taqī al-Majlisī and Safavid Shiʿism: Akhbarism and Anti-Sunni Polemic During the Reigns of Shah ʿAbbas the Great and Shah Safi', *Iran*, 55 (2017), pp. 24–34.

Niʿmat Allāh al-Jazāʾirī wrote several large commentaries on the canonical *ḥadīth* works, including *Ghāyat al-marām fī sharḥ Tahdhīb al-aḥkām* and *Kashf al-asrār fī sharḥ al-Istibṣār*, both commenting on the works of Muḥammad b. al-Ḥasan al-Ṭūsī. *Kashf al-asrār* includes a substantial introduction, divided into ten sections termed 'jewels', in which al-Jazāʾirī makes several fundamental points reflecting his goals and concerns. In his view, Shiʿi scholars who insisted on restricting the definition of sound *ḥadīth*s and restricting the definition of probity, thus removing many transmitters and many reports from being considered reliable, did not take into account the critical practices of the famous compilers of Shiʿi *ḥadīth* and the types of corroborating evidence that were available to them. The fact that a certain transmitter had belonged to a non-Imāmī sect, for example, did not disqualify him as a transmitter, particularly if he adopted the correct doctrine at a later point. Al-Jazāʾirī remarked that later scholars had been misled into thinking that they must adopt the material included in the canonical *ḥadīth* works on what appears to be blind faith, accepting only the authors' assurances that these works are based on earlier sources that are entirely reliable, on the grounds that the earlier sources are no longer available for inspection. In fact, he argued, there is a great deal of corroborating evidence that allowed later scholars to validate the authenticity of particular reports which appear to be inadequately documented. When al-Kulaynī did not provide full *isnād*s, for example, it was often because he supplied similar but more complete *isnād*s for other reports, so that familiarity with his *isnād*s generally enables one to fill in the ellipses. It is not that he was being lax or did not have well-documented material; rather, he did so merely to save space. Al-Ṭūsī followed a similar method, according to al-Jazāʾirī, and, in addition, his *isnād*s and his use of sources are confirmed by the material contained in his bibliographical work, *Fihrist kutub al-shīʿa*.[30] Overall, then, the Akhbārī method in such commentaries is clear: not only to explain the *ḥadīth* reports on which Shiʿi law is based but also to build up corroborating evidence and arguments to vindicate the methods of the

---

[30] Niʿmat Allāh al-Jazāʾirī, *Kashf al-asrār fī sharḥ al-Istibṣār*, ed. Al-Muftī al-Sayyid Ṭayyib al-Mūsawī al-Jazāʾirī (Qum, 1408/1987), vol. 2, pp. 39–93; Gleave, *Scripturalist Islam*, pp. 257–259.

compilers of the canonical *ḥadīth* works and to prove that the material they contained was generally authentic and reliable.

A prominent example of a commentary that does not hold to Akhbārī ideological positions is *Sharḥ Uṣūl al-Kāfī*, completed in 1044/1635 by the well-known philosopher Mullā Ṣadrā, that is Ṣadr al-Dīn Muḥammad b. Ibrāhīm al-Shīrāzī (d. 1045/1636).[31] In addition to this commentary, which addresses the *ḥadīth* of the imams, Mullā Ṣadrā also wrote three works that address Qur'anic studies: *Asrār al-āyāt*, *Mafātīḥ al-ghayb* and *Mutashābihāt al-Qur'ān*. In all these works, he used the commentary as a structure within which to address questions discussed in the scholarly tradition of Islamic philosophy without presenting it as material that falls outside the traditional religious sciences.[32] In *Sharḥ Uṣūl al-Kāfī*, Mullā Ṣadrā used the popularity of *ḥadīth* commentary that had been established by Akhbārī scholars in order to write, it would appear, in a manner in keeping with the general scholarly trends of his day. However, he also introduced important aspects of philosophical discourse through the commentary form, criticising exoteric scholars of law and theology and presenting a portrayal of the intellect drawing on the theories of earlier philosophers.

Al-Kulaynī's work is particularly suited to this approach, because it accords tremendous importance to reason (*al-ʿaql*) and knowledge, suggesting that reason, or 'the intellect', the term favoured by the philosophers, is central to the *ḥadīth* of the imams and to the Shiʿi faith in general. Andrew Newman has characterised *al-Kāfī* as a Qummī response to the rationalism of the Baghdadi Shiʿi scholars of the 3rd/9th and 4th/10th centuries, finding that al-Kulaynī stresses the point that all religious knowledge was based on revealed texts.[33] The

---

31 Mullā Ṣadrā, *Sharḥ Uṣūl al-Kāfī*, ed. Riḍā Ustādī et al. (Tehran, 1383–86 Sh./2003–08).

32 In general, see Seyyed Hossein Nasr, *Ṣadr al-Dīn Shīrāzī and His Transcendent Theosophy: Background, Life and Works* (Tehran, 1978); Sajjad Rizvi, *Mullā Ṣadrā Shīrāzī: His Life and Works and the Sources for Safavid Philosophy* (Oxford, 2007); Mohammad Rustom, *The Triumph of Mercy: Philosophy and Scripture in Mullā Ṣadrā* (Albany, NY, 2012).

33 Andrew J. Newman, *The Formative Period of Twelver Shīʿism: Ḥadīth as Discourse between Qum and Baghdad* (London, 2000), pp. 94–112.

appearance of a chapter on *ʿilm* at the outset of the work may be explained, in part, as an attempt to follow the example of the *Ṣaḥīḥ* of al-Bukhārī (d. 256/870), in which the *Kitāb al-ʿilm* is the third chapter, very near the beginning of the work, following chapters on 'the beginning of revelation' (*Kitāb badʾ al-waḥy*) and 'faith' (*Kitāb al-īmān*). The first section of this 'Chapter on Knowledge' is devoted to 'the merit of knowledge' (*faḍl al-ʿilm*), which is also found in al-Kulaynī's chapter on the same. Given this correspondence, the chapter on *ʿaql* in *al-Kāfī* stands out even more, because no such chapter occurs in al-Bukhārī's work. One might suppose that the use of the term here signals an engagement with the scholarship of the Muʿtazilī theologians, whose discussions revolved around dialectical reason. However, Mohammed-Ali Amir Moezzi argues that to interpret *ʿaql* in this fashion is misleading and anachronistic. In his view, that meaning became prominent only at a later historical period, while in early Shiʿism, and in most of al-Kulaynī's *Kitāb al-ʿaql wa'l-jahl*, *ʿaql* constituted a principal and essentially esoteric feature of early Shiʿi theological arguments regarding the imamate that may be rendered as 'hiero-intelligence'. According to Amir-Moezzi, in the term *ʿaql* are encapsulated cosmogonic, ethical-epistemological, spiritual and soteriological dimensions. The *ʿaql* is what God created before all else. It and its armies are parallel to the imams and their followers, and *jahl* and its armies are parallel to the inimical rulers and their followers. It is not an acquired skill, but a divine gift through which one may gain access to sacred knowledge. It is the thread that ultimately ties man to God, a cosmic entity, equivalent to the imam of the forces of Good.[34] Mullā Ṣadrā may have chosen to write a commentary on this work in particular because al-Kulaynī's chapter *Kitāb al-ʿaql wa'l-jahl* opened up the possibility of connections with the Neoplatonic concept of emanation and the active intellect.

Several scholars have argued that philosophy and mysticism constitute Mullā Ṣadrā's main concern in *Sharḥ Uṣūl al-kāfī*, while *ḥadīth* is instrumental to his presentation. Jari Kaukua has shown that Mullā Ṣadrā's work engages directly with the Islamic philosophical

[34] Mohammad Ali Amir-Moezzi, *The Divine Guide in Early Shi'ism: The Sources of Esotericism in Islam*, tr. David Streight (Albany, NY, 1994), pp. 6–13.

tradition in a manner that would be obvious to fellow philosophers but not to outsiders. In particular, his crucial discussion of 'the intellect' early on in the work draws extensively on the *Risāla fi'l-ʿaql* of al-Fārābī (d. 339/950), without citing it explicitly.[35] According to Maria Massi Dakake, the hierarchical epistemology and ontology he expounds in his commentary are essentially the same ones that appear in his expressly philosophical works. Attention to the *ḥadīth* corpus does not force him to adjust or accommodate his views. He expands the category of the *awliyā'*, 'God's wards', a traditional title accorded by the Shiʿis to the imams, to include others. The imams are thus in the company 'not of the exoteric Shiʿi religious scholars who claimed to be heirs to the knowledge and authority of the Imams, but of the saints and gnostics who in Ṣadrā's description look far more like Sufi mystics than Shīʿī devotees.'[36] It is clear, in this case, that adherence to the Akhbārī movement and a desire to support the Akhbārī ideological goals, especially the aim to bolster the authenticity of the canonical *ḥadīth* works, were not uppermost in Mullā Ṣadrā's mind when he wrote this work. Rather, his main goal was to expound and justify his philosophical system within an outwardly scriptural framework, drawing on a fundamental Shiʿi doctrinal work in the field of *ḥadīth*. Whereas most of Mulla Sadra's similar works focused on the Qur'an, the choice of *Uṣūl al-Kāfi* must have been conditioned by the popularity of commentaries on the canonical *ḥadīth* collections during this period, a result of the Akhbārī movement.

It is not surprising, then, that Mullā Ṣadrā's work drew the attention of his ideological opponents. Muḥammad Ṣāliḥ b. Aḥmad al-Sarawī al-Māzandarānī (d. 1086/1675) wrote another commentary on *Uṣūl al-kāfi*, in four large volumes. He also wrote a continuation, commenting on the later sections of *al-Kāfi*. He finished the commentary on the chapters devoted to reason and to the merits of knowledge, *Kitāb al-ʿaql wa-faḍl al-ʿilm*, on 14 Ṣafar 1063/14 January 1653. This commentary on *Uṣūl al-Kāfi* was primarily a sustained

---

[35] Jari Kaukua, 'The Intellect in Mullā Ṣadrā's Commentary on the *Uṣūl al-Kāfi*', in S. Nizamuddin Ahmad and Sajjad Rizvi, ed., *Philosophy and the Intellectual Life in Shiah Islam* (London, 2017).

[36] Maria Massi Dakake, 'Hierarchies of Knowledge in Mullā Ṣadrā's Commentary on *Uṣūl al-Kāfi*', *JIP*, 6 (2010), pp. 5–44, esp. p. 40.

refutation of Mullā Ṣadrā's work and formed part of a markedly anti-philosophical trend in Safavid Iran in the late 11th/17th century.[37]

C. *Re-collection of* hadīth *and related texts*

Perhaps the most striking effect of the Akhbārī movement was the production of extensive works that reframed the entire Shiʿi *ḥadīth* corpus. Among these were several that have remained extremely influential, despite the historical decline of the Akhbārī movement. Muḥammad b. al-Ḥurr al-ʿĀmilī (d. 1104/1693) completed the monumental work *Tafṣīl wasāʾil al-shīʿa ilā taḥṣīl masāʾil al-sharīʿa*, generally known as *Wasāʾil al-shīʿa*, which runs to thirty volumes in modern editions, in Mashhad in 1082/1671. It focuses on *ḥadīth* reports having to do with legal rulings, including all the legal *ḥadīth* reports of the four canonical *ḥadīth* collections in combination, as well as those from a large number of other early Shiʿi works. This work made it more convenient for any interested party to look up the *ḥadīth* reports related to a particular topic without having to consult multiple works and to go back and forth between them. In this it served a purpose similar to that of the gospel harmonies of the Christian tradition, such as Tatian's *Diatessaron*, which combined the four gospels into one text that could be read on its own. It also served a rhetorical and polemical purpose, which was to stress the idea that the canonical *ḥadīth* works corroborated each other and formed a unified and complete corpus. Together, the canonical *ḥadīth* collections were greater than the sum of their parts, and their combined effect was to bolster the authenticity of each individual work. The work includes a final section devoted to *ʿilm al-rijāl* and other related topics, also serving to support and justify the authenticity of the reports contained in the canonical works.[38] A similar objective may be ascribed to Muḥsin Fayḍ al-Kāshānī's major *ḥadīth* work *al-Wāfī*, which also brought together the material of the four canonical *ḥadīth* works.[39]

---

[37] Ata Anzali and S. M. Hadi Gerami, ed., *Opposition to Philosophy in Safavid Iran: Mulla Muḥammad-Ṭāhir Qummī's Ḥikmat al-ʿĀrifīn* (Leiden, 2018).

[38] Al-Ḥurr al-Āmilī and al-Muḥaddith Mīrzā Ḥusayn al-Nūrī, *Wasāʾil al-shīʿa wa-mustadrakuhā* (Qum, 1433/2011), vol. 22, pp. 404–765.

[39] Amin Ehteshami, 'The Pivot of Canonisation: Al-Fayḍ al-Kāshānī and the Safavid Ḥadīth Discourse' (PhD, University of California, Berkeley, 2019).

The largest and most ambitious of these monumental works was *Biḥār al-anwār* by Muḥammad Bāqir al-Majlisī (d. 1111/1699).[40] The work consisted of twenty-five large volumes in al-Majlisī's original plan, corresponding to 110 volumes in one of the modern editions. The work was a grand project involving not only al-Majlisī himself but also a number of students and assistants, including Niʿmat Allāh al-Jazāʾirī and Mīrzā ʿAbd Allāh b. ʿĪsā al-Iṣfahānī. The kernel of the project was a work al-Majlisī completed in 1070/1659, entitled *Fihrist biḥār al-anwār* or *Fihris muṣannafāt al-aṣḥāb*. What had begun as a historical catalogue of Shiʿi works evolved into a massive encyclopedia of Shiʿi lore based on nearly the entire corpus of Shiʿi literature as known in his day. The project continued for many decades. The earliest volume was completed on 1 Rabīʿ II 1077/1 October 1666, and the latest volumes – volumes 15–17, 19–20, 21–24 – were in an incomplete draft when al-Majlisī died in 1111/1699. These were eventually completed by al-Majlisī's student Mīrzā ʿAbd Allāh b. ʿĪsā al-Iṣfahānī.

The plan of the work according to the original volumes is as follows:

Volume I. Knowledge
Volume II. God's unicity and the divine attributes
Volume III. Free will and predestination; death and the afterlife
Volume IV. Defence of belief in the imamate
Volume V. Stories of the prophets
Volume VI. Biography of the Prophet Muhammad
Volume VII. The imamate (*Kitāb al-imāma*)
Volume VIII. The First *fitna*, or Civil War in the Muslim Community; the vices and nefarious deeds of the Sunni caliphs and others.
Volume IX. Biography of ʿAlī b. Abī Ṭālib, the First imam
Volume X. Biographies of Fāṭima, Ḥasan and Ḥusayn (Second and Third imams)

40 On this work, see Karl-Heinz Pampus, 'Die theologische Enzyklopädie Biḥār al-anwār des Muḥammad Bāqir al-Majlisī (1037–1110 A.H. = 1627–1699 A.D. Ein Beitrag zur Literaturgeschichte der Safawidenzeit' (PhD, Bonn, 1970); Etan Kohlberg, 'Beḥār al-anwār', *EIr*, vol. 4, pp. 90–93; Rainer Brunner, 'The Role of *Ḥadīth* as Cultural Memory in Shīʿī History', *JSAI*, 30 (2005), pp. 318–360; Rasūl Jafarian, 'The Encyclopaedic Aspect of *Biḥār al-anwār*, Part I', *JSIS*, 1 (2008), pp. 1–17; Jafarian, 'The Encyclopaedic Aspect of *Biḥār al-anwār*, Part II', *JSIS*, 1 (2008), pp. 55–69.

Volume XI. Biographies of the Imams Zayn al-ʿĀbidīn, Muḥammad al-Bāqir, Jaʿfar al-Ṣādiq and Mūsā al-Kāẓim (Fourth–Seventh imams)
Volume XII. Biographies of Imams ʿAlī al-Riḍā, Muḥammad al-Taqī, ʿAlī al-Naqī, and Ḥasan al-ʿAskarī (Eighth–Eleventh imams)
Volume XIII. 'The Proof', or the Twelfth imam, and the Occultation (*Kitāb al-ḥujja*)
Volume XIV. Cosmology and Natural History (*Kitāb al-samā' wa'l-ʿālam*)
Volume XV. Belief and Unbelief (*Kitāb al-īmān wa'l-kufr*)
Volume XVI. Proper Social Mores and Etiquette (*Kitāb al-ʿishra wa'l-ādāb wa'l-sunan*)
Volume XVII. Exhortations
Volume XVIII. Ritual Purity (*Kitāb al-ṭahāra*) and Prayer (*Kitāb al-ṣalā*)
Volume XIX. The Qur'an; Occasional Prayers (*duʿā'*) and Litanies (*dhikr*)
Volume XX. Alms; *Khums*; Fasting; Holy Days in the Calendar
Volume XXI. Pilgrimage to Mecca (*ḥajj* and *ʿumra*); Medina; *Jihād*, Enjoining Good and Forbidding Wrong (*al-amr bi'l-maʿrūf wa'l-nahy ʿan al-munkar*)
Volume XXII. Pilgrimages to the graves of the Prophet, the imams, and others (*Kitāb al-mazār*)
Volume XXIII. Sales, Lending, Endowments, Bequests, Marriage, Divorce, Slavery, Vows (*Kitāb al-ʿuqūd wa'l-īqāʿāt*)
Volume XXIV. Court Cases; Inheritance; Felonies (*Kitāb al-aḥkām*)
Volume XXV. Certificates of Study (*Kitāb al-ijāzāt*)[41]

Biḥār al-anwār thus includes sacred history, both before the rise of Islam and after, including the biographies of the Biblical prophets, along with those who entered the tradition from Arabian pagan lore such as Hūd, Ṣāliḥ and Shuʿayb, the Prophet Muhammad and his ancestors, the lives the twelve imams, together with Fāṭima, and discussion of the Occultation of the Twelfth imam. It covers the main topics of theology, including the unicity, nature, and attributes of God, predestination and free will, faith and unbelief, and the theory of the imamate. It covers the sacred law as well, including the three major categories of ritual obligations, transactions and judgments. Several volumes treat other

[41] al-Majlisī, *Biḥār al-anwār*, vol. 1, p. 231.

aspects of religious life that are not strictly legal, such as prayers for particular occasions, the special holy days of the Shiʿi calendar, proper social behaviour, ethics, and so on. Overall, the work covers four major areas of Shiʿi lore: history, theology, ritual and law.

Despite the enormous size of *Biḥār al-anwār* and the tremendous range of topics covered, certain subjects are omitted. A number of topics that appear in theological treatises that are traditionally termed *daqīq al-kalām* ('the fine points of theology'), and involve philosophical discussions of cosmology, theories of movement, and so on, do not appear. The legal material is decidedly skewed, partly on account of the source material but also partly because al-Majlisī did not have the opportunity to complete the later volumes of the work. A remarkable amount of material is devoted to daily prayer and other ritual obligations such as fasting and the pilgrimage to Mecca. Pilgrimages to the graves of the imams receive considerable attention as well, but the twenty-third and twenty-fourth volumes, which treat of transactions and judgments, are very slim in comparison to the other volumes. Al-Majlisī explicitly excluded discussions of philosophy and mysticism.[42] These last two lacunae are striking given the importance of such works in the Shiʿi tradition. The Shiʿi tradition of producing philosophical works goes all the way back to the writings of Hishām b. al-Ḥakam (d. after 187/803), a companion of Jaʿfar al-Ṣādiq, and include writings by such authors as Ibn Biṭrīq al-Ḥillī (d. 602/1203), Naṣīr al-Dīn al-Ṭūsī (d. 672/1274), and Mītham al-Baḥrānī (d. 680/1281), not to mention Ghiyāth al-Dīn al-Dashtakī (d. 948/1542), Mīr Dāmād (d. 1042/1631), and Mullā Ṣādrā (d. 1050/1640) from the Safavid period. On the Sufi side, one may mention *Asrār al-sharīʿa wa-aṭwār al-ṭarīqa wa-anwār al-ḥaqīqa* and other works by Ḥaydar al-Āmulī (d. after 787/1385).

The title of *Biḥār al-anwār* merits some attention. The full title is *Biḥār al-anwār al-jāmiʿa li-durar akhbār al-aʾimma al-aṭhār*. Etan Kohlberg has pointed out that the texts on which al-Majlisī drew as sources belonged to many genres: Qurʾanic exegesis, *ḥadīth* compilations, biographies of the imams, historical, theological, legal and polemical works, and so on. Nevertheless, they all depended, to varying extents, on reports of the imams, so that the entire collection is imbued with these

---

42 Etan Kohlberg, 'Beḥār al-anwār', *EIr*.

reports. As Kohlberg remarks, 'Most of this material consists of traditions from the Prophet and the imams, the significance of which was greatly enhanced by the growing influence of the Ak̲bārīs in the 11th/17th century; and Majlesī, though not a declared Ak̲bārī, was in sympathy with their belief that *ḥadīth* is the repository of all religious knowledge.'[43] I would only add that the fact that the title frames the work as a collection of reports of the imams should not be overlooked.

Karl-Heinz Pampus called *Biḥār al-anwār* a 'theological encyclopedia',[44] but while it certainly merits the label encyclopedia, the adjective 'theological' does not do justice to the work's contents overall and in particular to the centrality of *ḥadīth*. In the introduction to *Biḥār al-anwār*, al-Majlisī presents himself as a scripturalist, suggesting that he had undergone an experience of conversion that led him to focus exclusively on the *akhbār* of the imams.

> I found that all knowledge resided in the glorious Book of God, 'which no falsehood may approach, from before it or from behind' (Q 41–42), and in the reports of the people of the House of Messengership, whom God made the treasurer-keepers of His knowledge and the interpreters of His revelation. However, I realised that the rational capacities of the worshippers were not fully able to derive knowledge of the Qur'an from within it with certainty and that no one could encompass it save those whom God had selected for that purpose from among the leading figures of the faith, in whose House the trustworthy spirit had settled. I therefore abandoned that with which I had wasted a long period of my life, despite the fact that it is what is commonly appreciated in this age, and I turned to that which I knew would benefit me with regard to my afterlife, despite the fact that it garners little attention in our era. I chose to search for the reports of the pure, chaste imams, God's peace be upon them, and I began to investigate them, giving them their due in terms of inquiry, and their full measure of mental engagement. Upon my life! I found that they were the Ark of Salvation, laden with the treasures of real prosperity, and I found them to be adorned with shining stars that rescue from the murk of ignorance. I saw that

43 Etan Kohlberg, 'Beḥār al-anwār', *EIr*.

44 Ibid.

> their paths were clear and their roads manifest, with the landmarks of guidance and success raised up along their ways, and the voices of those who call to prosperity and salvation easily audible along their routes. Following their avenues, I arrived at lush meadows and verdant gardens, adorned with the flowers of every science and the fruits of every form of wisdom. Making the circuit of their stations, I witnessed well-travelled, populated routes that lead to every type of honour and high status. I stumbled across no piece of wisdom but that its clearest expression was to be found in those reports, and I attained no truth but that its origin lay in them.[45]

This extraordinary statement follows a passage in which al-Majlisī reports that in his youth he had spent a great deal of time and a considerable effort studying the sciences (*ṭalab al-ʿulūm*) in general. This passage then shows how his view of religious knowledge changed radically as a result of reflection. He came to realise the centrality of the *akhbār* among the other learned pursuits in which he had engaged, and which, he admits, proved to be a substantial waste of time. Now, in a new, enlightened state, he agrees with Akhbārī views to a surprising extent. In general, the most obvious concurrence is that al-Majlisī places an enormous emphasis on, indeed had an obsession with, the *ḥadīth* reports of the imams, making clear that in his conception, they are the most valuable element of Shiʿi scholarly tradition. He thereby implies that *Biḥār al-anwār* is based entirely on the Shiʿi *ḥadīth* corpus. In addition, though he states that knowledge lies in two 'scriptural' sources, the Qurʾan and the *akhbār*, he suggests that the content of the Qurʾan is not directly accessible to human reason. Consequently, human beings require additional guidance in order to understand and interpret the Qurʾan, and that is to be found in the interpretation of the imams, or more precisely, in their *akhbār*. It is striking that he does not mention any other sources of religious knowledge here. Indeed, he limits his attention to the two categories of the Qurʾan and the *akhbār* despite the fact that he uses several terms that are standard in the arsenal of the Uṣūlīs, *istinbāṭ* ('deduction') and *naẓar* ('rational speculation'). It is clear, then, that in al-Majlisī's opinion, *Biḥār al-anwār*

---

45 al-Majlisī, *Biḥār al-anwār* (Tehran, 1376–1405/1957–1985), vol. 1, p. 180.

is not a theological encyclopedia, but a *ḥadīth*-based encyclopedia of Shiʿism.

The outline of *Biḥār al-anwār* shows affinities with the organisation of the most famous canonical collection of Shiʿi *ḥadīth*, al-Kulaynī's work *al-Kāfī*. The fact that al-Majlisī devotes volume one to *ʿilm* seems to reflect the discussion of reason and knowledge at the beginning of *al-Kāfī*. The title of volume seventeen, devoted to exhortations, *Kitāb al-rawḍa,* recalls al-Kulaynī's use of the same title. The decision to term volume thirteen, which addresses the Twelfth imam, *Kitāb al-ḥujja*, may have been influenced by al-Kulaynī's prominent use of the term in his chapter titles. One may argue that the grand scheme of the work owes something to al-Majlisī's reading of *al-Kāfī*. This is not surprising, given that *Mir'āt al-ʿuqūl*, another of al-Majlisī's major works, is a twelve-volume commentary on *al-Kāfī*.

Even though it is clear that al-Majlisī was a *mujtahid* and fully endorsed their methods, *Biḥār al-anwār* includes sections that fit with the Akhbārīs' characteristic hermeneutics. The first volume of *Biḥār al-anwār* includes a section that addresses legal hermeneutics, including presentation of the traditional Shiʿi rejection of *qiyās* or legal analogy and sections devoted to the other principles of interpretation that may be derived from the *akhbār* of the imams. Indeed, this section is reminiscent of the work *al-Uṣūl al-aṣīla* by the well-known Akhbārī, Muḥsin Fayḍ al-Kāshānī, which similarly addressed legal hermeneutical principles that were endorsed by the imams, being sanctioned in their *akhbār*.

Biḥār al-anwār may be connected to an enhanced focus on the historiography of the Twelver Shiʿi learned tradition spurred by the Akhbārīs' overall goal of corroborating the authenticity of the Shiʿi *ḥadīth* corpus and of proving an unbroken connection between the early works and contemporary Shiʿi scholars. The work has an impressive scholarly apparatus. The introduction provides a long list of the sources used in its compilation.[46] Al-Majlisī explains, in each case, how he authenticated the copies he used.[47] He provides a table

[46] al-Majlisī, *Biḥār al-anwār*, vol. 1, pp. 183–196.

[47] Ibid., pp. 196–209.

of the abbreviations (*rumūz*) he used in the text to refer to these numerous sources without taking up too much space.[48] He describes how he refers to *isnād*s in an abbreviated manner to save space.[49] As is commonly found in works on *ḥadīth* criticism, he provides a section on names of transmitters and authorities that are easily confused.[50] At the end of his introduction, al-Majlisī provides his own chains of transmission to famous Sunni and Shiʿi works and explains how the authors he cites handled the citation of their sources.[51] The work also provides evidence of an enormous amount of archival research. Al-Majlisī mentions in his introduction to the *Biḥār* that he has had to travel far and wide to collect books; he was helped in this by friends and acquaintances.[52] These works had been ignored by his predecessors, who were convinced that they had been superseded by later works or did not contain anything of value. After an examination of the works in question, however, al-Majlisī found otherwise; they contained material not to be found elsewhere.[53]

The final volume of *Biḥār al-anwār*, *Kitāb al-ijāzāt*, merits special attention. It is devoted to *ijāza*s, certificates or diplomas of study from the Shiʿi tradition and also includes other texts that are not certificates of study in the strict sense but rather notes about paths of scholarly transmission or other aspects of the biographies and writings of earlier scholars. Overall the material has to do with the history of Shiʿi learning and the biographies of Shiʿi scholars of earlier periods. It is evident that these documents were collected from manuscripts found throughout Iran. The most important of colleagues who helped al-Majlisī collect rare books was his student Mīrzā ʿAbd Allāh al-Iṣfahānī, who, along with Niʿmat Allāh al-Jazāʾirī, worked for years on *Biḥār al-anwār*, as noted earlier. His biographical dictionary, *Riyāḍ al-ʿulamāʾ* and his anthological work *al-Fawāʾid al-ṭarīfa* show that he travelled widely in the Safavid empire, visiting dozens of libraries, *waqf*

48 Ibid., pp. 209–210.
49 Ibid., pp. 210–216.
50 Ibid., pp. 216–219.
51 Ibid., pp. 219–230.
52 Ibid., p. 180.
53 Ibid., pp. 180–181.

and private, throughout Iran.[54] He was evidently searching for manuscripts of rare works at the express request of his master, al-Majlisī. At the same time, he recorded marginalia from the manuscripts he encountered, including colopha, marginal notes and *ijāza*s, which were often written on the final pages or covers of books scholars had studied with a particular teacher. It was presumably he who collected large percentage of these *ijāza*s and other texts found in the *Kitāb al-ijāzāt* of the *Biḥār*. Scholars have only begun to investigate the movement of manuscripts from the periphery into Safavid Iran and the efforts that Mīrzā ʿAbd Allāh and other scholars like him made to locate, identify and record them.[55]

One enterprise that is emblematic of the considerable commitment to historical investigation in Shiʿi letters in late Safavid Iran was the search for *Madīnat al-ʿilm*, a major collection of Twelver *ḥadīth* by Ibn Bābawayh. This compendium was extant in earlier eras but had been lost by the 11th/17th century. Especially given the size of the work, this was viewed as a tragic loss. According to the report of al-Shaykh al-Ṭūsī in *Fihrist kutub al-shīʿa*, it was larger and more comprehensive than Ibn Bābawayh's other collection, *Man lā yaḥḍuruhu al-faqīh*. Ibn Shahrāshūb reported in *Maʿālim al-ʿulamā'* that while *Man lā yaḥḍuruhu al-faqīh* comprised four volumes, *Madīnat al-ʿilm* comprised ten, thus being two-and-a-half times its size. Ḥusayn b. ʿAbd al-Ṣamad mentions the work in *Wuṣūl al-akhyār* as one of the 'five' canonical *ḥadīth* books of the Twelver Shiʿis. The way in which he mentions it suggests that it was extant, but this is not at all certain since he does not cite any specific passages. The latest authors definitely to possess the work and cite it were Raḍī al-Dīn b. Ṭāwūs (d. 664/1266), who cited it in several works, and his student Yūsuf b. Ḥātim al-Shāmī (fl. 7th/13th c.), who cited it in his work *al-Durr al-naẓīm*. Muḥammad Bāqir al-Majlisī seems to have been convinced or at least hoped that it was extant, and he is reported to have expended large sums of money in his attempts to locate a manuscript of the work. He even enlisted the

---

54 Mīrzā ʿAbd Allāh al-Iṣfahānī, *al-Fawā'id al-ṭarīfa*, ed. Al-Sayyid Mahdī al-Rajā'ī (Qum, 1385 Sh./2006).

55 See, for example, Rasūl Jaʿfariyān, 'Mīrzā ʿAbd Allāh Afandī va-yāddāshthāyi vey dar bārayi mīrāth-i maktūb-i shīʿa dar Baḥrayn', *Ā'īna-yi mīrās*, 4 (1385 Sh./2006), pp. 178–196.

help of the throne when he tried to acquire a manuscript of it that was said to be in Yemen.[56]

D. Tafsīr *Based on* Ḥadīth *Reports*

Another distinctive facet of literary production of the late Safavid period is that of *ḥadīth*-based *tafsīr*, which Todd Lawson has addressed in an excellent study.[57] It was a tenet of the Akhbārīs that the Qur'an is best understood through the interpretation of the Shiʿi imams, and since their teachings are embodied in their reports, it follows that commentaries on the Qur'an ought to be based mostly, or even entirely, on the *ḥadīth* of the imams. It is no surprise, then, that several large Qurʾanic commentaries produced in the late Safavid period by Akhbārī scholars were devoted to a large extent to explanation of the Qurʾanic text through recourse to Shiʿi *ḥadīth*. The following are among the crucial works of this trend: ʿAbd ʿAlī b. Jumʿa al-ʿArūsī al-Ḥuwayzī (d. before 1105/1693) completed his *tafsīr*, *Nūr al-thaqalayn*, in the late 1060s/1650s.[58] Muḥsin Fayḍ al-Kāshānī completed his *tafsīr*, *al-Ṣāfī*, in 1074/1664, Hāshim al-Baḥrānī (d. 1106/1695 or 1108/1697) completed *Tafsir al-Burhān* in 1094/1683 and Mulla al-Sharīf Abu'l-Ḥasan b. Muḥammad Ṭāhir al-ʿĀmilī al-Futūnī al-Iṣfahānī completed *Mirʾāt al-anwār* in the 12th/18th century.[59] These commentaries on the Qur'an share more than simply a reliance on *ḥadīth*, and they are also quite different from their Sunni counterparts which rely on Prophetic *ḥadīth*, such as the famous work of Jalāl al-Dīn al-Suyūṭī, *al-Durr al-manthūr*. As Lawson points out, these commentators were not literalists in the ordinary meaning of the word. Rather, they exhibited veneration for the pronouncements of the imams on Qurʾanic texts, and they were concerned with promoting adherence to these among

---

[56] Āqā Buzurg, *al-Dharīʿa ilā taṣānīf al-shīʿa*, vol. 20, pp. 251–253; Etan Kohlberg, *A Medieval Muslim Scholar at Work: Ibn Ṭāwūs and His Library* (Leiden, 1992), pp. 240–241.

[57] B. Todd Lawson, 'Akhbārī Shīʿī Approaches to Tafsīr', in G.R. Hawting and Abdul-Kader A. Shareef, ed., *Approaches to the Qurʾān* (London, 1993), pp. 173–210.

[58] ʿAbd ʿAlī b. Jumʿa al-ʿArūsī al-Ḥuwayzī, *Tafsīr Nūr al-thaqalayn*, ed. Ḥāshim Rasūlī Maḥallātī (Qum, 1362 Sh./1983).

[59] Abu'l-Ḥasan b. Muḥammad Ṭāhir al-ʿĀmilī al-Futūnī, *Tafsīr al-Burhān al-musammā bi-Mirʾāt al-Anwār wa-mishkāt al-asrār fī tafsīr al-Qurʾān* (Beirut, 2006).

the believers. In this sense, he argues, their outlook might be termed 'fundamentalist'. They hoped to show the harmony of the exegetical structure, based on both scriptural text and religious authority. In their view, the authority of the Qur'an and the authority of the imams went hand-in-hand. Thus, according to Lawson, reliance on Shiʿi traditions and an unreserved approach to the imams' supranatural qualities led to a fusion of the sacred text and the imams, whereby the experience of reading and interpreting the Qur'an allowed one to participate in their charisma.

E. Biographical Dictionaries and Works on Ḥadīth *Transmitters*

The production of biographical works was given a major boost by the Akhbārī movement. Indeed, Muḥammad Amīn al-Astarābādī's mentor, Muḥammad b. ʿAlī al-Astarābādī, who urged him to write *al-Fawāʾid madaniyya*, was an expert in *rijāl*, that is the transmitters of *ḥadīth*, and wrote a biographical work, *Manhaj al-maqāl fī taḥqīq aḥwāl al-rijāl*.[60] Also before the Akhbārī manifesto was published, the students of ʿAbd Allāh b. al-Ḥusayn al-Tustarī in Iṣfahān showed a strong interest in the genre of biography. Muṣṭafā al-Tafrishī (fl. 11th/17th c.) completed *Naqd al-rijāl* in 1015/1606, and Zakī al-Dīn ʿInāyat Allāh b. ʿAlī al-Quhpāʾī (fl. 11th/17th c.) completed *Majmaʿ al-rijāl* in 1016/1607. A similar work, *Niẓām al-aqwāl fī aḥwāl al-rijāl*, was completed between Shawwāl 1021/November 1612 and Ṣafar 1022/March 1613 by a student of Bahāʾ al-Dīn al-ʿĀmilī, Niẓām al-Dīn Muḥammad b. Ḥusayn al-Qurashī al-Sāwajī (d. after 1038/1629), and includes all the transmitters from the four canonical Shiʿi *ḥadīth* works.[61] These biographical works focused relatively narrowly on *ḥadīth* transmitters. Similar in generic conventions and scope was Muḥammad b. ʿAlī al-Gharawī al-Ḥāʾirī al-Ardabīlī's (d. 1101/1690) *Jāmiʿ al-ruwāt*, a work which apparently took over twenty-five years to write.[62]

---

60 Muḥammad b. ʿAlī al-Astarābādī, *Manhaj al-maqāl fī taḥqīq aḥwāl al-rijāl* (Qum, 1380–1381 Sh./2001–2002).

61 Āqā Buzurg, *al-Dharīʿa ilā taṣānīf al-shīʿa*, vol. 24, p. 191.

62 Muḥammad b. ʿAlī al-Gharawī al-Ḥāʾirī al-Ardabīlī, *Jāmiʿ al-ruwāt* (Qum, 1403/1983).

Biographical dictionaries that were completed during this period and which may be said to have been inspired by the Akhbārī movement and their concerns include works that have become absolutely essential for the investigation of Shiʿi intellectual history during this and earlier periods. These include al-Ḥurr al-ʿĀmilī's *Amal al-āmil*, Mīrzā ʿAbd Allāh al-Iṣfahānī's *Riyāḍ al-ʿulamāʾ*, and Yūsuf b. Aḥmad al-Baḥrānī's *Luʾluʾat al-Baḥrayn*. Al-Baḥrānī's work above all others shows the intimate affinity between Akhbārī sensibilities and the production of biographical dictionaries, for the entire work is framed as an *ijāza* or certificate of transmission from the author, Yūsuf al-Baḥrānī himself, to his two nephews, Khalaf b. ʿAbd ʿAlī and Ḥusayn b. Muḥammad.[63] Here, it is as if the biographical dictionary *in toto* has been incorporated into a chain of *ḥadīth* transmission.

F. Autobiographies

In Islamic letters, most academic autobiographies are closely related to the genres of the biographical entry and the biographical dictionary. Some scholarly attention has been paid to Twelver Shiʿi autobiographies within the broader category of pre-modern Arabic and Persian autobiographies: the present author, Sabrina Mervin and Rainer Brunner have focused on various aspects of this topic.[64] I have pointed out previously, in a study of the autobiography of Yūsuf b. Aḥmad al-Baḥrānī, that the production of Shiʿi biographies in the 11th/17th and 12th/18th centuries appears to have been spurred on by the Akhbārī movement and the concomitant attention shown to *ḥadīth* studies.[65] Rainer

---

[63] Yūsuf b. Aḥmad al-Baḥrānī, *Luʾluʾat al-Baḥrayn fiʾl-ijāzāt wa-tarājim rijāl al-ḥadīth*, ed. Muḥammad Ṣādiq Baḥr al-ʿUlūm (Manama, 2008), pp. 6–7.

[64] Dwight F. Reynolds et al., *Interpreting the Self: Autobiography in the Arabic Literary Tradition* (Oakland, CA, 2001); Devin J. Stewart, 'The Humor of the Scholars: The Autobiography of Niʿmat Allāh al-Jazāʾirī', *IS*, 22 (1989), pp. 47–81; Devin J. Stewart, 'Capital, Accumulation, and the Islamic Academic Biography', *Edebiyat*, 7 (1997), pp. 345–362; Muḥsin al-Amīn, *Autobiographie d'un clerc chiite du Ǧabal ʿĀmil: Traduction et annotation par Sabrina Mervin et Haïtham al-Amīn* (Damascus, 1998); Rainer Brunner, '"Siehe, was mich an Ungluck und Schrecken trat!" Schiitische Autobiographien', in Rainer Brunner et al., ed., *Islamstudien ohne Ende—Festschrift für Werner Ende zum 65. Geburtstag* (Würzburg, 2002), pp. 59–68.

[65] Stewart, 'Capital, Accumulation, and the Islamic Academic Biography', pp. 347–348.

Brunner has also noted the connection between the production of autobiographies and the Akhbārī school, despite the fact that not all the authors of autobiographies were Akhbārīs themselves:

> It was not until the seventeenth century that autobiographical entries showed up in reference works, as at that time there occurred an enormous increase in biographical literature. This productivity went hand in hand with the revival of the Akhbārī school, which accorded the authoritative character of the entire Ḥadīṯ corpus far more weight than did their opponents, the Uṣūlīs, and therefore had the greatest interest in the academic careers of transmitters.[66]

The interest in autobiography appears to be closely related, in the first place, to the interest in biographical dictionaries. A number of the autobiographies that were produced appeared as autobiographical entries in biographical dictionaries: the autobiography of al-Ḥurr al-ʿĀmilī in *Amal al-āmil*, that of Mīrzā ʿAbd Allāh al-Iṣfahānī in *Riyāḍ al-ʿulamāʾ*, and that of Yūsuf b. Aḥmad al-Baḥrānī in *Luʾluʾat al-Baḥrayn*. Ultimately, these works were connected to the grand project of building up the scholarly apparatus around the canonical works of *ḥadīth*. It was only natural to extend the urge to record, collect and compile the biographical data of past participants in the Twelver Shiʿi scholarly tradition to contemporary Shiʿi scholars and thus to oneself. These were not the earliest autobiographies in the Twelver Shiʿis tradition, but they were certainly influential.

As in other aspects of the Akhbārīs' literary production, the 10th/16th-century scholar, Zayn al-Dīn al-ʿĀmilī, may be seen as influential. He believed that, in addition to studying the lives of earlier scholars, it was important for scholars to document and record events in their own careers and learned production. His student, Ḥusayn b. ʿAbd al-Ṣamad al-ʿĀmilī, refers to this several times as part of Zayn al-Dīn's advice to his students.[67] Zayn al-Dīn wrote an autobiography,

---

66 Brunner, "Siehe, was mich an Ungluck und Schrecken trat!", p. 61.

67 Devin J. Stewart, 'An Episode in the ʿĀmilī Migration to Safavid Iran: The Travel Account of Ḥusayn b. ʿAbd al-Ṣamad al-ʿĀmilī', *JIS*, 39 (2006), pp. 481–509, esp. pp. 497–99; Devin J. Stewart, 'Husayn b. ʿAbd al-Samad al-ʿAmili's Flight from Lebanon to Iraq', *SSR*, 3 (2019), pp. 59–106, esp. p. 83.

much of which is embedded in the hagiographical work *Bughyat al-murīd min al-kashf ʿan aḥwāl al-Shaykh Zayn al-Dīn al-Shahīd*, written around 966–980/1559–1573 by Zayn al-Dīn's long-time student-servitor (*khādim*), Bahāʾ al-Dīn Muḥammad b. ʿAlī b. Ḥasan b. al-ʿAwdī (d. after 970/1563).

At some point in 1078/1668 or later, Zayn al-Dīn's great-grandson, ʿAlī b. Muḥammad b. Ḥasan b. Zayn al-Dīn al-ʿĀmilī (d. 1103/1691-92), compiled a two-volume anthology titled *al-Durr al-Manthūr min al-maʾthūr wa-ghayr al-maʾthūr*. Part of the anthology consists of a family history presenting the biographies of five members of the author's family, including himself:

1. Zayn al-Dīn b. ʿAlī al-ʿĀmilī (d. 965/1558), great-grandfather.
2. Ḥasan b. Zayn al-Dīn (d. 1011/1602-03), grandfather.
3. Muḥammad b. Ḥasan b. Zayn al-Dīn (d. 1030/1621), father.
4. Zayn al-Dīn b. Muḥammad b. Ḥasan (d. 1064/1654), brother.
5. ʿAlī b. Muḥammad b. Ḥasan b. Zayn al-Dīn (d. 1103/1691-92), the author.[68]

The biography of Zayn al-Dīn included an incomplete version of *Bughyat al-murīd*, with as mentioned above the autobiography of Zayn al-Dīn, or at least a substantial part of it.[69]

Another source of inspiration was the well-known auto-bibliographies from the tradition. In his comprehensive bibliography of Shiʿi works, *Fihrist kutub al-shīʿa*, Muḥammad b. al-Ḥasan al-Ṭūsī included his auto-bibliography. Similar texts were well-known from the biographical works *Khulāṣat al-aqwāl fī aḥwāl al-rijāl*, by al-ʿAllāma al-Ḥillī, and the *Rijāl* of Ibn Dāwūd al-Ḥillī (d. after 707/1307). One indication of the popularity of the genre is the fact that Muḥsin Fayḍ al-Kāshānī actually wrote two auto-bibliographies, one in 1089/1678-79 and one in 1090/1679-80.[70]

68 Jaʿfar Muhājir, *Sittat fuqahāʾ abṭāl* (Beirut, 1994), p. 166.

69 Devin J. Stewart, 'The Ottoman Execution of Zayn al-Dīn al-ʿĀmilī', *Die Welt des Islams*, 48 (2008), pp. 289–347, here pp. 294–296.

70 Fayḍ al-Kāshānī, *Fihristhā-yi khudnivisht-i Fayḍ-i Kāshānī*, ed. Muḥsin Nājī Naṣrābādī (Mashhad, 1377 Sh./1998), pp. 73–108 and 111–125.

Another early work that was an important influence on the Akhbārīs in connection with autobiographies was the *Mashyakha* of Ibn Bābawayh al-Qummī, in which he presented an account of his teachers and the authorities from whom he transmitted *ḥadīth*. Ibn Bābawayh included this text as an appendix to his *ḥadīth* collection, *Man lā yaḥḍuruhu al-faqīh*, and it served the aims of the Akhbārīs exactly, for they wanted to argue that this text supplied all the necessary information regarding the transmission of the reports included in the collection, allowing modern scholars to restore the chains of transmission that appeared to be missing. The problem of documentation was thus only apparent, and the *Mashyakha* solved it. For this reason, al-Ḥurr al-ʿĀmilī included much of the information from Ibn Bābawayh's *Mashyakha* in the first sub-section of the concluding section of *Wasā'il al-shīʿa*, which addressed issues of *ḥadīth* criticism.[71] Similarly, Muḥammad Taqī al-Majlisī devoted the final section of his commentary on *Man lā yaḥḍuruhu al-faqīh* to a commentary on Ibn Bābawayh's *Mashyakha*. The result is a major biographical work, including not just entries on individual transmitters but also assessments of Ibn Bābawayh's various chains of transmission, over 700 pages of printed text in the modern published version.[72]

In addition to ʿAlī al-ʿĀmilī, prominent writers of autobiographies in late Safavid Iṣfahān include Muḥsin Fayḍ al-Kāshānī, al-Ḥurr al-ʿĀmilī, Niʿmat Allāh al-Jazā'irī and Mīrzā ʿAbd Allāh al-Iṣfahānī, all of whom were involved in writing works on Akhbārī method or ideas, commentaries on the Shiʿi *ḥadīth* corpus, or biographical works. Somewhat later Yūsuf b. Aḥmad al-Baḥrānī was engaged in similar work. Al-Baḥrānī's autobiography is particular revealing because it maintains a theme of accumulation, both of wealth and of learning, throughout the text. It is clear that, as far as he was concerned, wealth consists of two parts, one's inherited wealth (*tilād, talīd*) and one's newly acquired wealth (*ṭārif, ṭarīf*). In the realm of learning, one of the few things the effects of which can outlive this earthly existence and which provide one with a store (*dhakhīra, zād*) for the afterlife, are the

[71] Al-Ḥurr al-ʿĀmilī and al-Muḥaddith al-Nūrī, *Wasā'il al-Shīʿa wa-mustadrakuhā*, vol. 22, pp. 404–478.

[72] Muḥammad Taqī al-Majlisī, *Rawḍat al-muttaqīn fī sharḥ* Man lā yaḥḍuruhu al-faqīh *li'l-Ṣadūq* (Qum, 1387 Sh./2008), vol. 20.

books one writes. Inherited wealth is represented in a biography or autobiography by the *mashyakha* or catalogue of teachers, while newly acquired wealth is represented by the catalogue of one's own compositions.[73] The autobiographies of this period combine the two.

Particularly interesting are the autobiographies of Muḥsin Fayḍ al-Kāshānī and Niʿmat Allāh al-Jazāʾirī, both of which are rather more emotional than is common in Islamic scholarly biographies and autobiographies. Al-Kāshānī gave his autobiography the title *Sharḥ al-ṣadr*. In the introduction to the work, which he wrote in 1065/1654-55 at the age of 58, he claims that he had no one in whom he could confide and to whom he could complain of his many troubles. This particular situation, the lack of an effective network of emotional support, led him to compose the work. Unlike the other autobiographical texts discussed here, *Sharḥ al-ṣadr* is written in Persian, perhaps on account of its relatively intimate, emotional content. Niʿmat Allāh al-Jazāʾirī includes his autobiography as an appendix or epilogue to his anthology of general Shiʿi literature, *al-Anwār al-nuʿmāniyya*. In it, he includes much of the usual information, his teachers, travels and bibliography, but his humour is striking, as are his accounts of trials and tribulations in his youth, when he suffered acutely from poverty and exploitative teachers.[74] It becomes evident that a major rhetorical strategy in the text is to deflect envy, the evil eye, by putting the apparent attractiveness of his current success into perspective through revelation of the miseries he had to suffer to attain it.

G. Ḥadīth-*Based Legal Manuals*

Before al-Astarābādī wrote *al-Fawāʾid al-madaniyya*, Twelver scholars were already addressing the challenge to Twelver Shiʿi law, that is *fiqh*, the actual points of law, as opposed to *uṣūl al-fiqh*, legal hermeneutics, represented by the stringent application of *ḥadīth* criticism to the reports in the four canonical *ḥadīth* works. Ḥasan b. Zayn al-Dīn (d. 1101/1602) wrote *Muntaqā al-jumān* in 1006/1597-98 in order to

---

[73] Reynolds et al., *Interpreting the Self*, pp. 216–223; Stewart, 'Capital, Accumulation, and the Islamic Academic Biography'.

[74] Stewart, 'The Humor of the Scholars'; Brunner, "Siehe, was mich an Ungluck und Schrecken trat!"

present a restricted collection of *ḥadīth* reports that rose to the level of 'sound' (*ṣaḥīḥ*) or 'good, excellent' (*ḥasan*) according to the criteria of *ḥadīth* criticism but that would support the traditional Twelver positions on the main points of Islamic law. In 1007/1599, Bahā' al-Dīn al-ʿĀmilī wrote a similar work, *al-Ḥabl al-matīn,* and then *Mashriq al-shamsayn* in 1015/1607, which included not only the main *ḥadīth*s that served as the basis for legal rulings, but also Qur'anic verses. The Akhbārīs held a radically different view of the epistemological status of the reports of the imams, but they attempted to address the same hermeneutical situation that Ḥasan b. Zayn al-Dīn and Bahā' al-Dīn al-ʿĀmilī had faced, and this led them as well to write legal works that granted a larger and larger space to the oral reports of the imams, while also providing a critical analysis of the hermeneutical methods of their opponents.

The Akhbārīs' emphasis on adherence to *ḥadīth* reports and the rejection of legal analogy and similar rational methods led to distinct differences in the interpretation of some points of law. Muḥammad Amīn al-Astarābādī, the founder of the Akhbārī movement, gave greater attention to legal hermeneutics and legal theory than he did to the points of law but he did, nevertheless, address some particular legal issues in his writings, including the question of the ritual purity of wine. His treatise on this issue, in which he upheld the view that wine, despite the fact that its consumption is forbidden, is not a ritually impure substance, provides an example of Akhbārī legal intepretation. His evidence for this position is, first, reports of the imams that allow believers to pray in garments that have been spattered by wine. Secondly, he stressed the declaration that wine is impure has been concluded on the basis of an invalid legal analogy between ritual purity and the consumption of food and drink. Thirdly, the fact that the Sunni legal authorities all agree that wine is impure, going against the reports of the imams, should indicate to Shiʿis that the Sunni view is incorrect and that the opposite is in fact the true ruling.[75] Another example is the distinct ruling that a Muslim man cannot marry two women who are *sayyida*s, descendants of the Prophet through his

[75] See Gleave, *Scripturalist Islam*, pp. 97–99.

daughter Fāṭima, on the basis of a *ḥadīth* report. The logic behind this seems to be the analogy with sisters, for one cannot marry two sisters simultaneously, but this is not *qiyās* since it is based on an explicit report. Robert Gleave has analysed two treatises on this topic, the first by Yūsuf al-Baḥrānī, upholding this opinion on the basis of the report, and the other by Muḥammad Bāqir al-Bihbihānī, rejecting this opinion, largely on the basis of consensus and historical precedent.[76]

The prominent Akhbārī Muḥsin Fayḍ al-Kāshānī wrote two legal manuals which straddle his 'conversion' to the Akhbārī school. In Rajab 1029/June 1620, when he was still quite young, he wrote the legal manual *Muʿtaṣam al-shīʿa fī aḥkām al-sharīʿa*, adhering to what would come to be called the Uṣūlī method. In his later years he wrote a thoroughly Akhbārī elaboration of the law entitled *Mafātīḥ al-sharāʾiʿ*.[77] Another major work of Akhbārī law is Yūsuf al-Baḥrānī's *al-Ḥadāʾiq al-nāḍira fī aḥkām al-ʿitra al-ṭāhira*. This work is a thorough and extensive treatment of the law, in eight volumes or more in modern editions, based throughout on the Shiʿi *ḥadīth* corpus. Its introduction presents what is essentially a complete manual of legal hermeneutics or *uṣūl al-fiqh* from the Akhbārī point of view. The work may be fairly characterised as the culmination and high point of Akhbārī scholarship on the points of law.[78] It is likely that a number of additional, important Akhbārī legal works have not yet been recognised, in part because they may have been framed as commentaries on the standard legal works of the Shiʿi tradition, such as al-Fāḍil al-Tūnī's (d. 1071/1660-61) commentary on al-ʿAllāma al-Ḥillī's legal manual *Irshād al-adhhān ilā aḥkām al-īmān*.

[76] Robert Gleave, 'Marrying Fatimid Women: Legal Theory and Substantive Law in Shīʿī Jurisprudence', *Islamic Law and Society*, 6 (1999), pp. 38–68. Gleave discusses a number of other issues in his *Scripturalist Islam*, pp. 89–99.

[77] Muḥsin Fayḍ al-Kāshānī, *Muʿtaṣam al-shīʿa fī aḥkām al-sharīʿa*, ed. Masīḥ al-Tawḥīdī (Tehran, 1388 Sh./2009); Muḥsin Fayḍ al-Kāshānī, *Mafātīḥ al-sharāʾiʿ fī fiqh al-imāmiyya*, ed. Mahdī Rajāʾī (Qum, 1401/1981).

[78] Yūsuf b. Aḥmad al-Baḥrānī, *al-Ḥadāʾiq al-nāḍira fī aḥkām al-ʿitra al-ṭāhira*, ed. Muḥammad Taqī al-Īrwānī (Najaf, 1958–1962). See Gleave, *Inevitable Doubt*.

H. The Recuperation of Neglected and Marginalised Works

As mentioned above, the grand project to support the authenticity of the four canonical *ḥadīth* collections led to massive efforts to recollect *ḥadīth* and to locate early sources that could, potentially, provide corroboration of the material in these collections. Also mentioned above is the effort of Muḥammad Bāqir al-Majlisī to locate the lost work *Madīnat al-ʿilm*, by Ibn Bābawayh al-Qummī. In some cases, the historiographical aspects of these scholars' labours restored earlier works that had been rejected on ideological grounds. Muḥammad b. ʿAlī b. Abī al-ʿAzāqir al-Shalmaghānī was a jurist active in the 3rd/9th and 4th/10th centuries who served as an agent for Ḥusayn b. Rawḥ al-Nawbakhtī (d. 326/937-38), the third representative of the Hidden imam. When al-Nawbakhtī was imprisoned, al-Shalmaghānī claimed to be a representative of the imam. On account of this claim, he was denounced and executed in 322/934, and his book on Shiʿi law, *Kitāb al-taklīf*, was rejected by the subsequent legal tradition. Al-Sharīf al-Murtaḍā voiced the opinion that one ought not to consult the work, but the question to which his *fatwā* responded gives the impression that this work was still widely used in the early 5th/11th century. However, during the Safavid period, the book was recovered, edited and presented as *Fiqh al-Riḍā*, avoiding mention of al-Shalmaghānī and focusing on the figure of the Eighth imam as the supposed source of the legal rulings contained in the work. Both Muḥammad Taqī al-Majlisī and Muḥammad Bāqir al-Majlisī accepted the authenticity of the work, and it has remained a widely used text in Twelver Shiʿi legal circles.[79]

In addition to the monumental *ḥadīth* works and the commentaries on the individual canonical *ḥadīth* collections mentioned above, Akhbārī scholars also resurrected lesser-known *ḥadīth* works by writing commentaries on them. One notable example of this trend is

---

[79] *Al-Fiqh al-mansūb li al-Imām al-Riḍā al-mushtahir bi-*Fiqh al-Riḍā (Beirut, 1990); Devin J. Stewart, 'al-Sharīf al-Murtaḍā (D. 436/1044)', in Oussama Arabi et al., ed., *Islamic Legal Thought: A Compendium of Muslim Jurists* (Leiden, 2013), pp. 167–210, in particular pp. 180–181, 199; Wilferd Madelung, "Alī al-Reżā', *EIr*, vol. 1, pp. 877–880; al-Sayyid Ḥasan al-Ṣadr, 'Faṣl al-qaḍā' fi'l-kitāb al-muštahir bi-*Fiqh al-Riḍā*', in Riḍā al-Ustādī, ed., *Āshnā'ī bā chand nuskha-yi khaṭṭī* (Qum, 1355 Sh./1976), vol. 1, pp. 86–136.

Niʿmat Allāh al-Jazāʾirī's *al-Jawāhir al-ghawālī,* a commentary on *ʿAwālī al-laʾālī*, a *ḥadīth* compilation that Ibn Abī Jumhūr al-Aḥsāʾī (d. after 901/1506) completed in the winter of 897/1491-92.[80] Āyat Allāh al-Marʿashī al-Najafī (d. 1990) reported that despite the great value of the work, it had been abandoned in libraries and eaten by moths. The work was neglected for three main reasons: the lax manner of *ḥadīth* documentation in the work, its mystical, philosophical and *ghulāt* content, and the fact that it drew on Sunni sources. Accordingly, Ibn Abī al-Jumhūr was accused of being a Sufi mystic, a philosopher, or one of the *ghulāt* Shiʿis. In al-Marʿashī al-Najafī's view, none of these claims was true.[81]

Niʿmat Allāh al-Jazāʾirī had similar issues in mind when he wrote his commentary on *ʿAwālī al-laʾālī*. This was one of his late works; he completed the first volume of the book in Shūshtar in Rajab 1105/ February 1694.[82] He presented it as part of his larger project of commenting on the works of *ḥadīth*,[83] but it is clear that *ʿAwālī al-laʾālī* does not belong to the same category as the other works Niʿmat Allāh addressed, namely *Tahdhīb al-aḥkām* and *al-Istibṣār*. In the introduction, he makes it clear that the work had been viewed with some suspicion by earlier Twelver scholars. He reports that his teacher Muḥammad Bāqir al-Majlisī did not at first favour the work, particularly on account of Ibn Abī Jumhūr's treatment of *ḥadīth*. The work contains many *marāsīl*, that is, reports attributed to particular imams without specifying all of the intervening transmitters, and the author generally did not indicate the earlier sources from which he derived the reports that he cited. In addition, other scholars accused him of associating with Sunnis, philosophers and mystics. However, al-Majlisī changed his mind about the book because of the positive assessment of Ibn Abī Jumhūr's reliability and great learning by

80 Muḥammad b. ʿAlī b. Ibrāhīm b. Abī Jumhūr al-Aḥsāʾī, *ʿAwālī al-laʾālī al-ʿazīziyya fiʾl-aḥādīth al-dīniyya*, ed. Mujtabā al-ʿIrāqī (Qum, 1362 Sh./1983); Niʿmat Allāh al-Jazāʾirī, *Ghawālī al-laʾālī*, vol. 1, p. 117.

81 Āyat Allāh al-ʿUẓmā al-Sayyid Shihāb al-Dīn al-Ḥusaynī al-Marashī al-Nafajī, *Risālat al-Rudūd waʾl-nuqūd ʿalā al-kitāb wa-muʾallifihi waʾl-ajwiba al-shāfiya al-kāfiya ʿanhumā*, a treatise prefaced to Ibn Abī Jumhūr al-Aḥsāʾī, *ʿAwālī al-laʾālī*, vol. 1.

82 Niʿmat Allāh al-Jazāʾirī, *Ghawālī al-laʾālī*, vol. 1, p. 102.

83 Ibid., p. 110.

prominent Shiʿi biographers and other scholars and because of the quality of his other works. On these grounds, al-Majlisī felt that it was inappropriate to be suspicious of such an author's treatment of his sources.[84] Al-Jazāʾirī viewed his own task as restorative. First, his work would preserve the author's own glosses or marginal commentaries (*ḥawāshī*) on the text, which were in danger of being lost. This often happened, Niʿmat Allāh pointed out, because when later scholars copy works, they often omit the glosses. Though he had seen many copies of the work, only two copies included the glosses, one in the library of Muḥammad Bāqir al-Majlisī, and one, an autograph copy, in the library of a Shūshtarī *sayyid*.[85] In addition, through assiduous examination, Niʿmat Allāh was able to identify the sources for Ibn Abī Jumhūr's *ḥadīth*, including the four canonical *ḥadīth* collections and other works.[86] He passed over the particular issue of the radical content of the reports that are emphasised in the work. Overall, it is fair to say that the Akhbārīs' inclusive approach to *ḥadīth* reports re-integrated into mainstream scholarship aspects of the Shiʿi *ḥadīth* corpus that had been previously marginalised for centuries.

This reintegration was particularly important with regard to certain topics and ideological positions. Drawing especially on two works by Hāshim b. Sulaymān al-Baḥrānī (d. 1107/1695-96), Christian Lange has recognised that the Akhbārīs played a notable role in popularising a particular Shiʿi eschatology. He describes *Maʿālim al-zulfā fī maʿārif al-nashʾa al-ūlā waʾl-ukhrā* as a *summa* of eschatological traditions. A shorter treatise, *Nuzhat al-abrār wa-manār al-anẓār fī khalq al-janna waʾl-nār* brings together a smaller collection of traditions describing Paradise and Hell. These works include stories of a legendary and fantastical nature, including many that portray the involvement of the imams in Paradise. For example, two stories about the Prophet's *miʿrāj* connect Fāṭima with Paradise. In one, Gabriel gave the Prophet a date to eat in Paradise, and this date settled in his loins and later caused the conception of Fāṭima. In another report, Fāṭima existed in Paradise in the form of an apple that the Prophet consumed and then was born

84 Ibid., pp. 109–110.

85 Niʿmat Allāh al-Jazāʾirī, *Ghawālī al-laʾālī*, vol. 1, pp. 116–117.

86 Ibid., p. 110.

on earth.[87] An Akhbārī account of eschatology that Lange does not address is embedded in Niʿmat Allāh al-Jazāʾirī's work *al-Anwār al-nuʿmāniyya fiʾl-nashʾa al-insāniyya,* which he completed on 15 Ramaḍān 1089/31 October 1678.[88]

A number of other ideological emphases were associated with works inspired by Akhbārī methods and approaches. Etan Kohlberg has pointed out that the *ḥadīth* corpus collected in *Biḥār al-anwār* brought out three issues that had been suppressed in earlier centuries. The Akhbārīs revived significant material impugning the integrity of the Qurʾan, suggesting that the enemies of the Shiʿis had historically suppressed many Qurʾanic passages, most of which referred to the special status of the imams.[89] They also stressed derogatory reports concerning the status of the companions of the Prophet. Polemical works against the companions formed an important aspect of Safavid literary production in general, beginning long before rise of the Akhbārī movement, with ʿAlī b. ʿAbd al-ʿĀl al-Karakī's *Nafaḥāt al-lāhūt fī laʿn al-jibṭ waʾl-ṭāghūt,* a work dedicated to Shah Ismāʿīl I (r. 907–930/1501–1524) and justifying the practice of anathematising the Prophet's companions, especially Abū Bakr and ʿUmar. Other reports highlighted by the Akhbārīs stressed the suprahuman status and powers of the imams.[90]

Conclusion

The Safavid period saw a general increase in literary production of all kinds, particularly in the Shiʿi religious sciences, including law, theology, general devotional works, conversion narratives and polemical literature. Alongside this general trend, Akhbārī ideology played an important role in shaping directions of intellectual debate in

---

[87] Christian Lange, *Paradise and Hell in Islamic Traditions* (Cambridge, 2016), pp. 204–209.

[88] Niʿmat Allāh al-Jazāʾirī, *al-Anwār al-nuʿmāniyya fiʾl-nashʾa al-insāniyya,* ed. Muḥammad Alī al-Qāḍī al-Ṭabāṭabāʾī (Beirut, 2010), vol. 4, pp. 173–259.

[89] On the issue of the falsification of the Qurʾan in Shiʿi literature, see Rainer Brunner, *Die Schia und die Koranfälschung* (Würzburg, 2001); Etan Kohlberg and Mohammed Ali Amir-Moezzi, ed., *Revelation and Falsification: The* Kitāb al-Qirāʾāt *of Aḥmad b. Muḥammad al-Sayyārī* (Leiden, 2009).

[90] Kohlberg, 'Beḥār al-anwār'.

a number of specific genres. The Akhbārī movement strongly affected literary production in Twelver Shiʿi environments in the 11th/17th and 12th/18th centuries. It involved many areas and regions of the Islamic world, including Iraq, Lebanon, Bahrain, the Hijaz and Mashhad, but it was concentrated overwhelmingly in Iṣfahān, which was not only the Safavid capital from the late 10th/16th century onwards, but also the cultural capital of the Twelver Shiʿi Islamic world up until the fall of the dynasty in 1134/1722.

The literary production engendered by the Akhbārī movement involved a large number of genres, including some that are perhaps not obvious. Some were polemical and directly related to the Akhbārī-Uṣūlī controversy, like *al-Fawāʾid al-madaniyya* and *Safīnat al-najāt*, or the lists of differences between the Akhbārī and Uṣūlī schools. Some had to do directly with *ḥadīth* reports, such as the commentaries on the canonical *ḥadīth* works, the massive, comprehensive *ḥadīth* compilations such as *al-Wāfī*, *Wasāʾil al-shīʿa* and *Biḥār al-anwār*. Others were at one or more removes from *ḥadīth* works, such as Qurʾanic commentaries, biographical dictionaries and autobiographies. It is notable that the typical representatives of several of the genres produced, especially the commentaries on the canonical *ḥadīth* works and the comprehensive *ḥadīth* compilations, were large, multi-volume works. In some sense, the surge in production in Safavid Iṣfahān resembled that which had occurred in Baghdad in the 3rd/9th and 4th/10th centuries, involving many works running to ten, twenty, or more volumes.

Even though the Akhbārī movement had been defeated by the early 19th century and in most contexts disappeared completely thereafter, the literary production they had inspired lived on. If the explicitly polemical works lost popularity, others did not. Al-Ḥurr al-ʿĀmilī's *Wasāʾil al-shīʿa* has remained a fundamental reference work in Twelver Shiʿi legal scholarship. Muḥammad Bāqir al-Majlisī's *Biḥār al-anwār* is recognised as the premier encyclopedia of Shiʿi Islam. As Rainer Brunner argues, *Biḥār al-anwār* has taken on an emblematic function, representing the collective memory of Shiʿi society and standing as a monument to the Shiʿi tradition as a whole.[91]

[91] Brunner, 'The Role of *Ḥadīth* as Cultural Memory'.

The Akhbārī movement also played a crucial role in shaping the entire collective archive of Shiʿi religious literature. Emphasis on the centrality of the *ḥadīth* corpus for guidance of the believer resulted in an expansion in the interests of members of the religious establishment who, for centuries, had focused rather narrowly on legal studies and limited any forays into other fields that were considered ancillary to law. The Akhbārīs brought about a renewed interest in, and focused examination of, the Shiʿi *ḥadīth* legacy, thereby infusing a number of genres with innovative conceptions and methods. The insistence on bolstering the epistemological status of the canonical *ḥadīth* collections rendered the Akhbārī movement a restorative, historical project that involved locating, investigating, disseminating and commenting on those texts in the Shiʿi tradition that could provide context or corroboration for the Shiʿi *ḥadīth* corpus. Because the investigatory net was cast widely, the Akhbārīs ended up promoting the diversity of the tradition, resuscitating formerly marginalised works that had been considered doctrinally suspect. Throughout the Twelver Shiʿi world, the Akhbārī movement played a crucial role in the collection, cataloguing and preservation of manuscripts and the recovery of neglected works.

10

Postclassical Legal Commentaries: The Elaboration of Tradition in the Twelver Shiʿism of Safavid Times[1]

Robert Gleave

Islamic Postclassicism

The term 'Postclassical' has emerged in the study of Islamic intellectual history to describe (roughly) scholarly activity during the time between 9th–13th/15th–19th centuries.[2] The foremost genre of religious literary production was the commentary; the prevalent educational method was intense textual study in a scholar-led study circle; the principal institutional setting was the *madrasa*. All of these elements existed in the so-called 'classical' period (that is, between the 4th and 8th/10th and 14th centuries). There were commentaries, study circles

[1] Research for this paper was carried out under the auspices of the Law, Authority and Learning in Imami Shiite Islam project (www.lawalisi.eu), funded by the European Research Council (no.695245). I thank Drs Amin Ehteshami, Raha Rafii, Kumail Rajani and Cameron Zargar (of the LAWALISI project) for their helpful comments.

[2] Use of the timeframe of the 'postclassical' is not without its critics. Following the publications of Roger Allen et al., *Arabic literature in the post-classical period* (Cambridge and New York, 2006), Thomas Bauer embarked on a detailed critique of the use of the term in the field of Arabic and Islamic Studies: Thomas Bauer, 'In Search of "Post-Classical Literature": A Review Article', *Mamlūk Studies Review*, 11 (2007). On the other hand, we have the productive use of the time-period in Robert Wisnovsky, 'The Nature and Scope of Arabic Philosophical Commentary in Post-Classical (ca. 1100-1900 AD) Islamic Intellectual History: Some Preliminary Observations', *Bulletin of the Institute of Classical Studies*, 47 (2004), pp. 149–191. There is no equivalent term in use (apart from recent neologisms), as far as I can tell, in the various intellectual traditions of Islam, but that in itself does not make it a useful marker. See also, Robert Gleave and Asad Q. Ahmed, 'Rationalist Disciplines and Postclassical Islamic Legal Theories', *Oriens*, 46 (2018), pp. 1–5.

and *madrasas* during this period, though these features were not yet fully established as the prime elements of intellectual enquiry. Furthermore, the 'modern' period (from the 19th century onwards) was not devoid of these features: that is, there was no cliff-edge, sudden disappearance of these phenomena; they simply began to decline as the principal scholarly fora. What sets the postclassical period apart is the dominance (almost monopoly) of these modes of intellectual activity in the area of Islamic religious scholarship, and the stability of the institutional structures which supported them. This stability has sometimes been interpreted as unoriginality and stagnation giving rise to moribund, self-referential scholarship. One of the rallying calls of the so-called reform (*iṣlāḥī*) movements of the 19th century was that, intellectually speaking, 'Islam' had failed to advance due to the introspection of postclassical scholarship; this meant it was insufficiently robust to counteract new ('Western') forms of knowledge.[3] The supposed postclassical torpor needed to be swept away, and a renewed vision of Islamic scholarship was needed, the reformers argued – one which was more engaged with the needs of society, more dynamic in the face of social change and better equipped to rebuff both the military and intellectual challenges of imperial Western Europe.[4] This analysis was also promoted by early European academic

[3] An example of this attitude can be found in the approach of the famous reformer Muhammad Abduh, whose comment on his own postclassical (Azharī) education caused some controversy: 'whose comment have a portion of true knowledge, I got it through ten years of sweeping the dirt of the Azhar from my brain, and to this day it is not as clean as I would like.' See Mark Sedgwick, *Muhammad Abduh* (Oxford, 2010), p. 103.

[4] Jamāl al-Dīn al-Afghānī, one time associate (and perhaps mentor) of Abduh, viewed traditional Muslim education as a hindrance to scientific and political development. The traditional Muslim scholar is '[y]oked, like an ox to the plow, to the dogma whose slave he is, he must walk eternally in the furrow that has been traced for him in advance by the interpreters of the law. Convinced, besides, that his religion contains in itself all morality and all sciences, he attaches himself resolutely to it and makes no effort to go beyond.' See Sayyid Jamāl al-Dīn al-Afghānī, 'Answer to Renan', in *An Islamic Response to Imperialism: Political and Religious Writings of Sayyid Jamal al-Din al-Afghani*, tr. Nikki Keddie (Berkeley and Los Angeles, CA, 1968), pp. 181–187.

scholarship on Islamic intellectual history. There was a twin focus on the 'classical' period of Islam, and recent innovations in Muslim thinking; the period between (the 'postclassical', one might say) was viewed as repetitive, intellectually uninteresting and tediously casuistic. One thing the so-called 'Orientalist' scholarship and the Muslim modernists agreed upon was that the postclassical model was not only intellectually uninteresting; it was no longer fit for purpose.

There has, though, been a renewed appreciation for the postclassical period and its modes of knowledge production recently. There has been discussion over whether the term 'postclassical' devalues the phenomenon under discussion, and is best seen as an imposition of European modes of periodisation on the history of Islamic civilisation. Recently there has been the assertion of Muslim neo-traditionalism which features a nostalgia for the intellectual structures of the period before modernism, coupled with a frustration with a perceived superficiality (and overtly political agenda) of so-called 'Modernist Islam'. In the academic literature, there has also been a new focus on the complexity and sophistication found in 'postclassical' works in the various Islamic religious sciences. First, there is a growing recognition that these works were not simply unoriginal repetitions of the great works of the classical period: novel interpretations, along with intellectual advances did occur, albeit within a pedagogical framework which was usually rigid and unbending. Second, there is a rejection that originality (as conceived in European humanism) is necessarily the only marker of intellectual vibrancy: evaluating a cultural product solely in terms of a perceived 'originality' is to prioritise a particular notion of intellectual worth (i.e. 'novelty') over another (i.e. 'established tradition'). Some commentators appear to subscribe to the view that 'real' originality cannot take place in a 'traditional' framework. But it can be argued that 'postclassical' has moved from being a term with negative connotations, to one which usefully describes a particular cultural form which was common to the major Islamic empires of the time, encompassed various sectarian contexts and traversed the myriad societal settings of the period. What was previously described as 'late medieval' or 'early premodern' now has its own identity, facilitated by the development of the idea of a distinctive history of 'postclassical' Islamic intellectual activity. This renewed focus on the postclassical in the secondary literature may turn out to be a fad, and Islamicists shall, perhaps, return to the supposed excitement of the advances of earlier and later periods in time. But even if focus shifts, the current vogue for postclassical developments will leave a lasting mark, and it will no longer be acceptable for researchers to write with an implicit dismissal of half a millennium of Muslim scholarship.

In this chapter, I will endeavour to present a description and analysis of the postclassical legal literature of Twelver Shiʿism – both commentaries and monographs. In many ways the style of argument in these works is unsurprising, revealing features which one typically finds in postclassical legal works from different Muslim intellectual traditions and *madhāhib*; in other respects, the works are distinctly Ithnā ʿasharī Shiʿi, drawing on a history of scholarship which is exclusive, reserving a prominent place for particular works by Ithnā ʿasharī scholars for commentary. In the same vein, the works analysed below display characteristics which are not, in many ways, specifically 'legal'. The subject of these books may be *fiqh* (jurisprudence), but the mode of discourse is characteristic of postclassical works treating other subjects (philosophy, theology, mysticism, etc.). In other ways, the works described below are virtuoso works in the specific field of *fiqh*; they are deeply involved in explaning legal principles for legal scholars, and do not engage extensively with non-legal works. As we shall see, the invariably legal focus of these works is, in itself, a feature of postclassical works, which often plough a furrow within a genre or discipline reflecting and reinforcing disciplinary divisions in the seminary curriculum.

Postclassical Ithnā ʿasharī Shiʿi Legal Scholarship

Two political events fix the limitations of this study – the beginnings of the Safavid and Qājār periods (907/1501 and 1203/1789 respectively). These dates are partly convenient markers, but they do represent significant changes in the way Twelver Shiʿism was organised, this is reflected, in part, in the styles of scholarship in the period. This is not to say that scholarship did not take place outside the Iranian (or more broadly, Persianate) context – Arab Twelver scholars, in particular, were particularly active in areas under Ottoman control, and there was a developing tradition of Twelver scholarship in India.[5] However, the establishment of the Safavid dynasty as an avowedly Twelver Shiʿi political power changed the dynamic of Twelver Shiʿi scholarship. The patronage of religious learning by the Safavids facilitated the elaboration of established modes of scholarly enquiry in Iran and, to some extent, elsewhere. In *fiqh*, this meant the entrenchment of the *ijtihād*-based approach, initiated by the school of Ḥilla and led by the Ḥilla-based scholars al-Muḥaqqiq and al-ʿAllāma. Later, Safavid possibilities for scholarly endeavour led to the expansion of previously neglected scholarly disciplines in Shiʿism, most notably philosophy and the collection of and commentary on *ḥadīth* (the former associated with the so-called 'Iṣfahān school of philosophy', the latter with the Akhbārī movement). The increase in resources encouraged greater intellectual activity, which in time led to greater diversity in the religious outlook of the scholarly classes. For these reasons, then, the beginning of the Safavid period is a useful point at which to begin any study of postclassical Twelver legal scholarship, even if not all the scholarship under consideration here was written in Iran (or through Iranian patronage). At the other end of the period under consideration, the beginning of the Qājār period marks not only the beginning of a new relationship between the Twelver Shiʿi *ʿulamāʾ* and political power; it also coincides with (and is not unconnected to) the loss of the Akhbārī school's pre-eminence at the seminaries of Iraq and Iran.

[5] It is, though, worth remembering that whilst Shiʿi jurists may have been affected by the rise and fall of Iranian dynasties, much scholarship was taking place outside the Iranian realm. Shiʿi scholars living under Ottoman control were particularly active, notwithstanding regular instances of political pressure, and many of the works discussed in this chapter were composed outside the Iranian lands. See Devin Stewart, *Islamic Legal Orthodoxy: Twelver Shiite Responses to the Sunni Legal System* (Salt Lake City, UT, 1998). Furthermore, in the later part of the period, Indian Shiʿi scholars were active not only in the Iranian sphere of influence; there was also a burgeoning Shiʿi scholarly community emerging in India itself. The period, then, is chosen partly for convenience (the 19th century legal material is voluminous and would be impossible to cover adequately in a single chapter) – see Juan Cole, *Roots of North Indian Shiʿism in Iran and Iraq: Religion and State in Awadh, 1722-1859* (Berkeley and Los Angeles, CA, 1988); but also, in part, because there are significant intellectual markers (from the end of classicism to the revival of the Uṣūlī movement) and political changes (the rise of the Safavids and the establishment of the Qājārs) which bookend the period.

The much-discussed 'revival' of the Uṣūlī school under the leadership of al-Waḥīd al-Bihbahānī marked both a new relationship with political power and a major realignment of Twelver Shiʿi scholarship. Al-Bihbahānī's revival, though drawing on the tradition of *ijtihād*-based legal scholarship of preceding centuries, had a quite novel character described, albeit patchily, in the scholarship to date. The emergence of this revived Uṣūlī school makes an appropriate marker for the terminus of the period under examination here.

The principal surviving legal literature from this postclassical period of Ithnā ʿasharī scholarship consists of works of *fiqh* (including both the comprehensive works of jurisprudence and the shorter treatises on specific legal issues), works of legal theory (*uṣūl*) and legal *ḥadīth* collections and commentaries. There are few collections of Safavid *fatwā*s and the wealth of legal documentary evidence is yet to be made available for extensive scholarship. I have discussed postclassical Twelver *uṣūl* and *ḥadīth* scholarship elsewhere; the emergence of the *risāla* as a method of juristic expression deserves a discrete treatment.[6] The focus of this chapter is the composition of comprehensive (or unfinished attempts at) works on *fiqh* and their commentaries. In the Safavid period, the writing of works of *fiqh* by Twelver scholars increased at an almost industrial rate, mirroring the explosion of *fiqh* composition in non-Shiʿi postclassical settings elsewhere in the Muslim world, with a similar abundance of commentaries, super-commentaries and marginal glosses.[7] It is quite possible that *fiqh* works constitute the single largest genre of religious literary production in the postclassical Ithnā ʿasharī context, though there are yet to be available the bibliographic resources to confirm this. The Twelver legal works of the period can be divided between independent monographs

[6] See R. Gleave, 'Moral Assessments and Legal Categories: The Relationship between Rational Ethics and Revealed Law in Post-Classical Imāmī Shīʿī Legal Theory', in F. Bouhafa, 'Towards New Perspectives on Ethics in Islam: Casuistry, Contingency and Ambiguity', *Journal of Arabic and Islamic Studies*, themed issue, 21 (2021), pp. 183–207.

[7] See now Samy Ayoub, *Law, Empire, and the Sultan: Ottoman Imperial Authority and Late Hanafi Jurisprudence* (Oxford, 2020) and Alan Guenther, 'Ḥanafī Fiqh in Mughal India: The *Fatāwá-i ʿĀlamgīrī*', in Richard Eaton, ed., *India's Islamic Tradition, 711–1750* (New Dehli, 2003), pp. 207–230.

and commentaries, with the latter probably being more numerous. Independent monographs were, in the main, the prerogative of the established, respected scholar. To compose a monographic treatment of all areas of jurisprudence is, in a sense, to propose that one's new monograph should be the subject of subsequent teaching and commentarial activity. Writing such a monograph would, in the main, be attempted only by an established scholar who has a sufficient following not only to teach the text himself (perhaps thereby creating an 'auto-commentary'), but also for his students and their students to teach the text and produce subsequent commentaries.[8]

Commentaries, then, are often the product of teaching classes, where the base text (*matn*) was taught and explained by a teacher (sometimes the *matn*'s author) to a group of students. The teacher's comments formed the basis for the commentary (*sharḥ* or *ḥāshiya*). He (the teacher, almost all of whom were male) might commit these comments to the paper himself (often in the margins of the *matn* textbook), or one of the students would record them, and this became a new work which was then transmitted, copied and studied along with the *matn*. This new work was, sometimes, the subject of additional commentary (i.e. supercommentary) and on occasions the supercommentary itself was the subject of commentary (super-supercommentary, one might say).[9] Examples of the style and format of each of these different types of legal writing (monograph/*matn*, auto-commentary, commentary, supercommentary) are given in the exposition below, though it should be noted that the boundaries between these styles of writing were hardly fixed either in Twelver Shiʿi or other postclassical intellectual traditions.

---

[8] For example, al-ʿAllāma al-Ḥillī, who will be discussed in greater detail below, wrote a work of law titled *Talkhīṣ al-marām fī maʿrifat al-aḥkām*; he then wrote a commentary (*sharḥ*) on it called *Ghāyat al-Aḥkām fī taṣḥīḥ talkhīṣ al-marām*, Āqā Buzurg al-Ṭihrānī, *al-Dharīʿa ilā taṣānīf al-shīʿa* (Najaf, 1936), vol. 16, p. 6.

[9] For example, there is an astronomical work titled *al-Mulakhkhas* by Maḥmūd al-Jaghmīnī (whose death date is uncertain but who lived in the 8th/14th century); this was subject to a commentary by Qāḍīzāda al-Rūmī, a 9th/15th-century scholar. This commentary then received a supercommentary by al-Shaykh al-Bahāʾī, the great Safavid scholar, whose pupil wrote a *ḥāshiya* on al-Shaykh al-Bahāʾī's commentary, thereby creating a super-supercommentary on the base text. Ṭihrānī, *al-Dharīʿa*, vol. 6, p. 123.

***Fiqh* texts, Commentaries and Supercommentaries**

In the postclassical period, there were, broadly speaking, three types of *fiqh* literature being composed: (1) commentaries on existing *fiqh* works (and supercommentaries on those commentaries); (2) new, independent *fiqh* works and (3) short treatises (*rasāʾil*, sing. *risāla*) on specific (usually controversial) *fiqh* questions (e.g. a *risāla* on Friday prayer, a *risāla* on the permissibility of smoking tobacco, etc). The first of these literary activities (the production of commentaries and super-commentaries) comprise the bulk of legal literature from the period. It is this body of literature which is the focus of this chapter, as it reveals much about the dynamics of legal thinking during the period. The second category, new works of *fiqh*, were also the subject of commentary in the period and hence examples from new works and their commentaries are included below also. As these works became the standard textbooks in Shiʿi seminaries (which experienced a period of sustained growth in Safavid Iran), a series of supercommentaries (sometimes no more than teaching notes) are produced. In addition to all this, there is the rise of the legal *risāla* as a form of intellectual exchange in the Safavid period – this important development deserves a detailed separate study.

The terminology used for commentaries in the biobibliographical literature is reasonably stable, though not without occasional ambiguities. The base text is the *matn* (pl. *mutūn*); some *mutūn* are intentionally compressed (i.e. are *mukhtaṣars*) to aide memorisation and to invite commentary, making them intentionally difficult to read (or giving only partial understanding) without the assistance of a teacher and his commentary (oral or otherwise). Indeed, one of the four popular classical *mutūn* has the title *mukhtaṣar* – though this is because it is an abbreviation of another, already abbreviated, text. What should be noted about all these texts is the low level of rule justification found in them. As we shall see, these texts are characterised by a statement of the rules, with very little discussion of alternative rules, or explicit justification for the rules given. They are, in the main, compressed handbooks of regulations, and this is a phenomenon common to both the Ithnā ʿasharī jurists and those in other classical Islamic intellectual traditions. Whilst books from the classical period were the popular contenders for postclassical commentary, there were new *mukhtaṣar*s written in the postclassical period which spawned commentaries and occasionally supercommentaries. They represent a continuation rather than a break with practices established in the classical period.

In the Ithnā ʿasharī biobibliographical literature, the *sharḥ* (pl. *shurūḥ*) is probably the most common name for a commentary. The *sharḥ* is sometimes distinguished from the *ḥāshiya* (pl. *ḥawāshī*, occasional comments), of which there are also many listed. It is commonly said that a *sharḥ* commented on every element of the text, whilst a *ḥāshiya* focused on selected phrases deemed worthy of comment. Notwithstanding this distinction, the difference between a *sharḥ* and a *ḥāshiya* is not always clear, though, and sometimes the terms are used interchangeably. Biobibliographers sometimes make the point that an author's *ḥāshiya* might actually be the same as the author's *sharḥ*; on rare occasions (for this period at least), there is also a record of *taʿlīqāt* (sing. *taʿlīqa*) on a work ('occasional remarks', one might call them), which, the biobibliographers add, could actually be an indirect reference to the author's *ḥāshiya*, or even his *sharḥ*, rather than a separate work. Some authors are recorded as composing both a *sharḥ* and a *ḥāshiya* on the same work, and the biobibliographers are explicit in saying these are separate works, usually having seen copies of both works. Whilst there exist inconsistent formal definitions of each category of commentary (*sharḥ, ḥāshiya, taʿlīqa*), these do not always appear to correspond perfectly to how the terms are used in titles and descriptions found in biobibliographical sources. In the analysis below, works called by all these terms are given below: they may represent different forms of commentarial activity, but the various styles of commentary discussed below do not perfectly match up with the different titles given to books of commentary. In the biobibliographical literature, these broad categories are supplemented by various subcategories. For example, the *sharḥ bi'l-qawl* ('commentary by statement') is described as 'on the pattern of *his statement*, then *I say*' (*qawluhu aqūlu*).[10] *Sharḥ mamzūj* (also called *sharḥ mazj* and *sharḥ mazjī*, 'blended commentary') is glossed as 'the commentator mentions the phrase from the *matn* without indicating it with *qawluhu*,

[10] For example, Ṭihrānī, *al-Dharīʿa*, vol. 14, p. 50.

or *qāla* or *matn* or anything else; then he gives a commentary on it.'[11] Commonly, the *sharḥ mamzūj* is understood to be a commentary which is inserted between the words and phrases of the *matn* text which clarifies and expands on the *matn* but does not disrupt the grammatical flow of the original text. The effect is to create a new 'blended' text, which might then become the subject of additional commentary. The various terms appear reasonably fluid, as in the example 'this is a *sharḥ mazjī* in the form of a *taʿlīq*',[12] or more simply 'a *sharḥ* in the form of *taʿlīq*'[13] or 'a *sharḥ* in the form of a *taʿlīq*, abbreviated (*mukhtaṣar*) with the title *qawluhu aqūlu*'.[14] Some of these classifications and subclassifications can be seen to be useful when examining the commentaries themselves (see below).

In the 'postclassical' period, many commentaries were produced on 'classical' works of Ithnā ʿasharī *fiqh* (that is, works written in the preceding period; roughly speaking, before 800/1400). Four were the focus of extensive commentary – outstripping other classical works in popularity. These are:

1. *Sharāʾiʿ al-Islām* of al-Muḥaqqiq al-Ḥillī (Jaʿfar b. al-Ḥasan b. Yaḥyā b. Saʿīd al-Ḥillī, d. 676/1277).
2. *al-Mukhtaṣar al-nāfiʿ* of al-Muḥaqqiq al-Ḥillī – this, according to al-Muḥaqqiq himself is an abbreviation of the author's *Sharāʾiʿ al-Islām* (hence, so it is stated, the name, *mukhtaṣar*/legal breviary).
3. *Irshād al-adhhān* of al-ʿAllāma al-Ḥillī (al-Ḥasan b. Yūsuf b. al-Muṭahhar al-Ḥillī, d. 726/1325).
4. *Qawāʿid al-aḥkām* of al-ʿAllāma al-Ḥillī.

These works became the foremost base-texts for commentary in the postclassical period, although there are other texts which received commentary in this period.[15] A brief survey of selected biobibliographical data records over 110 commentaries on these four

11 Ibid., vol. 13, p. 54.
12 Ibid., p. 54.
13 Ibid., p. 293.
14 Ibid., vol. 14, p. 63.
15 Examples include al-ʿAllāma's *Mukhtalaf al-shīʿa* and his *Tabṣirat al-mutaʿallimīn*.

works alone in the Safavid period (along with many both before and after). Many others are unreferenced in these sources but are extant, listed in the manuscript catalogues. This indicates that there are probably many more waiting to be uncovered in library collections as yet uncatalogued. From the available data, the most popular work is *Irshād al-adhhān*, with nearly forty commentaries recorded in this period; if one includes the post-Safavid period, though, there is a shift to the *Sharāʾiʿ al-Islām*, which becomes, for reasons that are not entirely clear, the most popular by some margin. Some of these commentaries became so well known that their stature eclipsed that of the original *matn*.[16] In time, the commentary text became the focus of study, meaning any understanding of the *matn* was (almost) entirely refracted through the commentary and the *matn* was not considered an important object of direct study. The most widely-read and studied commentaries on the four classical texts mentioned above are probably the following five works:

- ʿAlī b. al-Ḥusayn al-Karakī's (d. 940/1534) *Jāmiʿ al-maqāṣid* (on al-ʿAllāma's *Qawāʿid*).
- Zayn al-Dīn b. ʿAlī al-Shahīd al-Thānī's (d. 965/1557 or 966/1558), *Masālik al-afhām* (on al-Muḥaqqiq's *Sharāʾiʿ al-Islām*).
- Aḥmad b. Muḥammad al-Muqaddas al-Ardabīlī's (d. 993/1585) *Majmaʿ al-fāʾida waʾl-bayān* (on al-ʿAllāma's *Irshād al-adhhān*).
- Muḥammad b. ʿAlī al-ʿĀmilī (d. 1009/1600), *Madārik al-aḥkām* (on al-Muḥaqqiq's *Sharāʾiʿ al-Islām*).[17]
- Muḥammad Bāqir al-Sabzawarī's (d. 1090/1679) *Dhakhīrat al-maʿād* (on al-ʿAllāma's *Irshād al-adhhān*).

Many of these commentaries achieved sufficient renown to become the base text for supercommentary. The most prominent example of this phenomenon are the commentaries on the *Madārik al-aḥkām* by

[16] It seems to have become common to read a base text (such as al-ʿAllāma's *Sharāʾiʿ*) alongside one of its widely respected commentaries (such as al-Shahīd al-Thānī's *Masālik al-afhām* and al-ʿĀmilī's *Madārik al-aḥkām*, discussed below).

[17] Muḥammad al-ʿĀmilī also wrote a brief commentary on al-Muḥaqqiq's *al-Mukhtaṣar al-nāfiʿ* titled *Ghāyat al-marām*, demonstrating again the clear preferences of these texts as *mutūn* for *sharḥ* in this period.

Muḥammad b. ʿAlī al-ʿĀmilī (known as *Ṣāhib al-Madārik*). The biobibliographical date records over twenty commentaries on the *Madārik* (which thereby form supercommentaries on the *Sharāʾiʿ*). Well-known supercommentaries, composed at the end of the period under examination here, include:

- the *Ḥāshiya Majmaʿ al-fāʾida waʾl-bayān* – a commentary on al-Ardabīlī's *Majmaʿ* (and therefore a supercommentary on al-ʿAllāma's *Irshād*) by Muḥammad Bāqir al-Bihbahānī (known as al-Waḥīd, d. ca. 1205/1791, described as the great reviver of the Uṣūlī school).
- *al-Fadhālik* by Muḥammad ʿAlī al-Kirmānshāhī (d. 1206/1795, son of al-Waḥīd), being a commentary on the *Madārik* (and thereby a supercommentary on the *Sharāʾiʿ*).[18]

Sometimes, a postclassical commentary on a classical work became so popular that it seemed to eclipse all other commentaries on the *matn*, and it appears that scholars felt any further commentaries would not be meaningful contributions. An example of this might be the extremely important *al-Rawḍa al-bahiyya*, a commentary by al-Shahīd al-Thānī on the condensed breviary (*mukhtaṣar*) of all areas of *fiqh*, *al-Lumʿa al-Dimashqiyya* by Muḥammad b. al-Makkī al-ʿĀmilī al-Shahīd al-Awwal (d. 786/1386). *Al-Rawḍa* itself became an important teaching text, and, in later years, became the principal guide for students studying *al-Lumʿa*. Despite the widespread popularity of *al-Lumʿa al-Dimashqiyya* as a teaching text, there are few postclassical commentaries on it. I have found only three references to commentaries on *al-Lumʿa* from the postclassical period.[19] None of these could compete with *al-Rawḍa*, though, for popularity and influence. *Al-Rawḍa*'s popularity, though, led to the production of

[18] Indeed, al-Waḥīd himself also wrote a commentary on the *Madārik*, and hence a supercommentary on the *Sharāʾiʿ*.

[19] One anonymous manuscript; one by a pupil of the famous Sulaymān al-Māḥūzī (d. 1121/1709); and another by Muʿizz al-Dīn al-Tūnī, a contemporary of Shahid II. Interestingly, there were a significant number of commentaries on *al-Lumʿa* in the 19th century indicating perhaps a wish to return to the original text and bypass *al-Rawḍa*. See Ṭihrānī, *al-Dharīʿa*, vol. 14, pp. 47–51.

supercommentaries in great number in the postclassical period, into the 19th century, with nearly 100 supercommentary titles (i.e., commentaries on *al-Rawḍa* which is a commentary on *al-Lumʿa*) being identified in the sources.[20] These are called both *ḥāshiya* and *sharḥ*. Most of these supercommentaries do not appear to have acquired widespread use in the seminary teaching circles, probably because many would have simply been comments gleaned from teaching sessions. Some works, though, achieved respect in their own right, including Muḥammad b. Ḥasan al-Fāḍil al-Hindī's (d. 1131/1718) *al-Manāhij al-sawiyya* (on which see below). These super-commentaries do not themselves, it appears, become the subject of commentary (forming 'super-supercommentaries'), as one sometimes sees in other postclassical fields of study.

Commentarial activity was also sparked by new monographic *fiqh* texts composed in the postclassical period (i.e. writing texts which hope to replace the breviary texts such as *al-Lumʿa*, *Qawāʿid* and *Sharāʾiʿ*). Examples include al-Sabzawārī's *Kifāyat al-aḥkām* and Muḥsin al-Fayḍ al-Kāshānī's (d. 1091/1680) *Mafātiḥ al-sharāʾiʿ*. Both attracted commentaries, though the *Mafātiḥ* was a more popular base text. *Mafātiḥ*, one can argue, is written in a style which, more or less, invites commentary (rules are stated, argument is minimal); the *Kifāya*'s style is more discursive (albeit argument is present). As is exemplified below, the ideal base text contains rule stipulation with little or no argument or elucidation. Explaining why rules are as they are and what they precisely mean is the task of the commentator – the less expansive the *matn*, the greater the scope of the *sharḥ*. This is not to say that *mukhtaṣar*s are merely lists of rules – the structure of their presentation often forms an argument without it being explicitly stated. The authors of *mukhtaṣar*s are not simply listing rules; they are, in large part, writing texts intended for commentary, and one gets the impression that is what Muḥsin al-Fayḍ was attempting to do in his *Mafātiḥ*.

Finally, note should be taken of the enormous *al-Ḥadāʾiq al-nādira* of Yūsuf b. Aḥmad al-Baḥrānī (d. 1186/1772). This work stands apart from the other monographs on *fiqh* of the period mentioned above. It

[20] There is an early translation of *al-Rawḍa* into Persian by Mīr Findiriskī (d. 1050/1640). Ṭihrānī, *al-Dharīʿa*, vol. 4, p. 105.

received hardly any commentary in the subsequent tradition, even though it remains hugely influential and much utilised. As demonstrated below, it is the only work of this period which attempts to work through *fiqh* using an Akhbārī juristic methodology. It was left unfinished at the author's death, though al-Baḥrānī's notes on the remaining chapters were collected from his sessions and notes by his students, and these works display a continuation of his manner of presentation and argumentation.[21]

In short, most who might pick up a work of postclassical Twelver *fiqh*, finding abbreviations for these works and their authors cited without explanation, the text turns into a secret code for the initiated, excluding all but the expert. The intensity of this self-referential tradition is a hallmark of the postclassical scholarly milieu. Nevertheless, this was what formed the intellectual space in which the art of commentary was performed. These authors and their works, for the commentary writer, exist in an arena outside the restrictions of time – they all speak at once in answer to a legal question. *Fiqh* discourse (and particularly postclassical *fiqh* discourse) features a plethora of opinions that are cited and analysed, supported or rebuffed. The discussion occurs (in the main) without reference to the context of the authors and jurists cited. It is, one might say, as if all the authors are equally present in an extended *majlis*; they are all simultaneously available to have their views interrogated and tested. To the unfamiliar ear, it can appear to be a cacophony of voices. In these *fiqh* works, there is almost no attention paid to historical development or contextualisation either in the history of the Twelver law or outside it. There may, at times, be a privileging of certain authorities and their opinions (al-Muḥaqqiq, al-ʿAllāma etc) since theirs is often the base text the writer is subjecting to commentary. The default position of the commentator is to defend the view of the *matn*'s author, though there are regular instances of divergence (often masked as 'clarifications'). However, as we shall see, the citations sometimes reveal an unexpressed hierarchy for some commentators. In terms of legal debate, though, all (qualifying) opinions are equal – all are tested by the same reasoning

[21] See Ḥusayn b. Muḥammad Āl ʿUṣfūr, *ʿUyūn al-ḥaqāʾiq al-nāẓira fi tatimmat al-Ḥadāʾiq al-nāḍira* (Qum, 1414/1993).

process. The works cited, and the jurists quoted, all form part of the canon of Twelver Shiʿi legal history and the opinions, creating an acceptable *ikhtilāf* ('difference of opinion') – the tradition's range of legal opinions which can be acceptably incorrect.

An Example: Sexual Intercourse and the End of Menstruation

An illustration of all the above phenomena can be seen in a series of examples from the discussions around menstruation and the menopause in *fiqh* works. The sections on menstruation (various called *kitāb al-ḥayḍ, bāb al-ḥayḍ, faṣl fi'l-ḥayḍ*) are found in the first section on ritual purity (*ṭahāra*) of any *fiqh* work.[22] Examples of discussions with the regulations around menstruation illustrate the dynamics of *matn, sharḥ, ḥāshiya* and other commentarial activity in postclassical Ithnā ʿasharī legal scholarship. Here I take examples from the question of permission for sexual intercourse after the end of the menstrual cycle but before the ritual body wash (*ghusl*) has taken place.

Post-menstruation sexual contact before full ritual washing (*ghusl*)

Refraining from sexual intercourse during the period of menstruation is stipulated in the Qur'an (albeit obliquely with the phrase in Q 2.222 'keep away (*faʿtazilū*) from women during menstruation, and do not go near them until they are pure. When they are pure, then go to them as God has commanded.'). It is such a well-known prohibition that the Ithnā ʿasharī legal tradition, along with Sunni legal scholarship, classes it as one of the indisputable religious rules (*min ḍarūriyyāt al-dīn*). To reject this rule and declare menstrual intercourse permitted (*istiḥlāl*) is an act of unbelief (*kufr*) carrying the appropriate punishment. Having

---

[22] An example from the discussions around purity is particularly convenient because regularly commentaries and supercommentaries were left unfinished at the commentator's death. In addition, there is often an express intention on the part of the commentator only to cover the early sections on devotional practices (*ʿibādāt*), ending with the book on pilgrimage (*kitāb al-ḥajj*). Hence, viewing the postclassical *fiqh* corpus as a whole, the early *fiqh* chapters receive disproportionate coverage.

sexual intercourse with one's menstruant wife (after having forgotten the rule, or never having heard it) makes one liable for a discretionary punishment (*taʿzīr*) and, according to many, a compensatory payment (*kaffāra*). During menstruation, the Ithnā ʿasharī authors permit certain sexual activity (kissing, touching, fondling, though there is discussion about each of these, and different opinions are taken). There must, though, be no contact with the protected area of the menstruating woman (and there is some debate as to the extent of this area of a woman's body).

When the period of menstruation is over, sexual contact of all permitted types can resume, and the regulations are presented as developing out of the phrase in the above cited Qur'anic verse, '. . .do not go near them until they are pure. When they are pure, then go to them as God has commanded'. The Sunni schools, generally, require the post-menstruation woman to perform full ritual body wash (*ghusl*) before sexual intercourse is permitted: some even require her to have performed a valid prayer before sexual intercourse is permitted. The Ithnā ʿasharī jurists, though, consider it permitted (though for most, discouraged) to have sexual intercourse after the end of the menstrual period without a ritual purification – a simple washing of the genital area (*ghasl al-faraj*) will suffice (note here the difference between *ghusl*/the ritual wash and *ghasl*/ordinary wash). This, it appears, was a minority view amongst some Mālikī scholars, though it was not accepted within any of the Sunni schools as a mainstream opinion.[23]

The four popular Ithnā ʿasharī *mukhtaṣar* works simply state the rule without any elaboration:

> *Sharāʾiʿ al-Islām*: After she is pure, it is permitted for her husband to have sexual intercourse with her before she washes, though it is discouraged (*ʿalā al-karāhiyya*).
>
> *al-Mukhtaṣar al-nāfiʿ*: It is discouraged. . . to have intercourse with her before full ritual washing (*ghusl*).
>
> *Irshād al-adhhān*: It is forbidden for her husband to have sexual intercourse with her [during menstruation]. . . . And it is discouraged after the end of it before *ghusl*.

[23] It does appear to have been an opinion amongst some Ẓāhirīs – Abū Muḥammad ʿAlī b. Aḥmad b. Ḥazm, *al-Muḥallā* (Beirut, 1998), vol. 2, p. 171.

> *Qawāʿid al-aḥkām*: It is permitted for her husband to have sexual intercourse with her before *ghusl*, though it is discouraged. He should have patience until she washes, but if desire overcomes him, he should tell her to wash her genital area.[24]

The other classical *mukhtaṣar* which concerns us here is *al-Lumʿa*:

> *al-Lumʿa*: Sexual intercourse with her is discouraged after the end but before the *ghusl*, as this is the clearest position (*al-aẓhar*).[25]

All of these mention that sexual intercourse before *ghusl* is discouraged, but the phrasing differs between indicating 'it is permitted but discouraged' (*Sharāʾiʿ*, *Qawāʿid*) and 'it is discouraged' (*Nāfiʿ*, *Irshād*, *Lumʿa*). The different phrasings might indicate levels of disapproval (with 'permitted but discouraged' being higher than the forceful 'it is discouraged'). The *Qawāʿid* is the only one to give additional information, giving details not only of how it is discouraged, but also an additional stipulation (the woman's washing of her genital area). It might constitute a more expansive presentation style, with the author being less interested in creating a highly abbreviated 'text for commentary/classroom exposition' and closer to a full exposition of the law and its details. For the other authors, the detail about the washing is not required in their text. It should be noted that, as is typical in the *fiqh* discourse, it is to the man that permission is given; it is he who is being overcome by desire; and it is he who orders her to wash. It is usual in *fiqh* works, except when a rule is specifically addressed to women, for men to be the assumed addressee of the text. Indeed, as in the Qur'an, one finds the second person plural ('you') to refer to men (or a mixed group), but almost always when women are the subject of a

---

24 Jaʿfar b. al-Ḥasan al-Muḥaqqiq al-Ḥillī, *Sharāʾiʿ al-Islām fī masāʾil al-ḥalāl wa'l-ḥarām* (Tehran, 1374 Sh./1995), vol. 1, p. 25; al-Muḥaqqiq al-Ḥillī, *al-Mukhtaṣar al-nāfiʿ fī fiqh al-imāmiyya* (Tehran, 1387 Sh./2008), p. 10; al-Ḥasan b. Yūsuf al-ʿAllāma al-Ḥillī, *Irshād al-adhhān ilā aḥkām al-aymān* (Qum, 1410/1989), vol. 1, p. 228; al-ʿAllāma al-Ḥillī, *Qawāʿid al-aḥkām* (Qum, 1413/1992), vol. 1, p. 218.

25 al-Shahīd al-Awwal Muḥammad b. Jamāl al-Dīn Makkī al-ʿĀmilī, *al-Lumʿa al-Dimashqiyya* (Qum, 1374 Sh./1995), vol. 1, p. 19. The last phrase *al-aẓhar* is an indication that there is a difference of opinion in the school and the author considers this position to be the soundest, though without recounting the other opinion(s). It forms a prompt for the commentator.

ruling, it is expressed in the third person feminine plural (*hunna*). This is clearly a stylistic convention which emerges out of the assumption that men (and specifically male jurists) are the addressees and conduits through which women gain knowledge of the law.

The various commentaries on these brief statements of the law explain the argument by which this position – which, it should be added, is held by the vast majority of Ithnā ʿasharī jurists across time – is justified. The commentaries, though, approach the presentation of the justification in distinctive ways. Some take the opportunity for an extended discussion (for example, the lengthy (8-page in the printed edition) exposition in al-Shahīd al-Thānī's *Rawḍ al-janān* on the above-cited passage from al-ʿAllāma's *Irshād*).[26] Others express the arguments in a highly condensed fashion[27] or even give the statement no attention at all.[28] Despite these various approaches, the arguments are quite standard across the commentaries.

If one drills down further, and examines the various commentaries on a single phrase from just one of these *mutūn*, there is a clear illustration of the various approaches to commentary. Here is the passage from the *Irshād* as an example:

> *Irshād al-adhhān*: it [i.e. sexual intercourse] is discouraged after the end of it [i.e. menstruation] before full ritual washing (*ghusl*).

Ibrāhīm al-Qaṭīfī's *al-Hādī ilā al-rashād fī bayān mujmalāt al-Irshād* – a title which could be translated 'The guide to the right path concerning the elucidation of the obscurities of the *Irshād*' – is the earliest of the commentaries employed here. The title indicates that there are elements in al-ʿAllāma's *Irshād* which need elucidation and al-Qaṭīfī, in this work, aims to provide much-needed clarification. On the precise passage under examination here, Qaṭīfī writes:

---

26 Zayn al-Dīn b. ʿAlī al-ʿĀmilī al-Shahīd al-Thānī, *Rawḍ al-janān fī sharḥ Irshād al-adhhān* (Qum, 1422/2001), vol. 1, pp. 224–232.

27 See, for example, the passage from al-Ardabīlī's *Majmaʿ al-fāʾida waʾl-burhān*, commenting on the passage in *Irshād* and explained in the Appendix to this chapter.

28 al-Shahīd al-Thānī, *Ḥāshiya sharāʾiʿ al-Islām* (Qum, 1422/2001), vol. 1, p. 62.

His statement (*qawluhu*): *it is discouraged after the end of it*
I say (*aqūlu*): this is the established position, on account of the statement 'until they are pure', read without a doubling [i.e. of the middle root letter]; and according to the report of ʿAlī b. Yaqṭīn from Abū ʿAbd Allāh [Jaʿfar al-Ṣādiq] who said, 'When the bleeding stops, even if she has not washed, then her husband can go to her when he wishes.' One should interpret other reports which contradict this as meaning discouragement in order to achieve a reconciliation.[29]

The *qawluhu* – *aqūlu* exchange demonstrates the 'commentary by statement' style (*sharḥ bi'l-qawl*) referred to in the formal lists of commentarial types. Even though the commentary is not comprehensive (i.e. not every phrase of the text is subject to commentary), the work is not considered one of *ḥāshiya* by the tradition – illustrating how the terms *ḥāshiya* and *sharḥ* are not always used with formalistic precision. Al-Qaṭīfī apparently did write a *ḥāshiya* on the *Irshād*, which is sometimes referred to by the abbreviated title '*taʿlīqa*' (once again, the use of terms appears imprecise), but this work, *al-Hādī*, is a quite separate work.[30]

Turning to this particular passage, the two pieces of evidence for the 'established' (*mashhūr*) position are adduced – the Qurʾanic verse and the report of ʿAlī b. Yaqṭīn. But the evidence cited appears to indicate simple permission without any hint of negativity (that is, discouragement). Al-Qaṭīfī refers to (but does not cite) other reports which are much more negative, and accepts the idea that in order to reconcile these differing reports, one needs to downgrade the permission for sexual intercourse to 'discouraged' (with the act remaining within the permitted realm).

---

[29] Ibrāhīm b. Sulaymān al-Qaṭīfī, *al-Hādī ilā rashād fī bayān mujmalāt al-Irshād* (Qum, 1429/2008), vol. 1, p. 194. The passage continues: God's statement 'until they have purified themselves' reading it with a *shadda* means – and God knows best here – that they have cleansed themselves – as when one says they have eaten well, and they have eaten – or it could mean they have washed their genital area, and therefore it can be understood to be discouraged. And there is debate on this.'

[30] The editor says forcefully the two should not be confused, al-Qaṭīfī, *al-Hādī ilā rashād*, vol. 1, p. 15.

Underpinning this theory is, of course, the notion that although texts have a *prima facie* meaning, this not necessarily their actual intended meaning. The language system employed in texts can regularly function such that, on the production of convincing evidence, the *prima facie* meaning can be set to one side and another possible meaning is then indicated. In this case, the sources indicating permission (Qur'an and the report of ʿAlī b. Yaqṭīn) could possibly indicate that the action is 'permitted but discouraged'; similarly, a source indicating prohibition (the other uncited report) could, possibly, indicate discouragement. To reconcile these contradictory sources, the compromise position is proposed: it is discouraged but nonetheless permitted to have sexual intercourse after the end of menstruation but before the full ritual wash.

Al-Qaṭīfī continues with another piece of counter-evidence which might indicate something stronger than discouragement here:

> God's statement could be read with a doubling of the middle root letter, and it would then mean – and God knows best – that they perform the act of purification – along the pattern of the phrase 'they perform' or 'they performed' the 'act of feeding'. Or it could mean 'until they have washed their genitals'. [The verse read in this way] would be understood as discouraged, and this can be debated.[31]

Here al-Qaṭīfī is dealing with the variant Qur'anic reading in which the verse in question is read as either *ḥattā yaṭhurna* ('until they are pure' – single middle root letter) or *ḥattā yaṭṭahharna* ('until they perform the act of purification' – doubled middle root letter). The two readings are, when written without vowel pointers, identical, and therefore form more convincing possible variants. This is clearly an argument employed by those who argue for a prohibition on sexual relations before full ritual washing. Their argument appears to be that a possible Qur'anic reading in which the requirement of 'purification' (i.e., full ritual wash) is stipulated clearly makes prohibition more likely than permission (or discouragement). Al-Qaṭīfī's response here is to argue that even if the verse is read in this way, *ḥattā yaṭṭahharna* need not mean the performance of the full ritual wash. It could mean simply washing the genitals. And even with this reading, the whole

[31] Ibid., vol. 1, p. 194.

verse could still be understood as indicating a 'discouraged' action because any negative imperative ('do not do X'), even though it might have a *prima facie* meaning of prohibition, can also, when there is sufficient evidence, be understood as a mere discouragement (since that is the way language works). His final phrase (*wa-fihi naẓar* – 'and this is can be debated') recognises this may not be the strongest argument, but implies also that the alternative reading is not the definitive proof the opponents are putting forward.

Al-Qaṭīfī's commentarial technique is, as noted above, compliant with one of the types of commentary formally laid out elsewhere (i.e. the *sharḥ bi'l-qawl* style). In terms of content, there is a defence of the opinion laid out in the *Irshād*, by the production of evidence. The argument is not fully explained (there are many instances of abbreviation which require full exposition), but the aim is to provide the reader with both the evidence and the arguments; there is even an exploration of counter-arguments. What is clear is that al-Qaṭīfī wishes to portray the agreed established position (of discouragement) as a compromise result. The evidence is far from clear: there are contradictory revelatory sources (opposing reports), ambiguity in the formal text of the Qur'an itself (the double v. single readings), and equivocality in what the sources might actual mean (even if their form were to be fixed). There is no source which indisputably indicates the 'discouraged' position; instead, this position is formed out of a combination of the evidence in an attempt to keep all sources in line with each other (through a preference for reconciliation).

This is a brief but efficient commentarial style which assumes background knowledge but is not overly referential. It contrasts with a roughly contemporary commentary the *Irshād* by Zayn al-Din al-Shahīd al-Thānī. Whilst in his commentary on the *Sharā'i'*, Zayn al-Din al-Shahīd al-Thānī passes over the topic without comment, in his commentary on the *Irshād* (titled *Rawḍ al-janān fī sharḥ Irshād al-adhhān*), he devotes a lengthy passage, as previously mentioned, to discussing the arguments for and against the positions of permission and prohibition, examining arguments for and against, making reference to positions in works of legal theory (*uṣūl al-fiqh*) and how they impact on the argumentation from this case. The lengthy exposition begins with a citation of the *Irshād* passage (here in italics) but with interspersed glosses (here in normal type):

> *It is discouraged* to have intercourse with the menstruant *after the end of it* whether it be during the normal period time or not *before the full ritual wash* but without being forbidden, in accordance with the more established of the two opinions, on account of indications from the Qur'an and reports concerning it.[32]

This is a convenient example of the above mentioned *sharḥ mamzūj* ('blended commentary'). The grammar of the *matn* is not disrupted (though the sentence becomes extremely lengthy through al-Shahīd al-Thānī's insertions). The precise reference of the verb *it is discouraged* is supplied by the commentator; a gloss on the phrase *the end of it* is given; and the final phrase *before full ritual wash* acts as a springboard for subsequent recounting of the argumentation for the position expressed in the *matn*. There is no need to run through the lengthy argumentation produced by al-Shahīd al-Thānī here. It should be noted, though, that there is regular reference to al-ʿAllāma's views as recounted in other works (*Mabādi' al-uṣūl, Mukhtalaf al-shīʿa* and the *Nihāyat al-aḥkām* are all referenced). These are used to try and understand what the arguments might be for the position he puts forward in the *Irshād*. There is also a respect given to the position that sexual intercourse is actually forbidden before *ghusl* – a view attributed to Ibn Bābawayh in the Ithnā ʿasharī legal tradition. This, al-Shahid al-Thānī indicates, is not an unreasonable position to hold since there are reports which could be seen as indicating prohibition. The main target of al-Shahīd al-Thānī's presentation, though, are those 'permitters' (*mujawwizūn*) who view it as not even discouraged to have sexual intercourse with a menstruant before *ghusl*. He lists eight arguments against the 'proof of permission' (*ḥujjat al-ḥill*), and though he does not list any jurists as 'Permitters', it is clear they are a real group whose view needs to be discredited. Al-Shahīd al-Thānī sees the discouragement as emerging out of the conflicting indicators: the Qur'an has two readings, and each one of them is ambiguous but might indicate prohibition before *ghusl*; the reports are contradictory, some indicating prohibitions, and others permission (with or without the genital washing). Conflicting indicators without clear advantage to one over the other means, for al-Shahīd al-Thānī, that the practice is discouraged. It is possible to interpret the 'permission' indicators as

---

32 al-Shahīd al-Thānī, *Rawḍ al-janān*, vol. 1, p. 224.

meaning discouragement; and likewise, the 'prohibition' indicators could mean discouragement. This combination (*jam*ʿ) means discouragement is the most appropriate ruling; not because it has the clearest indicators, but because it is the best combination of conflicting indicators. Whilst the argumentation does not contract that found in al-Qaṭīfī's presentation, the exposition is much fuller, and the evidence is cited in full, and examined in forensic detail. In both cases, the focus is directly on the text of al-ʿAllāma's *Irshād* – explaining how he and the rest of the scholars (with the notable exception of Ibn Bābawayh) have come to conclusion that this is a discouraged – rather than a 'permitted' or 'forbidden' – act.

This contrasts with the commentary of al-Qaṭīfī's pupil, al-Muqaddas al-Ardabīlī (d. 993/1585). His *Majma*ʿ *al-fā*ʾ*ida wa*ʾ*l-burhān*, a commentary on the *Irshād*, is a masterpiece of brevity, and the result is barely comprehensible in translation. Whilst he does cite the *Irshād*, his focus is not the text itself. On this occasion, the text itself is not even cited, or forensically examined (as it was with al-Qaṭīfī through *sharḥ bi*ʾ*l-qawl* or al-Shahīd al-Thānī through *sharḥ mamzūj*). Instead, the content of the *Irshād* statement is taken as clear and in no need of analysis – the focus for al-Ardabīlī is on the evidence, and the arguments which might be made from them:

> As for it being discouraged to have vaginal sexual intercourse with the menstruant after the end of bleeding and before the full ritual wash, then this is the clear position on the basis of
>
> [1] *al-aṣl*, and the lack of any statement that it is forbidden absolutely. Agreeably there is, in the text of *al-Faqīh* [of Ibn Bābawayh] something which indicates a prohibition [on intercourse] before washing without any precedent. But it does not have a strong indicator.
>
> [2] the apparent meaning of one of the verses, recited without doubling [the middle root letter] and
>
> [3] the combination of the indicators and the two recitations without any indication that reading [the verse] with doubling definitively requires a full body wash
>
> [4] the reason for the prohibition has been removed, as is understood from the apparent meaning of this verse and others.[33]

[33] Aḥmad b. Muḥammad al-Muqaddas al-Ardabīlī, *Majma*ʿ *al-fā*ʾ*ida* (Qum, 1403/1983), vol. 1, p. 152. Numbering is mine.

This commentary itself clearly requires extensive annotation. There needs, one might say, to be a commentary on the commentary.[34] A number of observations can be made. First, al-Ardabīlī puts forward a series of arguments for permission to have sexual intercourse before *ghusl*, but he does not explicitly address the position of the *Irshād* (the so-called *mashhūr* position) that it is discouraged to do so. His primary focus is to side-line the view that it is prohibited (which is the majority Sunni position, and that of Ibn Bābawayh). This contrasts with al-Shahīd al-Thānī's position, which argues that although Ibn Bābawayh's position that it is forbidden is based on a valid textual source (reports from the imams), other evidence requires one to understand this textual report as meaning discouraged rather than prohibited. For al-Ardabīlī, by contrast, Ibn Bābawayh does not have a strong indicator (*dalīl qawī*) for his view. It is clear that the *Irshād* says it is discouraged, but al-Ardabīlī only ever presents arguments to establish that it is permitted. Once again, the focus is not on al-ʿAllāma and his exposition in the *Irshād* but on something beyond that. The *Irshād* text seems bypassed in the presentation, whilst in the texts of al-Qaṭīfī and al-Ardabīlī, it held centre-stage.

Second, given the condensed nature of the argumentation, the reader needs to be relatively expert in *fiqh* before understanding it. Al-Ardabīlī's text itself is not sufficient (contrast this with al-Shahīd al-Thānī's full exposition referred to above). He assumes the reader already has a full understanding of the arguments, referring to them only obliquely. For example, 'the combination of the indicators and the two recitations' only makes sense if one already knows what the two Qur'anic readings are, why they might indicate different rulings, and why, despite this, the *ghusl* is not required (since variant Qur'anic rulings cannot be the sole basis for legal stipulations). Al-Ardabīlī is confident that his audience knows what he is talking about. This leads one to the question as to what the purpose of the commentary might be. It certainly does not appear to be to provide the non-expert reader with a guide to the contents of the *matn*. Rather, al-Ardabīlī is demonstrating his virtuosity as a jurist author by condensing four complex arguments into a few lines of commentarial text.

---

[34] I provide an exposition of the argumentation in the Appendix to this chapter.

Third, al-Ardabīlī's intention in employing this highly compressed form may itself be to attract commentaries (and there were numerous *ḥawāshī* on the *Majma*ʿ). The new 'supercommentary' need not be supplied in written form. The referential style might be thought to act as an aide memoir for the teacher when giving a textual exposition (either of the *matn*, or indeed of the *sharḥ*). Finally, and perhaps most significantly, the purpose of commentary is not, it seems, to make the *matn* more accessible, but rather to supply legal arguments relevant to the topic which is addressed in the quoted segment of the *matn*. It is not even necessarily to support the *matn*'s rule – since, as we can see here, the arguments produced support permission, but are not explicit on the 'discouraged' assessment. In this commentary at least, the *matn* appears as simply a prompt for a cataloguing of the relevant arguments. The target appears to be the law itself, not the *matn* – that is to say al-Ardabīlī is simply using the *matn* as a vehicle through which he might present his own legal thinking.

The next generation of commentaries on the *Irshād* included the *Dhakhīrat al-maʿād* of Muḥammad Bāqir al-Sabzawārī. This continues the full exposition of source citation and argumentation exemplified in al-Shahīd al-Thānī's exposition. His commentary on the *Irshād* passage is lengthy, with developed and precise examination of each source. He begins, like al-Shahīd al-Thānī, with a *sharḥ mamzūj* of the text:

> *It*, sexual intercourse *is discouraged* with her – that is the menstruant *after the end of it*, that is, the blood of menstruation *before full ritual washing*.[35]

Whilst formally a *sharḥ mamzuj*, one can see that the textual focus here is greater even than in al-Shahīd al-Thānī's attempt. All pronouns are spelled out:

it=sexual intercourse
her=the menstruating woman
it=the blood of menstruation.

[35] Muḥammad Bāqir al-Sabzawārī, *Dhakhīrat al-maʿād* (Qum, 1363 Sh./1984), p. 72.

This exposition of the text continues:

> This is the established position amongst the fellow scholars (i.e. the Ithnā ʿasharī jurists). It is transmitted from Ibn Bābawayh that he considered [sexual intercourse] forbidden before the full ritual wash, but its words in *Man lā yaḥduruhu al-faqīh* do not indicate this – rather their apparent meaning is the opposite. He says:
>
> > It is not permitted to have sexual intercourse with a woman during her period because God has prohibited this when he says: 'Do not go near them until they are pure' meaning by this 'until after they have done *ghusl* from menstruation'. If the man is overcome with lust, and the woman is pure from her menstruation, and her husband wants to have sexual intercourse before the *ghusl*, he orders her to wash her genitals, and then have sexual intercourse.
> >
> > Clearly this statement means that there is no prohibition on sexual intercourse without *ghusl*.[36]

Here we have something new – Ibn Bābawayh's view – which was accepted as unambiguous in the other commentaries, is here problematised. Al-Sabzawārī brings Ibn Bābawayh into the fold of the established opinion, by citing the passage itself and not being content with the manner in which his opinion has been caricatured in previous commentaries. The debate now moves on to the status of the genital washing – is this obligatory (*wujūb*) before sexual relations can commence (as is indicated by al-Muḥaqqiq in his *al-Muʿtabar*)? Is the permissibility of sexual relations dependant on the washing? For al-Sabzawārī, 'the most plausible answer (*al-aqrab*) is that the elimination of the prohibition on sexual intercourse is not dependent on washing', and he cites a series of reports from the imams which indicate this. Washing the genital area is recommended, but not a prerequisite for legitimate sexual relations. There follows a detailed discussion of the reports, whether their chains of transmission are reliable and whether they indicate what scholars have thought. Also included is a detailed discussion of the Qurʾanic variants and the correct hermeneutical tools whereby the intended meaning might be understood. In conclusion, al-Sabzawārī states that even though there

36 al-Sabzawārī, *Dhakhīrat*, pp. 72–73.

is a 'hint of prohibition' in the Qur'anic verse – that is, the Qur'an does not unambiguously say sexual intercourse is permitted before the ritual wash – the reports indicate that it is permitted. In the interest of reconciliation between the indicators, the interpretation should be that it is discouraged, but not forbidden; the washing of the genital area is encouraged but not required; and the man need not be overcome with lust, though this might explain why he might be unable to wait until the woman does the preferred course of action – namely carrying out the full ritual wash.

Concluding Remarks

There is nothing in the text of the *matn* which requires any of these authors to approach the act of commentary in this way. Some see their task as first filling out the potential ambiguities in the *matn*, and then providing argumentation for the established position put forward in the text (al-Sabzawārī: commentary as expansion). Others see the *matn* as an opportunity to explore all the arguments for the various possible positions on an issue, and to engage in a denunciation of those they consider bogus (al-Shahīd al-Thānī: commentary as polemic). Yet others see the *matn* as purely a prompt for a discussion around the law beyond the text, ostensibly ignoring the content of the text beyond the legal issue it raises (al-Ardabīlī: commentary as independent exposition). And finally, there are those who see the commentary as the opportunity to defend the scholarly tradition, and strengthen the established positions of the scholars (al-Qaṭīfī: commentary as school bulwark). These types of commentarial activity could be multiplied through the examination of additional commentaries; and any single commentary need not exclusively exhibit one attitude throughout all its comments. What the evidence does suggest though is that commentary is much more than a reiteration of the content of the *matn* text – it is a creative elaboration, in which the commentators have the opportunity to exhibit their skills. This could be in the production of highly compressed text which itself needs much commentary; or in the exposition of arguments, the citation of sources, and the debunking of deviant opinions. In this, the postclassical legal tradition of Ithnā ʿasharī Shiʿism reveals dynamics of commentary which can be identified across scholarly disciplines, from philosophy to *ḥadīth* commentary. In this sense it is both distinctive and conventional in the Islamic postclassical scholarly milieu.

APPENDIX: Explanation of al-Ardabīlī's Commentary on *Irshād*

He outlines four arguments (labelled [1] to [4], numbering is mine) and none of them can be understood simply from the text of al-Ardabīlī's commentary, so some explanation is required:

> [1] *al-aṣl*, and the lack of any statement that it is forbidden absolutely. Agreeably there is, in the text of *al-Faqīh* something which indicates a prohibition [on intercourse] before washing without any precedent. But it does not have a strong indicator.

The first argument requires the reader to know arguments from *al-aṣl* in *fiqh* texts. *Al-aṣl* denotes the 'original state of affairs': that is, the situation without (or even before) any law was revealed – the natural state of affairs one might say. In the absence of a rule, the assumption is that an action is permitted. In this case, there is a prohibition on intercourse during menstruation, but there is a permission for intercourse after menstruation. In the absence of a ruling about the period between the end of menstruation and the time of the ritual wash (*ghusl*), the assumption is that it is permitted.

Al-Ardabīlī next refers to the position indicated in *al-Faqīḥ* – by which he means the work *Man lā yaḥḍuruhu al-faqīh* by Ibn Bābawayh. The passage referred to there, but not cited by al-Ardabīlī is:

> It is not permitted to have intercourse with a woman during her period because God said, 'do not go near them until they are pure. . .' – this means until they have performed *ghusl* after menstruation.[37]

[37] Ibn Bābawayh, *Man lā yaḥduruhu al-faqīh* (Qum, n.d.), vol. 1, p. 95 – Ibn Bābawayh does go on to say that if the man is overcome by lust then he can ask her to wipe her genitals and then sexual intercourse can take place, but this I understood to be a ruling out of necessity (*ḍarūra*) brought about because of the man's lust, rather than a permission. That is, for Ibn Bābawayh, the ruling is that it is forbidden, but like many forbidden things, in extreme circumstances, they can become permitted. This state of affairs is different from saying that it is discouraged but permitted, as the various *mukhtaṣar*s do.

Ibn Bābawayh's deduction appears to be from an understanding of the Qur'anic verse where the phrase 'until they are pure' (*ḥattā yaṭhurna*) is taken to mean, 'until they have finished their menstruation and have performed the ritual *ghusl* wash'. Al-Ardabīlī, along with most Ithnā ʿasharī scholars before him, argues that this is not a strong indicator of prohibition, and the reason is given in his second argument:

> [2] the apparent meaning of one of the verses, recited without a *shadda*

There are two readings of this Qur'anic phrase: one 'reading without a *shadda*', namely, *ḥattā yaṭhurna* ('until they are pure'); and the other reading with a *shadda*, namely *ḥattā yaṭṭahharna* ('until they have ritually purified themselves'?). The preferred reading is the first, and the verse's obvious meaning is that the woman has finished her menstrual period (i.e. where 'to be *ṭāhir*' here means 'to be free of menstrual bleeding'). One might dispute whether this is the apparent meaning, but the structure of the legal argument is clear.

When there is an alternative reading of a verse, and when this might lead to a different ruling (i.e. the reading with a *shadda* rather than without it), then another procedure comes into play:

> [3] the combination of the indicators and the two recitations without any indication that reading [the verse] with a *shadda* definitively requires a *ghusl*

Al-Ardabīlī states that even the reading with a *shadda* – that is, *ḥattā yaṭṭahharna* ('until they have purified themselves') does not clearly indicate that a *ghusl* is required. The verb has changed from 'to be pure' to another form – which can mean 'to purify oneself', though it can also indicate an intensive meaning 'to be completely pure'). Since this alternative reading with this different verbal form does not definitively indicate the requirement to perform the *ghusl*, and given that there are other indicators (not only the first reading, but also other uncited reports), the permission to have sexual intercourse when menstruation has ended but before the *ghusl* has been performed stands.

The final argument is a logical argument:

> [4] the reason for the prohibition has been removed, as is understood from the apparent meaning of this verse and others.

From the Qur'anic verse in question (and from other, uncited, verses), it is clear that the reason for the prohibition on sexual intercourse is the presence of menstrual bleeding. When that reason has been removed (i.e. there is no longer menstrual bleeding), then the corresponding prohibition must also be removed. When the reason for a rule disappears, the rule must, logically, also disappear. One returns to the pre-regulative state of affairs – namely that it is permitted for a man to have sexual intercourse with his legitimate sexual partner after she has completed her period of menstruation but before she has performed the ritual wash known as the *ghusl*.

11

A View from the Periphery: The *Ijāza* as Polemic in Early 10th/16th-Century Twelver Shiʿism

Andrew J. Newman

In earlier research on the exchanges between Ibrāhīm b. Sulaymān al-Qaṭīfī (d. after 945/1539[1]) and ʿAlī al-Karakī (d. 940/1534) it was concluded that the composition and increasingly forthright and distinctly Akhbārī-style aspects of al-Qaṭīfī's criticisms of al-Karakī were most usefully understood in the context of the changing fortunes of the Safavid polity during the years these exchanges took place.[2]

The present paper examines al-Qaṭīfī's *ijāzāt* as preserved in *Biḥār al-anwār* of Muḥammad Bāqir al-Majlisī (d. 1110/1699),[3] to examine whether such a contextual approach also sheds light on the style and substance of these texts and thereby further contributes to the understanding of the al-Qaṭīfī/al-Karakī 'debates' and to the extant discussions on Twelver Shiʿi *ijāzāt* more generally.

The paper first addresses some of this literature and then discusses each of the extant *ijāzāt* in turn. Of the five texts in *Biḥār*, three are

---

[1] The editor of Yūsuf al-Baḥrānī's (d. 1186/1772) *Luʾluʾa*, on which see further below, says al-Qaṭīfī was alive in 951/1544, when he completed *al-Firqa al-nājiyya*. Āghā Buzurg al-Ṭihrānī says this work was completed in 945/1538. See al-Baḥrānī, *Luʾluʾat al-Baḥrayn* (Manama, 1429/2008), p. 154, n. 3; Āghā Buzurg al-Ṭihrānī, *al-Dharīʿa ilā taṣānīf al-shīʿa* (Beirut, 1403/1983), vol. 16, p. 177; al-Ṭihrānī, *Ṭabaqāt aʿlām al-shīʿa*, vol. 7 (Beirut, 1430/2009), p. 5.

[2] A. Newman, 'The Myth of the Clerical Migration to Safawid Iran: Arab Shi'ite Opposition to ʿAlī al-Karakī and Safawid Shī'ism', *Die Welt des Islams*, 33 (1993), pp. 78ff.

[3] On other dates for al-Majlisī's death, see our 'The Idea of Bāqer al-Majlesī in 'The Idea of Iran: The Safavid Era', in C. Melville, ed., *Safavid Persia in the Age of Empires* (*The Idea of Iran*, vol. X) (London, 2021), pp. 157 n. 1, 166 n. 56.

dated to 915/1509, 920/1514 and 944/1537 respectively, and the larger historical contexts of each will be discussed before the texts themselves. Of the two undated texts, the very short one merits only passing notice. The second, longer, undated *ijāza* is discussed and, on the basis of its style and substance, a relative date for its composition is offered.[4]

Al-Karakī's presence looms large, if indirectly, across the four. The complex blend of al-Qaṭīfī's jurisprudential criticisms in these texts – documents not necessarily intended for widespread circulation – complement his open critique of al-Karakī as discussed elsewhere even as al-Qaṭīfī's personal reflections attest to a sense of being an 'outsider' of lesser stature in comparison with al-Karakī, based on fewer opportunities, ill health and personal slights, all leading to a lack of self-confidence. As such, the paper suggests that in the context of the Western-language discussion of Shiʿi *ijāzāt* to date the combination of the jurisprudential with the personal on offer in al-Qaṭīfī's *ijāzāt* is distinctive.

The Extant Literature on Twelver *Ijāzāt*

With a few exceptions, the limited Western-language academic discussion in works dedicated specifically to Twelver *ijāzāt* has not generally recognised these documents as having the potential for an 'agenda' above and beyond that of the function for which they were, ostensibly, intended. Most focus on the information on scholarly networks contained in these texts and refer to post-Safavid *ijāzāt*. Al-Qaṭīfī's *ijāzāt* have been given little or no attention.

Vajda and others in the *Encyclopaedia of Islam* (2nd ed.) discuss the *ijāza* as the form in which an 'authorized guarantor of a text or of a whole book (his own work or a work received through a chain of transmitters going back to the first transmitter or to the author) gives a person the authorisation to transmit it in his turn so that the person

---

[4] Muḥammad Bāqir al-Majlisī, *Biḥār al-anwār*, ed. S. Ibrāhīm al-Miyānjī, et al. (n.p., 1403/1983), vol. 105, pp. 85–123. Four of the five *ijāzāt* can also be found in *Mawsūʿat al-fāḍil al-Qaṭīfī*, ed. Ẓiyāʾ Āl Sunbul (Qum, 1429/2008), vol. 4, pp. 205–270. For al-Qaṭīfī's seven *ijāzāt*, see al-Ṭihrānī, *al-Dharīʿa*, vol. 1, pp. 134–135.

authorised can avail himself of this transmission.' They note 'the pre-eminent value attached to oral testimony' and note, therefore, the value 'contained in the *isnāds* . . .in the *samā'*s ("certificates of hearing") and in the *idjāzas* —often having indications of dates and places and details of the names of the persons who formed links in the transmission'. Thus, 'Separate from the texts there appear the systematic lists of authorities.' They note that 'among the 'Twelver' Shī'īs the *idjāza* obtains its authority from the infallible imāms whose *ḥadīths* are scrupulously transmitted by their faithful supporters.'[5]

More recently Stewart noted 'three main types of certificate developed in the medieval period': 1. The certificate of audition (*samā'* or *ijāzat al-samā'*) or the certificate of transmission (*ijāzat al-riwāya*); 2. the certificate of memorisation (*'arḍ*, *'irāḍa*); and, 3. the license to teach law and issue legal opinions (*ijāzat al-tadrīs wa'l-iftā'*) and discusses each in turn. He notes while in Sunni circles use thereof 'seems to have lapsed', in Twelver circles the practice survives as *ijāzat al-ijtihād*, not extant in the Safavid period but prevalent by the mid-19th century.[6]

Gleave's detailed discussion of an *ijāza* of the Akhbārī Yūsuf al-Baḥrānī (d. 1186/1772), written between 1175/1761 and 1182/1768, delineates the main sections of the text – introductory prayers; an introduction to the text, to the *mujīz* (the giver of the *ijāza*) and to the *mujāz* (the recipient); a list of 35 *isnād*; a list of 19 works whose transmission is being authorised; closing prayers and praise for the *mujāz*. Here the shaykh refers to the different forms of transmission – *qirā'a*, *samā'* and *ijāza*. Citing Goldziher and Vajda, Gleave argues this text represents 'a late stage in the development of the *ijāza* system' and suggests it as a 'prototype' for al-Baḥrānī's *Lu'lu'at al-Baḥrayn*,

[5] G. Vajda et al., 'Idjāza', *EI2*. In *EI*, Goldziher defines the term as 'Permission. . . granted to any one by a competent "carrier" of a text or even a whole book — whether it is the latter's own or an older text which he is able to trace back by a reliable chain of transmitters to the original transmitter or to the author — to transmit further the work, and to quote the transmitter as an authority. The *idjāza* does not require immediate contact between the person receiving the permission and him who grants it.' Shi'i variants are not discussed. See I. Goldziher, 'Idjāza', *EI*.

[6] D. Stewart, 'Ejāza', *EIr*, vol. 8, pp. 273–275.

which Gleave describes as a biographical work with 'the external form of an *ijāza*'. As discussed, the text appears devoid of polemic.[7]

Schmidtke, discussing an 1128/1716 *ijāza* by the Akhbārī scholar ʿAbd Allāh b. Ṣāliḥ al-Samāhījī (d. 1135/1722), highlights the attention the latter gives, as *mujīz*, to scholarly networks, contemporary and older. She does not note any particular polemical tone in the text, beyond the author's reproaching two named 10th/16th-century scholars who were, in fact, Akhbārīs.[8]

Discussing a 1168/1755 *ijāza* composed by ʿAbd Allāh al-Tustarī (d. 1173/1759), Schmidtke refers to the several kinds of *ijāzāt*, *al-riwāya* ('to transmit') and *al-samāʿ* 'or' *al-qirāʾa*, the latter based on the 'kind of instruction', and describes the al-Tustarī *ijāza* as 'comprising the whole literature of a certain scholarly tradition (*ijāza kabīra* or *ijāza ʿāmma*)', these often issued by a 'scholar more advanced

7 R. Gleave, 'The *Ijāza* from Yūsuf al-Baḥrānī (d. 1186/1772) to Sayyid Muḥammad Mahdī Baḥr al-ʿUlūm (d. 1212/1797-8)', *Iran*, 32 (1994), esp. p. 115. On al-Baḥrānī, see E. Kohlberg, 'Baḥrānī, Yūsof', *EIr*, vol. 3, pp. 529–530; Newman, 'al-Baḥrānī, Yūsuf ibn Aḥmad', *EI3*.

The *Luʾluʾa*, composed in Karbala in 1182/1768 was, in fact, an *ijāza* given to al-Baḥrānī's two sons in the form of a biographical dictionary. See al-Ṭihrānī, *al-Dharīʿa*, vol. 18, pp. 379–380, and al-Baḥrānī's introductory comments to the text (5f).

Elsewhere we have noted the polemical nature of such biographical dictionaries in general and Gleave has noted these in the case of the *Luʾluʾa*'s biographical entries. See A. J. Newman, 'The Nature of the Akhbārī/Uṣūlī in Late-Safawid Iran. Part Two: The Conflict Reassessed', *BSOAS*, 55 (1992), pp. 252–253, 260; idem, 'Anti-Akhbārī Sentiments among the Qajar ʿ*Ulamā*', The Case of Muḥammad Bāqir al-Khwānsārī (d. 1313/1895)', in R. Gleave, ed., *Religion and Society in Qajar Iran* (London, 2005), p. 124; R. Gleave, *Scripturalist Islam. The history and doctrines of the Akhbārī Shīʿī school* (Leiden, 2007), s.v., esp. p. 56f.

On al-Baḥrānī, see also R. Gleave, 'The Akhbārī-Uṣūlī Dispute in *Ṭabaqāt* Literature: An Analysis of the Biographies of Yūsuf al-Baḥrānī and Muḥammad Bāqir al-Bihbihānī', *Jusūr*, 10 (1994), pp. 79–109.

8 S. Schmidtke, 'The *ijāza* from ʿAbd Allāh ibn Ṣāliḥ al-Samāhījī to Nāṣir al-Jārūdī al-Qaṭīfī: A Source for the Twelver Shiʿi Scholarly Tradition of Baḥrayn', in F. Daftary and J. Meri, ed., *Culture and Memory in Medieval Islam: Essays in Honour of Wilferd Madelung* (London, 2003), pp. 64–85, esp. 74. On al-Samāhījī, see also Gleave, *Scripturalist Islam*, s.v. and our contributions ad nn. 7, 66.

In passing Schmidtke (pp. 67, 67n7, 76n36) refers to al-Qaṭīfī's inclusion, in his 915/1509 *ijāza*, of the text of an *ijāza* of al-ʿAllāma al-Ḥillī's (d. 726/1325) son Fakhr al-Muḥaqqiqīn Muḥammad (d. 771/1369-70). The 915/1509 *ijāza* is discussed below.

in age'. Most *ijāzāt al-riwāya*, she says, 'follow a more or less fixed pattern': an opening prayer, an introduction on the *mujīz* and *mujāz*, a listing of 'the contents and extent of the *ijāza*', often with extensive coverage of the donor's own shaykhs, and an ending with a statement of 'conditions'. Al-Tustarī's text is typical of such 'text-independent', i.e. *ijāza kabīra* or *ijāza ʿāmma, ijāzāt*. The 'special features' she mentions include the author's many 'theoretical reflections', in one of which she notes he addresses 'the admissibility of transmission by means of licences . . . in comparison with other ways of transmission, particularly the *samāʿ*, and concludes the former are admissible 'beyond doubt'.[9] He does, she notes, criticise some of his contemporaries as having made little, if any, advancement beyond 'mere imitation (*taqlīd*)'.[10] Schmidtke does note, without unpacking it, al-Tustarī's discussion of conditions attached to receiving a licence.[11]

Kondo also focuses on post-Safavid period texts, discussing developments in the 12th/18th and 13th/19th centuries in *ijāzāt* and the practice of *ijāzāt* of *ijtihād* and *riwāya*. He presents two such texts of each type, all from the 19th century but notes the forms are basically the same as those of the 12th/18th and 11th/17th centuries.[12]

---

[9] S. Schmidtke, 'Forms and Functions of "Licenses to Transmit" (*Ijāzas*) in 18th-Century-Iran: ʿAbd Allāh al-Mūsawī al-Jazāʾirī al-Tustarī's (1112-73/1701-59) *Ijāza Kabīra*', in G. Kramer et al., ed., *Speaking for Islam: Religious Authorities in Muslim Societies* (Leiden, 2006), esp. pp. 96–97, 101–103, 109f, 111. See especially p. 109, citing *Ijāzat al-kabīra li'l-ʿAllāma . . . ʿAbd Allāh al-Mūsawī al-Jazāʾirī al-Tustarī*, ed. Muḥammad al-Samāmī al-Ḥāʾirī (Qum, 1409/1988-89), pp. 7–9. See, also, further below.

[10] Schmidtke, 'Forms', pp. 112–113.

[11] Schmidtke, 'Forms', p. 111, citing *Ijāzat al-kabīra*, pp. 212–215. See also below.

[12] N. Kondo, 'Shiʿi ʿUlama and *Ijāza* during the Nineteenth Century', *Orient*, 44 (2009), esp. pp. 63–64. Kondo references Gleave, above, for the 12th/18th century text, and Muḥammad Taqī al-Majlisī (d. 1070/1659-60)'s *ijāza* to his son, Muḥammad Bāqir, cited in M. M. Tunikābunī, *Qiṣaṣ al-ʿulamāʾ*, ed. Muḥammad Riḍā Barzigar Khāliqī et al. (Tehran, 1383 Sh./2004), pp. 266–281, as his 11th/17th-century example. Kondo refers (pp. 56, 59–61) to M. Litvak's discussion of *ijāzāt al-ijtihād* in the latter's *Shiʿi Scholars of Nineteenth-century Iraq: The 'Ulama' of Najaf and Karbala* (Cambridge, 1998), pp. 41–42 (that the *ijāza riwāya* was less prestigious and could be given to 'not direct disciples. . .primarily as a token of esteem'), pp. 104–106. Kondo references (p. 59, n. 4) Stewart on *ijāzat al-ijtihād* as not extant in the Safavid period but prevalent by the mid-19th century.

To date then, the dedicated Western-language literature on Shiʿi *ijāzāt* has mainly been interested in the aspects of these texts concerning scholarly networking, has highlighted these texts' tendency to exhibit a 'fixed pattern' in their organisation, has – aside from instances in respect of individuals specifically named by the *mujīz* – not noticed/highlighted any particularly polemical dimensions, and has mainly discussed late-Safavid and/or, especially, post-Safavid *ijāzāt*. In the process, across these works 10th/16th-century Twelver *ijāzāt* have received relatively little attention and the texts of al-Qaṭīfī's *ijāzāt* none at all.[13]

[13] Although, as Litvak, not a bespoke work on *ijāzāt*, Gleave (*Scripturalist Islam*, pp. 145–146), cites the introduction in Taqī al-Majlisī's *Lavāmiʿ-i ṣāḥibqirānī* in which he lists the seven forms of transmission: 1) the teacher reads a work to his pupil from beginning to end; 2) the teacher reads part of a work to his pupil – these being *qirāʾa* – and then 3) the pupil reads the work to the teacher; 4) the pupil is present when another pupil reads the work to the teacher; 5) the teacher gives a copy of the work to the pupil, telling him to relate this work to the teacher; 6) the teacher gives the pupil permission to relate a particular book on his authority; 7) the pupil finds a work in the possession of his teacher, and then relates the work with qualification. Gleave suggests this list reflects al-Majlisī's 'order. . .of preference'. See further below, ad n. 69.

See also Gleave's general remarks on Safavid-period *ijāzāt* (143f) though he seems especially interested in their information on scholarly networks (142f, 215).

Although also not *per se* a study of *ijāzāt*, in her *Formation of a Religious Landscape, Shiʿi Higher Learning in Safawid Iran* (Leiden, 2018), M. Moazzen does discuss *ijāzāt* generally (pp. 128–129) and Safavid-period *ijāzāt* (pp. 136ff, 208, 209 (where she says: 'The *ijāza* also guaranteed the integrity of a manuscript copy used by a scholar.'), p. 243 and s.v.). Moazzen is particularly interested in scholarly networking (p. 25) and what the texts reveal of Uṣūlī dominance of 'higher learning', especially in the 10th/16th century (pp. 28, 133, 136f, 244) and the next century (p. 153f), and of the *madrasa* curriculum and study processes (pp. 24–25, 142f, 153f, 161f, 168f, 206f, 243). Although Moazzen notes (146–147) Muḥammad Ṭāhir al-Qummī's (d. 1098/1687) refutation of philosophy in an *ijāza* to Bāqir al-Majlisī who, she notes also (p. 165, n. 10), taught the rational sciences to his students, she does not otherwise explore the potentially polemical nature of these texts. Al-Qaṭīfī and his *ijāzāt* receive but passing attention (p. 22, citing Bāqir al-Majlisī's student Afandī's biographical dictionary on al-Majlisī's apparent poor opinion of al-Qaṭīfī, pp. 133, 133, n. 24, 136, 165, n. 11). See also pp. 11–13, 29. See ʿAbd Allāh Afandī, *Riyāḍ al-ʿulamāʾ*, ed. A. Al-Ḥusaynī (Qum, 1403/1982), vol. 1, esp. 19.

On al-Qummī see A. J. Newman, 'Glimpses into Late-Safavid Spiritual Discourse: An 'Akhbārī' Critique of Sufism and Philosophy', in R. Tabandeh and L. Lewisohn, ed., *Sufis and Mullas: Sufis and Their Opponents in the Persianate World* (Irvine, CA, 2020), pp. 259–307.

Al-Qaṭīfī's 915/1509 Ijāza

The earliest dated *ijāza* of al-Qaṭīfī in *Biḥār* was composed in Najaf in 915/1509, the year after the Safavid conquest of the region.

By this point, al-Karakī's Safavid connections were well established. In 908/1503, he was present at Ismāʿīl I's capture of Kāshān. Al-Karakī settled in Najaf in 909/1504 with some financial support from the court. In 910/1505 he was in Iṣfahān with Ismāʿīl. Having returned to Iraq, he was imprisoned, with Baghdad's Shiʿi *naqīb*, by the Aq-Qoyunlu. When in 914/1508 Ismāʿīl took Baghdad they were released and joined him in touring al-Ḥilla and the shrine cities. Al-Karakī received land grants of several villages in Iraq in these years.

As early as 908/1503 or 909/1504 Arab clerics, probably based in Iraq, were voicing disquiet at his ties to court.

Al-Qaṭīfī himself arrived in Iraq in 913/1507 from al-Qaṭīf. He settled in Najaf, went to al-Ḥilla but then returned to Najaf. Between 914/1508 and 916/1510, he journeyed to Mashhad and there debated with al-Karakī on the matter of al-Qaṭīfī's refusal to accept gifts from Ismāʿīl.[14]

At eighteen pages, this is the longest of al-Qaṭīfī's *ijāzāt* in *Biḥār*.[15] Indeed, *Biḥār*'s editor cites the biographical dictionary of Muḥammad Bāqir al-Khwānsārī (d. 1313/1895) calling it an *ijāza kabīra*.[16]

---

[14] Newman, 'Myth', p. 78f. On the date of al-Qaṭīfī's arrival, see al-Baḥrānī, p. 160; Shaykh ʿAlī al-Bilādī al-Baḥrānī, *Anwār al-badrayn* (Qum, 1407/1986), p. 282. al-Ṭihrānī, *al-Dharīʿa*, vol. 1, p. 134, n. 56. On Persian Gulf scholars moving to Iraq in these centuries, see A.J. Newman, *Twelver Shiism: Unity and Diversity in the Life of Islam, 632 to 1722* (Edinburgh, 2013), pp. 148, 166. These included Aḥmad b. Fahd al-Ḥillī (d. 841/1437), from whom al-Qaṭīfī narrated via intermediaries. On al-Karakī's 909/1504 *ijāza* received in Najaf, see n. 67. As noted below, al-Qaṭīfī composed the 915/1509 and 920/1514 *ijāzāt* in Najaf.

[15] Al-Majlisī, *Biḥār*, vol. 105, pp. 89–106; Āl Sunbul, *Mawsūʿat*, vol. 4, pp. 209–242. See also al-Ṭihrānī, *al-Dharīʿa*, vol. 1, p. 134.

[16] Al-Majlisī, *Biḥār*, vol. 105, p. 83, n. 9. On this term, see ad n. 9; Moazzen, pp. 129, 133, n. 23.

Afandī (vol. 1, p. 15) and al-Baḥrānī (p. 159) do not use the term in reference to this work, but al-Ṭihrānī (*Ṭabaqāt*, vol. 7, p. 4) does. Muḥammad Bāqir al-Khwānsārī, *Rawḍat al-jannāt* (Tehran, 1390 Sh./2011), vol. 1, pp. 25–29) also applies the term *kabīra* to al-Qaṭīfī's *ijāzāt* to Shāh Mahmūd and al-Tustarī, but not that to al-Astarābādī, discussed below.

The *ijāza* is written to Shaykh Shams al-Dīn Muḥammad b. Turk.[17] It comprises one page of introductory prayers; one page of opening remarks; a three-page introduction with three *masāʾil* (sing. *masʾala*; issues, matters); and a seven-page listing of the materials for which the *ijāza* is being given – the longest part of the text. It concludes with a one-page *fāʾida* (benefit) and a four-page *waṣiyya* (admonition).

In his opening, al-Qaṭīfī recounts the promulgation of *al-sharāʾiʿ* and the role of the angels and *al-rusul* (prophets). When, he says, creation started to splinter and it was no longer possible for the *sufarā* (His envoys) to reach people directly, God commanded the *ḥifẓ* (memorisation) of *al-athār* (the words and actions of the Prophet), *al-aḥādīth al-sharīʿa* (the legalistic *ḥadīth*), and the Prophetic *sīra* (biography). Those who knew these were to hand them down to those who did not, he says. Those who understood these were to help those who did not.

The Qurʾanic verses 16: 43[18] and 9: 122,[19] he says, are confirmed by *al-akhbār al-mutawātira.*[20] He cites two texts from Imam Jaʿfar (d. 148/765), the Sixth imam. In the first al-Ṣādiq says, 'It is to us [i.e. the imams] to set forth the *uṣūl* (sing., *aṣl*, the core statements) and to you *tafarrʿūʾ* (pl., to derive/deduce – put forth branches, i.e. of the law).'[21] In the second, partially quoted, he says, 'Look to a man from

[17] The name is 'Turk' on vol. 105, p. 89, but 'Turkī' on vol. 105, p. 101. *Biḥār*'s editor (vol. 105, p. 89, n. 3) cites al-Khwānsārī (p. 27) as giving 'Turkī', as does al-Ṭihrānī (*al-Dharīʿa*, vol. 1, p. 134).

[18] 'Ask Ahl al-Dhikr if You Do Not Know.' The imams explain the term as referring to themselves. See al-Kulaynī, *al-Kāfī*, ed. ʿA. A. al-Ghaffārī (Tehran, 1365 Sh./1986), vol. 1, pp. 210–212/1–9.

[19] 'If a contingent from every expedition remained behind, they could devote themselves to studies in religion and admonish the people when they return to them that thus they (may learn) to guard themselves (against evil).' Not all of al-Qaṭīfī's Qurʾanic citations in these texts are noted. Qurʾanic translations are from https://quran.com/

[20] That is, a *ḥadīth* narrated by many narrators, not *khabar al-wāḥid*, a text narrated via but one narrator. See Gleave, *Scripturalist Islam*, s.v.

[21] *Furūʿ* referring to branches/ancillaries of the law, e.g. ritual cleanliness, prayer, fasting. On the text, see Muḥammad b. Manṣūr, Ibn Idrīs (d. 598/1202), *Musṭarafāt al-sarāʾir* (Qum, 1411/1990), p. 575.

among you who knows something of our *qaḍāya*' (judgements).[22] The *akhyār* (superior) *salaf* (forefathers) did this and, says al-Qaṭīfī, the imams assured them of *al-najāt* (salvation).

This process, he says, turns on *al-riwāya*. It is the path to truth and *dirāya* (understanding) and the path revealed by the Prophets and the Infallible imams. The only path to that is by *naql* (transmitting) from those of earlier generations who are trustworthy back to the 'successors of the progeny' [i.e. the imams]. *Ḥifẓ al-riwāya* (memorising/protection of the transmission) insures that the lowest (*al-adna*) and the highest equally understand.

In the first *mas'ala*, al-Qaṭīfī says that *ijtihād* is *bāṭil* (false) except in time of *ḍarūra* (necessity), such as the *ghayba* (absence) of the imam. It is not a *ṭarīq mustaqil* (independent path) but is to be traceable to the specific issue to hand, as the Prophet's companions would do.[23]

This is not *jāriy* (permitted) for all matters. This mandates that *istidlāl* (deduction) is based on the *dalāla* (evidence) of the *ḥadīth*, and its *'umūm* (generality), *ijmāl* (conciseness) and *bayān* (clarity), *iṭlāq* (not being restricted) and *taqyīd* (restriction) and what most people do by it.

Absent *naṣṣ* (specific designation), there is *al-barā'a al-aṣliyya* (the principle of presumed permission), *istiṣḥāb* (continuance of past practice) or derivation from suitable issues where there is an *aṣl* (original statement of an imam) or *athār* in the *ḥadīth* or a *fatwā* from one of the best of the *asḥābūn*.[24] Then *al-ẓann* (speculation), based on *sabab* (a cause, reason), prevails because the imams' statements are *ḥujuj* (proofs) in the *dalāla*.

All this is incumbent on one seeking a *fatwā* from a mufti who possesses *sharā'iṭ al-istiftā* (conditions of issuing a *fatwā*).[25]

---

[22] This was not the well-known narration cited via Ibn Ḥanẓala but that cited via Abū Khadīja. See al-Kulaynī (vol. 7, p. 412/4) in which the imam cautions believers against seeking recourse to the *qāḍī*s of *al-jawr* (tyranny, oppression). The Ibn Ḥanẓala text is 412/5. See A.J. Newman, *The Formative Period of Shi'i Law: Hadith as Discourse Between Qum and Baghdad* (Richmond, 2000), pp. 107–108, 180–181.

[23] Al-Qaṭīfī cites the example of the Prophet's companion 'Ammār b. Yāsir and *al-tayammum* (dry ablution). See al-Kulaynī, vol. 3, p. 62/4.

[24] On these Uṣūlī-style principles and exegetical pair of analysis, see Gleave, *Scripturalist Islam*, pp. 183–185, 269–270, 279, 290.

[25] This refers to the skill set and training on which, according to Uṣūlīs, the mufti's competence must be based. See Newman, *Twelver Shiism*, pp. 129, 136, 142.

The *fatwā* is acted upon as long as the mufti lives. At his death, one must refer to another mufti[26] because the latter might discover a *wajh* (aspect) of the Qur'an or the Sunna in which there is a *dalāla*, or whose *dalāla* is stronger. Ignoring the Qur'an and following the *fatwās* of *ahl al-ijtihād* is not the path to salvation.

The second *mas'ala* addresses the levels or degrees (*al-marātib*) of *al-riwāya*. The highest of these is that of *qirā'a* (reciting) to the shaykh. Then there is *qirā'a* to him, *samā'* (listening) to his reading, then *mukātiba* (exchanging of correspondence). 'The last', says al-Qaṭīfī, is the *ijāza*. Even then, he says, the *ijāza* is most common in terms of benefit (*naf'*), the most widespread, the most in terms of *fā'ida* and the strongest in terms of *'ā'ida* (advantage).

The *ijāza* may be *mursala* (transmitted with an interruption) from an *'adl* (just person) to another *'adl* or to a *mamdūḥ* (praiseworthy person) from a *mamdūḥ* to someone like him, or to an *'adl*. It might also be transmitted from [one who is] a *thiqa* (trustworthy person) from a *ḍa'īf* (weak person); this based on *iqsām* (divisions) of *al-riwāya*.

If the *riwāya* is to books of *fatwās*, then the transmission ends at their authors. If it relates to *ḥadīth*, then this line of transmission ends with the imam, then the Prophet.

In the last *masa'la* al-Qaṭīfī says *al-riwāya* has *marātib*, but it absolutely does not mandate *'amal* (action). It is based on what is being transmitted, so if action is being permitted then act, but if not, then do not.

This limits the authority of the *mujāz* to that for which he is authorised by the *riwāya* and *ijāza*. Al-Qaṭīfī notes it can be that someone who transmits acts on it without the latter having actually been transmitted to him. After all, he says, 'someone *ḥāmil* (bearing) *fiqh* (jurisprudence) may not be a *faqīh*.'[27]

An *ijāza* is from a *mujtahid* or ends with him. The *riwāya* stops with him. It is not continuous. The *mujtahid* is not authorising action except based on what he has shown of *dalīl* (proof) for it. This is so even if the

---

[26] On Uṣūlī opposition to *taqlīd al-mayyit* (following rulings of a dead *mujtahid*), see Gleave, *Scripturalist Islam*, pp. 188, 195, 296.

[27] For a fuller version of the text, see al-Kulaynī, vol. 1, p. 403/1, 2. Al-Qaṭīfī cites the text again in his 920/1514 *ijāza*.

ijāza comprises an authorisation of all writings; because the *ijāza* can contain what the *mujīz* himself may not do, he cannot permit that to someone else.

Because the *ijāza* is only *riwāya*, it is not invalid at the death of the *mujīz*, because *akhbār* are not invalid at the death of the person narrating them.

The longest section of the *ijāza*, at seven pages, delineates the items and/or authors being authorised.

This *ijāza* comprises books of 'our companions', what 'our *ʿulamāʾ*' compiled from the *akhbār* of the *muḥaddithīn* and their *ijāzāt* and that whose *naql* stands out from various *riwāyāt* in the works *mansūba* (ascribed, traced) to the Imāmī Shiʿa.

Al-Qaṭīfī says he approves narrating from his own shaykh Ibrāhīm b. al-Ḥasan al-Dhirāq, from other *thiqāt* from such as ʿAlī b. Hilāl, back through Aḥmad b. Muḥammad b. Fahd[28] and, via the same *ṭarīq* – and others are also cited – to yet others, including al-ʿAllāma 'and all of his [unnamed] writings' on *uṣūl*, *al-furūʿ*, *ḥadīth* and *tafsīr*, and Muḥammad b. al-Ḥasan al-Ṭūsī (d. 460/1067) and all of his, also uncited, works in *fiqh*, *tafsīr* and *ḥadīth*. Also cited, via various links, are Muḥammad b. Makkī, al-Shahīd al-Awwal (d. 786/1384), Muḥammad b. Muḥammad, al-Shaykh al-Mufid (d. 413/1022), whom he calls *raʾīs al-madhhab* (master of the faith), the works of Muḥammad b, ʿAlī, Ibn Bābawayh (d. 381/991) and al-Kulaynī's *al-Kāfī*. Al-Qaṭīfī also cites such figures and their works as Aḥmad b. ʿAlī al-Najāshī (d. after 463/1071), and his *rijāl* work and other, named works of this genre and now names *fiqh* works of al-ʿAllāma.

Here al-Qaṭīfī includes the 758/1357 *ijāza* given by al-ʿAllāma's son, Fakhr al-Muḥaqqiqīn, to one Muḥammad b. Ṣadaqa.[29] At four pages, this is longer than al-Qaṭīfī's three-page listing of his own *ṭuruq* to items and authors. Al-Qaṭīfī says he also authorises Turkī (sic) with all that is in Fakhr al-Muḥaqqiqīn's *ijāza*, so Turkī can narrate all this from him, i.e. al-Qaṭīfī, and can then himself pass it on.

[28] On these three, see al-Ṭihrānī, *Ṭabaqāt*, vol. 7, pp. 3 (where the name is 'al-Dirāq'), 169; 6: 9–10. Others (Afandī, vol. 1, p. 15; al-Baḥrānī, p. 159; al-Khwānsārī, *Rawḍa*, vol. 1, p. 16; al-Tihrānī, *al-Dharīʿa*, vol. 1, p. 135) call the first al-Warrāq. See n. 67 on his 909/1504 *ijāza* to al-Karakī.

[29] Al-Majlisī, *Biḥār*, vol. 105, pp. 97–101; n. 8.

The one-page *fāʾida*[30] addresses a question about an *ijāza*'s worth, that there could be no references to specific works or specific authors or there might be errors in the works being transmitted.

The *ʿāqil* (wise person), al-Qaṭīfī replies, has no doubts that a specific text is that of its author. *Ijtihād* depends on *al-riwāya* and if there are doubts about the *isnād* of a transmission, then one cannot make a deduction (*yastadal*) or undertake an action based on it. If someone says he found something in al-Ṭūsī's *Tahdhīb*, his first of two collections of the imams' *aḥādīth/akhbār* – that would be the 'weakest' of *al-murāsīl* (transmissions). Absent its being traced back to the imams, one cannot act on it.

If there is a *ḥadīth* that is *mutawātir* based on *sharāʾiṭ* of *tawātur* (successive transmission) then one can act on the basis of it. Absent successive transmission of meaning from the Qurʾan, however, it cannot be acted upon without *taṣḥīḥ* (verification) of the transmission as being from the imams. Anyone who does not proceed in this manner is an apostate, and he cites Qurʾan 3: 85.[31]

The four-page *waṣiyya* is the *ijāza*'s second longest section.[32]

Here al-Qaṭīfī refers to a Muslim who, he says, knows the faith and repeats the great verses of the Qurʾan but without these finding a place in his soul, owing to the *ḥijāb* (barrier) of his citing himself and his love of the world. Although he denies this, says al-Qaṭīfī, in fact, he is *makhdūʿ* (misled).

Al-Qaṭīfī then offers words on piety and what this love of the world should entail. Qurʾan 2: 165,[33] he says, refers to the *mushrikūn* (polytheists) and one should remember God is always with him

---

30 Ibid., pp. 101–102.

31 'And whoever desires other than Islam as religion – never will it be accepted from him, and he, in the Hereafter, will be among the losers.'

32 Al-Majlisī, *Biḥār*, vol. 105, pp. 102–106.

33 'And [yet], among the people are those who take other than God as equals [to Him]. They love them as they [should] love God. But those who believe are stronger in love for God. And if only they who have wronged would consider [that] when they see the punishment, [they will be certain] that all power belongs to God and that God is severe in punishment.'

and then cites 57: 16.[34] These remarks, he says, are *fi'l- 'umūm* (in general).

As for *al-khuṣūs* (specifically, i.e. to Shams al-Dīn), al-Qaṭīfī tells him to look out after his time and when he completes something then *idhkir* (invoke) God. He should not look to *ḥājāt al-dunyā* (the desires of the world) and should take care not to say something he would not want to see written down for judgment on *Yawm al-qiyāma*. 'What you do not like,' says al-Qaṭīfī, 'leave it off.' He should not give over to *ḥubb al-riyāsa* (love of being in a leading position). 'This is of the great things that God opposes.'

Finally, says al-Qaṭīfī, 'Do not hasten to *al-futyā* (legal opinion).' There is, he says, a *khabar* that the person reaching Hell the quickest is the speediest person to the *fatwā*.[35] He then cites Qur'an 69: 44–46,[36] 16: 116[37] and part of 10: 59.[38]

This, he says, is his admonition to himself and to his fellow-believers.

The First Undated Ijāza

The nine-line second *ijāza* in *Biḥār* is written to Manṣūr, the son of 'Shaykh Muḥammad b. Turkī (sic)', for whom al-Qaṭīfī wrote the aforementioned 915/1509 *ijāza*.

---

[34] 'Has the time not come for those who have believed that their hearts should become humbly submissive at the remembrance of God and what has come down of the truth? And let them not be like those who were given the Scripture before, and a long period passed over them, so their hearts hardened; and many of them are defiantly disobedient.'

[35] Although Āl Sunbul traces this text (*Mawsū'at*, vol. 4, p. 241, n. 1) to *al-Sunun al-kubra* (vol. 6, p. 402) of Aḥmad b. Ḥusayn al-Bayhaqī (d. 458/1066), a version is found in Ibn Bābawayh's *Man lā yaḥḍuruhu al-faqīh* (Qum, 1413/1992), vol. 4, p. 286.

[36] 'And if Muhammad had made up about Us some [false] sayings, We would have seized him by the right hand; Then We would have cut from him the aorta.'

[37] 'And do not say about what your tongues assert of untruth, "This is lawful and this is unlawful", to invent falsehood about God. Indeed, those who invent falsehood about God will not succeed.'

[38] 'Say, "Has God permitted you [to do so], or do you invent [something] about God?".'

Here al-Qaṭīfī says he gives him an *ijāza* for all that he cited in the *ijāza* to his father. There is no date or place of composition.[39]

Al-Qaṭīfī's 920/1514 Ijāza

This text is dated Muḥarram 920/March 1514, in Najaf, about four months before the battle of Chaldiran at which the Ottomans decisively defeated the Safavids.[40]

In the interim between the 915/1509 *ijāza* and this text, al-Karakī had been present at Ismāʿīl's seige of Herat which took place the following year. The same year al-Karakī authored 'Nafaḥāt al-Lāhūt', a tract approving the open anathematising of the first three caliphs; Twelver clerics in the Hijaz later complained they were 'chastised' as a result. In these years, also, he replied for Ismāʿīl to the Ottoman sultan Selim's questions as to why Ismāʿīl had destroyed the tomb of the Sunni jurist Abū Ḥanīfa (d. 150/767) in Baghdad when he took the city. The year 916/1510 also saw al-Karakī receive additional administrative authority in Arab Iraq and a large stipend he is said to have distributed among his students. In 916/1510 al-Karakī completed his 'Qāṭiʿat al-Lajāj', defending his receipt of *kharāj* land as a gift from Ismāʿīl by arguing that, as a *faqīh*, he possessed *ṣifāt al-niyāba* (the qualities of deputyship) and that based on the principle of *niyāba ʿāmma* (general deputyship – the general authority possessed by a *faqīh* as deputy of the Hidden imam), he was permitted to accept *kharāj* land from *sulṭān al-jawr* (a tyranical ruler). In an essay composed the next year, al-Karakī argued that in the absence of the imam the Friday prayer could be led by a *faqīh* possessing *al-sharāʾiṭ* (the qualifications for practising *ijtihād*).[41]

---

[39] Al-Majlisī, *Biḥār*, vol. 105, p. 107; Āl Sunbul, *Mawsūʿat*, vol. 4, p. 245. *Biḥār*'s editor notes (p. 107, n. 2) he found no further information on Manṣūr. See also al-Ṭihrānī, *al-Dharīʿa*, vol. 1, p. 135.

[40] Al-Majlisī, *Biḥār*, vol. 105, pp. 108–115; Āl Sunbul, *Mawsūʿat*, vol. 4, pp. 249–258; al-Ṭihrānī, *al-Dharīʿa*, vol. 1, p. 134. On Chaldiran (Rajab 920/August 1514), see Michael J. McCaffrey, 'Čālderān', *EIr*, vol. IV, pp. 656–658. See also A. J. Newman, *Safawid Iran: Rebirth of a Persian Empire* (London, 2006), pp. 20f, 24.

[41] Newman, 'Myth', pp. 78f, 82–85, 88. Al-Karakī's argument concerning the *jāʾir* was perhaps first offered by al-Sharīf al-Murtaḍā (d. 436/1044). See W. Madelung, 'A Treatise of the Sharīf al-Murtaḍā on the Legality of Working for the Government ("Masāla fī l-ʿAmal maʿal-ṣulṭān")', *BSOAS*, 43 (1980), pp. 28–29.

The seven and-a-half page *ijāza* is written for one Muḥammad b. al-Ḥasan al-Astarābādī. It is comprised of the standard opening prayers; two pages of prefatory remarks; a nearly three-page *muqaddima* (introduction), with five *fawāʾid*; a two-page listing of items and authors being authorised; and a one-page conclusion.

In his preface al-Qaṭīfī refers to the divisions and fighting which appeared in Islam. Each group adhered to different *wujūḥ* (aspects) of the Qurʾan. 'We', he says, 'took recourse to the Prophetic Sunna and the narrated *ḥadīth*.' These include the *ḥadīth* of the 'two precious things' that the Prophet said he left to the *umma*, referring to the Qurʾan and the Ahl al-Bayt – a text, he says, narrated by numerous narrators in various forms that mandated holding fast to the Ahl al-Bayt.[42] The Ahl al-Bayt must, therefore, be followed just as the Prophet, and he cites Qurʾan 25: 27 in respect of those who do not.[43]

However, al-Qaṭīfī continues, the people of *ḍalāl* (error) took over, and *fisād* (corruption) and *ẓulm* (oppression) spread. The Ahl al-Dhikr [the imams] and *dalāla* were hidden, and the muftis became confused by ignorance.

Al-Astarābādī was one who remained true to the faith, al-Qaṭīfī says. In Najaf, he says, where the recipient came on *ziyāra*, they studied the entirety of *al-Sharāʾī* (of al-Muḥaqqiq al-Ḥillī, Jaʿfar b. Ḥasan, d. 676/1277). At his return to Najaf, al-Astarābādī contacted al-Qaṭīfī to ask for an *ijāza* in what al-Qaṭīfī had by way of *al-riwāya* from the imams and to connect to the narration of *fatwā*s to narrate to students as he wishes. Here al-Qaṭīfī cites the text in his 915/1509 *ijāza* saying that not everyone who is a scholar of *fiqh* understood it.[44]

In his *muqaddima*, al-Qaṭīfī says the faithful take the *aḥkām* (legal rulings) only from *ṣādiq* (someone truthful) and that truthfulness is known by his being infallible [i.e. an imam].

Those who took the place of the Prophet, i.e. the imams, allowed their Shiʿa to act based on what which was narrated from them. They

---

On the Shiʿi concept of the *faqīh* as *nāʾib* of the Hidden imam, see Newman, *Twelver Shiism*, s.v.

[42] The version of this text cited here is particular to this *ijāza* (vol. 105, p. 109). See, however, Newman, *Twelver Shiism*, p. 19.

[43] 'And the Day the wrongdoer will bite on his hands [in regret] he will say, "Oh, I wish I had taken a path with the Messenger."'

[44] n. 27.

commanded the *tafrīʿ* (derivation) of the *aḥkām* from the *uṣūl*. The Shiʿa did this owing to necessity, i.e. the absence of the imam.

If there is an *aṣl* on the issue in question, he says, then there is nothing to be derived. They agreed on the falseness of acting on the statement of a dead person. The *ʿāqil* then turns to another of the heirs of al-Dhikr so as not to break from the Prophetic *athār* or abandon acting based on the Qurʾan and the narrated Sunna.

And this was custom of the *salaf* and on this there are, he says, clear *adilla* in the *uṣūl*.

This process depends on *sharāʾiṭ*. These include acquaintance with the *uṣūl al-ʿaqāʾid*, *sharāʾiṭ* of *al-ḥadd* and *al-burhān*, *al-uṣūl*, *al-adab* and grammar. Using these, the *masāʾil* can be derived. The process needs a *ṭarīq* connected to the Ahl al-Bayt. The majority of *furūʿ*, he says, are down to their *uṣūl*. That is, there is present in the *ḥadīth* an *aṣl* on which one relies and with an *isnād* that is known.

There are many *ṭuruq* (paths) to the *isnād*. The *ijāza* is the most general of these in terms of *nafʿ* and the easiest in term of *tanāwul* (comprehension).

Here al-Qaṭīfī offers five *fawāʾid*. First, he says the *ijāza* is *idhn* (permission) for the *naql* of *ḥadīth* or a *fatwā* from a person himself or someone who narrates from him via *wāsiṭa* (an intermediary) or intermediaries. Secondly, the *fāʾida* (of the *ijāza*) is the *tasalluṭ* (authority) of the *mujāz* over that which is authorised to him and its *isnād* to its author or to the narrator of the ḥadīth. Its *riwāya* from him is based on the *ṭarīq* being *ṣaḥīḥ* (correct), or *mawwathaq* (confirmed), or *ḥasan* (good) or something else.

Thirdly, if a *ḥadīth* lacks a *muʿāriḍ* (contradiction/objection) or a preference as to what is being objected, then action on it and reliance on it is *wajaba* (mandated), if it is one of the [above-mentioned] three categories. If the *ḥadīth* is weak, *mursil* or cut off (*maqṭūʿ*, i.e. in its link to the imam), then one must seek recourse from the *ʿumūm* of the Qurʾan, the Sunna, or what is well known among the *aṣḥāb*, or a *dalīl ʿāqlī* (rational proof) or the reasons for preponderance on it, and act on this. One cannot act on the basis of anything else.

Fourth, if there are two opposing *amāratān* (signs) and there is no preference, then, citing Qurʾan 17:36,[45] al-Qaṭīfī says *waqf* (hesitation) is mandated, given the absence of *ʿilm*.

45 'And do not pursue that of which you have no knowledge.'

Finally, the *ijāza*'s *fā'ida* is clear. A written work is confirmed in its attribution to its speaker and author, and so too is the *ḥadīth*. This is because it is *mutawātir*. So, in the *ijāza* there must be knowledge of that. If not, then *naql* is not permitted. Each *mujīz* must certify that the works in question are Imāmī.

As to the attributing of the book to its author, there is no problem in permitting it. But this is not part of *al-riwāya*. Action and *al-naql* depend on *al-riwāya* and the *adna* (lowest form) of this is the *ijāza*. Absent *al-riwāya* the item cannot be narrated. Otherwise, it would be as if one found a book that someone else wrote: even if he knows who wrote it is not correct to narrate it from him.

The *ijāza* of a scholar relates to the writings of all the *'ulamā'*. Since these include contradictory *fatwā*s, he says, how could one give an *ijāza* to act on these? How, he asks, can Ibn Idrīs (Muḥammad b. Manṣūr, d. 598/1202) give an *ijāza* of the books of al-Ṭūsī for action?[46] Indeed, the *ijāza* is given from one *mujtahid* to another.

Al-Qaṭīfī then offers a one-page enumeration of items and authors for which he is giving authorisation. These include *al-Sharā'ī* and its *ḥawāshī* (marginalia) that he and al-Astarābādī read, *al-Alfiyya* of al-Shahīd and its *ḥawāshī*, al-Qaṭīfī's own *al-Rasā'il al-najafiyya*, the books of Shi'i *fatwā*s that he narrated from his shaykhs, including al-'Allāma's *Qawā'id al-aḥkām*, and other named texts. These included the *ḥadīth* and non-*ḥadīth* works of al-Ṭūsī, and books of other of 'our *aṣḥāb*' such as al-Sharīf al-Murtaḍā (d. 436/1044), Ibn Bābawayh, al-Mufīd and al-Kulaynī.[47]

Al-Qaṭīfī closes this section saying that he authorises al-Astarābādī to give his *ijāza* to others as he wishes, based on the *sharā'iṭ* of the *ijāza* and *al-riwāya*.

In his conclusion al-Qaṭīfī says the *ṭuruq* of his own *fuqahā'* are well known. They include those noted by al-'Allāma in his *rijāl* work, *Khulāṣat al-aqwāl*, and those figures whom al-Ṭūsī names at the end of his *al-Istibṣār* (his second collection of the imams' *ḥadīth* after

---

[46] Ibn Idrīs's criticisms of al-Ṭūsī were well known. See A.J. Newman, *Twelver Shiism*, p. 109.

[47] On *Qawā'id* as the Twelver Shi'i text supposedly available to Ismā'īl I, see A.J. Newman, *Safawid Iran*, p. 151, n. 3. On al-Qaṭīfī's 927/1521 *al-Rasā'il* and his 939/1532 *sharḥ* (commentary) on *al-Alfiyya*, see al-Ṭihrānī, *al-Dharī'a*, vol. 11, p. 227; vol. 2, p. 296.

Tahdhīb), and Ibn Bābawayh at the end of *al-Faqīh*. He says his *ṭuruq* to these are many and include what had been authorised to him from his own teachers. The *awthaq* (most trustworthy) of these is Ibrāhīm al-Dhirāq from ʿAlī b. Hilāl al-Jazāʾirī from Aḥmad b. Fahd al-Ḥillī through to al-Shahīd. He cites other *ṭuruq* linking him to al-Ṭūsī to al-Murtaḍā and al-Mufīd to Ibn Bābawayh and al-Kulaynī and, thence, to the best of 'our *fuqahā*' whose *ṭuruq* end in the imams and thence the Prophet himself. This includes their *fatwā*s and, for the *ḥadīth*, links to the Prophet, to the angel Gabriel and thence to God.

Al-Qaṭīfī's 944/1537 Ijāza

In 924/1518, four years after Chaldiran, as the fate of the Safavids, and Ithnā ʿasharī Islam, in Iran continued to be uncertain, al-Qaṭīfī composed his 'al-Sirāj', rebutting al-Karakī's 916/1510 essay on *kharāj*, arguing that receipt of any items from a tyrannical ruler was illegal as these had certainly been taken improperly from their owner. Al-Karakī, said al-Qaṭīfī, should have hesitated to accept these but, in any case, gifts from a tyrannical ruler should be avoided. In 926/1520, al-Qaṭīfī composed an essay on *al-riḍāʿ* (wet-nursing), replying to 916/1520 al-Karakī's essay on the subject. Al-Qaṭīfī's essay rebutting al-Karakī's ruling that the *faqīh* might perform Friday prayer during the Imam's continued absence might also have been completed in these post-Chaldiran years.

Ismāʿīl I died in 930/1524. The year after his son Ṭahmāsp's accession, al-Karakī returned to Iran. There he became embroiled in two confrontations, first with the two co-*ṣadr*s – one of whom was a student of both himself and al-Qaṭīfī – with one of the points of dispute being al-Karakī's view that the *faqīh*, as *nāʾib al-Imām* (deputy of the imam), might lead the Friday prayer and the second regarding al-Karakī's formulations on the direction of the *qibla*.

Ismāʿīl's death, however, unleashed a civil war lasting over ten years, not regarding the legitimacy of the Safavid house but among Qizil-bāsh tribal elements and their Tajik associates over a new hierarchical alignment around the ten-year-old Shah Ṭahmāsp. The turmoil encouraged invasions by the Uzbeks from the East and the Ottomans from the West. The Ottomans seized Tabrīz and Kurdistān, and attracted support in Gīlān.

At the height of the civil war, around 936/1529, al-Karakī 'won' both confrontations: both his opponents were dismissed. Al-Qaṭīfī, in Iraq, was also formally admonished to cease his criticisms of al-Karakī.[48] In 939/1532 Ṭahmāsp issued the famous *firmān* appointing al-Karakī *nā'ib al-imām* with authority over the realm's religious affairs. He was also given additional holdings in eastern Iraq and other western Safavid lands. Al-Karakī subsequently issued a series of rulings including the appointment of a prayer-leader in every village to instruct the people in the tenets of the Ithnā 'asharī faith and the changing of the *qibla* direction throughout the realm.

Al-Karakī died in 941/1534. That year Baghdad and all of Arab Iraq, including the shrine cities of Najaf and Karbala, surrendered to the Ottomans. Basra surrendered four years later, the year after al-Qaṭīfī composed this *ijāza*. In Iran, although two of al-Karakī's students subsequently served as *ṣadr*, the observance of the Friday prayers that he had promoted was discontinued.[49]

If the Safavid project, and its support for the Twelver faith, had not collapsed with Chaldiran, as al-Qaṭīfī wrote the present text, the fall of the one and, in consequence, of the other, may well still have seemed possible.

The *ijāza* is written to Sayyid Jamāl al-Dīn b. Nūr Allāh b. Shams al-Dīn Muḥammad Shāh al-Ḥusaynī al-Tustarī. No place of composition is cited.[50]

The eight-page text contains no formally delineated sections. More than a page is devoted to opening prayers, about two pages to preliminary remarks, and four pages to a 'discussion'. Six lines concern that for which authorisation of transmission is being given.

After the prayers, al-Qaṭīfī, in what is likely to have been a reference to al-Karakī's death, notes that God decreed the *faqd* (loss) of

---

48 Newman, 'Myth', pp. 84–91, 99. On al-Qaṭīfī's *al-riḍā'* and Friday prayer essays, see also al-Baḥrānī, p. 155; al-Ṭihrānī, *al-Dharī'a*, vol. 11, p. 188; vol. 15, pp. 62, 75–76.

49 Newman, 'Myth', pp. 96–105; Newman, *Safawid Iran*, pp. 26f, 38.

50 Al-Majlisī, *Biḥār*, vol. 105, pp. 116–123; Āl Sunbul, *Mawsū'at*, vol. 4, pp. 261–270. Al-Ṭihrānī's entry on the *ijāza* (*al-Dharī'a*, vol. 1, p. 134) is cited by *Biḥār*'s editor, who notes that the recipient's name is given there as Ẓiyā' al-Dīn b. Nūr Allāh and that he is the father of Qāḍī Nūr Allāh al-Tustarī, killed in India in 1019/1610. See Newman, *Twelver Shiism*, p. 194.

'the *ʿulamāʾ* and *ahl al-faḍl* (people of virtue)', and refers to Qurʾan 13:41.[51]

Al-Qaṭīfī says he noted that he was a *mutaʾakhir* (late-comer), owing to the paucity of his *biḍāʿa* (resources) and many *iḍāʿa* (lost opportunities). But, he says, he was also fearful of the Lord of the *sharīʿa* and of such of the Prophetic *ḥadīth* as

> When *al-badʿ* (innovation) emerges in my community,
> it is obligatory for the scholar to make his knowledge
> public, otherwise, God will condemn him.[52]

Although al-Qaṭīfī says he also tended to be withdrawn from people, he therefore embarked on much reading and study. He remained without resources and weak in health and, he says, probably also referring to al-Karakī, he faced much resistance from *ahl al-ḍalāl*, *al-ḥāsidīn* (the jealous), widespread *fitna* (strife) and *al-qīl wa'l-qāl* (idle talk).

Sayyid Jamāl al-Dīn's reading of al-ʿAllāma's *al-Irshād* showed al-Qaṭīfī that this man was of *ahl al-ʿilm*. He asked al-Qaṭīfī for an *ijāza* in the text and the *ḥawāshī*. Al-Qaṭīfī gave him an *ijāza* in the *riwāya*, for him and whoever narrated from him via al-Qaṭīfī.

---

[51] 'Have they not seen that We set upon the land, reducing it from its borders?'

As noted in Āl Sunbul (*Mawsūʿat*, vol. 4, p. 262, n. 1), in *al-Kāfī* the verse refers to *faqd* as the 'death' of the *ʿulamāʾ*. See the six texts cited in al-Kulaynī, vol. 1, p. 38, esp. 2, 6; the latter referencing this verse.

[52] Al-Kulaynī, vol. 1, p. 54/2, citing the Prophet. Al-Qaṭīfī refers to, but does not cite, other, similar texts. See also ad n., 57.

Although the poetry cited by al-Qaṭīfī across these texts is not discussed here, here he cites the verse

I was late to keep life and I did not find
a life for myself that is like progressing.

by the Syrian poet Abu Tammām (d. ca. 845/1441), author of *al-Ḥamāsa*. The text can be found in ʿAbd al-Qādir al-Baghdādī, *Khazānat al-adab*, vol. 7, p. 465, for which see: http://www.shiaonlinelibrary.com/%D8%A7%D9%84%D9%83%D8%AA%D8%A8/4655_%D8%AE%D8%B2%D8%A7%D9%86%D8%A9-%D8%A7%D9%84%D8%A3%D8%AF%D8%A8-%D8%A7%D9%84%D8%A8%D8%BA%D8%AF%D8%A7%D8%AF%D9%8A-%D8%AC-%D9%A7/%D8%A7%D9%84%D8%B5%D9%81%D8%AD%D8%A9_0?pageno=465øp, (accessed 13.8.20).

This *ijāza*, al-Qaṭīfī says, entails both the teaching of the work but also the *taqrīr* (determination) of its meaning, since the sayyid had mastered both. He was authorised to do likewise for those who read it with him who were of such people, in all of this observing *al-iḥtiyāṭ* (caution); the one who does not *ḍalla* (stray from) the *ṣirāṭ* (the path), he says, is he who follows the path of *al-iḥtiyāṭ*.

An *ijāza*, al-Qaṭīfī says, is of the *iqsām* (parts) of *al-riwāya*, being the last of the *marātib* in strength although the most common in terms of *fā'ida* and the most complete with respect to *'a'ida* (benefit).

It is last because the highest degree of transmission was for the *rāwī* (transmitter) to hear his shaykh reading, to insure against errors. The second is the *rāwī* reading and hearing what is being read. Then there is the reading of someone other than the two of them and the *rāwī* hearing the reading. Then, there is the *ijāza*.

The *mujāz* has authority over what he narrates from the person who gave him authorisation. This, says al-Qaṭīfī, refers to the narration of *lafẓ* (the words). The *mujīz* is not establishing the meaning. The meaning might be *mawkūl* (assigned) to something on which there is *al-'itimād* (reliance) in relation to knowledge of the three *dalālāt* and its associated *mafhūmāt* (understandings)

The *ijāza* is not *mufīda* (useful) for action by the *mujāz*. It is not relevant to what rulings the *mujīz* had issued. If he was a *mujtahid* who was in substantial disagreement with another *mujtahid*, then the *ijāza* would be giving permission in relation to all the *fatwā*s of his opponent. If the *ijāza* allowed for action, then the *mujtahid* would be permitting action in accord with what his opponent had demonstrated to be true.

The *ijāza* covers only *al-riwāya* (the transmission) of that for which an individual had been given an *ijāza*, so the recipient might master that field and become associated with the transmitters. If the *ijāza* refers to written works composed by a scholar, the latter is at the end of the line of transmission. If the *ijāza* is for transmission of books of *ḥadīth*, the line of transmission must end with the imam who made the statement, from the Prophet, from the angel Gabriel and from God.

As to works being authorised that the *mujīz* corrected and gave to the recipient, there is no discussion on the *tasalluṭ* of these being related. The recipient can only narrate that which is corrected in books of *fatwā*s.

As for the *ijāza* in what was read and the *ʿilm* of its meaning from a specified shaykh, this is an *ijāza* of *riwāya* and action. So, that which he read and understood of its meaning is in books of *ḥadīths*. The *ḥadīths* are *thābita* (affirmed) and there is no intrusion of the life of the *mujīz* in their being correct or corrupt. Thus, the statement that so and so said this is not made false by his death.

Rather the matter turns on the probability of truthfulness or lying. If he was *ʿadl* then the *riwāya* is *ṣaḥīḥ*. If there are *wasāʾiṭ* and all are *ʿadl*, then it is also correct. If they or one is *mamdūḥ*, which does not relate to justness, the *riwāya* is *ḥasan*. If there is among them a transmitter who is *mukhālif al-dīn* (non-Imāmī) but a just individual and *ʿadl* in his *madhhab* (belief) and *mawthūq* in his *amāna* (reliability), and there is no lying, then the *riwāya* is *mawthūqa*. If not, it is weak. A *khabar* is *ḍaʿīf* if the transmitter is *majhūl* (unknown) or *majrūḥ* (unworthy of trust) even if other narrators are *ʿadl*.

If the *ijāza* relates to books of *fatwās*, if there is *ijmāʿ* (scholarly consensus) on the *fatwā*, the transmitters gain authority over the *riwāya* and action on it based on the *ijāza*. What is disputed in the *ḥukm* is *shādh* (anomalous) and not regarded or *munqariḍ* (outdated) owing to later *ijmāʿ*.

If, al-Qaṭīfī says, a *fatwā* is the source of well-known disagreement from two sides, or what was not known did not reach the point where we noted it, acting on it is correct for one who receives it from him and about him, either orally or by intermediary/ies. When the *mujtahid* dies, he says, no action is permitted because a dead man's ruling is invalid. So, even if the giver was a *mujtahid* there is no *taqlid* (emulation), as al-ʿAllāma said in *al-Irshād* and elsewhere.[53]

The *ijmāʿ* comes together after his death if there was no agreement with him in the *fatwā* of living *mujtahids*. If there was disagreement there is no *ijmāʿ* with his death as there was none when he was alive.

Al-sirr al-ẓāhir (the presenting issue) here is the necessity of considering (*murāʿāh*) the Qurʾan and the Sunna. This is because a person, being fallible, can err. Even if the word of the *mujtahid* is reliable, not reconsidering the Qurʾan and the Sunna of the Prophet is of the greatest religious corruptions.

---

[53] Āl Sunbul (*Mawsūʿat*, vol. 4, p. 268, nn. 3, 5) references *Irshād* and al-ʿAllāma's *Mabādiʾ al-Wuṣūl ilā ʿilm al-uṣūl*, but without citing editions.

Ijtihād among Imāmīs, he says, is not a permitted *ṭarīq* (path) by *bi'l-aṣāla* (in principle). It is permitted by necessity owing to the absence of the imam and the impossibility of knowing his *fatwā*. It is permitted to the *mujtahid* as long as he safeguards the Qurʾanic proofs, the Prophetic *aḥādīth* and the divine *athār*. If the *mujtahid* dies and someone else takes his place, then recourse to the other on the disputed issue is necessary.

If, al-Qaṭīfī says, any age is devoid of a *mujtahid*, reliance on the *fatwā* of a dead *mujtahid* is permissible as long as all who have the capacity (*qābiliyya*) for that strive day and night to attain *ijtihād*. *Ijtihād*, he concludes, is a word based on *tashkīk* (doubt/scepticism/questioning) and *yatajazi* (limited/specific) in the chosen faith to the Uṣūlīs.[54]

In the few lines in which he ends the *ijāza*, al-Qaṭīfī says he authorises the *riwāya* of all the writings of the Imāmī *ʿulamāʾ* on the *ḥadīth*, *tafsīr*, *fiqh* and others. Everything except the *ḥadīth* is traced to him and his shaykhs and thence to the author. The *ḥadīth* are narrated from him through to the imams. He cites no names of his shaykhs and their *isnād*, nor does he name any works.[55]

Al-Qaṭīfī's Second Undated Ijāza

The four-page *ijāza* to Khalīfa Shāh Maḥmūd, also lacking any place reference, comprises three lines of prefatory prayers; one page of introductory remarks; three *fawāʾid* over two pages, including one page on items and authors for which the *ijāza* is being given; and a four-line *khātima* (conclusion).[56]

Al-Qaṭīfī commences saying that looking about him he saw that those embracing the faith were either a *muddaʿin* (a pretender) who

---

[54] Āl Sunbul (*Mawsūʿat*, vol. 4, p. 269, n. 2) references al-ʿAllāma's *Mabādiʾ*.

[55] The citation here (vol. 105, p. 123) of al-Qaṭīfī's *ṭarīq al-riwāya* from al-Dhirāq (sic) from ʿAlī b. Hilāl to Muḥammad b. Makkī and to his shaykhs is a later addition, possibly by the copyist. See also Āl Sunbul, *Mawsūʿat*, vol. 4, p. 270.

[56] Al-Majlisī, vol. 105, pp. 85–88. This *ijāza* is not cited in Āl Sunbul's *Mawsūʿat*. Al-Ṭihrānī (*al-Dharīʿa*, vol. 1, p. 134) only notes there that al-Qaṭīfī arrived in Iraq in 913/1507. Unusually, *Biḥār*'s editor does not cite this *al-Dharīʿa* reference. See also n. 14.

has no ʿ*ilm* or a *nāqil* transmitting from someone from whom it is not correct to transmit.

Al-Qaṭīfī says that although he saw he was neither, he had faced issues of *biḍāʿa* and many *iḍāʿa*. He then cites the same text as he had in the 944/1537 *ijāza*, that when *al-badʿ* emerged, the learned man had to act.[57]

While in Najaf, he says, Khalīfa's study of some works of *fiqh* with him proved his astuteness. He requested, and al-Qaṭīfī wrote, an *ijāza*. Khalīfa sought, says al-Qaṭīfī, a path to the Prophet referenced in Qurʾan 34: 18.[58] The Ahl al-Bayt, al-Qaṭīfī says, explain that the 'blessed' cities referred to Prophet's family and the 'visible' cities to those who narrated from them.[59]

In the first *fāʾida*, he says the *ijāza* does not include the authorisation of action. It is the last of the *marātib* of *al-riwāya* and its most general in terms of benefit. It gives the recipient authority to transmit that for which he was given an *ijāza*, whether a book of *fatwā*s – which he narrates from its author – or a work which he narrates back to the imam and thence to the Prophet and thence to God.

Citing Qurʾan 53:3,[60] al-Qaṭīfī says the Prophet did not undertake *ijtihād*. The imams are *ḥafaẓa*, he says – that is, they know the Qurʾan by heart – from the Prophet.

If it were said, if this were so then there would not be differences 'among the Imāmīs' and their transmissions, al-Qaṭīfī says he would say that correctness does not prove clarity of meaning, such that something else is not probable. Even if it did, it does not necessitate the lack of the possibility of the opposite, given that the Arabic language and its *dalāla* are not devoid of differences.

The meaning turns on *al-ḥaqīqa* (the truth) and the *ḥikma* (rationale) requires the presence of the ʿ*umūm* (generality) and the *khuṣūṣ*

---

[57] In his only use of verse in this *ijāza*, al-Qaṭīfī then cites the same line of poetry from Abū Tammām as cited above. See n. 52.

[58] 'And We placed between them and the cities which We had blessed [many] visible cities. And We determined between them the [distances of] journey, [saying], "Travel between them by night or day in safety".'

[59] See, for example, Ibn Bābawayh, *Kamāl al-dīn* (Qum, n.d.), vol. 1, p. 395; vol. 2, p. 483.

[60] 'He did not speak of his own desire, it is an inspiration which inspires him.'

(specificity), *ijmāl* (abridged) and *bayān* (clear, obvious), *iṭlāq* (not being restricted) and *taqyīd* (restriction) (together, loosening and tying), and *al-nusukh* (abrogation), all present in the Qurʾan. He then cites Qurʾan 16: 43[61] and explains that 'Dhikr' refers to the Prophet, as in Qurʾan 65: 10[62] and that his Ahl are the Ahl al-Bayt.

In the second *fāʾida*, al-Qaṭīfī says it is inevitable that there be both correctness and error in the transmission of a work if it is not *maqrūʾ* (read) personally.

It might be said that, since the Imāmīs hold that the dead person's word cannot be followed, what is the *fāʾida* of narrating their writings?

Al-Qaṭīfī replies there are many. These include knowledge of where there is *ijmāʿ* and where *khilāf* (disagreement) and *tasalluṭ* over the narration of *masāʾil* (issues) on which there is no disagreement. There is no disputing, he says, that one does not follow the dead in that in which there is dispute. As for that on which there is no *khilāf*, the statement is not based on him at all but on the *madhhab*, and, he says, there are other benefits.

What is the benefit of an *ijāza* if the book is correct and its *tawātur* and the author are well known?

Al-Qaṭīfī says the *ijāza* allows its recipient to narrate the book. There is a difference, he says, between narrating the work from the author and *isnād* (tracing it to the author). Among the conditions of *ijtihād*, he adds, is the tracing of *al-riwāya*.

The one-page third *fāʾida* addresses his own *ṭuruq*. He says he narrates from many *thiqāt* orally, calling al-Dhirāq (sic) *awthaq*, thence from ʿAlī b. Hilāl, from his shaykh through Aḥmad b. Fahd, via Shaykh Fakhr al-Dīn (sic) to his father, al-ʿAllāma. Via Aḥmad b. Fahd he has links to al-Shahīd and via ʿAlī b. Hilāl also to al-ʿAllāma. Fakhr al-Dīn said he had 'more than 100' *ṭuruq* to Imam Jaʿfar. There also are *ṭuruq* from the latter's father, al-ʿAllāma, to al-Ṭūsī, to al-Mufid, to al-Kulaynī through to Imam Mūsā, from Imam Jaʿfar. These all end in God.

Khalīfa's *ijāza*, he says, entails *riwāya* of all the works he has mentioned including the *ḥadīth* collections of *al-Kāfi*, *al-Faqīh*,

61 'Ask *ahl al-dhikr* if you do not know.'

62 'O ye who believe! Now God hath sent down unto you a *Dhikr* (messenger).'

Tahdhīb and *al-Istibṣār*.[63] These *ṭuruq*, he says, are via Fakhr al-Dīn via his father and the aforementioned *ṭarīq* to al-Ṭūsī and thence al-Mufid as well as, via another *ṭarīq*, from Fakhr al-Dīn's grandfather Shaykh Yūsuf via a different path that, however, also ends in al-Ṭūsī, al-Mufīd and thence to the imams. These *ṭuruq* are enumerated in the *ḥadīth* collections he has cited.

In the four-line *khātima* al-Qaṭīfī, citing part of Qurʾan 3: 83[64] and 16: 53 [65] says one is to seek only the face of God and not to forget prayer. He apologises for the *ikhtiṣār* (brevity) and says there may soon be a *taṭwīl* (elaboration).

Summary and Conclusions

Al-Qaṭīfī's discourse across these *ijāzāt* might be described as one of limits, both jurisprudential and personal.

First, across all four al-Qaṭīfī argues for limits on the *ijāza* and the authority it bestows. He acknowledges the various *marātib* of the *ijāza* and that, in this hierarchy, the *ijāza* is the last even as, he adds, it is the most beneficial and the most common. In the process, he also consistently notes that the *ijāza* does not grant authority to act or, similarly, authorise the transmission of meaning. In the first instance, it only traces the chain of transmitters back to the author of the text, if it is work of *fatwās*, or, in relation to the imams' *ḥadīth*, back to the imam, the Prophet and, finally, God himself.

He refers also to the rules for categorising the named transmitters of the works authorisation for the transmission of which is being given and to the skills and learning needed to qualify as a *mujtahid*.

His references to the processes associated with *fiqh* and the *aḥkām*/*furūʿ* also highlight limits. Al-Qaṭīfī rejects the absolute legitimacy of *ijtihād*. He acknowledges that in the Imam's absence its exercise may be necessary and, in the process, refers to the various

[63] Although not named as such, these are the 'four books' of the imams' *ḥadīth* compiled before the Saljūq's arrival in Baghdad in 447/1055. See Newman, *Twelver Shiism*, pp. 62, 75, n. 30, 87, 179, 209.

[64] 'So is it other than the religion of God they desire'.

[65] 'And whatever you have of favour – it is from God. Then when adversity touches you, to Him you cry for help.'

exegetical pairs and principles of textual analysis generally associated, he notes, with the Uṣūlī school of Twelver jurisprudence. The latter, he carefully cautions, must be grounded in the Qurʾan, the Sunna and the imams' narrations. The resulting *fatwā* is valid only during the lifetime of the mufti/*mujtahid*. At the latter's death, recourse to a living mufti is mandated. The latter must start the process afresh, making sure to ground any resulting *fatwā* in recourse to the above sources. In all these discussions, however, he stresses the virtues of practicing *waqf* and *iḥtiyāṭ* – a very Akhbārī reference.[66]

As to the relevance of historical context, across the dated *ijāzāt*, these 'polemical' jurisprudential discussions receive approximately the same attention – seven, five and six pages respectively. Four pages are devoted thereto in the undated Khalīfa Shāh *ijāza*.

There are also personal limits in evidence in these texts and here context seems to play a role: that al-Karakī's presence looms large, if indirectly, here suggests that al-Qaṭīfī's jurisprudential and personal concerns with al-Karakī as an associate of the Safavid court were of a piece.

Al-Qaṭīfī's 915/1509 *ijāza* was composed two years after his arrival in Iraq, by which time, as noted, both al-Karakī's connections to Ismāʿīl's court and also his standing in Iraq were well established. Al-Qaṭīfī's *waṣiyya* in it, condemning over-attention to the Qurʾan by those whose souls are untouched by the faith, *ḥubb al-riyāsa* and hasty recourse to *fatwā*s certainly intends to refer to al-Karakī.

Al-Qaṭīfī's citing of Qurʾan 13:41 in his 944/1537 *ijāza* to refer to the death of the *ʿulamāʾ* clearly references al-Karakī's recent death. Al-Qaṭīfī's care to note, separately, that the verse also refers to the loss of the *ahl al-faḍl* implicitly excludes al-Karakī from their number.

It is only after al-Karakī's death, in the 944/1537 text, that al-Qaṭīfī makes reference to clearly still-painful memories of the distinct contrast between his situation and that of al-Karakī after his own arrival in Iraq three decades earlier, his lack of self-confidence, health issues and numerous personal slights.

66 A. J. Newman, 'The Nature of the Akhbārī/Uṣūlī Dispute in Late-Safawid Iran. Part One: ʿAbdallāh al-Samāhijī's "Munyat al-Mumārisīn"', *BSOAS*, 55 (1992), pp. 19, 46.

Secondly, as to those works for which transmission is being authorised in these *ijāzāt*, al-Qaṭīfī's lists include a wide range of material across such different genres as *fatwās*, *tafsīr*, *rijāl* and *ḥadīth*. His naming of individuals here demonstrates that his own *ṭuruq* to the works in question are *mutawātir* through his own shaykhs.

This said, across these texts, in comparison with those discussed in the field, al-Qaṭīfī offers quite limited reference to his own immediate network of teachers. While he alludes to having studied with others, of these only al-Dhirāq/al-Warrāq, cited as *awthaq*, is named as his 'direct' shaykh. Only via al-Dhirāq does al-Qaṭīfī trace his own *ṭuruq* back through generations of named scholars, to the earliest well-known works and figures of the faith. Perhaps, knowing that al-Karakī himself had studied with al-Dhirāq/al-Warrāq years before al-Qaṭīfī's arrival coupled with awareness that the pedigrees of others of his shaykhs were more limited drove al-Qaṭifī to seek out al-Karakī's teacher. Indeed, al-Qaṭīfī's references to him in his two early dated texts stand as statements of, if not pleas for, equal status with al-Karakī, attesting all the more to al-Qaṭīfī's lack of self-confidence.[67]

Further attesting thereto is that al-Qaṭīfī's devoted four of the seven pages on his *ṭuruq* in his 915/1509 text to a verbatim citation of the 758/1357 *ijāza* of Fakhr al-Muḥaqqiqīn.

This said, al-Qaṭīfī's attention to his *ṭuruq* markedly diminishes, from seven pages in the 915/1509 text, to two in the 920/1514 text, to – after al-Karakī's death – six lines in the 944/1537 text, the latter lacking any names at all.

---

67 On al-Dhirāq (sic)'s *ijāza*, see al-Baḥrānī, p. 159; al-Ṭihrānī, *al-Dharīʿa*, vol. 1, p. 133.

In the undated *ijāza* to Khalīfa Shāh, al-Qaṭīfī refers to his shaykhs as al-Dhirāq, 'orally', and one Shaykh ʿAlī b. Jaʿfar b. Abī but the latter as among the *awthaq* who narrated from al-Dhirāq. Al-Ṭihrānī, *al-Dharīʿa*, vol. 1, p. 133; al-Ṭihrānī, *Ṭabaqāt*, vol. 7, p. 5, notes that he narrates from 'al-Warrāq' directly and indirectly, the latter via Shaykh ʿAlī. Afandī (vol. 1, p. 18) refers to other *ʿulamāʾ* of Bahrain. See also al-Baḥrānī, pp. 155, 159. The latter suggests al-Qaṭīfī studied with al-Karakī himself, but al-Khwānsārī (vol. 1, p. 29) suggests al-Karakī also studied with al-Dhirāq/al-Warrāq. See the 909/1503 *ijāza* given to al-Karakī referenced in al-Ṭihrānī, *Ṭabaqāt*, vol. 7, p. 3; n. 28.

In the aftermath of al-Karakī's death in 941/1534 al-Qaṭīfī could reflect on, and commit to paper, in a document not immediately intended for widespread circulation, the painful memories of his early situation. Indeed, the recollections on offer in the 944/1537 *ijāza* may have been further stirred up by a sense that the impact of his discourse was perhaps limited, even if across the century, in and outside Iran, others also had had reservations about the Safavid association with the faith and al-Karakī's connections therewith.[68] The absence of a detailed *ṭuruq* in it suggests he felt the argument for equal status with al-Karakī was now less of a requirement. Al-Qaṭīfī's briefer references to his early situation in the Khalīfa Shāh *ijāza* and to those pretending to embrace the faith, his devotion of but a page in the text to his own *ṭuruq* and his apology for its brevity all intimate that this *ijāza* also post-dates al-Karakī's death, perhaps even the 944/1537 text.

By contrast, none of the Shiʿi *ijāzāt* discussed by the field to date suggest their authors expand on discussions in them to address such other associated jurisprudential issues as did al-Qaṭīfī, let alone to offer also such personal reflections.

Taqī al-Majlisī's listing of the seven forms of transmission in his 1066/1655 *Lavāmiʿ*, a Persian-language commentary on Ibn Bābawayh's *al-Faqīh*,[69] in a separate *fāʾida*, precedes a discussion of, in order, the necessity for recourse to the imams and their narrations and for verifying the texts in question, his own *ṭuruq* – citing the same *ḥadīth* as al-Qaṭīfī concerning the 'bearer' of *fiqh*, his caution that the

[68] In al-Qaṭīfī's post-Chāldirān 924/1518 'al-Sirāj' essay, there is the sense that he was, or at least perceived himself to be, not without allies (Newman, 'Myth', p. 87). His connection with one of the co-*ṣadrs* involved in the early Ṭahmāsp-period disputes with al-Karakī and his admonishment by the Safavid court in the aftermath of al-Karakī's 'win' in these years both attest to his having had some standing in Iran in these later years and also to the ending of it. Indeed, perhaps indicative of relative popularity over the period, Dirāyātī lists six copies of 'al-Sirāj', as extant today; only two are dated, to 1116/1704 and 1321/1903. Nearly 70 copies of al-Karakī's *al-kharāj* essay are extant; nos eleven and seven date to the 10th/16th and 11th/17th centuries respectively. See M. Dirāyatī et al., ed., *Fihristvārī-yi dastnivishtihā-yi Īrān* (Mashhad, n.d.), vol. 6, pp. 81–82; vol. 8, pp. 7–9. On later unease with Safavid Shiʿism, see also Newman, 'The Myth', pp. 91f, 104f.

[69] See Gleave (n. 13) citing Taqī al-Majlisī, *Lavāmiʿ-yi ṣāḥibqirānī* (Qum, 1414/1993), vol. 1, pp. 65–76, esp. pp. 65–67.

ḥadīth must be narrated in their original Arabic and recorded accurately, perhaps out of place in a commentary on *al-Faqīh*, bespeak Akhbārī-style concerns; indeed, elsewhere he does denounce *ijtihad*.[70]

Al-Tustarī's post-Safavid comments on *ijāzāt* seem relatively perfunctory – stressing the care to be used in the texts' transmission and the *isnād*, for example – and certainly not overly/overtly polemical.[71] Like al-Majlisī, al-Tustarī does not immediately address such related issues as the question of action on the basis on an *ijāza* and *taqlīd al-mayyit* that were addressed by al-Qaṭīfī.

Reference might be made to works in *dirāyat al-ḥadīth*, the discipline of criticism of the text and narrative chains of *ḥadīth* evolving in the early 10th/16th century. In his *Wuṣūl*, Ḥusayn b. ʿAbd al-Ṣamad, (d. 984/1576), the father of Shaykh Bahāʾī (d. 1030/1620), divides the *ijāza* into seven sections.[72] Ḥusayn's own teacher Shaykh Zayn al-Dīn b. ʿAlī al-ʿĀmilī (d. 966/1559), al-Shahīd al-Thānī, had, in fact, written on *ʿilm al-dirāya* and, briefly, the various forms of the *ijāza*.[73] Nevertheless, Shaykh Ḥusayn, born in 918/1512, apparently composed *Wuṣūl* after arriving in Iran,[74] after Shaykh Zayn al-Dīn's death. Shaykh Zayn al-Dīn was born in 911/1506, before al-Qaṭīfī arrived in Iraq.[75] Interestingly both, like al-Qaṭīfī, were mainly based to the west of Iran.[76]

---

[70] Taqī al-Majlisī, vol. 1, pp. 68–71, 45. On this text, see al-Ṭihrānī, *al-Dharīʿa*, vol. 18, pp. 369–370.

[71] Al-Tustarī, *Ijāza kabīra*, pp. 7–9, 212–215; nn. 9–11.

[72] Ḥusayn b. ʿAbd al-Ṣamad, *Wuṣūl al-akhyār ilā Uṣūl al-akhbār*, ed. J. al-Mujāhidī (Karbalā, 1436/2015), pp. 201f.

[73] ʿAbd al-Hādī al-Faḍlī, *Introduction to Ḥadīth, including Dirāyat al-Ḥadīth by al Shahīd al-Thānī*, tr. N. Virjee (London, 2002), pp. 35–36, 227–228. See al-Khwānsārī's reference to *ʿilm al-dirāya* ad n. 75.

[74] Ḥusayn b. ʿAbd al-Ṣamad, pp. 13, 17–18, 35 (some copies are said not to have the reference in question).

[75] In this same discipline, in the next century, Mīr Dāmād (d. 1041/1631) in his *al-Rawāshiḥ* also, briefly addresses the *iqsām*. See Muḥammad Bāqir al-Ḥusaynī, Mīr Ḍāmād, *al-Rawāshīh al-samāwiyya*, ed. Gh. Qaysariha et al. (Qum, 1422/2001), pp. 157–160. Al-Khwānsārī (*Rawḍa*, vol. 1, pp. 25–29) notes al-Qaṭīfī's *ijāza* to al-Tustarī is very useful on *funūn al-dirāya* and *al-rijāl* (biography) and cites from it.

[76] On the continued vitality of the western centres of the faith across the period, see Newman, *Twelver Shiism*, pp. 163f, 190f; n. 68.

By the 'standards' of al-Samāhījī's later evaluation of the state of the Akhbārī/Uṣūlī debate,[77] al-Qaṭīfī's jurisprudential reservations here together with those in other works of his, as discussed elsewhere, render it difficult to affix a label to him. His disavowal of *taqlīd al-mayyit* and references to exegetical pairs of analysis, *istiṣḥāb* and *al-barāʾa al-aṣliyya*, and *sharāʾiṭ al-istiftā*, for example, suggest Uṣūlī sympathies. His disavowal of absolute *ijtihād*, the *faqīh* as *nāʾib al-Imām* and association with the court/*ḥubb al-riyāsa*, with his insistence on recourse to the revealed 'texts' and references to *waqf* and *iḥtiyāṭ*, for example, all suggest Akhbārī proclivities. Nevertheless, it was precisely this combination of concerns and criticisms that al-Qaṭīfī deployed against al-Karakī as the 'face' of Safavid Shiʿism in these years.

Taken together, al-Qaṭīfī's contributions reflect both a profound unease with the directions in which the faith, as being carried forward by al-Karakī, seemed to be headed now that it had found official favour in Iran – an unease which others shared. On offer here, as well, is a profound sense of his own status as an outsider, coming from the Twelver periphery to the centres of the faith in Iraq.

Al-Qaṭīfī may not have been overly popular in his own century or – *pace* Bāqir al-Majlisī – the next. But his sentiments offer a different perspective on, and something of a corrective to views of, developments in Safavid-period Twelver thought and practice based on the privileging of scholarly works produced in Safavid Iran.

[77] See our 'The Nature'.

PART FOUR

PHILOSOPHY, THEOLOGY AND INTELLECTUAL HISTORY

12

Mīr Dāmād's 'Wisdom of the Right Side' (*al-ḥikma al-yamāniyya*)

Janis Esots

The founder of the so-called 'Iṣfahān philosophical school', Mīr Dāmād (969–1040/1561–1631), described his philosophical doctrine as the 'Wisdom of the Right Side' (*al-ḥikma al-yamāniyya*).[1] In this article, I will attempt to establish the principal characteristics of this doctrine and its key implications, in particular in metaphysics.

As attested by Mīr Dāmād himself, at the heart of his 'wisdom of the right side' lie two interrelated principles: 1) the Creator makes the quiddities (*māhiyāt*) of the things by simple making (*ja'l basīṭ*); their existence is then abstracted from this 'making', i.e., the establishment of a relationship with the Maker. Hence, existence must be treated as a derived meaning (*ma'nā maṣdarī*) which does not possess any

[1] The expression alludes to the Q. 19:52 'We called to him (Moses) from the right side of the Mount (*nadaynāhu min jānib al-ṭūr al-ayman*), and We brought him near in communion' and the *ḥadīth*: 'Faith is from the right side and wisdom is from the right side' (*al-īmān yamānī wa'l-ḥikma yamāniyya*) (Aḥmad b. Ḥanbal, *al-Musnad* (Beirut, 1990), vol. 2, pp. 277, 457; cf. Abū Ja'far al-Kulaynī, *al-Kāfī* (Tehran, 1357 Sh./1978), vol. 8, p. 70). Sajjad Rizvi translates the expression as 'Yemeni philosophy' (Sajjad H. Rizvi, 'Mīr Dāmād's (d. 1631) *al-Qabasāt*: The Problem of the Eternity of the Cosmos', in Khaled El-Rouayheb and Sabina Schmidtke, ed., *The Oxford Handbook of Islamic Philosophy* (Oxford–New York, 2016), pp. 438–464; Sajjad H. Rizvi, 'Mullā Shamsā al-Gīlānī and His Treatise on the Incipience of the Cosmos', in Mullā Shamsā al-Gīlānī, *Ḥudūth al-'ālam*, ed. 'A. Aṣgharī and Gh. Dādkhāh (Costa Mesa, CA, 2015), pp. 16–19 (of the English introduction)); I myself did so previously (Janis Esots, 'Mīr Dāmād's "Yemenī" Wisdom: A Variety of Platonism?', *Islamic Philosophy Yearbook Ishraq*, 8 (2017), pp. 34–46). However, it is not Yemen as a country/region what Mīr Dāmād has in mind primarily – rather, it is the source of legitimate and undistorted divine inspiration.

instances but only portions related to different quiddities[2] – the stance, which Mullā Ṣadrā (and, following him, most later Iranian philosophers), not quite precisely,[3] interpreted as the 'principality of the quiddity' or 'genuineness of the quiddity' (*aṣālat al-māhiya*) and 2) (apart from the receptacle of time,) there exist the receptacles of eternity (*sarmad*) and perpetuity (*dahr*).[4] The term 'eternity' (*sarmad*) refers to the relationship of the eternal to the eternal (say, the relationship of God's attributes to His essence); the term 'perpetuity' (*dahr*) refers to the relationship of the eternal to the temporal (which can be described as 'the eternal's being with (*maʿa*) the temporal' (but not in [*fī*] it), and the term 'time' (*zamān*) refers to the relationship of the temporal to the temporal. Taking a different point of view, it can be said that eternity is the realm of the necessity, perpetuity is the realm of the essential contingency or possibility (*al-imkān al-dhātī*), and time is the realm of the possibility of preparedness or predisposition (*al-imkān al-istiʿdādī*).[5]

For a wider educated public, Mīr Dāmād as a thinker is primarily associated with the theory of the 'perpetual inception' (*ḥudūth dahrī*),[6]

---

[2] Mīr Dāmād, *al-Ufuq al-mubīn*, ed. Ḥāmid Nājī (Tehran, 1391 Sh./2013), p. 114, n. 135. Sabzawārī associates this stance with Davānī's *dhawq al-mutaʾallihīn*: 'Those Theologicians who assert that "existence" is nothing but the portions would seem to have borrowed from the "tasting" of theosophy' (Ḥājj Mullā Hādī Sabzawārī, *Sharḥ al-manẓūma fi'l-manṭiq wa'l-ḥikma*, ed. Muḥsin Bīdārfarr (Qum, 1386 Sh./2007), vol. 1, pp. 210–211; the English translation by Mehdi Mohaghegh and Toshihiko Izutsu in *The Metaphysics of Sabzawārī* (Tehran, 1991), p. 51).

[3] Philosophy, simply because it is philosophy, deals with universals (i.e., quiddities), not particulars (regardless of whether it treats these universals as transcendent or immanent of their particulars. If we treat the universals as mere mental positions (*iʿtibārāt*) void of reality, this (as I will try to show) inevitably leads to treating the whole as a single individual, in which all distinctions are relative – i.e., to professing the individual oneness (*al-waḥda al-shakhṣiyya*) of the affair.

[4] Mīr Dāmād, *al-Ufuq al-mubīn*, p. 536.

[5] Mīr Dāmād, *al-Qabasāt*, ed. Mahdī Mohaghegh (2nd ed., Tehran, 1374 Sh./1995), p. 113.

[6] The term, apparently, was coined by Jalāl al-Dīn Davānī (see Jalāl al-Dīn Muḥammad Davānī, 'Nūr al-hidāya', in his *al-Rasāʾil al-mukhtāra*, ed. Sayyid Aḥmad Tūysirkānī (Isfahan, 1364 Sh./1985), pp. 114–116). In their recent article, 'Taʾammulī dar intisābi risāla-yi *Nūr al-hidāya* ba Jalāl al-Dīn Davānī: muṭāliʿa-yi matn-i mihwar bar bunyād-i naẓariyya-i "ḥudūth-i dahrī" wa āthār-i Mīr-i Dāmād',

according to which the quiddities are created in perpetuity by establishing a relationship between them and the Creator. This theory is sometimes conceived simply as a refutation of the Ashʿarī theory of illusory time (*zamān mawhūm*) allegedly existing before the creation of the world, which, like the hypothesis it refutes, must primarily be considered in the context of the *kalām* discourse of creation. Hence, it is claimed, it belongs to the domain of theology rather than to the realm of philosophy. I will attempt to show that this assumption is only partially correct, and to demonstrate the fundamental philosophical importance of the theory.

Metaphysics I: Making the Quiddities

According to Mīr Dāmād, previous to being made (*qabl an yakūna majʿūl*^{an}), quiddities enjoy a hypothetical (*taqdīrī*) existence in the Creator's knowledge; through the act of making, these hypothetical quiddities become related (*intasaba*) to the reality of being/existence, thus turning into realised (*taḥqīqī*) or established (*mutaqarrar*) ones.[7] This establishment of a relation is described by Mīr Dāmād as the 'perpetual inception' (*ḥudūth dahrī*) – which he believes to be an a-temporal and a-local act that occurs in the realm of the factuality (*fī nafs al-amr*),[8] and through which nothing (*lays*) becomes something (*ays*).

Āʾina-yi mīrāth, 65 (1398 Sh./2019), pp. 123–143), Ḥusayn Najafī and Ḥāmid Nājī question the authenticity of *Nūr al-hidāya*. However, while raising legitimate doubts, the article fails to convincingly disprove the authorship of Davānī. I have modified the English rendering suggested by Sajjad H. Rizvi ('perpetual incipience', see, Rizvi, 'Mīr Dāmād's (d. 1631) *al-Qabasāt*', pp. 439–461, passim).

[7] Mīr Dāmād, *al-Ufuq al-mubīn*, pp. 10, 53, 264, 412, 663; idem, *al-Qabasāt*, pp. 38–39, 73; idem, 'al-Taqdīsāt', in Mīr Dāmād, *Muṣannafāt*, ed. ʿAbd Allāh Nūrānī, 2 vols (Tehran, 1381–1385 Sh./2002–2006,), vol. 1, p. 171.

[8] For the key texts on the history of the problem of *nafs al-amr*, see Muḥammad ʿAlī Ardistānī, *Nafs al-amr dar falsafa-yi islāmī* (2nd ed., Tehran, 1392 Sh./2013), in particular part 2. *Tafāsīr-i nafs al-amr* (pp. 101–298), and Naṣīr al-Dīn al-Ṭūsī et al., *Risāla ithbāt al-ʿaql al-mujarrad wa shurūḥ-i ān*, ed. Ṭayyiba ʿĀrifniyā (Tehran, 1393 Sh./2014). As Sabzawārī explains, factual proposition (*qaḍiya nafs al-amriya*) is the proposition 'in which judgment is made concerning the instances which may exist in the external world, regardless of whether they are realised or hypothetical, like for instance: "Every

The principle of the Maker's making the quiddities by simple making can be treated as a variant of Ibn Sīnā's teaching on the necessitation (*ījāb*) of the existence of the contingents by the Necessary Existent.[9] As said, in Mīr Dāmād's view, before they are made, the quiddities enjoy a hypothetical (*taqdīrī*) being in the Creator's knowledge (one wonders if this hypothetical state is in any way different from Avicennan contingency?) Through the act of making, these hypothetical quiddities become related (*intasaba*) to the reality of existence, thus turning into realised (*muḥaqqaq*) or established (*mutaqarrar*) ones. To restate this in Avicennan terms, owing to the establishment of the relation with the Necessary, the contingents become necessarily-existent-through-the-other (*wājib al-wujūd bi ghayrihi*). Does the new terminology employed by Mīr Dāmād change, or make more perfect, the scheme outlined by Ibn Sīnā, which rests on the necessary-contingent dichotomy? I am not sure.[10]

Although Mīr Dāmād's principle of the double referent of the concept of existent (the reality of existence and the quiddity related to that reality) appears to ultimately go back to the Avicennan division of the necessary existent into the necessary by/through itself and the necessary by/through the other, its immediate source seems to have been Jalāl al-Dīn Davānī (although the founder of the Wisdom of the Right Side does not acknowledge this).

---

body is limited, or has a place, or is divisible *ad infinitum*" and other similar propositions used in sciences' (Sabzawārī, *Sharḥ al-manẓūma fi'l-manṭiq wa'l-ḥikma* (Qum, 1386 Sh./2007), vol. 1, p. 264; the English translation by Mehdi Mohaghegh and Toshihiko Izutsu (Mohaghegh and Izutsu, *The Metaphysics of Sabzawārī*, p. 87), modified by the present author). According to Sabzawārī, factuality (*nafs al-amr*) is the receptacle of the subjects of all factual propositions, regardless of whether they are real (realised) or hypothetical (Sabzawārī, *Sharḥ al-manẓūma*, vol. 1, p. 64; cf. Ardistānī, *Nafs al-amr*, p. 113). Hence, *ḥudūth dahrī* appears to be a change of the mode of the thing's/proposition's factuality, which does not affect its factual status (being the fact itself).

[9] For Ibn Sīnā's treatment of the matter, see, for example, Avicenna, *The Metaphysics of the Healing*, tr. Michael Marmura (Provo, UT, 2005), p. 31 (I.6.5–6).

[10] Cf. Henry Corbin, 'Confessions extatiques de Mîr Dâmâd, maître de théologie à Ispahan', in *Mélanges Louis Massignon* (Damascus, 1956), vol. 1, p. 74, where Corbin acknowledges the Avicennan foundations of Mīr Dāmād's doctrine, but simultaneously describes the teaching of Ibn Sīnā as 'un avicennisme théorique' and that of Mīr Dāmād – as 'un avicennisme éprouvé au fond de l'âme, jusqu'à l'extase'.

According to Davānī, there is one truly existent individual, which is identical with the Necessary Existent.[11] However, by extention, every quiddity related to this single individual can also be called 'existent'. Explaining his understanding of the individual unity of existence, Davānī writes:

> The existence, which is the source of the derivation of the [concept of] 'existent', is a single entity, and it is an external reality. Both this self-subsistent existence and the entity that is in some particular way related to it are called 'existents'.[12] But, while the reality of existence possesses existence truly and substantially, the entity which is related to it possesses existence only accidentally and metaphorically, owing to its relation (*intisāb*) to the reality of existence.[13]

He illustrates this with the example of light and an illuminated thing: the first is itself the light; the second is an entity related to it.[14]

Mīr Dāmād introduces his principle in a very similar way:

> If the reality [of the thing] is substantiated by itself, [the concept of] 'existent' is predicated of its reality as such, without taking into account any additional consideration, be it a delimitation or a causal inference. If, however, its reality is substantiated through its relation to the Maker, [the concept] 'existent' can be predicated of this established reality in the aspect of causal inference, i.e., in the aspect of its issue from the generosity of the Maker and its being based on the presence of the latter.[15]

---

[11] Reza Pourjavady, 'Jalāl al-Dīn al-Dawānī (d. 908/1502), "Glosses on 'Alā' al-Dīn al-Qūshjī's Commentary on Naṣīr al-Dīn al-Ṭūsī's *Tajrīd al-i'tiqād*"', in Sabine Schmidtke and Khaled El-Rouayheb, ed., *Oxford Handbook of Islamic Philosophy* (Oxford, 2016), p. 423.

[12] Jalāl al-Dīn Davānī, *Sab' rasā'il*, ed. Sayyid Aḥmad Tūysirkānī (Tehran, 1381 Sh./2002), p. 131.

[13] Or its participation in the latter. For relation in Davānī's thought, see the discussion in Munīra Palangī, 'Ma'nā-yi intisāb dar andīsha-yi Davānī', *Khiradnāma-i Ṣadrā*, 56 (Summer 1388 Sh./2009), in particular pp. 22–23.

[14] Ghiyāth al-Dīn Dashtakī, *Ishrāq hayākil al-nūr li kashf ẓulumāt shawākil al-ghurūr*, ed. 'Alī Awjabī (Tehran, 1382 Sh./2003), pp. 184–185; cf. Ḥusayn Muḥammadkhānī, 'Waḥdat-i wujūd nazd-i Davānī', *Faṣlnāma-i andīsha-yi dīnī dānishgāh-i Shīrāz*, 28 (1387 Sh./2008), p. 88.

[15] Mīr Dāmād, *al-Ufuq al-mubīn*, pp. 271–272.

As we see, both Davānī and Mīr Dāmād endorse the double meaning of the term 'existent', which divides into truth (the reality of existence) and metaphor (something related to that reality). The relationship between the two referents can be described as 'systematic ambiguity' (*tashkīk*).[16] Mīr Dāmād calls the transformation of the hypothetical quiddity into a real/realised essence, through establishing a relation with the reality of existence, 'substantiation' (*tajawhur*)[17] or (elsewhere in *al-Ufuq al-mubīn*) 'essentialisation' (*tadhawwut*)[18]– which means, there are no essences or substances proper before the realisation or necessitation of the hypothetical quiddities.[19]

[16] The terms *tashkīk* ('systematic ambiguity') and *mushakkak* ('systematically ambiguous') were coined by the Arab translators of Aristotle's works on logic and their Neoplatonic commentaries, as an attempt to render the Greek word *amphibolous* (a term which is used to describe a certain kind of homonym – a word which is used in one and the same sense, but in different ways) – for further details, see H. A. Wolfson, 'The amphibolous terms in Aristotle, Arabic philosophy and Maimonides', *Harvard Theological Review*, 31 (1938), p. 173; cf. C. Bonmariage, *Le Réel et les réalités : Mollâ Sadrâ Shîrâzî et la structure de la réalité* (Paris, 2007), pp. 54–55. For the list of examples of the usage of *tashkīk* and related terms (*shakk, tashakkuk, al-mashkūk fīhi*) in Arabic translations, see Alexander Treiger, 'Avicenna's Notion of Transcendental Modulation of Existence (*Taškīk al-Wuǧūd, Analogia Entis*) and Its Greek and Arabic Sources', in Felicitas Opwis and David Reisman, ed., *Islamic Philosophy, Science, Culture and Religion: Studies in Honor of Dimitri Gutas* (Leiden, 2012), p. 344, n. 31. Treiger's study, inter alia, demonstrates that in the late Greek and early Arabic commentary tradition of Aristotle's logical works the term 'existent' was typically treated as *ism mushakkak* ('a systematically ambiguous word').

[17] Which may have led his student Mullā Ṣadrā to the conclusion that the substance experiences some sort of motion or intensification, whereas Mīr Dāmād meant that the presence of the constituents (the genus and the differentia) of the substance necessitates the presence, or the 'establishment' (*taqarrur*) of the said substance (which entails the relationship of logical priority and posteriority between the substance and its constituents). See Saʿīd Anwārī and Khadīja Hāshimī ʿAṭṭār, 'Barrasī-yi taqaddum wa taʾakhkhur bi al-tajawhur wa sayr-i taʾrīkhī-yi ān dar falsafa-yi islāmī', *Taʾrīkh-i falsafa*, 10 (1398 Sh./2019), pp. 113–142.

[18] Mīr Dāmād, *al-Ufuq al-mubīn*, p. 370.

[19] Ibid., p. 406.

He typically describes the presence of the thing in the realm of perpetuity or factuality as its establishment (*taqarrur*),[20] or obtainment of actuality,[21] treating existence (*wujūd*) as a secondary intelligible (albeit the one which is extracted from an established/ realised thing before all other secondary intelligibles),[22] which imitates or explains the establishment of the quiddity or the ipseity[23] (which possibly made Mullā Ṣadrā view his teacher as an exponent of the 'principality of quiddity' [*aṣālat al-māhiya*]).

Metaphysics II: Perpetuity and Perpetual Inception

There can be little doubt that Mīr Dāmād believed his principal philosophical contribution to consist in making a clear-cut distinction between the realm of perpetuity (*dahr*), which he, apparently, identified with the domain of factuality (*nafs al-amr*) or occurrence (*wāqi'*),[24] and the realm of becoming, or generation and corruption, in which everything occurs in time, and which is divided into past, present and future. 'Realisation' (*taḥqīq*) and 'establishment' (*taqarrur*) (which Mīr Dāmād identifies with the activity of the quiddity [*fi'liyyat al-māhiya*]),[25] thus, refer to the emergence of the thing in the realm of perpetuity (*dahr*) or factuality (*nafs al-amr*, i.e. the area of the applicability/

---

[20] Mīr Dāmād understands *taqarrur* ('establishment') as the essence that is actually made (*maj'ūla bi'l-fi'l*). It is posterior to the constituents of the essence but prior to (any consideration regarding) its existence. For a detailed discussion, see Dā'ūd Ḥusaynī, '*Ḥaqīqat, wujūd* wa *taqarrur*: ta'ammulī-yi ta'rīkhī dar bārai naẓar-i Ṣadrā dar bāb-i taḥaqquq-i wujūd dar barābar-i naẓar-i Mīr-i Dāmād', *Ḥikmat-i mu'āṣir*, 7 (1395 Sh./2016), pp. 85–94. Based on Mīr Dāmād's remark in *al-Ufuq al-mubīn* (p. 19), the later philosophical tradition correlates *taqarrur* with the conceptualisation (*taṣawwur*) of the known object in the mind of the knowing subject and *wujūd* with the assent (*taṣdīq*).

[21] Mīr Dāmād, *al-Ufuq al-mubīn*, p. 663.

[22] Ibid., p. 53.

[23] Mīr Dāmād, *al-Qabasāt*, pp. 73, 196.

[24] Mīr Dāmād, *Muṣannafāt*, vol. 1, p. 9. Cf. al-'Alawī: 'the occurrence to which one refers as "perpetuity"' (*al-wāqi' mu'abbar 'anhu bi al-dahr*), see Mīr 'Abd al-Ḥasīb b. Aḥmad al-'Alawī, '*Arsh al-īqān fī sharḥ taqwīm al-īmān*, ed. 'Alī Awjabī and Akbar Thaqafiyān (Tehran, 1390 Sh./2011), p. 277.

[25] Mīr Dāmād, *al-Ufuq al-mubīn*, p. 663.

validity of logical and philosophical laws, which comprises both the external and mental existence).[26] This emergence occurs once and forever: once the thing has emerged in perpetuity, it cannot fall back into perpetual non-being (*ʿadam dahrī*), or become non-established (*ghayr mutaqarrar*). What remains outside the limits of *nafs al-amr* – e.g., such concepts as 'the Companion of the Creator' and 'the hybrid of camel and cat'– are phantoms of our imagination and/or estimative faculty, void of an intelligible quiddity, and cannot exist in the realm of perpetuity or factuality.

According to some thinkers, apart from the forms of the things, the realm of the factuality includes all unconditionally true propositions (such as 'the whole is bigger than its part'). The position of Mīr Dāmād, who defines the existence of the thing in the realm of factuality as 'its being established as such and its realisation as such',[27] is not sufficiently elucidated on this point. One tentatively concludes that the realm of perpetuity or factuality is, for him, inhabited by the intelligible forms of the things and the propositions that describe the relationships between these forms. To put this in terms of theology, the objective paradigms/models (*al-muthul al-ʿayniyya*) of the things, pertaining to the realm of God's decree (*qaḍāʾ*), are realised/established in perpetuity, while their material instances, pertaining to the realm of measuring out (*qadar*, i.e. gradual implementation of that decree), emerge in time.[28] Mīr Dāmād argues that the Platonic forms (which he identifies with the universal natures)[29] are nothing else but these models or paradigms, present in the objective (= external) Decree,

26 Mīr Dāmād, *al-Qabasāt*, p. 39.

27 Ibid. This point was taken over by Allāma Ṭabāṭabāʾī who treated *nafs al-amr* as the container (*ẓarf*) of unqualified affirmation (*thubūt muṭlaq*), or realisation (*taḥaqquq*), of both affairs/things (*umūr*) and propositions (*qaḍāyā*) – see his gloss on Ṣadrā's *Asfār* (Ṣadr al-Dīn Shīrāzī (Mullā Ṣadrā), *al-Ḥikma al-mutaʿāliyya fi'l-asfār al-ʿaqliyya al-arbaʿa*, ed. R. Luṭfī, I. Amīnī and F. Ummīd (3rd. ed., Beirut 1981), vol. 7, p. 271); cf. Muḥammad Ḥusayn Ṭabāṭabāʾī, *Nihāyat al-ḥikma* (Tehran, 1363 Sh./1984), pp. 2, 24–25; see also Ardistānī, *Nafs al-amr*, pp. 185–187.

28 Mīr Dāmād, *al-Ufuq al-mubīn*, p. 636.

29 Mīr Dāmād, *al-Qabasāt*, p. 159.

which is identical with *dahr* in a certain sense,[30] quoting the *Uthūlūjiyā* of Pseudo-Aristotle in support of his claim.[31]

On the other hand, as mentioned above, according to Ibn Sīnā, perpetuity is the relation of eternity to time.[32] Does this mean that the Platonic forms, according to Mīr Dāmād, must be treated as the relations between the eternal and the temporal, or between being and becoming? If yes, are they, as relations, dependent on the entities which they relate to each other? If so, they must, in a way, be dependent not only on being, but also on becoming, i.e., on their instances in the realm of becoming – at least, it appears that we cannot perceive them without taking into account these instances. To my knowledge, Mīr Dāmād does not address these questions.

In addition, in what sense exactly are these forms, or relations, created? We know that they are present as possibilities, or hypothetical entities, in God's mind before obtaining existence in perpetuity/factuality. In my view, their creation can be interpreted as an (atemporal) apprehension of the intelligible structure (the Paradigm) of the world in its entirety by God (which apprehension is a concomitant of His apprehension of Himself). Calling this atemporal apprehension 'perpetual inception' must be taken as a metaphor.

Mīr Dāmād also argues that whatever is contingent in its essence, cannot beginninglessly exist in perpetuity, since, in his words, 'it cannot bear the weight of eternity' (which he, presumably, identifies with necessity):[33] hence, it must be created not only in essence (i.e., be essentially contingent), but also in perpetuity (i.e., represent an object of knowledge that was previously absent from the knower). As mentioned above, this presupposes the existentiation of the given thing in God's mind (whereas, if considered as a purely hypothetical entity, the contingent thing has no beginning in perpetuity).

The relationship between perpetuity and temporality is sometimes interpreted as the relationship between God's decree (*qaḍā'*) and

---

30 Mīr Dāmād, *al-Ufuq al-mubīn*, pp. 636–637.

31 Ibid., p. 638. Cf. 'Abd al-Raḥmān Badawī, ed., *Uthūlūjiyā: Afluṭīn 'inda al-'arab* (2nd ed., Qum, 1413/1992), p. 68.

32 Ibn Sīnā, *al-Ta'līqāt*, ed. Sayyid Ḥusayn Mūsawiyān (Tehran, 1391 Sh./2013), p. 99 (§118).

33 Mīr Dāmād, *al-Qabasāt*, p. 226.

measuring out (*qadar*). This was the path taken by Naṣīr al-Dīn al-Ṭūsī in his concise discussion on *qaḍāʾ* and *qadar* in the commentary on Ibn Sīnā's *al-Ishārāt wa'l-tanbīhāt* (a corollary of a more extensive discussion on the Necessary's atemporal knowledge of the particulars), and Mīr Dāmād elaborated on it. According to al-Ṭūsī, *qaḍāʾ* consists in the summary existence of all existents in the world of the Intellect, which they obtain through their creation *ex nihilo*. In turn, *qadar* consists in their existence in the external matter, after the obtaining of the required conditions, in a detailed manner, and in a certain sequence (*wāḥidan baʿda wāḥid*). The intelligible substances come to exist at once (*marrat*^{an} *wāḥidat*^{an}) in both *qaḍāʾ* and *qadar* (which constitute two aspects of their single and simple existence), whereas the corporeal substances come to exist twice, in perpetuity and in time, in two different ways.[34]

Mīr Dāmād developed al-Ṭūsī's seminal discussion into a theory on two types of decree and measuring out, mental and external. According to this theory, both *qaḍāʾ* and *qadar* exist in two aspects or levels – namely, as the entity's existence in the Creator's knowledge and as its objective external existence.[35] The entities which become the objects of the decree and the measuring out, as he elucidates, are of three kinds: a) the world as a whole; b) the immaterial beings created *ex nihilo* (i.e. the intellects); c) material things, which are engendered from a prime-material substrate and pertain to the world of becoming. The world as a whole is envisaged only in the decree of God's knowledge (*al-qaḍāʾ al-ʿilmī*). It acquires existence in the Creator's knowledge in the aspect of His knowledge of His single and unique essence, which is the perfect efficient cause of the world, from the point of the view of His perfect knowledge of Himself being the cause of the most perfect order that the nature of the contingency can receive through His agency. The existence of the world decreed is posterior to the decree of God's knowledge in two aspects – essentially and perpetually.

In turn, the 'measuring out' of the world as a whole can occur only in the objective/external world, as a hierarchical arrangement of its

---

[34] Ibn Sīnā, *al-Ishārāt wa'l-tanbīhāt, maʿa sharḥ al-khwāja Naṣīr al-Dīn al-Ṭūsī wa* al-Muḥākamāt *li Quṭb al-Dīn al-Rāzī*, ed. Karīm Fayḍī (Qum, 1383 Sh./2004), vol. 3, p. 343; cf. Mīr Dāmād, *al-Qabasāt*, pp. 421–422.

[35] Ibid., pp. 420–421.

existence in the receptacle of factuality, created after its essential non-being and its explicit non-existence in *dahr*, in accordance with the Creator's knowledge and providence.[36] Its objective existence in perpetuity (*al-wujūd al-ʿaynī fi'l-dahr*) represents a detalisation (*tafṣīl*) of its existence in God's knowledge, implicitly present in His perfect knowledge of His true single essence, which is the paradigm of the knowledge of all existents.

As for the immaterial intellects, they are the objects of God's decree in His knowledge (*al-qaḍāʾ al-ʿilmī*) in the aspect of their presence in His knowledge, and in the aspect of His knowledge and providence being the cause of their creation from nothing, as well as in the aspect of their transition from (the state of) pure nothingness to the (state of) the actuality of somethingness and establishment (*taqarrur*). The immaterial entities are the objects of God's decree in the external world in the aspect of their issue from the Creator and their transition from absolute nothingness to somethingness in actuality, and in the aspect of their transition, as parts of the universal comprehensive single order, from pure non-existence to the existence in the receptacle of perpetuity. The objective/external measuring out (*al-qadar al-ʿaynī*) of the immaterial entities, in turn, is envisaged in the aspect of the issue of their existence from the Creator in perpetuity, both in their particularity and specificity. Thus, the existentiation of the intellects in the decree and in the measuring out occurs at once but must be considered in two different aspects.

As for the things generated in matter, they exist both in perpetuity and in time, and both in a summary manner (in the universal order) and in a detailed way (where their specific traits are manifested). In addition, they enjoy a formal universal existence, as impressions in the intellect, and a formal universal and particular existence as impressions in the minds of celestial souls. For this reason, they possess multiple levels of decree and measuring out (each of which relates as decree to the posterior and as measuring out to the prior).

---

[36] Which, according to Mīr Dāmād, is primarily related to the macrocosm – see Mīr Dāmād, *al-Qabasāt*, p. 172. According to some indications, Mīr Dāmād, like Plotinus (*Enn.* III, 3 (48), 1–2), appears to distinguish two levels of providence, universal and particular.

The last degree of measuring out, which cannot be treated as a decree at all, in view of its being the ultimate idealisation, is the existence of the temporal and material existents, originated in their particular places and times, gradually and in a certain sequence, as self-renewing and perishing affairs, in accordance with their predispositions that gradually manifest themselves in the course of time, through an orderly arranged chain of causes, preparing them.[37]

This theory (outlined by al-Ṭūsī and elaborated by Mīr Dāmād) attempts to integrate the approaches of *kalām* and *falsafa* (the path which was well trodden by Fakhr al-Dīn Rāzī and later Ashʿarīs), but, it seems, with only a partial success: the lucid and transparent division between perpetuity and time, and being and becoming, previously established by Mīr Dāmād, considered in the categories of decree and measuring out, becomes blurred. In particular, one wonders if the relationship between perpetuity and temporality can be adequately expressed in terms of summarising and detailing (*ijmāl – tafṣīl*), which is pivotal principle of the *qaḍāʾ – qadar* relationship. As *dahr* and *zamān* represent different modes of being (or, more precisely, being and becoming), it is difficult to argue that the latter (time) can be viewed as a detailing of the former (perpetuity) – because, properly speaking, perpetuity can be imitated but not detailed. In a way, the *kalām* doctrine of *qaḍāʾ* and *qadar* represents the reasoning of the commoners (people who have not received philosophical training); as such, it cannot be useful in elucidating philosophical tenets. Mīr Dāmād could not have been unaware of this – hence, it can be argued that the primary goal of his extensive discussion on *qaḍāʾ* and *qadar* was to boost the seemingness of the compatibility of religious dogma and philosophical thought, in order to secure the survival of the philosophical tradition.

On the other hand, Mīr Dāmād treats perpetuity (*dahr*, the term, which, as we have learnt, was used by Ibn Sīnā to denote the relationship between the domains of the immutable and the changing)[38] simultaneously as a relation, a receptacle and a mode of being, in which 'all existents and all multiple entities count as a single immutable existent in its completeness'.[39] As mentioned above, the first Muslim

37 Mīr Dāmād, *al-Qabasāt*, pp. 421–422.

38 Ibn Sīnā, *al-Taʿlīqāt*, p. 98, §117; p. 99, §118; p. 422, §757; p. 423, §762.

39 Mīr Dāmād, *al-Ufuq al-mubīn*, p. 632.

philosopher who introduced the concept of the 'perpetual inception' (*ḥudūth dahrī*) of the world (which he defined as its non-existence 'on the level of the essence of the Necessary Existent, which is identical with the external existence' – and, hence, as its being preceded by the external non-existence) – was Jalāl al-Dīn Davānī.[40] His theory of the perpetual inception represented a philosopher's response to the *kalām* discussions on the creation of the world: the Mutakallimūn, who spoke of the 'temporal inception' (*ḥudūth zamānī*) (believing that God has created the world in time, at a certain moment of it), found it difficult to prove that time had existed before the creation of the world, in particular since their opponents, the Peripatetic philosophers (who, in turn, admitted only the essential inception (*al-ḥudūth al-dhātī*) of the world, i.e. its contingency in relation to the Necessary Existent or God, which did not necessarily rule out its eternity) argued that time was created by the motion of the celestial spheres, which were part of the world. More precisely, they treated it as the measure of the motion of the outermost and all-encompassing sphere (known as the *falak al-aflāk*, *al-falak al-muḥīt*, or *muḥaddid al-jihāt*). As such, it could not have existed before the creation of the world, they claimed. Attempting to solve this difficulty, without renouncing their belief in the temporal

[40] Jalāl al-Dīn Muḥammad Davānī, 'Nūr al-hidāya', in Davānī, *al-Rasā'il al-mukhtāra*, ed. Sayyid Aḥmad Tūysirkānī (Iṣfahān, 1364 Sh./1985), pp. 114–116; cf. idem, 'Unmūdhaj al-'ulūm', in Jalāl al-Dīn Davānī, *Thalāth rasā'il*, ed. Sayyid Aḥmad Tūysirkānī (Mashhad, 1411/1991), pp. 310–311; idem, *Sharḥ al-'aqā'id al-'aḍudiyya*, with the appendices of Sayyid Jamāl al-Dīn Afghānī and Muḥammad 'Abdu, ed. Sayyid Hādī Khusrawshāhī (n.p., 1423/2002), p. 51. Ḥāmid Nājī and Ḥusayn Najafī, in their recent article ('Ta'ammulī dar intisābi risāla-yi *Nūr al-hidāya* ba Jalāl al-Dīn Davānī' – see note 6) and in separate personal conversations in Iṣfahān and Tehran in September 2019, questioned the authenticity of *Nūr al-hidāya*, because of the absence of manuscripts older than 1019/1610 and because the treatise is not mentioned in Qāḍī Shūshtarī's (d. 1019/1610) list of Davānī's works provided in his *Majālis al-mu'minīn*: Qāḍī Nūr Allāh Shūhstarī, *Majālis al-mu'minīn*, ed. Ibrāhīm 'Arabpūr et al. (Mashhad, 1392–1393 Sh./2013–2014), vol. 4, pp. 551–556. Nonetheless, to me, these objections do not amount to a refutation of its authenticity. In addition, the author of *Nūr al-hidāya* refers to his addenda to al-Ṭūsī's *Tajrīd* and 'Aḍudī's *al-'Aqā'id al-'aḍudiyya* (Davānī, *al-Rasā'il al-mukhtāra*, p. 114), two works which Davānī is known to have composed.

inception, some theologians proposed the existence of an illusory time (*zamān mawhūm*)[41] before the moment of the inception of the world.

Davānī's remarks on *ḥudūth dahrī*, scattered in his works, can be viewed as a harbinger that preceded for more than a century Mīr Dāmād's elaborated theory on the subject, which systematically disproved the *kalām* theory of illusory time (*zamān mawhūm*).[42] According to Davānī, perpetual inception should be understood as the establishment of a relationship between the reality of existence and the entities that are mere virtualities if considered as such and if they acquire their (relative and/or metaphorical) existence owing to the establishment of this relation.[43]

However, Mīr Dāmād apparently was the first Muslim philosopher who indicated the separative (*infikākī*) character of the essential posteriority of perpetuity in relation to the Creator (which was further elucidated by his disciples, in particular Mullā Shamsā Gīlānī).[44] In other words, he held that there was an ontological and epistemological gap between God and the world (including the Intellect). All Muslim Peripatetics share the opinion that the world, as a whole, relates to the Creator as the effect to its cause: however, Mīr Dāmād and his disciples appear to be unique in their belief in the unbridgeable rupture between the cause and the effect (a stance which places them close to Proclus[45]).

---

[41] On which, see Mullā Ismāʿīl Khāju'ī, 'Risālat ibṭāl al-zamān al-mawhūm', in Davānī, *Sabʿ rasā'il*, pp. 239–283, in particular pp. 253–256, 268–269 and 274.

[42] Dāmād's acquaintance with Davānī's theory is confirmed by numerous references to the latter in his works (in particular, by the quotation of the relevant passage from Davānī's *Unmūdhaj* in his *Qabasāt*, see Mīr Dāmād, *Qabasāt*, p. 109).

[43] Mahdī Dahbāshī, 'Taḥlīlī az andīshahā-yi falsafī wa kalāmī Jalāl al-Dīn Muḥaqqiq Davānī', *Khiradnāma-i Ṣadrā*, 3 (Farvardīn 1375 Sh./April 1996), p. 49. Since, due to our inability to separate the intelligible from the sensible and imaginable, it is difficult for us to grasp the totality of these entities as a unique entity (the world), we find it equally difficult to apprehend the nature of the perpetual inception, which consists in establishing a relationship between the reality of existence and this entity, argues Davānī (Jalāl al-Dīn Muḥammad Davānī, 'Risālat al-zawrā'', in idem, *Sabʿ rasā'il*, p. 177).

[44] Mīr Dāmād, *al-Qabasāt*, pp. 75, 250; idem, 'Ḥawāshī *Ilāhiyyāt al-Shifā*'', in Mīr Dāmād, *Awrāq-i parākanda az muṣannafāt*, ed. Ḥusayn Najafī (Tehran, 1396 Sh./2017), p. 253; Mullā Shamsā al-Gīlānī, *Ḥudūth al-ʿālam*, pp. 49, 53, 55, 56, 69.

[45] Proclus repeatedly emphasises the transcendence of the productive cause over its effect – see Proclus, *The Elements of Theology*, ed. and tr. Eric Robertson Dodds (2nd ed., Oxford, 1963), pp. 8–11, 71, 87 (propositions 7–10, 75, 98).

Mīr Dāmād, following Ibn Sīnā and al-Ṭūsī, distinguishes between the essential possibility (*al-imkān al-dhātī*) and the possibility of preparedness (or predisposition) (*al-imkān al-istiʿdādī*), which belongs to the category of quality. The essential possibility is abstracted from an essence that exists. It is an adjoined accident of the quiddity (and not a concomitant, caused by it),[46] to the effect that it is a concept which cannot be separated from the notion of quiddity: taken as such, the quiddity lacks any actuality and/or determination, be it the actuality and determination of realisation (*taḥqīq*), or that of invalidation (*buṭlān*). Its reality consists of a double negation, i.e. in its being neither 'non-establishment' (*lā taqarrur*), nor 'non-non-establishment' (*lā lā taqarrur*), or in its negating both the establishment and non-establishment, in the aspect of congruence or derivation.[47] In turn, the possibility of preparedness (or predisposition) pertains to the temporal material substance when it is considered in relation to something that is not existent *in actu*: when the potency is actualised, it disappears. It is the potency and preparedness of matter to produce something which it is prepared to produce and potent to make.[48] This possibility presupposes the pre-existence of matter to the creation of the thing. In turn, the nature of contingency as such demands that the establishment/realisation of all contingent essences in the external world be preceded by their invalidity in the realm of perpetuity (while in the mind they are eternally preceded by their essential non-existence), argues Mīr Dāmād.[49] Hence, perpetual inception is an indispensable requirement for the establishment of the world, dictated by the innate contingency of the essences: all contingent entities are created in perpetuity.[50]

Conclusion

Mīr Dāmād was a philosopher who focused mainly on one subject – perpetuity and perpetual inception, because he believed the correct understanding of it to be the precondition for the proper understanding

---

46 Mīr Dāmād, *al-Ufuq al-mubīn*, pp. 412–413.

47 Ibid., p. 414; cf. Mīr Dāmād, *al-Qabasāt*, p. 265.

48 Ibid., p. 265.

49 Mīr Dāmād, *al-Ufuq al-mubīn*, pp. 424–425.

50 Mīr Dāmād, 'al-Taqdīsāt', in *Muṣannafāt*, vol. 1, p. 176.

of all, or almost all, other philosophical problems. To put it differently, he held that, in order to properly perceive the world of time and becoming and its relation to the world of eternity, we need to duly apprehend the world of perpetuity and (intelligible) being. On the other hand, according to Mīr Dāmād, a careful and systematic examination of the phenomena of the world of time leads to the affirmation of the existence of the realm of perpetuity, inhabited by the universal natures of things.

It can be said that what is in perpetuity relates to what is in time as the point relates to the line drawn by it,[51] as the traversal motion (*al-ḥaraka al-qaṭʿiyya*) relates to medial motion (*al-ḥaraka al-tawassuṭiyya*),[52] and the flowing instant (*al-ān al-sayyāl*) – to extended contiguous time.[53] Hence, God/the reality of existence can be envisaged in two aspects – 1) as the creator of the intellect(s)/perpetual being(s) (referred to as the point, the spark, the traversal motion and the flowing instant), and 2) as its/their 'mover', i.e. the creator of the temporal manifestation of this/these perpetual beings.[54]

---

[51] This perhaps can be best illustrated by comparing the relation of the First Intellect (described by Mīr Dāmād as the 'prime element of the universal order' (= the world as a whole) and 'the *stoicheion* (*usṭuquss*) of the world of the contingency') to the lower parts of that order with the relation of the point to the line drawn by it, or with the relation of the spark rotating around the centre of the circle, which draws a circle perceived by the sense, to that circle. Cf. Aristotle, *De anima*, I.4, 409a3–6 (but Aristotle does not describe the now as the producer of time). However, Philoponus and Simplicius do: [John Philoponus] *Ioannis Philoponi in physicorum libros quinque posteriores commentaria*, ed. Hieronymos Vitelli (Berlin, 1888), p. 727, ll. 10–23 (the English translation in Philoponus, *On Aristotle Physics 4, 10–14*, tr. Sarah Broadie (London, 2014), pp. 30–31); Simplicius, *In Aristotelis Physicorum libros quattor priores commentaria*, ed. H. Diels (Berlin, 1882), p. 722, ll. 26–34 (the English translation in Simplicius, *On Aristotle Physics 4.1–5, 10–14*, tr. J. O. Urmson (London, 2014), pp. 131–132). Cf. Plotinus, *Enneads* I.7 [54].1.23–28; IV.4 [28].16.23–31; VI.8 [39].18.7–26. See also Dietrich Mahnke, *Unendliche Sphäre und Allmittelpunkt: Beiträge zur Genealogie der matematischen Mystik* (Halle-Saale, 1937), pp. 215–244, in particular 217–221, and the discussion in Andreas Lammer, 'The Elements of Avicenna's Physics: Greek Sources and Arabic Innovations' (PhD thesis, Ludwig-Maximilians-Universität, Munich, 2016), pp. 484–487.

[52] Mīr Dāmād believed that the medial motion 'draws', or 'engraves' (*rāsim*) the traversal motion and sustains its subject (Mīr Dāmād, *al-Qabasāt*, p. 405).

[53] Mīr Dāmād, *al-Qabasāt*, pp. 408–409.

[54] Ibid., p. 409.

From the point of the view of perpetuity, this motion/manifestation is illusory.[55] What really is, is the realm of the immutable perpetual essences, or universal natures, made (= existentiated) by the Creator; the temporal manifestations of these essences enjoy a quasi-existence, similar to the becoming of the reflections of motionless statues in a running stream.

If we consider the thought of Mīr Dāmād from this perspective, he appears to us as primarily a Platonic (and only secondarily – an Avicennan) philosopher, in spite of the ebbs and flows in his attitude towards another great Platonist, Shihāb al-Dīn al-Suhrawardī. This opinion is supported by the sheer number of quotations from Neoplatonic texts, first of all, from the *Uthūlūjiyā* of Pseudo-Aristotle, present in his works. Furthermore, his doctrine of causation, according to which the cause is independent from its effect, in all likelihood is based on Proclus Arabus (i.e. the *Kitāb maḥḍ al-khayr*). Hence, his 'Wisdom of the Right Side' may be considered as an alternative reading of the Plotinus and Proclus Arabi, and, ultimately, as an insightful reflection on the eternal themes of Platonism.[56]

---

[55] Cf. Mīr Dāmād, *Jadhawāt wa mawāqīt*, ed. ʿAlī Awjabī (Tehran, 1380 Sh./2001), pp. 204–205, where the point and the spark are said to resemble the inhabitants of the domain of the perpetuity, such as the immaterial intellects and the souls, and the line and the circle – the beings that inhabit the realm of the time, such as forms and matters, whereas the mover of the point and the spark is said to refer to God's Command (and not God Himself). Cf. also idem, *al-Ufuq al-mubīn*, pp. 481, 552 (where, in both cases, the point is compared with the instant, and the line with time).

[56] Dimitri Gutas has recently described Mīr Dāmād's theory on *ḥudūth dahrī* as a perfect example of what he calls 'paraphilosophy', because 'it has theological intent and motivation, it consists of abstruse arguments of little or no scientific substance, and, from what we know from Mīr Dāmād himself, it was acquired through supra-rational means' (Dimitri Gutas, 'Avicenna and After: The Development of Paraphilosophy. A History of Science Approach', in Abdelkader Al Ghouz, ed., *Islamic Philosophy from the 12th to the 14th Century* (Bonn, 2018), p. 50). To me, this statement serves as regrettable evidence of the shallowness of his positivist approach.

13

Some Aspects of the Reception of Suhrawardī's Philosophy by Mullā Ṣadrā

Christian Jambet

Shiʿi philosophers constructed some of the most famous metaphysical systems in Islamic philosophy under the Safavid dynasty in Persia, especially towards the end of the 10th/16th and throughout the 11th/17th century.[1] Mīr Dāmād (d. 1041/1631) and Mullā Ṣadrā (Ṣadr al-Dīn Muḥammad al-Shīrāzī, d. ca. 1050/1640), for instance, incorporated *ishrāqī* philosophy in their theological and metaphysical works. This paper deals with the reception of *ishrāqī* philosophy by Mullā Ṣadrā.

In the foreword to his glosses on *Ḥikmat al-ishrāq*, Mullā Ṣadrā explains why philosophy is necessary. Metaphysics is the highest happiness because it confers the highest authority. According to Ṣadrā, the ancient philosophers were faithful to the prophetic way whereas his contemporaries who were Peripatetic philosophers made many mistakes in the divine science (i.e., metaphysics). Mullā Ṣadrā said that he had revived the original gnosis of the ancients in his *Four Journeys*[2] and in other works, as did Suhrawardī before him. He spoke in defence of philosophy against the 'common people' who, he said, are unable to understand the truth because 'truth does not suit the intellects of the people (*qawm*) corrupted in their natural dispositions by the internal

[1] See Henry Corbin, *La philosophie Iranienne Islamique aux XVIIe et XVIIIe siècles* (Paris, 1981), and Sajjad H. Rizvi, *Mullā Ṣadrā Shīrāzī: His Life and works and the Sources for Safavid Philosophy* (Oxford, 2007).

[2] Ṣadr al-Dīn Muḥammad al-Shīrāzī (Mullā Ṣadrā), *al-Ḥikma al-mutaʿāliyya fi'l-asfār al-arbaʿa al-ʿaqliyya* (Tehran, 1397/1976). Henceforth abridged as *Asfār*.

diseases that cannot be cured by the healers of the soul.'[3] Mullā Ṣadrā claimed that whoever tried to acquire knowledge of the divine world (*ḥikma ilāhiyya*) had first to read Avicenna and Suhrawardī. Nevertheless, Mullā Ṣadrā credited himself with the foundation of the highest science in his *magnum opus*, the *Four Journeys*. However, even though he held Suhrawardī in high esteem, Mullā Ṣadrā was not a strict *ishrāqī*. In fact, he did not consider himself in any way an *ishrāqī*. Reading and explaining Suhrawardī is necessary, Mullā Ṣadra believed, not because one should accept his every word and thought but for the exegetic distance we should observe between him and us. Suhrawardī is a necessary step in the philosophical journey, but he is just a step and not the final end.

Henry Corbin was the pioneer in studies on Mullā Ṣadrā's commentary on *Ḥikmat al-ishrāq*, translating a significant part of it into French. The author of the present article edited and published the translation after Corbin's death,[4] and would respectfully suggest that the magnificent picture drawn by Henry Corbin has to be slightly altered. The metaphysical continuity between *ishrāqī* philosophy and Mullā Ṣadrā's metaphysics as depicted by Corbin needs to be reconsidered. According to Corbin, Mullā Ṣadrā's exegesis in his commentaries of *Ḥikmat al-ishrāq* fits in the continuous tradition of 'oriental' philosophy,[5] but this is not so manifestly evident to us. Of course, Suhrawardī inspired Mullā Ṣadrā to adopt many themes in ethics. His vocabulary, his esoteric notion of *ishrāq* and his illuminative knowledge influenced many of Mullā Ṣadrā's works, but Mullā Ṣadrā never considered himself a disciple or a reviver of Suhrawardī's philosophy. Rather, Mullā Ṣadrā considered *ishrāqī* philosophy an esoteric teaching whose meaning had to be disclosed by him according to the true signification of *walāya*.

---

[3] Mullā Ṣadrā, *Taʿliqāt ʿalā Sharḥ Ḥikmat al-ishrāq*, in Suhrawardī, *Ḥikmat al-ishrāq bā Sharḥ-e Quṭb al-Dīn Shīrāzī wa Taʿliqāt Ṣadr al-Dīn Muḥammad Shīrāzī* (Tehran, 1392/1972), vol. 2, *Manṭiq*, pp. 5–6.

[4] Shihāb al-Dīn Yahyā al-Suhrawardī, *Le Livre de la sagesse orientale*. Kitâb Ḥikmat al-Ishrâq. *Commentaires de Qoṭboddîn Shîrâzî et Mollâ Ṣadrâ* Shîrâzî, tr. Henry Corbin, ed. Christian Jambet (Lagrasse, 1986).

[5] Henry Corbin, *En Islam Iranien. Aspects spirituels et philosophiques: Sohrawardî et les Platoniciens de Perse* (Paris, 1971), vol. 2, pp. 346–381.

This is not the place to consider now the numerous quotations and allusions concerning *ishrāqī* philosophy in the works of Mullā Ṣadrā. Instead, this will be an endeavour to demonstrate that the interpretation of *ishrāqī* doctrine by Mullā Ṣadrā may be described as an exegesis which places Suhrawardī's theses in a new metaphysical domain. Therefore, the focus here will be on Ṣadrā's commentary on *Ḥikmat al-ishrāq*. It consists of glosses on the earlier literal explanation (*tafsīr*) of this synthetic book by Quṭb al-Dīn al-Shīrāzī (d. 710/1311). Unlike this well-known *ishrāqī* commentator, Mullā Ṣadrā often moves far away from the main theses of Suhrawardī's doctrine. He translates *ishrāqī* theses into his own ontology and eschatology. On the three main subjects of metaphysics — the nature of being, the universe and the soul—Mullā Ṣadrā disagrees with Suhrawardī. Before we briefly examine their disagreement over ontology, cosmology and psychology, we shall refer to Ṣadrā's reinterpretation of human perfection, the human caliphate of God.

A New Interpretation of the Human Caliphate of God

It is possible that Mullā Ṣadrā commented on *Ḥikmat al-ishrāq* for the following important reason: freedom of intellect is achieved through assimilation with the divine lights. It is the foundation of the authority given by God to the Perfect Man. The authority of the Perfect Man rests on his mystical knowledge. Only the true possessor of the supreme knowledge is free, absorbed in God and qualified to govern the community of believers.[6]

In his foreword to his commentary on Suhrawardī's *Ḥikmat al-ishrāq*, Mullā Ṣadrā listed his reasons for examining the book which exactly coincide with the traditional philosophical aims. As Mullā Ṣadrā says at the beginning of *Four Journeys*, 'Philosophy is the way to perfection (*istikmāl*) for the human soul through the acquisition of knowledge of the true realities.'[7] That is why experiential knowledge of

[6] See al-Suhrawardī, *Ḥikmat al-ishrāq* § 5, in *The Philosophy of Illumination. A New Critical Edition of the Text of Ḥikmat al-ishrāq with English Translation, Notes, Commentary and Introduction*, ed. John Walbridge and Hossein Ziai (Provo, UT, 1999), p. 3.

[7] Ṣadrā, *Asfār*, vol. 1, p. 23.

the intelligible world is the highest happiness. Such a definition of philosophy comes, obviously, from Avicenna.[8] Coming into possession of such knowledge, one acquires supreme authority and the highest rank (which, according to Mullā Ṣadrā, is that of the prophet or the imam). The most elevated knowledge is in attendance on the higher lights in the Kingdom (*malakūt*). The goal of that perfect knowledge is the true happiness of the afterlife.

Obviously, in his introduction Mullā Ṣadrā identifies the most educated philosopher, whose intellect is similar to the divine light as depicted by Suhrawardī, with the prophetic guide, Abraham, the possessor of the highest authority. Nevertheless, it seems that the levels of both prophet and imam are superior to that of the philosopher. A very interesting gloss on the governing light of the human species, on the archangelic light named Gabriel, describes the ascension and the rank of the prophet. As we know, what is said of the prophet can be said of the imam as well. Mullā Ṣadrā comments on what Suhrawardī says about Gabriel. The angel is 'the proximate father among the mighty lords of the Kingdom of Dominance. He is *Ravān-Bakhsh*, the Holy Spirit, the bestower of knowledge and certainty, the giver of life and virtue.'[9] The governor of man's soul or spirit does not belong to the lowest immaterial intellects which govern natural species. The dominating light which is the Holy Spirit rules over the pleroma of all other intellectual substances. He stands at the top of the angelic world, which is the intelligible world. The Holy Spirit, according Mullā Ṣadrā, is the first and universal Intellect, not the tenth intellect as in Avicenna's cosmology.[10] Accordingly, the Perfect Man, either a prophet or an imam, is able to ascend to a station situated beyond the stations of governing angels. The Perfect Man ascends to the intelligible world and receives a rank situated above the angelic world. He reaches the station of the universal Intellect, the Holy Spirit. Just as with the first Intellect, there is no intermediary between the Perfect Man and God. That is the special experience of Muhammad during his *miʿrāj*.[11]

---

[8] Ibn Sīnā (Avicenna), *al-Shifāʾ*, *al-Manṭiq*, *al-Madkhal*, ed. I. Madkour (Cairo, 1955), p. 12.

[9] Al-Suhrawardī, *Ḥikmat al-ishrāq*, ed. Walbridge and Ziai, p. 132, § 210,

[10] Mullā Ṣadrā, *Taʿliqāt ʿalā Sharḥ Ḥikmat al-ishrāq*, vol. 4, pp. 268–269.

[11] Ibid., p. 269.

Finally, Mullā Ṣadrā says that spiritual ascension of the Prophet is the pattern of human destiny. The human soul is freed by philosophical practice from corporeal links, and it rises up to all upper levels of the psychic life and to all intellectual degrees. That is the substantial motion (*al-ḥaraka al-jawhariyya*) of the human soul. When its ascent is completed, man's soul unifies with the first universal Intellect, and the rational soul becomes an active intellect. By the unification with the intelligible world, the rational soul becomes an intellective world and not only an acquired intellect.[12]

In this ultimate station, the Perfect Man abandons the potentiality of existence, he becomes a truly divinised being, he is actually free and lives the necessary divine life. That is the station of the 'ultimate proximity to God'. Sometimes Mullā Ṣadrā equates the *miʿrāj* of Imam ʿAlī b. Abī Ṭālib with Muhammad's ascension. Of course, Muhammad, the Perfect Man, returns to the human condition, to the 'station of human nature', just as the Platonic philosopher does upon his return to the Cave. Through the mediation of the first Intellect, the Holy Spirit, he is now able to give the people valid instructions. The divinised philosopher, entrusted to govern souls, is now the authentic gnostic (*ʿārif*), and this authentic gnostic is the Prophet Muhammad or his successor, the imam in his double mission, contemplation and pedagogical practice. When the time of legislative prophecy comes to an end, the master of contemplation, the educator of the elite, is the immaculate imam. The ancient pillars of wisdom, such as Plato and Empedocles inter alia, are placed in second rank, for they are conceived as students who receive their wisdom from the prophets and imams. The ancient sages of Persia have gone. So, philosophy and the esoteric teaching of the imams pursue the same goal, namely to guide mankind to its perfection. The Sufi Pole (*quṭb*) is assimilated to the esoteric figure of the imam.

Mullā Ṣadrā's Critical Approach to *Ishrāqī* Ontology

Suhrawardī is well known for his criticism of Avicenna's doctrine of existence and quiddity, *wujūd* and *māhiya*, according to which existence always has the same signification whether it is said of a

[12] Ibid., p. 270.

quality, for instance blackness, or of a substance, for example a man or a horse. Existence taken in the most general sense is an empty concept typically used as a predicate and hence it adds nothing to a universal quiddity. That is because all predicates, whatever they be, are abstract representations and so have no reality *in concreto*. The quiddity of Zayd is Zayd himself, and to say that Zayd exists is not different from saying that Zayd is Zayd. The concept of existence is a pure abstraction, a point of view on the concrete existent.[13]

According to Mullā Ṣadrā, we have to reverse all these propositions. Every existence is a concrete singularity, a singular degree in the intensity of being determining the reality of the essence. More precisely, the essential nature of an existent is its own existence; it is its own act of being. Quiddity is only the 'umbra'[14] of this act of being. When Mullā Ṣadrā comments on Suhrawardī's theses about 'the abstractions of the intellect' in the third discourse of the first part of *Ḥikmat al-ishrāq*, he demonstrates very clearly the nature of the misunderstanding. In accordance with the theory of the pre-eminence of the act of being, he says that existence is a concrete ipseity (*huwiyya ʿayniyya*). Common existence which is abstracted from real existents is only a representation and imitation (*ḥikāya*). It is impossible to grasp the concrete act of being by a representative thought, because the act of being is not similar to a common predicate. Mullā Ṣadrā says: 'According to our theses, truly the concept of existence has priority, because it possesses reality. The existence of blackness exists by essence, even though the blackness united with it exists by accident and not by essence.'[15]

In his commentary on the first propositions of the metaphysical part of *Ḥikmat al-ishrāq*, Mullā Ṣadrā dismisses Avicenna's treatment of existence and quiddity. In addition, he also dismisses the *ishrāqī* notion of existence.[16] Although it is not possible now to discuss in

---

13 Al-Suhrawardī, *Ḥikmat al-ishrāq*, ed. Walbridge and Ziai, p. 45, § 56.

14 In Latin, 'shadow'. In astronomy, refers to the innermost and darkest part of the shadow cast by a celestial body (ed.).

15 Mullā Ṣadrā, *Taʿliqāt ʿalā Sharḥ Ḥikmat al-ishrāq*, vol. 2, p. 245.

16 See Christian Jambet, *The Act of Being. The Philosophy of Revelation in Mullā Sadrā* (New York, 2006), pp. 77–78.

detail all the consequences of this interpretation, we must examine the most important of its implications. Suhrawardī says that 'anything in existence that requires no definition or explanation is evident. Since there is nothing more evident than light, there is nothing less in need of definition.'[17] In his masterly commentary, Mullā Ṣadrā proves first that both terms, apparition or evidence (*ẓuhūr*) and being (*wujūd*), have the same meaning. Sometimes we understand an intellectual concept. Sometimes we understand why something that is evident or existing is concretely true. Sometimes we understand that it is about the existing lights, sometimes that it is about the metaphysical nature of revelation and being. Consequently, the word 'light' in *ishrāqī* vocabulary means being. Mullā Ṣadrā says:

> All the things which have been said or will be said about being, all the questions and all the conclusions, for example, the simplicity, absence of need in definition, impossibility of a definition and of a description, affirmation of intensity or weakness, priority or posteriority, being the pure good and its contrary the pure evil [. . .] all of these predicates and the other modes of being are also predicated of light.[18]

Then Mullā Ṣadrā analyses the way in which Suhrawardī speaks about light: Suhrawardī prefers the word 'light' to the word 'being'. He limits the use of the term 'light' to the necessary being, to God, to the being of the intellects and to the being of the souls and their faculties of knowledge, and also to the visible qualities of the luminous bodies. On the other hand, Suhrawardī says that bodies, bodily qualities and bodily aspects are 'the obscure things' (*al-ghawāsiq*). The natural body is called *barzakh* due to its medial situation between intelligible light and material obscurity. The body is hidden to itself. Neither evidence, nor an apparition, nor any knowledge or consciousness is present in the body. So each body is inexistent. The equation between being and knowledge or self-consciousness means that the body cannot belong to the field of being.[19]

---

17 Al-Suhrawardī, *Ḥikmat al-ishrāq*, ed. Walbridge and Ziai, p. 76, § 107.

18 Mullā Ṣadrā, *Taʿliqāt ʿalā Sharḥ Ḥikmat al-ishrāq*, vol. 4, p. 6.

19 Mullā Ṣadrā, *Taʿliqāt ʿalā Sharḥ Ḥikmat al-ishrāq*, p. 7.

Mullā Ṣadrā approves of such a definition of the body. He often says that the sensible world (*al-dunyā*) is the realm of evil, of privation, suffering and Hell. The dualistic meaning of conflict between corporal inexistence and intelligible immaterial being is a major trend of his ethics and eschatology.[20] Nevertheless, Mullā Ṣadrā has inherited Ibn ʿArabī's conception of being.[21] He cannot agree with Suhrawardī's dualistic definition of light and obscurity. Being is principally God Himself, and being is by essence necessity and freedom. Just as existence is the Real (*al-ḥaqq*), so all existences proceeding from the Real are forms of reality which are variously powerful, intense or weak in their mode of existence. As a result of the body's unity, it participates in being and must be said to be existent. Light, being, unity and necessity are all the Real, which is the essence of God. And so, Mullā Ṣadrā dismisses radical dualistic theses while using the ontology he inherited from Ibn ʿArabī rather than Suhrawardī's definitions. Mullā Ṣadrā substitutes his doctrine of being for the *ishrāqī* metaphysics of light and darkness. Nevertheless, he preserves the dualist view which discriminates between the world of lights and the enigmatic darkness of matter. He writes that in its reality being is full light, even if some of the beings are mixed with non-existences and potentialities. The substitution of the language of ontology for *ishrāqī* doctrine allows Mullā Ṣadrā to reconcile Suhrawardī's thought with the most important inspiration that he received from the writings of Ibn ʿArabī.

The Conflict of Philosophy with Religious Dogma about the Eternity of the World

Suhrawardī's cosmology is faithful to the doctrine of the *falāsifa* about the eternity of the world. He summarises his thesis at the end of the third discourse of the second part of *Ḥikmat al-ishrāq*, saying that 'the Light of lights is the cause of existence and the cause of the permanence of all existents, and so are also the dominating lights.'[22] Hence, the

[20] Mullā Ṣadrā, *Tafsīr al-Qur'ān al-karīm*, ed. Muḥammad Khājavī (Qum, 1361 Sh./1982), vol. 6, pp. 142–143; idem, *Asfār*, vol. 6, p. 144 ff.

[21] Mullā Ṣadrā, *Taʿliqāt ʿalā Sharḥ Ḥikmat al-ishrāq*, vol. 4, pp. 27–29.

[22] Al-Suhrawardî, *Ḥikmat al-ishrāq*, ed. Walbridge and Ziai, p. 123, § 193.

Intellects are eternal. 'Since the celestial bodies are neither generated nor corrupted, their managing lights never depart from them, but, on the contrary, govern them perpetually.'[23] Hence the celestial souls are eternal. In his commentary, Mullā Ṣadrā reminds us of the conflict of this thesis, asserting the eternity of the world (which assertion is congruent to Suhrawardī's theory of causality), with the dogma of all religions: 'For it is a general belief in all true revealed religious laws (*sharā'i'*) that we must maintain the world's creation in accordance with the *ḥadīth* "God existed and nothing was existent with Him".'[24]

Philosophers maintain, just as Suhrawardī does, that the intellects, celestial souls, celestial bodies and universal essences of the elements are eternal. In turn, the revealed religions and Plato agree that the universe is created and that it will perish. Mullā Ṣadrā says that he is guided by the doctrine of the prophets and imams. Hence, according to him, the metaphysical interpretation of the world's creation must be congruent with the religious tenets of the prophetic discourse whilst it also contradicts the *falāsifa* and the *ishrāqī* philosophy. The subtle exposition of the problem appearing in an important gloss of Mullā Ṣadrā combines a range of arguments, such as a critical approach to the problem of existence and essence, the distinction between the intellects and other beings, the status of the wisdom of the ancient Greeks, the authoritative gnosis inherited from Ibn 'Arabī, and the refutation of the world's eternity by the essential movement in corporeal natures. The result of such a combination of arguments is the rejection of Suhrawardi's cosmology and his theological teaching about the destiny of created beings.[25]

According to Mullā Ṣadrā, when we ask if a thing can exist forever or comes to be in time, our question is about the act of being and not about the specific quiddity. Time or eternity is nothing by itself but is a determination of the act of being. Mullā Ṣadrā does not consider there to be an intermediate degree such as the perennial duration (*dahr*) between time (*zamān*) and eternity (*sarmad*). Hence, he has to distinguish the everlasting existent from the temporal existent, without

---

23 Ibid.

24 Mullā Ṣadrā, *Ta'liqāt 'alā Sharḥ Ḥikmat al-ishrāq*, vol. 4, p. 207.

25 Mullā Ṣadrā, *Ta'liqāt 'alā Sharḥ Ḥikmat al-ishrāq*, pp. 208–213.

any resort to the intermediate degree, as it was done by Mīr Dāmād.[26] All corporeal beings are differentiated into species by their specific form which is their nature. Every nature 'flows' into the body and is its principle of movement and rest. The movement's substratum is matter. Of course, we should admit that the concept of movement is equivocal. The term 'movement' refers to changes in the attributes of a substance and also refers to the substantial or essential movement of the substance itself. There is nothing ambiguous or subject to misunderstanding in the use of the term 'movement'. Essential movement is a concept inherited from Plotinus. Essential movement is the perpetual renewal of each nature. The accidental movements and the final and natural rest result from the nature of the corporeal substance, and so they are determined by its essential movement. To support his philosophical treatment of nature, Mullā Ṣadrā appeals to three authorities, quoting from Zeno of Citium,[27] Ibn ʿArabī and, of course, the Qur'an. All these demonstrations and quotations, and also the important *Risāla fī ḥudūth al-ʿālam*, allow Mullā Ṣadrā to summarise his thesis in few words:

> The corporeal world is never deprived of an origination (*ḥudūth*) and of corruption without interruption. But the divine world and the world of the incorporeal forms do not pertain to anything but God. They are the radiant lights of the Real, his attributes and his beautiful names and the forms existing in the knowledge and the decree of God.[28]

In Ṣadrā's cosmology, there is no place for *dahr*, perpetuity. However, we find there three modes of being and three degrees of reality. First, the divine world, including the essence of God and the intelligible world. This world is eternal. Secondly, we find the world of nature, including all the corporeal substances, namely the elementary and mineral bodies, the corporeal mode of being of the vegetative and of the animal forms and the natural part of the human being. This

---

[26] See Mathieu Terrier, 'De l'éternité ou de la nouveauté du monde : Parcours d'un problème philosophique d'Athènes à Ispahan', *Journal Asiatique*, 299 (2011), pp. 369–421.

[27] Al-Shahrastānī, *Kitāb al-milāl wa'l-niḥal*, tr. Jean Jolivet and Guy Monnot as *Livre des religions et des sectes* (Paris, 1986), vol. 2, pp. 239–244.

[28] Mullā Ṣadrā, *Taʿliqāt ʿalā Sharḥ Ḥikmat al-ishrāq*, vol. 4, p. 228.

world is temporal and temporary. Mullā Ṣadrā says that the world of bodies is continuously annihilating and passing from its present abode to the realm of rest. The essential movement proves that any kind of corporeal body, even if it is a celestial sphere, is a vanishing reality. It leaves no place for the celestial theology or a religious devotion to the world of stars. We will see that this point is of great importance in the interpretation of *ʿālam al-mithāl*. The essential movement has a goal, which is the afterlife, the world of Resurrection, that will manifest itself at the end of time, corresponding to the events of the Hour announced in Qurʾanic verses.

Between these two worlds, we find the *barzakh* (literally 'screen'), the isthmus between *al-mulk*, the sensible world of nature, and *al-malakūt* and *al-jabarūt*, the two stages of the intelligible world. It is not really an ontologically distinct world, even if it is invisible and separate from the inferior matter. It is the intermediate stage of the spiritual journey of all psychic realities. In the rational soul, every inferior soul finds its final stage of development. Hence, there we find rational souls, including the souls of the spheres and the lowest degree of man's rational soul. The rational and psychic mode of being is a double one. Rational souls have two dimensions or aspects. In the first one, they look to the upper world and are permanent. In the second, they look at the lower world and are transient. All Mullā Ṣadrā's ethical recommendations are given in view of this.

Of course, the status of the Intellects and the intelligible world is ambiguous. In one aspect, the Intellects are distinct from the essence of God, for they are emanations from the pure and everlasting absolute and the necessary Being. But, in another aspect, the Intellects are eternal for they draw their own eternity from God's eternity. Mullā Ṣadrā thinks that God does not *make* them permanent beings. Rather, they are permanent by themselves because they simultaneously vanish in God's essence by their love and are eternally permanent by their immateriality. The intelligible world proceeds from divine knowledge which is an attribute of God, united with God's essence. The intelligible world is the world of God's decree. It encompasses all the eternal forms and does not belong to the temporal universe. Unlike Mīr Dāmād who preserved the absolute One in its eternity (*sarmad*) and thought that the intelligible world was everlastingly coming to being in perpetuity (*dahr*), Mullā Ṣadrā unites the essence of God and the divine decree in the eternal divine world. He draws a strange correspondence between five denominations, which, to him, denote the same thing, namely the intelligible world: the cognitive forms of God's knowledge (wrongly attributed to Aristotle), divine archetypal forms (according to Plato), the divine attributes (according to the Ashʿarīs), the states or modes of being (according to the Muʿtazilīs), the divine names and eternal essences (according to Ibn ʿArabī).

As we can see, Mullā Ṣadrā's cosmology deals only with the world of nature. The intelligible world is the subject of metaphysics and theology. Psychology deals with the afterlife of rational souls, which is an ethical and eschatological subject dependent on comprehension of the Qurʾan and *ḥadīth*. Mullā Ṣadrā puts forward his positions and enlists his references, the ancients, the prophets, even Aristotle, to argue against Suhrawardī and the *falāsifa*. We cannot agree with Henry Corbin when he associates the *ishrāqiyyūn* with Mullā Ṣadrā against Avicenna's doctrine of the world's eternity.[29]

A New Definition of the Human Soul

Mullā Ṣadrā's rejection of Suhrawardī's concept of the rational soul stems from the fact that they were not speaking about the same reality. They defined the human soul in different ways and ascribed to it different properties. The difference in the definition of the soul is best seen in Mullā Ṣadrā's comments on two important topics: the immateriality of the soul and the psychic life before the body; and, the destiny of the soul in the afterlife and the so-called 'imaginal world'.

We know that, according to Suhrawardī, it is impossible to give a definition of the immaterial light which is the soul, including its existence before the body. Suhrawardī points to the simplicity and the singularity of each human soul in support of his thesis. The existence of a singular ego and the indistinct existence of all souls before the body are both inconsistent assertions. If all human souls constituted a unique universal soul before their government of bodies, they would not be able to divide themselves among the material bodies because only bodies are divisible. Suhrawardī was unwilling to accept the concept of

---

[29] Corbin, *Le Livre de la sagesse orientale*, p. 569.

the universal soul, which idea originated with Plotinus. Should the human soul exist before the body, the governing lights would lose their original singularity. Also, if souls could exist in an indistinct way in the universal soul, they would never multiply as they do after their descent into the bodily fortresses. Both states, before and after the body, the oneness of the soul and the multiplicity of souls, are inconsistent with the theory of the pre-existence of the soul to the body. As the immaterial souls cannot initially be a common or universal soul, they cannot be multiple. Therefore, Suhrawardī says that 'since they can neither be many nor one before managing the fortresses, they cannot exist.'[30] The impossibility of the existence of the immaterial soul would be a logical result of its assumed pre-existence.

In his commentaries, Mullā Ṣadrā does not assume, as Suhrawardī seems to do, that all individual existences of the human soul belong to one unique species. He also does not accept the idea that a soul, from the time it becomes linked to the embryo and until the time of its perfection, could remain at the same degree, having one substance or essence. The human soul is perfect through the perfection of its intelligible principle. It is temporal and subject to becoming when it lives as a corporeal substance, and it is perpetual and permanent in its afterlife. What depends on the disposition of body is only the natural condition of the soul. If the body were a condition of the soul's life, we could not imagine anything other than the soul's death when the managing or the government of the body ceases. The refutation by Suhrawardī of the pre-existence of the human soul endangers three important principles: 1) the invincible diversity of human souls predetermined in God's decree; 2) the modulated being of the changing/'flowing' soul; and 3) the soul's afterlife. One must note the complete disagreement between Mullā Ṣadrā's doctrine, founded on the priority of existence, and Suhrawardī's doctrine, founded on the specific immutable nature of each being.[31] In his commentaries on *Ḥikmat al-ishrāq*, Mullā Ṣadrā provides many arguments against Suhrawardī which are reproduced and developed in a chapter of his

---

30 Al-Suhrawardī, *Ḥikmat al-ishrāq*, ed. Walbridge and Ziai, p. 132, § 211.

31 Ṣadrā, *Ta'liqāt 'alā Sharḥ Ḥikmat al-ishrāq*, vol. 4, pp. 270–274.

masterwork, the *Asfār*, written after the commentaries.[32] His main thesis is: the rational soul is corporeal in its origination, and spiritual in its permanence. Hence, we can agree with the philosophers who assert the link between soul and body. It can be said that the rational soul passes through certain corporeal states before it actualises its rational power. However, in fact there is no link between soul and body, for corporeal existence is a transient state in the development of the soul. During its vegetative and animal life, the human soul lives as the body does, while in its essence it is an incorporeal and immaterial substance.

The foundation of Mullā Ṣadrā's doctrine is the substantial movement, the intensification in the category of substance. In *Asfār* he writes: 'The human soul originates as a body and during its government of a body. It is spiritual in her permanence and her intellection. Its government in the bodies is corporeal, but its intellection of its own essence and of its Creator's essence is spiritual.'[33]

The pattern of the soul's destiny is the existential permanent evolution from the immaterial intelligible origin to the immaterial return to the first Intellect, and then to God. That is the reason why Mullā Ṣadrā has many objections to Suhrawardī's arguments. All of them are damning. Of course, their credibility depends on the credibility of Ṣadrā's exegesis. For instance, Mullā Ṣadrā sees the proof of the soul's fall and ascent in several Qurʾanic verses (2: 36, 38; 7: 29–30; 19: 71–72; 95: 4–6; 102: 1–8). And he interprets some words of the Prophet in the prophetic *ḥadīth* as a proof of the pre-existence of the human soul, for instance: 'Men are mines similar to gold and silver mines' and, of course, 'I was a Prophet when Adam was between water and clay'. He also discerns such proof in the *ḥadīth*: 'We are what came before and what comes after.'

The most important philosophical proof given by an authoritative author, according to Mullā Ṣadrā, is found in the *Theology* of Pseudo-Aristotle. Mullā Ṣadrā comments on numerous quotations from the *Theology*. He thinks that Plotinus's doctrine, ascribed to Aristotle, is the true exegesis of the teaching of the Prophet and the imams

---

[32] Ṣadrā, *Asfār*, vol. 8, pp. 398–434, especially pp. 406–409. See also *Asfār*, vol. 8, pp. 385–397. *Taʿliqāt ʿalā Sharḥ Ḥikmat al-ishrāq*, vol. 4, pp. 274–285.

[33] Ṣadrā, *Asfār*, vol. 8, p. 402.

regarding the soul. The purpose of such an exegesis is to prove that the human soul is the rational soul that it descends to the sensible world.[34] Hence, as Mullā Ṣadrā writes in one of his glosses: 'Human souls have a mode of being in the world of Intellect and a mode of being in the sensible world, and their mode of being up there is not [identical with] their mode of being down here.'[35] One cannot provide a better proof that Ṣadrā's doctrine of the human soul is incompatible with Suhrawardī's doctrine. Suhrawardī dismisses Plotinus's understanding of Plato's doctrine of the soul, while Mullā Ṣadrā bases his interpretation of the true discourse, that of the Prophet and the imams, on it.

The transformation of the concept of the soul has great consequences for eschatology. Were it possible to go into detail, we would note that Mullā Ṣadrā disagrees with the earliest commentators concerning the interpretation of the imagination and imaginative forms.[36] Suhrawardī's statements on the reward in the afterlife are well known. As for the ascetics and 'those who have attained an intermediate bliss', he says they will escape from their corporeal bodies to the world of suspended images whose locus of manifestation is one of the celestial bodies. The damned are punished in a similar way: 'They will possess shadows of suspended forms in accordance with their moral qualities.'[37] Suhrawardī calls the locus of these suspended forms 'the world of immaterial figures' (*ashbāḥ*), and he adds: 'The resurrection of bodies,[38] the apparitions of the Lord, and all promises of prophecies find their reality through it.'[39]

---

[34] Ṣadrā, *Ta'liqāt 'alā Sharḥ Ḥikmat al-ishrāq*, vol. 4, pp. 278, 282–285. See 'Theology', in *Plotinus apud Arabes, Theologia Aristotelis et fragmenta quae supersunt*, ed. and introd., 'A. Badawi (Cairo, 1955), pp. 35–37, 38, 84, 87.

[35] Mullā Ṣadrā, *Ta'liqāt 'alā Sharḥ Ḥikmat al-ishrāq*, vol. 4, p. 277.

[36] Al-Suhrawardī, *Ḥikmat al-Ishrāq*, ed. Walbridge and Ziai, pp. 148–150, §§ 244–248; Mullā Ṣadrā, *Ta'liqāt 'alā Sharḥ Ḥikmat al-ishrāq*, vol. 4, pp. 408–447.

[37] Al-Suhrawardī, *Ḥikmat al-ishrāq*, ed. Walbridge and Ziai, pp. 148–149, §§ 244–245.

[38] We read *ajsād* and not *amthāl* as it is read in the Walbridge and Ziai edition.

[39] Al-Suhrawardī, *Ḥikmat al-ishrāq*, ed. Walbridge and Ziai, p. 150, § 248.

Conclusion

First, Suhrawardī seems to have placed in the same world the forms seen in mirrors, the forms perceived by the imagination and the separated forms of reward and punishment. Mullā Ṣadrā dismisses Suhrawardī's fanciful interest in forms seen in mirrors, an interest very close to the mysterious and horrific feeling of the modern writer, Jorge Luis Borges, referring to the Islamic conception of images. Forms seen in mirrors exist concretely but by accident, not by themselves.[40] In this way, Suhrawardī's conception of the afterlife and imaginal world depends on the astral religion of the ancient Greeks. Mullā Ṣadrā cannot agree with such an astral theology, for the celestial bodies are vanishing substances. An Islamic doctrine of reward and punishment cannot easily integrate ancient forms of devotion to the eternal celestial world into the dogma of man's future perennial destiny as Suhrawardī does in *Ḥikmat al-ishrāq*. Mullā Ṣadrā says:

> You know yet that forms which are present to the soul in the afterlife do not subsist by something belonging to the external bodies. The soul does not need any locus of manifestation that might be separate from it, as mirror or other similar things are. It does not have any need of that for the contemplation of forms which belong to the soul.[41]

Thus, Mullā Ṣadrā dismisses the *ishrāqī* celestial religion in its entirety, reminding us that those celestial bodies belong to the inferior sensible world and that celestial bodies do not differ from elementary bodies in their transient nature. Hence, we must dismiss the external existence of the imaginal world that is not situated inside the human soul.

Since Mullā Ṣadrā's lengthy and detailed glosses on the fifth discourse in the third section of the second part of *Ḥikmat al-ishrāq* are more explicit than the brief corresponding chapter in *Asfār*, it is necessary to be brief. The main sources Mullā Ṣadrā uses are the *Epistles of the Brethren of Purity*, Abū Ḥāmid al-Ghazālī and, curiously, Avicenna. However, the pattern of his conception of imaginal world is mostly borrowed from Plotinus and perhaps from Proclus's analysis of Plato's

[40] Mullā Ṣadrā, *Taʿliqāt ʿalā Ṣharḥ Ḥikmat al-ishrāq*, vol. 4, pp. 337–338.

[41] Mullā Ṣadrā, *Taʿliqāt ʿalā Sharḥ Ḥikmat al-ishrāq*, p. 416.

famous symbol of the line in the *Republic*. In his commentary on a gloss written by Quṭb al-Dīn al-Shīrāzī, Mullā Ṣadrā quotes some relevant passages from the *Theology* of [Pseudo-]Aristotle.[42] According to this paraphrase of Plotinus, Mullā Ṣadrā discerns three degrees in human reality: natural man whose faculties subsist by his body is the image of the median man, the psychic man, whose faculties, in turn, are the umbra and the image of intelligible man. Mullā Ṣadrā exalts the light of so-called Aristotle (in fact Plotinus) and his intelligence. He says that his rank in the luminous *walāya* is very high, and so Plotinus with Plato and Socrates can be treated as authoritative authors by Shiʿi believers. The world of imaginal forms which is the world of the afterlife is nothing other than the second man, the psychic man, corresponding to the second degree of cosmic being, the psychic world.

In conclusion, we have to say that Mullā Ṣadrā read Suhrawardī for himself, with the purpose of establishing his own doctrine firmly and without any concession to his illustrious predecessor. Of course, he writes with the aim of giving a place to Suhrawardī in his programme of gnosis and philosophy and he defends *ishrāqī* philosophy against the numerous attacks launched by the Shiʿi clerics of his time. His commentary on *Ḥikmat al-ishrāq* is an important element in his system of defence and an illustration of the real *walāya*, including metaphysics and Platonic gnosis. Mullā Ṣadrā has to defend his own philosophy against those he considers to be ignorant *fuqahā'* and bigots. So, he interprets *ishrāqī* philosophy in terms of his own doctrine, and he claims that his interpretation is the true meaning and the perennial truth taught by Suhrawardī and his disciples.

---

[42] Ibid., pp. 339–341.

14

A *Symphonia* of Shiʿism, Philosophy and Sufism from the Late Safavid Period: Quṭb al-Dīn Ashkivarī's Epistle on the Imaginal World (written in 1077/1667)

Mathieu Terrier

Safavid Iran, in the 10th to 11th/16th to 17th centuries, was the centre of three major evolutions in the intellectual history of Islam: the revival of the Imāmī Shiʿi tradition, with an increase of activity in the fields of *ḥadīth* and *tafsīr*; the renaissance of philosophy, through the schools of Iṣfahān and Shīrāz; and the mutation of Iranian Sufism, with the repression of the Sunni-minded brotherhoods on the one hand, and the widespread adoption and Shiʿitisation of a certain Sufi heritage on the other.[1] Quṭb al-Dīn Ashkivarī (d. between 1088 and 1095/1677 and 1684), who was active during the reign of Shah Sulaymān (r. 1077–1105/1666–1694), is a complex figure in this threefold process, being at the same time a traditionist (*muḥaddith*) and a member of the Shiʿi clergy, even if at a middle rank, a populariser of philosophy rather than being himself an original philosopher, and an open defender of Sufism, if not himself a Sufi.[2] Sent to Iṣfahān in his early youth, he was the pupil of the famous philosophers and theologians Shaykh Bahāʾī (d. 1030/1621) and Mīr Dāmād (d. 1040/1631); but he had to return early to his hometown of Lāhījān, in Gīlān, to assume the role of *shaykh al-Islām*. He seems to have spent most of his life there, away from the main centres of power. His own intellectual production dates from 1070/1660.

---

[1] See A. J. Newman, *Safavid Iran. Rebirth of a Persian Empire* (London and New York, 2006). On the school of Iṣfahān, see now Janis Esots, *Patterns of Wisdom: The Philosophical School of Isfahan and the Gnostic of Shiraz* (London, 2021).

[2] On this author, see Mathieu Terrier, *Histoire de la sagesse et philosophie shiʿite.* L'Aimé des cœurs *de Quṭb al-Dīn Ashkevarī* (Paris, 2016).

Ashkivarī's most famous work, the *Maḥbūb al-qulūb* (first written in 1077/1667, then completed in 1088/1677 or after), is an encyclopedia of all the sages from Adam to Mīr Dāmād;[3] it should be regarded as the last great opus in a genre that first appeared in the 4th/10th century, immediately after the Greek-Arabic *translatio studiorum*, and the first to be composed from an explicitly Shiʿi point of view.[4] Noteworthily, his final notice on Mīr Dāmād was the major source for Henry Corbin's pioneer study on the 'third master' (*al-muʿallim al-thālith*, Mīr Dāmād's epithet), and, significantly, of his founding of the 'Iṣfahān school of philosophy' paradigm.[5] Under the name of al-Sharīf al-Lāhījī, Ashkivarī was also the author of a commentary on the Qur'an consisting mainly of Imāmī *ḥadīth*s or *akhbār* translated into Persian.[6] His third work of importance is entitled *Fānūs al-khayāl fī irā'at ʿālam al-mithāl*, also referred to as *al-Risāla al-mithāliyya*, written in 1077/1667.

The concept of the *ʿālam al-mithāl* or 'imaginal world', according to Henry Corbin's famous translation, is undoubtedly a key topic in Islamic philosophy, first developed among Suhrawardī's (d. 587/1191) and Ibn ʿArabī's (d. 638/1240) disciples, then throughout Safavid times, notably by Mullā Ṣadrā (d. 1050/1640) and his student Muḥsin

---

3 *Maḥbūb al-qulūb, al-maqālat al-'ūlā*, ed. I. al-Dībājī and H. Ṣidqī (Tehran, 1378 Sh./1999); *Maḥbūb al-qulūb, al-maqālat al-thāniyya* (Tehran, 1382 Sh./2003); third part unpublished. First part translated into French in Terrier, *Histoire de la sagesse et philosophie shi'ite*.

4 On the history of this genre, see M. Terrier, 'Histoire de l'histoire de la sagesse en islam. Résumé des conférences 2015-2016', *AEPHE-SSR*, 124 (2015–16), pp. 363–372 https://journals.openedition.org/asr/1652 (accessed on 28 January 2021); idem, 'Histoire de l'histoire de la sagesse en islam. Résumé des conférences 2016-2017', *AEPHE-SSR*, 125 (2016–17), pp. 395–404 https://journals.openedition.org/asr/2115 (accessed on 28 January 2021); idem, 'Histoire de l'histoire de la sagesse en islam. Résumé des conférences 2017-2018', *AEPHE-SSR*, 126 (2017–18), pp. 365–374 https://journals.openedition.org/asr/2930 (accessed on 28 January 2021).

5 Henry Corbin, 'Confessions extatiques de Mīr Dāmād, maître de théologie à Ispahan (ob. 1041/1631-1632)', in H. Massé, ed., *Mélanges offerts à Louis Massignon* (Damascus, 1956), vol. 1, pp. 331–378; idem, *En Islam Iranien* (Paris, 1971–1972), vol. 4. For a critical study of this paradigm, see Sajjad Rizvi, 'Isfahan School of Philosophy', *EIr*, vol. 14, pp. 119–125 http://iranicaonline.org/articles/isfahan-school-of-philosophy (accessed on 28 January 2021).

6 *Tafsīr al-Sharīf al-Lāhījī*, ed. M. Urmawī (Tehran, 1340 Sh./1962).

Fayḍ Kāshānī (d. 1090/1679).[7] Noteworthily, Ashkivarī's *Fānūs al-khayāl* seems to have been the first monograph on the subject.[8] Despite this, maybe because its author is a rather obscure figure, it has not received any scholarly interest since a brief mention by Corbin, and still remains unpublished.[9] This paper, based on the study of its sole manuscript (MS 1615, Malek Library of Tehran), is conceived as a preliminary to a critical edition and French translation.[10] After a presentation of Ashkivarī's project and sources, an overview of this work will be presented by focusing first on the concept of the imaginal world and then on various themes of the convergence between Shiʿism, Sufism and philosophy addressed by the author throughout the epistle.

Ashkivarī's Project, Style and Sources

The Symphonic Project

In my study on the *Maḥbūb al-qulūb*, I was able to show that the aim of this encyclopedia of sages was to demonstrate the harmony between the Shiʿi esoteric tradition, Greek and Islamic philosophy, and a certain type of Sufism, clearly three separate and rival threads in the quest for truth in spiritual Islam. This aim of harmonisation or establishing *symphonia*, in the sense of the term in Greek literature and exegesis (Jewish, Christian and Neoplatonist), i.e., concordance or agreement between texts and doctrines,[11] is also at the core of the *Fānūs al-khayāl*. With this project, Ashkivarī follows the line of thinkers such as Sayyid Ḥaydar Āmulī (d. after 787/1385-86), Ibn Abī Jumhūr al-Aḥsāʾī (d. after 904/1499) and Qāḍī Nūr-Allāh Shūshtarī (d. 1019/1610), who

[7] See L.W.C. Van Lit, *The World of Image in Islamic Philosophy. Ibn Sīnā, Suhrawardī, Shahrazūrī, and beyond* (Edinburgh, 2017).

[8] Actually, another monograph on the imaginal world was composed in the same period by a mysterious namesake of our author, if not he himself: Bahāʾī Lāhījī, *al-Risāla al-nūriyya al-mithāliyya*, ed. J. Ashtiyānī (Tehran n.d.).

[9] Henry Corbin, *Histoire de la philosophie Islamique* (Paris, 1986), p. 465.

[10] Mathieu Terrier, *Le guide du monde imaginal. Présentation, édition et traduction de la Risāla mithāliyya de Quṭb al-Dīn Ashkevarī* (Turnout, forthcoming).

[11] On this notion, see Sébastien Morlet, *Symphonia. La concorde des textes et des doctrines dans la littérature grecque jusqu'à Origène* (Paris, 2019).

in particular sought to reconcile Shiʿism and Sufism.[12] However, this attitude is even more significant in Ashkivarī's time, marked by a severe reaction on the part of the Shiʿi clergy against Sufism and philosophy.[13] When most of his contemporaries were banishing the word 'Sufism' (*taṣawwuf*) from their vocabulary and preferred to refer to 'gnosis' (*ʿirfān*), Ashkivarī was openly praising the 'unitarian Sufis' (*al-ṣūfiyya al-muwaḥḥida*) and their masters (*mashāʾikh*), whom he considered as both disciples of the imams, following Āmulī's and Shūshtarī's historiography, and 'true philosophers' of the lineage of the ancient sages, in accordance with Suhrawardī's claim.[14]

Ashkivarī's mode of composition is not that of an 'author' in the modern sense of the word, but rather it is an assemblage of personal reflections and numerous quotations, including Qurʾanic verses, Prophetic and Imāmī *ḥadīth*s, extensive extracts from various philosophical works, as well as poetic verses. For this reason, like the *Maḥbūb al-qulūb*, the *Fānūs al-khayāl* is written in a mixed language of Arabic and Persian sometimes called *mulammaʿ*. Most of the verses quoted are in Persian; many of the *ḥadīth*s and Qurʾanic verses, after being quoted in Arabic, are also translated into Persian; and some philosophical ideas are also expressed in turn in both languages. This reflects the diglossia of Safavid learned society as well as Ashkivarī's particular willingness to address the Persian-speaking population and not only the elite that was well acquainted with Arabic.

However, this kind of compilation by 'cut and paste' is far from being a formal exercise. In the *Fānūs al-khayāl* as well as in the *Maḥbūb al-qulūb*, Ashkivarī displays not only a fantastic degree of erudition and a 'rhapsodic art', as noted by Corbin,[15] but also real philosophical

[12] On this tradition of reconciliation, see Mathieu Terrier, 'The Defence of Sufism among Twelver Shiʿi Scholars of the Early Modern and Modern Times: Topics and Arguments', in D. Hermann and M. Terrier, ed., *Shiʿi Islam and Sufism: Classical Views and Modern Perspectives* (London, 2020), pp. 27–63.

[13] See on this Leonard Lewisohn, 'Sufism and the School of Iṣfahān: Taṣawwuf and ʿIrfān in Late Safavid Iran (ʿAbd al-Razzāq Lāhījī and Fayḍ Kāshānī on the Relation of Taṣawwuf, Ḥikmat and ʿIrfān)', in L. Lewisohn and D. Morgan, ed., *The Heritage of Sufism* (Oxford, 1999), vol. 3, pp. 63–134; Ata Anzali, *'Mysticism' in Iran: The Safavid Roots of a Modern Concept* (Columbia, SC, 2017).

[14] Shihāb al-Dīn Suhrawardī, *Kitāb al-talwīḥāt*, in his *Œuvres philosophiques et mystiques*, vol. 1, ed. H. Corbin (Tehran and Paris, 1952), pp. 73–74.

[15] Corbin, *En Islam Iranien*, vol. 4, p. 27.

and historical ambition. By compiling different sources and setting them in sequence, his purpose is not only to defend the idea of an agreement between the three main spiritual currents of Islam in theory, but also to make their harmony or *symphonia* actually heard.

The Argument of the Fānūs al-khayāl

Unlike the *Maḥbūb al-qulūb*, the *Fānūs al-khayāl* is a concise epistle that deals with an issue that is specifically both theological and philosophical. The introduction clearly states the motive behind the work, its project and what could be called its methodology:

> As the immaterial human souls, after their separation from the material bodies referred to as 'natural death' in the noble teachings reported from the Impeccable beings [i.e. the imams], attach themselves to imaginal shapes (*ashbāḥ mithāliyya*) similar to these bodies, they experience bliss or punishment in [these shapes] until the advent of the hour [of Resurrection]; then, they will go back into these bodies as they were, with the permission of their Giver of Existence. I was then called to write a brief epistle on the verification (*taḥqīq*) of the imaginal world and the shapes to which souls are attached after being delivered from bodily receptacles and sensitive attachments. We will first mention a handful of *ḥadīth*s confirming this view (. . .); then we will explain the reality of this world according to what the philosophers of Illumination (*ḥukamāʾ al-ishrāq*) professed, as well as what the deified men among the unitarian Sufi sects (*al-mutaʿalliha min al-firaq al-ṣūfiyya al-muwaḥḥida*) have made known through their spiritual struggles and contemplations (*mujāhadātihim wa mushāhadātihim*). You are [already] aware that the masters of spiritual observation (*al-irṣād al-rūḥānī*) have a higher rank than the masters of material observation. So, since you give credit to the latter in what they give you from the secrets of astronomy, it is right that you also give credit to the former in what they reveal to you from the secrets of the angelic worlds.[16]

[16] *Fānūs al-khayāl*, MS 1615, Malek Library Tehran, pp. 1–2. The last argument is an echo of Suhrawardī's *Kitāb hikmat al-ishrāq*, in idem, *Œuvres philosophiques et mystiques*, vol. 1, pp. 155–156, § 165; Suhrawardī, *The Philosophy of Illumination*, ed. and tr. J. Walbridge and H. Ziai (Provo, UT, 1999), pp. 107–108.

The argument of the epistle, stated from the outset, lies therefore at the crossroads of eschatology and metaphysics: human souls, between death and the greatest Resurrection, will experience at first reward or suffering in the grave, designated as a *barzakh* ('isthmus') in reference to Q 23:100, an intermediary world between the sensory and the intelligible one, labelled by the philosophers as 'the imaginal world'. Introduced by the first sentence, the distinction and the justification of these two bodies of Resurrection, that of the 'lesser Resurrection' in the grave, and that of the 'greatest Resurrection' at the end of time, is actually one of the main topics of the epistle. Since the beginning, this conception is presented as shared by the Impeccable beings (i.e. the Prophet Muhammad, his daughter Fāṭima and the Twelve imams), the *ishrāqī* philosophers and 'unitarian' Sufis.

Despite the announcement of a structured plan in which the three major currents are separated, the epistle constantly cross-references the Shiʿi sacred scriptures (i.e. the Qurʾan and Imāmī *ḥadīth*), philosophy and Sufism. It is also not divided into isoform parts (*faṣl* or *bāb*) but proceeds by free association. In its form and content, the *Fānūs al-khayāl*, like the *Maḥbūb al-qulūb*, is both an anthology and a personal work, a syncretic proposal and a work combatting the dominant exoteric and legalist trend of his time.

The Sources of the Symphonia

As demonstrated by his *Tafsīr*, Ashkivarī can himself be considered an expert in Imāmī *ḥadīth*, concerned with the conservation of the genuine esoteric tradition of the imams. Of the earlier sources, he borrows from al-Kulaynī's (d. 329/940-41) *Kitāb al-Kāfī* and Shaykh Ṣadūq's (d. 381/991) works such as *Kamāl al-dīn*, *al-Āmālī* and *ʿUyūn akhbār al-Riḍā*. Out of the medieval sources (5th–6th/11th–12th centuries), the *Nahj al-balāgha* compiled by al-Sharīf al-Raḍī (d. 406/1015); Shaykh Ṭabarsī's (d. 548/1153-54) *Iʿlām al-warā*, and al-Rāwandī's (d. 573/1177-78) *al-Kharāʾij waʾl-jarāʾiḥ* are frequently quoted. Last, among the late works on *ḥadīth*, Ibn Abī Jumhūr's *ʿAwālī al-liʾālī*, a collection often considered unorthodox, and Shaykh Bahāʾī's *al-Arbaʿūn ḥadīth* are also used. It should be noted that Ashkivarī's works predate the three main encyclopedias of Imāmī *ḥadīth* composed in the Safavid era by some of his contemporaries, namely Fayḍ

Kāshānī's *al-Wāfī*, Ḥurr ʿĀmilī's (d. 1104/1693) *Wasāʾil al-shīʿa*, and Muḥammad Bāqir al-Majlisī's (d. 1111/1699) *Biḥār al-anwār*.

Regarding philosophy, Ashkivarī mentions ancient sages such as Hermes Trismegistus, Pythagoras, Thales, Plato, Aristotle and Theophrastus, taking his information from medieval bio-doxographies as he does in his *Maḥbūb al-qulūb*.[17] From the Islamic period, Ibn Sīnā's (d. 428/1037) *al-Najāt* and *al-Shifāʾ* are quoted, as well as al-Ghazālī's (d. 505/1111) *al-Maḍnūn bihi ʿalā ghayr ahlihi*, an epistle of Avicennian inspiration.[18] Shihāb al-Dīn al-Suhrawardī is directly quoted several times. However, most of the *ishrāqī* material is borrowed from his major commentators, Shams al-Dīn Shahrazūrī (d. between 687/1288 and 704/1305), Quṭb al-Dīn al-Shīrāzī (d. 710/1311) and Ghiyāth al-Dīn Dashtakī (d. 949/1538). Shahrazūrī's philosophical encyclopedia *Rasāʾil al-shajara al-ilāhiyya* is one of the main philosophical sources used in the epistle. In addition to Dashtakī, Shams al-Dīn al-Khafrī (d. between 942/1535 and 946/1539), one of the first Shiʿi philosophers of 10th/16th-century Iran, is also mentioned. Last, among his early contemporaries, Ashkivarī quotes at length, without mentioning their names, his former teacher Mīr Dāmād – mainly his Persian *Jadhawāt wa mawāqīt*, but also his *Risāla al-khalʿiyya*, the notoriety of which is mostly due to his report in the *Maḥbūb al-qulūb* – and, more surprisingly, Mullā Ṣadrā – mainly *al-Shawāhid al-rubūbiyya* and *Sharḥ al-hidāya al-athīriyya*.[19]

As for Sufism, Ashkivarī draws from several traditions. Rabīʿa al-ʿAdawiyya (d. 185/801) and Junayd al-Baghdādī (d. 298/911) are briefly mentioned as spiritual authorities. Ibn ʿArabī and the Akbārī school are widely represented through a Persian translation of *al-Futūḥāt al-makkiyya*, the commentary on *Fuṣūṣ al-ḥikam* by Dāwūd al-Qayṣarī (d. 751/1350), and various works by ʿAbd al-Razzāq al-Qāshānī (d. between 730-6 /1329-35). The commentary of Kamāl al-Dīn Maybudī (d. 907/1501-2) on the *Dīwān* attributed to the First imam,

[17] On these sources, see Terrier, *Histoire de la sagesse et philosophie shi'ite*, pp. 124–137; on Suhrawardī's representation of the ancients, see John Walbridge, *The Leaven of the Ancients: Suhravardî and the heritage of the Greeks* (Albany, NY, 1999).

[18] On this, see Jean Michot, 'Avicenne et le *Kitāb al-Madnūn* d'al-Ghazālī', *Bulletin de philosophie médiévale*, 18 (1976), pp. 51–59.

[19] The latter is a commentary on Athīr al-Dīn al-Abharī's (d. ca. 663/1265) philosophical textbook. Noteworthily, Mullā Ṣadrā is never mentioned by name in Ashkivarī's works.

ʿAlī b. Abī Ṭālib, a synthesis of Shiʿi and Sufi doctrines, is frequently employed as a poetic archive. However, the most frequently cited work remains the *Mafātīḥ al-iʿjāz* of Shams al-Dīn Lāhījī (d. 912/1506-7), a commentary on Maḥmūd Shabistarī's (d. ca. 720/1317) poem *Gulshān-i rāz*. This work is marked by Nūrbakhshī Shiʿi Sufism, an influential though repressed tradition in Safavid Iran, and is undoubtedly a significant indication of Ashkivarī's spiritual and social attitudes.[20]

In Ashkivarī's symphonic device, poetry plays an important role. Out of the Persian mystical poets, Jalāl al-Dīn Rūmī (d. 672/1273) is widely cited as a spiritual authority and designated as a 'gnostic' (*ʿārif*), although he was not a Shiʿi. ʿAṭṭār al-Nīshābūrī (d. ca. 618/1221) and Ḥāfiẓ (d. ca 792/1390) are also included. Of the Arabic poems quoted, those attributed to ʿAlī b. Abī Ṭālib have the lion's share. Last, Ashkivarī also scattered his own Persian verses throughout the text, and poetry is obviously the only literary genre in which he laid claim to write.

The Imaginal World: A Syncretic Concept

The Temporal Definition: The Barzakh *or the Lesser Resurrection*

Ashkivarī introduces the imaginal world as an equivalent of the Isthmus (*barzakh*), the interregnum between natural death and the greatest Resurrection. He therefore cites several *ḥadīth*s of the Prophet as confirming the existence of Heaven and Hell in the 'imaginal Isthmus' (*barzakh-i mithālī*), two of them borrowed from al-Qāshānī's definition of the 'first [i.e. lesser] Resurrection'. From the Prophet: 'The grave is a garden from among the gardens of paradise, [or] a pit from among the pits of hell'; 'As you live, you will die, and as you die, you will rise again'; 'When someone dies, his resurrection has come'.[21]

Several *ḥadīth*s attributed to the imams describe more precisely the forms in which believers will experience their first resurrection. From Jaʿfar al-Ṣādiq, the sixth Imam: '[The spirits of the believers] are in

---

[20] About the Nūrbakhshī order, see Shahzad Bashir, *Messianic Hopes and Mystical Visions: the Nurbakhshiya Between Medieval and Modern Islam* (Columbia, SC, 2003); Hamid Algar, 'Nūrbakhshiyya', *EI2*, http://dx.doi.org.prext.num.bulac.fr/ 10.1163/ 1573-3912_islam_SIM_5992 (accessed on 28 January 2021).

[21] *Fānūs al-khayāl*, p. 5; the last two are quoted from ʿAbd al-Razzāq al-Kāshānī, *Iṣṭilāḥāt al-ṣūfiyya*, ed. A. al-Kayālī (Beirut, 2005), p. 66.

Paradise in the forms of their bodies. If you could see it, you would say: "It's so-and-so!".'[22] And from ʿAlī b. Abī Ṭālib: 'When God takes back [the soul of] the believer, He carries his spirit in a frame (*qālab*) similar to the one he had in this world. That is why [believers] eat and drink, and when a newcomer comes along, they recognise him by this form that he had in this world.'[23] Ashkivarī considers these forms as 'imaginal' or 'isthmic' bodies, intermediate between the sensory and the intelligible, neither having the rudeness of the former, nor the subtleness of the latter, and does not hesitate to attribute this philosophical conception to the imams.[24]

Quite surprisingly, Ashkivarī deemed it necessary to distinguish this conception from the heresy of transmigration (*tanāsukh*). The concept of the imaginal world as separated from the sensory world is a key to the argument:

> Some people imagine that to profess that human spirits, after separation from their original bodies, attach themselves to imaginal shapes, as we understand from these *ḥadīth*s, is to profess transmigration. It is an unfounded presumption. For the transmigration rejected by all sects of Islam means that spirits, after separation from their original bodies, attach themselves to other bodies composed of the four elements, in this very world of generation and corruption. [. . .] But to profess that in another world, different from this birth (*nash'a*), [spirits] will attach themselves to imaginal bodies; that in the duration of the *barzakh*, between the time of death and the coming of the [greatest] Resurrection, they will perform in these bodies the service of God; and that after the advent of the [greatest] Resurrection, they will return to their first bodies by the power of God (. . .), no one would call this transmigration.[25]

However, in a quotation from Mullā Ṣadrā, the 'lesser resurrection' of evildoers is identified with a legal meaning of *tanāsukh*, understood as a human-to-animal metamorphosis (*maskh*), as attested in the Qur'an (2:65; 5:60; 7:166):

---

22 *Fānūs al-khayāl*, p. 5.

23 Ibid., p. 10. The source: al-Kulaynī, *Furūʿ al-Kāfī* (Beirut, 1426/2005), p. 125.

24 A similar interpretation of these traditions can also be found in Mullā Muḥsin Fayḍ Kāshānī, *Kalimāt maknūna*, ed. ʿA. ʿAlīzāda (Qum, 1390 Sh./2011), p. 148.

25 *Fānūs al-khayāl*, pp. 10–11.

> The second meaning [of *tanāsukh*] (...) is the migration of the soul from this body to the body of the afterlife (*ukhrawī*), corresponding to the qualities and mores that have dominated it in this world. This is confirmed by the guides of unveiling and contemplation [i.e. the imams], reported by the bearers of revelations and religions [i.e. the prophets]. This is why it is said that there is no religion in which transmigration is not firmly rooted.[26] This is confirmed by many verses in the Qurʾan. It is in this meaning, I think, that the doctrine of transmigration is attributed to the pillars of wisdom such as Plato and his predecessors among the sages who drew the lights of wisdom from the niche of the lights of the prophets.[27] For, with their foresight, these sages have contemplated the interiors of souls and the forms in which they will be resurrected according to their intentions and deeds, as in His word: '*And We shall muster them on the Resurrection Day upon their faces*' (17:97) [...]. This is the metamorphosis of the interiors (*maskh al-bawāṭin*) without the form being changed on the outside: you see human forms, but inside there is a form of angel, demon, dog, pig, lion, or another animal appropriate to the interior.[28]

The imaginal body is therefore a subtle embodiment of the interior, by which the soul of the deceased may take the form of an individual of another species. This body will 'rise' or appear in the grave to experience, or constitute itself as, the soul's first reward or punishment. This conception is confirmed by a *ḥadīth* dealing with the supranatural attributes of the imams, characteristic of the so-called 'excessive' Shiʿis (*ghulāt*):

> I said to the sixth Imam, 'O son of the Prophet, we [the Shiʿis] see ourselves as having no superiority over our enemies (...); they are more favoured than us, more fortunate, better dressed and better prepared.' The imam became angry and said, 'Do you want me to show you your superiority over these perverse creatures?' (...) He passed his hand over his face and said, 'Look at these

[26] The formula is borrowed from al-Shahrastānī, *Kitāb al-milal waʾl-niḥal*, ed. M. Badrān (Cairo, 1366–1375/1947–1955), vol. 2, p. 262.

[27] This includes certainly Pythagoras, Thales and Empedocles.

[28] *Fānūs al-khayāl*, pp. 17–18. The source: Ṣadr al-Dīn Shīrāzī (Mullā Ṣadrā), *al-Shawāhid al-rubūbiyya*, ed. S.J. Ashtiyānī (Mashhad, 1360 Sh./1981), pp. 231–233.

> ones.' I turned to a group of Umayyads in front of the city gate, looked at them and saw monkeys, pigs, dogs and jackals in their place. I said to the imam, 'O son of the Prophet, what a great affair! By God! Make me return to my former condition or I will lose my mind!' He passed his hand over his face and I saw them again as human as before. Then he said, 'Soon, their condition will be as they saw it. [. . .] Here is your superiority over them.'[29]

Obviously, the *ḥadīth* quoted supports a literalist and non-allegorical approach to metamorphosis. However, Ashkivarī assimilated it to the reign of the imaginal world, itself based on the Platonic distinction between the intelligible and the sensible worlds. That is to say, he not only reactivated the most esoteric and seemingly non-rational Imāmī tradition, but also drew it closer to philosophical and mystical conceptions that were highly controversial.

Cosmo-Ontological Definitions: The Imaginal World in the Hierarchy of Worlds

Ashkivarī stresses that the concept reported in the *ḥadīth* of the imam, according to which rational souls, after their separation from their bodies and during their stay in the Isthmus, attach themselves to shapes substantially different from natural bodies, is similar to that of 'a group of leading sages' saying:

> There is in existence a measured world (*ʿālam-i miqdārī*) which is not the sensory world but an intermediate one between the world of immaterial realities and the world of material things, without having either the subtlety of the former, or the denseness of the latter. In this world, all bodies, species and accidents – including movements, rest, sounds, tastes and smells – have imaginal shapes. [These shapes] subsist by themselves; they have an attachment, but not to a matter. It is a huge world whose inhabitants are of different classes and unequal ranks of subtlety and coarseness, beauty and ugliness. In these imaginal bodies, [men] possess all the external and internal senses through which they perceive pain and pleasure and enjoy physical and spiritual happiness (*naʿīm*).[30]

---

29 *Fānūs al-khayāl*, p. 19.

30 Ibid., p. 22.

Having been introduced into the temporal or diachronic framework of eschatology, throughout the epistle the concept of the imaginal world also receives various synchronic, cosmo-ontological definitions and descriptions. As seen before, the attribute of 'imaginal' is first related to Heaven and Hell, as well to the bodies of their respective inhabitants. In this regard, the imaginal world is situated in the hierarchy of worlds and also possesses an internal hierarchical structure. It lies above the world of sensation and location (*ʿālam al-ḥiss wa'l-makān*) and below the world of the Intellect (*ʿālam al-ʿaql*), being intermediary between these two worlds. It has many layers (*tabaqāt*) that are beyond the count of all but the Creator. Its upper layers, which are noble, bright and pleasant, are those of the Paradise that is enjoyed by the mid-ranked rewarded souls. Its lower layers are dark and painful; they are the layers of Hell (*al-nār*) where the souls of the damned suffer. The uppermost and brightest layer is contiguous with the world of the Intellect; the lowest and darkest layer is at the semblance and the nearness of the sensory world.[31] It is called the imaginal world because it comprehends the forms of every existent of the sensory world, as well as the images of the true entities and realities (*aʿyān wa ḥaqāʾiq*) which are found in the Presence of Divine Science. It is also called the eighth clime, because the measured world is divided into eight climes: seven encompassing the sensory measures and the eighth one encompassing the imaginal ones.[32] In order to attest the existence of the imaginal world as so defined, Ashkivarī refers to Suhrawardī's report on the testimonies of Ādharbāyjānī villagers, as well as a direct testimony from Ibn ʿArabī during the *ḥajj*.[33]

According to an Akbārī concept, the imaginal world has its own place in the esoteric structure of the unique divine reality, as an isthmus between the world of Testimony (*ʿālam al-shahāda*), that of nature, and the world of Mystery (*ʿālam al-ghayb*), that of the true realities. In this understanding, 'the world of Testimony is a cover (*ghiṭāʾ*) for the

---

[31] Ibid., p. 26; Shams al-Dīn Shahrazūrī, *Rasāʾil al-shajara al-ilāhiyya fī ʿulūm al-ḥaqāʾiq al-rabbāniyya*, ed. N. Ḥabībī (Tehran, 1383 Sh./2004), vol. 3, p. 457.

[32] *Fānūs al-khayāl*, p. 26.

[33] Ibid., pp. 26–27. Quṭb al-Dīn Shīrāzī, *Sharḥ Ḥikmat al-ishrāq*, ed. ʿA. Nūrānī and M. Muḥaqqiq (Tehran, 1383 Sh./2004), p. 490; Ibn ʿArabī, *al-Futūḥāt al-makkiyya* (Beirut, 1331/2010), vol. 6, ch. 390, pp. 458–459.

world of the Image; the world of the Image is a cover for the divine Attributes and Names; the world of divine Attributes and Names is a cover for the divine Essence.'[34] This is confirmed by a *ḥadīth* from the Sixth imam, maybe the sole one in which the notion of 'image' (*mithāl*) appears: 'Of every believer, there is an image on the [divine] Throne. When he prostrates himself in prayer, his image acts like his act; then the angels see him and pray for his forgiveness. If [the believer] commits an act of disobedience, God casts a veil over his image so that the angels do not know about it.'[35]

Ashkivarī then presents a cartography of the imaginal world drawn from various sources. 'This world contains images of every immaterial and material reality, such as the Throne, the Pedestal, the seven skies and the two earths.' It also possesses countless cities, including three said to have been known to the Prophet: Jābalqā and Jābarṣā, which belong to its elementary (*ʿunṣurī*) part, and Hūrqalyā, which lies in the heavens of the same world.[36] Jābalqā is located to the east of the spirits and Jābarṣā is in front of it, to the west of the bodies. The imaginal world itself lies to the west of the world of Lordship (*ʿālam al-rubūbiyya*), so that the divine Effusion flows onto it from the latter, and to the east of the world of Testimony, so that the divine Effusion flows from it onto the latter.[37]

In the framework of the correspondence between macrocosm and microcosm, a philosophical commonplace especially adhered to by Ashkivarī's master Mīr Dāmād, the imaginal world plays a role similar to that of the animal spirit (*al-rūḥ al-ḥayawānī*), which ensures the first attachment of the spirit to the body. Quoting an anonymous source, Ashkivarī asserts that the creation of the imaginal world is

---

[34] *Fānūs al-khayāl*, p. 32; the source: *Tafsīr Ibn ʿArabī* (*Taʾwīlāt ʿAbd al-Razzāq Qāshānī*), ed. S. M. Rabbāb (Beirut, 1422/2001), vol. 1, p. 148.

[35] *Fānūs al-khayāl*, p. 34; the source: Shaykh Bahāʾī, *Miftāḥ al-falāḥ fī ʿamal al-yawm waʾl-layla min al-wājibāt waʾl-mustaḥabbāt* (Beirut, 1405/1984), p. 201.

[36] *Fānūs al-khayāl*, pp. 34–35. Source: Ghiyāth al-Dīn Dashtakī Shīrāzī, *Ishrāq hayākil al-nūr*, ed. A. Awjabī (Tehran, 1382 Sh./2003), pp. 255–256. These three cities are mentioned in Suhrawardī, *Ḥikmat al-ishrāq*, in *Œuvres*, vol. 2, p. 254, and Hūrqalyā specifically in *Kitāb al-mashāriʿ waʾl-muṭāraḥāt*, *Œuvres*, vol. 1, p. 494.

[37] *Fānūs al-khayāl*, pp. 35–36; Shams al-Dīn Muḥammad al-Lāhījī, *Mafātīḥ al-iʿjāz fī sharḥ Gulshan-i rāz*, ed. M. R. Barzagar Khāliqī and I. Karbāsī (Tehran, 1391 Sh./2012), p. 52.

relevant to God's wisdom (*ḥikma*). Since spirits are prior to bodies in existence and quiddity, because they are simple while bodies are composite, their government of bodies would be impossible without an intermediary, for otherwise there would be no relationship at all between them. Thus 'God, exalted be He, created the imaginal world as an isthmus uniting the worlds of spirits and bodies, so that the relationship between the two could be established, the influence exercised and experienced, the help provided and requested. And this is conceivable [only] in the imaginal world.'[38]

Objections to the Imaginal World

Ashkivarī also mentions philosophical objections to the concept of imaginal world. The first appears when the concept is introduced, in a quotation of Shams al-Dīn Khafrī:

> As for the world of the Image, for the *ishrāqī*s it is an existent world that does not subsist through bodily faculties [of the soul], which are only loci of manifestation for it. What man sees in a dream only happens in this world. However, according to those other than [the *ishrāqī*s], this world only happens [to exist] by means of the bodily faculties, and therefore is not to be counted among the four [categories of] substances that are the intelligences, souls, natures and hyletic realities.[39]

A second series of objections appears at the end of the epistle, in a section entitled 'the problems raised by the concept of the imaginal world according to the masters of examination and deduction' (*arbāb al-naẓar wa'l-istidlāl*), i.e. the Peripatetic and non-*ishrāqī* philosophers. It contains a long anonymous quotation from Mīr Dāmād's *Jadhawāt wa mawāqīt*. His first argument is actually of Peripatetic inspiration: 'The imaginal world and the suspended images of imagination, if they are pleasantly suited to the faculty of intuitive tasting (. . .), to rhetorical disposition and poetic syllogisms, remain problematic according to the

---

38 *Fānūs al-khayāl*, pp. 57–58, source unknown.

39 Ibid., p. 26. Shams al-Dīn Khafrī, *Tafsīr āyat al-kursī*, ed. A. Awjabī, summarised in Manūchihr Ṣadūqī Sahā, ed., *Tafāsīr ʿaqliyya li-falāsifa ilāhiyyīn* (Tehran, 1389 Sh./2010), pp. 269–290, here p. 276.

method of examination and demonstrative proof? The second criticism, theologically based, seems in direct contradiction to Ashkivarī's thesis in this epistle: 'The issues of corporal resurrection, promises of rewards and corporal punishment, authentication of dreams and miracles, do not depend on the burden of proof of this world and these images'. The last argument, which draws on an Akbārī inspiration, one originally more Platonic than Aristotelian, results in the rescuing of the concept of the imaginal world by denying its ontological independence:

> Considering existence, there is no intermediary between the immaterial and the material. For the individualised existent is either dependent, in its existence, on the world of time and place (. . .), or free from these chains and links (. . .). Yes, the kinds of attachments, the ranks of subtlety and coarseness of material things actually differ in intensity and weakness. If they apply this to the [whole world of] Testimony and materiality, and if they regard the world of the Image as the most subtle layer and the noblest rank in the world of Testimony, it would have sense.[40] As for their saying, 'These images are suspended forms (*ṣūwar-i muʿallaqa*), not in a matter or a substrate', it does not fit with the balance of demonstrative evidence. For just as every form of the sensory world, i.e. the world of Testimony, has an image in the imaginal world – which they consider related to the Testimony (*muḍāfash*) – so every material of that world necessarily has an image in this world. Consequently, the imaginal form must be actualised by imaginal matter. The imaginal matter and forms of the world of the Isthmus are in correspondence with the hyletic matter and the material forms of the sensory world.[41]

This quotation of Mīr Dāmād's only significant text on the imaginal world is especially revealing of Ashkivarī's independence from his former master, since the epistle clearly supports, on the contrary, the *ishrāqī* conception of this world as a genuine intermediary between the intelligible and the sensible. However, as we shall see, Ashkivarī attests elsewhere to his spiritual respect for the 'third master'.

---

[40] A somewhat parallel Arabic text in Mīr Dāmād's *Kitāb al-qabasāt*, ed. M. Muḥaqqiq (Tehran, 1977), p. 167, ll. 6–12.

[41] *Fānūs al-khayāl*, pp. 104–105; Mīr Dāmād, *Jadhawāt wa mawāqīt*, ed. A. Awjabī (Tehran, 1380 Sh./2001), pp. 65–67.

Subaltern Theories and Themes of Convergence

The Companion of the Grave

Apart from the concept of the imaginal body which is to be resurrected, Ashkivarī supports the idea that man's actions and beliefs in life take on an individual form after death that accompanies the departed soul to the grave. This understanding of the 'embodiment of beliefs and actions' (*tajassud al-ʿaqāʾid waʾl-aʿmāl*), he argues, is held by intellectual philosophers (*al-ḥukamāʾ al-ʿuqalāʾ*) as well as by the Prophet and the imams: 'According to the opinion of the gnostic sages, when freed from bodies human souls possess shadows that derive from the imaginal forms, consecutive with their mores and habits, by means of which they enjoy or suffer.' As an argument of authority, Ashkivarī quotes a saying attributed to Pythagoras, 'the deified sage' (*al-ḥakīm al-mutaʾallih*), and a *ḥadīth* of the Prophet, whose congruence is indeed striking. From the former:

> Know that you will be facing your actions, words and thoughts. From each movement of thought, speech or action, spiritual and bodily forms will be manifest for you. If the movement is of the irascible or concupiscible [part of the soul], it becomes matter for a demon who will make you suffer in this life and veil your perception of light after death. If the movement is of the intellectual [part of the soul], it becomes an angel of which you will enjoy the company in this world and which will guide you in the last world.[42]

From the Prophet:

> O Qays, you must have a companion (*qarīn*), that he be buried alive with you, that you be buried dead with him; if he is noble, he will honour you, if he is guilty he will submiss you (. . .). So make sure he is wholesome, because if he is, you will enjoy his familiarity, but if he is corrupt, you will suffer from loneliness with him. [This companion] is your action.[43]

---

[42] *Fānūs al-khayāl*, pp. 40–41. Among the possible sources: Dashtakī, *Ishrāq hayākil al-nūr*, pp. 264–265; Mullā Ṣadrā, *Mafātiḥ al-ghayb*, ed. N. Ḥabībī (Tehran, 1386 Sh./2007), vol. 2, p. 1041.

[43] *Fānūs al-khayāl*, pp. 41–42; the source: Shaykh Bahāʾī, *al-Arbaʿūn ḥadīth* (Qum, 1431/2009), p. 493.

A quotation from the *ishrāqī* Shahrazūrī draws out the philosophical consequences of this doctrine:

> The suffering that happens to the soul after the separation of the body results from its own defect and error and not, as the ordinary person imagines, like in this world where punishment occurs through external causes, from an external avenger who would punish it and take revenge on it. But this is not the case [in the other world]. For this suffering happens to [the soul] because of [its] vile forms and wicked mores. Thus, [the soul] is the bearer of its own punishment that it requires through these forms: it is itself that requires its punishment.[44]

One could remark that the same comment is appropriate for the conception of the 'lesser resurrection' presented above, of which this appears as an alternative. What is more, in contrast with the initial denials concerning transmigration, Shahrazūrī's reasoning fits with the fundamental idea of the Hindu and Pythagorean doctrine that the retribution of the soul after death is an immanent justice, not the act of a transcendent avenger, as obviously understood by monotheist religions.[45]

Apparitions, Miracles and Wonders

According to the *ishrāqī* tradition, in the city of Hūrqalyā human souls possess imaginal bodies which they dispose of at will and through which they manifest miracles (*muʿjizāt*) or breaches in the customary course of things (*khawāriq al-ʿādāt*).[46] It permits the explanation of the apparition of the angel Gabriel to the Prophet in the form of his young companion Daḥya al-Kalbī, and to Mary '*in the form of a perfect man*' (Q 19:17). Ashkivarī stresses that 'the meaning of this form is not the essence because the essence has no form', and that 'this change of state

---

[44] *Fānūs al-khayāl*, pp. 42–43. The source: Shams al-Dīn al-Shahrazūrī, *Rasāʾil al-shajara al-ilāhiyya*, vol. 3, p. 619.

[45] On the ambiguous positions of *ishrāqī* philosophers on this issue, see Sabine Schmidtke, 'The Doctrine of the Transmigration of Soul according to Shihāb al-Dīn al-Suhrawardī (killed 587/1191) and his Followers', *Studia Iranica*, 28 (1999), pp. 237–254.

[46] *Fānūs al-khayāl*, pp. 37–38. The source: al-Dashtakī, *Ishrāq hayākil al-nūr*, pp. 255–256.

(*istiḥāla*) in the angel is not a transformation (*inqilāb*), Gabriel remaining in his reality and his true attributes while he manifested himself to the Prophet in the form of Daḥya al-Kalbī.'[47] Likewise, it enables Ashkivarī to justify rationally the wonders attributed to the imams as well as to the Sufi saints, i.e. the *awliyā'*, in the respective views of Shiʿism and Sufism. The first of these wonders is the gift of ubiquity. According to a tradition, during the month of Ramadan, Imam ʿAlī broke the fast in different companions' houses before the Prophet declared that he was his guest and had broken the fast with him at his home.[48] Similarly, some Sufi saints were held to have been simultaneously in their country and in Mecca on the *ḥajj*.

Ashkivarī also supports a tenet at the core of the doctrine of the Nūrbakhshī order, that of *burūz* (technically 'projection'), according to which the spirit of a deceased master can return to dwell in the body of an heir.[49] From Shams al-Dīn Lāhījī, he quotes Muḥammad Nūrbakhsh, the founder of the order, without mentioning his name. It appears that this tenet, like that of the imaginal body of the lesser resurrection, has to be distinguished from transmigration:

> The difference between transmigration (*tanāsukh*) and projection (*burūz*) (. . .) is that transmigration occurs when a spirit departs from one body and joins an embryo ready for a spirit, in the fourth month from the time when the sperm settled in the womb. This removal of the spirit from one body and its junction with the other occur simultaneously. However, projection occurs when a perfect spirit pours (*yafīḍu*) into [another] individual in the same way that the theophanies (*tajalliyyāt*) pour into him: [this individual] then becomes his locus of manifestation (*maẓhar*).[50]

---

47 *Fānūs al-khayāl*, p. 36.

48 Ibid., p. 35. The original source for this tradition is unknown but a Persian version of this account can be found in Mīr Dāmād, *Jadhawāt wa mawāqīt*, p. 63, before the passage quoted above.

49 Bashir, *Messianic Hopes and Mystical Visions*, pp. 53–54.

50 *Fānūs al-khayāl*, p. 52. The source: Qāḍī Mīr Ḥusayn Maybudī, *Sharḥ Diwān mansūb bih Amīr al-mu'minīn*, ed. Ḥ. Raḥmānī and I. Ashkishīrīn (Tehran, 1390 Sh./2011), p. 124; obviously borrowed from Muḥammad Nūrbakhsh's *Risālat al-hudā*, quoted in Bashir, *Messianic Hopes*, pp. 98–99.

This is illustrated by three accounts resulting in an original synthesis of Sufism and philosophy. First comes a quotation from Ibn ʿArabī reporting, in his *Futūḥāt makkiyya*, a story from the mystic Awḥad al-Dīn Kirmānī (d. 636/1238). While he was on the pilgrimage route with his shaykh, the latter became ill. Awḥad al-Dīn asked him for permission to go in search of a medicine and the shaykh gave him permission to do so. He finally found a hospital, whose head received him with great honour and gave him the medicine he was asking for. When he returned to his shaykh, the latter told him that after his departure, for fear that his search would fail, he had himself seized the body of the head of the hospital to satisfy his request, and that he did not need medicine any more. To verify this, Awḥad al-Dīn returned to the hospital, whose head did not recognise or receive him.[51] Remarkably, this example confers the gift of *burūz* to the living perfect master as well as the deceased one, and allows the projection of the perfect spirit in an imperfect being.

Ashkivarī continues with a personal anecdote that suggests his family affiliation to Nūrbakhshī Sufism, and in a reference to his master opus, integrates Peripatetic philosophy in Shiʿi gnosis:

> My brother told me that after our father's death, he sent a letter of request to the sovereign's camp (. . .) in order to recover the paternal charge [of the *Shaykh al-Islām* of Lāhījān] (. . .). The night after receiving the news of the fulfilment of his wish, he saw our father in a dream and asked him, 'In the books of the masters of Sufism, I have read that the refined soul has the power to seize certain bodies in order to ensure the fulfilment of men's wishes in this life. If the soul has this ability when it lies in the dwelling of attachment, it must be able to do so even more after breaking its ties with the body. Are the fulfilment of my wish and the success of my request due to your help and assistance in accordance with their saying?' [Our] father answered him, 'Such a state only occurs to powerful, refined and holy souls. I have no capacity of this kind, neither power of this rank. However, the fulfilment of your wish is only due to my supplication to these masters.' Long after my brother's dream, I found in the speech of the wise Theophrastus, cousin, disciple and legatee of the very great and wise Aristotle, that the soul is able to fly and descend (*ḥulūl*) in all

[51] *Fānūs al-khayāl*, pp. 52–53; Ibn ʿArabī, *Futūḥāt makkiyya*, vol. 1, p. 339.

that it wants by means of its real wings, as we have reported in our book the *Maḥbūb al-qulūb*.[52]

The Progress after Death

The theory that presents the imaginal body as the subject of the lesser Resurrection also enables Ashkivarī to justify an idea commonly rejected, that of a moral acquisition (*kasb*) and progression (*taraqqā*) of the soul after death. Many theologians, he says, argue this world is the only place to acquire acts of merit, referring to Q 2:254: 'O believers, expend of that wherewith We have provided you, before there comes a day wherein shall be neither traffic, nor friendship, nor intercession; and the unbelievers – they are the evildoers',[53] and to a Prophetic *ḥadīth*: 'When man dies, his action separates from him'. However, the belief in a post-mortem progress of the soul has been held by Sufis such as Ibn ʿArabī and Rūmī, from whom this verse is quoted: 'Learn such a trade that hereafter gain, earning and knowledge may come in as revenue (to thee) / Yonder world is a city full of trafficking and earning: think not that the earnings here (in this world) are a sufficiency.'[54]

Ashkivarī reports from Ibn ʿArabī that he not only supported this tenet, but also proved it by a personal experience: 'I have helped Junayd, Shiblī and Bāyazid and they did progress; however, this progress does not concern the knowledge of God.'[55] This precision is confirmed by Q 17:72–74: 'And whosoever is blind in this world shall be blind in the world to come, and he shall be even further astray from the way'. According to al-Qayṣarī, blindness here only concerns the knowledge of God.[56] As for the *ḥadīth* mentioned above, Ashkivarī argues that it does not contradict Ibn ʿArabī when including the

[52] *Fānūs al-khayāl*, pp. 53–54; see also Ashkivarī, *Maḥbūb al-qulūb*, al-maqāla al-thāniyya, p. 404.

[53] Arberry's translation of the Qur'an, amended.

[54] *Fānūs al-khayāl*, p. 62; Jalāl al-Dīn Muḥammad b. Muḥammad Mawlavī (Rūmī), *Mathnavī-yi maʿnavī*, ed. R. Nicholson (Tehran, 1390 Sh./2011), p. 284; Nicholson's translation modified according to the text of the MS.

[55] The famous Sufis, Junayd al-Baghdādī, Abū Bakr al-Shiblī (d. 334/945–46) and Abū Yazīd Basṭāmī (d. 234/848 or 261/874).

[56] *Fānūs al-khayāl*, pp. 62–63; Dāwūd b. Maḥmūd Qayṣarī, *Sharḥ bar Fuṣūṣ al-ḥikam-i Ibn ʿArabī*, Persian tr. M. Khwājavī (Tehran, 1387 Sh./2008), p. 787.

addition reported by some traditionists: 'excepting a current donation, a science from which he has benefited (through action), and a virtuous child praying for his forgiveness.'[57]

This is in turn confirmed by a Shiʿi *khabar* borrowed from al-Kulaynī's *Kitāb al-ḥujja* and obviously altered. Imam Jaʿfar related that on Friday nights, the spirits of the deceased Prophets and imams, as well as the spirit of the living imam, perform a celestial ascent to the divine Throne, turn around it and pray before returning to their bodies; then in the morning, when the living imam rises his action (*ʿamaluhu*) is considerably increased. In the original *ḥadīth* as it appears in al-Kulaynī, this is the imam's learning (*ʿilmuhu*), not his action, that has been increased. Ashkivarī's comment shows that he had another version of the *ḥadīth* on his desk: 'As this ascent is spiritual, the spirit must be attached to an imaginal body in order to perform the acts of worship, being impossible to pray without bodily members. The imaginal body is therefore, like the material body, a means of acquiring practical perfections (*kamālāt-i ʿamalī*).'[58] One may remark that the *ḥadīth* attests to the progression of the living imam, not to that of the deceased ones; however, its interpretation clearly reinforces the concept of the imaginal body by conferring on it a religious legitimacy.

Voluntary Death and Ecstatic Experiences

An important commonplace between Shiʿism, Sufism and philosophy, is the notion of 'voluntary death' (*mawt irādī*) and the ability of the men of God to leave their body at will. This theme appears in a sequence taken from Mullā Ṣadrā and Mīr Dāmād, although without their names being mentioned, and concludes with a famous verse by Manṣūr al-Ḥallāj (d. 309/922):

---

[57] *Fānūs al-khayāl*, p. 63. The sources: *Tuḥaf al-ʿuqūl ʿan Āl al-rasūl*, ed. A. al-Ghiffārī (Qum, 1436/2014), p. 363; al-Shaykh Tāj al-Dīn Muḥammad b. Muḥammad al-Shaʿīrī, *Jāmiʿ al-akhbār* (Beirut, 1420/1999), p. 101; Ibn Abī Jumhūr al-Aḥsāʾī, *ʿAwālī al-liʾālī al-ʿazīziyya fi'l-aḥādith al-dīniyya* or *ʿAwālī al-liʾālī al-ḥadīthiyya ʿalā madhab al-imāmiyya*, ed. M. al-ʿIrāqī (Beirut, 1430/2009), vol. 1, p. 97; vol. 2, p. 53.

[58] *Fānūs al-khayāl*, p. 64; al-Kulaynī, *Uṣūl al-Kāfī* (Beirut, 1426/2005), pp. 144–145; Mohammad Ali Amir-Moezzi, *La preuve de Dieu. La mystique shiʿite à travers l'œuvre de Kulaynī (IXᵉ-Xᵉ siècle)* (Paris, 2018), p. 214.

> It is no secret to you that the Creator (. . .), as required by His all-encompassing Mercy and universal Grace, established all bodily and sensory things as images and signs of spiritual and intellective beings; that He made the sensory experience a means of elevation and progression towards the knowledge of intellectual beings. This is the ultimate goal of the advent of the soul among sensory things, of its appearance at the horizon of the material things. Just as material things are deprived in essence and in need of the intelligible beings, the latter being the sudations of the Light of lights and the shadows of its radiations, so the knowledge of bodily and sensory things needs the body and its organs to perceive these things by their means. However, after what it has acquired by sensory experience and through the body, [the soul] does not need anything, except its own essence and substance, in order to perceive the spiritual realities. When it succeeds, it becomes in actuality both Intellect and intellective, and then no longer needs senses or any attachment to the body. Therefore, make efforts to seek the [true] wealth before the extinction of time, the expiration of life and the corruption of [your] body. Thus, the voluntary death, whose attainment is spurred on by the words of the masters of clear vision (*akābir ahl al-baṣāʾir*), must be grasped and attained: 'Die by will and you will live by nature',[59] that is, it is necessary to kill the bond of formal attachments before natural death, to rise from the rank of animality, which is the lowest pit of the Sijjīn, to the highest degree of the angel, and to sit on a place on the Throne of contemplation. [. . .] 'Kill me, my faithful friends / For in my being killed is my life'.[60]

Ashkivarī was inspired by Plato and al-Ḥallāj in regarding death as the source of perfect certitude, quoting a *ḥadīth* attributed to Imam ʿAlī: 'People are asleep, they wake up when they die'.[61] However, he argues, the human rational soul is already able, during its life, to

[59] This sentence is commonly attributed to Plato.

[60] *Fānūs al-khayāl*, pp. 59–60; Ṣadr al-Dīn Shīrāzī, *al-Ḥikma al-mutaʿāliyya fiʾl-asfār al-ʿaqliyya al-arbaʿa*, ed. M. ʿAqīl (Beirut, 1432/2011), vol. 1, p. 352; Mīr Dāmād, *Jadhawāt wa mawāqīt*, p. 79.

[61] *Fānūs al-khayāl*, p. 64; *Miʾa kalimāt liʾl-imām amīr al-muʾminīn ʿAlī b. Abī Ṭālib, sharaḥā Kamāl al-Dīn Maytham al-Baḥrānī* (Beirut, 1412/1992), pp. 54–57.

abstract itself from attachment to the body and the temporal world. The one who acquires the habit (*malaka*) of divesting himself of his body (*khalʿ-i badan*) and attains the level of the perfection of the acquired intellect (*ʿaql-i mustafād*), can thus make his *hijra* from the material world, designated as the 'city of evildoers' (*al-qariya al-ẓālima ahluhā*) according to Q 2:75: 'Our Lord, bring us forth from this city whose people are evildoers' (2:75). Such a man merits the appelation of 'pure intellect' (*ʿaql khāliṣ*) and engages himself in the higher rank of the Malakūt.[62] The ecstatic state of the perfect men is described in a long sequence borrowed from Shahrazūrī and Mullā Ṣadrā, giving another synthesis of philosophy and mysticism under the authority of a *ḥadīth qudsī*:

> Thus, the intellective lights become places of manifestation for the separated souls; these ones are seized by the intellective illuminations and then find themselves in a pleasurableness, a love and a brightness unrelated to the pleasures of this world. [...] Such is the state of the perfect men who have disposed themselves to immateriality after separation [from their bodies].[63] [...] This reveals the secret of what a certain man of spiritual realisation has said: 'When the soul reaches its intellectual perfection, free from any movement and reflection, its faculties become one, so that its science becomes action and its action becomes science, just as the science and power of separate entities, in their relationship with what is subordinate to them, are one.'[64]
>
> Then, when the soul is united to certain immaterial lights and of a sudden is stripped of its body, through the power of intellectual delectations and spiritual elations which adhere to it, through the intensity of the shining auroras, it withdraws from its essence and from the consciousness of its essence. The sovereign of the immaterial and intellectual lights takes hold of it and it then disappears from its own essence (*tafnā ʿan dhātihā*). They describe this state as 'unification' (*ittiḥād*). [...] When the journeying soul reaches the station of unification, so that the weaker light is extinguished in the more powerful and intense light, so that he becomes intoxicated with the pleasures of the

---

62 *Fānūs al-khayāl*, pp. 65–66.

63 Ibid., p. 66; Shahrazūrī, *Rasāʾil al-shajara al-ilāhiyya*, vol. 3, pp. 600–601.

64 *Fānūs al-khayāl*, p. 66; Mullā Ṣadrā, *al-Shawāhid al-rubūbiyya*, p. 200.

> lights of Victory, such that these immaterial lights become the epiphanic forms where rational minds unite, then this soul is in such a state that it only sees the epiphanic form, and speaks only with the language of this epiphanic form, as it says in the *ḥadīth qudsī*: 'My servant draws not near to Me with anything more loved by Me than the religious duties I have enjoined upon him, and My servant continues to draw near to Me with supererogatory works so that I shall love him. When I love him, I am his hearing with which he hears, his seeing with which he sees, his hand with which he grasps (. . .). Were he to ask [something] of Me, I would surely give it to him.'[65]

It is notable that this argument is used in the *Maḥbūb al-qulūb* in order to justify the ecstatic utterances (*shaṭaḥāt*) of Sufis such as Basṭāmī and Ḥallāj against an accusation of heresy;[66] here, it enables the author to validate the ecstatic reports of reputed philosophers past and present.

Ashkivarī gives three testimonies confirming that, in Suhrawardī's words, 'the divine sage is the one for whom the body has become like a tunic, which he sometimes puts on and at other times casts off, and who rises when he wants to the world of Light.'[67] First comes the divine sage Pythagoras, who ascended (*ʿaraja*) by his soul to the higher world until he heard the music of the spheres, and then returned to his body.[68] Then there is the famous account of the *Theology* of the Pseudo-Aristotle, adapted from Plotinus's *Enneads* (IV, 8, 1), beginning with 'often have I been alone with my soul and have doffed my body and laid it aside. . .'.[69] Askhiwarī, quoting it from Suhrawardī,[70] attributes this to Plato but mentions that 'in some books' it is attributed to Aristotle: even more, he considers that both attributions may be

[65] *Fānūs al-khayāl*, p. 67; Shahrazūrī, *Rasā'il al-shajara al-ilāhiyya*, vol. 3, pp. 474–475.

[66] See Terrier, 'The Defence of Sufism', pp. 91–93.

[67] *Fānūs al-khayāl*, p. 37. The source: Shahrazūrī, *Rasā'il al-shajara al-ilāhiyya*, vol. 3, p. 471.

[68] *Fānūs al-khayāl*, p. 29.

[69] *Aflūṭīn ʿinda al-ʿArab – Plotinus apud Arabes*, ed. A. Badawī (Kuwait, 1977), p. 22.

[70] Suhrawardī, *al-Talwīḥāt*, in *Œuvres*, vol. 1, pp. 112–113.

reliable as both sages were prepared to reach such a spiritual level.[71] The third testimony, not attributed by name, is Mīr Dāmād's narrative known as *al-Risāla al-khalʿiyya*, in which he declares: 'It was as if I had divested myself of my body (. . .), as if I had withdrawn from the domain of time to enter the world of sempiternity (*ʿālam al-dahr*).'[72] As in the *Maḥbūb al-qulūb*, Ashkivarī comments on these two last reports by saying that such experience is not 'proper to a people [i.e. the ancient Greeks] at the exclusion of another [i.e. the Muslim 'moderns']', an argument confirmed by a verse of Ḥāfiẓ: 'If the bounty of the Holy Spirit would assist once more / Others would do that which Jesus Christ did.'[73] It should be noted, in all the three cases mentioned, the ecstatic experience comes to corroborate theoretical views on true reality, in accordance with Suhrawardī's claim, quoted in the introduction, that spiritual observation is more trustworthy than any physical kind. In other words, with the concept of imaginal world, metaphysics becomes an empirical discipline, eluding in advance its death as pronounced in Kant's criticism of it.[74]

The Corporal Resurrection

In the last part of the epistle, philosophers, Sufis and men of Revelation (prophets and imams) are brought together in the statement of the twofold Return (*maʿād*) of body and spirit (*jismānī wa rūḥānī*). It is well known that philosophers were frequently accused of denying this tenet, especially since al-Ghazālī's *Tahāfut al-falāsifa*. Ashkivarī aims to defend the first two groups against the charge of unbelief:

---

[71] *Fānūs al-khayāl*, p. 68. Symmetrically, in *Maḥbūb al-qulūb*, vol. 2, p. 139, the same account is attributed to Aristotle, but the hypothesis that it could be from Plato is mentioned.

[72] On this text, see Corbin, *En Islam Iranien*, vol. 4, pp. 43–53; Terrier, 'Mīr Dāmād (m. 1041/1631), philosophe et mujtahid. Autorité spirituelle et autorité juridique en Iran safavide shīʿite', *Studia Islamica*, 113 (2018), pp. 121–165, see pp. 152–156.

[73] *Fānūs al-khayāl*, pp. 69–70. Translation of Ḥāfiẓ taken from Dominic Parviz Brookshaw, *Hafiz and His Contemporaries: Poetry, Performance and Patronage in Fourteenth-Century Iran* (London and New York, 2019), p. 263.

[74] E. Kant, *Critique of Pure Reason, Second Edition*, English tr. N. Kemp Smith (London, 2007), Preface, pp. 17–37.

> Men of weak intelligence assume that the people of *ishrāq*, the Peripatetic philosophers and the Sufi masters do not profess the resurrection of the body. This is far from being the case! Contrary to these erroneous assumptions, all of them explicitly professed this tenet by referring to and conforming themselves to the divine Revelations. (. . .) What they said is that the resurrection of the body cannot be proved by the way of demonstrative syllogisms. That is why they have only expressed themselves on the resurrection of the soul (*al-maʿād al-nafsānī*), in terms of the support provided for this view by demonstrative syllogisms.[75]

A passage of Ibn Sīnā's *Kitāb al-Najāt* is quoted as evidence for this statement.[76] Then, Ashkivarī reproduces a lengthy section of Mullā Ṣadrā's commentary on *al-Hidāya al-athīriyya*, in which Ibn Sīnā and al-Ghazālī are quoted in turn in order to provide a distinction between sensory, imaginal (*khayālī*) and intellectual pleasures.[77] The reconciliation of these two thinkers over the concept of the 'imaginal' can seem like an ironic glance at the controversy about the *Tahāfut al-falāsifa*. To be sure, in the thought of the Shiʿi gnostics such as Mullā Ṣadrā and Ashkivarī, the quarrel between the philosophers, theologians and mystics is definitely over.

The argument continues with the issue of the resurrected body. The *ishrāqī* notion of prime matter (*hayūlā*) as a continuous and infinite subtle body (*jism*), allows for conservation in the grave until the Day of the Resurrection, of certain particles of the original body. These original particles (*al-ajzāʾ al-aṣliyya*) are designated in the *akhbār* as the clay (*ṭīna*) or the sacrum bone (*ʿajb al-dhanab*), from which the individual body will be recreated after the time of the Isthmus (the interregnum of the Grave).[78] Ashkivarī argues that this also

---

[75] *Fānūs al-khayāl*, pp. 76–77.

[76] Ibid., p. 77; Ibn Sīnā, *Kitāb al-Najāt*, ed. M. Fakhrī (Beirut, 1405/1985), p. 326; idem, *Ilāhiyyāt al-Shifāʾ*, ed. G. C. Anawati and S. Zāyid (Qum, 1404/1983), p. 423.

[77] *Fānūs al-khayāl*, pp. 78–81. Mullā Ṣadrā, *Sharḥ al-hidāya al-athīriyya*, ed. M. Muḥammadī (Tehran, 1393 Sh./2014), vol. 2, pp. 315–323. Ibn Sīnā, *Ilāhiyyāt al-Shifāʾ*, p. 432; al-Ghazālī, *Risālat al-maḍnūn bihi ʿalā ghayr ahlihi*, in idem, *Majmūʿat rasāʾil al-imām al-Ghazālī* (Beirut, 2011), vol. 4, pp. 111–113.

[78] *Fānūs al-khayāl*, pp. 85–89.

corroborates the belief in *rajʿa*, i.e. the resurrection of certain deceased individuals, among the people of *walāya* and their enemies, for the manifestation of the Redeemer (*al-qāʾim*). This tenet, he says, distinguishes the people of the 'saved sect' (*al-firqa al-nājiya*), i.e., the Imāmī Shiʿis, from the people of 'the sect of the hypocrites and of the infidels', i.e., the Sunnis.[79] The ecumenism of our thinker here reveals its limits. It should be noted that the doctrine of *rajʿa* is known to be supported by the *ghulāt*, probably more faithful to the original doctrine than the so-called 'moderate' Shiʿi scholars, who generally tended to overlook the messianic doctrine. In a tour de force that can also be found in his contemporary Muḥsin Fayḍ Kāshānī,[80] Ashkivarī defends this ancient, pre-philosophical and non-rational tenet of Shiʿi Islam, by suggesting that its reality has to be situated in the imaginal world as defined by the *ishrāqī* philosophers.

In his conclusion, Ashkivarī stresses that asceticism and spiritual exercises (*riyāḍāt*), i.e. autodeification (*taʾalluh*), are necessary in order to be able to apprehend the imaginal world.[81] This philosophical concept having been itself regarded necessary to interpret correctly the Revelation (i.e. Qurʾan and Imāmī *ḥadīth*), one may understand that for Ashkivarī, to paraphrase Sayyid Ḥaydar Āmulī, the true Shiʿi has to be a philosopher and a Sufi, just as the true philosopher and the true Sufi have to be Shiʿis in order to achieve their perfection and fulfill their salvation.

Conclusion

Ashkivarī's *Fānūs al-khayāl* is not only the first monograph on the imaginal world; it is also one of the few works of the Safavid period to openly defend Shiʿi esotericism, philosophy and Sufism all together. No doubt the decision to dedicate this epistle to the concept of the imaginal world was not in any way accidental. Indeed, it responded to major challenges of his time, both theoretical and practical: on the one hand, rationalising the most esoteric material of the ancient Imāmī

---

79 Ibid., pp. 89–93.

80 Fayḍ Kāshānī, *Kalimāt maknūna*, pp. 88–89.

81 *Fānūs al-khayāl*, pp. 109–111.

tradition in order to better preserve it; on the other, and as if in exchange, to integrate *ishrāqī* philosophy and theoretical Sufism into the heritage of the Imāmī Shiʿi understanding of Islam. In so doing, the concept of the imaginal world itself plays the role of an isthmus connecting the main spiritual trends of Islam.

15

Shah Ṭahmāsp's View of Nature, as Reflected in his *Shāhnāma*[1]

Sheila R. Canby

Shah Ṭahmāsp, the second Safavid shah who ruled from 930/1524 to 984/1576, has been widely acknowledged as an inspired patron of the arts of the book, particularly in the first half of his reign. Despite acceding to the throne at the tender age of ten, Ṭahmāsp engaged a team of artists, binders, calligraphers and others to produce a magnificent *Shāhnāma* manuscript consisting of 759 folios and 258 illustrations.[2] The manuscript's illustrations not only represent the finest, most inspired paintings of their day, but also provide insights into myriad physical features of early Safavid Iran, ranging from dress and armour to architecture, flora and fauna. This paper will focus on the flora and fauna that appear in a selection of the *Shāhnāma* paintings in order to investigate whether they reflect the actual environment of Iran in the 10th/16th century and by extension the Safavid attitude to the land and its stewardship. If such an outlook can be determined, to what extent did it reflect the Safavids' Shiʿi faith or is it simply an extension of a long-standing approach to Iranian resource management? Needless to say, 10th/16th century illustrations to a

---

[1] I would like to thank The Institute of Ismaili Studies for inviting me to deliver the paper on which this chapter is based at the London conference, 'The Renaissance of Shiʿi Islam in the 15th–17th Centuries: Facets of Thought and Practice', in October 2018.

[2] The manuscript's illustrations are published in full in Martin Bernard Dickson and Stuart Cary Welch, *The Houghton Shahnameh* (Cambridge, MA, 1981) and Sheila R. Canby, *The Shahnama of Shah Tahmasp* (New York, 2011, 2nd ed. 2014). The *Shāhnāma*, or Book of Kings, was composed by Abu'l-Qāsim Firdawsī and completed in 400/1010.

literary work are not photographs. Artists were just as likely to base their depiction of a horse or a flower on a pictorial prototype as an actual living example, especially in the case of certain wild animals. Thus, underlying any discussion of flora and fauna in the *Shāhnāma* paintings is the question of naturalism and how faithfully the artists reproduced the details of their world.

In 'The Feast of Sada' (fig. 15.1), attributed to Sulṭān Muḥammad who was Ṭahmāsp's teacher, Hūshang, the grandson of the first Iranian legendary king, Gāyumars, is depicted at the beginning of a feast on a mountainside celebrating the discovery of fire. This king is credited in the *Shāhnāma* with the development of metalworking and animal husbandry, a subject woven into the composition of this painting. Wild animals appear in the mountains at the top of the painting. In addition, faces of lions and other creatures are embedded in the rocks at the lower right and in combination with human forms in the outcrops above Hūshang. At the upper left and right are groups of men, some of whom clutch animals in their arms. Held as if they were pets, a young fox and a marmot at the left and a leopard cub and another marmot appear in the story as 'furry rovers' who were slain for their skins to clothe men. Oxen, asses and sheep, however, were domesticated and 'turned to good use . . . for toil, . . . [and] their produce' and taxes were paid on profits made from them.[3]

Along the lower edge of the painting appear a number of animals that were domesticated and some that were not. At the right a red deer with a magnificent set of antlers turns back towards his doe, while at the lower right edge a pair of young deer peek out behind the rocks. These, of course, are animals that were never tamed. Moving to the left along the lower edge of the image, we see a herdsman with four goats and a mouflon sheep with s-shaped horns and at the far left a bullock and cow and a mule braying. Although mouflon sheep appear on Sasanian dishes of the 5th–6th century,[4] they are shown hunted in the wild. Interestingly, they are now considered the ancestors of domestic

---

[3] Firdawsi, *Shahnama*, tr. Arthur George Warner and Edmond Warner (London, 1905–1929) https://persian.packhum.org/main, v. 19, (accessed on 28 March 2019).

[4] Prudence Oliver Harper and Pieter Meyers, *Silver Vessels of the Sasanian Period* (New York, 1981), vol. 1, pp. 64–66, pl. 17.

sheep, but the appearance of the mouflon in this painting may have more to do with Sulṭān Muḥammad's desire to suggest the transition from wild to domestic that took place during the reign of Hūshang. If that is a subtext of this painting, the range from wild to tame would occur across the lower edge of the image from right to left.

Firdawsī's mention of taxes paid on income from rearing animals reflects the longevity of an organised system of agriculture in Iran. The Turko-Mongol occupation of the country from the 5th/11th to the 9th/15th century introduced new ways of distributing land such as the *iqṭā* in which tribal leaders whose followers were conscripted to fight for the reigning sultan were rewarded with land grants. In the early Safavid period the Qizil-bāsh Turkomans who supported the shahs also received land as payment. However, the shahs additionally converted certain lands into crown property and collected taxes from sharecroppers and the landed gentry. Although Ṭahmāsp was a teenager during the period in which this *Shāhnāma* was produced, he would have understood that his dominion depended on agriculture supported by the domestic animals – cattle, donkeys, and sheep – depicted in 'The Feast of Sada'.

As for produce from the land, the pomegranates and apples or guava fruit on a dish at the right allude to the orchards found in various parts of Iran. Otherwise, the notable plants in this painting are flowers and trees. Aside from the small conifers along the ridges of the mountains, the few deciduous trees include a flowering prunus at the left and lower down a couple of leafy trees without flowers. Prunus, a member of the rose family, includes some of the fruit most favoured in Iran such as peaches, apricots and almonds. Although they can grow wild, they were cultivated in domestic gardens and often appear in this *Shāhnāma*'s illustrations in tamer settings than this one. The flowers include a pair of hollyhocks on either side of Hūshang, suggesting an arch or niche to frame him. At the base of the hollyhock spray at the right are blue and white six-petalled flowers that are most likely primulas. Next to the trunk of the prunus tree grows a red lily, while in the lower part of the painting a large blue iris appears next to the fire with small yellow and white flowers sprouting around its base, apparently primroses or cowslips. While all of these plants and flowers can be found in Iran and were presumably familiar to the artist, some of them recur repeatedly throughout the manuscript in scenes set in the wild or in palace gardens. Unlike the animals, the story line rarely hangs on an individual flower or tree. Yet, Persian poetry abounds with floral imagery and like an underlying melody, flowers appear in almost every illustration of Ṭahmāsp's *Shāhnāma*.

One problem with trying to connect the depictions of flora and fauna in Ṭahmāsp's *Shāhnāma* with his view of nature is that the written information about him is mostly second-hand, written by historians concerned with politics and regional power struggles, chroniclers writing after Ṭahmāsp's death or composers of poetical panegyrics. None of the sources dates exactly to the period in which the manuscript was produced, roughly between 930 and 941/1524 and 1535. On the one hand, this increases the importance of the *Shāhnāma* illustrations as documents of their time, and on the other it forces one to look outside that decade for relevant texts. One of these is the five-part poem *Jannat-i ʿadn* or 'The Garden of Eden', from 965–7/1557–60, by ʿAbdī Beg Shīrāzī, a longstanding Safavid government administrator and poet. This five-part poem was commissioned by Shah Ṭahmāsp to celebrate the building of his new palace at Qazvīn between the late 950s–965/early 1550s and 1558–59. In addition to descriptions of the wall paintings in the palace buildings and the general relationship of palace buildings to one another, the poet provides a detailed account of its various gardens. While the whole poem praises Shah Ṭahmāsp's taste and the wondrous artists who realised his vision, it also provides a sense of the combination of elements in an ideal garden, with lovely, scented flowers and delicious fruit.

In addition to small gardens associated with the main palace buildings, a pavilion, the Chihil Sutūn, sat in the centre of a large formal garden with other small buildings and gardens around it. (fig. 15.2) In his lyrical, somewhat extravagant poem ʿAbdī Beg describes the shah's garden as consisting of two avenues that cross and just below the intersection stands a pavilion, the Chihil Sutūn. On either side of the perpendicular avenues ran water channels along which were planted trees, bushes and flowers. Called Saʿādatābād, this garden included the Dawlat-khāna where the shah lived as well as lodgings for government and military employees, smaller gardens and water courses. While only the Chihil Sutūn remains today, the description seems to indicate that the shah's garden was constructed along the lines of the *chahār bāgh*, a formal garden with rectangular plots intersected by water channels forming four, or multiples of four, sections. According to the poem apples, plums, peaches and 'hundreds of kinds of flowers' grew in the garden along with red and yellow roses that 'make the grieving hearts bloom'.[5] A modern reconstruction of another 10th/16th-century garden, described in the *Irshād al-zirā'a*, a 10th/16th-century treatise on cultivation and agriculture, shows how trees, bushes and flowers were planted in square plots on either side of a central channel.[6]

Two illustrations from the *Shāhnāma*, 'Siyāvush and Farangīs Wedded' (fig. 15.3) and 'The Coronation of the Infant Shāpūr II' (fig. 15.4) are both set in gardens, but the gardens do not conform to the *chahār bāgh* plan. Instead, in both of them a pavilion stands before a hillside through which flows a stream, once silver, now tarnished to black. The brick structure in the painting of Siyāvush and Farangīs has a window next to their bed through which we see a large hollyhock on a gold ground. Presumably the artist, Qāsim b. 'Alī, intended to imply that the hill dropped off so steeply that one could only see the sky from the window, not the earth from which the flower springs. Despite the flowers, clumps of vegetation and the flowering tree, why would we consider this to be a cultivated garden and not just a meadow with wild flowers, shrubs and trees? The gate at the right through which young women crowd onto the terrace where musicians play is one indication that they are coming from another part of the royal precinct. Moreover, the permanence of the structure and the high wall at the left of the picture imply that uninhabited or at least undeveloped space lies beyond the wall, in contrast to the greensward at the right. Most convincing is the figure in the red tunic turning to look at a greybeard who offers him a round yellow object, perhaps one of the gold coins thrown to the crowd at the wedding of Farangīs and Siyāvush. Over the shoulder of the younger man is a spade, its business end now oxidised and misshapen. A gardener with a spade would have no role on an uncultivated hillside. Even if the vegetation around him is

[5] Paul E. Losensky, 'The Palace of Praise and the Melons of Time: Descriptive Patterns in 'Abdī Bayk Šīrāzī's *Garden of Eden*', *Eurasian Studies*, 1 (2003), p. 12.

[6] D. Fairchild Ruggles, *Islamic Gardens and Landscapes* (Philadelphia, PA, 2008), p. 60, fig. 36.

rendered in a conventional style, the presence of what appears to be a Rose of Sharon seems to conform to one type of garden found in late 9th/15th and early 10th/16th century paintings.

'The Coronation of the Infant Shāpūr II' presents a variation on the garden and pavilion theme of 'Siyāvush and Farangīs Wedded'. Instead of placing the protagonist, the infant king Shāpūr II, in a permanent structure, he has been seated on an ornate throne within a portable pergola. Out of the tiled building at the right emerges a servant with a platter of gems to be presented to the new king, while young ladies regard the scene from an upstairs window. The garden extends up a hill beyond a red fence. Once again, the scene contains a gardener holding his spade, beside a small stream. Here the artist, Muẓaffar ʿAlī, who would go on to decorate the walls of Shah Ṭahmāsp's new palace in Qazvīn, has taken care to depict the flowers and trees accurately. The pink flower at the right appears to be a variety of primula, while the flowering tree is probably an almond. At the foot of a pair of cypresses with differently coloured trunks to the right of the throne are a purple iris and a red lily while slightly higher up on the hill is what appears to be a variety of wallflower. The tall cypress behind the throne may be a reference to the future stature of the king, but it is also one of the trees most closely associated with the *chāhar bāgh* type garden. Nonetheless, the gardens in these illustrations conform to a type found in painting from the 9th/15th and into the 10th/16th century that presents the garden as a pleasant place in the countryside surrounded by a fence. Although gardeners may have tended the plants, they were not grown in beds or lined up along straight canals. Rigidly planned *chāhar bāgh* gardens only begin to appear in Persian painting in the second half of the 11th/17th century, as in the 1074/1663 *Shāhnāma* illustration of 'Siyāvush Captive before Afrāsiyāb' (fig. 15.5) by Muḥammad Zamān.[7] Even though the *chāhar bāgh* type garden is attested in Iran by the Mughal Bābur by 912/1506, the concept of the ideal garden with a natural stream outside an enclosure

[7] B.W. Robinson, 'The Shahnameh Cochran 4 in the Metropolitan Museum of Art', in Richard Ettinghausen, ed., *Islamic Art in the Metropolitan Museum of Art* (New York, 1972), p. 76 attributes the painting to Muḥammad Zamān on the basis of the inscription 'Yā sāhib al-zamān' that appears below the curtain.

remained stubbornly current for over a century and a half. Since Shah Ṭahmāsp spent a great deal of time moving around his kingdom, trying to quell rebellions or fighting against the Uzbeks in the east, he would have been familiar with the variety of landscapes in Iran. While his construction of a new palace in Qazvīn and the transfer of the administrative capital there were part of a strategic move away from the border with the Ottomans, ʿAbdī Beg Shīrāzī's detailed description of the buildings and the grounds of Saʿādatābād Garden suggests that Ṭahmāsp appreciated his natural surroundings and was so pleased with his new capital that he commissioned a long poem praising it.

Whether the depiction of animals and landscapes in the *Shāhnāma* produced for Shah Ṭahmāsp can be linked to a Shiʿi point of view is almost impossible to prove. According to Ann Lambton, 'early Shiʿi authorities [were] even more theoretical than the Sunni authorities, since the Shiʿi, except for certain isolated instances such as the Zaydīs in the Caspian provinces and the Būyids, did not achieve political power until the Safavid period, and there was no imperative need for them . . . to reconcile theory with practice.'[8] In the six hundred years between the Būyids and the Safavids the systems of land tenure in Iran mentioned earlier became well established. Following on from the position of the Safavid shahs as divinely ordained spiritual and temporal leaders, the lands they ruled were theoretically owned by them as well, though in practice this took the form of appropriating privately owned land to use it for land grants to tribal leaders and their militias. We would call this redistribution. Moreover, land given in *waqf* to Shiʿi shrines by landowners in the early Safavid period attests to the continuation of the traditional system of land ownership.

Shah Ṭahmāsp's well-known aversion to hunting – he apparently only liked to fish – may also reflect a dislike of the large-scale carnage that occurred in big organised hunts with scores of participants. What this antipathy to killing animals actually means and if it was based in the religious belief that animals have souls and by extension should not be slaughtered for sport or was a basic distaste for hunting as a pastime remains a matter of debate. Where the land was concerned,

---

[8] A. K. S. Lambton, *Landlord and Peasant in Persia: A Study of Land Tenure and Land Revenue Administration* (London, 1953), p. xx.

ʿAbdī Beg Shīrāzī's poem equates Ṭahmāsp's new garden with the garden of Paradise and calls him the 'king of power and faith' and states 'The King of Kings has spread out a cradle [*mahd*] of security.'[9] Certainly, he was viewed as a righteous temporal and spiritual leader and descendant of the Shiʿi imams. Through his sparing of wild animals and his commissioning of a major garden, can he be considered a responsible steward of the natural world?

To a certain extent the paintings in Ṭahmāsp's *Shāhnāma* represent the environment of Iran as it must have existed in the early 10th/16th century. Yet, even details such as a day lily sprouting next to an iris at the foot of a pair of cypresses suggest that Ṭahmāsp's artists manipulated nature to their own pictorial needs. Thus, they placed botanically correctly drawn flowers in artistically expedient situations. Similarly, in 'The Feast of Sada' the placement of wild and domesticated animals in close proximity to one another serves a narrative purpose but compresses the natural setting so all the different creatures are found in one place at the same time. What the manuscript succeeds in doing is conjuring up the many environments of Iran as a charming and believable backdrop for the myriad episodes of the *Shāhnāma* without necessarily respecting the temporality or spatial unity of the natural world. While the depiction of flora and fauna may have been primarily in the service of pictorial necessities or predilections in Ṭahmāsp's *Shāhnāma*, the level of verisimilitude strongly suggests not only a high level of awareness of plants and animals but the desire on the part of the artists and their patron to render them faithfully and thus respectfully.

---

[9] Paul E. Losensky, 'The Palace of Praise', p. 28.

Selected Bibliography

Works of Reference

Encyclopaedia of Islam, ed. M. Th. Houtsma et al. 1st edition, Leiden-London, 1913–1938; reprinted, Leiden, 1987.
Encyclopaedia of Islam, ed. H. A. R. Gibb et al. New edition, Leiden, 1960–2006.
Encyclopaedia of Islam, ed. Kate Fleet et al. 3rd ed., Leiden, Boston, 2007—
Encyclopaedia Iranica, ed. E. Yarshater. London and New York, 1982—
Encyclopaedia Islamica, ed. W. Madelung and F. Daftary, Leiden, 2008—
Daftary, Farhad. *Ismaili Literature: A Bibliography of Sources and Studies*. London, 2004.
Ivanow, Wladimir. *Ismaili Literature: A Bibliographical Survey*. Tehran, 1963.
Kaḥḥāla, ʿUmar Riḍā. *Muʿjam al-muʾallifīn: tarājim muṣannifī al-kutub al-ʿArabiyya*. Damascus, 1957–1961, 13 vols.
Khuyī, ʿAlī Ṣadrāyī. *Kitābshinās-yi Tajrīd al-iʿtiqād*. Qum, 2003.
Modarressi, Hossein. *Tradition and Survival: A Bibliographical Survey of Early Shīʿite Literature*. Oxford, 2003.
al-Mudarris, Mīrzā Muḥammad ʿAlī. *Rayḥānat al-adab: dar tarājim-i aḥwāl-i maʿrūfīn bi-kunya aw laqab yā kunan wa alqāb*. Tehran, 1967, 6 vols.
al-Najāshī, Abu'l-ʿAbbās. *Fahrasat asmāʾ muṣannifī al-shīʿa al-mushtahiru bi*-Rijāl al-Nahāshī, ed. Mūsā al-Shubayrī al-Zanjānī. Qum, 1995.
al-Ṭihrānī, Āghā Buzurg. *al-Ḍarīʿa ilā taṣānīf al-shīʿa*. Beirut, 1403/1983, 26 vols.
——. *Ṭabaqāt aʿlām al-shīʿa*, ed. ʿAlī Naqī Munzawī. Beirut, 1971, 26 vols.

Texts and Translations

Abū Isḥāq Quhistānī. *Haft bāb*, ed. and tr. W. Ivanow. Bombay, 1959.
al-Afandī (Efendī), ʿAbd Allāh b. ʿĪsā. *Riyāḍ al-ʿulamāʾ*. Qum, 1401/1981.
Afūshta-yi Naṭanzī, Maḥmūd b. Hidāyat Allāh. *Naqāvat al-āthār fī dhikr al-akhyār dar tārīkh-i ṣafaviyya*, ed. Iḥsān Ishrāqī. Tehran, 1373 Sh./1994.
Āl ʿAṣfūr, Ḥusayn b. Muḥammad. *ʿUyūn al-ḥaqāʾiq al-nāẓira fī tatimmat al-ḥadāʾiq al-Nāḍira*. Qum, 1414/1993.
Āl Sunbul, Ḍiyāʾ, ed. *Mawsūʿat al-Fāḍil al-Qaṭīfī*. Qum, 1429/2008.
al-ʿĀmilī, ʿAlī. *al-Durr al-manthūr min al-maʾthūr wa-ghayr al-maʾthūr*. Qum, 1398/1978, 2 vols.
al-ʿĀmilī, Zayn al-Dīn. *Sharḥ al-Bidāya fī ʿilm al-dirāya*, ed. Muḥammad Riḍā al-Ḥusaynī al-Jalālī. Qum, 1432/2011.
al-Ardabīlī, Aḥmad b. Muḥammad al-Muqaddas. *Majmaʿ al-fāʾida*. Qum, 1403/1983.
al-Astarabādī, Muḥammad Amīn. *al-Fawāʾid al-madaniyya* wa bi-dhaylihi *al-Shawāhid al-Makkiyya li-Nūr al-Dīn al-Mūsawī al-ʿĀmilī*. 2nd ed., Qum, 2005.
Ashkivarī, Quṭb al-Dīn. *Fānūs al-khayāl*, MS 1615, Malek Library, Tehran.
——. *Maḥbūb al-qulūb*, ed. I. al-Dībājī and H. Ṣidqī. Tehran, 1378–1382 Sh./1999–2003, 2 vols.

Badawī, ʿAbd al-Raḥmān, ed. *Uthūlūjiyā: Afluṭīn ʿinda al-ʿArab*. 2nd ed., Qum, 1413/1992.
al-Baḥrānī, Yūsuf. *al-Ḥadāʾiq al-nāḍira*. Qum, 1363–1367 Sh./1985–1987.
———. *Luʾluʾat al-Baḥrayn*, ed. Muḥammad Ṣādiq Baḥr al-ʿUlūm. Tehran, n.d.
Dihdār Shīrāzī, Muḥammad. *Rasāʾil-i dihdār*, ed. Muḥammad Ḥusayn Akbarī Sāvī. Tehran, 1375 Sh./1996.
Fāḍilī, ʿAlī, ed. ʿal-Ḥāshiya ʿalā *Uṣūl al-Kāfī* li Muḥammad Amīn al-Astarabādī, jamaʿahā wa-rattabahā Mawlā Khalīl Qazwīnī (d. 1089AH/1678AD)', *Mīrāth-i ḥadīth-i shīʿa*, 8 (2001), pp. 229–410.
———. 'Ḥāshiyat *Man lā yaḥḍuruhu al-faqīh*, Mawlā Muḥammad Amīn Astarabādī (d. 1036)', *Mīrāth-i ḥadīth-i shīʿa*, 10 (2003), pp. 449–513.
———. '*Ḥāshiyat al-Istibṣār*, Muḥammad Amīn Astarabādī (d. 1036) wa Muḥammad Astarabādī, collected by Muḥammad b. Jābir Najafī', *Mīrāth-i ḥadīth-i shīʿa*, 13 (1384 Sh./2005), pp. 35–125.
al-Faḍlī, ʿAbd al-Hādī. *Introduction to Ḥadīth, including* Dirāyat al-Ḥadīth *by al Shahīd al-Thānī*, tr. N. Virjee. London, 2002.
Fidāʾī Khurāsānī, Muḥammad b. Zayn al-ʿĀbidīn. *Hidāyat al-muʾminīn al-ṭālibīn*, ed. Aleksandr A. Semenov. Moscow, 1959.
al-Fiqh al-mansūb li'l-Imām al-Riḍā al-mushtahir bi-Fiqh al-Riḍā. Beirut, 1411/1990.
Firdawsī, Abu'l-Qasim. *Shahnama*, tr. Arthur George Warner and Edmond Warner. London, 1905–1929, 9 vols.
Ḥāfiẓ-i Ābrū, ʿAbd Allāh b. Luṭf Allāh al-Bihdādīnī. *Zubdat al-tawārīkh*, ed. Sayyid Javādī. Tehran, 1380 Sh./2001, 4 vols.
Ḥājjī Khalīfa, Kâtip Çelebi. *Kashf al-ẓunūn ʿan asāmī al-kutub wa'l-funūn* [with introduction by Āyāt Allāh Sayyid Shihāb al-Dīn Najafī Marʿashī]. Beirut, n.d., 2 vols.
Ḥasan-i Maḥmūd-i Kātib. *Dīwān-i qāʾimiyyāt*, ed. S.J. Badakhchani. Tehran, 1390 Sh./2011; 2nd ed., 1395 Sh./2016.
al-Ḥillī, al-Ḥasan b. Yūsuf, al-ʿAllāma. *Irshād al-adhhān ilā aḥkām al-aymān*. Qum, 1410/1989.
———. *Qawāʿid al-aḥkām*. Qum, 1413/1992.
al-Ḥillī, Jaʿfar b. al-Ḥasan, al-Muḥaqqiq. *al-Mukhtaṣar al-nāfiʿ fī fiqh al-imāmiyya*. Tehran, 1387/1967.
———. *Sharāʾiʿ al-Islām fī masāʾil al-ḥalāl wa'l-ḥarām*. Tehran, 1374 Sh./1995.
al-Ḥurr al-Āmilī and Mīrzā Ḥusayn al-Nūrī. *Wasāʾil al-shīʿa wa-mustadrakuhā*. Qum, 1433/2011, 22 vols.
Ḥusaynī Qummī, Qāḍī Aḥmad. *Khulāṣat al-tawārīkh*, ed. Iḥsān Ishrāqī. Tehran, 1980.
Ibn Abī Jumhūr al-Aḥsāʾī, Muḥammad b. ʿAlī. *ʿAwālī al-laʾālī al-ʿazīziyya fi'l-aḥādīth al-dīniyya*, ed. Mujtabā al-ʿIrāqī. Qum, 1983, 4 vols.
———. *Mujlī mirʾat al-munjī fi'l-kalām wa'l-ḥikmatayn wa'l-taṣawwuf*, ed. R. Y. Fārmad. Beirut, 2013.
Ibn Bābawayh, Abū Jaʿfar Muḥammad b. Abu'l-Ḥasan ʿAlī. *Kamāl al-dīn*. Qum, 1380 Sh./2001.
———. *Man lā yaḥḍuruhu al-faqīh*. Qum, 1414/1994.
Ibn Idrīs, Muḥammad b. Manṣūr al-Ḥillī. *Musṭarafāt al-sarāʾir*. Qum, 1411/1990.
Ibn Sīnā, Abū ʿAlī al-Ḥusayn b. ʿAbd Allāh. *al-Ishārāt wa'l-tanbīhāt, maʿa sharḥ al-Khwāja Naṣīr al-Dīn al-Ṭūsī wa'l- Muḥākamāt li Quṭb al-Dīn al-Rāzī*, ed. Karīm Fayḍī. Qum, 1383 Sh./2004.
———. *al-Shifāʾ: al-Manṭiq*, vol. 1, *al-Madkhal*. Cairo, n.d.
———. *al-Taʿlīqāt*, ed. Sayyid Ḥusayn Mūsawiyān. Tehran, 1391 Sh./2013.
al-Iṣfahānī, Mīrzā ʿAbd Allāh. *Riyāḍ al-ʿulamāʾ wa-ḥiyāḍ al-fuḍalāʾ*, ed. Aḥmad al-Ḥusaynī. Qum, 1982, 6 vols.
al-Jazāʾirī, Niʿmat Allāh. *Kashf al-asrār fī sharḥ al-Istibṣār*, ed. Al-Muftī al-Sayyid Ṭayyib al-Mūsawī al-Jazāʾirī. Qum, 1408/1987, 3 vols.
al-Kāshānī, Mullā Muḥsin Fayḍ. *Kalimāt maknūna*, ed. ʿA. ʿAlīzāda. Qum, 1390 Sh./2011.

———. *Mafātīḥ al-sharā'i' fī fiqh al-imāmiyya*, ed. Mahdī Rajā'ī. Qum, 1402/1982, 3 vols.
———. *Mu'taṣam al-shī'a fī aḥkām al-sharī'a*, ed. Masīḥ al-Tawḥīdī. Tehran, 1387 Sh./2008, 3 vols.
Khākī Khurāsānī, Imām Qulī. *An Abbreviated Version of the Diwan of Khaki Khorasani*, ed. Wladimir Ivanow. Bombay, 1352/1933.
Khūzānī Iṣfahānī, Faḍlī Beg. *A Chronicle of the Reign of Shah 'Abbas [Afḍal al-tawārīkh]*, ed. Kioumars Ghereghlou. Cambridge, 2015, 2 vols.
Khwāfī, Aḥmad Faṣīḥ. *Mujmal-i faṣīḥī*, ed. Sayyid Muḥsin Nājī Naṣrābādī. Tehran, 1386 Sh./2007, 3 vols.
al-Khwānsārī, Muḥammad Bāqir. *Rawḍāt al-jannāt*. Qum, 1390–1392/1970–1972.
al-Kulaynī, Abū Ja'far Muḥammad b. Ya'qūb. *Uṣūl al-kāfī*. Beirut, 1426/2005
al-Majlisī, Muḥammad Bāqir. *Biḥār al-anwār*. Beirut, 1403/1983, 110 vols.
Majlisī, Muḥammad Taqī. *'Ayn al-ḥayāt*, ed. 'Alī Muḥammad Rafī'ī. Tehran, n.d.
———. *Mir'āt al-'uqūl*, ed. Sayyid Hāshim Rasūlī Maḥallātī. 2nd ed., Tehran, 1404/1984.
al-Maqrīzī, Taqī al-Dīn Aḥmad b. 'Alī. *Durar al-'uqūd al-farīda fī tarājim al-a'yān al-mufīda*. Beirut, 1423/2002, 4 vols.
Mīr Dāmād, Muḥammad Bāqir b. Shams al-Dīn Muḥammad al-Astarābadī. *Jadhawāt wa mawāqīt*, ed. 'Alī Awjabī. Tehran, 1380 Sh./2001.
———. *Muṣannafāt*, ed. 'Abd Allāh Nūrānī. Tehran, 1381–1385 Sh./2002–2006, 2 vols.
———. *al-Qabasāt*, ed. Mahdī Mohaghegh. 2nd ed., Tehran, 1374 Sh./1995.
———. *al-Rawāshīh al-samāwiyya*, ed. G. Qaysariha et al. Qum, 1422/2001.
———. *al-Ufuq al-mubīn*, ed. Ḥāmid Nājī. Tehran, 1391 Sh./2013.
Mīr Khwānd, Ghiyāth al-Dīn Muḥammad b. Khwandshāh. *Ḥabīb al-siyar*. Tehran, 1954.
Munshī, Iskandar Beg. *Tārīkh-i 'ālamārā-yi 'Abbāsī*, tr. R. Savory and R. Bernhard as *History of Shah 'Abbas the Great*. Boulder, CO, 1978, 2 vols.
Mustanṣir bi'llāh (II). *Pandiyāt-i javānmardī*, ed. and tr. W. Ivanow. Leiden, 1953.
Mustawfī Qazwīnī, Ḥamd Allāh. *Nuzhat al-qulūb*, ed. M. Dabīr Siyāqī. Qazvin, 1381 Sh./2002.
Mullā Ṣadrā, Ṣadr al-Dīn Muḥammad al-Shīrāzī. *Sharḥ Uṣūl al-kāfī*, ed. Riḍā Ustādī et al. Tehran, 1384–1387 Sh./2003–2008, 4 vols.
———. *al-Ḥikma al-muta'āliya fi'l-asfār al-'aqliyya al-arba'a*, ed. R. Luṭfī, I. Amīnī and F. Ummīd. 3rd ed., Beirut, 1981.
———. *al-Shawāhid al-rubūbiyya*, ed. S.J. Ashtiyānī. Mashhad, 1360 Sh./1981.
Nāṣir-i Khusraw, Ḥakīm Abū Mu'īn. *Kitab-e Jami' al-Hikmatain: Le livre réunissant les deux sagesses; ou harmonie de la philosophie Grecque et de la théosophie Ismaélienne*, ed. Henry Corbin and M. Mu'in. Tehran and Paris, 1953.
———. *Wajh-i dīn*, ed. Ghulām Riḍā A'wānī. Tehran, 1977.
Navā'ī, Mīr 'Alī Shīr. *Majālis al-nafā'is*. Ankara, 2001, 2 vols.
al-Qazwīnī, 'Abd al-Nabī. *Tatmīm Amal al-āmil*, ed. Sayyid Aḥmad al-Ḥusaynī. Qum, 1986.
Qazwīnī Iṣfahānī, Muḥammad Yūsuf Wālih. *Khuld-i barīn: Sections 6–7*, ed. Mīr Hāshim Muḥaddith. Tehran, 2001.
al-Qummī, 'Abbās b. Muḥammad Riḍā. *al-Kunā wa'l-alqāb*. Najaf, 1970, 3 vols.
al-Risāla al-Jāmi'a, ed. Jamīl Ṣalībā. Damascus, 1949.
Rūmlū, Ḥasan. *Aḥsan al-tawārīkh*, ed. 'Abd al-Ḥusayn Navā'ī. Tehran, 2005.
Sabzawārī, Ḥājj Mullā Hādī. *Sharḥ al-manẓūma fi'l-manṭiq wa'l-ḥikma*, ed. Muḥsin Bīdārfarr. Qum, 1386 Sh./2007.
al-Sabzawārī, Muḥammad Bāqir. *Dhakhīrat al-ma'ād*. Qum, 1984.
al-Sakhawī, Shams al-Dīn. *al-Ḍaw' al-lāmi' li ahl al-qarn al-tāsi'*. Beirut, 1412/1992, 6 vols.
Samarqandī, Kamāl al-Dīn 'Abd al-Razzāq. *Matla' al-sa'dayn wa majma' al-baḥrayn*, ed. 'Abd al-Ḥusayn Navā'ī. Tehran, 1372 Sh./1993, 4 vols.

al-Shahīd al-Awwal, Muḥammad b. Jamāl al-Dīn Makkī al-ʿĀmilī. *al-Lumʿa al-dimashqiyya*. Qum, 1374 Sh./1995.
al-Shahīd al-Thānī, Zayn al-Dīn b. ʿAlī al-ʿĀmilī. *Rawḍat al-janān fī sharḥ* Irshād al-Adhhān. Qum, 1422/2001.
———. *Ḥāshiya Sharāʾiʿ al-Islām*. Qum, 1422/2001.
al-Shahrastānī, Abu'l-Fatḥ Muḥammad b. ʿAbd al-Karīm. *Kitāb al-milal wa'l-niḥal*, translated into French as *Livre des religions et des sects*, by Daniel Gimaret and Guy Monnot. Paris and Leuven, 1986–1993, 2 vols.
al-Shūshtarī, Qāḍī Nūr Allāh. *Majālis al-muʾminīn*, ed. Ibrāhīm ʿArabpūr et al. Mashhad, 1392–1393 Sh./2013–2014, 7 vols.
al-Sijistānī, Abū Yaʿqūb Isḥāq b. Aḥmad. *Kitāb al-Yanābīʿ*, ed. and French trans. Henry Corbin, in his *Trilogie Ismaélienne*. Tehran and Paris, 1961, text, pp. 1–97, translation, pp. 5–127.
al-Suhrawardī, Shihāb al-Dīn Yaḥyā. *Ḥikmat al-ishrāq bā sharḥ-i Quṭb al-Dīn Shīrāzī wa taʿliqāt-i Ṣadr al-Dīn Muḥammad Shīrāzī*. Tehran, 1392 Sh./2013, 4 vols; ed and English trans. as *The Philosophy of Illumination* by John Walbridge and Hossein Ziai. Provo, UT, 1999; French tr. as Sohrawardî, Shihâboddîn Yahyâ, *Le Livre de la sagesse orientale*. Kitâb Ḥikmat al-ishrâq. *Commentaires de Qoṭboddîn Shîrâzî et Mollâ Sadrâ Shîrâzî*, by Henry Corbin, ed. Christian Jambet. Lagrasse, 1986; 2nd ed., Paris, 2003.
Tabrīzī b. al-Karbalāʾī, Ḥāfiẓ Ḥusayn. *Rawḍat al-jinān wa jannāt al-janān*, ed. Jaʿfar Sulṭān al-Qurrāʾī. Tehran, 1970, 2 vols.
al-Tafrishī, Muṣṭafā b. Ḥusayn. *Naqd al-rijāl*. Qum, 1997, 5 vols.
Turka-yi Iṣfahānī, Ṣāʾin al-Dīn ʿAlī b. Muḥammad. *Chahārdah risāla-yi fārsī*, ed. S. A. M. Bihbahānī, S. I. Dībājī and Taqī Sharīf Riḍāʾī. Tehran, 1351 Sh./1972.
al-Ṭūsī, Naṣīr al-Dīn Abū Jaʿfar b. Muḥammad. *Rawḍa-yi taslīm*, ed. and tr. S. J. Badakhchani as *Paradise of Submission: A Medieval Treatise on Ismaili Thought*. London, 2005.
———. *Sayr wa sulūk*, ed. and English tr. S. J. Badakhchani as *Contemplation and Action: The Spiritual Autobiography of a Muslim Scholar*. London, 1998.
Yazdī, Mullā Jalāl al-Dīn Munajjim. *Tārīkh-i ʿAbbāsī*, ed. Sayf Allāh Waḥīd-niyā. Tehran, 1366 Sh./1987.

Studies

Abisaab, Rula Jurdi. *Converting Persia: Religion and Power in the Safavid Empire*. London, 2004.
———. 'Shīʿī Jurisprudence, Sunnism, and the Traditionist Thought (Akhbārī) of Muḥammad Amīn Astarābādī (D. 1626–27)', *IJMES*, 47 (2015), pp. 5–23.
———. 'Was Muḥammad Amīn al-Astarābādī (d. 1036/1626–27) a Mujtahid?', *SSR*, 2 (2018), pp. 38–61.
Algar, Hamid. 'The Revolt of Āghā Khān Maḥallātī and the Transference of the Ismāʿīlī Imamate to India', *Studia Islamica*, 29 (1969), pp. 55–81.
———. 'Nūrbakhshiyya', *EI2*.
Allen, Roger, and D. S. Richards. *Arabic Literature in the Post-Classical Period*. Cambridge, 2006.
Amanat, Abbas. *Apocalyptic Islam and Iranian Shiʿism*. London, 2009.
Amir-Moezzi, M.A. *The Divine Guide in Early Shiʿism: The Sources of Esotericism in Islam*, tr. David Streight. Albany, NY, 1994.
———. *La preuve de Dieu. La mystique shiʿite à travers l'œuvre de Kulaynī (IXᵉ-Xᵉ siècle)*. Paris, 2018.
———. *La religion discrète. Croyances et pratiques spirituelles dans l'islam shi'ite*. Paris, 2006; English tr. by Hafiz Karmali as *The Spirituality of Shiʿi Islam: Beliefs and Practices*. London, 2011.

—— and Christian Jambet. *Qu'est-ce que le shî'isme?*. Paris, 2004; English tr. By K. Casler and E. Ormsby as *What is Shi'i Islam?*. London, 2018.
Anṣārī, Ḥasan. *Tashayyu'-i imāmī dar bistar-i taḥawwul. Tārīkh-i maktabhā wa bāvarhā dar Īrān wa Islām*. Tehran, 1395 Sh./2016.
Anthony, Sean. 'Ghulāt', *EI3*.
Anzali, Ata. *"Mysticism" in Iran: The Safavid Roots of a Modern Concept*. Columbia, SC, 2017.
—— and S. M. Hadi Gerami, ed. *Opposition to Philosophy in Safavid Iran: Mullā Muḥammad Ṭāhir Qummī's* Ḥikmat al-ʿĀrifīn. Leiden, 2018.
Ardistānī, Muḥammad ʿAlī. *Nafs al-amr dar falsafa-yi Islāmī*. 2nd ed., Tehran, 1392 Sh./2013.
Arjomand, Saïd Amir. *The Shadow of God and the Hidden Imam*. Chicago, 1984.
——. *Sociology of Shiʿite Islam*. Leiden and Boston, 2016.
Ayoub, Samy. *Law, Empire, and the Sultan: Ottoman Imperial Authority and Late Hanafi Jurisprudence*. Oxford, 2020.
Āzhand, Yaʿqūb. *Ḥurūfiyya dar tārīkh*. Tehran, 1369 Sh./1990.
Babayan, Kathryn. *Mystics, Monarchs and Messiahs: Cultural Landscapes of Early Modern Iran*. Cambridge, MA, 2002.
——. 'The Safavid Synthesis: From Qizilbash Islam to Imamite Shiʿism', *IS*, 27 (1994), pp. 135–161.
Bashir, Shahzad. 'Enshrining Sainthood: The Death and Memorialization of Faḍlallāh Astarābādī in Ḥurūfī Thought', *MW*, 90 (2000), pp. 289–308.
——. *Fazlallah Astarabadi and the Hurufis*. Oxford, 2005.
——. 'The Imam's Return: Messianic Leadership in Late Medieval Shiʿism', in Linda Walbridge, ed., *The Most Learned of the Shiʿa: The Institution of* Marjaʿ Taqlid. New York, 2001, pp. 21–33.
——. *Messianic Hopes and Mystical Visions: The Nurbakhshiya Between Medieval and Modern Islam*. Columbia, SC, 2003.
Bauer, Thomas. 'In Search of "Post-Classical Literature"', *Mamlūk Studies Review*, 11 (2007), pp. 137–167.
Binbaş, I. Evrim. 'The Anatomy of a Regicide Attempt: Shāhrukh, the Hurufis, and the Timurid Intellectuals in 830/1426–27', *JRAS*, 23 (2013), pp. 391–428.
Bonmariage, Cécile. *Le Réel et les réalités: Mollâ Sadrâ Shîrâzî et la structure de la réalité*. Paris, 2007.
Brummett, Palmira. 'The Myth of Shah Ismail Safavi: Political Rhetoric and "Divine" Kingship', in John Victor Tolan, ed., *Medieval Christian Perceptions of Islam: A Book of Essays*. New York, 1996, pp. 331–360.
Brunner, Rainer. *Die Schia und die Koranfälschung*. Würzburg, 2001.
——. 'Majlesī, Moḥammad Bāqer', *EIr*.
Canby, Sheila R. *The Shahnama of Shah Tahmasp: The Persian Book of Kings*. New York and New Haven, CT, 2011.
Cole, Juan. *Roots of North Indian Shiʿism in Iran and Iraq: Religion and State in Awadh, 1722–1859*. Berkeley and Los Angeles, 1988.
——. 'Shiʿi Clerics in Iraq and Iran, 1722–1780: The Akhbari-Usuli Conflict Reconsidered', *IS*, 18 (1985), pp. 3–34.
Corbin, Henry. 'Confessions extatiques de Mîr Dâmâd, maître de théologie à Ispahan', in *Mélanges Louis Massignon*. Damascus, 1956, vol. 1, pp. 278–331.
——. *En Islam Iranien. Aspects spirituels et philosophiques*. Paris, 1971–1972, 4 vols.
——. *Histoire de la philosophie Islamique*. Paris, 1986.
——. *La philosophie Iranienne Islamique aux XVIIe et XVIIIe siècles*. Paris, 1981.
Csirkés, Ferenc. 'Messianic Oeuvres in Interaction: Misattributed Poems by Shah Esmāʿīl and Nesimi', *JPS*, 8 (2015), pp. 155–194.
Dabashi, Hamid. 'Mīr Dāmād and the Founding of the "School of Isfahan"', in S. H. Nasr and O. Leaman, ed., *History of Islamic Philosophy*. London, 2001, vol. 1, pp. 597–634.

——. 'The Philosopher/Vizier: Khwāja Naṣīr al-Dīn al-Ṭūsī and the Isma'ilis', in F. Daftary, ed., *Mediaeval Isma'ili History and Thought*. Cambridge, 1996, pp. 231–245.
Daftary, Farhad. 'Ismā'īlī-Sufi Relations in Early Post-Alamūt and Safavid Persia', in L. Lewisohn and D. Morgan, ed., *The Heritage of Sufism*. Oxford, 1999, vol. 3, pp. 275–289; reprinted in his *Ismailis in Medieval Muslim Societies*. London, 2005, pp. 183–203.
——. 'Khayrkhwāh-i Harātī and the Post-Mongol Revival in Nizārī Ismaili Literary Activities in Persia', in M. A. Amir-Moezzi, ed., *Raison et quête de la sagesse. Hommage à Christian Jambet*. Turnhout, 2020, pp. 215–227.
——. *A History of Shi'i Islam*. London, 2013.
——. *A Short History of the Ismailis*. Edinburgh, 1998.
——. *The Ismā'īlīs: Their History and Doctrines*. 2nd ed., Cambridge, 2007.
Dakake, Maria Massi. 'Hierarchies of Knowledge in Mullā Ṣadrā's Commentary on *Uṣūl al-Kāfī*', *JIP*, 6 (2010), pp. 5–44.
D'Ancona, Cristina. 'Plotinus, Arabic', in H. Lagerlund, ed., *Encyclopedia of Medieval Philosophy*. Dordrecht, 2020, pp. 1546–1557.
——. 'Porphyry, Arabic', in H. Lagerlund, ed., *Encyclopedia of Medieval Philosophy*, pp. 1576–1584.
——. 'Translations from Greek into Arabic', in H. Lagerlund, ed., *Encyclopedia of Medieval Philosophy*, pp. 1940–1959.
Dargāhī, Ḥusayn and 'Alī Akbar Talāfī Dāriyānī. *Kitāb shināsī-yi Majlisī*. Tehran, 1370 Sh./1991; 2nd ed. 1385 Sh./2006.
De Smet, Daniel. 'L'auteur des *Rasā'il Ikhwān al-Ṣafā'* selon les sources ismaéliennes ṭayyibites', *SSR*, 1 (2017), pp. 151–166.
——. *La philosophie ismaélienne. Un ésotérisme chiite entre néoplatonisme et gnose*. Paris, 2012.
——. *La quiétude de l'intellect. Néoplatonisme et gnose ismaélienne dans l'œuvre de Ḥamîd ad-Dîn al-Kirmânî (X*e*/XI*e*s)*. Leuven, 1995.
——. 'The Religious Applications of Philosophical Ideas', in Ulrich Rudolph, Rotraud Hansberger and Peter Adamson, ed., *Philosophy in the Islamic World. Volume 1: 8th – 10th Centuries*. Leiden and Boston, 2017, pp. 733–758.
Dressler, Markus. *Writing Religion: The Making of Turkish Alevi Islam*. Oxford, 2013.
El-Bizri, Nader, ed. *Epistles of the Brethren of Purity. The Ikhwān al-Ṣafā' and their* Rasā'il*: An Introduction*. Oxford, 2008.
El-Rouayheb, Khaled, and Sabina Schmidtke, ed. *The Oxford Handbook of Islamic Philosophy*. Oxford, 2016.
Ettinghausen, Richard, ed. *Islamic Art in the Metropolitan Museum of Art*. New York, 1972.
Goldziher, Ignác. 'Idjāza', *EI*.
Guenther, Alan. 'Ḥanafī *Fiqh* in Mughal India: The *Fatāwá-i 'Ālamgīrī*', in Richard Eaton, ed., *India's Islamic Tradition, 711–1750*. New Delhi, 2003, pp. 207–230.
Gutas, Dimitri. 'Avicenna and After: The Development of Paraphilosophy', in Abdelkader Al Ghouz, ed., *Islamic Philosophy from the 12th to the 14th Century*. Bonn, 2018, pp. 19–72.
——. *Greek Thought, Arabic Culture*. London, 1998.
Gallagher, Amelia. 'The Apocalypse of Ecstasy: The Poetry of Shah Ismā'īl Revisited', *IS*, 51 (2018), pp. 363–366.
——. 'Poetry Attributed to Shah Ismail in the Study of Anatolian Alevism', *Turcica*, 49 (2019), pp. 61–83.
——. 'Shah Isma'il's Poetry in the *Silsilat al-Nasab-i Safaviyya*', *IS*, 44 (2011), pp. 895–911.
——. 'Shāh Ismā'īl Ṣafevī and the *Mi'rāj*: Ḫaṭā'ī's Vision of a Sacred Assembly', in Christiane Gruber and Frederick Colby, ed., *The Prophet's Ascension: Cross-Cultural Encounters with the Islamic Mi'rāj Tales*. Bloomington, IN, 2010, pp. 313–329.
——. 'The Transformation of Shah Ismail Safevi in the Turkish *Hikâye*', *JFR*, 46 (2009), pp. 173–195.

Gleave, Robert. 'Akhbārī Shīʿī *Uṣūl al-fiqh* and the Juristic Theory of Yūsuf b. Aḥmad al-Baḥrānī', in Robert Gleave and E. Kermeli, ed., *Islamic Law: Theory and Practice*. London, 1997, pp. 24–45.

———. 'The Akhbārī-Uṣūlī Dispute in *Ṭabaqāt* Literature: An Analysis of the Biographies of Yūsuf al-Baḥrānī and Muḥammad Bāqir al-Bihbihānī', *Jusur: UCLA Journal of Middle Eastern Studies*, 10 (1994), pp. 79–109.

———. 'Compromise and Conciliation in the Akhbārī–Uṣūlī Dispute: Yūsuf al-Baḥrānī's Assessment of ʿAbd Allāh al-Samāhījī's *Munyat al-Mumārisīn*', in Omar Alí-de-Unzaga, ed., *Fortresses of the Intellect: Ismaili and Other Islamic Studies in Honour of Farhad Daftary*. London, 2011, pp. 491–520.

———. *Inevitable Doubt: Two Theories of Shīʿī Jurisprudence*. Leiden, 2000.

———. 'The Qadi and the Mufti in Akhbari Shiʿi Jurisprudence', in Wolfhart Heinrichs, Peri Bearman and Bernard Weiss, ed., *The Law Applied: Contextualizing the Islamic Shariʿa, Studies in Honor of Frank Vogel*. London, 2007, pp. 235–258.

———. 'Questions and Answers in Akhbari Jurisprudence', in A. Christmann, R. Gleave and C. Imber, ed., *Studies in Islamic Law*. Oxford, 2007, pp. 73–122.

———. *Scripturalist Islam. The History and Doctrines of the Akhbārī Shīʿī School*. Leiden, 2007.

Halm, Heinz. *Shiism*, tr. J. Watson. Edinburgh, 1991.

Hermann, Denis, and Mathieu Terrier, ed. *Shiʿi Islam and Sufism: Classical Views and Modern Perspectives*. London, 2020.

Hıyāvī, Rawshan. *Ḥurūfiyya*. Tehran, 1378 Sh./1999.

Hodgson, Marshall G.S. *The Order of Assassins: The Struggle of the Early Nizārī Ismāʿīlīs against the Islamic World*. The Hague, 1955.

———. *The Venture of Islam: Conscience and History in a World Civilization*. Chicago, 1974, 3 vols.

Huseynova, Aida. *Music of Azerbaijan: from Mugham to Opera*. Bloomington, IN, 2016.

Jaʿfariyān, Rasūl. *Dīn va siyāsat dar ʿaṣr-i Ṣafavī*. Qum, 1370 Sh./1991.

Jambet, Christian. *L'acte d'être. La philosophie de la révélation chez Mollâ Sadrâ*. Paris, 2002; English tr. Jeff Fort as *The Act of Being: The Philosophy of Revelation in Mullā Ṣadrā*. New York, 2006.

Kākāʾī, Qāsim. *Ghiyāth al-Dīn Manṣūr Dashtakī wa falsafa-yi ʿirfān*. Tehran, 2008.

Karakaya-Stump, Ayfer. 'Documents and Buyruk Manuscripts in the Private Archives of Alevi Dede Families: An Overview', *BJMES*, 37 (2010), pp. 273–286.

Karamustafa, Ahmet T. 'In His Own Voice: What Hatayi Tells us about Şah İsmail's Religious Views', in M.A. Amir-Moezzi et al., ed., *L'Ésotérisme shi'ite, ses racines et ses prolongements*. Turnhout, 2016, pp. 601–612.

Kiyā, Ṣādiq. *Nuqṭawiyān yā Pasīkhāniyān*. Tehran, 1320 Sh./1941.

———. *Wāzhanāma-yi gurgānī*. Tehran, 1330 Sh./1951.

Kohlberg, Etan. 'Aspects of Akhbārī Thought in the Seventeenth and Eighteenth Centuries', in Nehemia Levtzion and John O. Voll, ed., *Eighteenth Century Renewal and Reform in Islam*. Syracuse, NY, 1987, pp. 133–160.

———. 'Akbārīya', *EIr*.

———. 'Baḥrānī, Yūsof', *EIr*.

Lambton, A. K. S. *Landlord and Peasant in Persia: A Study of Land Tenure and Land Revenue Administration*. London, 1953.

Lawson, B. Todd. 'Akhbārī Shīʿī Approaches to Tafsīr', in G.R. Hawting and Abdul-Kader A. Shareef, ed., *Approaches to the Qur'ān*. London, 1993, pp. 173–210.

Lewisohn, Leonard. 'Sufism and the School of Iṣfahān: *Taṣawwuf* and *ʿIrfān* in Late Safavid Iran (ʿAbd al-Razzāq Lāhījī and Fayḍ Kāshānī on the Relation of *Taṣawwuf*, *Ḥikmat* and *ʿIrfān*)', in L. Lewisohn and D. Morgan, ed., *The Heritage of Sufism*. Oxford, 1999, vol. 3, pp. 63–134.

Lockhart, Laurence. *The Fall of the Ṣafavī Dynasty and the Afghan Occupation of Persia*. Cambridge, 1958.

Losensky, Paul E. 'The Palace of Praise and the Melons of Time: Descriptive Patterns in 'Abdī Bayk Šīrāzī's *Garden of Eden*', *Eurasian Studies*, 2 (2003), pp. 1–29.
Madelung, Wilferd. *Religious Schools and Sects in Medieval Islam*. London, 1985.
———. 'al-Karakī', *EI2*.
Mahdavī, Muṣliḥ al-Dīn. *Zindagī-nāma-yi 'Allāma Majlisī*. Isfahan, n.d.; repr. Tehran, 1378 Sh./1999.
Mazzaoui, Michel M. *Origins of the Ṣafawids: Šī'ism, Ṣūfism, and the Ġulāt*. Wiesbaden, 1972.
Mélikoff, Irène. 'Le problème Bektaşi-Alévi: quelques dernières considérations', *Turcica*, 31 (1999), pp. 7–34.
Melville, Charles P. 'Sarbadārids', *EI2*.
Minorsky, Vladimir. 'The Poetry of Shāh Ismā'īl I', *BSOAS*, 4 (1942), pp. 1006–1029.
Mir-Kasimov, Orkhan. 'The Nizārī Ismaili Theory of the Resurrection (*Qiyāma*) and Post-Mongol Iranian Messianism', in O. Mir-Kasimov, ed., *Intellectual Interactions in the Islamic World: The Ismaili Thread*. London, 2020, pp. 323–352.
———. *The Words of Power: Ḥurūfī Teachings Between Sufism and Shi'ism in Medieval Islam*. London, 2015.
Moazzen, Maryam. *Formation of a Religious Landscape: Shi'i Higher Learning in Safawid Iran*. Leiden, 2018.
Moin, Azfar. *The Millennial Sovereign: Sacred Kingship and Sainthood in Islam*. New York, 2014.
———. 'Dabistān-i madhāhib', *EI3*.
Momen, Moojan. *An Introduction to Shi'i Islam*. New Haven and London, 1985.
Morton, Alexander H. 'The Early Years of Shah Isma'il in the *Afżal al-Tavārīkh* and Elsewhere', in Charles Melville, ed., *Safavid Persia: The History and Politics of an Islamic Society*. London, 1996, pp. 27–52.
———. 'The Chub-i Tariq and Qizilbash Tirual in Safavid Persia', in J. Calmard, ed., *Études Safavides* (Tehran/Paris, 1993), pp. 225–245.
Nasr, Seyyed Hossein. 'The School of Ispahan', in M. M. Sharif, ed., *A History of Muslim Philosophy*. Wiesbaden, 1963–1966, vol. 2, pp. 904–932.
———. *Islamic Philosophy from its Origins to the Present*. Albany, NY, 2006.
Newman, Andrew J. 'Fayḍ al-Kāshānī and the Rejection of the Clergy/State Alliance: Friday Prayer as Politics in the Safavid Period', in Linda S. Walbridge, ed., *The Most Learned of the Shi'a. The Institution of the Marja' Taqlīd*. New York, 2001, pp. 34–52.
———. *The Formative Period of Twelver Shī'ism: Ḥadīth as Discourse between Qum and Baghdad*. London, 2000.
———. 'Glimpses into Late-Safavid Spiritual Discourse: An "Akhbārī" Critique of Sufism and Philosophy', in R. Tabandeh and L. Lewisohn, ed., *Sufis and Mullas: Sufis and Their Opponents in the Persianate World*. Irvine, CA, 2020, pp. 259–307.
———. 'The Idea of Bāqer al-Majlesī', in C. Melville, ed., *Safavid Persia in the Age of Empires (The Idea of Iran. Volume X)*. London, 2021, pp. 190–221.
———. 'The Myth of the Clerical Migration to Safawid Iran: Arab Shi'ite Opposition to 'Alī al-Karakī and Safawid Shī'ism', *Die Welt des Islams*, 33 (1993), pp. 66–112.
———. 'The Nature of the Akhbārī/Uṣūlī Dispute in Late-Safavid Iran', *BSOAS*, 55 (1992), pp. 22–52 and 250–262.
———. *Safavid Iran: Rebirth of a Persian Empire*. London, 2006.
———. *Twelver Shi'ism: Unity and Diversity in the Life of Islam, 632 to 1722*. Edinburgh, 2013.
———. 'al-Baḥrānī, Yūsuf ibn Aḥmad', *EI3*.
Pourjavady, Reza. *Philosophy in Early Safavid Iran: Najm al-Dīn Maḥmūd al-Nayrīzī and His Writings*. Leiden, 2011.
Rizvi, Sajjad H., ed. *Mullā Ṣadrā Shīrāzī: His Life and Works and the Sources for Safavid Philosophy*, *Journal of Semitic Studies*, Supplement 18 (2007).

——. 'Isfahan School of Philosophy', *EIr*.
Roemer, H. R. 'The Safavid Period', in *The Cambridge History of Iran*, Volume 6, *The Timurid and Safavid Periods*, ed. P. Jackson and L. Lockhart. Cambridge, 1986, pp. 189–212.
Ruggles, D. Fairchild. *Islamic Gardens and Landscapes*. Philadelphia, PN, 2008.
Rustom, Mohammad. *The Triumph of Mercy: Philosophy and Scripture in Mullā Ṣadrā*. Albany, NY, 2012.
Savory, Roger. *Iran under the Ṣafavids*. Cambridge, 1980.
Saatchian, Firouzeh. *Gottes Wesen-Gottes Wirken: Ontologie und Kosmologie im Denken von Šams-al-Dīn Muḥammad al-Ḫafrī*. Berlin, 2011.
Scarcia Amoretti, Biancamaria. 'Religion in the Timurid and Safavid Periods', in *The Cambridge History of Iran*, Volume 6, *The Timurid and Safavid Periods*, ed. P. Jackson and L. Lockhart. Cambridge, 1986, pp. 610–634.
Schmidtke, Sabine. 'Forms and Functions of "Licenses to Transmit" (*Ijāzas*) in 18th-Century-Iran: ʿAbd Allāh al-Mūsawī al-Jazā'irī al-Tustarī's (1112–73/1701–59) *Ijāza Kabīra*', in G. Kramer et al., ed., *Speaking for Islam: Religious Authorities in Muslim Societies*. Leiden, 2006, pp. 95–127.
——. *The Theology of ʿAllāma al-Ḥillī (d. 726/1325)*. Berlin, 1991.
Sedgwick, Mark. *Muhammad Abduh*. Oxford, 2010.
al-Shaybī, Kāmil Muṣṭafā. *al-Ṣila bayna al-taṣawwuf wa'l-tashayyuʿ*, 2 vols. Beirut, 1982.
Stern, Samuel M. *Studies in Early Ismāʿīlism*. Jerusalem and Leiden, 1983.
Stewart, Devin J. 'The Genesis of the Akhbārī Revival', in Michel Mazzaoui, ed., *Safavid Iran and Her Neighbors*. Salt Lake City, UT, 2003, pp. 169–193.
——. *Islamic Legal Orthodoxy: Twelver Shiite Response to the Sunni Legal System*. Salt Lake City, UT, 1998.
——. 'Ejāza', *EIr*.
Taşgin, Ahmet, Ali Yaman, and Namiq Musalı, ed. *Safevîler ve Şah İsmail*. Istanbul, 2014.
Terrier, Mathieu. 'The Defence of Sufism among Twelver Shiʿi Scholars of Early Modern and Modern Times: Topics and Arguments', in D. Hermann and M. Terrier, ed., *Shiʿi Islam and Sufism: Classical Views and Modern Perspectives*. London, 2020, pp. 27–63.
——. *Histoire de la sagesse et philosophie shi'ite. "L'Aimé des cœurs" de Quṭb al-Dīn Aškevarī*. Paris, 2016.
Thackston, Wheeler. 'The Diwan of Khata'i: Pictures for the Poetry of Shah Ismaʿil I', *Asian Art*, 1 (1989), pp. 37–63.
Vajda, George, Ignac Goldziher and Seeger A. Bonebakker. 'Idjāza', *EI2*.
Van Bruinessen, Martin. 'Between Dersim and Dâlahû: Reflections on Kurdish Alevism and the Ahl-i Haqq religion', in Shahrokh Raei, ed., *Islamic Alternatives: Non-Mainstream Religion in Persianate Societies*. Wiesbaden, 2017, pp. 65–93.
Virani, Shafique N. *The Ismailis in the Middle Ages*. Oxford, 2007.
——. 'The Right Path: A Post-Mongol Persian Ismaili Treatise', *JIS*, 43 (2010), pp. 197–221.
——. 'Surviving Persecution: Ismailism and *Taqiyyah* after the Mongol Invasions', in Leonard Lewisohn and Reza Tabandeh, ed., *Sufis and their Opponents in the Persianate World*. Irvine, CA, 2020, pp. 205–236.
——. 'Khayrkhvāh-i Harātī', *EI3*.
Usluer, Fatih. *Hurufilik: Ilk Elden Kaynaklarla Doguşundan Itibaren*. Istanbul, 2009.
Wisnovsky, Robert. 'The Nature and Scope of Arabic Philosophical Commentary in Post-Classical (ca. 1100–1900 AD) Islamic Intellectual History: Some Preliminary Observations', *Bulletin of the Institute of Classical Studies*, 47 (2004), pp. 149–191.
Wood, Barry. 'The *Târîkh-i jahânârâ* in the Chester Beatty Library: An Illustrated manuscript of the "Anonymous Tales of Shah Ismaʿil"', *IS*, 37 (2004), pp. 89–107.
Woods, John E., ed. *Faḍlullāh b. Rūzbihān Khunjī-Isfahānī, Tārīkh-i ʿĀlam-ārā-yi Amīnī*. London, 1992.
Yaman, Mehmet, ed. *Buyruk: Alevî İnanç-İbâdet ve Ahlâk İlkeleri*. Mannheim, 2000.

Yıldırım, Rıza. 'In the Name of Hosayn's Blood: The Memory of Karbala as Ideological Stimulus to the Safavid Revolution', *JPS*, 8 (2015), pp. 127–154.

———. 'Literary Foundations of the Alevi Tradition: Mainstream, Canon, and Orthodoxy', in Benjamin Weineck and Johannes Zimmermann, ed., *Alevism between Standardisation and Plurality: Negotiating Texts, Sources and Cultural Heritage*. Berlin, 2018, pp. 61–96.

———. 'Red Sulphur, the Great Remedy and the Supreme Name: Faith in the Twelve Imams and Shiʿi Aspects of Alevi-Bektashi Piety', in Denis Hermann and Mathieu Terrier, ed., *Shiʿi Islam and Sufism: Classical Views and Modern Perspectives*. London, 2020, pp. 255–290.

Zarcone, Thierry. 'Bektaşiyye', *EI3*.

Index

'A Servant of 'Alī, king of men, am I' (Khālū Maḥmūd)
  composition, 40–2
  context, 60–5
  Ghulām-i Shāh-i mardān-am, 43–50
  manuscripts and studies, 37–40, 66
  prosody, 40–2
  reading, 41–2
  rhythm, 51n139
  syllables, 41, 42
  translation, 51–9
  trilling metre, 40–1
Abaqa, Īlkhān, 2
'Abbās I, Safavid shah, 14, 202
  legitimacy, 154, 172–3
  Munshī's account, 156–8
  Naṭanzī's account, 151–5
  Nuqṭavīs, threat, 154–5, 155–6, 159
  and the Nuqṭavīs, 131, 133, 135n12, 136, 150–60, 161, 167, 172–3, 173–4, 174–5
  pious motivations, 160
  religious authority, 172, 173–4
  sources, 150–1
  Yazdī's narrative, 155–6
Abbasid caliphate, 2, 18
'Abd Allāh al-Mahdī, Fatimid imam-caliph, 33
'Abd al-Ḥayy, Sayyid Niẓām al-Dīn, 117
'Abd al-Vahhāb Darvīshzāda, 122
Abraham, 326
Abū Isḥāq, Nizārī Ismaili author, *Haft bāb-i Abū Isḥāq*, 22–5
Abu'l-Sha'thā' Qanbar b. Kādān al-Dawsī, 51n140
Adam, 82–8, 90, 169, 170
'Aḍud al-Dīn, Khwāja, 119, 125–6
al-Afghānī, Jamāl al-Dīn, author and reformer, 243n4
Afshārid dynasty, 143
afterlife, the, 333, 337
Afūshta-yi Naṭanzī, historian, 151–5, 157
Aga Khan I, Ḥasan 'Alī Shāh, Ismaili imam, 70–1
Aga Khan III, Sultan Muhammad Shah, Ismaili imam, 70–2
agriculture, 371
al-Aḥsā'ī, Muḥammad b. 'Alī, Ibn Abī Jumhūr, 9, 147, 236–7, 343,
'Ajamī cycles, 163–8
Akbar, Mughal emperor, 173, 173–5
akhbār (reports), 222–3, *see also, ḥadīth*
Akhbārī movement, 180, 186–9, 191–2, 198–204, 238–40, 245, 301
  adherence to *ḥadīth*, 233
  autobiographies, 228–32
  biographical dictionaries, 227, 229

canonical *ḥadīth* commentaries, 207–17
defeat, 239
ḥadīth-based *tafsīr*, 226–7
ḥadīth re-collection, 217–26
ḥadīth resurrection, 234
ḥadīth-based legal manuals, 232–4
juristic methodology, 254
legal hermeneutics, 204–7, 223
literary production, 197–8, 204–40
role, 240
Akhūnd, Mawlāna Mīrzā Ḥusayn, 66–7
Alamūt, fortress and seat of the Ismaili state, in northern Iran, 1–2, 10, 19, 25, 34
alcohol, 123, 127, 157, 233–4
Alevi, the, 102–6
ʿAlī b. Abī Ṭālib, first Shiʿi imam and fourth caliph, 349
ʿAlī-centred theology, 110
ʿAlid mysticism, 103
al-ʿĀmilī, al-Ḥasan b. Zayn al-Dīn, 203, 205–6, 207 232–3
al-ʿĀmilī, Bahāʾ al-Dīn Muḥammad b. Ḥusayn, Imāmī scholar, 233
al-ʿĀmilī, Muḥammad b. al-Ḥurr, 217
Amir-Moezzi, Mohammed-Ali, 215
Amīr Nūr Allāh, 116–17, 122–6, 127–8, 130
Āmulī, Sayyid Ḥaydar, Twelver Shiʿi theologian, 8–9, 343, 367
Āmulī, Sharīf, 175
angels, 278, 326, 357–8
animals, domestication, 370–1, 376
Anjudān, village in central Iran, 13
Anwār, Qāsim, 119
apparitions, 357–8
Arab cycle, 163–7
Arabic Plotinus, 75
Ardabīl, 7
al-Ardabīlī, Aḥmad b. Muḥammad al-Muqaddas, 263–5
commentary on *Irshād*, 268–70
Aristotle, 310n16, 336–7, 338–9, 364–5
Ashkivarī, Quṭb al-Dīn, known also as Sharīf Lāhijī,
argument, 345–6
cartography of the imaginal world, 353
conclusion, 367
division of sciences, 79–80
ecumenism, 367
Fanūs al-khayāl, 341–68
imaginal world syncretic concept, 348–55
intellectual production, 341–2
Maḥbūb al-qulūb, 75–91, 342, 343, 344
mode of composition, 344
objections to the imaginal world, 354–5
project, 343–5
on Pythagoras, 80
and the *Rasāʾil Ikhwān al-Ṣafāʾ*, 76–81
and the *Risālat al-Jāmiʿa*, 81–90
sources, 76, 81, 344–5, 346–8
status, 341
story of Adam, 82–8, 90
subaltern theories, 356–67
Zoroaster and the origin of evil, 88–90, 90
al-Astarābādī, Muḥammad Amīn, founder of the Akhbārī school, 179, 186, 190, 198–9, 199–200, 204–5, 211–12, 227, 233–4

al-Astarābādī, Muḥammad b. ʿAlī, 227
al-athār, memorisation of, 278–9
ʿAṭṭār, Farīd al-Dīn, Sufi poet, 12
Aubin, Jean, 136–7
autobiographies, 228–32
Avicenna, 326, 327–8, 328–9, see also Ibn Sīnā
Awḥad al-Dīn, 359
awliyā' (lit. 'friends of God'), 216

Bada'ūnī, ʿAbd al-Qādir, 175
Balāghī, Ḥujjat, 191–2
al-Baḥrānī, Hāshim b. Sulaymān, 237–8
al-Baḥrānī, Yūsuf, 189–90, 191, 231–2, 234, 253–4, 273–4
balance, search for, 189–93
Bāysunghur, Tīmūrid prince 118
being, 329–30
  modes of, 332–3
Bektashi, Sufi order, 104
Bichara, the, 54n144
al-Bihbahānī, al-Waḥīd, 246
biographical dictionaries, 227, 229
blackness, 328
blindness, 360
body, the
  definition of, 329–30
  imaginal, 350–1, 356–7, 357–60, 360–1
  resurrected, 355, 365–7
Borges, Jorge Luis, 338
Brunner, Rainer, 228, 228–9, 239
Bursī, Rajab, 148
burūz, 358–60

Cahen, Claude, 6
causality, 331
celestial souls, 330–1
Chaldirān, battle of, 284, 289
charisma, 96
Chingiz Khan, 1
Companion of the Grave, the, 356–7
confessional universalism, 148
Corbin, Henry, 31, 324, 342–3, 344
'The Coronation of the Infant Shāpūr II', 373, 374–5
corporal Resurrection, 355, 365–7
cosmic hierarchy, 80n21
cosmology, 330–4, 338
cultural transformation, 113

Daftary, Farhad, 21, 34
dāʿī (summoner, religious missionary or propagandist), 30–1
Dakake, Maria Massi, 216
Davānī, Jalāl al-Dīn, 308–9, 317–18
Darvīsh Najm al-Dīn, 122
Darvīsh Quṭb al-Dīn, 17, 26–7
death
  progress after, 360–1
  voluntary, 361–2
Dervish Khusraw, 151–9, 175
Dihdār Shīrāzī, Muḥammad b. Maḥmūd, 135, 175
divine balance, 169
double negation, 319
dualism, 90, 330
Duldul, 57n150
düvaz imam poetry, 106–12

ecstatic experiences, 363–5
Empedocles, Pre-Socratic philosopher, 327
Emre, Yunus, 105
Encyclopaedia of Islam, 272–3
esoteric Shiʿism, 145–9, 179, 183, 343, 367–8
eternity, 306, 313, 331–2, 333–4
Eve, 87

evil, origin of, 88–90, 90
existence
  individual unity of, 309
  signification, 327–30
experiential knowledge, 325–6

factuality, realm of, 312
Faḍl Allāh Astarābādī, founder of Ḥurūfism, 116, 117, 122, 124, 127, 130 133, 147n35, 161, 162, 170
Faḍlī Beg Khūzānī Iṣfahānī, historian, 158–9
Fakhr al-Muḥaqqiqīn, 281–2, 298
falsafa (philosophy), 75, 79, 316
Fanūs al-khayāl (Ashkivarī), 341–68
  argument, 345–6
  conclusion, 367
  imaginal world syncretic concept, 348–55
  mode of composition, 344
  objections to the imaginal world, 354–5
  project, 343–5
  sources, 344–5, 346–8
  subaltern theories, 356–67
Fatimid caliphate, 33, 63
fatwās, 246, 279–80, 291–3
fawā'id, 286–7
'The Feast of Sada' (Sulṭān Muḥammad), 370–2, 376
Fihrist biḥār al-anwār or *Fihris muṣannafāt al-aṣḥāb* (al-Majlisī), 218–25
fiqh literature, 248–55
flora and fauna, *Shāhnāma*, 369–76
floral imagery, 371–2, 376

Gabriel, 326, 357–8
gardens, 372–6
Ghālib, Muṣṭafā, 82
al-Ghazālī, Abū Ḥamīd Muḥammad, Sunni theologian, 365–6
Ghiyāth al-Dīn, Amīr, 128
  letter, 120–1, 122–6, 127
ghulāt (pl. of *ghālī*, exaggerator, extremist), 149
ghuluww (exaggeration in religion), 146
Glassen, Erika, 98n9
Gleave, Robert, 202, 205, 212, 234, 273–4, 276n13
God, 82, 87, 278, 282, 320–1
  and being, 330
  essence, 333–4
  human caliphate of, 325–7
  knowledge, 314–15, 334
  wisdom, 354
God's decree, 313–14, 315
Gölpýnarlý, Abdülbaki, 121
greater Resurrection, 346
Gutas, D., 321n56

ḥadīth (report, Tradition), 163–4, 180, 188–9, 190, 240, 278, 285, 286–7, 292, 341, 344, 348–9, 351, 353, 360–1, 361
  adherence to, 233
  authenticity, 199, 199–200, 203–4
  canonical commentaries, 207–17
  criticism, 199–204, 300
  legal manuals, 232–4
  line of transmission, 280, 282
  re-collection, 217–26
  resurrection, 235–8
  tafsīr, 226–7
al-Ḥallāj, Ḥusayn b. Manṣūr, Sufi master, 35, 99, 361–3
Ḥasan Rūmlū, historian, 126
Ḥasan-i Maḥmūd-i Kātib, Nizārī Ismaili author, 22, 24, 25, 26–7

Ḥasan-i Ṣabbāḥ, founder of the Nizārī Ismaili state, 33, 60
Ḥaydar, Ṣavafī Sufi master, 7, 96
Hell, 237–8, 348, 352
heretics, 151–5, 155–6, 364
Hermes, 82
Hidden imam, the, 8, 140n19, 141, 146–7, 150n46, 182, 184, 192
Hierarchy of Worlds, 351–4
Ḥikmat al-ishrāq (al-Suhrawardī), 324–39
  cosmology, 330–4, 338
  ishrāqī ontology, 327–30, 339
  and the soul, 334–7
Ḥilla, School of, 182
al-Hindī, Muḥammad b. Ḥasan al-Fāḍil, *al-Manāhij al-sawiyya*, 253
Hindus, expulsion of, 183
Hodgson, Marshall, 4
Holy Spirit, 326, 327
Hülegü, founder of Īlkhānid dynasty, 1, 1–2
human caliphate, of God, 325–7
hunting, 375–6
al-Ḥurr al-ʿĀmilī, Twelver Shiʿi scholar, 186, 202, 207, 228, 229, 231, 239
Ḥurūfism, 115–30, 133, 161, 162, 164–5, 170, 172
  adherence increased, 128–9
  and alcohol, 123
  Amīr Ghiyāth al-Dīn letter, 120–1, 122–6, 127
  basic themes, 124
  era of sainthood, 120
  expansion, 117
  ignorance of, 124, 130
  poetic images, 129
  Qara-Qoyunlu state, 126–9, 130
  rebellion, 127
  Ṣaḥīfat al-istikhlāṣ, analysis, 122–6
  Shāhrukh Era, 117–21
Ḥusayn b. ʿAbd al-Ṣamad, Twelver Shiʿi scholar, 201, 203, 300
Ḥusayn b. Yaʿqūb Shāh, Mīrzā, Aq-Qoyunlu prince, 61

Iblīs, 85–6, 87
Ibn al-ʿArabī, Sufi master, 2, 166–7, 330, 332, 359, 360
Ibn al-Qifṭī, author, 77–8, 91
Ibn Bābawayh al-Qummī, Muḥammad, Imāmī scholar, also known as Ibn Bābūya, 225–6, 231, 235, 264, 266, 268–9, 288, 299–300
Ibn Muṭahhar al-Ḥillī, Ḥasan b. Yūsuf, ʿAllāma, Twelver Shiʿi theologian, 2–3, 198, 199, 230, 234, 245, 250–1, 252, 254, 258, 262, 263, 264, 281, 287, 290–1, 292, 295
Ibn Sīnā, philosopher, 2 308, 313, 316, 319, 366, *see also* Avicenna
Ibn Turk, Shaykh Shams al-Dīn Muḥammad, 278
ijāza (diploma, certificate), 224–5, 290–3, 293–6
ijāzāt (al-Qaṭīfī)
  915/1509, 277–83, 297, 298
  920/1514, 284–8, 298
  944/1537, 288–93, 297, 298, 299
  first undated, 283–4
  second undated, 293–6
ijmāʿ (consensus), 292
ijtihād (independent legal reasoning), 3
Īlkhānid dynasty, 1–3

Ikhwān al-Ṣafā' (Brethren of Purity), 76–9, 81, 91
Image, world of the, 353, 354
imaginal body, the, 350–1, 356–7, 357–60, 360–1
imaginal world, the, 342
  cartography, 353
  cosmo-ontological definitions, 351–4
  creation, 353–4
  in the Hierarchy of Worlds, 351–4
  as intermediary world, 346
  objections to, 354–5
  progress after death, 360–1
  syncretic concept, 348–55
  temporal definition, 348–51
Impeccable beings, the, 346
India, 70–2, 173–5, 245
intellect, role in religion, 32
Intellects, the, 333
Iṣfahān, School of, 9–10, 245, 341
ishrāq (illuminationism), 75
ishrāqī ontology, 323–4, 327–30, 339
Iskandar Beg Munshī, historian, 156–8, 174
Iskandar, Mīrzā, Qara-Qoyunlu prince, 127–8
Ismāʿīl, Safavid shah, 7–8, 95–113, 137–43, 185, 288
  ʿAlī-centred theology, 110
  attributions, 95
  and broader esoteric Shiʿi Islam, 95–6, 102–6, 113
  düvaz imam poetry, 106–12
  humility, 111
  image, 97
  immortality, 95
  inherits leadership, 96
  later attributions, 105–6
  manuscripts, 102
  pen-name, 95, 106
  poetic persona, 100, 105, 113
  poetry, 95–6, 97–102, 105–6, 113
  role, 96–7, 98n9, 106, 113
Ismāʿīl II, Safavid shah, 143
Ismāʿīl b. Jaʿfar al-Ṣādiq, al-Mubarak, Ismaili imam, 32
al-Istibṣār, 210, 211–12
Ithnā ʿasharī Shiʿi legal commentaries, 244–8, 249–50
Ivanow, W., Russian orientalist, 20, 22, 24, 30, 31, 74

Jabal ʿĀmil, Twelver Shiʿi centre in southern Lebanon, 197
Jaʿfar al-Ṣādiq, Shiʿi imam, 32, 278–9, 348–9
Jahānshāh, Qara-Qoyunlu ruler, 128–9, 130
Jalāl al-Dīn Ḥasan, Ismaili imam, 18
Jalāl al-Dīn Rumī, Sufi master and poet, 12, 41, 360
Jannat-i ʿadn (Shīrāzī), 372–3, 375
al-Jazāʾirī, Niʿmat Allāh, 206, 213, 232, 236–7, 238
Jesus, 145n34, 167, 169, 170
Junayd, Ṣafavī Sufi master, 7
jurisprudence, Twelver Shiʿism, 3
juristic Islam, 173–4
jurist-theologian, the, 181–2
justice, 193

al-Karakī, ʿAlī, Twelver Shiʿi jurist, 272, 273, 277, 284, 288–90, 299
al-Karakī, al-Muḥaqqiq, Twelver Shiʿi scholar, 196
al-Kāshānī, Muḥsin Fayḍ, Shiʿi philosopher and mystic, 186, 217, 232, 234, 367
al-Khafrī, Shams al-Dīn, Shiʿi philosopher, 354

Khākī Khurāsānī, Nizārī Ismaili poet, 36
Khālū, Maḥmūd ʿAlī, Nizārī poet, 31–2, 34, 37, 73–4
  ʻA Servant of ʻAlī, king of men, am I', 40–2, 51–9, 60, 67–8
  Ghulām-i Shāh-i mardān-am, 43–50
  identity, 65–73, 74
  letter symbolism, 69
  manuscripts and studies, 38–40
Khaṭṭāṭ, Mawlānā Maʿrūf, 118, 125
Khayrkhwāh-i Harātī, Nīzārī Ismaili *dāʿī* and author, 24–5, 34–5, 37
Khunjī, Rūzbihān, historian, 98
Khurāsānī, Yūsifī, 153, 154–5
al-Khwānsārī, Muḥammad Bāqir, Twelver Shiʿi scholar, 277
Kohlberg, Etan, 188, 220–1, 238
Kondo, N., 275
al-Kulaynī, Muḥammad b. Yaʿqūb, Imāmī scholar, 223, 361
Kurdish Alevism, 103

Lāhījī, Shams al-Dīn, 358, *see also* Ashkivarī
Lambton, Ann, 375
land stewardship, 369–76
land tenure, 375
Lange, Christian, 237–8
law, 193
  and philosophy, 77–8
Lawson, Todd, 226–7
leaders, hidden, 29–37, 74
legal commentaries, Postclassical, 241–70
  background, 241–4
  base-texts, 249–52
  'commentary by statement' style, 259, 261
  exposition, 255–67
  fiqh literature, 248–55
  ijtihād-based approach, 245–6
  Ithnā ʿasharī Shiʿi, 244–8, 249–50, 256–7
  meaning, 260
  popularity, 252–3
  presentation style, 257–8, 261, 267–8
  role, 247
  supercommentaries, 251–2, 253, 265
  terminology, 248–50
legal hermeneutics, 199, 204–7, 223, 232–4
legal manuals, *ḥadīth*-based, 232–4
legitimacy, 140
lesser Resurrection, 346, 348–51, 357, 360–1
letter symbolism, 69
literary production, 195–8, 232, 238–40
  Akhbārī school, 197–8, 204–40
  autobiographies, 228–32
  biographical dictionaries, 227–8, 229
  canonical *ḥadīth* commentaries, 207
  ḥadīth based *tafsīr*, 226–7
  ḥadīth re-collection, 217–26
  ḥadīth resurrection, 234
  legal hermeneutics, 204–7, 223
literature, 17–27
  annihilation, 18
  bibliographical sources, 21–2
  classification, 21
  content, 22–7
  heritage, 17–18
  ijāzāt, 272–6
  interpolations, 20, 23–4
  repositories, 17–18

scope and extent, 21–2
Sufi terminology, 26
word-count comparison, 23–4
Lūrī, Aḥmad, 117, 118–19, 130

Madīnat al-ʿilm, 225–6
madrasa, 241–2
Maḥbūb al-qulūb (Ashkivarī), 75–91, 342, 343, 344
division of sciences, 79–80
on Pythagoras, 80
and the *Rasāʾil Ikhwān al-Ṣafāʾ*, 76–81
and the *Risālat al-Jāmiʿa*, 81–90
sources, 76, 81, 91
story of Adam, 82–8, 90
Zoroaster and the origin of evil, 88–90, 90
Mahdi, the, 97–102, 145n34
Maḥmūd-i Shabistarī, *Gulshan-i rāz*, 11, 12
al-Majlisī, Muḥammad Bāqir, Twelver Shiʿi scholar, 179–93, 212, 225–6, 231, 235, 236–7, 239, 276n13
Akhbarī tendencies, 186–9
Biḥār al-anwār, 187–9, 272
career, 181
defence of official Shiʿism, 182–4
Fihrist biḥār al-anwār or *Fihris muṣannafāt al-aṣḥāb*, 218–25
goal, 191–2
mysticism, 186–7
position, 181–6
search for balance, 189–93
al-Majlisī, Muḥammad Taqī, Majlisī the First, 186, 187, 299
making, act of, 307–11
al-Majrīṭī, Maslama, 81
man, as a microcosm, 83–4
Man lā yaḥḍuruhu al-faqīh (Ibn Bābawayh), 209–10, 212
Matter, and Nature, 80
Māzandarānī, Mullā Muḥammad Ṣāliḥ, Akhbārī scholar, 186, 208, 209, 210, 212,
measuring out, 313–16
Melville, Charles, 158
menstruation, 255–67, 268–70
Mervin, Sabrina, 228
messianic expectations, 140, 144, 145–9
metamorphosis, 349–51
middle way, the, 191
Minorsky, Vladimir, Russian orientalist, 95n2, 97, 99, 101, 106
Mīr Dāmād, philosopher, 91, 323, 342, 353, 354–5, 365
making the quiddities, 305–6, 307, 307–11
perpetuity and perpetual inception, 306–7, 311–19, 320–1
Platonism, 321
'Wisdom of the Right Side', 305–21
miracles, 357
Mīrshāhī, Ghiyāth al-Dīn, 38, 39, 39–40
Moazzen, M., 276n13
Modernist Islam, 244
Mongol invasions, 1, 19, 34, 148
Moses, 169, 170
movement, essential, 332, 333
Muhammad, cycle of, 168
Muhammad, the Prophet, 32, 162, 163–4, 169, 170, 171–2, 219, 294, 326–7, 356
Muhammad Abduh, 242n3

Mu'izzī, Maryam, 38–9, 54n144, 57n152, 66–7, 70
mujtahids, 3
muqallids, 3
Mullā Ṣadrā, *see* Shīrāzī, Ṣadr al-Dīn
Mūsā al-Kāẓim, 7th Ithnā 'asharī Shi'i imam, 32
Mustanṣir bi'llāh, Fatimid imam-caliph, 35
al-Mustanṣir bi'llāh II, Nizārī Ismaili imam and author of *Pandiyāt-i javānmardī*, 13
Mustanṣir bi'llāh III, Nizārī Ismaili imam, 25

Nādir Shāh Afshār, founder of the Afshārid dynasty,143
Nasafī, 'Azīz al-Dīn, Sufi master, 12–13
Nature, and Matter, 80
nature, view of, 369–76
Necessary Existent, the, 309, 317
Neo-Akhbārism, 186
Neoplatonism, 84
neo-traditionalism, 244
Nesīmī, poet, 99, 129
Newman, Andrew, 144, 205, 214–15
al-Nīsābūrī, Ismaili *dā'ī*, 30–1
Nizār, al-Muṣṭafā li-Dīn Allāh b. al-Mustanṣir, Nizārī Ismaili imam, 33
Nizārī Ismailis, 10–13, 14, 18, 21, 22
non-existence, 317
nothingness, 315
Nizārī Quhistānī, Nizārī Ismaili poet, 11–12, 21
al-Nu'mān, al-Qāḍī Abū Ḥanīfa, Ismaili jurist and author, 61–2
Nuqṭavī, Nuqṭaviyya,
  and Akbar, 173–5
  antinomianism, 161–2
  appeal, 152–3, 159
  and Buddhist concepts, 135
  doctrinal positions, 132, 160–73
  heresy, 151, 155–6
  historical narrative, 150–60
  Munshī's account, 156–8
  Naṭanzī's account, 151–5
  persecution, 153, 158
  political success, 173–6
  Qazvīn circle, 134, 136
  Qizil-bāsh involvement, 154n57
  and the Safavids, 131–76
  sources, 131–5, 150–1
  threat to Shah 'Abbās, 154–5, 155–6, 159
  universal language, 170
  universalism, 169
  Yazdī's narrative, 155–6
Nūr al-Dahr 'Alī, Nizārī Ismaili imam, 35, 60, 65–6, 67
Nūrbakhsh, Muḥammad, founder of the Nūrbakhshī Sufi order, 358
Nūrbakhshī order, 358–60

Occultation, the, 183–4, 184, 193, 199, 219
Ögedei, Mongol Great Khān, 1
Öljeitü, Īl Khān, 2
ontological dot, the, 163–70
oral testimony, 273
Ottoman Empire, 244, 284, 288, 289

Padwick, Constance, 60
painting, 369–76
Pampus, Karl-Heinz, 221
Paradise, 237–8, 348–9, 352
Pasīkhānī, Maḥmūd, Nuqṭavī leader, 131, 132, 133, 136, 162–7, 167, 170, 172
Perfect Man, the, 325–7
perfection, loss of, 89–90

Peripatetic philosophers, 317, 318
perpetual inception, 306–7, 307, 317–19
perpetuity and perpetual inception, 306–7, 311–19, 320–1, 332
Persian alphabet, 163–4
philosophers, source of wisdom, 78–9
philosophical Shiʿism, 10
philosophy
  conflict with religion, 330–4
  and law, 77–8
Plato, 327, 334, 339, 350, 362, 364–5
Platonic forms, the, 312–13
Platonism, 321
Plotinus, 332, 336–7, 339
poetry, 11–12, 348
  düvaz imam, 106–12
  floral imagery, 371–2
  ghazal, 99
  Ḥurūfi images, 129
  Khālū Maḥmūd ʿAlī, 37–74
  letter symbolism, 69
  in praise of the imams, 25–6
  prosody, 40–2
  Shah Ismāʿīl I, 95–6, 97–102, 105–6, 113
  Sufi terminology, 26
  trilling metre, 40–1
political power, 185–6
Postclassicism, 241–4
power, right to, 193
prayers of proximity, 60–5, 73–4
Principlists (*uṣūliyya*), 179–80
projection, 358–60
prophets, the, 78–9, 278
Pseudo-Aristotle, 313, 321, 336–7, 339, 364
punishment, 338
Pythagoras, 80, 356, 364
qaḍāʾ, 314, 316
al-Qaṭīfī, Ibrāhīm b. Sulaymān, Twelver Shiʿi scholar, 258–61
  915/1509 *ijāzāt*, 277–83, 297, 298
  920/1514 *ijāzāt*, 284–8, 298
  944/1537 *ijāzāt*, 288–93, 297, 298, 299
  admonition, 283
  arrival in Iraq, 277
  authorisations, 287–8
  contributions, 301
  fawāʾid quotes, 286–7
  first undated *ijāzāt*, 283–4
  ijāzāt, 271–301
  jurisprudential criticisms, 273
  jurisprudential reservations, 301
  second undated *ijāzāt*, 293–6
  sources, 281–2, 298
  teachers, 298
Qājār dynasty, legal commentaries, 245–6
Qarā Meḥmed, Qara-Qoyunlu khān, 127
Qarā Yūsuf, Qara-Qoyunlu khān,115, 127, 130
Qarāguzlū, ʿAlī Riḍā Dhakāvatī, Iranian scholar, 132
Qara-Qoyunlu state, 126–9, 130
Qāsim Shāh, Nīzārī Ismaili imam, 21
Qavāmī Shīrāzī, ʿAbdī Beg, historian,144
Qazvīn, 18
al-Qazwīnī, ʿAbd al-Jalīl, 179
qiyāma (resurrection), 22–3
Qizil-bāsh, the, 96, 101, 102–6, 112, 113, 136–7, 138–43, 154n57, 159, 288, 371
quiddity, 305–6, 307, 307–11, 327–8
Quinn, Sholeh A., 150n46
Qummī, Azīz Allāh, 35–6

al-Qummī, Muḥammad Ṭāhir, 186, 276n13
Qur'an, 82, 161–2, 163–4, 170, 222–3, 226, 255, 256, 266–7, 269, 278, 282–3, 285, 294, 332, 336, 349–50

Rasā'il Ikhwān al-Ṣafā', 75, 76, 76–81
rationalist Shi'ism, 179
reading, 324
reality, degrees of, 332–3
Redeemer, the, 367
religious authority, 172–3, 199, 200
religious jurisdiction, 183
religious manuals, 23
Resurrection, 333, 337
  the Companion of the Grave, 356–7
  corporal, 355, 365–7
  greater, 346
  lesser, 346, 348–51, 357, 360–1
  progress after death, 360–1
  two bodies, 346
rewards, 338, 355
al-Riḍawī, 'Abd al-Ḥayy, 184
Risālat al-Jāmi'a, 76, 81–90, 90–1
ritual body wash, 255–67
ritual purification, 255–67
ritual purity, 233–4

al-Sabzawārī, Muḥammad Bāqir, Twelver Shi'i scholar, 265–7
Ṣafī al-Dīn Ardabīlī, eponymous founder of the Ṣafavī order, 7
Ṣafavīs, Ṣafaviyya, Sufi order, 6, 7–8
Safavid dynasty, 3–4, 13–14, 75, 96–7, 99, 150–60, 195–8, 204–40
  fatwās, 246
  legal commentaries, 244–5
  legitimacy, 140, 141–2, 150n46, 154, 184–5
  and Nuqṭavī doctrinal positions, 160–73
  Nuqṭavī political success, 173–6
  and the Nuqṭavī, 131–76
  power structure, 131
  religious authority, 172–3, 173–4
  Shi'i revival, 179–93
  Shi'ism, 136, 136–50
  Twelver Shi'ism, 137–44
Ṣaḥīfat al-istikhlāṣ, 122–6
Ṣā'in al-Dīn, *Nafsat al-maṣdūr-i thānī*, 119–20
sainthood, era of, 120
Saljūqs, 33–4
al-Samāhījī, 'Abd Allāh, 205, 274, 301
Sarbadārs, 4, 140n18, 148
satr (concealment), 19, 21
Saviour of the End of Time, 192
Sayyid Imām Shāh, Ismaili poet, 63
Schmidtke, S., 274–5
sciences, division of, 79–80
scripture, understandings of, 32
self-referential scholarship, 242
Seth, 82
sexual intercourse, 255–67, 268–70
Shāh Muḥammad b. Qarā Yūsuf, 128
Shāhnāma (Ṭahmāsp), 369–76
al-Shahrastānī, *Kitāb al-Milal wa'l-niḥal*, 88, 89
Shāhrukh, Tīmūrid ruler, 4, 115–16, 117
  Amīr Ghiyāth al-Dīn and Amīr Nūr Allāh interrogations, 122–4, 130
  assassination attempt, 117–20, 126–7

al-Shalmaghānī, ʿAlī b. Abī al-ʿAzāqir, 235
Shams al-Dīn Muḥammad, Nīzārī Ismaili imam, 11
Sharḥ Uṣūl al-Kāfī, 214, 215–16
sharīʿa (lit. path, way), 77–8
Shiʿi Islam, broader esoteric, 95–6, 102–6, 113
Shiʿitisation, 4–8, 14
Shīrāz, 118
Shīrāzī, ʿAbdī Beg, 372–3, 375
Shīrāzī, Ṣadr al-Dīn (Mullā Ṣadrā), 9, 75, 91, 306, 310n17, 349–50, 366
  Asfār, 336, 338
  cosmology, 330–4, 338
  critical approach to *ishrāqī* ontology, 323–4, 327–30, 339
  definition of the body, 329–30
  Four Journeys, 323–4, 325–6
  Ḥikmat al-ishrāq, 323–39
  and philosophy, 323, 325–6
  Sharḥ Uṣūl al-Kāfī, 214, 215–17
  and the soul, 334–7
  sources, 338–9
ṣifāt al-niyāba, 284
'Siyāvush and Farangīs Wedded', 373–4
'Siyāvush Captive before Afrāsiyāb', 374
Socrates, 339
souls,
  abstraction from body, 363–5
  ascent of, 327
  celestial, 330–1
  cycle of occultation, 86–7
  destiny, 336
  human-to-animal metamorphosis, 349–51
  imprisonment, 83–4
  lower faculties, 85
  mode of being, 337
  perfection, 335
  rational, 84–6, 327, 333, 334–6, 351, 362–3
  singularity, 334–5
  transmigration, 81, 90
  universal, 334–5
spiritual guides, 63–5
spiritual observation, 365
stewardship, 369–76
Stewart, D., 273
Ṣūfī b. Ṣādiq, 36, 60, 63
Sufism, 2, 4–5, 62–3, 75, 91, 137, 182–3, 341, 343–4, 358–60, 364
al-Suhrawardī, Shihāb al-Dīn Yaḥyā, philosopher, 147, 324–39
Sunni Islam, 5, 137, 143, 189, 199, 233
Sulṭān Muḥammad, artist, 370–2
systematic ambiguity, 310

Tabrīz, 124, 128–9
Tabrīzī, Ḥaṣrī, 129
Tabrīzī, Ḥusayn, 129
tafsīr (Qurʾanic exegesis), 226–7, 341, 346
Tahdhīb al-aḥkām, 210–11, 211–12
Ṭahmāsp, Safavid shah, 144, 153, 158, 179, 182, 288–9
  aversion to hunting, 375–6
  gardens, 372–3, 376
  Shāhnāma, 369–76
taʿlīm (authoritative teaching, instruction), 26–7
tanāsukh (metempsychosis), 349–51
taqiyya (precautionary dissimulation), 10, 13, 19, 34–5
al-Tawḥīdī, Abū Ḥayyān, philosopher and author, 77–8
temporality, 313–14, 316, 321, 331–2, 376

Terrier, Mathieu, 75–6, 80, 81, 91
Testimony, world of, 353–3
theosophy, 10
al-Ṭihrānī, Āqā Buzurg, Twelver Shiʿi scholar, 206, 211
Tīmūr, founder of the Tīmūrid dynasty and empire, 4
Tīmūrids, 4, 116, 121, 130
Traditionalists, 179
transmigration, 349, 358, see also *tanāsukh*
al-Ṭūsī, Khwāja Naṣīr al-Dīn Muḥammad, Shiʿi scholar, 1–2, 25, 314, 316, 319
  Awṣāf al-ashrāf, 8
  Rawḍa-yi taslīm, 22, 24
al-Ṭūsī, Abū Jaʿfar Muḥammad, al-Shaykh al-Ṭāʾifa, Twelver Shiʿi scholar, 225
al-Tustarī, ʿAbd Allāh b. al-Ḥusayn, 201–2, 274–5, 300
al-Tustarī, Sayyid Jamāl al-Dīn b. Nūr Allāh, 289–90
Twelver Shiʿism, 2–3, 13–14, 20, 96, 167, 198–9
  jurisprudence, 3
  Safavid, 137–44
  and Sufism, 8–12

universal language, 170–1
Universal Soul, fall of, 81, 83–4, 90
universality, 170
Uṣūl al-Kāfī, 207–8, 208, 209, 211–12, 214–15, 223
Uṣūlī school, the, 180, 204–7

voluntary death, 361–2

wealth, 231–2
Weber, Max, 96
wine, 123, 127, 157, 233–4
wisdom, source of, 78–9
'Wisdom of the Right Side' (Mīr Dāmād), 305–21
  making the quiddities, 305–6, 307, 307–11
  perpetuity and perpetual inception, 306–7, 311–19, 320–1
  Platonism, 321
women, ritual body wash, 255–67, 268–70
wonders, 358–60

Yazdī, Jalāl al-Dīn Munajjim, chronicler, 155–6

Zayn al-Dīn ʿAlī al-ʿĀmilī, al-Shahīd al-Thānī, Twelver Shiʿi scholar, 200–1, 203, 207, 229–30, 261–3, 264, 265
Zeno of Citium, Hellenistic philosopher, 332
Zoroaster, and the origin of evil, 88–90, 90

Figure 15.1. 'The Feast of Sada', folio 22v from the *Shāhnāma* of Shah Ṭahmāsp, attributed to Sulṭān Muḥammad, Tabrīz, ca. 1525, opaque watercolour, ink, silver and gold on paper, Painting: H. 9 1/2 in. (24.1 cm), W. 9 1/16 in. (23 cm); Page: H. 18 1/2 in. (47 cm), W.12 1/2 in. (31.8 cm), Metropolitan Museum of Art, New York, Gift of Arthur A. Houghton Jr., 1970 1970.301.2

Figure 15.2. Chihil Sutūn, Qazvin, Safavid, built mid-10th/16th century, with 18th and 19th-century alterations. Behnam Minaei, CC BY-SA 4.0 <https://creativecommons.org/licenses/by-sa/4.0>, via Wikimedia Commons

Figure 15.3. 'Siyāvush and Farangīs Wedded', folio 185v, from the *Shāhnāma* of Shah Ṭahmāsp, attributed to Qāsim b. ʿAlī, ca. 1525-30, opaque watercolour, ink, silver and gold on paper, Painting: H. 11 3/8 in. (28.9 cm), W. 7 1/4 in. (18.4 cm); Page: H. 18 5/8 in. (47.3 cm), W. 12 5/8 in. (32.1 cm), Metropolitan Museum of Art, New York, Gift of Arthur A. Houghton Jr 1970. 1970.301.28

Figure 15.4. 'The Coronation of the Infant Shāpūr II', folio 538r, from the *Shāhnāma* of Shah Ṭahmāsp, attributed to Muẓaffar 'Alī, ca. 1525-30, opaque watercolour, ink, silver and gold on paper, Painting: H. 13 1/4 (33.7cm.), W. 8 11/16 in. (22.1 cm); Page: H. 18 9/16 (47.1 cm.), W. 12 1/2 in. (31.8 cm), Metropolitan Museum of Art, New York, Gift of Arthur A. Houghton Jr 1970. 1970.301.59

Figure 15.5. 'Siyāvush Captive before Afrāsiyāb', fol. 110b, from a *Shāhnāma* of Firdawsī, probably Isfahan, dated A.H. 1074–79/A.D. 1663–69, signed by Muhammad Zaman, Opaque watercolour, ink, silver and gold on paper, H. 18 1/2 in. (47 cm), W. 11 1/8 in. (28.2 cm), Gift of Alexander Smith Cochran, 1913. 13.228.17

www.ingramcontent.com/pod-product-compliance
Lightning Source LLC
Chambersburg PA
CBHW051802230426
43672CB00012B/2608